Contents

INTERMEDIATE MATHEMATICS FOR GCSE

A complete course for the Intermediate Tier

Written for AQA specifications A & B

Brian Speed

Keith Gordon

Kevin Evans

Collins

Published by Collins Educational
An imprint of HarperCollins*Publishers* Ltd
77–85 Fulham Palace Road
Hammersmith
London W6 8JB

www.**Collins**Education.com
Online Support for Schools and Colleges

© HarperCollins*Publishers* Ltd 2001

10 9 8 7 6 5 4

ISBN 0 00 711509 1

British Cataloguing in Publication Data
A catalogue record for this book is available from the
British Library

Edited by Michael Fitch
Typesetting by Ken Vail Graphic Design
Expert Reader: Peter Clarkson
Additional proofreading by Angus Boyd-Heron
Illustrations by Moondisks, Cambridge
and Ken Vail Graphic Design
Cover by Sylvia Kwan
Index by Susan Leech
Production by Kathryn Botterill
Commissioned by Mark Jordan
Printed and bound by Scotprint, Haddington

Acknowledgements

We are grateful to the following Examination Groups for
permission to reproduce questions from their past
examination papers and from specimen papers. Full
details are given with each question. The Examination
Groups accept no responsibility whatsoever for the
accuracy or method of working in the answers given,
which are solely the responsibility of the authors and the
publisher.

Assessment and Qualifications Alliance (AQA)
EDEXCEL Foundation (formerly ULEAC)
Midland Examining Group (MEG)
Northern Examinations and Assessment Board
  (NEAB)
Northern Ireland Council for the Curriculum
  Examinations and Assessment (NICCEA)
Oxford, Cambridge and RSA examinations (OCR)
Southern Examining Group (SEG)
Welsh Joint Education Committee (WJEC)

Every effort has been made to contact all copyright
holders. If any have been inadvertently overlooked, the
publisher would be pleased to make full
acknowledgement at the first opportunity.

You might also like to visit:
www.**fire**and**water**.com
The book lover's website

Introduction

This book is the title's second edition, specifically tailored to meet the requirements of the GCSE mathematics specifications which come into force in September 2001, to be first examined in June 2003.

All the changes to content for examination from 2003 onwards are covered, including the non-calculator component (which first appeared as a separate examination paper in June 2000).

Non-calculator questions

 Throughout the book, the non-calculator questions are flagged by the non-calculator icon. The icon indicates that the numerical demands of the question are such that it could appear in Paper 1, which is the non-calculator paper. Questions not flagged may be solved with the help of a calculator.

Syllabus changes

Coursework

All specifications now have a coursework component. There is no end-of-course examination paper to test coursework. A minimum of two coursework tasks must be done. One of these can be on Number, Algebra or Shape and Space (or a combination of them), but the other must be on Handling Data.

In most chapters, there are ideas for coursework tasks. These can be done by the students and marked by their teachers. However, some boards will be setting their own tasks, which will be marked by the boards. Whichever way coursework is marked, it is assessed by the same criteria. These are explained in the Appendix, and worked examples of coursework tasks are given. After Chapters 4, 11 and 17, there are Algebra/Number/Shape and Space examples; and after Chapter 22, there is a Statistics example.

Content

The extent of the Handling Data which is examined has been reduced. This accounts for the introduction of the coursework task on Handling Data. Some of the material in this book (the section on tangents, for example) is not examined in the two end-of-course papers. However, the ideas may be used in a coursework example, or help with the overall understanding of a topic, and so have been included. The fact that a topic is not part of the content examined is announced where this occurs.

Using and Applying Maths

In the previous specifications, Using and Applying Mathematics (UAM) was tested by coursework in school, or in the end-of-course coursework paper. Some questions on UAM are now included in the end-of-course examinations. Examples of these are included throughout the book and are flagged with the UAM icon. Generally, these will test a student's ability to think a problem through and may expect the student to use his or her mathematics in an unfamiliar context.

Proof

Proof has been introduced for examination from 2003 onwards. Chapter 27 is devoted to proof, but questions on proof appear throughout the book. These are flagged with the proof icon. Because proof is not a separate topic, the chapter on it comes after most of the proof questions. It may, therefore, be preferable to leave some of these questions until later and then revisit them. The authors want to leave the decision on this to teachers, who will best be able to decide what their students need.

Other matters

As in the first edition, each chapter opens with a 'What you should already know' section and closes with a list of the skills needed to get each grade. There have been a few changes in the latter due to some topics being graded differently. For example, trigonometry is now regarded as a grade B topic, whereas before it was regarded as grade C topic.

At the end of each chapter is a selection of questions from recent higher-tier examination papers. Where possible these are arranged in order of difficulty so that the earlier questions are aimed at lower grades than the later ones. Some questions cover more than one grade and some questions involve topics learnt earlier. This is because examination questions cover more than one topic.

Using the internet

Through the internet, students have access to a vast amount of data which they could use in a variety of activities, particularly their coursework on Handling Data.

Addresses of appropriate website sources are available from the Collins Educational maths website:

> www.**Collins**Education.com/maths
> Online Support for Schools and Colleges

We hope that everyone who uses this book enjoys it, and we wish them the best of luck with their examinations!

Brian Speed, Keith Gordon, Kevin Evans.

1 Number

This chapter is going to ...

remind you of some of the arithmetic that you have already done. It will also show you which arithmetic you need to be able to do on a calculator and which *without* a calculator.

Arithmetic occurs in many different places in your GCSE examination papers, so it is most important that you are completely familiar with all the different techniques.

What you should already know

It really does help you if you know your times tables! Yes, you can always find the answer on a calculator, but it is much more efficient if you know the tables.

Much of this chapter reminds you of things learned earlier, so we expect you to have some experience of the following arithmetical techniques.

✔ Long multiplication
✔ Long division
✔ Calculating with fractions
✔ Adding and subtracting negative numbers
✔ Multiplying and dividing with negative numbers
✔ Rounding off

If you feel you need to revise any of these techniques, you should work through the rest of this chapter, starting from here.

Long multiplication and division

You will have learnt long multiplication before, but on the non-calculator paper in your GCSE examinations you will be asked to do some long multiplication and division.

Long multiplication

Do you remember how to work out 357×24? You could do

$$300 \times 24 = \quad 7200$$
$$50 \times 24 = \quad 1200$$
$$7 \times 24 = \quad \underline{168}$$
$$\text{add up to} \quad \underline{8568}$$

EXERCISE 1A

Calculate the following. Check your answers on a calculator *afterwards*.

1	357×34	**2**	724×63	**3**	714×42	**4**	898×23
5	958×54	**6**	676×37	**7**	239×81	**8**	437×29
9	539×37	**10**	477×55	**11**	371×85	**12**	843×93
13	507×34	**14**	810×54	**15**	905×73	**16**	1435×72
17	2504×56	**18**	4037×23	**19**	8009×65	**20**	2070×38

Long division

There are several different ways of doing long division. It is quite acceptable to use any method as long as it gets the right answer. The method used in this book is called the *Italian Method*.

For example, to work out $840 \div 24$, you could do a sum like the one below. Remember to show all your working.

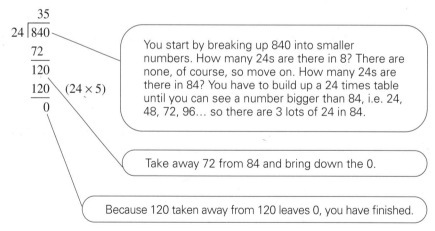

You start by breaking up 840 into smaller numbers. How many 24s are there in 8? There are none, of course, so move on. How many 24s are there in 84? You have to build up a 24 times table until you can see a number bigger than 84, i.e. 24, 48, 72, 96... so there are 3 lots of 24 in 84.

Take away 72 from 84 and bring down the 0.

Because 120 taken away from 120 leaves 0, you have finished.

So the answer to $840 \div 24$ is 35.

Let's take another example: 1655 ÷ 35. You could do this as follows:

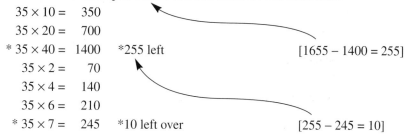

$35 \times 10 =$ 350

$35 \times 20 =$ 700

* $35 \times 40 = 1400$ *255 left   [1655 − 1400 = 255]

$35 \times 2 =$ 70

$35 \times 4 =$ 140

$35 \times 6 =$ 210

* $35 \times 7 =$ 245   *10 left over   [255 − 245 = 10]

This is the end of the line. You have 10 left over.

So the answer to 1655 ÷ 35 is 47, remainder 10   [40 + 7 = 47]

EXERCISE 1B

Work out these sums without a calculator. (Of course, you can check your answers with a calculator afterwards.)

1 525 ÷ 21	**2** 480 ÷ 32	**3** 925 ÷ 25	**4** 645 ÷ 15
5 621 ÷ 23	**6** 576 ÷ 12	**7** 1643 ÷ 31	**8** 728 ÷ 14
9 832 ÷ 26	**10** 2394 ÷ 42	**11** 829 ÷ 22	**12** 780 ÷ 31
13 895 ÷ 26	**14** 873 ÷ 16	**15** 875 ÷ 24	**16** 225 ÷ 13
17 759 ÷ 33	**18** 1478 ÷ 24	**19** 756 ÷ 18	**20** 1163 ÷ 43

Solving real problems

In your GCSE examination you may not be given simple, straightforward problems like Exercises **1A** and **1B** but **real** problems that you have to **read**, **think about** and then **sort out** without using a calculator. Try working out this next example.

How many coaches holding 53 people each will be needed to take a school party of 672 children on a day out?

We read the problem and realise that we have to do a division sum: the number of children into the number of coaches. This is 672 ÷ 53.

$53 \times 10 =$ 530   142 left

$53 \times 2 =$ 106   36 left

The answer is 12, remainder 36. So there will be 12 full coaches and one coach with 36 children on. So we would have to book 13 coaches.

EXERCISE 1C

Read the problem carefully and then do the calculation to solve the problem.

1   There are 48 tins of soup in a crate. If a supermarket has a delivery of 125 crates of soup, how many tins of soup will that be?

2   Greystones Primary School has 12 classes all with 26 pupils in. How many pupils are there at Greystones Primary School?

3   3600 supporters of Arsenal want to go to an away game by coach. Each coach can hold 53 passengers. How many coaches will the supporters need altogether?

4   How many stamps costing 23p each can I buy for £10?

5   Joseph walks to school each morning and back in the afternoon. The distance to school is 450 m. How far will he walk in a school term that has school on 64 days?

6   On one page of a newspaper there are 7 columns. In each column there are 172 lines and in each line there are an average of 50 letters. How many letters are there on the page?

7   A tank of water was being emptied into casks. Each cask held 81 litres. 71 casks were filled, with 68 litres left over. How much water was in the tank to start with?

8   Joy was going to do a sponsored walk for the Macmillan Nurses. She managed to get 18 people to sponsor her, each for 35p per kilometre. She walked a total of 68 kilometres. How much sponsor money should she expect to collect?

9   Kirsty collected small models of animals; each one cost 45p. She was given £10 a month pocket money. How many model animals could Kirsty buy with one month's pocket money?

10   Eunice wanted to save up to go to a concert. Her pocket money was £3.50 a week. If a ticket for the concert was £25, how many weeks would Eunice have to save her pocket money for to be able to buy the ticket?

11   The magazine *Teen Dance* is paid for annually (once a year). The annual subscription for the magazine is £21, but you do get a magazine every month of the year. How much does each magazine cost per month?

12   Paula buys a music centre from her club at a cost of £3.96 per week for 48 weeks. How much will she actually pay for this music centre?

13   The youth club leader buys a box of 50 crisps for £6.80.
   a   What is the least that she can sell each packet of crisps for in order not to make a loss on the box?
   b   What profit will be made if she sells the crisps at 19p per packet?

14   Lee Hung opened his new Chinese Restaurant and had 53 customers on the first night, each paying a modest £6.50. How much money did he take that night?

Fractions

A fraction is a part of a whole.

Like $\frac{3}{4}$

The top number is called the **numerator**.

The bottom number is called the **denominator**.

$\frac{3}{4}$ means divide a whole thing into 4 portions and take 3 of them.

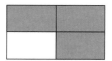

Equivalent fractions

Look at the circles below.

In **a** the circle has been cut into four equal pieces. One piece is $\frac{1}{4}$ of the circle.

In **b** the circle has been cut into eight equal pieces. Two pieces are $\frac{2}{8}$ of the circle.

In **c** the circle has been cut into sixteen equal pieces. Four pieces are $\frac{4}{16}$ of the circle.

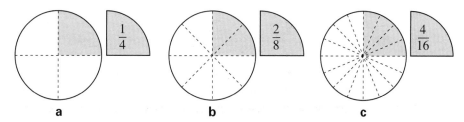

a   b   c

We can see that the same amount of the circle has been shaded each time.

So $\frac{1}{4} = \frac{2}{8} = \frac{4}{16}$ which are called **equivalent fractions**, because they all equal each other.

There are of course many other fractions that are equivalent to any particular fraction.

In fact the value of a fraction remains the same if both the numerator and the denominator are multiplied by the same number. In other words we can find equivalent fractions by multiplying the numerator and the denominator by the same number.

For example, let's look at $\frac{2}{5}$

This could be expressed as:

$$\frac{2 \times 2}{5 \times 2} = \frac{4}{10} \quad \text{or} \quad \frac{2 \times 3}{5 \times 3} = \frac{6}{15} \quad \text{or} \quad \frac{2 \times 4}{5 \times 4} = \frac{8}{20} \quad \text{and so on.}$$

So, $\frac{4}{10}$, $\frac{6}{15}$ and $\frac{8}{20}$ are just a few of the thousands of fractions all equivalent to $\frac{2}{5}$.

EXERCISE 1D

1 Copy and complete each of these statements.

a $\dfrac{2}{5} \longrightarrow \dfrac{\times 4}{\times 4} = \dfrac{\square}{20}$ **b** $\dfrac{1}{4} \longrightarrow \dfrac{\times 3}{\times 3} = \dfrac{\square}{12}$ **c** $\dfrac{3}{8} \longrightarrow \dfrac{\times 5}{\times 5} = \dfrac{\square}{40}$

d $\dfrac{4}{5} \longrightarrow \dfrac{\times 3}{\times 3} = \dfrac{\square}{15}$ **e** $\dfrac{5}{6} \longrightarrow \dfrac{\times 3}{\times 3} = \dfrac{\square}{18}$ **f** $\dfrac{3}{7} \longrightarrow \dfrac{\times 4}{\times 4} = \dfrac{\square}{28}$

g $\dfrac{3}{10} \longrightarrow \dfrac{\times \square}{\times 2} = \dfrac{\square}{20}$ **h** $\dfrac{1}{3} \longrightarrow \dfrac{\times \square}{\times \square} = \dfrac{\square}{9}$ **i** $\dfrac{3}{5} \longrightarrow \dfrac{\times \square}{\times \square} = \dfrac{\square}{20}$

j $\dfrac{2}{3} \longrightarrow \dfrac{\times \square}{\times \square} = \dfrac{\square}{18}$ **k** $\dfrac{3}{4} \longrightarrow \dfrac{\times \square}{\times \square} = \dfrac{\square}{12}$ **l** $\dfrac{5}{8} \longrightarrow \dfrac{\times \square}{\times \square} = \dfrac{\square}{40}$

m $\dfrac{7}{10} \longrightarrow \dfrac{\times \square}{\times \square} = \dfrac{\square}{20}$ **n** $\dfrac{1}{6} \longrightarrow \dfrac{\times \square}{\times \square} = \dfrac{4}{\square}$ **o** $\dfrac{3}{8} \longrightarrow \dfrac{\times \square}{\times \square} = \dfrac{15}{\square}$

2 Copy and complete each of these statements.

a $\dfrac{1}{2} = \dfrac{2}{\square} = \dfrac{3}{\square} = \dfrac{\square}{8} = \dfrac{\square}{10} = \dfrac{6}{\square}$

b $\dfrac{1}{3} = \dfrac{2}{\square} = \dfrac{3}{\square} = \dfrac{\square}{12} = \dfrac{\square}{15} = \dfrac{6}{\square}$

c $\dfrac{3}{4} = \dfrac{6}{\square} = \dfrac{9}{\square} = \dfrac{\square}{16} = \dfrac{\square}{20} = \dfrac{18}{\square}$

d $\dfrac{2}{5} = \dfrac{4}{\square} = \dfrac{6}{\square} = \dfrac{\square}{20} = \dfrac{\square}{25} = \dfrac{12}{\square}$

e $\dfrac{3}{7} = \dfrac{6}{\square} = \dfrac{9}{\square} = \dfrac{\square}{28} = \dfrac{\square}{35} = \dfrac{18}{\square}$

3 We use fractions to give us an answer to a problem such as $3 \div 4$.

This does not divide exactly; the answer is part of a number; in fact it is

$3 \div 4 = \dfrac{3}{4}$

Give the answer to each of the following problems in the form of a fraction.

   a $5 \div 6$ **b** $3 \div 5$ **c** $1 \div 8$ **d** $2 \div 3$ **e** $7 \div 10$

4 Write down the problem (as above) that would give the following answers.

   a $\dfrac{3}{8}$ **b** $\dfrac{2}{7}$ **c** $\dfrac{5}{12}$ **d** $\dfrac{7}{8}$ **e** $\dfrac{9}{11}$

Cancelling down a fraction

In the same way as making equivalent fractions by multiplying both top and bottom by the same number, we can make a fraction look simpler by dividing both top and bottom by the same number. This is called **cancelling down**.

For example

Look at $\dfrac{10}{15}$; we can divide both top and bottom by 5, which will give us $\dfrac{10 \div 5}{15 \div 5} = \dfrac{2}{3}$.

EXERCISE 1E

1 Copy and complete each of these statements.

a $\dfrac{10}{15} = \dfrac{10 \div 5}{15 \div 5} = \dfrac{\square}{\square}$

b $\dfrac{12}{15} = \dfrac{12 \div 3}{15 \div 3} = \dfrac{\square}{\square}$

c $\dfrac{20}{28} = \dfrac{20 \div 4}{28 \div 4} = \dfrac{\square}{\square}$

d $\dfrac{12}{18} = \dfrac{12 \div \square}{\square \div \square} = \dfrac{\square}{\square}$

e $\dfrac{15}{25} = \dfrac{15 \div 5}{\square \div \square} = \dfrac{\square}{\square}$

f $\dfrac{21}{30} = \dfrac{21 \div \square}{\square \div \square} = \dfrac{\square}{\square}$

2 Cancel down each of these fractions.

a $\dfrac{4}{6}$　　b $\dfrac{5}{15}$　　c $\dfrac{12}{18}$　　d $\dfrac{6}{8}$　　e $\dfrac{3}{9}$

f $\dfrac{5}{10}$　　g $\dfrac{14}{16}$　　h $\dfrac{28}{35}$　　i $\dfrac{10}{20}$　　j $\dfrac{4}{16}$

k $\dfrac{12}{15}$　　l $\dfrac{15}{21}$　　m $\dfrac{25}{35}$　　n $\dfrac{14}{21}$　　o $\dfrac{8}{20}$

p $\dfrac{10}{25}$　　q $\dfrac{7}{21}$　　r $\dfrac{42}{60}$　　s $\dfrac{50}{200}$　　t $\dfrac{12}{18}$

u $\dfrac{6}{9}$　　v $\dfrac{18}{27}$　　w $\dfrac{36}{48}$　　x $\dfrac{15}{21}$　　y $\dfrac{12}{42}$

3 Copy and complete the following.

a $\dfrac{2}{3} = \dfrac{\square}{6} = \dfrac{\square}{9} = \dfrac{\square}{12}$

b $\dfrac{2}{5} = \dfrac{\square}{10} = \dfrac{12}{\square} = \dfrac{16}{\square}$

c $\dfrac{7}{10} = \dfrac{\square}{30} = \dfrac{49}{\square} = \dfrac{\square}{100}$

d $\dfrac{5}{8} = \dfrac{15}{\square} = \dfrac{\square}{40} = \dfrac{20}{\square}$

4 Which is the larger fraction in each of the following pairs?

a $\dfrac{5}{6} , \dfrac{7}{8}$　　b $\dfrac{5}{9} , \dfrac{3}{5}$　　c $\dfrac{3}{4} , \dfrac{2}{3}$　　d $\dfrac{7}{10} , \dfrac{5}{8}$

5 Put the correct sign, $>$, $=$, $<$ in the box between each of the following pairs.

a $\dfrac{2}{3} \ \square \ \dfrac{4}{9}$　　b $\dfrac{3}{4} \ \square \ \dfrac{6}{8}$　　c $\dfrac{5}{6} \ \square \ \dfrac{4}{5}$　　d $\dfrac{5}{8} \ \square \ \dfrac{7}{10}$

e $\dfrac{2}{7} \ \square \ \dfrac{1}{3}$　　f $\dfrac{3}{4} \ \square \ \dfrac{5}{8}$　　g $\dfrac{4}{9} \ \square \ \dfrac{1}{2}$　　h $\dfrac{2}{3} \ \square \ \dfrac{3}{5}$

i $\dfrac{3}{5} \ \square \ \dfrac{4}{7}$　　j $\dfrac{1}{4} \ \square \ \dfrac{3}{10}$　　k $\dfrac{4}{5} \ \square \ \dfrac{8}{10}$　　l $\dfrac{5}{6} \ \square \ \dfrac{7}{8}$

m $\dfrac{3}{8} \ \square \ \dfrac{2}{5}$　　n $\dfrac{2}{3} \ \square \ \dfrac{6}{9}$　　o $\dfrac{5}{9} \ \square \ \dfrac{3}{5}$　　p $\dfrac{7}{10} \ \square \ \dfrac{2}{3}$

To find a fraction of a quantity

To do this, you simply multiply the number by the fraction. For example, find $\frac{3}{4}$ of £196.

First, find $\frac{1}{4}$ by dividing by 4. Then find $\frac{3}{4}$ by multiplying your answer by 3.

$196 \div 4 = 49$　then　$49 \times 3 = 147$

The answer is £147.

Of course, you can do this problem using your calculator by simply either

- pressing the sequence   [1] [9] [6] [÷] [4] [×] [3] [=]
- or using the [aᵇ/c] key   [3] [aᵇ/c] [4] [×] [1] [9] [6] [=]

EXERCISE 1F

1 Calculate these fractions.

    a $\frac{3}{5} \times 30$ **b** $\frac{2}{7} \times 35$ **c** $\frac{3}{8} \times 48$ **d** $\frac{7}{10} \times 40$ **e** $\frac{5}{6} \times 18$

    f $24 \times \frac{3}{4}$ **g** $60 \times \frac{4}{5}$ **h** $72 \times \frac{5}{8}$

2 Calculate these fractions.

    a $\frac{3}{4}$ of £2400   **b** $\frac{2}{5}$ of 320 grams   **c** $\frac{5}{8}$ of 256 kilograms

    d $\frac{2}{3}$ of £174   **e** $\frac{5}{6}$ of 78 litres   **f** $\frac{3}{4}$ of 120 minutes

    g $\frac{4}{5}$ of 365 days   **h** $\frac{7}{8}$ of 24 hours   **i** $\frac{3}{4}$ of 1 day

    j $\frac{5}{9}$ of 4266 miles

3 In each case, find out which is the larger number.

    a $\frac{2}{5}$ of 60 or $\frac{5}{8}$ of 40   **b** $\frac{3}{4}$ of 280 or $\frac{7}{10}$ of 290   **c** $\frac{2}{3}$ of 78 or $\frac{4}{5}$ of 70

    d $\frac{5}{6}$ of 72 or $\frac{11}{12}$ of 60   **e** $\frac{4}{9}$ of 126 or $\frac{3}{5}$ of 95   **f** $\frac{3}{4}$ of 340 or $\frac{2}{3}$ of 381

4 A director was entitled to $\frac{2}{15}$ of his firm's profits. The firm made a profit of £45 600 in one year. What was the director's income from this profit?

5 A woman left $\frac{3}{8}$ of her estate to the local Methodist Church. What amount is this if her estate totalled £8400?

6 There were 36 800 people at Hillsborough to see Sheffield Wednesday play Manchester United. We know that $\frac{3}{8}$ of this crowd were female. How many males were at the ground?

7 Two-thirds of a person's weight is water. Paul weighed 78 kg. How much of his body weight was water?

8   **a**   Information from the first census in Singapore suggests that $\frac{2}{25}$ of the population were then Indian. The total population was 10 700. How many people were Indian?

      b   By 1990 the population of Singapore had grown to 3 001 800. Only $\frac{1}{15}$ of this population were Indian. How many Indians were living in Singapore in 1990?

9 Which is the bigger: three-quarters of two-thirds of six million *or* two-thirds of three-quarters of six million?

Top-heavy fractions and mixed numbers

A **top-heavy fraction** is one in which the numerator is larger than the denominator, for example $\frac{11}{4}$.

A **mixed number** is a number that is made up of some whole ones and a fraction, for example $3\frac{4}{5}$.

We change top-heavy fractions into mixed numbers by dividing the numerator by the denominator to see how many whole ones we have and how many left over for the fraction part.

For example:

$\frac{11}{4}$ can make 2 whole ones with three left over to make $\frac{3}{4}$

This then gives the mixed number as $2\frac{3}{4}$

We change mixed numbers into top-heavy fractions by changing the whole parts to the same denominator, and then adding the two together.

For example:

$3\frac{4}{5}$ will make $\dfrac{3 \times 5}{5} + \dfrac{4}{5} = \dfrac{19}{5}$

EXERCISE 1G

Try this exercise **without** your calculator.

Change each of these top-heavy fractions into a mixed number.

1 $\frac{7}{3}$	**2** $\frac{8}{3}$	**3** $\frac{9}{4}$	**4** $\frac{10}{7}$	**5** $\frac{12}{5}$	**6** $\frac{7}{5}$
7 $\frac{13}{5}$	**8** $\frac{15}{4}$	**9** $\frac{10}{3}$	**10** $\frac{15}{7}$	**11** $\frac{17}{6}$	**12** $\frac{18}{5}$
13 $\frac{19}{4}$	**14** $\frac{22}{7}$	**15** $\frac{14}{11}$	**16** $\frac{12}{11}$	**17** $\frac{28}{5}$	**18** $\frac{19}{7}$
19 $\frac{40}{7}$	**20** $\frac{42}{5}$	**21** $\frac{21}{10}$	**22** $\frac{5}{2}$	**23** $\frac{5}{3}$	**24** $\frac{25}{8}$
25 $\frac{23}{10}$	**26** $\frac{23}{11}$	**27** $\frac{38}{5}$	**28** $\frac{38}{7}$	**29** $\frac{40}{8}$	**30** $\frac{12}{6}$

Change each of these mixed numbers into a top-heavy fraction.

31 $3\frac{1}{3}$	**32** $5\frac{5}{6}$	**33** $1\frac{4}{5}$	**34** $5\frac{2}{7}$	**35** $4\frac{1}{10}$	**36** $5\frac{2}{3}$
37 $2\frac{1}{2}$	**38** $3\frac{1}{4}$	**39** $7\frac{1}{6}$	**40** $3\frac{5}{8}$	**41** $6\frac{1}{3}$	**42** $9\frac{8}{9}$
43 $11\frac{4}{5}$	**44** $3\frac{1}{5}$	**45** $4\frac{3}{8}$	**46** $3\frac{1}{9}$	**47** $5\frac{1}{5}$	**48** $2\frac{3}{4}$
49 $4\frac{2}{7}$	**50** $8\frac{1}{6}$	**51** $2\frac{8}{9}$	**52** $6\frac{1}{6}$	**53** $12\frac{1}{5}$	**54** $1\frac{5}{8}$
55 $7\frac{1}{10}$	**56** $8\frac{1}{9}$	**57** $7\frac{5}{8}$	**58** $10\frac{1}{2}$	**59** $1\frac{1}{16}$	**60** $4\frac{3}{4}$

Addition and subtraction of fractions

Fractions can only be added or subtracted after we have changed them to equivalent fractions, both having the same denominator.

For example:

i $\frac{2}{3} + \frac{1}{5}$; note we can make both fractions equivalent with a denominator of 15

This then becomes $\dfrac{2 \times 5}{3 \times 5} + \dfrac{1 \times 3}{5 \times 3} = \dfrac{10}{15} + \dfrac{3}{15} = \dfrac{13}{15}$

ii $\frac{3}{4} + \frac{5}{6}$; note we can make both fractions equivalent with a denominator of 12

This then becomes $\dfrac{9}{12} + \dfrac{10}{12} = \dfrac{19}{12} = 1\frac{7}{12}$.

EXERCISE 1H

1 Evaluate the following:

   a $\frac{1}{3} + \frac{1}{5}$ b $\frac{1}{3} + \frac{1}{4}$ c $\frac{1}{5} + \frac{1}{10}$ d $\frac{2}{3} + \frac{1}{4}$

   e $\frac{3}{4} + \frac{1}{8}$ f $\frac{1}{3} + \frac{1}{6}$ g $\frac{1}{2} - \frac{1}{3}$ h $\frac{1}{4} - \frac{1}{5}$

   i $\frac{1}{5} - \frac{1}{10}$ j $\frac{7}{8} - \frac{3}{4}$ k $\frac{5}{6} - \frac{3}{4}$ l $\frac{5}{6} - \frac{1}{2}$

   m $\frac{5}{12} - \frac{1}{4}$ n $2\frac{1}{7} + 1\frac{3}{14}$ o $6\frac{3}{10} + 1\frac{4}{5} + 2\frac{1}{2}$ p $3\frac{1}{2} - 1\frac{1}{3}$

2 Evaluate the following:

   a $\frac{1}{3} + \frac{4}{9}$ b $\frac{1}{4} + \frac{3}{8}$ c $\frac{7}{8} - \frac{1}{2}$ d $\frac{3}{5} - \frac{8}{15}$

   e $\frac{11}{12} + \frac{5}{8}$ f $\frac{7}{16} + \frac{3}{10}$ g $\frac{4}{9} - \frac{2}{21}$ h $\frac{5}{6} - \frac{4}{27}$

   i $1\frac{7}{18} + 2\frac{3}{10}$ j $3\frac{2}{6} + 1\frac{9}{20}$ k $1\frac{1}{8} - \frac{5}{9}$ l $1\frac{3}{16} - \frac{7}{12}$

   m $\frac{5}{6} + \frac{7}{16} + \frac{5}{8}$ n $\frac{7}{10} + \frac{3}{8} + \frac{5}{6}$ o $1\frac{1}{3} + \frac{7}{10} - \frac{4}{15}$ p $\frac{5}{14} + 1\frac{3}{7} - \frac{5}{12}$

3 In a class of children, three-quarters are Chinese, one-fifth are Malays and the rest are Indians. What fraction of the class are Indians?

4 In a class election, half of the people voted for Aminah, one-third voted for Janet and the rest voted for Peter. What fraction of the class voted for Peter?

5 A group of people travelled from Hope to Castletown. One-twentieth of them decided to walk, one-twelfth went by car and all the rest went by bus. What fraction went by bus?

6 A one-litre flask filled with milk is used to fill two glasses, one of capacity half a litre, and the other of capacity one-sixth of a litre. What fraction of a litre will remain in the flask?

7 A boy had 930 stamps in his collection. $\frac{2}{15}$ of them were British stamps. How many British stamps did he have?

8 Because of illness, $\frac{2}{5}$ of a school was absent one day. If the school had 650 pupils on the register, how many were absent that day?

9 Which is the biggest: half of 96, one-third of 141, two-fifths of 120, or three-quarters of 68?

10 To increase sales, a shop reduced the price of a car stereo radio by $\frac{2}{5}$. If the original price was £85 what was the new price?

11 Two-fifths of a class were boys. If the class contained 30 children, how many were girls?

12 At a burger-eating competition, Lionel ate 34 burgers in 20 minutes while Brian ate 26 burgers in 20 minutes. How long after the start of the competition would they have consumed a total of 21 burgers between them?

Multiplication of fractions

Look at the problem:

$\frac{3}{4} \times \frac{2}{5}$ or put another way find $\frac{3}{4}$ of $\frac{2}{5}$

If we shade $\frac{2}{5}$ of a rectangle, we get a diagram like

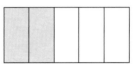

Now shade in $\frac{3}{4}$ of the $\frac{2}{5}$ and we get the situation shown:

You can see that $\frac{3}{10}$ of the diagram is shaded.

This illustrates that $\frac{3}{4} \times \frac{2}{5} = \frac{3 \times 2}{4 \times 5} = \frac{6}{10}$ which cancels to $\frac{3}{10}$

So, to multiply two fractions, multiply each numerator and each denominator and cancel.

Some helpful reminders:
- You will find with practice that it is often helpful to cancel before you start multiplying.
- When multiplying with a mixed number, change the mixed number to a top-heavy fraction before you start multiplying.

EXERCISE 1I

1 Evaluate the following, leaving your answer in its simplest form:

a $\frac{1}{2} \times \frac{1}{3}$ b $\frac{1}{4} \times \frac{2}{5}$ c $\frac{3}{4} \times \frac{1}{2}$ d $\frac{3}{7} \times \frac{1}{2}$

e $\frac{2}{3} \times \frac{4}{5}$ f $\frac{1}{3} \times \frac{3}{5}$ g $\frac{1}{3} \times \frac{6}{7}$ h $\frac{3}{4} \times \frac{2}{5}$

i $\frac{5}{16} \times \frac{3}{10}$ j $\frac{2}{3} \times \frac{3}{4}$ k $\frac{1}{2} \times \frac{4}{5}$ l $\frac{9}{10} \times \frac{5}{12}$

m $\frac{14}{15} \times \frac{3}{8}$ n $\frac{8}{9} \times \frac{6}{15}$ o $\frac{6}{7} \times \frac{21}{30}$ p $\frac{9}{14} \times \frac{35}{36}$

2 Evaluate the following, leaving your answer as a mixed number where possible:

a $1\frac{1}{4} \times \frac{1}{3}$ b $1\frac{2}{3} \times 1\frac{1}{4}$ c $2\frac{1}{2} \times 2\frac{1}{2}$ d $1\frac{3}{4} \times 1\frac{2}{3}$

e $3\frac{1}{4} \times 1\frac{1}{5}$ f $1\frac{1}{4} \times 2\frac{2}{3}$ g $2\frac{1}{2} \times 5$ h $7\frac{1}{2} \times 4$

3 I walked two-thirds of the way along Pungol Road which is four and a half kilometres long. How far have I walked?

4 One-quarter of Alan's stamp collection were given to him by his sister. Unfortunately two-thirds of these were torn. What fraction of his collection were given to him by his sister and which were not torn?

5 A greedy girl eats one-quarter of a cake, and then half of what is left. How much cake is left uneaten?

6 Kathleen spent three-eighths of her income on rent, and two-fifths of what was left on food. What fraction of her income was left after buying her food?

7 A merchant buys 28 crates, each containing three-quarters of a tonne of waste metal. What is the total weight of this order?

8 Which is larger, $\frac{3}{4}$ of $2\frac{1}{2}$ or $\frac{2}{5}$ of $6\frac{1}{2}$?

9 After James spent $\frac{2}{5}$ of his pocket money on magazines, and $\frac{1}{4}$ of his pocket money at a football match, he had £1.75 left. How much pocket money did he have in the beginning?

10 Eileen lost $\frac{3}{4}$ of her money in the market, but then found $\frac{3}{5}$ of what she had lost. She now had £21. How much did she start with?

11 If £5.20 is two-thirds of three-quarters of a sum of money, what is the sum?

Dividing fractions

Let's look at the problem $3 \div \frac{3}{4}$. This is like asking, 'how many $\frac{3}{4}$'s are there in 3?'

Look at the diagram

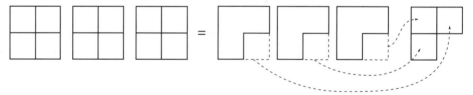

We have divided each of the three whole shapes into quarters, and wish to see how many 3's go into this number.

It helps us to see that we could fit the 4 shapes on the right-hand side of the = sign into the 3 shapes on the left-hand side.

i.e. $3 \div \frac{3}{4} = 4$

or $3 \div \frac{3}{4} = 3 \times \frac{4}{3} = \frac{3 \times 4}{3} = \frac{12}{3} = 4$

So, to divide by a fraction, we turn the fraction upside down (finding its reciprocal), and then multiply.

EXERCISE 1J

1 Evaluate the following, leaving your answer as a mixed number where possible.

a $\dfrac{1}{4} \div \dfrac{1}{3}$ **b** $\dfrac{2}{5} \div \dfrac{2}{7}$ **c** $\dfrac{4}{5} \div \dfrac{3}{4}$ **d** $\dfrac{3}{7} \div \dfrac{2}{5}$

e $5 \div 1\dfrac{1}{4}$ **f** $6 \div 1\dfrac{1}{2}$ **g** $7\dfrac{1}{2} \div 1\dfrac{1}{2}$ **h** $3 \div 1\dfrac{3}{4}$

i $1\dfrac{5}{12} \div 3\dfrac{3}{16}$ **j** $3\dfrac{3}{5} \div 2\dfrac{1}{4}$

2 A grain merchant has only thirteen and a half tonnes in stock. He has several customers who are all ordering three-quarters of a tonne. How many customers can he supply?

3 For a party, Zahar made twelve and a half litres of lemonade. His glasses could each hold five-sixteenths of a litre. How many of the glasses could he fill from the twelve and a half litres of lemonade?

4 How many strips of ribbon, each three and a half centimetres long, can I cut from a roll of ribbon that is fifty-two and a half centimetres long?

5 Joe's stride is three-quarters of a metre long. How many strides does he take to walk along a bus twelve metres long?

6 Evaluate the following, leaving your answers as mixed numbers wherever possible

a $2\dfrac{2}{9} \times 2\dfrac{1}{10} \times \dfrac{16}{35}$ **b** $3\dfrac{1}{5} \times 2\dfrac{1}{2} \times 4\dfrac{3}{4}$ **c** $1\dfrac{1}{4} \times 1\dfrac{2}{7} \times 1\dfrac{1}{6}$ **d** $\dfrac{18}{25} \times \dfrac{15}{16} \div 2\dfrac{2}{5}$

e $\left(\dfrac{2}{5} \times \dfrac{2}{5}\right) \times \left(\dfrac{5}{6} \times \dfrac{5}{6}\right) \times \left(\dfrac{3}{4} \times \dfrac{3}{4}\right)$ **f** $\left(\dfrac{4}{5} \times \dfrac{4}{5}\right) \div \left(1\dfrac{1}{4} \times 1\dfrac{1}{4}\right)$

7 An investigation.

a Calculate $\dfrac{1}{1+1}$. This is the first term in a series.

To calculate $\dfrac{1}{1 + \dfrac{1}{1+1}}$ you need to start at the bottom;

so $\dfrac{1}{1 + \dfrac{1}{1+1}} = \dfrac{1}{1 + \dfrac{1}{2}} = \dfrac{1}{\dfrac{3}{2}} = 1 \div \dfrac{3}{2} = 1 \times \dfrac{2}{3} =$

b Calculate

i $\dfrac{1}{1 + \dfrac{1}{1 + \dfrac{1}{1+1}}}$ **ii** $\dfrac{1}{1 + \dfrac{1}{1 + \dfrac{1}{1 + \dfrac{1}{1+1}}}}$

iii the next two terms in this series.

c Look for the pattern in the answers and see if you can predict the next one. Test this out.

Negative numbers

You meet negative numbers in winter-time when the temperatures fall below freezing (0 °C). Negative numbers are those less than 0.

You also meet negative numbers on graphs and will have plotted co-ordinates with negative numbers many times.

You need to be able to do simple arithmetic with negative numbers, as in Examples 1 to 3 below.

1 The temperature at midnight was 2 °C but then it fell by 5 °C. What was the new temperature?

$$-10 \quad 0 \quad 10 \quad 20 \quad 30 \quad 40 \quad 50 \quad 60 \quad 70 \quad 80 \quad 90 \quad 100 \quad 110$$
$$°C$$

We have the problem of $2° - 5°$, which is equal to $-3°$.

2 The temperature drops from -4 °C by a further 5°. What does the temperature drop to?
We have the problem of $-4° - 5°$, which is -9 °C.

3 The temperature is -3 °C and rises by 7 °C. What is the new temperature?
We have the problem of $-3° + 7°$, which is 4 °C.

These examples illustrate the arithmetic that you need to be able to do. This can be summarised by three simple rules.

- To **add two negative numbers…**
  … add the numbers and make the answer negative.
  Example: $-3 + -2$ or $-3 - 2 = -5$

- To **add a negative number and a positive number…**
  … take the smaller number away from the bigger and give the answer the sign of the bigger number.
  Examples: $-8 + 3 = -(8 - 3) = -5$
  $\qquad\qquad\quad 2 + -6$ or $2 - 6 = -(6 - 2) = -4$

- To **subtract a negative number…**
  … you read the '$- -$' (minus a minus) as a plus (+).
  Example: $4 - -2 = 6$

You will find, after practice, that you will be able to do many of these problems simply by looking at the numbers and having a feel for the right sign and the difference.

Negative numbers on a calculator

You can enter a negative number into your calculator and check the result. You enter, say, -5 by pressing the keys **5** and **+/−**. (You may need to press **+/−** followed by **5**, depending on the type of calculator that you have.)

Try this on your calculator. You will see the calculator shows -5. Then try these two sums:

$-8 - 7 \rightarrow$ **8** **+/−** **−** **7** **=** -15

$6 - -3 \rightarrow$ **6** **−** **3** **+/−** **=** 9

EXERCISE 1K

1 Write down the answers to the following.

a −3 − 5 =	**b** −2 − 8 =	**c** −5 − 6 =	**d** 6 − 9 =
e 5 − 3 =	**f** 3 − 8 =	**g** −4 + 5 =	**h** −3 + 7 =
i −2 + 9 =	**j** −6 + −2 =	**k** −1 + −4 =	**l** −8 + − 3 =
m 5 − −6 =	**n** 3 − −3 =	**o** 6 − − 2 =	**p** 3 − −5 =
q −5 − −3 =	**r** −2 − −1 =	**s** −4 − 5 =	**t** 2 − 7 =
u −3 + 8 =	**v** −4 + −5 =	**w** 1 − −7 =	**x** −5 − −5 =

2 The temperature at midnight was 4 °C. Find the temperature if it **fell** by

a 1 °C **b** 4 °C **c** 7 °C **d** 9 °C **e** 15 °C

3 What is the **difference** in temperature between

a 4 °C and −6 °C **b** −2 °C and −9 °C **c** −3 °C and 6 °C

4 Rewrite the following list putting the numbers in order of size, lowest first.

1 −5 3 −6 −9 8 −0.5 1.8

5 Write down the answers to the following.

a 2 − 5 =	**b** 7 − 11 =	**c** 4 − 6 =	**d** 8 − 15 =
e 9 − 23 =	**f** −2 − 4 =	**g** −5 − 7 =	**h** −1 − 9 =
i −4 + 8 =	**j** −9 + 5 =	**k** 9 − −5 =	**l** 8 − −3 =
m −8 − −4 =	**n** −3 − −2 =	**o** −7 + −3 =	**p** −9 + 4 =
q −6 + 3 =	**r** −1 + 6 =	**s** −9 − −5 =	**t** 9 − 17 =

6 Find what you have to **add to** 5 to get

a 7 **b** 2 **c** 0 **d** −2 **e** −5 **f** −15

7 Find what you have to **subtract from** 4 to get

a 2 **b** 0 **c** 5 **d** 9 **e** 15 **f** −4

8 Find what you have to **add to** −5 to get

a 8 **b** −3 **c** 0 **d** −1 **e** 6 **f** −7

9 Find what you have to **subtract from** −3 to get

a 7 **b** 2 **c** −1 **d** −7 **e** −10 **f** 1

10 Write down 10 different addition sums that give the answer 1.

11 Write down 10 different subtraction sums that give the answer 1. (There must be one negative number in each sum.)

Multiplying and dividing with negative numbers

The rules for multiplying and dividing with negative numbers are very easy.

- When the signs of the numbers are the **same**, the answer is **positive**.
- When the signs of the numbers are **different**, the answer is **negative**.

Here are some examples.

$$2 \times 4 = 8 \qquad 12 \div -3 = -4$$
$$-2 \times -3 = 6 \qquad -12 \div -3 = 4$$

EXERCISE 1L

1 Write down the answers to the following.

a	-3×5	**b**	-2×7	**c**	-4×6	**d**	-2×-3	**e**	-7×-2
f	$-12 \div -6$	**g**	$-16 \div 8$	**h**	$24 \div -3$	**i**	$16 \div -4$	**j**	$-6 \div -2$
k	4×-6	**l**	5×-2	**m**	6×-3	**n**	-2×-8	**o**	-9×-4
p	$24 \div -6$	**q**	$12 \div -1$	**r**	$-36 \div 9$	**s**	$-14 \div -2$	**t**	$100 \div 4$
u	-2×-9	**v**	$32 \div -4$	**w**	5×-9	**x**	$-21 \div -7$	**y**	-5×8

2 Write down the answers to the following.

a	$-3 + -6$	**b**	-2×-8	**c**	$2 + -5$	**d**	8×-4	**e**	$-36 \div -2$
f	-3×-6	**g**	$-3 - -9$	**h**	$48 \div -12$	**i**	-5×-4	**j**	$7 - -9$
k	$-40 \div -5$	**l**	$-40 + -8$	**m**	$4 - -9$	**n**	$5 - 18$	**o**	$72 \div -9$
p	$-7 - -7$	**q**	$8 - -8$	**r**	6×-7	**s**	$-6 \div -1$	**t**	$-5 \div -5$
u	$-9 - 5$	**v**	$4 - -2$	**w**	$4 \div -1$	**x**	$-7 \div -1$	**y**	-4×0

3 What number do you multiply -3 by to get the following?

a	6	**b**	-90	**c**	-45	**d**	81	**e**	21

4 What number do you divide -36 by to get the following?

a	-9	**b**	4	**c**	12	**d**	-6	**e**	9

5 Evaluate the following.

a	$-6 + (4 - 7)$	**b**	$-3 - (-9 - -3)$	**c**	$8 + (2 - 9)$

6 Evaluate the following.

a	$4 \times (-8 \div -2)$	**b**	$-8 - (3 \times -2)$	**c**	$-1 \times (8 - -4)$

7 What do you get if you divide -48 by the following?

a	-2	**b**	-8	**c**	12	**d**	24

8 Write down six different multiplication sums that give the answer -12.

9 Write down six different division sums that give the answer -4.

10 Find the answers to the following.

a	-3×-7	**b**	$3 + -7$	**c**	$-4 \div -2$	**d**	$-7 - 9$	**e**	$-12 \div -6$
f	$-12 - -7$	**g**	5×-7	**h**	$-8 + -9$	**i**	$-4 + -8$	**j**	$-3 + 9$
k	-5×-9	**l**	$-16 \div 8$	**m**	$-8 - -8$	**n**	$6 \div -6$	**o**	$-4 + -3$
p	-9×4	**q**	$-36 \div -4$	**r**	-4×-8	**s**	$-1 - -1$	**t**	$2 - 67$

Rounding off

We use rounded-off information all the time. Look at these examples. All of these statements are using rounded-off information. Each actual figure is either above or below the approximation shown here. But if the rounding off is done correctly, we can find out what the maximum and the minimum figures really are. For example, if we know that the number of matches in the book is rounded off to the nearest 10,

- the smallest figure to be **rounded up** to 30 is 25, and

• the largest figure to be **rounded down** to 30 is 34 (because 35 would be rounded up to 40).

So there could actually be from 25 to 34 matches in the book.

What about the number of runners in the marathon? If we know that 23 000 people is the number to the nearest 1000,

• the smallest figure to be rounded up to 23 000 is 22 500, and

• the largest figure to be rounded down to 23 000 is 23 499.

So there could actually be from 22 500 to 23 499 people in the marathon.

EXERCISE 1M

1 Round off these numbers to the nearest 10.

a 24	**b** 57	**c** 78	**d** 54	**e** 96
f 112	**g** 645	**h** 35	**i** 998	**j** 1017

2 What is the least and the greatest number of people that can be found in these villages? The data are given to the nearest 100.

Elsecar	population	800
Hoyland	population	1200
Jump	population	600

3 What is the least and the greatest number of sweets that can be found in these jars?

a

80 sweets (to the nearest 10)

b

120 sweets (to the nearest 10)

c

190 sweets (to the nearest 10)

4 Round off these figures to the nearest 100.

a 240	**b** 570	**c** 780	**d** 504	**e** 967
f 112	**g** 645	**h** 350	**i** 998	**j** 1050

5 Round off these numbers to the nearest 1000.

a 2400	**b** 5700	**c** 7806	**d** 5040	**e** 9670
f 1120	**g** 6450	**h** 3500	**i** 9098	**j** 1500

6 What is the least and the greatest number of people that could have been at these football matches? (All data are given to the nearest 1000.)

a	Rotherham	12 000	**b**	Barnsley	17 000
c	Doncaster	5 000	**d**	Sheffield Wed.	28 000
e	Sheffield Utd	19 000	**f**	Chesterfield	10 000

7 Round off each of these numbers to

i the nearest 10   **ii** the nearest 100   **iii** the nearest 1000

a	3467	**b**	1027	**c**	8764	**d**	12 649	**e**	9999
f	1989	**g**	1209	**h**	998	**i**	12 991	**j**	347

8 Give these cooking times to the nearest 5 minutes.

a	24 min	**b**	57 min	**c**	18 min	**d**	54 min	**e**	9 min
f	12 min	**g**	44 min	**h**	32.5 min	**i**	3 min	**j**	50 s

9 The times in question **8 i** and **j** are from microwave meals. Why is it not a good idea to give these to the nearest 5 minutes?

10 Round off these times to the nearest half-hour.

a	43 minutes	**b**	1 hour 20 minutes	**c**	2 hours 10 minutes
d	100 minutes	**e**	5 hours 35 minutes	**f**	3 hours 50 minutes

11 Look at these signs posted in three villages.

Welcome to Castleton
Population 600
(to the nearest 100)

Welcome to Bakewell
Population 1200
(to the nearest 100)

Welcome to Heathersage
Population 800
(to the nearest 100)

Which of the following sentences could be true and which must be false?

a There are 789 people in Heathersage. **b** There are 1278 people in Bakewell.
c There are 550 people in Castleton.   **d** There are 843 people in Heathersage.
e There are 1205 people in Bakewell.   **f** There are 650 people in Castleton.

12 These were the crowds at nine Premier Division games on a weekend in September 1995.

Bolton v QPR	17 362
Chelsea v Arsenal	31 048
Coventry v Aston Villa	20 987
Leeds v Sheffield Wednesday	34 076
Middlesborough v Blackburn	29 462
Notts Forest v Man. City	25 620
Tottenham v Wimbledon	25 321
Everton v Newcastle	33 080
Manchester Utd v Liverpool	34 934

a Which match was the best attended?

b Which was the worst attended?

c Round off all the attendance figures to the nearest 1000.

d Round off all the attendance figures to the nearest 100.

e Add up all the crowds at all the games.

f Round off your answer to part **e** to the nearest 1000.

g Add up all your answers in part **c**.

h Are your answers to parts **f** and **g** the same?

Rounding off to decimal places

There are two other important ways of rounding off. One of them is rounding off to **decimal places**, the other is rounding off to **significant figures**.

When a number is written in decimal form, the digits on the right-hand side of the decimal point are called the decimal places. For example,

6.83 is written to two decimal places

79.4 is written to one decimal place

0.526 is written to three decimal places

To round off a decimal number to a particular number of places, take these steps.

- Count down the decimal places from the point and look at the first digit you are going to remove.
- When this digit is less than 5, then just remove the unwanted places.
- When this digit is 5 or more, then add 1 to the last decimal place digit.

Here are some examples.

5.852 will round off to 5.85 to two decimal places

7.156 will round off to 7.16 to two decimal places

0.274 will round off to 0.3 to one decimal place

15.3518 will round off to 15.4 to one decimal place

EXERCISE 1N

1 Round off each of the following numbers to one decimal place.

a 4.83	**b** 3.79	**c** 2.16	**d** 8.25	**e** 3.673
f 46.935	**g** 23.883	**h** 9.549	**i** 11.08	**j** 33.509
k 7.054	**l** 46.800	**m** 0.057	**n** 0.109	**o** 0.599
p 64.99	**q** 213.86	**r** 76.07	**s** 455.177	**t** 50.999

2 Round off each of the following numbers to two decimal places.

a 5.783	**b** 2.358	**c** 0.977	**d** 33.085	**e** 6.007
f 23.5652	**g** 91.7895	**h** 7.995	**i** 2.3096	**j** 23.9158
k 5.9999	**l** 1.0075	**m** 3.5137	**n** 96.508	**o** 0.009
p 0.065	**q** 7.8091	**r** 569.899	**s** 300.004	**t** 0.0009

3 Round off each of the following to the number of decimal places (dp) indicated.

a	4.568 (1 dp)	**b**	0.0832 (2 dp)	**c**	45.715 93 (3 dp)
d	94.8531 (2 dp)	**e**	602.099 (1 dp)	**f**	671.7629 (2 dp)
g	7.1124 (1 dp)	**h**	6.903 54 (3 dp)	**i**	13.7809 (2 dp)
j	0.075 11 (1 dp)	**k**	4.001 84 (3 dp)	**l**	59.983 (1 dp)
m	11.9854 (2 dp)	**n**	899.995 85 (4 dp)	**o**	0.0499 (1 dp)
p	0.009 87 (2 dp)	**q**	0.000 78 (1 dp)	**r**	78.3925 (3 dp)
s	199.9999 (2 dp)	**t**	5.0907 (1 dp)	**u**	0.0953 (2 dp)

Rounding off to significant figures

We often use significant figures when we want to approximate a number with quite a few digits in it.

Look at the following table which illustrates some numbers rounded off to one, two and three significant figures (sf).

One sf	8	50	200	90 000	0.000 07	0.003	0.4
Two sf	67	4.8	0.76	45 000	730	0.006 7	0.40
Three sf	312	65.9	40.3	0.0761	7.05	0.003 01	0.400

The steps taken to round off a number to a particular number of significant figures are very similar to those used for decimal places.

- From the left, count down the number of digits of the given significant figure. When the original number is less than 1, start counting from the first non-zero digit.
- Look at the next digit.
- When the next digit is less than 5, leave the digit on the left the same.
- When the next digit is equal to or greater than 5, add 1 to the digit on the left.
- Put in enough zeros to keep the number the right size.

For example, look at the following table which shows some numbers rounded off to one, two and three significant figures, respectively.

Number	Rounded to 1 sf	Rounded to 2 sf	Rounded to 3 sf
45 281	50 000	45 000	45 300
568.54	600	570	569
7.3782	7	7.5	7.38
8054	8000	8100	8050
99.8721	100	100	99.9
0.7002	0.7	0.70	0.700

EXERCISE 1P

1   Round off each of the following numbers to 1 significant figure.

    a 46 313   **b** 57 123   **c** 30 569   **d** 94 558   **e** 85 299

    f 54.26   **g** 85.18   **h** 27.09   **i** 96.432   **j** 167.77

    k 0.5388   **l** 0.2823   **m** 0.005 84   **n** 0.047 85   **o** 0.000 876

    p 9.9   **q** 89.5   **r** 90.78   **s** 199   **t** 999.99

2   What is the least and the greatest number of sweets that can be found in these jars?

a 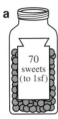   **b**    **c**

3   What is the least and the greatest number of people that can be found in these towns?

    Elsecar   population 800 (to 1 significant figure)

    Hoyland   population 1200 (to 2 significant figures)

    Barnsley   population 165 000 (to 3 significant figures)

4   What is the least and the greatest number of people that could have been at concerts at the following venues?

    Huddersfield   11 000 (to 2 significant figures)

    Leeds   27 500 (to 3 significant figures)

    Middlesborough 20 000 (to 1 significant figure)

5   Round off each of the following numbers to 2 significant figures.

    a 56 147   **b** 26 813   **c** 79 611   **d** 30 578   **e** 14 009

    f 5876   **g** 1065   **h** 847   **i** 109   **j** 638.7

    k 1.689   **l** 4.0854   **m** 2.658   **n** 8.0089   **o** 41.564

    p 0.8006   **q** 0.458   **r** 0.0658   **s** 0.9996   **t** 0.009 82

6   Round off each of the following to the number of significant figures (sf) indicated.

    a 57 402 (1 sf)   **b** 5288 (2 sf)   **c** 89.67 (3 sf)

    d 105.6 (2 sf)   **e** 8.69 (1 sf)   **f** 1.087 (2 sf)

    g 809.8 (3 sf)   **h** 4710 (1 sf)   **i** 66.51 (2 sf)

    j 0.9785 (1 sf)   **k** 8.663 (1 sf)   **l** 9.7454 (3 sf)

    m 12.65 (2 sf)   **n** 18.31 (1 sf)   **o** 869.89 (3 sf)

    p 26.99 (1 sf)   **q** 0.073 61 (2 sf)   **r** 0.00999 (2 sf)

    s 0.0905 (1 sf)   **t** 0.070 87 (3 sf)   **u** 9.813 (2 sf)

Approximation of calculations

How do we approximate the value of a calculation? What do we actually do when we try to approximate an answer to a problem?

For example, what is the approximate answer to 35.1×6.58?

To approximate the answer in this and many other similar cases, we simply round off each number to 1 significant figure, then work out the sum. So in this case, the approximation is

$$35.1 \times 6.58 \approx 40 \times 7 = 280$$

Sometimes, especially when dividing, we round off a number to something more useful at 2 sf instead of at 1 sf. For example,

$$57.3 \div 6.87$$

Since 6.87 rounds off to 7, then round off 57.3 to 56 because 7 divides exactly into 56. Hence,

$$57.3 \div 6.87 \approx 56 \div 7 = 8$$

A quick approximation is always a great help in any calculation since it often stops your writing down a silly answer.

EXERCISE 1Q

1 Find approximate answers to the following sums.

a 5435×7.31	**b** 5280×3.211	**c** $63.24 \times 3.514 \times 4.2$
d 3508×2.79	**e** $72.1 \times 3.225 \times 5.23$	**f** $470 \times 7.85 \times 0.99$
g $354 \div 79.8$	**h** $36.8 \div 1.876$	**i** $5974 \div 5.29$
j $208 \div 3.78$	**k** $1409 \div 64.28$	**l** $53.94 \div 8.502$
m $14.74 \div 2.65$	**n** $28.673 \div 7.24$	**o** $406.9 \div 23.78$
p $0.584 \div 0.0216$		

(Check your answers on a calculator to see how close you were.)

2 By rounding off, find an approximate answer to these sums.

a $\dfrac{573 + 783}{107}$ **b** $\dfrac{783 - 572}{24}$ **c** $\dfrac{352 + 657}{999}$ **d** $\dfrac{1123 - 689}{354}$

e $\dfrac{589 + 773}{658 - 351}$ **f** $\dfrac{793 - 569}{998 - 667}$ **g** $\dfrac{354 + 656}{997 - 656}$ **h** $\dfrac{1124 - 661}{355 + 570}$

i $\dfrac{28.3 + 19.5}{87.4}$ **j** $\dfrac{78.3 - 22.6}{2.69}$ **k** $\dfrac{3.52 + 7.95}{9.9}$ **l** $\dfrac{11.78 + 67.8}{39.4}$

m $\dfrac{84.7 + 12.6}{65.7 - 11.2}$ **n** $\dfrac{32.8 + 71.4}{9.92 + 11.7}$ **o** $\dfrac{14.9 + 27.9}{62.3 - 15.3}$ **p** $\dfrac{12.7 + 34.9}{78.2 - 29.3}$

3 Find the approximate monthly pay of the following people whose annual salary is
    a Paul £35 200   **b** Michael £25 600   **c** Jennifer £18 125
    d Ross £8420

4 Find the approximate annual pay of the following people who earn:
    a Kevin £270 a week   **b** Malcolm £1528 a month
    c David £347 a week

5 A litre of paint will cover an area of about 8.7 m². Approximately how many litre cans will I need to buy to paint a room with a total surface area of 73 m²?

6 A farmer bought 2713 kg of seed at a cost of £7.34 per kg. Find the approximate total cost of this seed.

7 A greengrocer sells a box of 450 oranges for £37. Approximately how much did each orange sell for?

8 Approximately how many 19p stamps can be bought for £5?

9 If a fuel is £3.15 per kilogram, about how much can I buy for £86?

10 It took me 6 hours and 40 minutes to drive from Sheffield to Bude, a distance of 295 miles. My car uses petrol at the rate of about 32 miles per gallon. The petrol cost £3.51 per gallon.
    a Approximately how many miles did I do each hour?
    b Approximately how many gallons of petrol did I use in going from Sheffield to Bude?
    c What was the approximate cost of all the petrol I used in the journey to Bude and back again?

11 Mr Bradshaw wanted to find out how many bricks were in a chimney he was about to knock down. He counted 187 bricks in one row all the way round the chimney. He counted 53 rows of bricks up the chimney. Each brick weighed about 3.2 kg.
    a Approximately how many bricks were in the chimney?
    b Approximately how much did all the bricks weigh?

12 Kirsty arranges for magazines to be put into envelopes. She sorts out 178 magazines between 10.00 am and 1.00 pm. Approximately how many magazines will she be able to sort in a week in which she works for 17 hours?

13 An athlete trains often. Brian's daily training routine is to run 3.75 km every day. Approximately how far does he run in
    a a week   **b** a month   **c** a year?

14 A box full of magazines weighs 8 kg. One magazine weighs about 15 g. Approximately how many magazines are in the box?

15 An apple weighs about 280 grams.
    a What is the approximate weight of a bag containing a dozen apples?
    b Approximately how many apples will there be in a sack weighing 50 kg?

16 When typing, John manages 85 words a minute. How long approximately will it take him to type a 2000 word essay?

Sensible rounding

You will be required to round off answers to problems to a suitable degree of accuracy without being told specifically what that is.

Generally, you can use common sense. For example, you would not give the length of a pencil as 14.574 cm; you would round off to something like 14.6 cm. If you were asked how many tins you need to buy to do a particular job, then you would give a whole-number answer and not something such as 5.91 tins.

It is hard to make rules about this, as there is much disagreement even among the 'experts' as to how you ought to do it. But, generally, when you are in any doubt as to how many significant figures to use for the final answer to a problem, round off to no more than one extra significant figure to the number used in the original data. (This particular type of rounding is used throughout the book.)

EXERCISE 1R

1 Round off each of the following figures to a suitable degree of accuracy.
  a I am 1.7359 metres tall.
  b It took me 5 minutes 44.83 seconds to mend the television.
  c My kitten weighs 237.97 grams.
  d The correct temperature at which to drink Earl Grey tea is 82.739 °C.
  e There were 34 827 people at the Test Match yesterday.
  f In my collection I have 615 theatre programmes.
  g The distance from Wath to Sheffield is 15.528 miles.
  h My telephone number is 284519.
  i The area of the floor is 13.673 m².

2 Rewrite the following article, rounding off all the numbers to a suitable degree of accuracy if they need to be.
  It was a hot day, the temperature was 81.699 °F and still rising. I had now walked 5.3289 km in just over 113.98 minutes. But I didn't care since I knew that the 43 275 people watching the race were cheering me on. I won by clipping 6.289 seconds off the record time. This was the 67th time it had happened since records first began in 1788. Well, next year I will only have 15 practice walks beforehand as I strive to beat the record by at least another 4.673 seconds.

3 About how many test-tubes each holding 24 cm³ of water can be filled from a 1 litre flask?

4 If I walk at an average speed of 70 metres per minute, approximately how long will it take me to walk a distance of 3 km?

5 Keith earns £27 500 a year. About how much does he earn in
    a   1 month   **b**   1 week   **c**   1 day?

6 About how many stamps at 21p each can I buy for £12?

7 I travelled a distance of 450 miles in 6.4 hours. What was my approximate average speed?

8 You need 1 teaspoon of cocoa to make a chocolate drink. Each teaspoon of cocoa is about 2.75 cm^3. Approximately how many chocolate drinks could you make from a tin that had 200 cm^3 of cocoa in it?

9 At Manchester United, it takes 160 minutes for 43 500 fans to get into the ground. On average, about how many fans are let into the ground every minute?

10 A 5p coin weighs 4.2 grams. Approximately how much will one million pounds worth of 5p pieces weigh?

Possible coursework tasks

A number trick

Pick any 3-digit number, for example 741.

Repeat it to make a 6-digit number: 741 741.

Divide this 6-digit number by 7: 741 741 ÷ 7 = 105 963

Divide the answer by 11: 105 963 ÷ 11 = 9633

Divide again by 13: 9633 ÷ 13 = ...

What do you notice?

Will this always happen?

Why does this happen?

Invent a number trick of your own.

Elizabethan multiplication

Look at how the Elizabethans worked out 412 × 237.

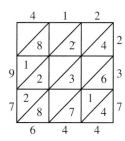

Investigate and see if you can find out

- how it works

- why it works

- how to work it yourself.

➤ *Russian multiplication*

Look at this popular Russian way to do long multiplication.

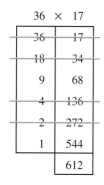

36 × 17

36	17
18	34
9	68
4	136
2	272
1	544
	612

27 × 19

27	19
13	38
6	76
3	152
1	304
	513

Investigate and see if you can find out

- how it works

- why it works

- how to work it yourself.

Squares on a chessboard

There are 5 squares in this diagram. How many squares are there on a chessboard?

A full digit sum

This sum uses all ten digits from 0 to 9.

$$
\begin{array}{r}
423 \\
675 \\
\hline
1098
\end{array}
$$

Can you make up at least ten different sums that also use all ten digits?

Examination questions: coursework type

1 Two brothers, Michael and Paul, usually save £1 each per week. Paul gets fed up with that and suggests changing to save

1p for the first week

2p the week after

4p the week after

8p the week after

so that each week he doubles what he saved the previous week. Michael continues to save £1 each week. Investigate

i   the amounts saved by each over various times and comment

ii what might happen with different patterns of saving.

2 A long street of terraced houses has been changed into flats. Each house has three flats – basement, middle and top. The flats are numbered as shown in the diagram. (Only the first five are given.)

a   Investigate any number patterns you might find when completing the numbering of the flats in the whole street.

b   Miss Ling visited her friend who lived at flat 94. She thought it was a middle flat. Is she correct? Explain your answer.

Examination questions

1 A shopkeeper wishes to store 500 marbles into boxes. Each box can store 36 marbles. How many boxes can he fill and how many marbles will be left over?

WJEC, Question 1, Specimen Paper 1, 1998

2 Write down two different fractions that lie between $\frac{1}{4}$ and $\frac{1}{2}$.

EDEXCEL, Question 2, Intermediate Paper 3, June 2000

3 **a** Estimate the values of:
   i 25.1×19.8
   ii $119.6 \div 14.9$

b Jonathan uses his calculator to work out the value 42.2×0.027
   The answer he gets is 11.394
   Use approximation to show that his answer is wrong.

NEAB, Question 7, Intermediate Paper 1, June 2000

4 An orange drink is made by mixing water with concentrated orange juice. $\frac{3}{4}$ of the orange drink is water. How many litres of water will be in 12 litres of orange drink?

MEG, Question 1, Specimen Paper 2, 1998

5 The temperatures of three food cabinets in a shop are 2 °C, –5 °C and –1 °C.
   a Write down these temperatures, in order, with the coldest first.
   b What is the difference in temperature between the coldest and the hottest cabinet?

WJEC, Question 5, Paper B1, June 1994

6 Calculate an estimate of $\sqrt{(5.84^2 - 3.19^2)}$.

OCR, Question 11, Intermediate Paper 3, June 2000

7 Write as a single fraction
   a $\left(\frac{1}{2} + \frac{1}{3}\right) \times \frac{1}{4}$
   b $\frac{1}{2} - \left(\frac{1}{3} \times \frac{1}{4}\right)$
   c $\frac{1}{2} \times \frac{1}{3} \div \frac{1}{4}$

8 At 1 pm the temperature in Birmingham was 5 °C. According to the weather forecast, the temperature at midnight was expected to be –4 °C.
   a By how many degrees was the temperature expected to fall?
   b In fact the temperature at midnight was 2 °C lower than expected. What was the temperature that night?

MEG, Question 1, Specimen Paper 3, 1998

9 The size of the crowd at a football match is given as 34 700 to the nearest hundred.

    a What is the lowest number that the crowd could be?

    b What is the largest number that the crowd could be?

NEAB, Question 2, Specimen Paper 1I, 1998

Summary

How well do you grade yourself?

To gain a grade **E**, you need to be able correctly to perform long multiplication and division without a calculator, showing clearly your method. You also need to be able to add and subtract negative numbers.

To gain a grade **D**, you need to be able to evaluate fractions of amounts, round off numbers to a specific number of decimal places or significant figures, and make estimates of problems by suitable rounding off.

To gain a grade **C**, you need to be able to round off your answers to a suitable degree of accuracy without being asked. You also need to be able to multiply and divide by negative numbers.

What you should know after you have worked through Chapter 1

- How to calculate multiplication and division with and without a calculator.
- How to find a fraction of an amount. For example,
  $\frac{2}{3}$ of X
  You find one-third first, then multiply by 2. That is,
  $(X \div 3) \times 2$
- How to add, subtract, multiply and divide with fractions.
- That > means 'is greater than', and < means 'is less than'.
- How to round off to the nearest unit, ten, hundred, etc.
- What is meant by significant figures and decimal places.
- How to operate the four rules of arithmetic with negative numbers.

2 Percentage

This chapter is going to ...

remind you of the principles of percentage and introduce you to the types of everyday problem you may meet which involve percentages. It will also show you how to calculate percentages using a calculator.

What you should already know

✔ 'Per cent' means 'out of 100'. So a statement such as 32% means 32 out of 100.

✔ To find $P\%$ of an amount T, you calculate
$(P \times T) \div 100$
For example, 4% of 30 kg is
$(4 \times 30) \div 100 = 1.2$ kg

✔ Any percentage can be represented as a decimal by dividing by 100. For example,
$65\% = 65 \div 100 = 0.65$

✔ The common fractions expressed as percentages:
$\frac{1}{2} = 50\%$ $\frac{1}{4} = 25\%$ $\frac{3}{4} = 75\%$
$\frac{1}{10} = 10\%$ $\frac{1}{5} = 20\%$ $\frac{1}{3} = 33\frac{1}{3}\%$

All these techniques are revised at various places in this chapter.

EXERCISE 2A

1   Write each percentage as a fraction in its lowest terms.

a	8%	**b**	50%	**c**	20%	**d**	5%	**e**	10%
f	75%	**g**	25%	**h**	85%	**i**	60%	**j**	40%
k	35%	**l**	90%	**m**	4%	**n**	30%	**o**	100%

2   Write each percentage as a decimal.

a	27%	**b**	85%	**c**	13%	**d**	6%	**e**	8%
f	2%	**g**	34.6%	**h**	12.5%	**i**	98.4%	**j**	200%
k	125%	**l**	175%	**m**	34%	**n**	26.8%	**o**	112%

3   Of the 300 members of a social club 50% are male. How many members are female?

4 Gillian came home and told her dad that she got 100% of her spellings correct. In total there were 25 spellings to learn. How many spellings did Gillian get wrong?

5 Every year a school library likes to replace 1% of its books. One year the library had 1879 books. How many should it replace?

6 **a** If 23% of pupils go home for lunch, how many do not go home for lunch?
   b If 61% of the population take part in the National Lottery, how many do not take part?
   c If 37% of the Church are males, how many of the Church are females?

7 28% of my time is spent sleeping, 45% is spent working. How much time is left to spend doing something else?

8 24.7% of the population is aged 16 or below. 13.8% of the population is aged 65 or over. How much of the population is aged between 16 and 65?

9 Approximately what percentage of each bottle is filled with water?

a   **b**   **c**

10 Helen made a cake for James. The amount of cake left each day is shown in the diagram.
   a What percentage of the original cake is left each day?
   b What percentage of the original cake has been eaten each day?

Monday   Tuesday   Wednesday   Thursday   Friday

Calculating a percentage of a quantity

To calculate a percentage of a quantity, we multiply the quantity by the percentage. That is, *P*% of an amount *T* is calculated as

$$\frac{P}{100} \times T \quad \text{or} \quad (P \times T) \div 100$$

For example, calculate 12% of 54 kg.

$(12 \times 54) \div 100 = 6.48 \text{ kg}$

Use of calculators and percentage

All calculators have a percentage key %. The problem is that, for different types of calculator, there are different ways to use the percentage key.

You need to investigate how to use the percentage key on your calculator. For example, to calculate 15% of 120

you could try   **1** **5** **%** **×** **1** **2** **0** **=**

or   **1** **2** **0** **×** **1** **5** **%** **=**

Maybe both of these ways work for your calculator, or only one of them. The correct answer is 18.

On some calculators you will need to press the **=** key, while on others you won't.

It is important for you to be familiar with your calculator and to use it whenever it is sensible to do so. With percentages, it is often sensible to use a calculator.

EXERCISE 2B

1 Calculate the following.
a	15% of £300	**b**	6% of £105	**c**	23% of 560 kg
d	45% of 2.5 kg	**e**	12% of 9 hours	**f**	21% of 180 cm
g	4% of £3	**h**	35% of 8.4 m	**i**	95% of £8
j	11% of 308 minutes				

2 15% of the pupils in a school bring sandwiches with them. If there are 640 pupils in the school, how many bring sandwiches?

3 An estate agent charges 2% commission on every house he sells. How much commission will he earn on a house that he sells for £60 250?

4 A department store had 260 employees. During one week of a flu epidemic the shop had 15% of its employees absent. How many employees managed to get to work?

5 It is thought that about 20% of fans at a rugby match are female. For a match at Twickenham there were 42 600 fans. How many of these do you think would be female?

6 At St Pancras Railway Station one week 240 trains arrived. 5% of these trains arrived early, 13% of them arrived late. How many arrived on time?

7 For the FA Cup Final at Wembley each year the 75 000 tickets are split up as follows.
   Each of the teams playing gets 30% of the tickets.
   The referees' association gets 1% of the tickets.
   The other 90 teams get 10% of the tickets between them.
   The FA associates get 20% of the tickets between them.
   The rest are for the special celebrities.
   How many tickets go to each set of people?

8 For a Y10 parents evening, a school decides that if the teachers see the parents of 60% or more of the students, the turnout of parents is *good*. If the turnout is 40% or less, it is *poor*. Otherwise, the turnout is *only satisfactory*.

One year there are 120 Y10 students. How many of these need to have parents attending the parents evening for the turnout to be

  a good   **b** poor   **c** only satisfactory?

9 A school had 780 pupils, and the attendance record in the week before Christmas was

Monday 96% Tuesday 97% Wednesday 99% Thursday 94% Friday 89%

How many pupils were present each day?

10 Soft solder consists of 60% lead, 35% tin and 5% bismuth (by weight). How much of each metal is in 250 grams of solder?

11 Calculate the following.
  a 12.5% of £26   **b** 6.5% of 34 kg   **c** 26.8% of £2100
  d 7.75% of £84   **e** 16.2% of 265 m   **f** 0.8% of £3000

12 Air consists of 80% nitrogen and 20% oxygen (by volume). A man's lungs have a capacity of 600 cm^3. How much of each gas will he have in his lungs when he has just taken a deep breath?

13 A factory estimates that 1.5% of all the garments they produce will have a fault in them. One week they make 850 garments. How many are likely to have a fault?

14 An insurance firm sells house insurance and the premiums are usually at a cost of 0.3% of the value of the house. What will be the annual premium for a house valued at £90 000?

Percentage increase and decrease

Increase

There are three methods for increasing by a percentage.

Method 1

Find the increase and add it to the original amount. For example, to increase £6 by 5%
  find 5% of £6: $(5 \times 6) \div 100 = £0.30$
  add the £0.30 to the original amount: $£6 + £0.30 = £6.30$

Method 2

Change the percentage to a decimal, add 1, then multiply by the amount to be increased. For example, to increase £6 by 5%
  change 5% to a decimal, add 1, then multiply by £6: $1.05 \times 6 = £6.30$

Method 3

Using the calculator % key.

As you saw earlier, each type of calculator can operate percentage quite differently. So you have to find out how your calculator deals with percentage increase (if it does at all – since some don't).

For example, to increase £6 by 5%

you could try 6 + 5 % =

Check that you get the answer £6.30.

EXERCISE 2C

1 Increase each of the following by the given amount. (Use any method you like.)
  a £60 by 4%   **b** 12 kg by 8%   **c** 450 g by 5%
  d 545 m by 10%   **e** £34 by 12%   **f** £75 by 20%
  g 340 kg by 15%   **h** 670 cm by 23%   **i** 130 g by 95%
  j £82 by 75%

2 Kevin, who was on a salary of £27 500, was given a pay rise of 7%. What was his new salary?

3 In 1990 the population of Melchester was 1 565 000. By 1995 that had increased by 8%. What was the population of Melchester in 1995?

4 A small firm made the same pay increase for all its employees: 5%.
  a Calculate the new pay of each employee listed below. Each of their salaries before the increase is given.
  Bob, caretaker, £16 500   Jean, superviser, £19 500
  Anne, tea lady, £17 300   Brian, manager, £25 300
  b Is the actual pay increase the same for each worker?

5 A bank pays 7% interest on the money that each saver keeps in the bank for a year. Allison keeps £385 in this bank for a year. How much will she have in the bank after the year?

6 In 1980 the number of cars on the roads of Sheffield was about 4200. Since then it has increased by 80%. Approximately how many cars are on the roads of Sheffield now?

7 An advertisement for a breakfast cereal states that a special offer packet contains 15% more cereal for the same price than a normal 500 g packet. How much breakfast cereal is in a special offer packet?

8 A headteacher was proud to point out that, since he had arrived at the school, its population then of 680 students had increased by 35%. How many students are now in the school?

9 At a school disco there are always about 20% more girls than boys. If at one disco there were 50 boys, how many girls were there?

10 VAT is a tax that the Government adds to the price of most goods and services. At the moment, it is 17.5% (except for fuel at 8%).
Calculate the price of the following goods in a shop after VAT of 17.5% has been added.

Goods	Pre-VAT price
TV set	£245
Microwave oven	£72
Desk	£115
Rug	£19.50

11 Since Newcastle United were promoted to the Premier Division, the crowds at their ground have increased by 65%. If the average-sized crowd before Newcastle were promoted was 21 800, what is the average-sized crowd now they are in the Premier Division?

Decrease

There are three methods for decreasing by a percentage.

Method 1

Find the decrease and take it away from the original amount. For example, to decrease £8 by 4%

find 4% of £8: $(4 \times 8) \div 100 = £0.32$

take the £0.32 away from the original amount: $£8 - £0.32 = £7.68$

Method 2

Change the percentage to a decimal, take it away from 1, then multiply by the amount to be decreased. For example, to decrease by £8 by 4%

change 4% to a decimal and take from 1: $1 - 0.04 = 0.96$

multiply 0.96 by the original amount: $0.96 \times £8 = £7.68$

Method 3

Using the calculator **%** key.

You tried the percentage increase with your calculator, now try percentage decrease by, perhaps, using subtraction instead of addition. For example, to decrease £8 by 5%

you could try **8** **−** **5** **%** **=**

Check that you get the answer £7.60.

EXERCISE 2D

1 Decrease each of the following by the given amount. (Use any method you like.)

a £10 by 6%   **b** 25 kg by 8%   **c** 236 g by 10%

d 350 m by 3%   **e** £5 by 2%   **f** 45 m by 12%

g 860 m by 15%   **h** 96 g by 13%   **i** 480 cm by 25%

j 180 minutes by 35%

2 A car valued at £6 500 last year is now worth 15% less. What is its value now?

3 A new P-plan diet guarantees that you will lose 12% of your weight in the first month. How much did the following people weigh after 1 month on the diet?

a Gillian, who started at 60 kg

b Peter, who started at 75 kg

c Margaret, who started at 52 kg

4 A motor insurance firm offers no-claims discounts off the given premium, as follows:

1 year no claim	15% discount
2 years no claim	25% discount
3 years no claim	45% discount
4 years no claim	60% discount

Mr Speed and his family are all offered motor insurance from this firm:

Mr Speed, who has 4 years no-claim discount, is quoted a premium of £140.

Mrs Speed, who has 1 year no-claim discount, is quoted a premium of £350.

James, who has 3 years no-claim discount, is quoted a premium of £230.

John, who has 2 years no-claim discount, is quoted a premium of £450.

Calculate the actual amount each member of the family has to pay for the motor insurance.

 5 A large factory employed 640 people. Then management decided to streamline its workforce and lose 30% of the workers. How big is the workforce now?

6 On the last day of the Christmas term, a school expects to have an absence rate of about 6%. If the school population is 748 pupils, how many pupils will the school expect to see on the last day of the Christmas term?

7 Since the start of the National Lottery a particular charity called Young Ones said they now have a decrease of 45% in the money raised by scratch cards. If before the Lottery the charity had an annual income of £34 500 from their scratch cards, how much do they collect now?

 8 Most speedometers in cars have an error of about 5% from the true reading. When my speedometer says I am driving at 70 mph,

a what is the slowest speed I could be doing?

b what is the fastest speed I could be doing?

9 You are a member of a club which allows you to claim a 12% discount on marked price in shops. What will you pay in total for the following goods.

Sweatshirt £19

Track suit £26

10 I read an advertisement in my local newspaper last week which stated: 'By lagging your roof and hot water system you will use 18% less fuel.' Since I was using an average of 640 units of gas a year, I thought I would lag my roof and my hot water system. How much gas would I expect to use now?

Compound interest

Compound interest is where the interest due at the end of a year on, for example, an amount of money in a savings account, is added to that amount and the new total amount then earns further interest at the same rate in the following year. This pattern is repeated year after year while the money is in the account. Therefore, the original amount grows bigger by the year, as does the actual amount of interest. In compound interest, the interest rate is always set at a fixed percentage for the whole period.

Example

A bank pays 6% compound interest per year on all amounts in a savings account for that year. What is the final amount that Elizabeth will have in her account if she has kept £400 in her bank for 3 years?

The amount in the bank increases by 6% each year, so

after 1 year she will have £400 × 1.06 = £424

after 2 years she will have 424 × 1.06 = £449.44

after 3 years she will have £449.44 × 1.06 = £476.41 (rounded)

As you can see, the actual increase gets bigger and bigger.

The idea of compound interest does not only concern money. It can be about, for example, the growth in populations, increases in salaries and increases in body weight or height. Also the idea can involve reduction by a fixed percentage each time: for example, car depreciation, pollution losses, population losses and even water losses. Work through the next exercise and you will see the extent to which compound interest ideas are used.

EXERCISE 2E

1 A baby octopus increases its body weight by 5% each day for the first month of its life. In a safe ocean zoo, a baby octopus was born weighing 10 kg.

a What is its weight after

i 1 day **ii** 2 days **iii** 4 days **iv** 1 week?

b After how many days will the octopus first weigh over 15 kg?

2 A certain type of conifer hedging increases in height by 17% each year for the first 20 years. When I bought some of this hedging, it was all about 50 cm tall. How long will it take to grow 3 m tall?

3 The manager of a small family business offered his staff an annual pay increase of 4% every year they stayed with the firm.

    a Gareth started work at the business on a salary of £8200. What salary will he be on after 4 years?

    b Julie started work at the business on a salary of £9350. How many years will it be until she is earning a salary of over £20 000?

4 Scientists have been studying the shores of Scotland and estimate that due to pollution the seal population of those shores will decline at the rate of 15% each year. In 2000 they counted around 3000 seals on those shores.

    a If nothing is done about pollution, how many seals will they expect to be there in

        i 2001   **ii** 2002   **iii** 2005?

    b How long will it take for the seal population to be less than 1000?

5 I am told that if I buy a new car its value will depreciate at the rate of 20% each year. I buy a car in 2000 priced at £8500. How much will the car be valued at in

    a 2001   **b** 2004   **c** 2009?

6 At the peak of the drought during the summer of 1995, a reservoir in Derbyshire was losing water at the rate of 8% each day as the water-saving measures were being taken. On 1 August this reservoir held 2.1 million litres of water.

    a At this rate of losing water, how much would have been in the reservoir on the following days?

        i 2 August   **ii** 4 August   **iii** 8 August

    b The danger point is when the water drops below 1 million litres. When would this have been if things had continued as they were?

7 Talvin put a gift of £400 into a special savings account that offered him 9% compound interest if he promised to keep the money in for at least 2 years. How much was in this account after

    a 2 years   **b** 4 years   **c** 6 years?

8 The population of a small country, Yebon, was only 46 000 in 1990, but it steadily increased by about 13% each year during the 1990s.

    a Calculate the population in

        i 1991   **ii** 1995   **iii** 1999

    b If the country keeps increasing at this rate, when will its population be half a million?

9 How long will it take to accumulate one million pounds in the following situations?

    a An investment of £100 000 at a rate of 12% compound interest.

    b An investment of £50 000 at a rate of 16% compound interest.

10 A tree increases in height by 18% per year. When it is 1 year old, it is 8 cm tall. How long will it take the tree to grow to 10 m?

Expressing one quantity as a percentage of another

We express one quantity as a percentage of another by setting up the first quantity as a fraction of the second, and then converting that fraction to a percentage by simply multiplying it by 100.

For example, to express £5 as a percentage of £40

set up the fraction $\frac{5}{40}$ and multiply by 100

which becomes $(5 \times 100) \div 40 = 12.5\%$

We can use the method to calculate gain or loss in a financial transaction. For example, Bert buys a car for £1500 and sells it at £1800. What is his percentage gain?

The gain is £300, so the percentage gain is

$$\frac{300}{1500} \times 100 = 20\%$$

Notice how the percentage gain was found by

$$\frac{\text{Difference}}{\text{Original}} \times 100$$

Using your calculator

Here is another place you can use the % key on your calculator. For example, to express 5 as a percentage of 40

try 5 ÷ 4 0 % =

You should get the answer 12.5%. You may not have to press the = key, depending on how your calculator works this out.

EXERCISE 2F

1   Express the following as percentages. (Give suitably rounded-off figures where necessary.)

a	£5 of £20	**b**	£4 of £6.60	**c**	241 kg of 520 kg
d	3 hours of 1 day	**e**	25 minutes of 1 hour	**f**	12 m of 20 m
g	125 g of 600 g	**h**	12 minutes of 2 hours	**i**	1 week of a year
j	1 month of 1 year	**k**	25 cm of 55 cm	**l**	105 g of 1 kg
m	5 oz of 16 oz	**n**	2.4 litres of 6 litres	**o**	8 days of 1 year
p	25p of £3	**q**	18p of £2.50	**r**	40 seconds of 1 day
s	8 hours of 1 year	**t**	5 mm of 4 cm		

2 Find, to 1 decimal place, the percentage profit on the following.

	Item	Retail price (selling price)	Wholesale price (price the shop paid)
a	CD player	£89	£60
b	TV set	£345	£210
c	Computer	£829	£750
d	Video player	£199.99	£110
e	Microwave oven	£98.50	£78

3 John came home from school one day with his end-of-year test results. Change each result of John's results to a percentage.

Maths	56 out of 75
English	46 out of 60
Science	78 out of 120
French	43 out of 80
Geography	76 out of 90
History	34 out of 40

4 There were 3 pupils absent from a class of 27. What percentage were absent?

5 In 1995 the Melchester County Council raised £14 870 000 in council tax. In 1996 it raised £15 597 000 in council tax. What was the percentage increase?

6 In Greece in 1893, there were 5 563 100 acres of agricultural land. Of this

olives occupied	432 000 acres
currants occupied	168 000 acres
figs occupied	52 000 acres

a What percentage of the agricultural land was occupied by each commodity?

In Greece in 1993, there were 3 654 000 acres of agricultural land. Of this

olives occupied	237 000 acres
currants occupied	92 000 acres
figs occupied	51 000 acres

b What percentage of the agricultural land was occupied by each commodity in 1993?

c What changes are there in the percentage of the agricultural land occupied by each commodity?

7 Martin had an annual salary of £22 600 in 1999, which was increased to £23 100 in 2000. What percentage increase does this represent?

8 During the wet year of 1981, it rained in Manchester on 123 days of the year. What percentage of days were wet?

9 When Blackburn Rovers won the championship in 1995, they lost only 4 of their 42 league games. What percentage of games did they not lose?

10 In the year 1900 Britain's imports were as follows:

British Commonwealth	£109 530 635
USA	£138 789 261
France	£53 618 656
Other countries	£221 136 611

What percentage of the total imports came from each source?

Finding the original quantity (reverse percentage)

There are situations when we know a certain percentage and wish to get back to the original amount. For example, the 70 men who went on strike represented only 20% of the workforce. How large was the workforce?

Since 20% represents 70 people, then

1% will represent 70 ÷ 20 people [Don't work it out.]

so 100% will represent (70 ÷ 20) × 100 = 350

Hence the workforce is 350.

Using your calculator

You need to check this with your own calculator and see how it works. For example, if 42 represents 15% of an original amount, then

the original amount will be   42 ÷ 15 × 100 = 280

or on the calculator try   **4** **2** **÷** **1** **5** **%** **=**

(Again, the **=** key may not be needed.)

EXERCISE 2G

1 Find what 100% represents when

a	30% represents 63 kg	**b**	20% represents £45
c	40% represents 320 g	**d**	25% represents 3 hours
e	5% represents £23	**f**	14% represents 35 m
g	45% represents 27 cm	**h**	4% represents £123
i	2.5% represents £5	**j**	12.5% represents 60 g
k	8.5% represents £34	**l**	12.5% represents 115 m

2 On a gruelling army training session, only 28 youngsters survived the whole day. This represented 35% of the original group. How large was the original group?

3 VAT is a government tax added to goods and services. With VAT at 17.5%, what is the pre-VAT price of the following priced goods?

T shirt	£9.87	Tights	£1.41
Shorts	£6.11	Sweater	£12.62
Trainers	£29.14	Boots	£38.07

4 Ruth spends £8 each week on her social activities. This is 40% of her weekly income. How much is Ruth's weekly income?

5 Howard spends £200 a month on food. This represents 24% of his monthly take-home pay. How much is his monthly take-home pay?

6 Tina's weekly pay is increased by 5% to £81.90. What was Tina's pay before the increase?

7 Dave sold his car for £2940, making a profit of 20% on the price he paid for it. How much did Dave pay for the car?

8 A particular rock is made up by weight of: 18% sandstone, 52% shale and 30% limestone. A sample of this rock was found to contain 375 grams of limestone. How heavy was the sample?

9 If 38% of plastic bottles in a production line are blue and the remaining 7750 plastic bottles are brown, how many plastic bottles are blue?

10 I received £3.85 back from the tax office, which represented the 17.5% VAT on a piece of equipment. How much did I pay for this equipment in the first place?

11 A man's salary was increased by 5% in one year and reduced by 5% in the next year. Is his final salary greater or less than the original one and by how many per cent?

Possible coursework tasks

Double your money

If you put £100 in a building society deposit account that pays compound interest at 8% per annum and leave it there for a number of years, how long will it take to double your money?

Snails in the well

A snail tries to climb out of a well 10 m deep. It climbs 60 cm in 1 hour, but for every 1 m that it climbs it falls back 5% of the total height climbed. Approximately how long will it take for the snail to climb out of the well?

Which percentage is bigger?

a If I make something 10% bigger, then make it 10% smaller, what happens to the original? Is it bigger, smaller or what?

b If I make something 10% smaller, then make it 10% bigger, is it the same as in part **a**? If not, why not?

Examination questions

1 In a General Election, a candidate loses his deposit if he does not get at least 5% of the votes cast. After the votes were counted in the General Election in Bradworth,

6540 people voted for Mary Ashworth

5235 people voted for John Barnard

425 people voted for Bill Crowther

Calculate the percentage of the vote that Bill Crowther got and state whether he lost his deposit or not.

NEAB, Question 16, Specimen Paper 11, 1998

2 Elizabeth earned £350 each week. She gets a pay increase of 3%. How much is her weekly pay now?

NEAB, Question 7, Specimen Paper 21, 1998

3 David is a scout leader. He is calculating the cost of a day trip to a theme park for 182 scouts. The cost of entry to the theme park is £13 per person.

  a Calculate, by writing down in full, how he works out the total cost of entry for 182 scouts **without** using a calculator.

  b For scout groups the theme park gives a 15% discount on the £13 cost of entry. What is the cost of entry for each scout?

SEG, Question 4, Paper 3, June 1994

4 List the following in size, starting with the smallest.

  $\frac{2}{3}$ 0.6 0.59 65%

MEG, Question 3, Specimen Paper 3, 1998

5 Bill is given £150. He gives £45 of this to charity. What percentage is this of his share?

MEG, Question 7, Specimen Paper 3, 1998

6 **a** In a survey of 2400 adults, 72% said they were in favour of people carrying donor cards. Calculate the number of adults who said they were in favour.

  b In a certain region, only 180 000 adults carry donor cards. This is 8% of the adults in the region. Calculate the total number of adults in the region.

MEG, Question 1, Specimen Paper 4, 1998

7 Kathy earned £27 000 in 1995. Her tax allowance was £3525. She did not pay tax on this amount of her income.

On a further £2570 of her income she did not pay tax, because she paid this amount into a pension fund. She paid tax on the rest of her income.

a How much of her income was taxable?

She paid tax at 20% on the first £3200 of her taxable income.

She paid tax at 25% on the next £21100 of her taxable income.

She paid tax at 40% on the rest of her income.

b Calculate the total amount of tax that she paid in 1995.

SEG, Question 3, Specimen Paper 10, 1998

8 When 15 oranges are bought individually the total cost of the 15 oranges is £1.20. When 15 oranges are bought in a pack the cost is £1.14

a Express the amount saved by buying the pack as a percentage of the cost of buying the oranges individually.

b A special offer pack of these oranges has 20% extra free. How many oranges are in the special offer pack?

c What fraction of the oranges in the special offer pack are free?

SEG, Question 9, Specimen Paper 10, 1998

9 A joint of lamb costs £5.95 per kg. The price per kilogram is reduced. A joint weighing 1.2 kg is reduced by 50p.

a What is the reduced price per kilogram?

b Calculate the reduction in price as a percentage of the previous price. Give your answer correct to two significant figures.

SEG, Question 2, Specimen Paper 11, 1998

10 At the end of 1993 there were 5000 members of a certain rare breed of animal remaining in the world. It is predicted that their number will decrease by 12% each year.

a How many will be left at the end of 1996?

b By the end of which year will the number first be less than 2500?

MEG, Question 19, Specimen Paper 3, 1998

11 Nerys bought some wood which was priced at £8. When she went to pay for the wood, the shopkeeper added VAT at 17.5%. How much VAT did Nerys have to pay?

WJEC, Question 2, Paper 1, June 1994

12 Tony bought a second-hand car for £7500. It decreased in value each year by 8% of its value at the beginning of that year. Calculate the value of the car 2 years after he bought it.

WJEC, Question 10, Paper 1, June 1994

13 a A particular CD costs a shopkeeper £9.20 from the wholesaler. The shopkeeper wants to make a profit of 35% on his cost. What price will the CD be in the shop.

b Another CD is offered in a sale at a discount of 15%. The sale price is £12.41. What was the price of the CD before the sale discount?

WJEC, Question 13, Specimen Paper 1, 1998

Summary

How well do you grade yourself?

To gain a grade **E**, you need to be able to calculate percentage parts of quantities.

To gain a grade **C**, you need to be able to express one number as a percentage of another and to understand the equivalences between fractions, decimals and percentages.

To gain a grade **B**, you need to be able to use percentages to solve problems involving repeated changes and the calculation of the original quantity given a particular percentage value.

What you should know after you have worked through Chapter 2

- To find $P\%$ of an amount T, you calculate
  $(P \times T) \div 100$
- To calculate A as a percentage of B, you calculate

  $$\frac{A}{B} \times 100$$

- To calculate percentage gain, you calculate

  $$\frac{\text{Gain}}{\text{Original amount}} \times 100$$

- To calculate 100% when you know that $P\%$ represents an amount M, you calculate

  $$\frac{M}{P} \times 100$$

3 Ratio

EXERCISE 3A

1 Express the following ratios in their simplest form.

    a   6 : 18   **b**   15 : 20   **c**   16 : 24   **d**   24 : 36   **e**   20 to 50

    f   12 to 30   **g**   25 to 40   **h**   125 to 30   **i**   15 : 10   **j**   32 : 12

    k   28 to 12   **l**   100 to 40   **m**   0.5 to 3   **n**   1.5 to 4   **o**   2.5 to 1.5

    p   3.2 to 4

2 Express the following ratios of quantities in their simplest form. (Remember always to get a common unit.)

    a   £5 to £15   **b**   £24 to £16   **c**   125 g to 300 g

    d   40 minutes : 5 minutes   **e**   34 kg to 30 kg   **f**   £2.50 to 70p

    g   3 kg to 750 g   **h**   50 minutes to 1 hour   **i**   1 hour to 1 day

    j   12 cm to 2.5 mm   **k**   1.25 kg : 500 g   **l**   75p : £3.50

    m   4 weeks : 14 days   **n**   600 m : 2 km   **o**   465 mm : 3 m

3 A length of wood is cut into two pieces in the ratio 3 : 7. What fraction of the original length is the longer piece?

4 Jack and Thomas find a bag of marbles which they divide between them in the ratio of their ages. Jack is 10 years old and Thomas is 15. What fraction of the marbles did Jack get?

5 One morning a farmer notices that her hens, Gertrude, Gladys and Henrietta, have laid eggs in the ratio 2 : 3 : 4.

    a   What fraction of the eggs did Gertrude lay?

    b   What fraction of the eggs did Gladys lay?

    c   How many more eggs did Henrietta lay than Gertrude?

6 In a circus at feeding time, the elephants, the lions and the chimpanzees are given food in the ratio 10 to 7 to 3. What fraction of the total food is given to

    a   the elephants   **b**   the lions   **c**   the chimpanzees?

7 Three brothers, James, John and Joseph, share a huge block of chocolate in the ratio of their ages. James is 20, John is 16 and Joseph is 10. What fraction of the bar of chocolate does each brother get?

8 The recipe for a pudding is 125 g of sugar, 150 g of flour, 100 g of margarine and 175 g of fruit. What fraction of the pudding is each ingredient?

9 The goals scored by members of the Sheffield Wednesday squad in a promotion year were

    David Hirst 28   Paul Williams 15   John Sheridan 11

    Carlton Palmer 8   Paul Warhurst 17   Nigel Worthington 7

    Nigel Pearson 6   Peter Shirtliff 5   Others 13

    a   What fraction of the total goals were scored by John Sheridan?

    b   What percentage of the total goals were scored by David Hirst?

10 The money received from a lottery is divided between the organisers, the charity and the administration in the ratio 50 : 8 : 6. What percentage of the money received is given to
   a the organisers   **b** the charity?

Dividing amounts by ratios

To divide an amount into portions according to a given ratio, you first change the whole numbers into fractions with the same bottom number, then multiply the amount by each fraction.

For example, divide £40 between Peter and Hitan in the ratio 2 : 3.

Changing the ratio to fractions gives

Peter's share $= \dfrac{2}{(2 + 3)} = \dfrac{2}{5}$

Hitan's share $= \dfrac{3}{(2 + 3)} = \dfrac{3}{5}$

So Peter receives $£40 \times \frac{2}{5} = £16$ and Hitan receives $£40 \times \frac{3}{5} = £24$.

EXERCISE 3B

1 Divide the following amounts in the given ratios.
   a 400 g in the ratio 2 : 3   **b** 280 kg in the ratio 2 : 5
   c 500 in the ratio 3 : 7   **d** 1 km in the ratio 19 : 1
   e 5 hours in the ratio 7 : 5   **f** £100 in the ratio 2 : 3 : 5
   g £240 in the ratio 3 : 5 : 12   **h** 600 g in the ratio 1 : 5 : 6
   i £5 in the ratio 7 : 10 : 8   **j** 200 kg in the ratio 15 : 9 : 1

2 The ratio of female to male members of Banner Cross Church is about 5 : 3. The total number of members of the church is 256.
   a How many members are female?
   b What percentage of members are male?

3 A supermarket tries to have in stock branded goods and their own goods in the ratio 2 : 5. They stock 350 kg of breakfast cereal.
   a What percentage of the cereal stock is branded?
   b How much of the cereal stock is their own?

4 The Illinois Department of Health reported that, for the years 1981 to 1992 when they tested a total of 357 horses for rabies, the ratio of horses with rabies to those without was 1 : 16.
   a How many of these horses had rabies?
   b What percentage of the horses did not have rabies?

5 Being overweight increases the chances of an adult suffering from heart disease.
The table headings below show a way to test whether an adult has an increased risk.

Waist W and hip H measurements

For women, increased risk when $W/H > 0.8$

For men, increased risk when $W/H > 1.0$

a Find whether the following people have an increased risk of heart disease or not.

Miss Mott	waist 26 inches	hips 35 inches
Mrs Wright	waist 32 inches	hips 37 inches
Mr Brennan	waist 32 inches	hips 34 inches
Ms Smith	waist 31 inches	hips 40 inches
Mr Kaye	waist 34 inches	hips 33 inches

b Give three examples of waist and hip measurements which would suggest no risk of heart disease for a man, but would suggest a risk for a woman.

6 Rewrite the following scales as ratios as simply as possible.

a 1 cm to 4 km   **b** 4 cm to 5 km   **c** 2 cm to 5 km   **d** 4 cm to 1 km
e 5 cm to 1 km   **f** 2.5 cm to 1 km   **g** 8 cm to 5 km   **h** 10 cm to 1 km
i 5 cm to 3 km

7 A map has a scale of 1 cm to 10 km.

a Rewrite the scale as a ratio in its simplest form.

b How long is a lake that is 4.7 cm on the map?

c How long will an 8 km road be on the map?

8 A map has a scale of 2 cm to 5 km.

a Rewrite the scale as a ratio in its simplest form.

b How long is a path that measures 0.8 cm on the map?

c How long should a 12 km road be on the map?

9 The scale of a map is 5 cm to 1 km.

a Rewrite the scale as a ratio in its simplest form.

b How long is a wall that is shown as 2.7 cm on the map?

c The distance between two points is 8 km; how far will this be on the map?

10 You can simplify a ratio by changing one of the numbers to 1. For example, 5 : 7 can be rewritten as

$$\frac{5}{5} : \frac{7}{5} = 1 : 1.4$$

Rewrite each of the following as 1 : a number.

a 5 : 8   **b** 4 : 13   **c** 8 : 9
d 25 : 36   **e** 5 : 27   **f** 12 : 18
g 5 hours : 1 day   **h** 4 hours : 1 week

Calculating in a ratio when only part of the information is known

For example, two business partners, John and Ben, divided their total profit in the ratio 3 : 5. John received £2100. How much did Ben receive?

John's £2100 was $\frac{3}{8}$ of the total profit. (Check you know why.) So

$\frac{1}{8}$ of the total profit = £2100 ÷ 3 = £700

Therefore, Ben's share, which was $\frac{5}{8}$, amounted to £700 × 5 = £3500.

EXERCISE 3C

1 Derek, aged 15, and Ricki, aged 10, shared, in the same ratio as their ages, all the conkers they found in the woods. Derek had 48 conkers.
   a Simplify the ratio of their ages.
   b How many conkers did Ricki have?
   c How many conkers did they find altogether?

2 The soft drinks Coke, Orange and Vimto were bought for the school disco in the ratio 10 : 5 : 3. They bought 80 cans of Orange.
   a How much Coke did they buy?
   b How much Vimto did they buy?

3 Gwen is making a drink from lemonade, orange and ginger in the ratio 40 : 9 : 1. If Gwen has only 4.5 litres of orange, how much of the other two ingredients does she need to make the drink?

4 When I harvested my apples I found some eaten by wasps, some just rotten and some good ones. These were in the ratio 6 : 5 : 25. Eighteen of my apples had been eaten by wasps.
   a What percentage of my apples were just rotten?
   b How many good apples did I get?

5 A 'good' children's book is supposed to have pictures and text in the ratio 17 : 8. In a book I have just looked at, the pictures occupy 23 pages.
   a Approximately how many pages of text should this book have to be deemed a 'good' children's book?
   b What percentage of a 'good' children's book will be text?

6 Three business partners, Kevin, John and Margaret, put money into a venture in the ratio 3 : 4 : 5. They shared any profits in the same ratio. Last year, Margaret made £3400 out of the profits. How much did Kevin and John make last year?

7 'Proper tea' is made by putting milk and tea together in the ratio 2 : 9. How much 'proper tea' can be made by using 1 litre of milk?

8 A blend of tea is made by mixing Lapsang with Assam in the ratio 3 : 5. I have a lot of Assam tea but only 600 g of Lapsang. How much Assam do I need to make the blend with all the Lapsang?

9 The ratio of male to female spectators at ice hockey games is 4 : 5. At the Steelers' last match, 4500 men watched the match. What was the total attendance at the game?

10 A teacher always arranged each of his lessons to Y10 as 'teaching' and 'practising learnt skills' in the ratio 2 : 3.

   a If a lesson lasted 35 minutes, how much teaching would he do?

   b If he decided to teach for 30 minutes, how long would the lesson be?

   c For what percentage of his lessons would the pupils practise learnt skills?

Rates of change

Speed, time and distance

Speed is a rate of change, not a ratio.

Rates always have units such as km per hour or £ per kg. Many rates are commonsense and simply arithmetical. Speed, however, is a particular rate that can be used in different ways.

The relationship between speed, time and distance can be expressed in three ways:

$$\text{Speed} = \frac{\text{Distance}}{\text{Time}} \qquad \text{Distance} = \text{Speed} \times \text{Time} \qquad \text{Time} = \frac{\text{Distance}}{\text{Speed}}$$

When we refer to speed, we usually mean **average** speed, as it is unusual to maintain one exact speed for the whole of a journey.

The relationships between distance D, time T and speed S can be recalled using this diagram.

$$D = T \times S \qquad S = \frac{D}{T} \qquad T = \frac{D}{S}$$

Use the above relationships to help you to answer the following problems.

EXERCISE 3D

1 A cyclist travels a distance of 90 miles in 5 hours. What was her average speed?

2 How far along a motorway will you travel if you drive at 70 mph for 4 hours?

3 I drive to Bude in Cornwall from Sheffield in about 6 hours. The distance from Sheffield to Bude is 315 miles. What is my average speed?

4 The distance from Leeds to London is 210 miles. The train travels at an average speed of 55 mph. If I catch the 9.30 am train in London, at what time would you expect me to get into Leeds?

5 How long will an athlete take to run a 2000 m race at an average speed of 8 m/second?

6 Complete the following table.

	Distance travelled	Time taken	Average speed
a	150 miles	2 hours	
b	260 miles		40 mph
c		5 hours	35 mph
d		3 hours	80 km/h
e	540 km	8 hours 30 minutes	
f		3 hours 15 minutes	100 km/h
g	215 km		50 km/h

7 A train travels at 50 km/h for 3 hours, then slows down to do the last 30 minutes of its journey at 40 km/h.
  a What is the distance of this journey?
  b What is the average speed of the train?

8 Jane runs and walks to work each day. She runs the first 2 miles at a speed of 9 mph and then walks the next $1\frac{1}{2}$ miles at a steady 4 mph.
  a How long does it take Jane to get to work?
  b What is her average speed?

9 Change the following speeds to metres per second.
  a 36 km/h **b** 12 km/h **c** 60 km/h **d** 150 km/h **e** 75 km/h

10 Change the following speeds to kilometres per hour.
  a 25 m/s **b** 12 m/s **c** 4 m/s **d** 30 m/s **e** 0.5 m/s

11 A train travels at an average speed of 18 m/s.
  a Express its average speed in km/h.
  b Find the time taken to travel 500 m.
  c The train set off at 7.30 on a 40 km journey. At what time will it arrive?

12 A cyclist is travelling at an average speed of 24 km/h.
  a What is this speed in metres per second?
  b What distance does he travel in 2 hours 45 minutes?
  c How long does it take him to travel 2 km?
  d How far does he travel in 20 seconds?

Density

Density is another rate of change. It is the mass of a substance per unit volume, usually expressed in grams per cm^3. The relationship between the three quantities is

$$\text{Density} = \frac{\text{Mass}}{\text{Volume}}$$

This is often remembered with a triangle similar to that for distance, speed and time.

Mass = Density × Volume   Density = Mass ÷ Volume

Volume = Mass ÷ Density

Note Density is defined in terms of mass, which is commonly referred to as 'weight', although, strictly speaking, there is a difference between them (you may already have learnt about it in science). In this book, the two terms are assumed to have the same meaning.

Example 1 A piece of metal weighing 30 g has a volume of 4 cm^3. What is the density of the metal?

$$\text{Density} = \frac{30}{4} = 7.5 \, \text{g/cm}^3$$

Example 2 What is the weight of a piece of rock which has a volume of 34 cm^3 and a density of 2.25 g/cm^3?

Weight = 34 × 2.25 = 76.5 g

EXERCISE 3E

1   Find the density of a piece of wood weighing 6 g and having a volume of 8 cm^3.

2   Calculate the density of a metal if 12 cm^3 of it weighs 100 g.

3   Calculate the weight of a piece of plastic, 20 cm^3 in volume, if its density is 1.6 g/cm^3.

4   Calculate the volume of a piece of wood which weighs 102 g and has a density of 0.85 g/cm^3.

5   Find the weight of a marble model, 56 cm^3 in volume, if the density of marble is 2.8 g/cm^3.

6   Calculate the volume of a liquid weighing 4 kg and having a density of 1.25 g/cm^3.

7   Find the density of the material of a pebble which weighs 34 g and has a volume of 12.5 cm^3.

8   It is estimated that the statue of Queen Victoria in Endcliffe Park, Sheffield, has a volume of about 4 m^3. The density of the material used to make the statue is 9.2 g/cm^3. What is the estimated weight of the statue?

9 I bought a 50 kg bag of coal, and estimated the total volume of coal to be about 28 000 cm³. What is the density of coal in g/cm³?

10 A 1 kg bag of sugar has a volume of about 625 cm³. What is the density of sugar in g/cm³?

Possible coursework tasks

Half-time scores

The final score in a football match was 3 – 2. Some possible half-time scores were 0 – 0, 0 – 1, 0 – 2, 1 – 0, 1 – 1, …

a Find all the possible half-time scores for this match.

b Investigate the total number of half-time scores possible if you know the final score.

Paper sizes

Obtain a sheet of paper in each of these sizes: A3, A4 and A5.

a How are the sheets related to each other?

b Investigate the ratio of the length to the width for each size.

Grandmother's last will and testament

In her will a grandmother has left £120 every year to be divided among her three grandchildren in the ratio of their ages in that year. At the moment, the three grandchildren are aged 2, 5 and 8 years.

Investigate how the amounts for each grandchild change each year.

The billiard-table

On a billiard-table of size 1 : 2, the ball starts at pocket A, rebounds from the cushion once and ends up in pocket D.

a What happens if the ball rebounds at other points on the table?

b Investigate for a billiard-table of size $a : b$.

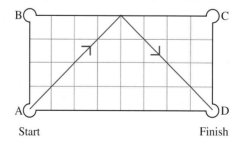

Examination questions

1 A full skip holds $19.7\,m^3$ if filled level with the top. If this skip is filled with earth of density $700\,kg/m^3$, what is the weight of the earth in the skip?

WJEC, Question 11, Specimen Paper 2, 1998

2 Recipe for Bread and Butter Pudding.

  6 slices of bread

  2 eggs

  1 pint of milk

  150 g raisins

  10 g margarine

This recipe is for four people.

Work out the amounts needed so that there will be enough for 6 people.

  .... slices of bread

  .... eggs

  .... pints of milk

  .... g raisins

  .... g margarine

EDEXCEL, Question 7, Paper 4, June 1999

3 Harry draws a plan of his classroom. He uses a scale of 1 : 40. The classroom is 12 m long. What will be its length on the plan? Give your answer in cm.

NEAB, Question 7, Specimen Paper 2, 1998

4 Kylie, Lucas and Daniel share £972 in the ratio of 11 : 9 : 7. How much does each one get?

WJEC, Question 7, Paper 2, June 1999

5 Anne and Bill share £400 in the ratio 5 : 3. How much does each of them receive?

MEG, Question 7, Specimen Paper 3, 1998

6 a Joyce cycled to work at an average speed of 15 km/h. She took 20 minutes for the journey. What distance did she travel to work?

  b The distance travelled by Alan was 7.5 km. It took Alan 15 minutes to travel to work. Calculate his average speed in km/h.

SEG, Question 16, Specimen Paper 10, 1998

7 On a motorway there are three lanes: an inside lane, a middle lane and an outside lane. One day, at midday, the speed of the traffic on these three lanes was in the ratio 3 : 4 : 5. The speed on the outside lane was 70 mph. Calculate the speed on the inside lane.

NEAB, Question 12, Specimen Paper 1, 1998

8 Ann, Beth and Cheryl share the total cost of a holiday in the ratio of 6 : 5 : 4. Ann pays £294.

   a Work out the total cost of the holiday.

   b Work out how much Cheryl pays.

EDEXCEL, Question 15, Intermediate Paper 4, June 2000

9 To be on time a train must complete a journey of 210 miles in 3 hours.

   a Calculate the average speed of the train for the whole journey when it is on time.

   b The tran averages a speed of 56 mph over the first 98 miles of the journey. Calculate the average speed for the remainder of the journey so that the train arrives on time.

WJEC, Question 7, Intermediate Paper 2, June 1999

10 In 1993 Nouredinne Morcelli's time for running the mile was 225 seconds. By taking 5 miles to be equal to 8 kilometres, calculate what his time for the 1500 metres would have been, assuming that his average speed was the same.

SEG, Question 13, Specimen Paper 11, 1998

11 Jack shares £180 between his two children Ruth and Ben. The ration of Ruth's share to Ben's share is 5 : 4.

   a Work out how much each child is given.

Ben then gives 10% of his share to Ruth.

   b Work out the percentage of the £180 that Ruth now has.

EDEXCEL, Question 10, Intermediate Paper 3, June 1999

Summary

How well do you grade yourself?

To gain a grade **E**, you need to be able to simplify a ratio.

To gain a grade **D**, you need to be able to calculate average speeds from given data.

To gain a grade **C**, you need to be able to calculate using ratios in appropriate situations.

To gain a grade **B**, you need to be able to calculate with density.

What you should know after you have worked through Chapter 3

- To divide any amount in a given ratio, multiply the amount by each fraction of the ratio. For example, to divide £6 in the ratio 3 : 5
  multiply £6 by $\frac{3}{8}$ to give £2.25
  and multiply £6 by $\frac{5}{8}$ to give £3.75

- The relationships between speed, time and distance are

$$\text{Speed} = \frac{\text{Distance}}{\text{Time}} \qquad \text{Distance} = \text{Speed} \times \text{Time} \qquad \text{Time} = \frac{\text{Distance}}{\text{Speed}}$$

- Density is a rate. It is the mass per unit volume, usually expressed in grams per cm^3. The relationships between the three quantities involved are

$$\text{Density} = \frac{\text{Mass}}{\text{Volume}} \qquad \text{Mass} = \text{Density} \times \text{Volume} \qquad \text{Volume} = \frac{\text{Mass}}{\text{Density}}$$

4 Shape

This chapter is going to ...

remind you how to calculate the perimeters and the areas of common shapes you have met before. It will introduce you to calculating the area of a circle and that of a trapezium, and will look at the types of problem you will be able to solve with knowledge of area.

What you should already know

✔ Perimeter is the distance all the way round a 2-D shape. When the shape is a circle, the perimeter has a special name – circumference.
✔ The area of a rectangle is given by Area = Length × Breadth.
✔ The circumference of a circle is given by $C = \pi D$, where D is the diameter of the circle.
✔ The most accurate value of π that you can use is on your calculator. You should use it every time you have to work with π.
✔ The length of the diameter of a circle is twice the length of its radius. When you are given a radius in order to find a circumference, first double the radius to get the diameter.

EXERCISE 4A

1   Write down the perimeter and the area of each of these rectangles.

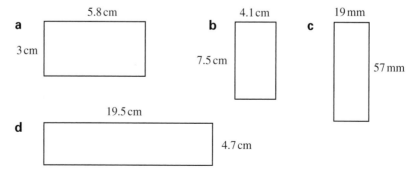

2 Copy and complete the following table for rectangles **a** to **g**.

	Length	Breadth	Perimeter	Area
a	13 cm	4 cm		
b	5 cm		30 cm	
c		6 cm	28 cm	
d	4 cm			28 cm^2
e		5 cm		30 cm^2
f	3 cm		10.2 cm	
g		4 cm		21.2 cm^2

3 Find the total perimeter and the total area of each of these shapes.

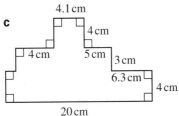

4 a Draw a square centimetre.
   b How many square millimetres are there in one square centimetre?
   c How many mm^2 are there in 5 cm^2?

5 a Sketch a square metre.
   b How many square centimetres are there in one square metre?
   c How many cm^2 are there in 6 m^2?
   d How many mm^2 are there in 1 m^2?

6 Convert the following.
   a 4 cm^2 to mm^2 **b** 8 m^2 to cm^2 **c** 3 km^2 to m^2

7 A rectangular field is 150 m long and 45 m wide.
   a What length of fencing is needed to go all the way round the field?
   b What is the area of the field?

8 A rugby pitch is 160 m long and 70 m wide.
   a Before a game, the players have to run all the way round the pitch twice to help them loosen up. What is the distance that they have to run?
   b The groundsman waters the pitch at the rate of 100 m^2 per minute. How long will it take him to water the whole pitch?

9   How much will it cost to buy enough carpet for a rectangular room 12 m by 5 m, if the carpet costs £13.99 per m²?

10   What is the perimeter of a square with an area of 100 cm²?

11   A gardener can mow his lawn in strips 40 cm wide. His lawn is rectangular, measuring 6 m by 14 m.
     a   If it takes him 1 minute 20 seconds to mow one long strip of his lawn, how long will it take him to mow the whole lawn?
     b   After mowing the lawn, the gardener puts down lawn feed. It says on the packet of feed that he should apply 50 g of feed to every square metre of lawn. How much feed does he need for the whole lawn?

12   A room measures 5.6 m by 7.2 m. The floor of the room is to be covered with carpet tiles, each 40 cm square.
     a   What is the area of the room?
     b   How many carpet tiles will be needed to cover the floor?

13   What is the area of one page of this book?

14   A square lawn of side 5 m has a path, 1 m wide, running all the way round the outside of it. What is the area of this path?

15   The floor of a room, 4.7 m by 6.8 m, is to be covered with carpet tiles. Square carpet tiles of side 50 cm are bought in packs of 5 at £15.99 each. These carpet tiles cannot be bought singly, only in packs of 5.
     a   How many packs must be bought to make sure the floor is covered completely?
     b   How many tiles will actually be needed to cover the floor completely?
     c   Explain how many whole tiles will be used and the size of the tiles needed to fill the gaps.

Circumference of a circle

Do remember that the value for π is best found by pressing the $\boxed{\pi}$ key on your calculator. If at any time you do not have access to a scientific calculator, 3.14 is a good approximation to use.

Here are two examples of calculating a circumference.
   1   Find the circumference of a circle with a diameter of 4 cm.
       You can immediately use the formula $C = \pi D$:
       $\pi \times 4 = 12.6$ cm (rounded)
   2   Find the circumference of a circle with a radius of 3.7 cm.
       First you need to double the radius to get the diameter. Only then can you use $C = \pi D$, which gives
       $\pi \times 7.4 = 23.2$ cm (rounded)

Exercise 4B

1 Find the circumference of the following circles. Round off your answers to 1 dp.

  a Diameter 5 cm   **b** Diameter 8.2 cm   **c** Radius 4 cm

  d Radius 5.8 cm   **e** Diameter 12 m   **f** Radius 9 m

  g Diameter 1.3 cm   **h** Radius 3.7 m   **i** Radius 1.9 cm

  j Diameter 4.6 mm   **k** Diameter 5.8 m   **l** Radius 0.8 cm

2 A bicycle wheel has a radius of 30 cm. The bicycle is cycled 50 km.

  a What is the circumference of the bicycle wheel?

  b How many complete revolutions will the wheel make over the 50 km?

3 A rope is wrapped 8 times round a capstan (cylindrical post), the diameter of which is 35 cm. How long is the rope?

4 On my watch the hour hand is 0.9 cm long, the minute hand 1.4 cm long.

  a How far does the end of the minute hand travel in

    i 1 minute   **ii** 1 hour   **iii** 1 day?

  b How far does the end of the hour hand travel in

    i 1 hour   **ii** 1 week   **iii** 1 minute?

5 A circular racing track has 5 lanes. Each lane is 1 m wide, and the radius of the inner lane is 32 m. In one race, the competitors have to run all the way round the track once, keeping in the same lanes in which they started.

  a How far would each competitor run in each lane?

  b Express the ratio of shortest run : longest run as a percentage.

6 The roller used on a cricket pitch has a radius of 70 cm.

  a What is the circumference of the roller?

  b How many revolutions does it make when rolling the pitch – a length of 20 m?

7 A semicircle is, as shown, exactly half a circle.

If a semicircle has a diameter of 6 cm, calculate

  a its arc length   **b** its total perimeter.

6 cm

8 What is the total perimeter of a semicircle of diameter 15 cm?

9 What is the total perimeter of a circle of radius 7 cm?

10 How many complete revolutions will a car wheel, radius 25 cm, make in a journey of 285 km?

11 Assume that the human waist is circular.

  a What are the distances around the waist of the following people?

    Sue   waist radius of 10 cm   Dave   waist radius of 12 cm

    Julie   waist radius of 11 cm   Brian   waist radius of 13 cm

  b What interesting fact do the answers to the above tell you?

  c What would be the difference in length between a rope stretched tightly round the earth and another rope always held 1 m above it?

12 A hamster has a treadmill of radius 6 cm.

   a How far has he run when the wheel has made 100 complete revolutions?

   b How many revolutions will be needed to cover 1 km?

Areas of triangles and trapeziums

Area of a right triangle

The area of a right triangle (one containing a right angle) is easily seen to be half the area of the rectangle it comes from. Hence the area is

$\frac{1}{2} \times$ Base length $\times$ Height

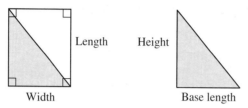

For example, find the area of this triangle.

Area $= \frac{1}{2} \times 7\,\text{cm} \times 4\,\text{cm} = 14\,\text{cm}^2$

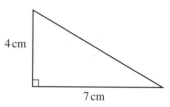

EXERCISE 4C

1 Write down the area and the perimeter of each triangle.

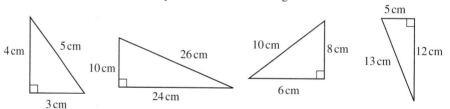

2 Find the area of the shaded part of each triangle.

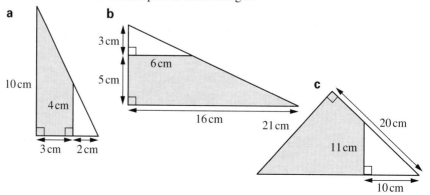

3 A tree is in the middle of a garden. Around the tree there is a square region where nothing will be planted. The dimensions of the garden are shown in the diagram.

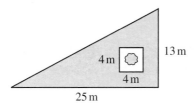

How much area can be planted?

4 This is the flag of an island. The dimensions of the actual flag are 50 cm by 75 cm.

    a The larger triangle is blue. What is the area of the blue triangle?

    b The smaller triangle is yellow. The rectangular sides of this triangle are respectively $\frac{2}{5}$ the length and width of the whole flag. What is the area of the yellow part of the flag?

5 Find the area of the shaded triangle RST.   **6** Find the area of triangle ELF.

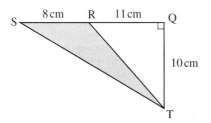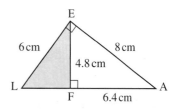

7 Calculate the area of each of these shapes.

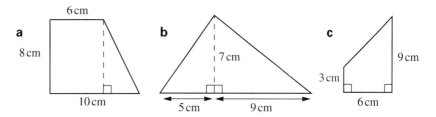

8 Which of these three triangles has the largest area?

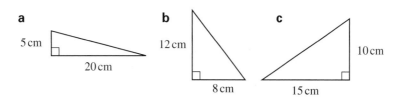

Area of any triangle

The area of any triangle is given by
$\frac{1}{2} \times$ Base length $\times$ Vertical height

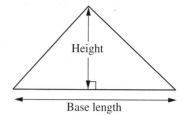

EXERCISE 4D

1   What is the vertical height of a triangle with an area of 48 cm² and a base length of 6 cm?

2   Copy and complete the following table for triangles **a** to **f**.

	Base	Vertical height	Area
a	8 cm	7 cm	
b		9 cm	36 cm²
c		5 cm	10 cm²
d	4 cm		6 cm²
e	5 cm		16.5 cm²
f	7 cm	13 cm	

3   Find the area of these shapes.

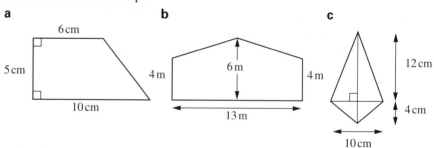

4   Find the area of the shaded shapes.

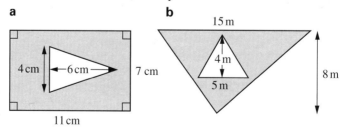

5   Write down the dimensions of two different-sized triangles that have the same area of 50 cm².

6 A triangle of base length 5 cm and vertical height 9 cm is cut from a rectangle 12 cm by 13 cm.

    a What area has been left in the rectangle?

    b What percentage of the original rectangle has been cut out?

7 Write down the perimeter and the area of each triangle.

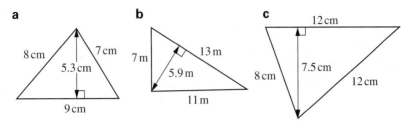

8 Find the area of the shaded part of each diagram.

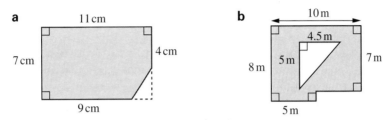

Area of a trapezium

The area of a trapezium is calculated by finding the average of the lengths of its parallel sides and multiplying this by the perpendicular distance between them.

$$\text{Area} = h\left(\frac{a+b}{2}\right)$$

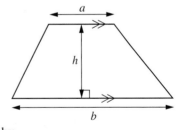

For example, the area of the trapezium ABCD is given by

$$\text{Area} = 3 \times \left(\frac{4+7}{2}\right)$$

which equals 16.5 cm².

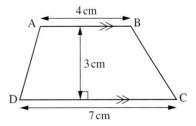

EXERCISE 4E

1   Copy and complete the following table for each trapezium.

	Parallel side 1	Parallel side 2	Vertical height	Area
a	8 cm	4 cm	5 cm	
b	10 cm	12 cm	7 cm	
c	7 cm	5 cm	4 cm	
d	5 cm	9 cm	6 cm	
e	3 m	13 m	5 m	
f	4 cm	10 cm		42 cm^2
g	7 cm	8 cm		22.5 cm^2
h	6 cm		5 cm	40 cm^2
i		7 cm	1.5 cm	7.5 cm^2
j		7.5 cm	6 cm	30 cm^2
k	4.8 cm	9.4 cm		85.2 cm^2

2   Calculate the perimeter and the area of each of these trapeziums.

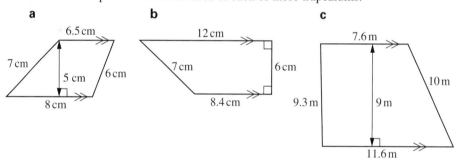

3   Calculate the area of each of these shapes.

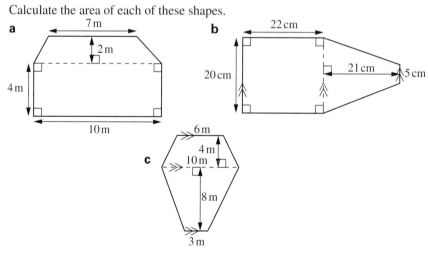

4 Calculate the area of the shaded part in each of these diagrams.

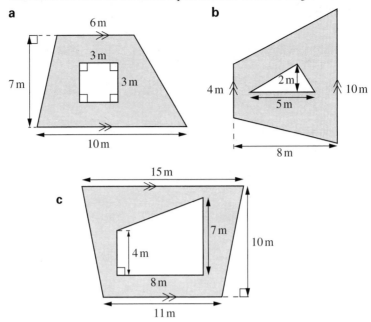

5 A trapezium has an area of 25 cm². Its vertical height is 5 cm. Write down 5 different possible pairs of lengths which the two parallel sides could be.

6 Which of the following shapes has the largest area?

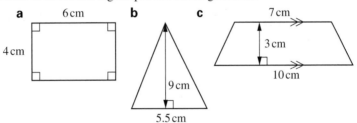

7 Which of the following shapes has the smallest area?

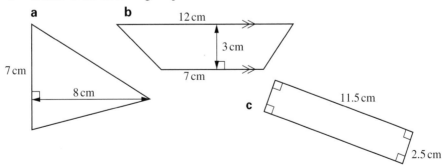

8 What percentage of this shape has been shaded?

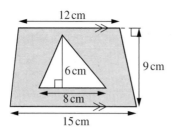

9 The shape of most of Egypt (see map) roughly approximates to a trapezium. The north coast is about 900 km long, the south boundary is about 1100 km long, and the distance from north to south is about 1100 km.

What is the approximate area of this part of Egypt?

10 Find the perimeter and the area of each parallelogram.

a

b

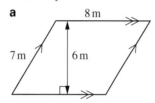
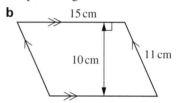

Area of a circle

The area of a circle is given by

Area = πr^2

But be careful because this formula uses radius. So when you are given the diameter of a circle, do remember to halve it to get the radius.

Example 1: radius given   Find the area of a circle with a radius of 7 cm.

Area = $\pi r^2 = \pi \times 7^2 = \pi \times 49$ (Use π on the calculator)
$= 154 \, cm^2$ (rounded)

Example 2: diameter given   Find the area of a circle with a diameter of 6 cm.

First, halve the diameter to get the radius of 3 cm. Then find the area.

Area = $\pi r^2 = \pi \times 3^2 = \pi \times 9$
$= 28.3 \, cm^2$ (rounded)

EXERCISE 4F

1   Copy and complete the following table for each circle.

	Radius	Diameter	Circumference	Area
a	5 cm			
b	4.5 cm			
c		8 cm		
d			22 cm	
e	2.9 m			
f			110 m	
g		7.6 m		
h			121 m	
i	0.08 mm			

2   Calculate the area of each of these circles, giving your answers to 1 decimal place.

    a   Radius 8 cm   **b**   Diameter 9 m   **c**   Radius 13 cm

    d   Diameter 1 m   **e**   Radius 11 m   **f**   Diameter 67 cm

3   The diameter of each of these coins is

    1p...2 cm   2p...2.6 cm   5p...1.7 cm   10p...2.4 cm

    Calculate the area of one face of each coin.

4   Calculate the area of these shapes.

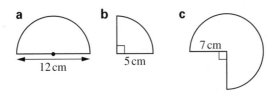

5   Calculate the area of these shapes.

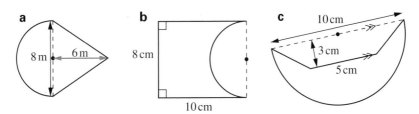

6   A garden has a circular lawn of diameter 30 m. There is a path 2 m wide all the way round the circumference. What is the area of this path?

7 Calculate the area of the shaded part of each of these diagrams.

a   **b**   **c**

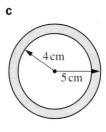

8 Metal discs are stamped from a rectangular sheet of metal, as shown in the diagram.

   a What is the largest number of discs 3 cm in diameter that can be cut from a sheet which measures 10 cm by 16 cm?

   b What would be the percentage wasted from the original sheet of metal?

9 The whole area of a circular playground, radius 10 m, is to be covered in a rubber solution. This solution comes in cartons. Each carton contains enough solution to cover 2 m². How many cartons are needed?

10 The shaded shape consists of three semicircles. Calculate the perimeter and the area of the whole shape.

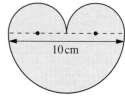

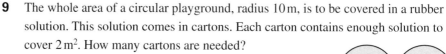

Answers in terms of π

There are times when we do not want a numerical answer to a circle problem, but need to evaluate the answer in terms of π. (The numerical answer could be evaluated later.)

For example: What is the circumference and area of this circle?

Leave your answers in terms of π.

Circumference $= \pi \times 14 = 14\pi$

Area $= \pi \times 7^2 = 49\pi$

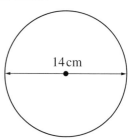

If a question asks you to leave it in terms of π it is most likely to be on the non-calculator paper and hence saves you the trouble of using your calculator.

But if you did, and calculated the numerical answer, you could well lose a mark.

EXERCISE 4G

Leave all your answers in terms of π

1 State the circumference of the following circles:
    a diameter 4 cm   **b** radius 10 cm   **c** diameter 15 cm   **d** radius 2 cm

2 State the area of the following circles:
    a radius 4 cm   **b** diameter 10 cm   **c** radius 3 cm   **d** diameter 18 cm

3 State the diameter of the circle with a circumference of 50 cm.

4 State the radius of the circle with an area of 100 cm².

5 Complete the following table

Radius	Diameter	Circumference	Area
1 cm			
	1 cm		
	200 cm		
50 cm			
		10 cm	
			36 cm²

6 State the area of the following shapes
    a   **b**   **c**

7 State the area of each diagram
    a   **b**   **c**

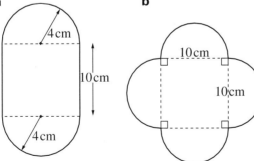 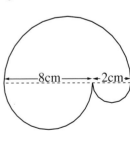

8 State the area of a circle with a circumference of 10 cm.

9 State the circumference of a circle with an area of 64 cm².

10 What are the radii of the circles with the same area as the following squares?
    a side length 5 cm   **b** side length 7 cm   **c** side length 20 cm

Possible coursework tasks

A farmer's problem

A farmer uses 60 metres of fencing to build an enclosure against a wall.

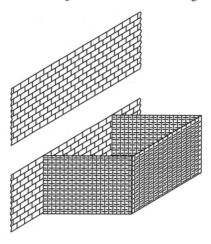

Find the largest area that can be made for the enclosure.

Pick's theorem

This quadrilateral has an area of $16\frac{1}{2}$ square units.

The perimeter of the quadrilateral passes through 9 dots. Thirteen dots are contained within the perimeter of the quadrilateral.

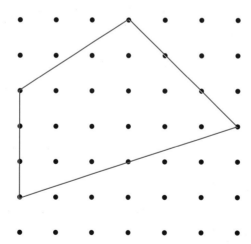

Investigate for quadrilaterals of different shapes and sizes.

➤ Flower beds

In a park, hexagonal flower beds are surrounded by hexagonal paving stones.

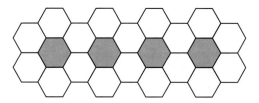

In the diagram, 4 flower beds are surrounded by 18 paving stones. Investigate to find how many paving stones are needed to surround 100 flower beds.

Equable shapes

An 'equable shape' is defined as a shape for which the numerical value of its area is equal to the numerical value of its perimeter. Investigate for different shapes.

A problem with waste

Different sizes of coin are stamped from a square sheet of metal.

Investigate the percentage wasted for each size of coin.

Examination questions: coursework type

1   The diagram shows a grid which has 6 dots along its length, 4 dots along its width. There are 8 dots inside the rectangle and 16 dots around its perimeter. Investigate the numbers of dots inside and on the perimeter of other rectangles which can be drawn on this grid.

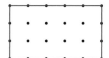

2 Suzie wants a new desk for her bedroom. She has seen one that she likes in a store. The kit costs £59.99.

The desk top measures 120 cm × 60 cm and is 72 cm high. The back panel is 40 cm high.

Parts list

01	Top
02	Left side
03	Right side
04	Back panel

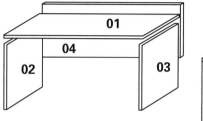
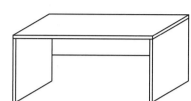

In a second store, Suzie has found that a similar black-ash effect board is available in 8 feet lengths and several widths. Here are some prices.

Width in cm	30	40	50	60
Price	£8.29	£11.79	£15.49	£18.99

The store will cut boards to size free of charge. (Suzie also knows that 1 foot is just over 30 cm.)

Write your advice to Suzie.

- Should she buy the kit or make the desk herself?
- If she decides to make it herself, how should she ask for the boards to be cut?

NEAB, Question 1, Specimen Paper 3F, 1998

3 Square panes of glass, 10 cm by 10 cm, are held together by thin strips of lead to form rectangular panels. Each panel also has a thin lead strip around its perimeter.

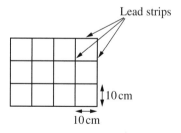

a Explain why arranging the panes of glass in a long thin rectangular panel uses more lead than arranging the same panes in other rectangular panels.

The rectangular panels made from the square panes of glass are also edged around the perimeter by a wooden strip.

Lead strip costs 28.3p per 10 cm

Wood strip costs 7.8p per 10 cm

10 cm by 10 cm panes of glass cost 12.5p each.

The rectangular panels have wooden and lead strips around the perimeter, with lead strips holding all the panes of glass together.

b Find the minimum cost of making a panel using 156 panes of glass. You must give your reasons for your choice of dimensions for the panel.

WJEC, Question 4, Paper A3, June 1995

Examination questions

1 This diagram shows the floor plan of a room.

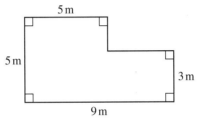

Work out the area of the floor.

Give the units with your answer.

EDEXCEL, Question 9, Intermediate Paper 4, June 1999

2 The radius of the wheel of a bike is 34 cm. Calculate the circumference of the wheel.

MEG, Question 2c, Specimen Paper 4, 1998

3 The radius of a circle is 8 cm. Work out the area of the circle.

ULEAC, Question 12, Paper 7, June 1994

4 A mat is made in the shape of a rectangle with a semicircle added at one end.

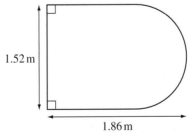

Diagram **NOT** accurately drawn

The width of the mat is 1.52 metres.

The length of the mat is 1.86 metres.

Calculate the area of the mat.

Give your answer in square metres, correct to 2 decimal places.

EDEXCEL, Question 10, Intermediate Paper 4, November 1999

5 Andrea is rolling a hoop along the ground. The hoop has a diameter of 60 cm.

   a What is the circumference of the hoop?

   b What is the minimum number of complete turns the hoop must make to cover a distance of 5 m?

SEG, Question 4, Specimen Paper 10, 1998

6 A circle has a radius of 3.3 cm. Calculate the area of the circle.

WJEC, Question 11a, Specimen Paper 3, 1998

7 A circular mirror is mounted on a square wooden frame of side 12 cm so that it touches the sides of the frame as shown in the diagram.

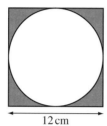

Calculate the area of the wooden frame not covered by the mirror (the shaded part of the diagram).

Give your answer to an appropriate degree of accuracy.

WJEC, Question 18, Intermediate Paper 2, June 1998

8 The diagram shows a running track. BA and DE are parallel and straight. They are each of length 90 metres. BCD and EFA are semicircular. They each have a diameter of length 70 metres.

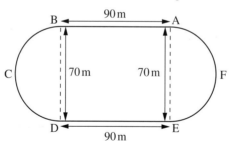

   a Calculate the perimeter of the track.

   b Calculate the total area inside the track.

NEAB, Question 4, Paper 2, June 1995

9 a Calculate the area of a circle of radius 4 cm.
Give your answer in terms of π.

b A square is drawn inside the circle, as shown in the diagram.

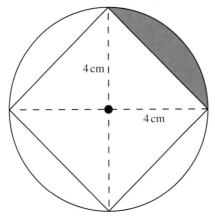

Diagram **NOT** accurately drawn

i Calculate the area of the square.
Remember to state the units in your answer.

ii Calculate the area of the shaded segment.
Give your answer in terms of π.

NEAB, Question 20, Intermediate Paper 1, June 2000

Summary

How well do you grade yourself?

To gain a grade **E**, you need to know what a perimeter is and be able to calculate the area of a rectangle.

To gain a grade **D**, you need to be able to calculate the area of a triangle and the area of a trapezium.

To gain a grade **C**, you need to be able to calculate the circumference and the area of a circle.

What you should know after you have worked through Chapter 4

- The area of a rectangle is Length × Breadth.
- The area of a triangle is $\frac{1}{2}$ × Base × Vertical height
- The circumference of a circle is πD, where D is the diameter.
- The area of a circle is πr^2, where r is the radius.
- The area of a trapezium is its vertical height h, multiplied by the average of the lengths of the two parallel sides a and b:

$$A = h\left(\frac{a+b}{2}\right)$$

Coursework example **1**

Diagonals

Refer to the Appendix for a summary of coursework marks.

Problem statement

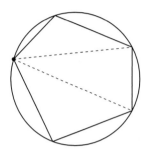

Take any 5 points on the circumference of a circle and join them to make a five-sided polygon. Two diagonals can be drawn from any corner of the polygon.

Investigate the number of diagonals that can be drawn from a corner of any polygon.

Possible solution

I am going to draw some more examples.

i	ii	iii	Notes
3			Examples show that the necessary information has been obtained.

3 sides   4 sides   6 sides   7 sides
0 diagonals   1 diagonal   3 diagonals   4 diagonals

I am now going to put my results in a table.

i	ii	iii	Notes
4			The problem has been broken down into easy stages.
	3		The results are shown in a table
		3	A correct pattern has been explained.

No. of sides	No. of diagonals
3	0
4	1
5	2
6	3
7	4

From my table of results, I have spotted a pattern.

The number of diagonals is always 3 less than the number of sides.

To show my rule works, I am going to test it with a polygon of 10 sides. I predict that there will be 7 diagonals.

i	ii	iii	Notes
		4	The further example has shown that the rule works.
	4		The explanation links the table and the diagrams.
5			A new question has been introduced to find out more about the problem.
	5		The rule has been explained by using an example and by using algebra.
	5		The use of algebra to show the rule has improved the mathematical presentation. **Final marks:** **(i) 5 (ii) 5 (iii) 5**

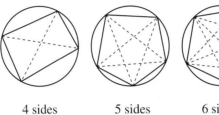

From my diagram, I have shown that my prediction was correct.

I am going to use algebra to show this rule. If a polygon has n sides then there will be $n - 3$ diagonals from any corner. This is because if I had 10 corners, I could only draw lines to 9 other points and 2 of these lines are the sides of the polygon. So there will be only 7 diagonals.

Now I have found this rule, I am going to see if I can find the total number of diagonals inside any polygon.

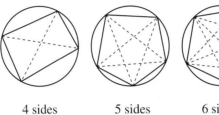

4 sides — 2 diagonals

5 sides — 5 diagonals

6 sides — 9 diagonals

7 sides — 14 diagonals

Again I am going to put my results in a table and try to find a rule.

No. of sides	No. of diagonals
4	2
5	5
6	9
7	14

The pattern is more difficult to spot but I think it will have something to do with my first rule.

If, for each corner, there are 3 less diagonals than the number of sides, then I will have to multiply this by the number of corners to get all the diagonals. So if I had a 6-sided polygon, then from each corner there would be 3 diagonals. So for 6 corners there would be 6×3 diagonals which is 18. But this is double, since I've counted each diagonal twice. I've now found the rule for 6 sides:

$$\text{Total number of diagonals} = \frac{6 \times 3}{2}$$

I can now show this rule using algebra, which will make it clearer and easier to understand.

$$\text{Total number of diagonals} = \frac{\text{Number of sides} \times (\text{Number of sides} - 3)}{2}$$

So for a polygon with n sides:

$$\text{Total number of diagonals} = n\left(\frac{n-3}{2}\right)$$

5 Volume and surface area

This chapter is going to ...

remind you how to calculate the volume of a cuboid, and introduce you to calculating the volume of a cylinder and that of prisms. It will also revise area through problems about the surface area of regular 3-D shapes.

What you should already know

✔ The volume of a cuboid is given by
Volume = Length × Breadth × Height
For example, find the volume
of the cuboid shown below.

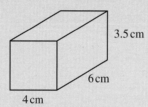

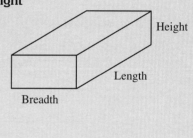

Volume = Length × Breadth × Height
= 6 cm × 4 cm × 3.5 cm = 84 cm³
Note: Sometimes 'height' will be referred to as 'depth'.

EXERCISE 5A

1 Find the volume of each of these cuboids.

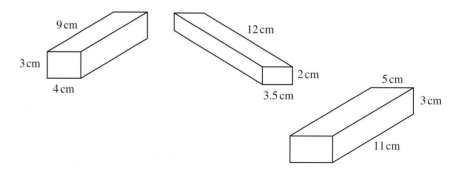

2 Complete the table below for cuboids **a** to **e**.

	Length	Breadth	Height	Volume
a	8 cm	5 cm	4.5 cm	
b	12 cm	8 cm		480 cm³
c	9 cm		5 cm	270 cm³
d		7 cm	3.5 cm	245 cm³
e	7.5 cm	5.4 cm	2 cm	

3 Give the volume inside the boxes with these dimensions.
  a Length 6 cm, width 3 cm and depth 4 cm.
  b Width 12 cm, length 6 cm and depth 2.25 cm.
  c Depth 10 cm, width 8 cm and length 15 cm.

4 Find the total surface area of each box in question **3**.

5 Give the volume of the cuboid in each of the following cases.
  a The area of the base is 40 cm² and the height is 4 cm.
  b The base has one side 10 cm, another side 2 cm longer, and the height is 4 cm.
  c The area of the top is 25 cm² and the depth is 6 cm.

6 a Calculate the volumes of cubes with these sides.
    i 4 cm   **ii** 7 cm   **iii** 10 cm   **iv** 1.4 m   **v** 5.6 m
  b What are the total surface areas of these cubes?

7 How many square centimetres are equivalent to one square metre?

8 How many square millimetres are equivalent to one square centimetre?

9 How many square metres are equivalent to one square kilometre?

10 The safety regulations say that in a room where people sleep there should be at least 12 m³ for each person. A shed is 20 m long, 13 m wide and 4 m high. What is the greatest number of people who can safely sleep in the shed?

11 Calculate the volume of each of these shapes.

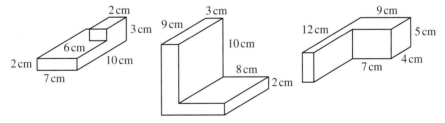

12 What is the weight of a plastic brick whose dimensions are 2 cm by 4 cm by 1.5 cm if the density of the plastic is 1.4 g/cm³?

13 What is the weight of a bar of metal which is 15 cm by 6 cm by 4 cm if the density of the metal is 2.7 g/cm³?

14 A block of wood, 12 cm by 7 cm by 5 cm, weighs 380 g. What is the density of the wood?

15 A flagstone, 60 cm by 60 cm by 4 cm, was made from material which had a density of 2.4 g/cm³. A truck carried 240 of these flagstones to a park. How heavy was this load?

16 Sugar cubes are 1 cm³. I dissolve 5 of these lumps in a glass holding 450 cm³ of water, which has a density of 1 g/cm³. Given that the density of sugar is 1.6 g/cm³, what will be the density of the solution assuming that the volume stays the same at 450 cm³?

17 Find the depth of a tank which contains 3.6 m³ of water, the area of the base being 7500 cm².

18 A tank contains 32 000 litres of water. The base of the tank measures 6.5 m by 3.1 m. Find the depth of water in the tank.

19 A room contains 168 m³ of air. The height of the room is 3.5 m. What is the area of the floor?

20 Find the weight of an iron bar 1.2 m long, 11 cm wide and 6 cm deep, given that the density of iron is 7.9 g/cm³.

21 What are the dimensions of a cube with a volume of
    a   27 cm³   **b**   125 m³   **c**   8 mm³   **d**   1.44 m³?

Volume of cylinders and prisms

Volume of a cylinder

The volume of a cylinder is found by multiplying the area of its circular end by the length of the cylinder. That is,

Volume = $\pi r^2 h$

where r is the radius of the cylinder and h is its height or length.

For example, what is the volume of a cylinder having radius 5 cm and height 12 cm?

Volume = Base area × Height
$$= \pi r^2 \times h = \pi \times 5^2 \times 12 = 942 \text{ cm}^3$$

EXERCISE 5B

1 Find the volume of each of these cylinders.
    a   Base radius 4 cm and height 5 cm.
    b   Base diameter 9 cm and height 7 cm.
    c   Base diameter 13.5 cm and height 15 cm.
    d   Base radius 1.2 m and length 5.5 m.

2 Find the volume of each of these cylinders.

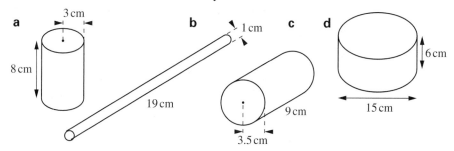

3 The diameter of a cylindrical marble column is 60 cm and its height is 4.2 m. The cost of making this column is quoted as £67.50 a cubic metre. What is the estimated total cost of making the column?

4 Find the weight of a solid iron cylinder 55 cm high with a base diameter of 60 cm. The density of iron is 7.9 g/cm³.

5 What is the radius of a cylinder 7 cm long and with a volume of 200 cm³?

6 What is the diameter of a cylinder 12 cm long and with a volume of 150 cm³?

7 A cylindrical container is 65 cm in diameter. Water is poured into the container until it is 1 metre deep. How much water is in the container? (Remember 1000 cm³ = 1 litre.)

8 A cylindrical can of soup has a diameter of 7 cm and a height of 9.5 cm. It is full of soup which weighs 625 g. What is the density of the soup?

9 An iron drainpipe has an outer diameter of 12 cm and an inner diameter of 11.5 cm.
  a What volume of iron is in the 4 m long drainpipe?
  b What is the mass of the drainpipe, given that iron has a density of 7.9 g/cm³?

10 15 cm³ of gold are rolled and made into wire 90 m long. Calculate the diameter of the wire.

11 A metal bar, 1 m long, and with a diameter of 6 cm, weighs 22 kg. What is the density of the metal from which the bar is made?

12 A solid iron cylinder of diameter 15 cm and height 12 cm is melted down to make wire 0.01 cm thick (diameter). What length of wire will be made?

13 What is the length of 0.015 cm thick wire made from a block of copper measuring 40 cm by 15 cm by 10 cm?

14 Give the answers to this question in terms of π.
  What are the volumes of the following cylinders?
  a With a base radius of 6 cm and a height of 11 cm.
  b With a base diameter of 10 cm and a height of 12 cm.

Volume of prisms

A prism is a 3-D shape which has the same cross-section running all the way through it.

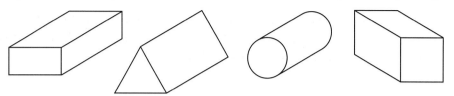

The volume of a prism is found by multiplying the area of its regular cross-section by the length of the prism (or height if the prism is stood on end). That is,

Volume of prism = Area of cross-section × Length

For example, this diagram shows a prism with a triangular cross-section.

The area of its cross-section is the area of its triangular end, which is

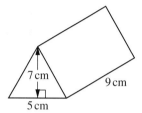

$$\frac{5 \times 7}{2} = 17.5 \text{ cm}^2$$

The volume is the area of its cross-section × its length, which is

$$17.5 \text{ cm}^2 \times 9 \text{ cm} = 157.5 \text{ cm}^3$$

EXERCISE 5C

1 For each prism shown
  i sketch the cross-section   **ii** calculate the area of the cross-section
  iii calculate the volume.

a
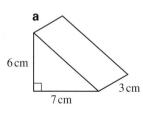

b
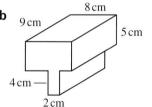

c
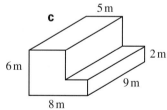

d
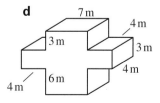

e
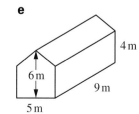

f
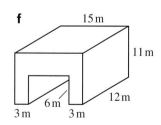

2 The uniform cross-section of a swimming pool is a trapezium with parallel sides, 1 m and 2.5 m, with a perpendicular distance of 30 m between them. The width of the pool is 10 m. How much water is in the pool when it is full?

3 A container is made in the shape shown. The top and bottom are the same size, both consisting of a rectangle, 4 cm by 9 cm, with a semicircle at each end. The depth is 3 cm. Find the volume of the container.

4 Each of these prisms has a regular cross-section in the shape of a right-angled triangle.
    a Find the volume of each prism.
    b Find the total surface area of each prism.

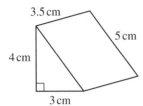
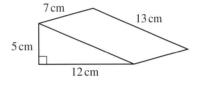

5 A lean-to is a prism as shown. Calculate the volume of air inside the lean-to.

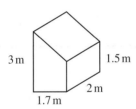

6 A tunnel is in the shape of a semicircle of radius 5 m, running for 500 m through a hill. Calculate the volume of soil removed when the tunnel was cut through the hill.

7 A horse trough is in the shape of a semicircular prism as shown. What volume of water will the trough hold when it is filled to the top?

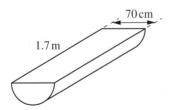

8 The dimensions of the cross-section of a girder, 2 m in length, are shown on the diagram. The girder is made of iron with a density of 7.9 g/cm³. What is the weight of the girder?

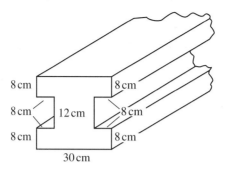

8 cm   8 cm
8 cm   12 cm   8 cm
8 cm   8 cm
30 cm

9 Which of these solids is
   a the heaviest   **b** the lightest?

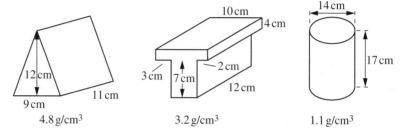

12 cm   9 cm   11 cm
4.8 g/cm³

10 cm   4 cm
3 cm   7 cm   2 cm
12 cm
3.2 g/cm³

14 cm
17 cm
1.1 g/cm³

10 A block of wood has a hole of radius 2.5 cm drilled out as shown in the diagram. Calculate the weight of the wood if its density is 0.95 g/cm³.

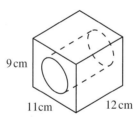

9 cm
11 cm   12 cm

11 I have a length of guttering 3 metres long. Its regular cross-section is a semicircle of radius 7 cm. What is the volume of water that this gutter could hold if the ends were blocked off?

Give your answer in terms of π.

Possible coursework tasks

Heat loss and office blocks

This office loses 5 units of heat. Investigate how much heat is lost for office blocks containing two or more offices. Each office must have at least one external window.

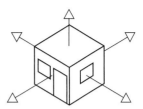

Cubes

Take 4 cubes. How many different solids can you make using all 4 cubes?
Investigate the minimum and maximum surface areas for the solids you have made.

The open box problem

A rectangular piece of card is made into an open box by cutting a square from each corner, as shown.

Investigate how to obtain a box which has the maximum volume. (You may find it easier to solve this problem using a spreadsheet.)

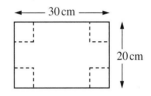

The guttering problem

A length of guttering is made from a rectangular sheet of plastic, 20 cm wide.

What is the best position for the folds so that the guttering carries the maximum amount of water?

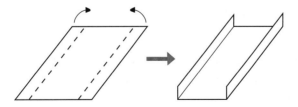

Cylinders

The rectangle can be rolled into a cylinder in two different ways. Which way gives the larger volume?

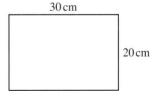

Examination questions: coursework type

1 Cheesecake recipe

Base 6 oz crushed digestive biscuits Filling 12 oz soft cheese

2 oz butter   2 oz sugar

2 oz chopped nuts   2 teaspoons of cornflour

Grease a $7\frac{1}{2}$ inch diameter cake tin. Cover the base of the tin with the chopped nuts. Melt the butter and mix with the crushed biscuits. Spoon the mixture …

The recipe continues to explain how to make the cheesecake.

a A 15 inch diameter cheesecake is to be made for a party. It is not simply a matter of doubling the quantities of ingredients. Find the quantity of chopped nuts needed to make the cheesecake for the party. You must show your working.

b Individual cheesecakes are made using $\frac{1}{2}$ oz of chopped nuts. Suggest three different shapes and sizes of cake tins suitable for making the individual cheesecakes. You must show your working.

WJEC, Question 5, Specimen Paper 3, 1998

2 Air passengers are allowed to take one item of hand luggage on the flight. Airlines have different rules about the size of the hand luggage.

Airline 1 Length + width + height of hand luggage must not be more than 150 cm.

Airline 2 The volume of hand luggage must not be more than 60 000 cm³.

Investigate, for each airline, suitable designs of hand luggage which will satisfy the rule and be as large as possible, but made from the smallest amount of material.

SEG, Intermediate Coursework Task B, Specimen Paper, 1998

Examination questions

1 Jeni is making a range of vases from thin metal.

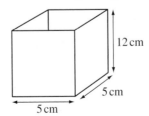

12 cm

5 cm

5 cm

a One vase, in the shape of a cuboid, has the measurements shown.

What volume of water can it hold? State the units of your answer.

b Jeni wants to make a cylindrical vase to hold 500 ml

If it has a radius of 3.5 cm, what height should it be?

Give your answer to a suitable degree of accuracy.

OCR, Question 14, Intermediate Paper 4, June 2000

Examination questions

2 A rubbish skip is a prism. The cross-section is an isosceles trapezium. This diagram shows the inside measurements of the cross-section.

  a The internal width of the skip is 2 m. It is filled with earth. The earth is level with the top of the skip. What is the volume of the earth in the skip?

  b The density of the earth in the skip is 700 kg/m³. What is the weight of the earth in the skip?

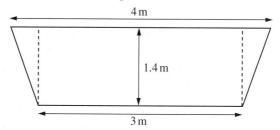

WJEC, Question 11ed, Specimen Paper 2, 1998

3 A rectangular tank has length 60 cm, breadth 40 cm and height 36 cm. It is placed on a horizontal table. Water is poured into the tank until it is three-quarters full.

  a Calculate the depth of water in the tank.

  b Calculate the volume, in cubic centimetres, of water in the tank.

  c Express your answer to part **b** in litres.

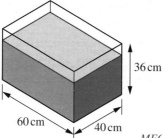

MEG, Question 2, Specimen Paper 3, 1998

4 A motorist fills the fuel tank of his car and a petrol can with petrol.

  a The petrol can is cylindrical. It has a diameter of 16 cm and a height of 24 cm. Calculate, to the nearest litre, the amount of petrol in a full can.

  b The motorist takes 20 seconds to fill the can. The motorist uses the same pump to fill the fuel tank in his car. It takes him 1 minute 48 seconds to fill the tank. How many litres of petrol did he put in the tank?

Petrol can

24 cm

16 cm

SEG, Question 7, Specimen Paper 10, 1998

5 A cylindrical tin of soup is 8.4 cm tall and has a base diameter of 7.0 cm.
   a Calculate the area of the base of the tin.
   b Calculate the capacity of the tin.

NEAB, Question 16, Specimen Paper 2, 1998

6 In Jane's classroom there is a bin. The bin is a
   cylinder with an open top. Jane uses the
   formula $A = \pi r(r + 2h)$ to calculate the surface
   area of the bin. The bin has a radius of 0.48 m
   and a height of 0.76 m. By using suitable
   approximations, show that the surface area of
   the bin is roughly 3 square metres.

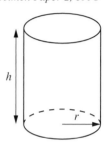

SEG, Question 11b, Specimen Paper 10, 1998

7 Abdul is cooking. He has a pan that has a circular base of radius 12 cm
   filled with water to a depth of 11 cm. He places a sealed cylindrical can
   of radius 4 cm and height 10 cm in the water. It sinks to the bottom of the
   pan. Calculate the new height of the water in the pan.

SEG, Question 20, Specimen Paper 11, 1998

8 The diagram shows a block of Starlight soap. Its volume is 48 cm³.

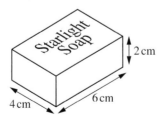

   i Sketch another block of soap with
   different dimensions which also
   has a volume of 48 cm³.
   ii Give the dimensions of your block of
   soap.

NEAB, Question 6, Specimen Paper 1, 1998

Summary

How well do you grade yourself?

To gain a grade E, you need to be able to find the volume of a cuboid.

To gain a grade C, you need to be able to find the volumes of 3-D shapes such as cylinders, cuboids and other regular prisms.

To gain a grade B, you need to be able to use volume and density to find weight, and to use other combinations of these three quantities.

What you should know after you have worked through Chapter 5

- The volume of a cuboid is Length × Breadth × Height.
- The volume of a prism is (the regular) Cross-sectional area × Length.
- The volume of a cylinder is given by $\pi r^2 h$, where r is the radius and h is the height or length of the cylinder.

6 Algebra 1

This chapter is going to ...

remind you about the basic language of algebra and the algebraic processes that you will meet through this book. It will lead you through simple linear equations to equations which are not so simple, including those that need to be solved through the method of trial and improvement.

What you should already know

✔ The basic language of algebra. For example,

$x + 4$ means add 4 to the number x

$x - 2$ means take 2 away from the number x

$a + b$ means add the number b to the number a

$7x$ means 7 multiplied by the number x

$\frac{x}{5}$ means the number x divided by 5

r^2 means the number r multiplied by itself

✔ Like terms only can be added or subtracted to simplify an expression.

For example,

$2x + 3x$ can be added to give $5x$

but $2x + 3y$ cannot give anything simpler

✔ Expressions can be simplified by collecting like terms together.

For example,

$2x + 3y + 3x - y = 5x + 2y$

(dealing with the x's first, then the y's).

✔ A number next to a bracket indicates a multiplication, and everything in the bracket can be multiplied by that number.

For example,

$3(2t - 5) = 3 \times 2t - 3 \times 5$

$\qquad\qquad = 6t - 15$

EXERCISE 6A

1 Write down the algebraic expression that says

    a   2 more than x **b**   6 less than x **c** k more than x

    d t less than x **e** x added to 3   **f** d added to m

    g y taken away from b **h** p added to t added to w **i**   8 multiplied to x

    j h multiplied to j **k** x divided by 4   **l**   2 divided by x

    m y divided by t **n** w multiplied to t **o** a multiplied to a

    p g multiplied by itself

2 Write down the perimeter of each of these shapes.

    a    **b**   **c**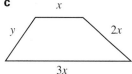

3 Write these expressions in a shorter form.

    a $a+a+a+a+a$ **b** $b+b+b+b$ **c** $c+c+c+c+c+c$

    d $2d+3d$ **e** $4e+5e$ **f** $f+2f+3f$

    g $g+g+g+g-g$ **h** $h+h+h-h-h$ **i** $3i+2i-i$

    j $5j+j-2j$ **k** $4k+5k-2k$ **l** $3l-2l+4l$

    m $4m-5m+3m$ **n** $n+5n-6n$ **o** $20x+14x$

    p $16p+4p-2p$ **q** $9q-3q-3q$ **r** $3r-3r$

    s $6s+s+s-5s$ **t** $5t+5t+5t$ **u** $5u-4u+u+u$

    v $2v-3v$ **w** $2w+4w-7w$ **x** $5x+6x-7x+2x$

    y $8y+5y-7y-y$ **z** $2z-2z+3z-3z$

4 Simplify the following expressions.

    a $3x+4x$ **b** $4y+2y$ **c** $5t-2t$

    d $3m-m$ **e** $k+7k$ **f** $3x-5x$

    g $t-4t$ **h** $-2x-3x$ **i** $-k-4k$

    j $-3x+7x$ **k** $2a+a+6a$ **l** $4t+2t-t$

    m $m+2m-m$ **n** $2y+3y-5y$ **o** $-f+4f-2f$

5 Simplify the following expressions.

    a $4y+2x+5y+3x$ **b** $3m+p-m+4p$ **c** $5x+8+2x-3$

    d $7-2x-1+7x$ **e** $4p+2t+p-2t$ **f** $8+x+4x-2$

    g $5p-4-p-2$ **h** $x+4y+3x+y+2x-3y$ **i** $3+2t+p-t+2+4p$

    j $5w-2k-2w-3k+5w$ **k** $7+4x-8-6x+4$ **l** $5x+2y+5-y-5x-y$

    m $a+b+c+d-a-b-d$ **n** $9k-y-5y-k+10$

6 Write these in a shorter form. (Careful – three of them will not simplify.)

a $a + b + a + b + a$

b $b + c + b + c + c$

c $c + d + d + d + c$

d $2d + 2e + 3d$

e $4e + 5f + 2f + e$

f $f + 3g + 4h$

g $g + h + g + h - g$

h $h + j + h - j + j - h$

i $3i + 2k - i + k$

j $5j + 3k - 2j + 4k$

k $4k + 5p - 2k + 4p$

l $3k + 2m + 5p$

m $4m - 5n + 3m - 2n$

n $n + 3p - 6p + 5n$

o $20x + 14y$

p $19p + 4q - 2p + 5q$

q $9q - 3r - 3r + 7q$

r $3r - 3s + 3s - 3r$

s $6s + t + s - 5t$

t $5t + 5s + 5t$

u $5u - 4v + u + v$

v $2v - 5w + 5w$

w $2w + 4y - 7y$

x $5x + 6x - 7y + 2y$

y $8y + 5z - 7z - 9y$

z $2z - 2x + 3x - 3z$

7 Find the perimeter of each of these shapes in its simplest form.

a

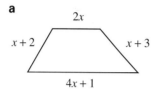

b

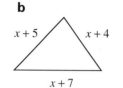

c

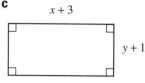

8 Multiply out the following brackets, leaving the answer as simple as possible.

a $2(f + 3)$

b $3(k - 4)$

c $4(t + 1)$

d $3(2d + 3)$

e $4(3t - 2)$

f $2(5m + 3)$

g $4(5 + 2w)$

h $2(3 - 4x)$

i $3(4 + 5p)$

j $5(2t + 3w)$

k $4(3m - 2d)$

l $3(2x + 5y)$

m $2(4f + 3)$

n $5(8 - 2t)$

o $3(4g + 2t)$

9 Give the total cost of

a 5 pens at 15p each

b x pens at 15p each

c 4 pens at Ap each

d y pens at Ap each

10 A boy went shopping with £A. He spent £B. How much has he got left?

11 Five ties cost £A. What is the cost of one tie?

12 My dad is 72 and I am T years old. How old will we both be in x years time?

13 I am twice as old as my son. I am T years old.

a How old is my son?

b How old will my son be in 4 years time?

c How old was I x years ago?

14 Joseph is given £t, John has £3 more than Joseph, Joy has £$2t$.

a How much more has Joy than Joseph?

b How much have they got altogether?

15 What is the total perimeter of these figures?

a A square of side $2x$.

b An equilateral triangle of side $4m$.

c A regular hexagon with a side $3t$.

Substitution

One of the most important features of algebra is the use of expressions and formulae and the substitution of real numbers into them.

The value of an expression, such as $3x + 2$, will change with the different values of x substituted into it. For example, the expression $3x + 2$ has the value

5 when $x = 1$ 14 when $x = 4$

and so on. A formula, too, is used to express the value of one variable as the others in the formula change. For example, the formula for the area of a trapezium is

$$A = h\left(\frac{a+b}{2}\right)$$

When $a = 4$, $b = 7$ and $h = 8$

$$A = 8\,\frac{(4+7)}{2} = 44$$

EXERCISE 6B

1 Find the value of $3x + 2$ when   **i** $x = 2$ **ii** $x = 5$ **iii** $x = 10$

2 Find the value of $4k - 1$ when   **i** $k = 1$ **ii** $k = 3$ **iii** $k = 11$

3 Find the value of $5 + 2t$ when   **i** $t = 2$ **ii** $t = 5$ **iii** $t = 12$

4 Evaluate $15 - 2f$ when   **i** $f = 3$ **ii** $f = 5$ **iii** $f = 8$

5 Evaluate $5m + 3$ when   **i** $m = 2$ **ii** $m = 6$ **iii** $m = 15$

6 Evaluate $3d - 2$ when   **i** $d = 4$ **ii** $d = 5$ **iii** $d = 20$

7 Find the value of $\dfrac{8 + 4h}{5}$ when   **i** $h = 3$ **ii** $h = 7$ **iii** $h = 31$

8 Find the value of $\dfrac{25 - 3p}{2}$ when   **i** $p = 4$ **ii** $p = 8$ **iii** $p = 10$

9 Find the value of $2x + 3$ when   **i** $x = -1$ **ii** $x = -3$ **iii** $x = 1.5$

10 Evaluate $3w - 4$ when   **i** $w = -1$ **ii** $w = -2$ **iii** $w = 3.5$

11 Evaluate $8 + 4g$ when   **i** $g = -2$ **ii** $g = -5$ **iii** $g = 2.5$

12 Evaluate $10 - x$ when   **i** $x = -2$ **ii** $x = -4$ **iii** $x = 5.6$

13 Find the value of $4b + 3$ when   **i** $b = 2.5$ **ii** $b = -1.5$ **iii** $b = \frac{1}{2}$

14 Find the value of $6t - 5$ when   **i** $t = 3.4$ **ii** $t = -2.5$ **iii** $t = \frac{3}{4}$

15 Find the value of $1 + 5y$ when   **i** $y = 2.5$ **ii** $y = -3.4$ **iii** $y = \frac{1}{3}$

16 Evaluate $8 - 2t$ when   **i** $t = 1.5$ **ii** $t = -2.3$ **iii** $t = \frac{3}{4}$

17 Evaluate $\frac{x}{3}$ when   **i** $x = 6$ **ii** $x = 24$ **iii** $x = -30$

18 Evaluate $\frac{A}{4}$ when   **i** $A = 12$ **ii** $A = 10$ **iii** $A = -20$

19 Find the value of $\frac{12}{y}$ when   **i** $y = 2$ **ii** $y = 4$ **iii** $y = -6$

20 Find the value of $\frac{24}{x}$ when   **i** $x = -5$ **ii** $x = \frac{1}{2}$ **iii** $x = \frac{3}{4}$

Using your calculator

You could try working out a solution on your calculator, remembering to put in the brackets as required.

Take the expression

$$t = 5 \left(\frac{w + 2d}{4} \right)$$

To find t when, for example, $w = 6$ and $d = 3.5$, you put this into your calculator as

You should get the answer 16.25.

When you have to work out the bottom part of a fraction, you will also need to use brackets to do this part separately. For example, take

$$k = \frac{a + c}{b - d}$$

To evaluate k when $a = 8$, $c = 3$, $b = 7$ and $d = 3$, you put this into your calculator as

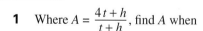

You should get the answer 2.75.

Notice that the expression doesn't include brackets, but you need to use them on your calculator.

EXERCISE 6C

1 Where $A = \frac{4t + h}{t + h}$, find A when

     a $t = 2$ and $h = 3$ **b** $t = 3$ and $h = 5$ **c** $t = 1$ and $h = 9$

2 Where $P = \frac{5w - 4y}{w + y}$, find P when

     a $w = 3$ and $y = 2$ **b** $w = 6$ and $y = 4$ **c** $w = 2$ and $y = 3$

3   Where $T = \dfrac{2x + 3}{2 + x}$, find T when

   a $x = 3$ **b** $x = -3$ **c** $x = 2.5$

4   Where $Y = x^2$, find Y when

   a $x = 3$ **b** $x = -5$ **c** $x = 1.2$

5   Where $Z = \dfrac{y^2 + 3}{4 + y}$, find Z when

   a $y = 4$ **b** $y = -6$ **c** $y = 8.5$

6   Where $A = b^2 + c^2$, find A when

   a $b = 2$ and $c = 3$ **b** $b = 5$ and $c = 7$ **c** $b = -1$ and $c = -4$

7   Where $L = f^2 - g^2$, find L when

   a $f = 6$ and $g = 3$ **b** $f = -3$ and $g = -2$ **c** $f = 5$ and $g = -5$

8   Where $C = \dfrac{N^2 + N}{N + 1}$, find C when

   a $N = 4$ **b** $N = -3$ **c** $N = 1.5$

9   Where $T = P - n^2$, find T when

   a $P = 100$ and $n = 5$ **b** $P = 17$ and $n = 3$ **c** $P = 10$ and $n = 4$

10   Where $A = \dfrac{180\,(n - 2)}{n + 5}$, find A when

   a $n = 7$ **b** $n = 3$ **c** $n = 1$

In questions **11** to **15**, give your answers correct to a suitable degree of accuracy.

11   Where $A = \pi r^2$, find A when

   a $r = 1.7$ **b** $r = 4.5$ **c** $r = 7.8$

12   Where $t = 10 - \sqrt{P}$, find t when

   a $P = 10$ **b** $P = 25$ **c** $P = 8$

13   Where $W = \dfrac{v + 5}{m + 2}$, find W when

   a $v = 3$ and $m = 7$ **b** $v = 2$ and $m = 3$ **c** $v = -3$ and $m = 8$

14   Where $K = \sqrt{(a + 3b)}$, find K when

   a $a = 5$ and $b = 2$ **b** $a = 8$ and $b = -1$ **c** $a = 9$ and $b = 2.5$

15   Where $h = \sqrt{(a^2 + b^2)}$, find h when

   a $a = 4$ and $b = 6$ **b** $a = 4.5$ and $b = 7.5$ **c** $a = -3$ and $b = -7$

Solving equations

The first type of equation we need to be able to solve is the **linear equation**.
Here are some examples of the linear equation:

$$2x + 1 = 1 \qquad 5y - 2 = 3 \qquad 9 - 4t = 5$$

Notice that there are no powers or roots of the variables (x, y and t) in these equations.

We solve an equation by rearranging its terms until eventually we get the variable (letter) we want on its own – usually on the left-hand side of the 'equals' sign.

Example 1

Solve $4x + 3 = 23$.

We move 3 to give $\qquad\qquad\qquad\qquad 4x = 23 - 3 = 20$

We now divide both sides by 4 to give $\qquad x = \dfrac{20}{4} = 5$

So the solution is $\qquad\qquad\qquad\qquad x = 5$

Example 2

Solve $\dfrac{y}{5} - 4 = 3$.

We move 4 to give $\qquad\qquad\qquad\qquad \dfrac{y}{5} = 3 + 4 = 7$

We now multiply both sides by 5 to give $\quad y = 7 \times 5 = 35$

So the solution is $\qquad\qquad\qquad\qquad y = 35$

EXERCISE 6D

Solve the following equations.

1 $3x + 5 = 11$	**2** $3x - 13 = 26$	**3** $3x - 7 = 32$	**4** $4y - 19 = 5$
5 $3a + 8 = 11$	**6** $2x + 8 = 14$	**7** $6 + y = 18$	**8** $8x + 4 = 12$
9 $2x - 10 = 8$	**10** $x + 4 = 60$	**11** $3y - 2 = 4$	**12** $3x - 4 = 11$
13 $5y + 3 = 18$	**14** $7 + 3t = 19$	**15** $5 + 4f = 15$	**16** $3 + 6k = 24$
17 $4x + 7 = 17$	**18** $5m - 3 = 17$	**19** $3t + 17 = 29$	**20** $6d + 3 = 30$
21 $5x + 2.5 = 10$	**22** $3y - 1.5 = 9$	**23** $5p + 4 = 10$	**24** $5t - 4 = 5$

EXERCISE 6E

Solve the following equations.

1 $\dfrac{x}{5} = 3$	**2** $\dfrac{t}{3} = 2$	**3** $\dfrac{y}{4} = 7$	**4** $\dfrac{k}{2} = 8$
5 $\dfrac{h}{8} = 5$	**6** $\dfrac{w}{6} = 4$	**7** $\dfrac{x}{4} + 5 = 7$	**8** $\dfrac{y}{2} - 3 = 5$

9 $\dfrac{f}{5} + 2 = 8$ **10** $\dfrac{w}{3} - 5 = 2$ **11** $\dfrac{x}{8} + 3 = 12$ **12** $\dfrac{m}{7} - 3 = 5$

13 $\dfrac{2x}{5} + 3 = 7$ **14** $\dfrac{4y}{3} - 2 = 6$ **15** $\dfrac{5t}{4} + 3 = 18$ **16** $\dfrac{3y}{2} - 1 = 8$

17 $\dfrac{2x}{3} + 5 = 12$ **18** $\dfrac{4x}{5} - 3 = 7$ **19** $\dfrac{5x}{2} + 3 = 2$ **20** $\dfrac{5x}{7} + 4 = 3$

EXERCISE 6F

Solve the following equations.

1 $2x + 8 = 6$ **2** $2t + 7 = 1$ **3** $10 + 3x = 4$ **4** $15 + 4y = 3$

5 $8 - 2x = 10$ **6** $9 - 4t = 17$ **7** $6 - 5x = 21$ **8** $\dfrac{x}{3} + 7 = 5$

9 $\dfrac{t}{5} + 3 = 1$ **10** $\dfrac{x+3}{2} = 5$ **11** $\dfrac{t-5}{4} = 3$ **12** $\dfrac{x+10}{2} = 3$

13 $\dfrac{2x+1}{3} = 5$ **14** $\dfrac{5y-2}{4} = 3$ **15** $\dfrac{4t+3}{2} = 5$ **16** $\dfrac{3x-1}{10} = 2$

17 $\dfrac{5x-2}{7} = 4$ **18** $\dfrac{6y+3}{9} = 1$ **19** $\dfrac{2x-3}{5} = 4$ **20** $\dfrac{5t+3}{4} = 1$

Brackets

When we have an equation which contains brackets, we have a choice. We can either
- first multiply out the brackets, then solve the equation, or
- first work out the value of the brackets, then solve the equation.

Example 1

Solve $3(2x - 7) = 15$.

If we first multiply out the brackets, we get

$$6x - 21 = 15$$
$$6x = 15 + 21 = 36$$
$$\Rightarrow \quad x = \frac{36}{6} = 6$$

If we use the second method and first work out the value of the brackets, we get

$$2x - 7 = \frac{15}{3} = 5$$
$$2x = 5 + 7 = 12$$
$$\Rightarrow \quad x = \frac{12}{2} = 6$$

As you see, you will always get the same answer. The only difference is that sometimes you will find it easier first to multiply out the brackets, and at other times easier first to work out the value of the brackets.

EXERCISE 6G

Solve the following equations.

1 $2(x+5)=16$	**2** $5(x-3)=20$	**3** $3(t+1)=18$	**4** $4(2x+5)=44$
5 $2(3y-5)=14$	**6** $5(4x+3)=135$	**7** $4(3t-2)=88$	**8** $6(2t+5)=42$
9 $2(3x+1)=11$	**10** $4(5y-2)=42$	**11** $6(3k+5)=39$	**12** $5(2x+3)=27$
13 $5(3y-2)=26$	**14** $2(7t-3)=57$	**15** $4(5x-4)=54$	**16** $9(3x-5)=9$
17 $2(x+5)=6$	**18** $5(x-4)=-25$	**19** $3(t+7)=15$	**20** $2(3x+11)=10$
21 $4(5t+8)=12$	**22** $5(2x-1)=-45$	**23** $7(3y+5)=-7$	**24** $2(3x+8)=7$

Trial and improvement

Certain equations cannot be solved exactly. However, a close enough solution to such an equation can be found by the trial-and-improvement method. (Sometimes wrongly called the trial-and-error method.)

The idea is to keep trying different values in the equation which will take it closer and closer to its 'true' solution. This step-by-step process is continued until a value is found which gives a solution that is close enough to the accuracy required.

The trial-and-improvement method is the way in which computers are programmed to solve equations.

Example

Solve the equation $x^3 + x = 100$, giving the solution to 2 decimal places.

Step 1   We must find the two consecutive whole numbers between which x lies. We do this by intelligent guessing.

Try $x = 5$: $125 + 5 = 130$ Too high – next trial needs to be much smaller.

Try $x = 4$: $64 + 4 = 68$ Too low.

So we now know that the solution lies between $x = 4$ and $x = 5$.

Step 2   We now must try 4.5, which is halfway between 4 and 5.

Try 4.5: $91.125 + 4.5 = 95.625$ Too small but very close.

So we attempt to improve this by trying 4.6.

Try 4.6: $97.336 + 4.6 = 101.936$ Too high.

We now know the solution lies between 4.5 and 4.6.

Step 3 We now have to try 4.55, which is halfway between 4.5 and 4.6.

Try 4.55:   94.1964 + 4.55 = 98.746 (rounded)   Too low.

So we next try between 4.55 and 4.6 (close to halfway).

Try 4.57:   95.444 + 4.57 = 100.014 (rounded) Too high (just).

Try 4.56:   94.8188 + 4.56 = 99.3788 (rounded) Too low.

We now know the solution lies between 4.56 and 4.57, but which is closer?

Step 4 We cannot find which of these numbers is closer by just looking at them, because the differences between the values of the equation do not go up equally. So again we try the halfway value, which is 4.565.

Try 4.565:   95.131 + 4.565 = 99.696   Too low.

So 4.57 is nearest to the true solution (to 2 decimal places).

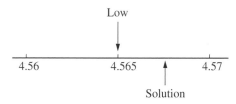

If the question had asked for the solution to be given to 1 decimal place, we should have stopped at 4.55 because this value immediately shows us that 4.6 is the nearest solution to 1 decimal place.

EXERCISE 6H

1 Without using a calculator, find the two consecutive whole numbers between which the solution to each of the following equations lies.

   a $x^3 = 20$ **b** $x^3 = 80$ **c** $x^3 = 200$ **d** $x^3 = 450$

2 Find a solution to each of the following equations to 1 decimal place. Do not use the cube-root key on your calculator.

   a $x^3 = 30$ **b** $x^3 = 90$ **c** $x^3 = 250$ **d** $x^3 = 500$

3 Find a solution to each of the following equations to 2 decimal places. Do not use the cube-root key on your calculator.

   a $x^3 = 40$ **b** $x^3 = 70$ **c** $x^3 = 180$ **d** $x^3 = 600$

4 Without using the cube-root key on your calculator, find the cube root of the following numbers, giving your answer to 1 decimal place.

   a 55   **b** 75   **c** 175

5 Find the two consecutive **whole numbers** between which the solution to each of the following equations lies.

a $x^3 + x = 24$ **b** $x^3 + x = 61$ **c** $x^3 + x = 575$

6 Find a solution to each of the following equations to 1 decimal place.

a $x^3 + x = 33$ **b** $x^3 + x = 52$ **c** $x^3 + x = 79$

7 Find a solution to each of the following equations to 1 decimal place.

a $x^3 = 20$ **b** $x^3 - x = 28$ **c** $x^3 + x = 7$

8 Find a solution to each of the following equations to 1 decimal place.

a $x(x^2 + 5) = 110$ **b** $x(x^2 + 10) = 61$ **c** $x(x^2 + 8) = 109$

EXERCISE 6I

1 A rectangle has an area of $100\,cm^2$. Its length is $5\,cm$ longer than its width. Find, correct to 1 decimal place, the dimensions of the rectangle.

2 A gardener wants his rectangular lawn to be $10\,m$ longer than the width, and the area of the lawn to be $550\,m^2$. What are the dimensions he should make his lawn? (Give your solution to 1 decimal place.)

3 A triangle has a vertical height $1\,cm$ longer than its base length. Its area is $19\,cm^2$. What are the dimensions of the triangle? (Give your solution to 2 decimal places.)

4 A rectangular picture has a height $1\,cm$ shorter than its length. Its area is $96\,cm^2$. What are the dimensions of the picture? (Give your solution to 1 decimal place.)

5 What are the dimensions, to 1 decimal place, of a cube that has a volume of $475\,cm^3$?

6 A square piece of card, whose area is $100\,cm^2$, has a square cut out from its middle so that the two pieces of card have the same area. What is the size of the cut-out square? (Give your answer to 1 decimal place.)

7 A square piece of card, whose area is $100\,cm^2$, is to have a square cut out at each corner, as in the diagram. What size must each cut-out square be if the area left is to be $50\,cm^2$? (Give your answers to 1 decimal place.)

8 What is the length of a cube with volume $5.8\,cm^3$? (Give your answer to 2 decimal places.)

9 Find, correct to 1 decimal place, the solution to each of these equations.

a $x^2 - \dfrac{1}{x} = 5$ **b** $x^2 + \dfrac{1}{x} = 10$ **c** $x^3 - \dfrac{1}{x} = 2$

10 Find, correct to 1 decimal place, the solution to $x^4 = 46$.

Possible coursework tasks

School dinners

For dinners a school arranges square tables in a row and places chairs around the tables, as in the diagram.

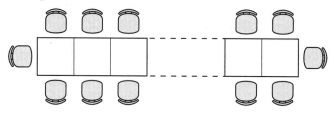

Find a formula for the number of chairs needed when n tables are arranged in a single row.

Handshakes

At a meeting, there are n people who introduce themselves to everyone else in the room. How many handshakes will there be if every person shakes hands with every other person?

A number chain

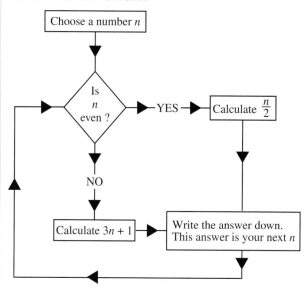

Investigate for n, where n is a whole number.

A prime example

Evaluate the expression $x^2 + x + 41$ for different values of x. Investigate whether the expression generates prime numbers.

Round and round we go

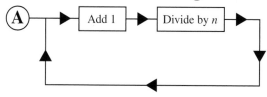

Investigate.

Examination questions: coursework type

1 Investigate the truth of this statement.

There are no numbers x and y such that $x^2 - 2y^2 = 1$.

WJEC, Question 3b, Paper 3, June 1995

2 Pam is using straws and drawing pins to make a row of triangles.

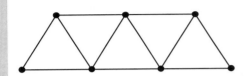

I used 7 drawing pins and 11 straws to make this row of 5 triangles.

a Complete Pam's table.

Number of triangles	1	2	3	4	5	6
Number of drawing pins					7	

b What do you notice about the number of drawing pins needed?

c Write down a rule for working out the number of drawing pins needed for n triangles.

d Pam decides to use straws and drawing pins to make a row of squares. Investigate this situation.

3 Fred decides to cover the kitchen floor with tiles of different colours.
He starts with a row of four tiles of the same colour.
He surrounds these four tiles with a border of tiles of a different colour.
The design continues as shown.

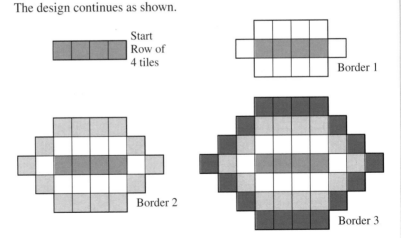

Start
Row of
4 tiles

Border 1

Border 2

Border 3

Fred makes a table to show how many different tiles he needs for each border.

Border number	1	2	3
Number of tiles in border	10	14	18

He writes $t = 4b + 6$, where t is the number of tiles and b is the border number.

a Check whether Fred's formula is correct if he continues this pattern.

b Check Emma's statement (see below) and show that it is not correct.

> Fred started with four tiles and his formula was
> $t = 4b + 6$
> So if I start with five tiles, my formula will be $t = 5b + 6$.

c Find the correct formula for starting with five tiles.

Examination questions

1 This is an approximate rule to change a temperature in degrees Celsius (C), into one in degrees Fahrenheit (F).

Double the Celsius temperature, then add 30.

  a Write this approximate rule as a formula for F in terms of C.

  b Use your formula, or otherwise, to find

    i F when $C = 54$ **ii** C when $F = 54$

NEAB, Question 7, Specimen Paper 1, 1998

2 The diagram shows a cuboid with length l, breadth b, and height h. Write in its simplest form an expression for the total length of all the edges of the cuboid in terms of l, b and h.

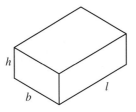

SEG, Question 4a, Specimen Paper II, 1998

3 Solve the equations

  a $7x = 56$ **b** $6y + 5 = 14$ **c** $2z + 6 = 21 - z$

MEG, Question 6, Specimen Paper 3, 1998

4 Solve the equation $3(x - 1) = 15$.

WJEC, Question 8, Specimen Paper 1, 1998

5 The diagram shows a square and a rectangle. The square has sides of length $2y$ metres. The rectangle has length $3y$ metres and breadth 3 metres.

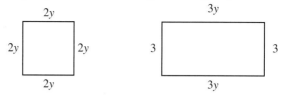

a **i** Find, in terms of y, the perimeter of the square.
  ii Find, in terms of y, the perimeter of the rectangle.
b The perimeter of the square is equal to the perimeter of the rectangle. Work out the value of y.
c The areas of these two rectangles are the same.

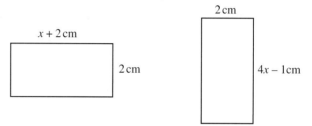

By solving the equation $2(x + 2) = 2(4x - 1)$ find the area of one of these rectangles.

SEG, Question 9, Specimen Paper 11, 1998

6 This picture shows some packets of rice in the pans of a weighing machine. Each packet of rice weighs x kg.

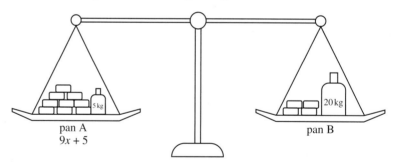

In pan A there are 9 packets of rice and a weight of 5 kg. An expression for the total weight in kg in pan A is $9x + 5$. In pan B there are 4 packets of rice and a weight of 20 kg.
a Write down in terms of x an expression for the total weight in pan B.
The total weight in each pan is the same.
b Write down an equation in terms of x to represent this information.
c Use your equation to calculate the weight, x kg, of one packet of rice.

ULEAC, Question 3, Paper 4, June 1994

7 **a** Solve

    i $2x = 7$ **ii** $3x - 5 = 13$ **iii** $6x - 9 = x + 26$

  b Simplify

    i $4q + 9q + 3q$ **ii** $6n + 5p + 2n - p$

OCR, Question 3, Intermediate Paper 3, June 2000

8 The length of a rectangle is 2 cm more than its width.

  a Calculate the area of the rectangle

    i when the width is 4 cm   **ii** when the width is 5 cm.

  b Using a trial-and-improvement method, find the width of the rectangle given that its area is 32 cm². (Give your answer in centimetres correct to one decimal place.)

MEG, Question 9, Specimen Paper 3, 1998

9 This question is about finding a solution to the equation $x^3 + 2x = 7$ by a trial-and-improvement method.

  a Complete the entries in the following table.

x	$x^3 + 2x$
1.4	5.544
1.5	
1.6	
1.7	8.313

  b Between which two consecutive values of x used in the table in **a** does the solution to the equation lie?

  c Using a value for x with 2 decimal places, determine which of your two values in **b** is the solution to the equation to 1 decimal place.

WJEC, Question 16, Specimen Paper 1, 1998

10 The length of a man's forearm (f cm) and his height (h cm) are approximately related by the formula

    $h = 3f + 90$

  a Part of the skeleton of a man is found and the forearm is 20 cm long. Use the formula to estimate the height of the man.

  b A man's height is 162 cm. Use the formula to estimate the length of his forearm.

  c George is 1 year old and he is 70 cm tall. Find the value the formula gives for the length of his forearm and state why this value is impossible.

MEG, Question 7, Specimen Paper 4, 1998

11 Paul is solving the equation $x^4 = 37$ by a trial-and-improvement method. He sees that

    $2.1^4 = 19.4481$ $2.6^4 = 45.6976$

Show how you would continue in this way to find the solution to the equation, correct to 1 decimal place.

WJEC, Question 14, Paper 1, June 1994

12 The number x satisfies the equation $x^3 = 20$.

   i Between which two consecutive whole numbers does x lie?

   ii Use a trial and improvement method to find this value of x correct to one decimal place. Show all your working clearly.

NEAB, Question 11, Paper 2, June 1995

13 A student conducts a survey of the heights of fathers and their adult daughters. From the data collected she finds that the height, f inches, of a father is related to the height, d inches, of his adult daughter by the formula $f = 32 + 0.6d$

   a Calculate the height of a daughter whose father is 68 inches tall.

   b A father and daughter are the same height.

     By putting $f = d$, find this height.

   c Rearrange the original formula to make d the subject.

OCR, Intermediate Paper 3, June 2000

14 A rocket is fired vertically upwards with velocity u metres per second. After t seconds the rocket's velocity, v metres per second, is given by the formula $v = u + gt$ (g is a constant)

   a Calculate v when $u = 100$, $g = -9.8$ and $t = 5$.

   b Calculate t when $u = 93.5$, $g = -9.8$ and $v = 20$.

NEAB, Question 15, Specimen Paper 2, 1998

Summary

How well do you grade yourself?

To gain a grade **E**, you need to be able to write simple algebraic expressions from simple situations, and use simple formulae.

To gain a grade **C**, you need to be able to solve equations and problems by trial and improvement. You also need to be able to make simple equations from simple situations and be able to solve them.

To gain a grade **B**, you need to be able to substitute fractions and negative values into expressions and formulae.

What you should know after you have worked through Chapter 6

- How to read and write simple algebraic expressions.
- How to substitute fractional and negative values into different expressions and evaluate them.
- How to solve simple linear equations.
- How to solve equations by trial and improvement.

7 Geometry

This chapter is going to ...

remind you of some of the geometrical terms you have met before, as
well as show you the rules of geometry you need to be familiar with. It
will also revise some of the properties of polygons and show you how
to find the size of their angles.

What you should already know

✔ How to use a protractor to find the size of any angle.

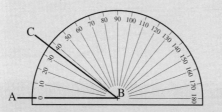 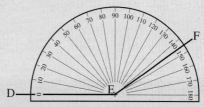

For example, ∠ABC is 35° and ∠DEF is 145°

✔ How to estimate the sizes of angles, and be able to draw an angle
close to a given size.

✔ The meaning of the terms 'acute', 'obtuse', 'reflex', 'right', and be
able to describe angles using these terms.

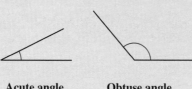 

Acute angle
Less than 90°

Obtuse angle
Greater than 90°
but less than 180°

Right angle
90°

Reflex angle
Greater than 180°
but less than 360°

✔ A polygon is a many-sided plane shape.

✔ A diagonal is a line joining two vertices (corners)
of a polygon, as shown in this diagram.

✔ The dashed lines show two of the four
diagonals of this polygon.

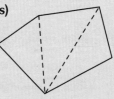

EXERCISE 7A

1 Use a protractor to find the size of each marked angle.

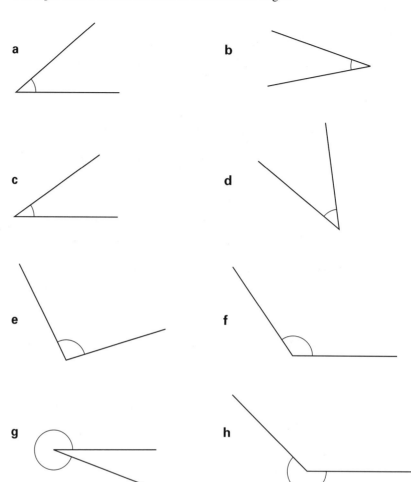

2 a By estimation, try to draw angles of the following sizes.

    i 30° **ii** 60° **iii** 90° **iv** 100° **v** 20° **vi** 45° **vii** 75°

  b Now accurately measure your angles to see how much out you were.

  c **i** What percentage error did you have for each angle?

    ii Which angles were your most accurate?

  d Try drawing these again to see whether you can improve your accuracy.

3 a **i** Draw any three acute angles.

    ii Estimate their size.

    iii What is your total percentage error?

  b Repeat parts **i–iii** using three obtuse angles.

  c Repeat parts **i–iii** using three reflex angles.

  d Which type of angle are you most accurate with, and which type are you least accurate with?

4 Sketch the following triangles without measuring. Then measure and see how close you were.

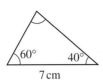
60° 40°
7 cm

40°
6 cm

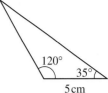
120° 35°
5 cm

Angles

Vertically opposite angles

Vertically opposite angles are equal. You can easily draw this situation for yourself to show that the statement is true.

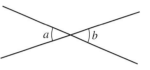

The angles labelled a and b are vertically opposite.

Angles on a line

The angles on a straight line add up to 180°, that is $a + b = 180°$. Check this for yourself, too.

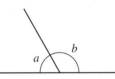 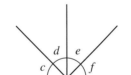

This is true for any number of angles on a line.
For example,

$c + d + e + f = 180°$

Angles around a point

The sum of the angles around a point is 360°.
For example,

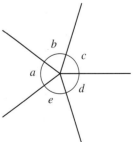

$a + b + c + d + e = 360°$

Also check this for yourself.

Angles in a triangle

The three angles in a triangle add up to 180°, that is

$a + b + c = 180°$

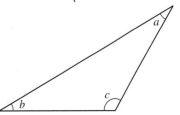

Again, check this for yourself.

EXERCISE 7B

1 Calculate the value of *x* in each of these situations.

a **b** **c** **d**

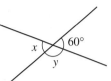 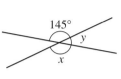 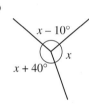 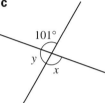

2 Calculate the value of *x* and *y* in each of these situations.

a **b** **c**

  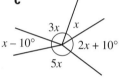 

3 Calculate the value of *x* in each of these situations.

a **b** **c**

 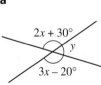

4 Calculate the value of *x* in each of these situations.

a **b** **c**

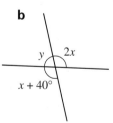 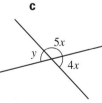

5 Calculate the value of *x* and *y* in each of these situations.

a **b** **c**

6 Calculate the value of *x* in each of these triangles.

a **b** **c** **d**

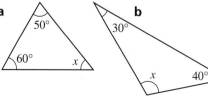 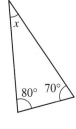 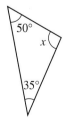

7 Calculate the values of x and y in each of these situations.

a

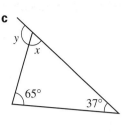

50° x 130° y

b

y 55° 115° x

c

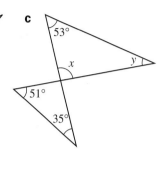

y x 65° 37°

8 Calculate the values of x and y in each of these shapes.

a

70° 60° x y 64°

b

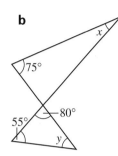

x 75° 55° 80° y

c

53° x y 51° 35°

9 The three angles of a triangle are given by $x + 10°$, $x + 30°$, $x + 50°$. What are the actual angles of the triangle?

10 A triangle has angles given by $2x$, $2x + 5°$, $3x$. What are the actual angles?

Parallel lines

Draw this for yourself to check that it works.

The diagram shows two parallel lines cut by a third line. (The arrowheads indicate that the lines are parallel.) The line which cuts the parallel lines is called a **transversal**.

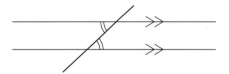

You can see in the diagram that equal angles are formed. The correct name for these is **alternate angles** but they are also popularly known as Z angles, because that is what they look like. This name also reminds us that alternate angles are equal. (Another name for them is F angles.)

All corresponding angles

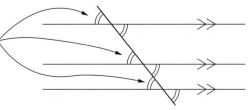

The previous diagram shows three parallel lines cut by a transversal. In this case, either set of equal angles in similar positions on the same side of the transversal are called **corresponding angles**.

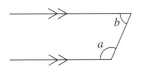

Two angles positioned like *a* and *b*, which add up to 180°, are called **allied** angles.

EXERCISE 7C

1 State the size of the lettered angles in each diagram.

a

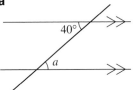

b

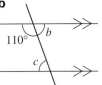

c

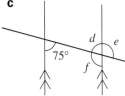

d

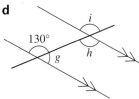

e

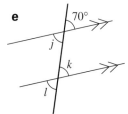

f

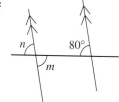

2 State the size of the lettered angles in each situation.

a

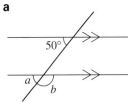

b

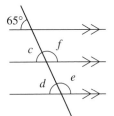

c

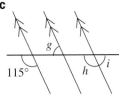

d

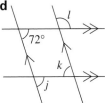

e

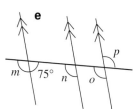

f

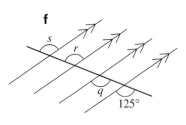

3 Two angles whose sum is 180° and which form a straight line are called
supplementary angles. Write down **all** the pairs of angles in the diagram that are
supplementary.

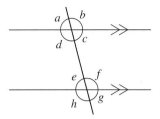

4 State the size of the lettered angles in these diagrams.

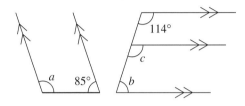

5 Calculate the values of *x* and *y* in these diagrams.

a 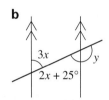 **b** 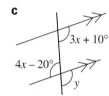 **c**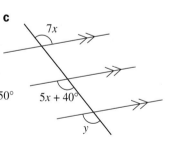

6 Calculate the values of *x* and *y* in these situations.

a 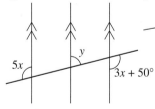 **b** **c**

7 Redraw these diagrams, labelling each angle with its actual value.

a 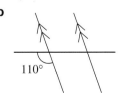 **b** **c**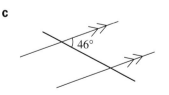

8   Redraw these diagrams, labelling each angle with its actual value.

a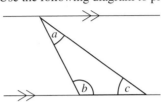

b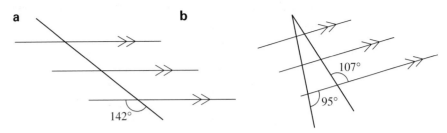

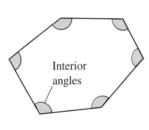

!PROOF

9   Use the following diagram to prove that the three angles in a triangle add up to 180°.

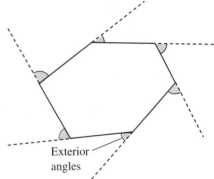

Angles in a polygon

A polygon has two kinds of angle:

Interior angles

Exterior angles

- interior angles (angles made by adjacent sides of the polygon and lying inside the polygon)
- exterior angles (angles lying on the outside of the polygon)

The exterior angles of **any** polygon add up to 360°.

Interior angles

You can find the sum of the interior angles of any polygon by splitting it into triangles.

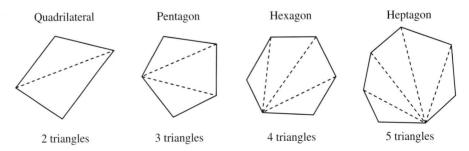

Quadrilateral   Pentagon   Hexagon   Heptagon

2 triangles   3 triangles   4 triangles   5 triangles

Since we already know that the angles in a triangle add up to 180°, the sum of the interior angles in a polygon is found by multiplying the number of triangles in the polygon by 180°, as shown in this table.

Shape	Name	Sum of interior angles
4-sided	Quadrilateral	$2 \times 180° = 360°$
5-sided	Pentagon	$3 \times 180° = 540°$
6-sided	Hexagon	$4 \times 180° = 720°$
7-sided	Heptagon	$5 \times 180° = 900°$
8-sided	Octagon	$6 \times 180° = 1080°$

As you can see from the table, for an N-sided polygon, the sum of the interior angles is $(N - 2) \times 180°$.

As you see from the diagram, the sum of an exterior angle and its adjacent interior angle is 180°.

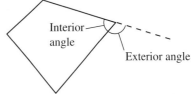

Regular polygons

A polygon is regular if all its interior angles are equal and all its sides have the same length.

Here are two simple rules for calculating the interior and the exterior angles of regular polygons.
- The exterior angle of a regular N-sided polygon $= 360° \div N$
- The interior angle of a regular N-sided polygon $= 180° -$ exterior angle
$$= 180° - (360° \div N)$$

EXERCISE 7D

1 Calculate the sum of the interior angles of polygons with
   a 10 sides   **b** 15 sides   **c** 100 sides   **d** 45 sides

2 Calculate the size of the interior angle of regular polygons with
   a 12 sides   **b** 20 sides   **c** 9 sides   **d** 60 sides

3 Find the number of sides of the polygon with the interior angle sum of
   a 1260°   **b** 2340°   **c** 18 000°   **d** 8640°

4 Find the number of sides of the regular polygon with an exterior angle of
   a 24°   **b** 10°   **c** 15°   **d** 5°

5 Find the number of sides of the regular polygon with an interior angle of
   a 150°   **b** 140°   **c** 162°   **d** 171°

6 Calculate the size of the unknown angle in each of these polygons.

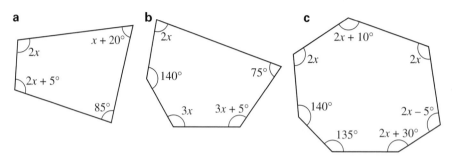

a
95° ? 65° 70°

b
100° 105° 140° 160° 120° ?

c
? 150° 160° 140° 110° 100° 170° 120°

7 Find the value of x in each of these polygons.

a
$2x$ $x + 20°$ $2x + 5°$ 85°

b
$2x$ 140° 75° $3x$ $3x + 5°$

c
$2x + 10°$ $2x$ $2x$ 140° $2x - 5°$ 135° $2x + 30°$

8 What is the name of the regular polygon whose interior angles are twice its exterior angles?

9 Calculate the interior angles of a quadrilateral which are given by
$x + 15°$ $\quad$ $x - 5°$ $\quad$ $2x$ $\quad$ $2x - 10°$

10 Wesley measured all the interior angles in a polygon. He added them up to make 991°, but he had missed out one angle.
a What type of polygon did Wesley measure?
b What is the size of the missing angle?

11 The exterior angles of a polygon are in the ratio 6 : 7 : 8 : 9 : 10.
a What type of polygon is this?
b What are the actual sizes of the exterior angles of this polygon?

Special triangles

Equilateral triangle

An equilateral triangle is a triangle with all its sides equal.
Therefore, all three interior angles are 60°.

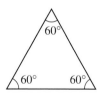

Isosceles triangle

An isosceles triangle is a triangle with two equal sides, and therefore with two equal angles (at the foot of the equal sides). Notice how we mark the equal sides and equal angles.

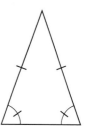

1 Calculate the lettered angles in each triangle.

  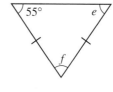

2 Calculate the two identical angles in an isosceles triangle when the other angle is

    a   30°   **b**   80°   **c**   56°   **d**   100°

3 An isosceles triangle has an angle of 50°. Sketch the two different possible triangles that match this description, showing what each angle is.

4 The three angles of an isosceles triangle are $2x$, $x - 10°$ and $x - 10°$. What is the actual size of each angle?

5 Calculate the lettered angles in these diagrams.

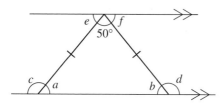 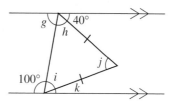

6 Given that ABCDE is a regular pentagon, calculate

    a   angle BCD   **b**   angle BCA   **c**   angle ACD

7 Given that ABCDEF is a regular hexagon, calculate

    a   angle ABC   **b**   angle ACD   **c**   angle ADE

8 Given that ABCDEFGH is a regular octagon, calculate

    a   angle DEF   **b**   angle AEF   **c**   angle EAF

Special quadrilaterals

You should know the names of the following quadrilaterals, and be familiar with all their angle properties.

Trapezium

- A trapezium has two parallel sides.
- The sum of the interior angles at the ends of each non-parallel side is 180°, that is
  $$\angle A + \angle D = 180° \quad \text{and} \quad \angle B + \angle C = 180°$$

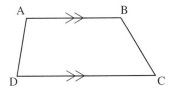

Parallelogram

- A parallelogram has opposite sides parallel.
- Its opposite sides are equal.
- Its diagonals bisect each other.
- Its opposite angles are equal, that is
  $$\angle A = \angle C \quad \text{and} \quad \angle B = \angle D$$

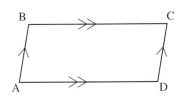

Rhombus

- A rhombus is a parallelogram with all its sides equal.
- Its diagonals bisect each other at right angles.
- Its diagonals also bisect the angles.

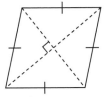

Kite

- A kite is a quadrilateral with two pairs of equal adjacent sides.
- Its longer diagonal bisects its shorter diagonal at right angles.
- The opposite angles between the sides of different lengths are equal.

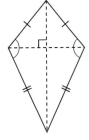

EXERCISE 7F

1 For each of these trapeziums, calculate the value of the lettered angles.

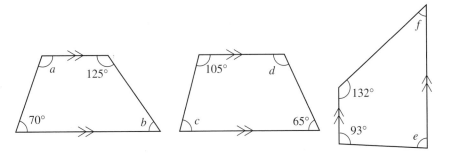

2 For each of these parallelograms, calculate the value of the lettered angles.

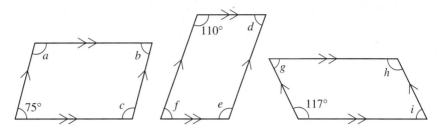

3 For each of these kites, calculate the value of the lettered angles.

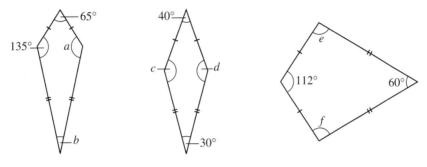

4 For each of these rhombuses, calculate the value of the lettered angles.

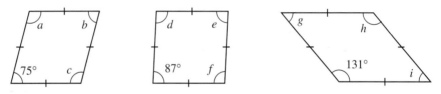

5 For each of these shapes, calculate the value of the lettered angles.

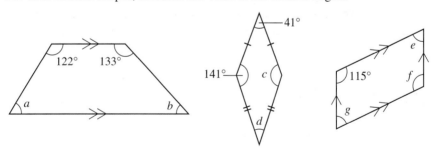

6 For each of these shapes, calculate the value of the lettered angles.

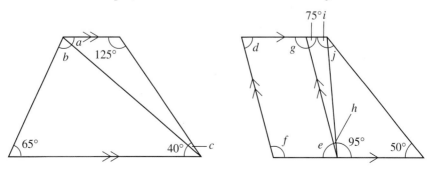

7   Calculate the values of x and y in each of these trapeziums.

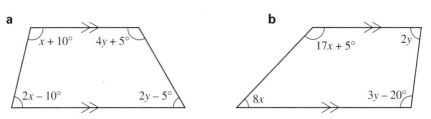

a $x + 10°$ $4y + 5°$ $2x - 10°$ $2y - 5°$

b $17x + 5°$ $2y$ $8x$ $3y - 20°$

8   Calculate the values of x and y in each of these parallelograms.

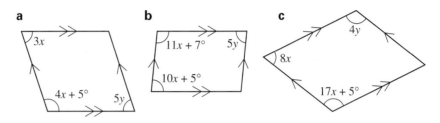

a $3x$ $4x + 5°$ $5y$

b $11x + 7°$ $5y$ $10x + 5°$

c $4y$ $8x$ $17x + 5°$

9   Calculate the value of x in each of these rhombuses.

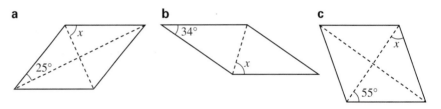

a x $25°$

b $34°$ x

c x $55°$

10   Calculate the values of the letters in each of these shapes.

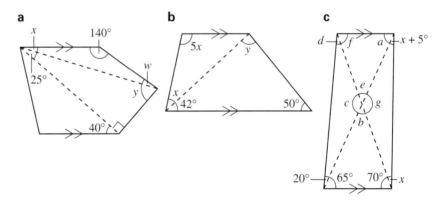

a x $140°$ w $25°$ y $40°$

b $5x$ y x $42°$ $50°$

c d f a $x + 5°$ e c g b $20°$ $65°$ $70°$ x

11   Find the value of x in each of these quadrilaterals and hence state the type of quadrilateral it is.

   a   One with angles $x + 10°$, $x + 20°$, $2x + 20°$, $2x + 10°$

   b   One with angles $x - 10°$, $2x + 10°$, $x - 10°$, $2x + 10°$

   c   One with angles $x - 10°$, $2x$, $5x - 10°$, $5x - 10°$

   d   One with angles $4x + 10°$, $5x - 10°$, $3x + 30°$, $2x + 50°$

Possible coursework tasks

Everywhere triangles

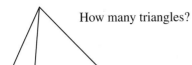

How many triangles?

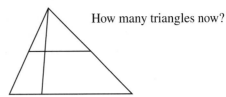

How many triangles now?

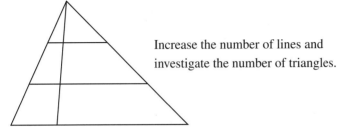

Increase the number of lines and investigate the number of triangles.

Dotty parallel lines

How many lines can be drawn on the grid which are parallel to line A and have the same length as line A?

Investigate for different lines and grids.

Interior and exterior right angles

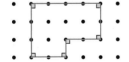

The shape is made by drawing only horizontal and vertical lines.

There are five right angles inside the shape and one outside the shape.

Investigate for other shapes.

Star patterns

Draw a pentagon and put in all its diagonals.
How many diagonals have you drawn?

Investigate for other polygons.

Squares in polygons

How many right angles can be drawn inside an *N*-sided polygon?

Examination questions

1 A regular octagon, drawn opposite, has eight sides. One side of the octagon has been extended to form angle *p*.

  a Work out the size of angle *p*.

  b Work out the size of angle *q*.

Not to scale

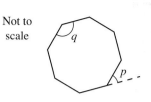

SEG, Question 14, Paper 3, June 1994

2 i What is the special name given to this quadrilateral?

  ii Write the letter A in one acute angle in the diagram.

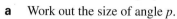
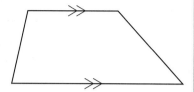

NEAB, Question 10, Specimen Paper 1, 1998

3 Find the sizes of the angles marked by the letters in these diagrams.

a   **b**   **c**

Not to scale

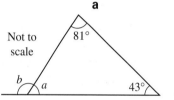
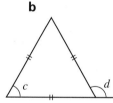
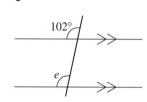

  d Give a reason for your answer to part **c**.

NEAB, Question 11, Specimen Paper 2, 1998

4 The diagram represents a regular pentagon with 2 of its lines of symmetry shown.

  a Write down the value of angle *p*.

  b Find the size of angle

  i *q*   **ii** *r*

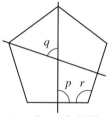

NEAB, Question 13, Specimen Paper 2, 1998

5 PQR is an equilateral triangle. PRS is an isosceles triangle with PR = RS.

  a When SPR = 20°, what is the size of angle QRS?

  b i When PQ is parallel to RS, what name is given to quadrilateral PQSR?

  ii Give a reason for your answer.

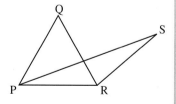

SEG, Question 5, Specimen Paper 10, 1998

6 The framework for some staging consists of three equilateral triangles ABE, EDB and DBC as shown in the diagram.
You must give a reason for each of your answers in this question.

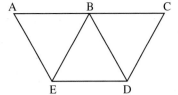

a What is the size of angle ABE?

b What is the size of angle ABD?

c What does your answer to part **b** tell you about the points A, B and C?

d What is the size of angle BED?

e What does your answer to part **d** tell you about the lines AB and ED?

WJEC, Question 4, Specimen Paper 2, 1998

7 The diagram shows the positions of three places A, B and C. AB is the same length as AC.

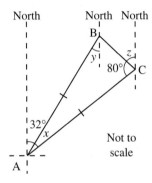

Not to scale

i Calculate the size of the angle marked *x*.

ii Explain why the angle marked *y* is equal to 32°.

iii Calculate the size of the angle marked *z*.

NEAB, Question 5, Paper 2, June 1995

8 PQRS is a parallelogram.
angle QSP = 47°
angle QSR = 24°
PST is a straight line.

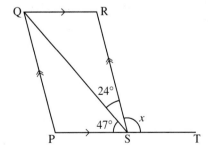

a **i** Find the size of the angle marked *x*.

ii Give a reason for your answer.

b **i** Work out the size of angle PQS.

ii Give a reason for your answer.

EDEXCEL, Question 14, Intermediate Paper 3, June 2000

Summary

How well do you grade yourself?

To gain a grade **E**, you need to be able to measure and draw angles accurately and to use the language associated with angles.

To gain a grade **D**, you need to be familiar with the different types of triangle and to know the names of the different polygons.

To gain a grade **C**, you need to be able to solve problems using the angle properties of polygons and the properties of intersecting and parallel lines.

To gain a grade **B**, you need to be familiar with the properties of each different type of quadrilateral and be able clearly to give reasons to support your answers to problems involving angles.

What you should know after you have worked through Chapter 7

- Vertically opposite angles are equal. The sum of the angles on a straight line is 180°. The sum of the angles around a point is 360°. The sum of the three interior angles of a triangle is 180°.
- A line which intersects parallel lines is called a transversal. The alternate angles formed by a transversal are equal. Corresponding angles are equal. The sum of allied angles is 180°.
- For an N-sided polygon, the sum of the interior angles = $(N - 2) \times 180°$. The exterior angle of a regular N-sided polygon = $360° \div N$. Its interior angle = $180° - (360° \div N)$.
- An equilateral triangle has all its sides equal and all its interior angles equal to 60°. An isosceles triangle is a triangle with two equal sides and two equal angles.
- A trapezium is a quadrilateral with two parallel sides. The sum of the interior angles at the ends of each non-parallel side is 180°.
- A parallelogram is a quadrilateral whose opposite sides are parallel and equal. Its diagonals bisect each other. Its opposite angles are equal.
- A rhombus is a parallelogram with all its sides equal. Its diagonals bisect each other at right angles and bisect the angles.
- A kite is a quadrilateral with two pairs of equal adjacent sides. Its longer diagonal bisects its shorter diagonal at right angles. The opposite angles between the sides of different lengths are equal.

Revision paper for Chapters 1 to 7

Answer **all** questions, showing your methods of solution.

1 Write down the answer to

    a $6 - 10$ **b** $-2 - 8$ **c** $-7 + 4$ **d** $-2 - 5$ **e** $-3 + 7$

    f -2×6 **g** 5×-4 **h** -4×-3 **i** $-20 \div 4$ **j** $-24 \div -6$

2 Round off the following numbers.

    a 6817 to 1 significant figure   **b** 452 to 2 significant figures

    c 0.0625 to 1 significant figure   **d** 0.009 74 to 2 significant figures

    e 3.7846 to 1 decimal place   **f** 0.2853 to 2 decimal places

    g 0.009 34 to 1 decimal place   **h** 9.915 to 2 decimal places

3 A certain bacterium increases at the rate of 15% per hour. A sample of it contained 6000 cells at 9.00 am. How many cells were there at

    a 10.00 am   **b** 11.00 am   **c** 1.00 pm?

4 a A circle has a radius of 4 cm. What is

        i its circumference   **ii** its area?

    b Another circle has a diameter of 12 cm. What is

        i its circumference   **ii** its area?

5 Calculate the area of each shape.

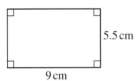 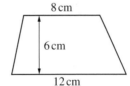

6 a Divide 360 in the ratio 4 : 5.

    b A drink is made by mixing orange, lemon and lemonade in the ratio 5 : 1 : 14.

        i How much could you make if you had only 50 ml of orange?

        ii How much could you make if you had 5 litres of lemonade?

7 What is the weight of a block of wood measuring 12 cm by 9 cm by 30 cm, when the density of the wood is 0.8276 g/cm³?

8 Expand and simplify $5(x + 3y) - 3(4x - 5y)$.

9 Solve these equations.

    a $5x + 7 = 22$ **b** $\dfrac{4x - 3}{3} = 7$

10 Solve, by trial and improvement, the equation $x^3 + x = 18$.
Give your solution to 1 decimal point.

11 Find the volume of this triangular prism.

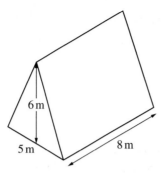

12 **a** Sketch a pentagon.
  b What is the angle sum of a pentagon?
  c **i** What is a regular decagon?
   ii What is the exterior angle of a regular decagon?
   iii What is the interior angle of a regular decagon?

13 A class has 30 pupils in it. Twelve of these pupils are boys.
  a What percentage of the class are girls?
  b Two new pupils join the class, one a boy, the other a girl. What has now
   happened to the percentages of the class? Has the boys' percentage increased
   or decreased? Explain all your working.

14 Calculate the value of x in each of these diagrams.

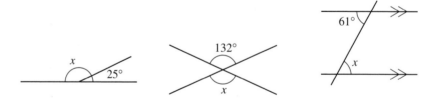

Transformation geometry

This chapter is going to ...

show you what is meant by congruency and then introduce you to geometric transformation, which involves the movement and enlargement of shapes.

What you should already know

✔ How to identify simple line graphs and their equations, such as these two, which occur often.

✔ How to recognise the equations of lines such as those below.

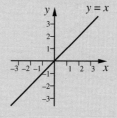

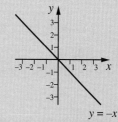

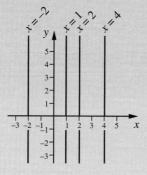

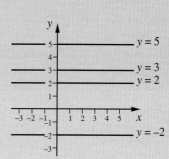

Congruence

Two shapes are congruent if they fit exactly on each other. For example, these triangles are all congruent.

Notice that the triangles can be differently orientated (turned in different directions) or flipped over.

EXERCISE 8A

1   State whether each pair of shapes **a** to **f** are congruent or not.

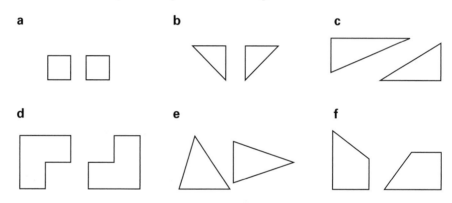

2   Which figure in each group **a** to **c** is not congruent to the other two?

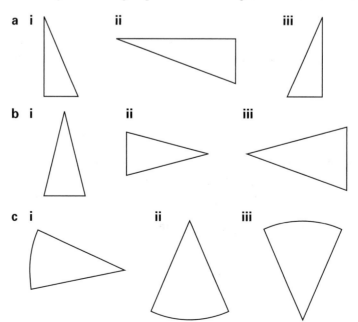

3　State whether each pair of triangles **a** to **h** is congruent.

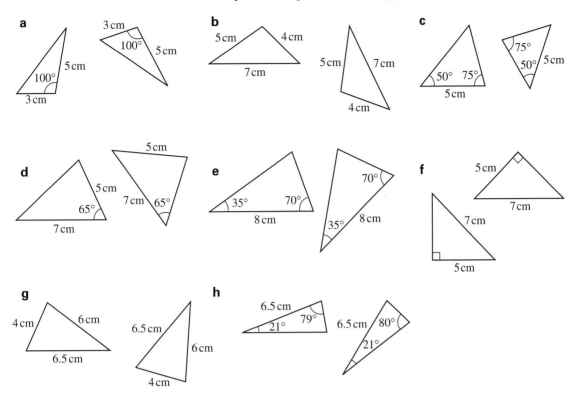

4　Draw a square PQRS. Draw in the diagonals PR and QS. Which triangles are congruent to each other?

5　Draw a rectangle EFGH. Draw in the diagonals EG and FH. Which triangles are congruent to each other?

6　Draw a parallelogram ABCD. Draw in the diagonals AC and BD. Which triangles are congruent to each other?

7　Draw an isosceles triangle ABC where AB = AC. Draw the line from A to the mid-point of BC. Which triangles are congruent to each other?

Transformations

Geometrical transformation changes the positions, or sizes, of shapes on a plane in particular ways. We shall deal with the four basic ways of changing the position and size of shapes: **translation**, **reflection**, **rotation** and **enlargement**.

All of these transformations, except enlargement, keep a shape congruent with itself.

Translation

Translation is the movement of a shape from one place to another without reflecting it or rotating it. It is sometimes called a 'glide', since the shape appears to glide from one place to another. Every point in the shape moves in the same direction and through the same distance.

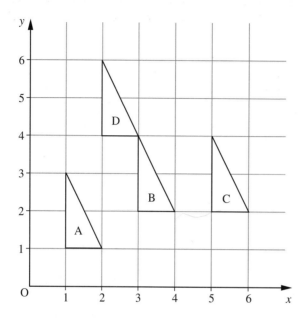

We describe such changes of position using vectors. In such a vector, the move from one point to another is represented by the combination of a horizontal shift and a vertical shift. For example, take the case, shown in this diagram, of a triangle being moved from A to D, via B and C, and then back to A.

The vector describing the translation from A to B is $\begin{pmatrix} 2 \\ 1 \end{pmatrix}$.

The vector describing the translation from B to C is $\begin{pmatrix} 2 \\ 0 \end{pmatrix}$.

The vector describing the translation from C to D is $\begin{pmatrix} -3 \\ 2 \end{pmatrix}$.

The vector describing the translation from D to A is $\begin{pmatrix} -1 \\ -3 \end{pmatrix}$.

Notice

* The top number describes the horizontal movement. To the right +, to the left −.

* The bottom number describes the vertical movement. Upwards +, downwards −.

EXERCISE 8B

1 Describe with vectors these translations.
- **a** **i** A to B   **ii** A to C   **iii** A to D   **iv** A to E   **v** A to F   **vi** A to G
- **b** **i** B to A   **ii** B to C   **iii** B to D   **iv** B to E   **v** B to F   **vi** B to G
- **c** **i** C to A   **ii** C to B   **iii** C to D   **iv** C to E   **v** C to F   **vi** C to G
- **d** **i** D to E   **ii** E to B   **iii** F to C   **iv** G to D   **v** F to G   **vi** G to E

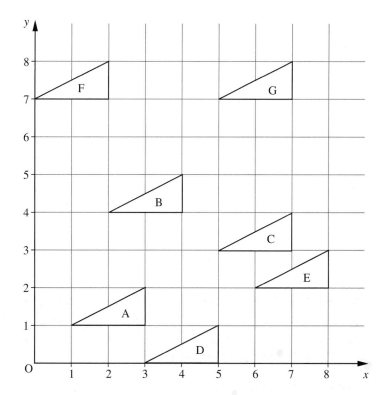

2 **a** Draw the triangle with co-ordinates A(1, 1), B(2, 1) and C(1, 3).

   b Draw the image of ABC after a translation with vector $\begin{pmatrix} 2 \\ 3 \end{pmatrix}$. Label this P.

   c Draw the image of ABC after a translation with vector $\begin{pmatrix} -1 \\ 2 \end{pmatrix}$. Label this Q.

   d Draw the image of ABC after a translation wih vector $\begin{pmatrix} 3 \\ -2 \end{pmatrix}$. Label this R.

   e Draw the image of ABC after a translation with vector $\begin{pmatrix} -2 \\ -4 \end{pmatrix}$. Label this S.

3 Using your diagram from question **2**, describe the translation that will move
- **a** P to Q   **b** Q to R   **c** R to S   **d** S to P
- **e** R to P   **f** S to Q   **g** R to Q   **h** P to S

4 Take a 10×10 grid and the triangle A(0, 0), B(1, 0) and C(0, 1). How many different translations are there that use integer values only and will move the triangle ABC to somewhere in the grid? (Do not draw them all.)

Reflection

Reflection is the movement of a shape so that it becomes a mirror image of itself. For example,

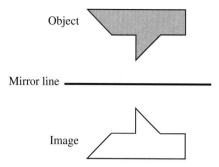

Object

Mirror line

Image

Notice the reflection of each point in the original shape (called the object) is perpendicular to the mirror line. So if you 'fold' the whole diagram along the mirror line, any object point will coincide with its reflection (also called its image point).

EXERCISE 8C

1 Draw these figures on squared paper and then draw the reflection of each in the given mirror line.

a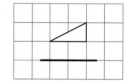

b

c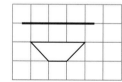

d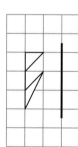

e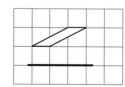

f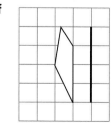

g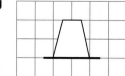

2 Draw these figures on squared paper and then draw the reflection of each in the given mirror line.

a   b   c

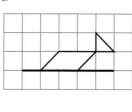 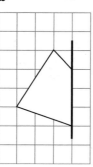 

3 a Draw a pair of axes: *x*-axis from −5 to 5, *y*-axis from −5 to 5.
   b Draw the triangle with co-ordinates A(1, 1), B(3, 1), C(4, 5).
   c Reflect the triangle ABC in the *x*-axis. Label the image P.
   d Reflect triangle P in the *y*-axis. Label the image Q.
   e Reflect triangle Q in the *x*-axis, label it R.
   f Describe the reflection that will move triangle ABC to triangle R.

4 a Repeat the steps of question **3** but start with any shape you like.
   b Is your answer to part **f** the same as before?
   c Would the final answer in part **d** always be the same no matter what shape you started with?

5 Draw these figures on squared paper and then draw the reflection of each in the given mirror line.

a   b   c

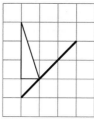  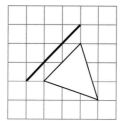

6 Draw these figures on squared paper and then draw the reflection of each in the given mirror line.

a   b   c

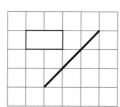   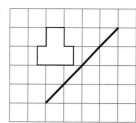

7 **a** Draw a pair of axes and the lines $y = x$ and $y = -x$, as shown.

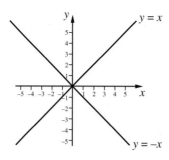

b Draw the triangle with co-ordinates A(2, 1), B(5, 1), C(5, 3).

c Draw the reflection of triangle ABC in the x-axis and label the image P.

d Draw the reflection of triangle P in the line $y = -x$ and label the image Q.

e Draw the reflection of triangle Q in the y-axis and label the image R.

f Draw the reflection of triangle R in the line $y = x$ and label the image S.

g Draw the reflection of triangle S in the x-axis and label the image T.

h Draw the reflection of triangle T in the line $y = -x$ and label the image U.

i Draw the reflection of triangle U in the y-axis and label the image W.

j What single reflection will move triangle W to triangle ABC?

8 **a** Repeat the steps of question **7** but start with any shape you like.

b Is your answer to part **j** the same as before?

c Would your answer to part **j** always be the same no matter what shape you started with?

9 **a** Draw a pair of axes where both the x and y values are from −5 to 5.

b Draw, in the first quadrant, any triangle ABC and write down the co-ordinates of each vertex.

c **i** Reflect triangle ABC in the x-axis and label the image A′B′C′, where A′ is the image of A, etc.

ii Write down the co-ordinates of A′, B′ and C′.

iii What connection is there between A, B, C and A′, B′, C′?

iv Will this connection always be so?

10 Repeat question **9**, but reflect the triangle ABC in the y-axis.

11 Repeat question **9**, but reflect the triangle ABC in the line $y = x$.

12 Repeat question **9**, but reflect the triangle ABC in the line $y = -x$.

Rotation

Rotation moves a shape to a new position by turning it about a fixed point called the
centre of rotation.

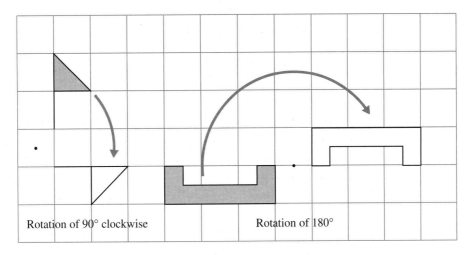

Rotation of 90° clockwise   Rotation of 180°

Notice

- The angle of rotation has direction, usually expressed as clockwise or anticlockwise.

- The position of the centre of rotation is always specified.

    The rotations which most often appear in examination questions are 90° and 180°
    about the origin.

EXERCISE 8D

1   On squared paper, draw these shapes and centres of rotation.

a   b   c 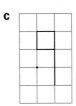   d

e 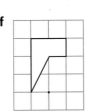   f

   a   Rotate each shape about its centre of rotation
     i   first by 90° clockwise   **ii**   then by a further 180°
   b   Describe, in each case, the transformation that would take the original shape to
     the final image.

2 On squared paper draw these shapes and centres of rotation.

a **b** **c** 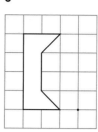 **d**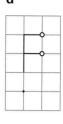

    a Rotate each shape about its centre of rotation

        i first by 90° anticlockwise   **ii** then by a further 180°

    b Describe, in each case, the transformation that would take the original shape to the final image.

3 What other rotations are equivalent to these rotations?

    a 270° clockwise   **b** 90° clockwise

    c 60° anticlockwise   **d** 100° anticlockwise

4 **a** Draw a pair of axes where both the x and y values are from −5 to 5.

    b Draw, in the first quadrant, any triangle ABC and write down the co-ordinates of each point.

    c **i** Rotate triangle ABC 90° clockwise about the origin (0, 0) and label the image A′, B′, C′, where A′ is the image of A, etc.

        ii Write down the co-ordinates of A′, B′, C′.

        iii What connection is there between A, B, C and A′, B′, C′?

        iv Will this connection always be so?

5 Repeat question **4**, but rotate triangle ABC 180° clockwise.

6 Repeat question **4**, but rotate triangle ABC 90° anticlockwise.

7 **a** Draw a pair of axes where both the x and y values are from −5 to 5.

    b Draw the triangle with vertices A(2, 1), B(3, 1), C(3, 5).

    c Reflect ABC in the x-axis, then reflect the image in the y-axis. Label the final position A′B′C′.

    d Describe the transformation that will take ABC directly to A′B′C′.

    e Will this always happen no matter what shape you start with?

    f Will this still happen if you reflect in the y-axis first, then reflect in the x-axis?

8 **a** Draw a regular hexagon ABCDEF with centre O.

    b Using O as the centre of rotation, describe a transformation that will move

        i triangle AOB to triangle BOC   **ii** triangle AOB to triangle COD

        iii triangle AOB to triangle DOE   **iv** triangle AOB to triangle EOF

    c Describe the transformations that will move the rhombus ABCO to

        i rhombus BCDO   **ii** rhombus DEFO

9 ABCDE is a regular pentagon with centre O.
   a What transformation will move
      i   triangle DOE to triangle EOA
      ii quadrilateral ABCO to quadrilateral BCDO?
   b Name all the triangles congruent to
      i   AOB   ii ADC

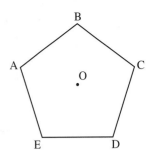

Enlargement

Enlargement changes the size of a shape to give a similar image. It always has a centre of enlargement and a scale factor. Every length of the enlargement will be

   Original length × Scale factor

The distance of each image point on the enlargement from the centre of enlargement will be

   Distance of original point from centre of enlargement × Scale factor

For example, this diagram shows an enlargement by scale factor 3 of a triangle ABC.

Notice

- Each length on the enlargement A′B′C′ is three times the corresponding length on the original shape.

- The distance of any point on the enlargement from the centre of enlargement is three times longer than the corresponding distance on the original shape.

There are two distinct ways to enlarge a shape: the ray method and the co-ordinate method.

Ray method

This is the **only** way to construct an enlargement when the diagram is not on a grid. The example below shows an enlargement by scale factor 3 made by the ray method.

Notice that the rays have been drawn from the centre of enlargement to each vertex and beyond.

The distance from each vertex on triangle ABC to the centre of enlargement was measured and multiplied by 3 to give the distance of each image vertex from the centre of enlargement. Once each image vertex has been found, the whole image shape can then be drawn.

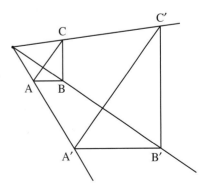

Check the measurements and see for yourself how the calculations have been done. Notice again that each line is three times longer in the enlargement.

Co-ordinate method

In the diagram below, an enlargement has been made by scale factor 3 from the centre of enlargement, (1, 2).

The co-ordinates of each image vertex were found as follows.

First, we worked out the horizontal and vertical distances from each original vertex to the centre of enlargement.

Then we multiplied each of these distances by 3 to find the position of each image vertex.

For example, take the calculations to find the co-ordinates of C′.

From the centre of enlargement (1, 2) to point

  C (3, 5)

  horizontal distance = 3 − 1 = 2

  vertical distance = 5 − 2 = 3

Make these 3 times longer to give

  new horizontal distance = 6

  new vertical distance = 9

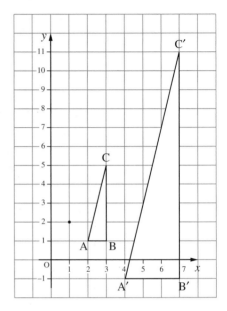

So the co-ordinates of C′ = (1 + 6, 2 + 9) = (7, 11)

Notice again that each line is three times longer in the enlargement.

EXERCISE 8E

1 Copy each of these figures with its centre of enlargement. Then enlarge it by the given scale factor, using the ray method.

 a   **b**   **c**   **d**

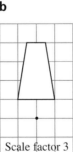
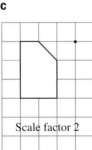
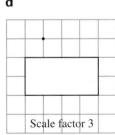

 Scale factor 2   Scale factor 2   Scale factor 3

    Scale factor 3

2 Copy each of these shapes on squared paper and enlarge it from the given centre of enlargement by the given scale factor. Use the co-ordinate method.

a   **b**   **c**   **d**

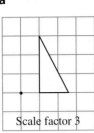
Scale factor 3

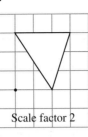
Scale factor 2

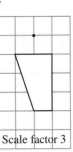
Scale factor 3

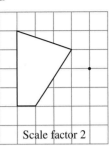
Scale factor 2

3 **a** Draw on squared paper a triangle ABC.

    b Mark four different centres of enlargement on your diagram:

        one above your triangle

        one below your triangle

        one to the left of your triangle

        one to the right of your triangle.

    c From each centre of enlargement draw an enlargement by scale factor 2.

    d What do you notice about each enlarged shape?

4 'Strange but True'… you can have an enlargement in mathematics that is actually smaller than the original shape! This happens when you 'enlarge' a shape by a fractional scale factor. For example, try 'enlarging' the shapes in the lower diagram by scale factor $\frac{1}{2}$.

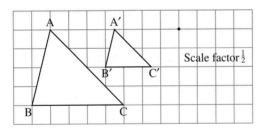
Scale factor $\frac{1}{2}$

a   **b**

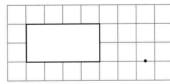
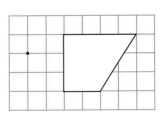

c   **d**

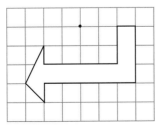
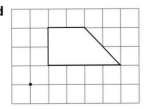

5 Draw the enlargement of each shape at the given scale factor.

a

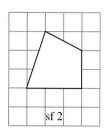

sf 2

b

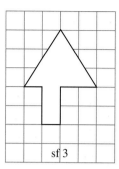

sf 3

c

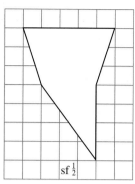

sf ½

d

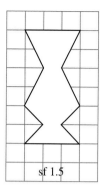

sf 1.5

6 When you draw an enlargement:

a What effect does moving the centre of enlargement have on the enlarged shape?

b What is not affected by moving the centre of enlargement?

EXERCISE 8F

1 Describe fully the transformation that will move the shaded triangle to each of the positions A–F.

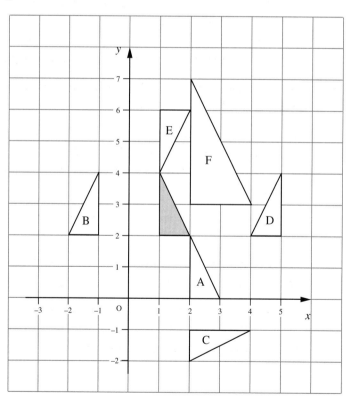

2 Describe fully the transformation that will move

   a T_1 to T_2

   b T_1 to T_6

   c T_2 to T_3

   d T_6 to T_2

   e T_6 to T_5

   f T_5 to T_4

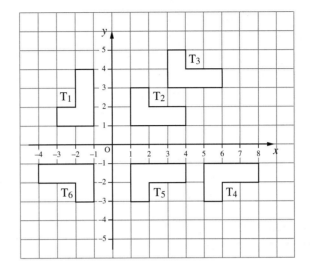

3 **a** Plot a triangle T with vertices (1, 1), (2, 1), (1, 3).

   b Reflect triangle T in the y-axis and label the image T_b.

   c Rotate triangle T_b 90° anticlockwise about the origin and label the image T_c.

   d Reflect triangle T_c in the y-axis and label the image T_d.

   e Describe fully the transformation that will move triangle T_d back to triangle T.

4 The point P (3, 4) is reflected in the x-axis, then rotated by 90° clockwise about the origin. What are the co-ordinates of the image of P?

5 A point Q (5, 2) is rotated by 180°, then reflected in the x-axis.

   a What are the co-ordinates of the image point of Q?

   b What single transformation would have taken point Q directly to the image point?

6 Find the co-ordinates of the image of the point (3, 5) after a clockwise rotation of 90° about the point (1, 3).

7 Describe fully at least three different transformations that could move the square labelled S to the square labelled T.

8 The point A (4, 4) has been transformed to the point A′ (4, –4). Describe as many different transformations as you can that could transform point A to point A′.

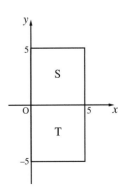

Possible coursework tasks

Keep turning left

The shape is made by following the instructions.

** • Draw a line 1 cm long.
• Rotate left 90° and draw a line 3 cm long.
• Rotate left 90° and draw a line 2 cm long.
• Rotate left 90° and draw a line 1 cm long.
• Go back to **.

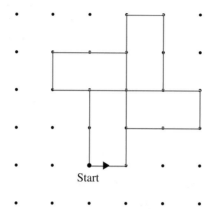

Start

Call this pattern (1, 3, 2). What other patterns can you make using different numbers?

Vectorial areas

The vector describing the translation from O to A is $\begin{pmatrix} 3 \\ 4 \end{pmatrix}$.

The vector describing the translation from O to B is $\begin{pmatrix} 6 \\ 4 \end{pmatrix}$.

The area of the triangle is 6 square units.

Can you find a connection between the two vectors and the area of the triangle?

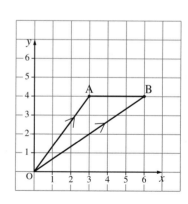

What's the change?

There are 4 different transformations which leave a rectangle in the same position although its vertices may have changed.

a   Can you find all four?
b   Can you find this property for other shapes?

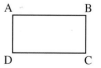

Examination questions

1   On a copy of the
    grid, draw the
    reflection of
    triangle PQR in
    the line AB.

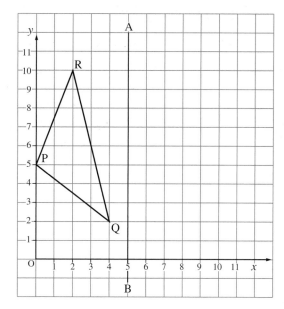

EDEXCEL, Question 2, Intermediate Paper 3, June 1999

2   **a**   Describe fully the single
            transformation that maps
            shape P onto shape Q.
    b   On a copy of the
            diagram, rotate shape P
            90° anticlockwise about
            the point A (1, 1).

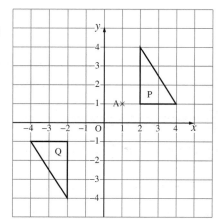

EDEXCEL, Question 22, Intermediate Paper 3, June 2000

3   **a**   A translation moves (3, 4) to (7, −2).
            The same translation moves (2, 1) to point P.
            i   Write down the co-ordinates of point P.
            ii   Write down the column vector which describes this translation.
    b   A reflection moves (9, 1) to (9, 5).
            The same reflection moves (11, 7) to point Q.
            i   Write down the co-ordinates of point Q.
            ii   Write down the equation of the mirror line of this reflection.

OCR, Question 10, Intermediate Paper 3, June 2000

4 **a** Write down the co-ordinates of point A.

b Rotate triangle ABC 90° clockwise about (0, 0). Label the new triangle A′B′C′.

c Reflect triangle A′B′C′ in the *x*-axis. Label the new triangle A″B″C″.

d Which transformation maps triangle ABC onto triangle A″B″C″?

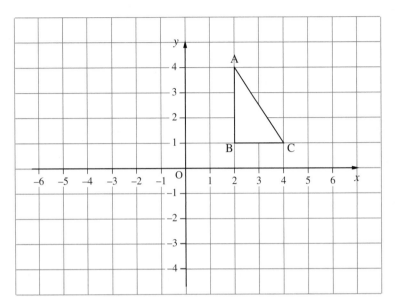

WJEC, Question 1, Specimen Paper 2, 1998

5 The parallelogram ABCD has vertices at (6, 3), (9, 3), (12, 9) and (9, 9) respectively.

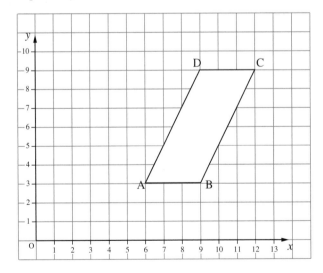

An enlargement, scale factor $\frac{1}{3}$ and centre (0, 0), transforms parallelogram ABCD onto parallelogram $A_1B_1C_1D_1$. Draw the parallelogram $A_1B_1C_1D_1$.

SEG, Question 16, Specimen Paper 11, 1998

6 The sketch shows the position of a rectangle ABCD.

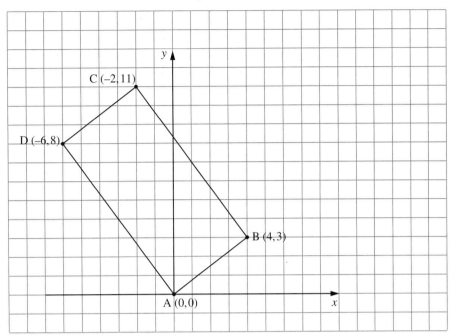

a The rectangle ABCD is reflected in the line $x = 4$ to give rectangle $A_1B_1C_1D_1$. What are the co-ordinates of C_1?

b The rectangle ABCD is rotated about A anticlockwise through $90°$ to give $A_2B_2C_2D_2$. What are the co-ordinates of B_2?

c The rectangle is enlarged by scale factor 2, centre of enlargement A. What are the co-ordinates of the new position of B?

SEG, Question 2, Specimen Paper 10, 1998

7 The diagram shows a regular pentagon ABCDE. List all the triangles in the pentagon congruent to ADC.

NEAB, Question 8, Paper 1Q, June 1994

Summary

How well do you grade yourself?

To gain a grade **E**, you need to be able to translate a shape using a vector. You also need to be able to recognise congruent shapes.

To gain a grade **D**, you need to be able to reflect a shape in any given line and be able to rotate a shape about a centre of enlargement.

To gain a grade **C**, you need to be able to enlarge a shape by a positive whole-number scale factor and a fraction scale factor.

What you should know after you have worked through Chapter 8

- Congruence: Two or more shapes are congruent if they fit exactly on one another.
- Translation: This is the movement of a shape from one place to another without reflecting it or rotating it. Every point in the shape moves in the same direction and through the same distance. Such changes of position are described using vectors which express the move from one point to another in terms of a horizontal shift and a vertical shift.
- Reflection: This is the movement of a shape so that it becomes a mirror image of itself. The reflection of each point in the original shape (the object) is perpendicular to the mirror line.
- Rotation: This moves a shape to a new position by turning it about a fixed point, called the centre of rotation.
  - The angle of rotation has direction – clockwise or anticlockwise.
  - The position of the centre of rotation is always specified.
- Enlargement: This changes the size of a shape (object) to give a similar image. The original lengths are multiplied by a scale factor to obtain the image lengths.

  The enlargement is always made from a centre of enlargement. The distance of each image point from the centre of enlargement is the distance of each object point from the centre of enlargement multiplied by the scale factor.

9 Constructions

This chapter is going to ...

show you how to construct triangles from given information, using a ruler, a pair of compasses and a protractor.
It will also show you how to construct line bisectors, angle bisectors, right angles, and angles of 60°, using only a pencil, a ruler and a pair of compasses.

What you should already know

✔ How to use a protractor.
✔ How to use a pair of compasses.
✔ How to work out simple problems involving bearings.

Bearings

The bearing of a point B from a point A is the angle through which you turn clockwise as you change direction from due north to the direction of B.

For example, in this diagram the bearing of B from A is 60°.

As a bearing can have any value from 0° to 360°, it is customary to give all bearings as three-digit numbers. So in the example above, the bearing becomes 060° using three digits. Here are three more examples.

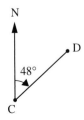

D is on a bearing of 048° from C

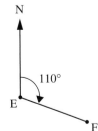

F is on a bearing of 110° from E

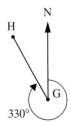

H is on a bearing of 330° from G

There are eight bearings with which you should be familiar. Here they are.

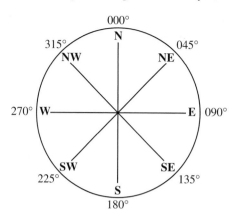

Back bearings

The back bearing of a point B from a point P is the bearing of P from B. So suppose the bearing of B from P is 065°, then we can calculate the back bearing as follows.

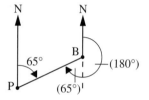

The back bearing is the clockwise angle from north round to the direction of P from B. From the diagram, you can see that this angle is

$$65° + 180° = 245°$$

So it follows that for any bearing $x°$, the back bearing is given by $x° + 180°$.

When this gives an answer that is greater than 360°, you have to subtract 360° to obtain the **correct** back bearing.

EXERCISE 9A

1   Draw sketches to illustrate the following situations and then give the back bearing for each one.

   a   Rotherham is on a bearing of 025° from Sheffield.

   b   Castleton is on a bearing of 170° from Hope.

   c   Bude is on a bearing of 310° from Wadebridge.

   d   Liverpool is on a bearing of 265° from Manchester.

2   A is due north from C. B is due east from A. B is on a bearing of 045° from C. Sketch the layout of the three points A, B and C.

3   An aircraft is flying on a bearing of 125° when the pilot is told to fly straight back. On what bearing should the pilot return the aircraft?

4 Look at the following sketch map.

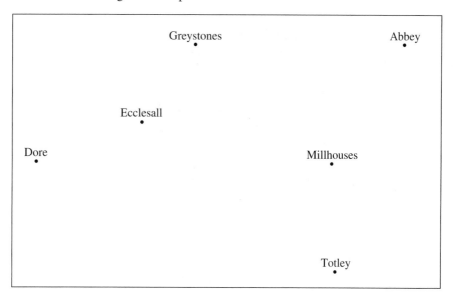

Without measuring, try to estimate the approximate bearing of

a Totley from Dore

b Dore from Ecclesall

c Millhouses from Dore

d Greystones from Abbey

e Millhouses from Greystones

f Totley from Millhouses

5 Captain Bird decided to sail his ship in square formation: that is, to sail around the sides of a square kilometre.

a Assuming he started sailing due north, give two different ways in which he could complete the square formation.

b Assuming he started sailing on a bearing of 040°, give two different ways in which he could complete the square formation.

Constructing triangles

There are three different ways of constructing a triangle. Which one we use depends on what information we are given about the triangle.

All three sides known

Example Draw a triangle with sides 5 cm, 4 cm and 6 cm long.

- First, draw the longest side as the base. In this case, the base will be 6 cm, which you draw using a ruler. (The diagrams in this example are drawn at half-size.)

- Next, deal with the second longest side, in this case the 5 cm side. Open the compasses to a radius of 5 cm (the length of the side), place the point on one end of the 6 cm line and draw a short feint arc, as shown here.

- Then, deal with the shortest side, in this case the 4 cm side. Open the compasses to a radius of 4 cm, place the point on the other end of the 6 cm line and draw a second short feint arc to intersect the first arc, as shown below.

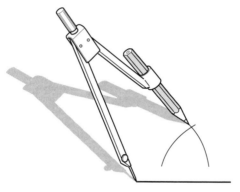

- Finally, complete the triangle by joining each end of the base line to the point where the two arcs intersect.

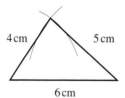

4 cm   5 cm

6 cm

Note   The arcs are construction lines and so are always drawn lightly. They **must** be left in an answer to an examination question to show the examiner how you constructed the triangle.

Two sides and the included angle known

Example Draw a triangle ABC, where AB is 6 cm, BC is 5 cm and the included angle ABC is 55°. (The diagrams in this example are drawn at half-size.)

- First, draw the longest side, AB, as the base. Label the ends of the base A and B.

  A ——————————— B

- Next, place the protractor along AB with its centre on B, and make a point on the diagram at the 55° mark.

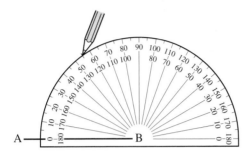

- Then draw a **feint** line from B through the 55° point. From B measure 5 cm along this line and mark the point. Label it C.

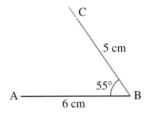

- Finally, join A and C and make AC and CB into bolder lines.

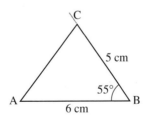

Note The construction lines are drawn lightly and left in to demonstrate how the triangle has been constructed.

Two angles and a side known

When we know two angles of a triangle, we also know the third.

Example Draw a triangle ABC, where AB is 7cm, angle BAC is 40° and angle ABC is 65°.

- As before, start by drawing the base, which here has to be 7cm. Label the ends A and B.

- Next, centre the protractor on A and mark the angle of 40°. Draw a feint line from A through this point.

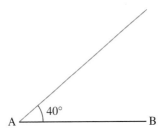

- Then centre the protractor on B and mark the angle of 65°. Draw a feint line from B through this point, to intersect the 40° line drawn from A. Label the point of intersection as C.

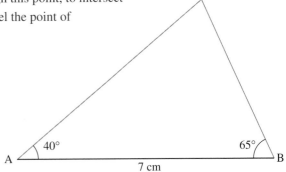

- Complete the triangle by making AC and BC into bolder lines.

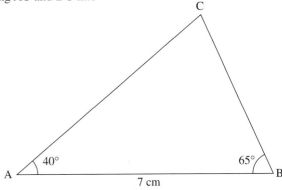

EXERCISE 9B

1   Draw the following triangles accurately and measure the sides and angles not given in the diagram.

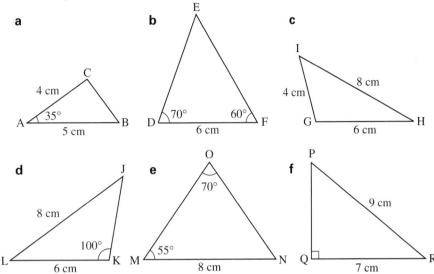

2   a   Draw a triangle ABC, where AB = 7cm, BC = 6cm and AC = 5cm.
    b   Measure the sizes of the angles ∠ABC, ∠BCA and ∠CAB.

3   Draw an isosceles triangle that has two sides of length 7cm and one angle of 50°.
    a   Measure the length of the base of the triangle.
    b   What is the area of the triangle?

4   A triangle ABC has ∠ABC = 30°, BC = 8cm and AC = 5cm. Draw two different triangles from this information. What are the two different lengths that AB can be?

5   Construct an equilateral triangle of side length 5cm. What is the area of this triangle?

6   Construct a parallelogram whose two side lengths are 5cm and 8cm with an angle of 120° between them.

Solve each of the following problems by drawing the situation to a suitable scale. (Remember to show your scale at the side, e.g. 1cm represents 1km.)

7   When I stood 50 metres from a tall building I estimated that the angle from my eye to the top of the building was about 30°. Estimate the height of the building.

8   A ship set off from port and sailed due north for 80km. It then changed course to a bearing of 040° for a further 70km before landing at the Isle of Doe. How far is it from the port to the Isle of Doe?

9   A ship is about 200 metres away from a lighthouse known to be about 50 metres above sea level. At what angle will someone on the ship have to look up in order to see the top of the lighthouse?

10 A plane left Melchester Airport and flew due east for 150 km before turning onto a bearing of 120° and flying for a further 100 km to land at Billsbury Airport.

    a What is the distance from Melchester to Billsbury?

    b What is the bearing of Billsbury from Melchester?

11 How far up a wall will a 6 metre ladder reach if its foot is 1 metre from the wall?

12 Sohan is flying his kite on a 50 metre string. The string is held tight by Sohan standing on its end. The angle between the string and the ground is 65°. How high is the kite flying?

13 The back of a lorry has a floor of 20 m by 3 m.

    a What is the length of the longest piece of metal that can be placed on the floor of the lorry?

    The back of the lorry is enclosed to a height of 3.5 m.

    b What is the length of the longest piece of metal that can be put into the back of the lorry?

14 Sally wanted to know the height of the tall tree in the park. She stood quite a way from the tree, looked up at its top and estimated that the angle at which she had to look up was 20°. Sally then took 50 paces towards the tree, where she again looked up at its top. This time she reckoned she had looked up at an angle of 40°. Sally estimated that her average pace was 40 cm. Use Sally's estimates to find the height of the tree.

Bisectors

To bisect means to divide in half. So a bisector divides something into two equal parts.
- A line bisector divides a straight line into two equal lengths.
- An angle bisector is the straight line which divides an angle into two equal angles.

To construct a line bisector

It is usually more accurate to construct a line bisector than to measure its position (the midpoint of the line).
- Here is a line to bisect. ⎯⎯⎯⎯⎯⎯

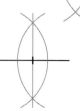

- Open your compasses to a radius of about three-quarters of the length of the line. Using each end of the line as a centre, draw two intersecting arcs without changing the radius of your compasses.

- Join the two points at which the arcs intersect. This line is the **perpendicular bisector** of the original line.

To construct an angle bisector

It is much more accurate to construct an angle bisector than to measure its position.

- Here is an angle to bisect.

- Open your compasses to any reasonable radius
  that is less than the length of the shorter line. If in
  doubt, go for about 3 cm. With the vertex of the
  angle as centre, draw an arc through both lines.
- With centres at the two points at which this arc
  intersects the lines, draw two more arcs so that they
  intersect. (The radius of the compasses may have to
  be increased to do this.)
- Join the point at which these two arcs intersect
  to the vertex of the angle.

This line is the **angle bisector**.

EXERCISE 9C

1 Draw a line 7 cm long. Bisect it with a pair of compasses. Check your accuracy by
seeing if each half is 3.5 cm.

2 **a** Draw any triangle whose sides are between 5 cm and 10 cm.
   b On each side construct the line bisector.
      All your line bisectors should intersect at the same point.
   c Use this point as the centre of a circle that only touches each vertex of the
      triangle. Draw this circle.

3 Repeat question **2** with a different triangle and check that you get a similar result.

4 **a** Draw a quadrilateral whose opposite angles add up to 180°.
   b On each side construct the line bisector.
      They all should intersect at the same point.
   c Use this point as the centre of a circle that only touches the quadrilateral at
      each vertex. Draw this circle.

5 **a** Draw an angle of 50°.   **b** Construct the angle bisector.
   c Check how accurate you have been by measuring each half. Both should be 25°.

6 **a** Draw any triangle whose sides are between 5 cm and 10 cm.
   b At each angle construct the angle bisector.
      All three bisectors should intersect at the same point.
   c Use this point as the centre of a circle that only touches the sides of the triangle
      without cutting through them.

Constructing 90° and 60° angles

The 90° angle

The following method will produce an angle of
90° at a particular point on a line.

- Open your compasses to about 2 or 3 cm. With the given point as centre, draw two
  short arcs to intersect the line each side of the point.
- Now extend the radius of your compasses to
  about 3 or 4 cm. With centres at the two points at
  which the arcs intersect the line, draw two arcs to
  intersect each other above the line.

- Join the point at which these two arcs intersect to the given point on the line.

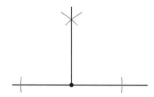

The two lines form the required angle of 90°.

Note that if you needed to construct a 90° angle at the end of a line, you would first have
to extend the line.

You could be even more accurate by also drawing two arcs underneath the line, which
would give three points in line.

The 60° angle

An angle of 60° is usually wanted at an end of a line, so here is a method for constructing
it in that position.

- Open your compasses to about 3 cm. With the end of the line as centre, draw an arc
  from above to intersect the line.

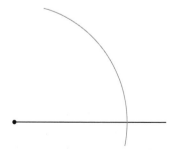

- With this point of intersection as centre, draw a second arc which passes through the end of the line to intersect the first arc.

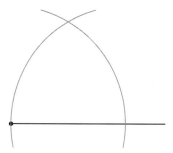

- Join the point of intersection of the arcs to the end of the line. The two lines make an angle of 60°.

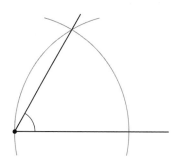

Examination note When a question says '*construct*', you must use **only** compasses – no protractor. When it says '*draw*', you may use whatever you can to produce an accurate diagram.

But **note**, when constructing you may use your protractor to check your accuracy.

EXERCISE 9D

1 Construct these triangles accurately without using a protractor.

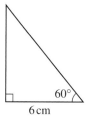 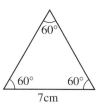

2 **a** Without using a protractor, construct a square of side 6 cm.
   b See how accurate you have been by constructing an angle bisector on any of the right angles and seeing whether this also cuts through the opposite right angle.

3 **a** Construct an angle of 90°.
   b Bisect this angle to construct an angle of 45°.

4 **a** Construct these angles.

    i 30°   **ii** 15°   **iii** 22.5°   **iv** 75° [30° + 45°]

    b Calculate your percentage error of each angle constructed.

5 With ruler and compasses only, construct these triangles.

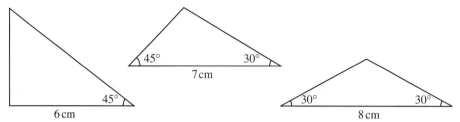

6 Construct an isosceles triangle ABC, where AB = AC = 7 cm and ∠CAB = 120°.

7 Construct a trapezium whose parallel sides are 8 cm and 6 cm, and having an angle of 60° at each end of the longer side.

8 **a** Construct the triangle ABC, where AB = 7 cm, ∠BAC = 60° and ∠ABC = 45°.

    b Measure the lengths of AC and BC.

9 **a** Construct the triangle PQR, where PQ = 8 cm, ∠RPQ = 30° and ∠PQR = 45°.

    b Measure the lengths of PR and RQ.

10 Construct the parallelogram which has sides of 6 cm and 8 cm with an angle of 105°.

Possible coursework tasks

More polygons

Investigate which regular polygons can be constructed using a ruler and compasses only.

Perpendicular lines

• P

A ———————————————————————— B

Using a ruler and compasses only, construct a line which passes through P and is perpendicular to the line AB.

Find the centre

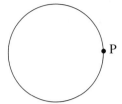

P is a point on the circumference of a circle whose centre is unknown.

Show how you can construct a diameter passing through P.

Show how to locate the centre of the circle.

You should use ruler and compasses only.

Bisect every angle

Draw a triangle and extend its sides.

Construct the lines which bisect the interior and the exterior angles at each vertex of the triangle.

By extending them, the angle bisectors should meet three at a time at various points. Comment.

Examination question: coursework type

a 'The perpendicular bisector of any chord in a circle is a diameter of that circle.'

b 'The angle bisector of any two chords in a circle is a diameter of that circle.'

Test each statement out and state whether you can say for each one:

    i   it may be true   **ii**   it is always true

    iii it is sometimes not true   **iv** it is never true.

Examination questions

1   Ceri and Diane want to find out how far away a tower (T) is on the other side of a river. To do this they mark out a base line, AB, 100 metres long as shown on the diagram. Next they measure the angles at the ends A and B between the base line and the lines of sight of the tower. These angles are 30° and 60°. Using ruler and compasses to make a scale drawing, find the shortest distance of the tower (T) from the base line AB. Use a scale of 1 cm to represent 10 metres. Show clearly all your construction lines.

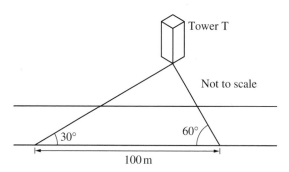

NEAB, Question 20, Specimen Paper 11, 1998

2   The diagram below is drawn accurately. It shows two straight lines AB and BC. P is a point such that P is equidistant from points A and B. P is also 2 cm from the line BC.

Copy the diagram below and plot the point P accurately on the diagram. You should show how you find the position of point P.

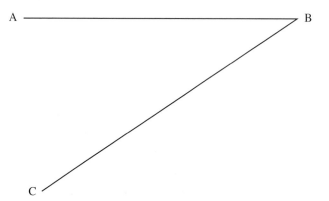

WJEC, Question 8, Intermediate Paper 2, June 1999

3 The diagram shows a map of part of the North Devon coast. The bearing of a ship from Hartland Point is 070°. Its bearing from Appledore is 320°. Showing your construction lines, mark the position of the ship on the map. Label the position with the letter S.

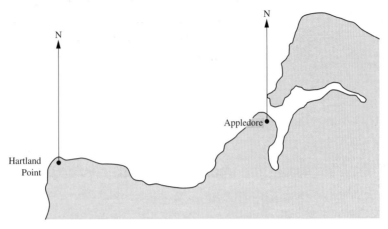

MEG, Question 7, Paper 2, 1994

4 The diagram shows a regular tetrahedron. Each edge is 5 cm long. Draw an accurate net of the tetrahedron.

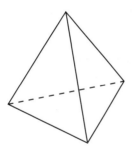

NEAB, Question 7, Paper 1Q, November 1995

5 The front of the main building of Andrew's school is parallel to the edge of the playing field and 100 metres from it. Andrew stands at a point A on the edge of the playing fields. He measures the bearing of one corner of the front of the building as 015° and the bearing of the other corner as 330°.

a Using the scale of 1 cm to 10 metres, construct a scale drawing to show the positions of the two corners relative to the edge of the playing fields.

b From the scale drawing find the length of the building.

NICCEA, Question 7, Paper 3, June 1995

Summary

How well do you grade yourself?

To gain a grade **E**, you need to be able to sketch a situation involving bearings, and to be comfortable with constructing angles.

To gain a grade **D**, you need to be able to recognise when to use a protractor and when not to use it. You need to be accurate to within 2°.

To gain a grade **C**, you need to be able to calculate a back bearing and to construct accurately to the nearest degree. You also need to be able to draw good scale diagrams when necessary.

What you should know after you have worked through Chapter 9

- What bearings are and how to calculate back bearings.
- How to draw a triangle from partial information.
- How to construct a line bisector and an angle bisector.
- How to construct angles of 90° and 60°.

10

Shape and symmetry

This chapter is going to ...

remind you about line symmetry and rotational symmetry. It will revise some 3-D shapes and show you how to represent them in a 2-D picture, and how to draw their nets so that you could make the actual shapes. It will then introduce you to 3-D symmetry.

What you should already know

✔ How to recognise reflections and to draw the images of reflected shapes.
✔ The property of line symmetry and how to recognise it.
✔ The names of 3-D shapes such as cube, cuboid, prism, pyramid, cone and sphere.

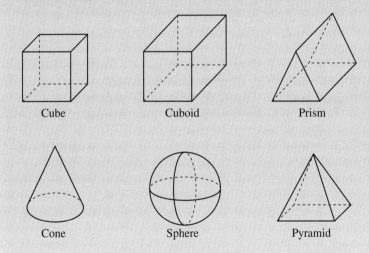

| Cube | Cuboid | Prism |
| Cone | Sphere | Pyramid |

Lines of symmetry

Many flat (plane) shapes have one or more lines of symmetry. A line of symmetry is a line that can be drawn through a shape so that one side of the line is the mirror image of the other side.

It is also the line along which a shape can be folded exactly onto itself.

Look at these shapes. Each has one line of symmetry. Can you see where it is?

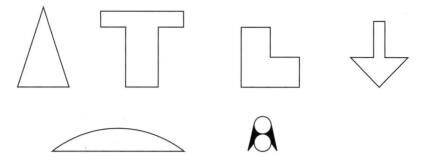

Now look at these shapes. Each has more than one line of symmetry. Can you spot them?

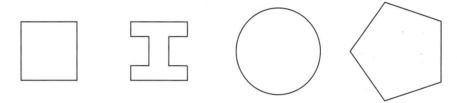

Rotational symmetry

A plane shape has rotational symmetry if it can be rotated about a point to look exactly the same in a new position.

Look at these shapes. Each has rotational symmetry, as you can rotate it about the given point to look the same in another position. This point is called the **point of symmetry**.

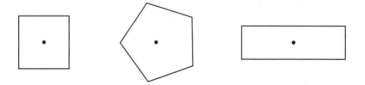

Order of rotational symmetry

The order of rotational symmetry of any shape is the number of different positions in which the shape looks the same, when it is rotated about its point of symmetry (which is like the centre of rotation in transformation geometry).

For example, a rectangle has rotational symmetry of order 2:

a parallelogram has rotational symmetry of order 2:

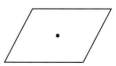

and a regular pentagon has rotational symmetry of order 5:

Note Every shape has an **order** of rotational symmetry, but a shape can only have **rotational symmetry** if its **order is 2** or higher. For example, even though the shape on the right has no symmetry, it can be rotated through 360° back to its original position to look exactly the same. So it is seen to have rotational symmetry of order 1. But we still say it has no symmetry.

EXERCISE 10A

1 Sketch each of these shapes.

   i Show each line of symmetry with a dashed line.

   ii State the order of rotational symmetry.

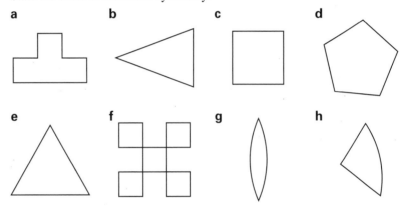

2 Below is the alphabet of capital letters.

   a State how many lines of symmetry each letter has.

   b State the order of rotational symmetry for each letter.

A B C D E F G H I J K L M N O P Q R S T U V W X Y Z

3 Which capital letters have no lines of symmetry?

4 For each shape listed below, find out how many lines of symmetry it has and what the order of rotational symmetry is.

   a Equilateral triangle   **b** Regular hexagon

   c Square   **d** Isosceles triangle with one angle 100°

   e Regular octagon   **f** Circle   **g** Semicircle

5 What is the connection between an isosceles triangle, a perpendicular bisector and a line of symmetry?

6 What connection is there between the number of lines of symmetry and the order of symmetry for regular polygons?

7 **i** Sketch the following diagrams.
  ii Write down under each shape its order of rotational symmetry.
  iii Mark clearly on each of your diagrams where the point of symmetry is.

a 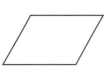 **b**  **c**

d **e** 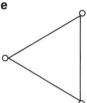 **f**

8 Many wallpapers are designed with symmetry. State the symmetries you can see in the following wallpaper patterns.

a  **b**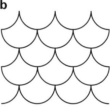

9 Try to draw the following. If you think it's impossible, say so.
  A trapezium with one line of symmetry
  A trapezium with no lines of symmetry
  A trapezium with two lines of symmetry
  A trapezium with three lines of symmetry

10 See if you can draw the following. (Or are some impossible?)
  a A shape with one line of symmetry but
    i rotational symmetry of order 1   **ii** rotational symmetry of order 2
    iii rotational symmetry of order 3   **iv** rotational symmetry of order 4.
  b A shape with two lines of symmetry and the above rotational symmetries.

11 **a** Draw some shapes with only two lines of symmetry.
  b What is the order of rotational symmetry for each shape?
  c Comment on the answers to part **b**.

12 'A line of symmetry always divides a shape into two congruent halves.'
  a Is this statement true?
  b Give clear reasons to support your answer to part **a**.

13 Look at several crosswords in some newspapers. If you ignore the numbers, what are the symmetries of each of the crosswords? Are they all the same?

14 Draw a shape with four lines of symmetry and, if possible,

    a no rotational symmetry   **b** rotational symmetry of order 2

    c rotational symmetry of order 3   **d** rotational symmetry of order 4.

Three-dimensional shapes

The problem with a 3-D shape is that we have to draw it on a flat surface so that it looks like the 3-D shape we want to represent. We have to give the diagram the appearance of depth by slanting the view.

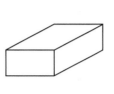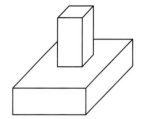

Look at the shapes above and try to draw them yourself without simply copying.

One easy way to draw a 3-D shape is to use a square grid or an isometric grid (a grid of equilateral triangles), as shown below.

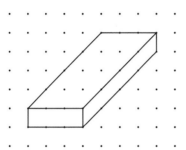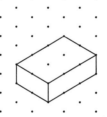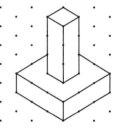

Notice that the dimensions of a 3-D object can easily be seen on the isometric grid but not on the square grid.

When using isometric paper, you **must** make sure that it is the **correct way round** – as shown here.

Nets of 3-D shapes

A net of a 3-D shape is an outline drawn on paper or card in such a way that it can be cut out and folded into the 3-D shape. For example, look at this net for a cube. When cut out, it can be folded into a cube.

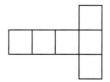

If you intend to make this cube, you will have to put tabs on some sides to be able to glue the thing together. But for nets in examination questions you do **not** need to put on the tabs.

EXERCISE 10B

1 On isometric paper, draw these shapes.

a b   c

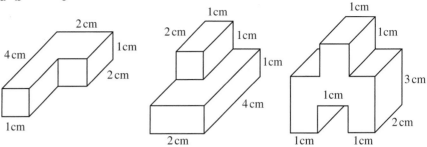

2 Imagine that this shape falls and lands on the side shaded. Draw, on isometric paper, the position of the shape after it has landed.

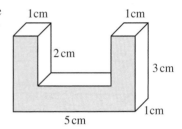

3 The firm TIL want their name made into a solid shape from 1 m³ blocks of concrete. Draw, on isometric paper, a representation of these letters made from the blocks.

4 **a** Sketch a square-based pyramid.
b Sketch the pyramid after it has been tipped over and lies on one of its triangular faces.
c Two of these same pyramids have been stuck together, base to base. Draw the shape they now make.

5 **a** Draw a net of a cube (1 cm³).
b Draw a net of a 1 cm³ cube that is different from the first one you drew.
c How many different nets of the 1 cm³ cube can you draw?

6 A tetrahedron is a pyramid made up of four equilateral triangles. Draw two different nets of a tetrahedron.

7 Draw the net of a square-based pyramid whose vertex is perpendicularly above one corner of the base.

8 Explain why it is impossible to draw a net of a cone or a cylinder.

9 A tent is usually in the shape of a prism whose cross-section is an isosceles triangle. Sketch the net of such a tent.

10 Sketch nets of these shapes.

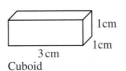

1cm
1cm
3 cm
Cuboid

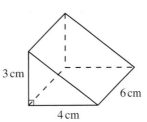

4 cm
4 cm
4 cm
4 cm
4 cm
Square-based pyramid

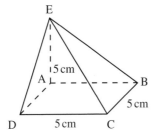

E
5 cm
A
B
5 cm
D   5 cm   C

Square-based pyramid, with
point E directly above point A

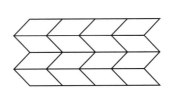

3 cm
6 cm
4 cm
Prism

Tessellations

A tessellation is a regular pattern made on a plane (flat) surface with identical shapes which fit together exactly, leaving no gaps. It is another form of symmetry in a plane. For example, these three patterns are tessellations.

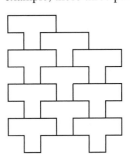
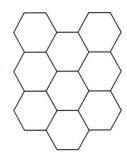

EXERCISE 10C

1 **a** Draw a sketch to illustrate a tessellation using a square.

   b Draw another tessellation using the same square.

   c How many different tessellations could be made using a square?

2 **a** Draw a sketch to illustrate a tessellation using an equilateral triangle.

   b Draw another tessellation using an equilateral triangle.

   c How many different tessellations could be made using an equilateral triangle?

3 How many different tessellations can be made from a rectangle?

4 **a** Why can you **not** sketch a tessellation using a regular pentagon?

   b Can you sketch a non-regular pentagon that would tessellate?
       Sketch the tessellation.

5 a Sketch a tessellation using a regular hexagon.

b How many different tessellations are there using a regular hexagon?

6 Which of the following shapes will tessellate?

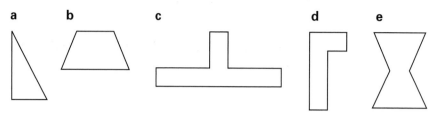

a   **b**   **c**   **d**   **e**

i Draw simple sketches to illustrate those tessellations that can be made.

ii For those shapes that do not tessellate, give clear reasons why they do not.

7 Why won't a circle tessellate?

8 Does a kite tessellate?

9 Draw an octagon that will tessellate. [Hint: not regular, use right angles.]

10 Show that a tessellation can always be made using a trapezium.

11 'Every quadrilateral will form a tessellation.'

a Investigate this statement to see whether it is true.

b Draw some tessellations with quadrilaterals that contain

i only one obtuse angle   **ii** two obtuse angles   **iii** a reflex angle

Symmetry of 3-D shapes

Planes of symmetry

Because of their 'depth', 3-D shapes have **planes of symmetry**, instead of the lines of symmetry found in 2-D shapes.

A plane of symmetry divides a 3-D shape into two identical parts or halves. That is, one half of the shape is the reflection of the other half in a plane of symmetry.

For example, a cuboid has three planes of symmetry. That is, it can be sliced in halves in three different ways.

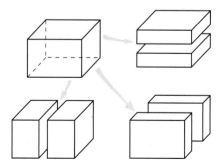

Rotational symmetry

This is like the rotational symmetry of plane shapes but, because of their 'depth', 3-D shapes are rotated about a line, called the **axis of symmetry**, instead of about the point of symmetry found in plane shapes.

A 3-D shape has an axis of symmetry if it can be rotated about that axis to look exactly the same in a new position. For example, a cuboid has three axes of symmetry.

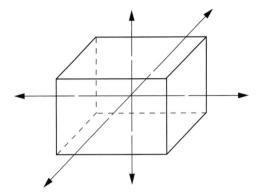

Note how the axes are such that the shape can rotate about each one and appear to remain unaltered. For the cuboid shown, each axis of symmetry is of order 2 since the cuboid can occupy two different places about each axis without changing its appearance.

This is not easy to see on a diagram. So do try to get an actual cuboid and see where these axes of rotation symmetry are located.

EXERCISE 10D

1   For each shape given below describe each plane of symmetry and axis of symmetry. Use the letters on the diagrams to help you. A cross in a circle indicates the centre of a surface. A dot on a line indicates the mid-point of the line.

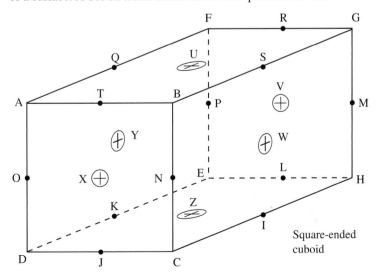

Square-ended cuboid

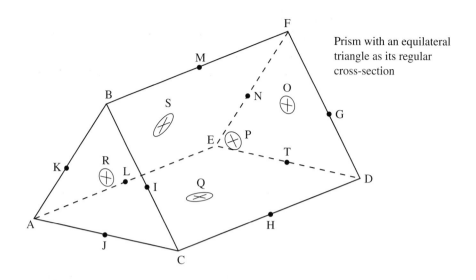

Prism with an equilateral triangle as its regular cross-section

2 Describe the symmetries of
  a a prism with an isosceles triangle as its regular cross-section
  b a prism with a regular hexagon as its regular cross-section.

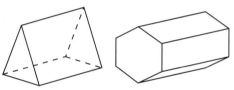

3 Describe the symmetries of
  a a cylinder   **b** a cone   **c** a sphere

4 **a** Sketch a prism with two planes of symmetry.
  b How many axes of symmetry does this shape have?

5 How many planes of symmetry do the following have?
  a Your thumb   **b** A shovel   **c** A chair
  d A teaspoon   **e** A milk bottle   **f** A knife

6 A tetrahedron is a pyramid made up from four equilateral triangles.
  It has six planes of symmetry and four axes of symmetry. Describe each symmetry using the letters on the shape.

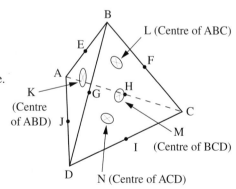

7 If the following solids were put on a mirror, describe the new shape that would appear.
  a Cuboid   **b** Cube
  c Cylinder (one end on the mirror)
  d Hemisphere

8 Sketch a solid that has the following rotational symmetries (ignore plane symmetry).
  a One axis of symmetry of order 2.
  b Four axes of symmetry, one order 3 and the others order 2.

9 Why is a house brick such a good shape to build with? (Use symmetry in your answer.)

10 Imagine the shell of a car.

    a Is the shell symmetrical? Describe the symmetries if there are any.

    b Are all the doors on the car the same?

    c Could you put the driver's door on the passenger's side?

Possible coursework tasks

Mirror images

How many different words can you make which look the same when read in a mirror?

Symmetrical tiles

On this 3×3 tile, three squares are shaded so that the tile has one line of symmetry. Investigate the symmetry of the tile by shading different numbers of squares.

Quadrilateral tessellation

    a Every quadrilateral will tessellate. Show why this is true.

    b By giving the sides of a quadrilateral rotational symmetry, create some tessellations of your own.

Pentomino patterns

Pentominoes are shapes made with five adjoining squares. Investigate line symmetry and rotational symmetry for different pentominoes.

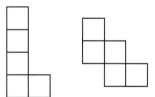

Four cubed

How many symmetrical shapes can be made from four cubes placed face to face?

Build the pyramids

The pyramid shown is constructed from 10 cubes and has one plane of symmetry. Investigate the number of planes of symmetry for different types of pyramid.

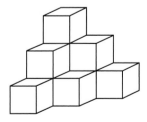

Tessellating transformations

Make your own tessellating patterns using rotations, reflections or translations.

Examination questions: coursework type

1 A shape is folded exactly onto itself.
This is what it looks like now.

The starting shape could have been this.

a On squared paper, draw other possible starting shapes.

b How many lines of symmetry has each of the starting shapes?

NEAB, Question 3, Paper 3I, June 1996

2 Show that a triangle will always tessellate.

3 Is it true that all tessellations will have
a at least one line of symmetry,
b rotational symmetry of at least order 2?

4 Which regular polygons
a will tessellate **b** will not tessellate?

Examination questions

1 The diagram shows three identical rhombuses P, Q and T.

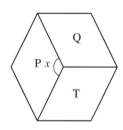

a Explain why angle *x* is 120°.
b Rhombus Q can be rotated onto rhombus T.
　i Copy the diagram and mark a centre of rotation on the diagram.
　ii State the angle of rotation.
c Write down the order of rotational symmetry of
　i a rhombus **ii** a regular hexagon
d The given shape could also represent a three-dimensional shape. What is this shape?

NEAB, Question 2, Paper 1Q, June 1995

2 The diagram shows a regular hexagon.
O is the point at the centre of the hexagon.
A and B are two vertices.

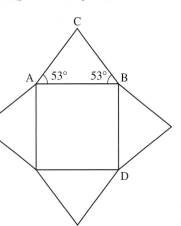

a Write down the order of rotational symmetry of the regular hexagon.

b Draw the lines from O to A and from O to B.

   i Write down the size of angle AOB.

   ii Write down the mathematical name for triangle AOB.

ULEAC, Question 1, Paper 4, June 1994

3 This diagram is not drawn to scale, it shows the net of a square-based pyramid. The line AB is 6 cm long. Angles CAB and CBA are each 53°. The four triangles are congruent.

a On the net, draw all its lines of symmetry.

b Explain why AC and BC must have the same length.

c Find the size of angle CBD.

d Draw the triangle ABC full size.

WJEC, Question 2, Paper 2, June 1994

4 Complete the drawing of a cuboid. One edge is drawn for you.

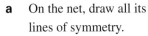

SEG, Question 14, Paper 4, June 1994

5 The diagram shows a regular tetrahedron. Each edge is 5 cm long. Draw an accurate net of the tetrahedron.

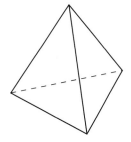

NEAB, Question 7, Paper 1Q, June 1995

6   The solid shape shown falls over onto the shaded face.
On an isometric grid, draw the shape after it has fallen over.

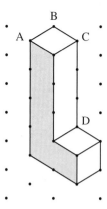

NEAB, Question 11, Paper 1Q, June 1995

7   On a copy of the diagram below, show how the shaded shape will tessellate. You should draw at least 5 shapes.

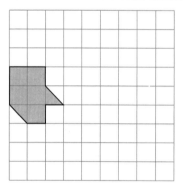

EDEXCEL, Question 5, Paper 3, June 2000

8   Draw diagrams to illustrate one plane of symmetry for each of the following shapes.

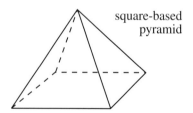

cube   square-based pyramid

EDEXCEL, Question 7, Paper 3, June 2000

9   A builder is putting a square piece of plain glass into a window.
His labourer says, 'There's four ways you can put that in, Guv.'
The builder says, 'No, there's not, there are...'
a   Complete what the builder could correctly say.
b   Give clear reasons to justify your answer.

Summary

How well do you grade yourself?

To gain a grade **E**, you need to be able to identify all the symmetries of 2-D shapes, and to sketch nets for simple 3-D shapes.

To gain a grade **D**, you need to be able accurately to draw 2-D representations of 3-D shapes, and accurately to draw nets of simple 3-D shapes, and to show clearly why particular shapes (such as octagons) will not tessellate.

To gain a grade **C**, you need to be able to identify all the symmetries of 3-D shapes.

What you should know after you have worked through Chapter 10

- How to recognise lines of symmetry and draw them on plane (flat) shapes.

- How to recognise whether a plane (flat) shape has rotational symmetry and how to find its order of rotational symmetry.

- How to draw 2-D representations of 3-D shapes.

- How to draw nets of certain common 3-D shapes.

- What tessellations are and how to construct them.

- How to recognise the symmetry of 3-D shapes.

11 Properties of number, indices & standard form

This chapter is going to ...

remind you of some of the special types of number, show you how to write and manipulate numbers given as indices, and introduce you to standard form, which is a way of writing and dealing with very large or very small numbers.

What you should already know

✔ **Multiples of numbers** These are often called the 'times tables'. For example, a multiple of 7 is any number that can be written as $n \times 7$, where n is a whole number. So the multiples of 7 are 7, 14, 21, 28, 35, 42, ... Likewise, the multiples of 5 are 5, 10, 15, 20, ...

✔ **Factors of numbers** A factor of a number is any number that divides into it exactly. For example, the factors of 20 are 1, 2, 4, 5, 10, 20; the factors of 12 are 1, 2, 3, 4, 6, 12. This is where it helps to know your tables.

1 is always a factor and so is the number itself. When you find a factor, there is always another number that must go with it. For example,

$1 \times 20 = 20 \quad 2 \times 10 = 20 \quad 4 \times 5 = 20$

Example 1 Find the factors of 32.

Look for 'pairs' of numbers that make 32. For example,

$1 \times 32 = 32 \quad 2 \times 16 = 32 \quad 4 \times 8 = 32$

The factors of 32 are

1, 2, 4, 8, 16, 32

Example 2 Find the factors of 36.

$1 \times 36 = 36 \quad 2 \times 18 = 36 \quad 3 \times 12 = 36 \quad 4 \times 9 = 36 \quad 6 \times 6 = 36$

The factors of 36 are

1, 2, 3, 4, 6, 9, 12, 18, 36

✔ **Square numbers** What is the next number in this sequence?

1, 4, 9, 16, 25, ...

You may have spotted that the difference increases by 2 each time, i.e. the pattern is up 3, up 5, up 7 etc. So the next number is 36. Another way of working this out is to write the sequence as

$1 \times 1, 2 \times 2, 3 \times 3, 4 \times 4, 5 \times 5, ...$ which is $1^2, 2^2, 3^2, 4^2, 5^2, ...$

So the next number is $6^2 = 36$.

They are called square numbers because they make patterns of squares.

$1^2 = 1$ $2^2 = 4$ $3^2 = 9$ $4^2 = 16$ $5^2 = 25$

✔ **Triangle numbers**   What is the next number in this sequence?

   1, 3, 6, 10, 15, ...

You may have spotted that the difference increases by 1 each time, i.e. the pattern is up 2, up 3, up 4, etc. So the next number is 21. They are called triangle numbers because they make triangular patterns.

1   3   6   10   15

✔ **Prime numbers**   What are the factors of 2, 3, 5, 7, 11, 13?

These are examples of prime numbers. A prime number has only two factors: 1 and itself.

Note: 1 is **not** a prime number, since it has only one factor.

EXERCISE 11A

1   Write out the first five multiples of

   a   3   **b**   7   **c**   9   **d**   11   **e**   16

   Remember: the first multiple is the number itself.

2   Write out the first three numbers that are multiples of both of the numbers shown.

   a   3 and 4   **b**   4 and 5   **c**   3 and 5   **d**   6 and 9   **e**   5 and 7

3   What are the factors of these numbers?

   a   10   **b**   18   **c**   25   **d**   30   **e**   24
   f   32   **g**   17   **h**   40   **i**   45   **j**   16

4   In question **3**, part **g**, there were only two factors. Why?

5   In question **3**, every number had an even number of factors except parts **c** and **j**. What sort of numbers are 25 and 16?

6   What are the prime numbers up to 20?

7 What are the square numbers up to 100?

8 What are the triangle numbers up to 100?

9 If hot-dog sausages are sold in packs of 10 and hot-dog buns are sold in packs of 8, how many of each do you have to buy to have complete hot dogs with no wasted sausages or buns?

10 Rover barks every 8 seconds and Spot barks every 12 seconds. If they both bark together, how many seconds will it be before they both bark together again?

11 A bell chimes every 6 seconds. Another bell chimes every 5 seconds. If they both chime together, how many seconds will it be before they both chime together again.

12 Fred runs round a running track every 4 minutes. Debbie runs round every 3 minutes. If they both start on the line at the end of the finishing straight, when will they both be on the line together again? How many laps will Debbie have done? How many laps will Fred have done?

13 From this box choose one number that fits each of these descriptions.

12		21
	8	15
13		17
9		18
	10	6
14	16	

    a A multiple of 3 and a multiple of 4.

    b A square number and an odd number.

    c A factor of 24 and a factor of 18.

    d A prime number and a factor of 39.

    e An odd factor of 30 and a multiple of 3.

    f A number with 4 factors and a multiple of 2 and 7.

    g A number with 5 factors exactly.

    h A triangle number and a factor of 20.

    i An even number and a factor of 36 and a multiple of 9.

    j A prime number that is one more than a square number.

    k If you write the factors of this number out in order they make a number pattern in which each number is twice the one before.

    l An odd triangle number that is a multiple of 7.

14 Copy these sums and write out the **next four** lines.

$$1 = 1$$
$$1 + 3 = 4$$
$$1 + 3 + 5 = 9$$
$$1 + 3 + 5 + 7 = 16$$

Prime factors

Start with a number – say 110 – and find two numbers which, when multiplied together, give that number, e.g. 2×55. Are they both prime? No. So take 55 and repeat the operation, to get 5×11. Are these prime? Yes. So

$$110 = 2 \times 5 \times 11$$

These are the prime factors of 110.

This method is not very logical and needs good tables skills. There are, however, two methods that you can use to make sure you do not miss any of the prime factors.

The next two examples show you how to use the first of these methods.

Example 1   Find the prime factors of 24.

Divide 24 by any prime number that goes into it. (2 is an obvious choice.) Divide the answer (12) by a prime number. Repeat this process until you have a prime number as the answer.

$$\begin{array}{c|c} 2 & 24 \\ \hline 2 & 12 \\ \hline 3 & 6 \\ \hline & 2 \end{array}$$

So the prime factors of 24 are $2 \times 2 \times 2 \times 3$.

A quicker and neater way to write this answer is to use index notation, expressing the answer in powers. (Powers are dealt with on pages 193–204.)

In index notation, the prime factors of 24 are $2^3 \times 3$.

Example 2   Find the prime factors of 96.

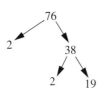

So, the prime factors of 96 are $2 \times 2 \times 2 \times 2 \times 2 \times 3 = 2^5 \times 3$.

The second of these methods is called **prime factor trees**. You start by splitting the number into a multiplication sum. Then you split this, and carry on splitting until you get to prime numbers.

Example 3   Find the prime factors of 76.

We stop splitting the factors here because 2, 2 and 19 are all prime numbers.

So, the prime factors of 76 are $2 \times 2 \times 19 = 2^2 \times 19$.

Example 4   Find the prime factors of 420.

The process can be done upside down to make an upright tree.

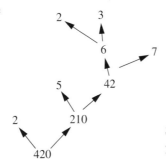

So, the prime factors of 420 are $2 \times 5 \times 2 \times 3 \times 7 = 2^2 \times 3 \times 5 \times 7$.

EXERCISE 11B

1 Copy and complete these prime factor trees.

a

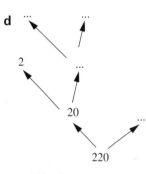

$84 = 2 \times 2 \ldots \times \ldots$

b

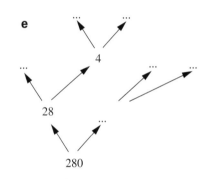

$100 = 5 \times 2 \ldots \times \ldots$

c

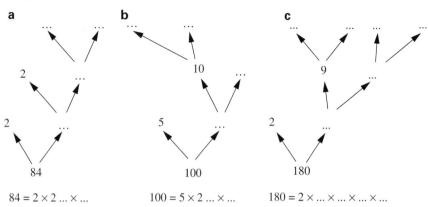

$180 = 2 \times \ldots \times \ldots \times \ldots \times \ldots$

d

$220 = 2 \times \ldots \times \ldots \times \ldots$

e

$280 = \ldots \times \ldots \times \ldots \times \ldots \times \ldots$

f

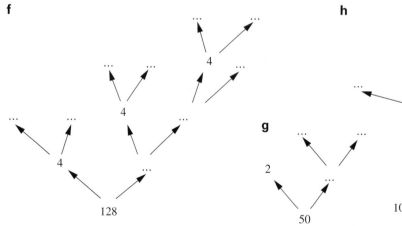

$128 = \ldots \times \ldots \times \ldots \times \ldots \times \ldots \times \ldots \times \ldots$

g

$50 = \ldots \times \ldots \times \ldots$

h

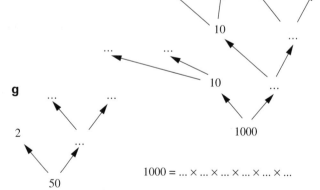

$1000 = \ldots \times \ldots \times \ldots \times \ldots \times \ldots \times \ldots$

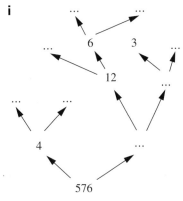

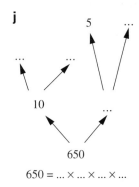

i

j

$$576 = \ldots \times \ldots \times \ldots \times \ldots \times \ldots \times \ldots \times \ldots \times \ldots$$

$$650 = \ldots \times \ldots \times \ldots \times \ldots$$

2 Using index notation, for example,
$$100 = 2 \times 2 \times 5 \times 5 = 2^2 \times 5^2$$
and $540 = 2 \times 2 \times 3 \times 3 \times 3 \times 5 = 2^2 \times 3^3 \times 5$

rewrite the answers to question **1** parts **a** to **j**.

3 Write the numbers from 1 to 50 in prime factors. Use index notation. For example,
$$1 = 1 \quad 2 = 2 \quad 3 = 3 \quad 4 = 2^2 \quad 5 = 5 \quad 6 = 2 \times 3 \quad \ldots$$

4 **a** What is special about the answers to 2, 4, 8, 16, 32, …?

  b What are the next two terms in this series?

  c What are the next three terms in the series 3, 9, 27, …?

  d Continue the series 4, 16, 64, …, for three more terms.

  e Write all the above series in index notation. For example, the first series is
$2^2, 2^3, 2^4, 2^5, 2^6, 2^7, \ldots$.

Powers

Powers are a convenient way of writing repetitive multiplication sums. (Powers are also called 'indices' – singular 'index'.)

The most common power is 2, which has the special name 'square'. The only other power with a special name is 3, which is called 'cube'.

Examples

1 The value of 7 squared is $7^2 = 7 \times 7 = 49$
The value of 5 cubed is $5^3 = 5 \times 5 \times 5 = 125$

2 Write out in full: **a** 4^6, **b** 6^4, **c** 7^3, **d** 12^2.

  a $4^6 = 4 \times 4 \times 4 \times 4 \times 4 \times 4$ **b** $6^4 = 6 \times 6 \times 6 \times 6$

  c $7^3 = 7 \times 7 \times 7$ **d** $12^2 = 12 \times 12$

3 Write **a** to **d** in index form.

  a $3 \times 3 \times 3 \times 3 \times 3 \times 3 \times 3 \times 3 = 3^8$ **b** $13 \times 13 \times 13 \times 13 \times 13 = 13^5$

  c $7 \times 7 \times 7 \times 7 = 7^4$ **d** $5 \times 5 \times 5 \times 5 \times 5 \times 5 \times 5 = 5^7$

Working out powers on your calculator

For example, how do we work out the value of 5^7 on a calculator?

We could do the sum as $5 \times 5 \times 5 \times 5 \times 5 \times 5 \times 5 = $. But if we tried to key this sum, we would probably end up missing a number or pressing a wrong key. Instead, we use the power key $\boxed{x^y}$ or, on some calculators, $\boxed{y^x}$. So

$5^7 = \boxed{5} \ \boxed{x^y} \ \boxed{7} \ \boxed{=}$ 78 125

Make sure you know where to find the power key on your calculator. It may be an INV or SHIFT function.

Try to work these out on your calculator : 3^4, 7^8, 23^4, 72^3.

Check that you get 81, 5 764 801, 279 841 and 373 248.

Two special powers

Choose any number, say 5, and use your calculator to raise it to the power 1. You will find that $5^1 = 5$. That is, a number raised to the power 1 stays the same number. This is true for **any** number, so we do not normally write down the power 1.

Choose any number, say 9, and use your calculator to raise it to the power 0. You will find that $9^0 = 1$. This is true for **any** number raised to the power 0. The answer is **always** 1.

EXERCISE 11C

1 Write these sums using power notation. Do not work them out yet.
   a $2 \times 2 \times 2 \times 2$
   b $3 \times 3 \times 3 \times 3 \times 3$
   c 7×7
   d $5 \times 5 \times 5$
   e $10 \times 10 \times 10 \times 10 \times 10 \times 10 \times 10$
   f $6 \times 6 \times 6 \times 6$
   g 4
   h $1 \times 1 \times 1 \times 1 \times 1 \times 1 \times 1$
   i $0.5 \times 0.5 \times 0.5 \times 0.5$
   j $100 \times 100 \times 100$

2 Write these power terms out in full. Do not work them out yet.
   a 3^4 b 9^3 c 6^2 d 10^5 e 2^{10}
   f 8^1 g 0.1^3 h 2.5^2 i 0.7^3 j 1000^2

3 Using the power key on your calculator (or another method), work out the values of the power terms in question **1**.

4 Using the power key on your calculator (or another method), work out the values of the power terms in question **2**.

5 Without using a calculator, work out the values of these power terms.
   a 2^0 b 4^1 c 5^0 d 1^9 e 1^{235}

6 The answers to question **5**, parts **d** and **e**, should tell you something special about powers of 1. What is it?

7 Write the answer to question **1**, part **j** as a power of 10.

8 Write the answer to question **2**, part **j** as a power of 10.

9 Using your calculator, or otherwise, work out the values of these power terms.
    a $(-1)^0$ **b** $(-1)^1$ **c** $(-1)^2$ **d** $(-1)^4$ **e** $(-1)^5$

10 Using your answers to question **9**, you should be able to write down the answers to these.
    a $(-1)^8$ **b** $(-1)^{11}$ **c** $(-1)^{99}$ **d** $(-1)^{80}$ **e** $(-1)^{126}$

11 Copy this pattern of powers of 2 and continue it for another five terms.

2^2	2^3	2^4	...	...	...	...	...
4	8	16	...	...	...	...	...

12 What would be the terms **before** the terms in question **11**?

...	2^2	2^3
...	4	8

13 Continue the pattern in questions **11** and **12** backwards for three more terms.

...	...	...	2^2	2^3
...	...	...	4	8

14 Copy the pattern of powers of 10 and fill in the previous five and the next five terms.

...	...	...	...	...	10^2	10^3	...	...	...	...	...
...	...	...	...	...	100	1000	...	...	...	...	...

The last question uses powers of 10, which we have already seen are special.

How many noughts does a million have? What is a million as a power of 10? This table shows some of the pattern of the powers of 10.

Number	0.001	0.01	0.1	1	10	100	1000	10 000	100 000
Powers	10^{-3}	10^{-2}	10^{-1}	10^0	10^1	10^2	10^3	10^4	10^5

What pattern is there in the top row?
What pattern is there to the powers in the bottom row?

Rules for multiplying and dividing powers

When we multiply together powers of the same variable or number, something unexpected happens. For example,

$$a^2 \times a^3 = (a \times a) \times (a \times a \times a) = a^5$$
$$3^3 \times 3^5 = (3 \times 3 \times 3) \times (3 \times 3 \times 3 \times 3 \times 3) = 3^8$$

Can you see the rule? We can do these sums just by **adding** the powers. For example,

$$a^3 \times a^4 = a^{3+4} = a^7$$
$$b^4 \times b^7 = b^{11}$$
$$2^3 \times 2^4 \times 2^5 = 2^{12}$$
$$10^4 \times 10^{-2} = 10^2$$
$$10^{-3} \times 10^{-1} = 10^{-4}$$

A similar rule applies when we divide powers of the same variable or number. For example,

$$a^5 \div a^2 = (a \times a \times a \times a \times a) \div (a \times a) = a \times a \times a = a^3$$
$$7^6 \div 7 = (7 \times 7 \times 7 \times 7 \times 7 \times 7) \div (7) = 7 \times 7 \times 7 \times 7 \times 7 = 7^5$$

Can you see the rule? We can do these sums just by **subtracting** the powers. For example,

$$a^4 \div a^3 = a^{4-3} = a^1 = a$$
$$b^4 \div b^7 = b^{-3}$$
$$10^4 \div 10^{-2} = 10^6$$
$$10^{-2} \div 10^{-4} = 10^2$$

When we raise a power term to a further power, a third rule applies. For example,

$$(a^2)^3 = a^2 \times a^2 \times a^2 = a^6$$
$$(b^4)^5 = b^4 \times b^4 \times b^4 \times b^4 \times b^4 = b^{20}$$

Can you see the rule? We can do these sums just by **multiplying** together the powers. For example,

$$(a^3)^3 = a^{3 \times 3} = a^9$$
$$(a^{-2})^4 = a^{-8}$$
$$(a^2)^6 = a^{12}$$

Here are some examples of different kinds of power sums.

$$2a^2 \times 3a^4 = (2 \times 3) \times (a^2 \times a^4) = 6 \times a^6 = 6a^6$$

$$4a^2b^3 \times 2ab^2 = (4 \times 2) \times (a^2 \times a) \times (b^3 \times b^2) = 8a^3b^5$$

$$12a^5 \div 3a^2 = (12 \div 3) \times (a^5 \div a^2) = 4a^3$$

$$(2a^2)^3 = (2)^3 \times (a^2)^3 = 8 \times a^6 = 8a^6$$

EXERCISE 11D

1 Write these as single powers of 5.
   a $5^2 \times 5^2$ **b** $5^4 \times 5^6$ **c** $5^2 \times 5^3$ **d** 5×5^2 **e** $5^6 \times 5^9$
   f 5×5^8 **g** $5^{-2} \times 5^4$ **h** $5^6 \times 5^{-3}$ **i** $5^{-2} \times 5^{-3}$

2 Write these as single powers of 6.
   a $6^5 \div 6^2$ **b** $6^7 \div 6^2$ **c** $6^3 \div 6^2$ **d** $6^4 \div 6^4$ **e** $6^5 \div 6^4$
   f $6^2 \div 6^4$ **g** $6^4 \div 6^{-2}$ **h** $6^{-3} \div 6^4$ **i** $6^{-3} \div 6^{-5}$

3 Write these as single powers of 4.
   a $(4^2)^3$ **b** $(4^3)^5$ **c** $(4^1)^6$ **d** $(4^3)^{-2}$ **e** $(4^{-2})^{-3}$ **f** $(4^7)^0$

4 Simplify these and write them as single powers of a.
   a $a^2 \times a$ **b** $a^3 \times a^2$ **c** $a^4 \times a^3$ **d** $a^6 \div a^2$ **e** $a^3 \div a$ **f** $a^5 \div a^4$

5 Simplify these expressions.
   a $2a^2 \times 3a^3$ **b** $4a^3 \times 5a$ **c** $2a^{-2} \times 4a^5$ **d** $3a^4 \times 3a^{-2}$ **e** $3a^2 \times 5a^{-2}$
   f $(2a^2)^3$ **g** $-2a^2 \times 3a^2$ **h** $-4a^3 \times -2a^5$ **i** $-2a^4 \times 5a^{-7}$

6 Simplify these expressions.

   a $6a^3 \div 2a^2$ **b** $12a^5 \div 3a^2$ **c** $15a^5 \div 5a$ **d** $18a^{-2} \div 3a^{-1}$

   e $24a^5 \div 6a^{-2}$ **f** $30a \div 6a^5$

7 Simplify these expressions.

   a $2a^2b^3 \times 4a^3b$ **b** $5a^2b^4 \times 2ab^{-3}$ **c** $6a^2b^3 \times 5a^{-4}b^{-5}$ **d** $12a^2b^4 \div 6ab$

   e $24a^{-3}b^4 \div 3a^2b^{-3}$

8 Simplify these expressions.

   a $\dfrac{6a^4b^3}{2ab}$ **b** $\dfrac{2a^2bc^2 \times 6abc^3}{4ab^2c}$ **c** $\dfrac{3abc \times 4a^3b^2c \times 6c^2}{9a^2bc}$

Multiplying and dividing by powers of 10

The easiest number to multiply by is zero, because any number multiplied by zero is zero. The next easiest number to multiply by is 1, because any number multiplied by 1 stays the same.

After that it is a matter of opinion, but it is generally accepted that multiplying by 10 is simple. So try these on your calculator.

   a 7×10 **b** 7.34×10 **c** 43×10

   d 0.678×10 **e** 0.007×10 **f** 34.5×10

Can you see the rule for multiplying by 10? You may have learnt that when you multiply a number by 10, you add a nought to the number. This is only true when you start with a whole number. It is not true for a decimal. The rule is

> Every time you multiply a number by 10, move the digits in the number one place to the left.

Check to make sure that this happened in examples **a** to **f** above.

It is almost as easy to multiply by 100. Try these sums on your calculator.

   a 7×100 **b** 7.34×100 **c** 43×100

   d 0.678×100 **e** 0.007×100 **f** 34.5×100

This time you should find that the digits move two places to the left.

We can write 100, 1000, 10 000 as times sums in 10. For example,

$$100 = 10 \times 10 = 10^2$$
$$1000 = 10 \times 10 \times 10 = 10^3$$
$$10\,000 = 10 \times 10 \times 10 \times 10 = 10^4$$

Can you see a connection between the number of zeros and the power of 10? Try these on your calculator. See if you can decide what the rule is.

   a 12.3×10 **b** 3.45×1000 **c** 3.45×10

   d $0.075 \times 10\,000$ **e** 2.045×10 **f** 6.78×1000

   g 25.67×10 **h** 34.21×100 **i** $0.0324 \times 10\,000$

Can you find a similar rule for division? Try these on your calculator. See if you can decide what the rule is.

a $12.3 \div 10$ **b** $3.45 \div 1000$ **c** $3.45 \div 10$

d $0.075 \div 100$ **e** $2.045 \div 10$ **f** $6.78 \div 1000$

g $25.67 \div 10$ **h** $34.21 \div 100$ **i** $0.0324 \div 1000$

This principle can be used to multiply together multiples of 10, 100 and so on. We use this method in estimation. You should have the skill to do this mentally so that you can check that your answers to calculations are about right. (Approximation of calculations is covered on page 22.)

Work out these sums.

a $200 \times 300 =$ **b** $100 \times 40 =$ **c** $2000 \times 3000 =$

d $200 \times 50 =$ **e** $200 \times 5000 =$ **f** $300 \times 40 =$

Can you see a way of doing these without using a calculator or pencil and paper?

Dividing is almost as simple. Try doing these sums.

a $400 \div 20 =$ **b** $200 \div 50 =$ **c** $1000 \div 200 =$

d $300 \div 30 =$ **e** $250 \div 50 =$ **f** $30\,000 \div 600 =$

Once again, there is an easy way of doing these 'in your head'. Look at these examples.

$$300 \times 4000 = 1\,200\,000 \qquad 5000 \div 200 = 25$$
$$200 \times 50 = 10\,000 \qquad 60 \times 5000 = 300\,000$$
$$400 \div 20 = 20$$

Can you see the connection between the method of combining powers and the way in which these sums are worked out?

EXERCISE 11E

1 Write down the value of

  a 3.1×10 **b** 3.1×100 **c** 3.1×1000 **d** $3.1 \times 10\,000$

2 Write down the value of

  a 6.5×10 **b** 6.5×10^2 **c** 6.5×10^3 **d** 6.5×10^4

3 In questions **1** and **2** there is a connection between the multipliers. (It isn't that the first number is the same.) What is the connection?

4 This list of answers came from a very similar set of sums to those in questions **1** and **2**. Write down what the sums must have been, using numbers written out in full and powers of 10. (There is a slight catch!)

  a 73   **b** 730   **c** 7300   **d** 730 000

5 Write down the value of

  a $3.1 \div 10$ **b** $3.1 \div 100$ **c** $3.1 \div 1000$ **d** $3.1 \div 10\,000$

6 Write down the value of

  a $6.5 \div 10$ **b** $6.5 \div 10^2$ **c** $6.5 \div 10^3$ **d** $6.5 \div 10^4$

7 In questions **5** and **6** there is a connection between the divisors. What is it?

8 This list of answers came from a very similar set of sums to those in questions **5** and **6**. Write down what the sums must have been, using numbers written out in full and powers of 10. (There is a slight catch!)

    a 0.73   **b** 0.073   **c** 0.0073   **d** 0.000 073

9 Without using a calculator, write down the answers to these sums.

a 2.5×100	**b** 3.45×10	**c** 4.67×1000
d 34.6×10	**e** 20.789×10	**f** 56.78×1000
g 2.46×10^2	**h** 0.076×10	**i** 0.076×10^3
j 0.897×10^5	**k** 0.865×1000	**l** 100.5×10^2
m 0.999×10^6	**n** 234.56×10^2	**o** 98.7654×10^3
p 43.23×10^6	**q** 78.679×10^2	**r** 203.67×10^1
s 76.43×10	**t** 34.578×10^5	**u** $0.003\,4578 \times 10^5$
v 0.0006×10^7	**w** $0.005\,67 \times 10^4$	**x** 56.0045×10^4
y $0.909\,07 \times 10^4$	**z** 70.086×10^3	

10 Without using a calculator, write down the answers to these sums.

a $2.5 \div 100$	**b** $3.45 \div 10$	**c** $4.67 \div 1000$
d $34.6 \div 10$	**e** $20.789 \div 100$	**f** $56.78 \div 1000$
g $2.46 \div 10^2$	**h** $0.076 \div 10$	**i** $0.076 \div 10^3$
j $0.897 \div 10^5$	**k** $0.865 \div 1000$	**l** $100.5 \div 10^2$
m $0.999 \div 10^6$	**n** $234.56 \div 10^2$	**o** $98.7654 \div 10^3$
p $43.23 \div 10^6$	**q** $78.679 \div 10^2$	**r** $203.67 \div 10^1$
s $76.43 \div 10$	**t** $34.578 \div 10^5$	**u** $0.003\,4578 \div 10^5$
v $0.0006 \div 10^7$	**w** $0.005\,67 \div 10^4$	**x** $56.0045 \div 10^4$
y $0.909\,07 \div 10^4$	**z** $70.086 \div 10^3$	

11 Without using a calculator, write down the answers to these sums.

a 200×300	**b** 30×4000	**c** 50×200
d 60×700	**e** 70×300	**f** 10×30
g 3×50	**h** 200×7	**i** 200×500
j 100×2000	**k** 20×1400	**l** 30×30
m $(20)^2$	**n** $(20)^3$	**o** $(400)^2$
p 30×150	**q** 40×200	**r** 50×5000
s 40×250	**t** 300×2	**u** 6×500
v 30×2000	**w** $20 \times 40 \times 5000$	**x** $20 \times 20 \times 900$
y $200 \times 4000 \times 60\,000$	**z** $20 \times 50 \times 400 \times 3000$	

12 Without using a calculator, write down the answers to these sums.

a $2000 \div 400$	**b** $3000 \div 60$	**c** $5000 \div 200$
d $6000 \div 200$	**e** $2100 \div 300$	**f** $9000 \div 30$
g $300 \div 50$	**h** $2100 \div 70$	**i** $2000 \div 500$
j $10\,000 \div 2000$	**k** $2800 \div 1400$	**l** $3000 \div 30$
m $2000 \div 50$	**n** $80\,000 \div 400$	**o** $400 \div 20$
p $3000 \div 150$	**q** $400 \div 200$	**r** $5000 \div 5000$
s $4000 \div 250$	**t** $300 \div 2$	**u** $6000 \div 500$

    v $30\,000 \div 2000$ **w** $2000 \times 40 \div 2000$ **x** $200 \times 20 \div 800$

    y $200 \times 6000 \div 30\,000$ **z** $20 \times 80 \times 600 \div 3000$

13 Without using a calculator, work out the answers to these sums.

    a 2.3×10^2 **b** 5.789×10^5 **c** 4.79×10^3 **d** 5.7×10^7

    e 2.16×10^2 **f** 1.05×10^4 **g** 3.2×10^{-4} **h** 9.87×10^3

14 Which of these statements is true about the numbers in question **13**?

    a   The first part is always a number between 1 and 10.

    b   There is always a times sign in the middle of the sum.

    c   There is always a power of 10 at the end.

    d   Calculator displays sometimes show numbers in this form.

Standard form

This is also known as standard index or SI form. On calculators, it is usually called Scientific Notation.

Standard form is a way of writing large and small numbers using powers of 10. In this form, a number is given a value between 1 and 10 multiplied by a power of 10. That is,

    $a \times 10^n$ where $1 \leq a < 10$, and n is a whole number

This is the way you will find standard form defined in your examination formula sheet.

Follow through these examples to see how numbers are written in this way.

    $52 = 5.2 \times 10 = 5.2 \times 10^1$

    $73 = 7.3 \times 10 = 7.3 \times 10^1$

    $625 = 6.25 \times 100 = 6.25 \times 10^2$

    $389 = 3.89 \times 100 = 3.89 \times 10^2$

    $3147 = 3.147 \times 1000 = 3.147 \times 10^3$

The numbers at the right are in standard form.

When writing a number in this way, two rules must always be followed:

● The first part must be a number between 1 and 10 (1 is allowed but 10 isn't).

● The second part must be a whole number (negative or positive) power of 10. Note that we would **not normally** write the power 1.

In the examples above, each starting number is a whole number, whose decimal point (which isn't shown) comes after the last digit. How many places does each decimal point move?

Can you see the connection between the number of places that the point moves and the power?

What about $753.2 = 7.532 \times 10^2$? Does the rule still work?

These numbers are written in standard form. Make sure that you understand how they are formed.

a $23 = 2.3 \times 10$ **b** $345 = 3.45 \times 10^2$

c $2300 = 2.3 \times 10^3$ **d** $45.7 = 4.57 \times 10$

e $2134 = 2.134 \times 10^3$ **f** $12.17 = 1.217 \times 10$

g $345.2 = 3.452 \times 10^2$ **h** $567.132 = 5.671\ 32 \times 10^2$

i $3.4 = 3.4 \times 1 = 3.4 \times 10^0$ **j** $4567.32 = 4.567\ 32 \times 10^3$

Standard form on a calculator

A number such as 123 000 000 000 is obviously difficult to key into a calculator. Instead, you enter it in standard form (assuming you are using a scientific calculator):

$$123\,000\,000\,000 = 1.23 \times 10^{11}$$

The key strokes to enter this into your calculator will be

   (On some calculators EXP is EE.)

Your calculator display should now show

1.23 $^{\boxed{11}}$ or   1.23 $\boxed{11}$

Be careful when you get an answer like this on your calculator. It needs to be written properly in standard form with × 10, not copied exactly as shown on the calculator display.

Try putting examples **a** to **j** into your calculator.

Look at the following examples.

$0.7 = 7 \times 0.1 = 10^{-1}$

$0.03 = 3 \times 0.01 = 3 \times 10^{-2}$

$0.456 = 4.56 \times 0.1 = 4.56 = 10^{-1}$

$0.0006 = 6 \times 0.0001 = 6 \times 10^{-4}$

What is the rule this time? When we move the decimal point to the left, the power becomes negative.

These numbers are written in standard form. Make sure that you understand how they are formed.

a $0.4 = 4 \times 10^{-1}$ **b** $0.05 = 5 \times 10^{-2}$

c $0.007 = 7 \times 10^{-3}$ **d** $0.123 = 1.23 \times 10^{-1}$

e $0.0085 = 8.5 \times 10^{-3}$ **f** $0.0032 = 3.2 \times 10^{-3}$

g $0.007\ 65 = 7.65 \times 10^{-3}$ **h** $0.9804 = 9.804 \times 10^{-1}$

i $0.0098 = 9.8 \times 10^{-3}$ **j** $0.000\ 0078 = 7.8 \times 10^{-6}$

On a calculator you will enter 1.23×10^{-6}, for example, as

or **1** **.** **2** **3** **EXP** **+/−** **6**

or **1** **.** **2** **3** **EXP** **6** **+/−**

Try to enter some of the numbers **a** to **j** (above) into your calculator.

EXERCISE 11F

1 Write down the value of

    a 3.1×0.1 **b** 3.1×0.01 **c** 3.1×0.001 **d** 3.1×0.0001

2 Write down the value of

    a 6.5×10^{-1} **b** 6.5×10^{-2} **c** 6.5×10^{-3} **d** 6.5×10^{-4}

3 **a** What is the largest number you can enter into your calculator?

    b What is the smallest number you can enter into your calculator?

4 Work out the value of

    a $3.1 \div 0.1$ **b** $3.1 \div 0.01$ **c** $3.1 \div 0.001$ **d** $3.1 \div 0.0001$

You will probably need a calculator for this question.

5 Work out the value of

    a $6.5 \div 10^{-1}$ **b** $6.5 \div 10^{-2}$ **c** $6.5 \div 10^{-3}$ **d** $6.5 \div 10^{-4}$

You will probably need a calculator for this question.

6 Write these numbers out in full.

a	2.5×10^2	**b**	3.45×10	**c**	4.67×10^{-3}
d	3.46×10	**e**	2.0789×10^{-2}	**f**	5.678×10^3
g	2.46×10^2	**h**	7.6×10	**i**	7.6×10^3
j	8.97×10^5	**k**	8.65×10^{-3}	**l**	1.005×10^2
m	9.99×10^{-6}	**n**	2.3456×10^2	**o**	$9.876\,54 \times 10^3$
p	4.323×10^6	**q**	7.8679×10^{-2}	**r**	2.0367×10^{-1}
s	7.643×10	**t**	3.4578×10^{-5}	**u**	3.4578×10^5
v	6×10^7	**w**	5.67×10^{-4}	**x**	$5.600\,45 \times 10^4$
y	9.0907×10^4	**z**	7.0086×10^{-3}		

7 Write these numbers in standard form.

a	250	**b**	0.345	**c**	46700
d	340	**e**	207 800	**f**	0.000 5678
g	2460	**h**	0.076	**i**	0.000 76
j	0.897	**k**	8650	**l**	100.5
m	0.999	**n**	234.56	**o**	98.7654
p	43.23	**q**	7867.9	**r**	203.67
s	76.43	**t**	34.578	**u**	0.003 4578
v	0.0006	**w**	0.005 67	**x**	56.0045
y	0.909 07	**z**	70.086		

In questions **8** to **11**, write the numbers given in each question in standard form.

8 One of the busiest bridges in the world is the Howrah Bridge in Calcutta. It is 72 feet wide and 1500 feet long. It carries 57 000 vehicles a day.

9 One year, 27 797 runners completed the New York Marathon.

10 The largest number of dominoes ever toppled by one person is 281 581, although 30 people set up and toppled 1 382 101.

11 The asteroid Phaethon comes within 12 980 000 miles of the Sun, whilst the asteroid Pholus reaches at its furthest point a distance of 2 997 million miles from the Earth. The closest asteroid ever to Earth came within 93 000 miles.

12 These numbers are not in standard form. Write them in standard form.

a 56.7×10^2	**b** 234.6×10^3	**c** 0.06×10^4
d 34.6×10^{-2}	**e** 0.07×10^{-2}	**f** 56×10
g $2 \times 3 \times 10^5$	**h** $2 \times 10^2 \times 35$	**i** 35×10^{-7}
j 160×10^{-2}	**k** 100×10^{-2}	**l** 10×10^2
m 23 million	**n** 0.0003×10^{-2}	**o** 25.6×10^5
p $2 \times 10^4 \times 54 \times 10^3$	**q** $16 \times 10^2 \times 3 \times 10^{-1}$	**r** $2 \times 10^4 \times 56 \times 10^{-4}$
s $54 \times 10^3 \div 2 \times 10^2$	**t** $18 \times 10^2 \div 3 \times 10^3$	**u** $56 \times 10^3 \div 2 \times 10^{-2}$

Calculations with standard form without the calculator

We can calculate with numbers written in standard form by separating the problem into the two separate parts, calculating them and then putting the result back into standard form.

Examples

1 The value of
$$3 \times 10^5 \times 6 \times 10^7 = (3 \times 6) \times (10^5 \times 10^7)$$
$$= 18 \times 10^{12}$$
$$= 1.8 \times 10^1 \times 10^{12}$$
$$= 1.8 \times 10^{13}$$

2 The value of
$$(2.1 \times 10^8) \div (3 \times 10^{-3}) = (2.1 \div 3) \times (10^8 \div 10^{-3})$$
$$= 0.7 \times 10^{11}$$
$$= 7 \times 10^{-1} \times 10^{11}$$
$$= 7 \times 10^{10}$$

EXERCISE 11G

1 Find the results of the following, leaving your answers in standard form.

a $(4 \times 10^6) \times (7 \times 10^9)$		**b** $(7 \times 10^5) \times (5 \times 10^7)$
c $(3 \times 10^5) \times (8 \times 10^8)$		**d** $(2.1 \times 10^7) \times (5 \times 10^8)$
e $(9 \times 10^7) \times (5 \times 10^3)$		**f** $(7 \times 10^3) \times (6 \times 10^5)$
g $(5 \times 10^3) \times (3 \times 10^7)$		**h** $(9 \times 10^{11}) \times (3 \times 10^{19})$
i $(2 \times 10^9) \times (9 \times 10^{-8})$		**j** $(6 \times 10^{13}) \times (7 \times 10^{-9})$

2 Find the results of the following, leaving your answers in standard form.

a $(9 \times 10^8) \div (3 \times 10^4)$		**b** $(2.7 \times 10^7) \div (9 \times 10^3)$
c $(8 \times 10^7) \div (2 \times 10^3)$		**d** $(9 \times 10^{-8}) \div (5 \times 10^5)$
e $(1.2 \times 10^9) \div (3 \times 10^2)$		**f** $(7 \times 10^{11}) \div (2 \times 10^{-4})$
g $(9.6 \times 10^6) \div (8 \times 10^3)$		**h** $(3.6 \times 10^{12}) \div (6 \times 10^5)$
i $(5.5 \times 10^4) \div (1.1 \times 10^{-2})$		**j** $(4.2 \times 10^{-9}) \div (3 \times 10^{-8})$

3 Find the results of the following, leaving your answers in standard form.

a $\dfrac{8 \times 10^9}{4 \times 10^7}$ **b** $\dfrac{12 \times 10^6}{3 \times 10^4}$ **c** $\dfrac{8.1 \times 10^{19}}{9 \times 10^7}$

d $\dfrac{2.8 \times 10^7}{7 \times 10^{-4}}$ **e** $\dfrac{4.2 \times 10^8}{7 \times 10^7}$ **f** $\dfrac{4 \times 10^{-6}}{5 \times 10^{-9}}$

4 $p = 8 \times 10^5$ and $q = 2 \times 10^7$

Find the value of the following, leaving your answer in standard form.

a $p \times q$ **b** $p \div q$ **c** $p + q$ **d** $q - p$ **e** $\frac{q}{p}$

5 $p = 4 \times 10^{-2}$ and $q = 5 \times 10^{-3}$

Find the value of the following, leaving your answer in standard form.

a $p \times q$ **b** $p \div q$ **c** $p + q$ **d** $q - p$ **e** $\frac{q}{p}$

6 $p = 8 \times 10^5$ and $q = 5 \times 10^7$

Find the value of the following, leaving your answer as an ordinary number.

a $p \times q$ **b** $p \div q$ **c** $p + q$ **d** $q - p$ **e** $\frac{q}{p}$

7 $p = 2 \times 10^{-2}$ and $q = 4 \times 10^{-3}$

Find the value of the following, leaving your answer as an ordinary number.

a $p \times q$ **b** $p \div q$ **c** $p + q$ **d** $q - p$ **e** $\frac{q}{p}$

Possible coursework tasks

Last digit

$18^2 = 324$ The last digit is 4.
Investigate the last digits for all square numbers.

Cans to the moon

In an advertisement, an American brewery claimed that if all the cans of beer it produced were stacked end to end, they would stretch 2 million miles. This is four return trips to the moon. Investigate their claim.

Prime time

Consider the formula $P = n^2 - n + 17$.
When $n = 1$, $P = 17$, which is a prime number.
Investigate for other values of n.

Fermat's primes

The mathematician Pierre de Fermat (1601–65) discovered that some prime numbers are the sum of two square numbers. For example,

$29 = 2^2 + 5^2$

Investigate this for other prime numbers.

Escape

A prison consisted of a long corridor of 100 cells manned by 100 warders. During an inspection:

The first warder walked along the corridor and unlocked all the cell doors.
The second warder then went along and locked every second door.
The third warder changed the state of every third door, i.e. if it was locked, he unlocked it, but if it was unlocked, he locked it.
The fourth warder walked along and changed the state of every fourth door.
The fifth warder changed the state of every fifth door.
And so on for the rest of the warders.
When the hundredth warder had changed the state of the hundredth door, all the warders went home.
How many prisoners escaped?

Examination questions: coursework type

1 The sets {11, 13, 17} and {23, 29, 31} are examples of sets of three consecutive prime numbers. For **each** of the following statements, investigate its validity, giving an explanation, an example and a conclusion.

   a 'The sum of the numbers in any set of three consecutive prime numbers is always odd.'

   b 'In any set of three consecutive prime numbers the difference between the largest and the smallest is less than 10.'

   WJEC, Question 8, Specimen Paper 1998

2 a The number 169 is a square number. It has factors 1, 13, and 169. Investigate the truth of the statement:

   'All square numbers have only three factors.'

   b Investigate the truth of this statement:

   'There are no numbers x and y such that $x^2 - 2y^2 = 1$.'

   WJEC, Question 4, Paper 3, June 1995

3 Tessa and Ronnie are working on the following problem.

> Which whole numbers can be written as the difference of two square numbers?
>
> For example $\quad 7 = 16 - 9 \qquad$ and $\quad 20 = 36 - 16$
>
> $\qquad\qquad\qquad = (4 \times 4) - (3 \times 3) \qquad\quad = (6 \times 6) - (4 \times 4)$
>
> $\qquad\qquad\qquad = 4^2 - 3^2 \qquad\qquad\qquad\quad = 6^2 - 4^2$
>
> So both 7 and 20 can be written as the difference of two square numbers.

This is the written work Ronnie has produced.

$5 = 3^2 - 2^2 \qquad\qquad\qquad 7 = 4^2 - 3^2 \qquad\qquad\qquad 9 = 5^2 - 4^2$

a State the generalisations you can make using diagrams like Ronnie's.

Here is what Tessa has written.

> I made a table with the square numbers along the edge.
>
> The numbers in the middle are the differences of the square numbers

	0	1	4	9	16		
0	0	1	4	9	16		
1	1	0	3	8	15		
4	4	3	0	5	12		
9	9	8	5	0	7		
16	16	15	12	7	0		

> I cannot see any patterns in the numbers in my table.

Ronnie said, 'Because of my work, I can see at least one pattern.'

b Examine Tessa's work carefully. Comment on what she could do and say using her table.

NEAB, Question 3, Paper 3Q, June 1995

Examination questions

1 a Express 540 as a product of powers of its prime factors.

b What is the lowest number which 540 must be multiplied by to become a square number?

WJEC, Question 7, Specimen Paper 1, 1998

2 Find the value of $\qquad$ **i** $9^4 \qquad$ **ii** 5^{-2}.

NEAB, Question 22, Specimen Paper 2, 1998

3 The National Lottery uses balls with the numbers from 1 to 49 on them.

    a From these numbers write down

        i a square number   **ii** a factor of 100, other than 1

        iii a multiple of 5   **iv** a prime number

    b Paul makes a set of cards with instructions on them. He takes two cards at a time to decide which lottery numbers to choose. Write down his first three numbers.

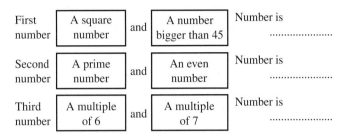

First number	A square number	and	A number bigger than 45	Number is ....
Second number	A prime number	and	An even number	Number is ....
Third number	A multiple of 6	and	A multiple of 7	Number is ....

NEAB, Question 3, Specimen Paper 1, 1998

4 **a** Evaluate 3^{-2}.

    b Write the following expression as a power of 2: $\dfrac{2}{2^4 \times 2^3}$

    c Evaluate each of the following. Give your answers in standard form.

        i $(3 \times 10^5) \times (6 \times 10^4)$

        ii $\dfrac{2 \times 10^6}{5 \times 10^2}$

OCR, Question 18, Intermediate Paper 3, June 2000

5 **a** At certain times Jupiter is approximately 775 000 000 kilometres from the Sun. Express this distance in standard form.

    b The mass of a proton is 1.67×10^{-24} grams and the mass of an electron is 9.109×10^{-28} grams. Evaluate

$$\frac{\text{Mass of proton}}{\text{Mass of electron}}$$

correct to the nearest whole number.

WJEC, Question 14, Specimen Paper 1, 1998

6 In the box are six numbers written in standard form.

| 8.3×10^4 | 3.9×10^5 | 6.7×10^{-3} |
| 9.245×10^{-1} | 8.36×10^3 | 4.15×10^{-2} |

    a **i** Write down the largest number.

       ii Write your answer as an ordinary number.

    b **i** Write down the smallest number.

       ii Write your answer as an ordinary number.

AQA (North), Question 16, Intermediate Paper 1, June 2000

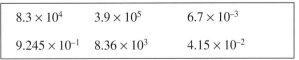

7 **a** Write each of the following numbers in standard form.

     i   734 800 000   **ii**   0.000 57

   b Find, in standard form, the value of each of the following.

     i $(3.42 \times 10^4) \times (5.91 \times 10^{-11})$

     ii $\dfrac{4.69 \times 10^{-6}}{7.45 \times 10^4}$

WJEC, Question 21, Intermediate Paper 2, June 1999

8 A light year is the distance travelled by light in 365 days. The speed of light is 3.0×10^5 kilometres per second. The distance to the nearest star is 4.0×10^{13} kilometres. How many light years is it to the nearest star? Give your answer to an appropriate degree of accuracy.

SEG, Question 17, Specimen Paper 13, 1998

9 $p = 8 \times 10^3$ $q = 2 \times 10^4$

   a Find the value of $p \times q$. Give your answer in standard form.

   b Find the value of $p + q$. Give your answer as an ordinary number.

EDEXCEL, Question 21, Intermediate Paper 3, June 2000

Summary

How well do you grade yourself?

To gain a grade E, you need to be able to multiply and divide whole numbers and decimals by 10, 100, and 1000.

To gain a grade C, you need to be able to multiply and divide numbers in index form.

To gain a grade B, you need to be able to write numbers in standard form and use these in various problems.

What you should know after you have worked through Chapter 11

- How to express a number in its prime factors.

- How to divide or multiply a number by 10, 100, or 1000.

- How mentally to multiply and divide numbers rounded to 1 significant figure.

- How to write numbers in standard form and compare their size.

- How to solve problems using numbers in standard form.

Coursework example 2

Tiling patterns

Refer to the Appendix for a summary of coursework marks.

Problem statement

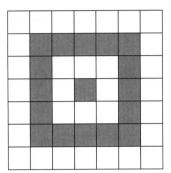

This pattern is composed of grey and white squares on a 7 by 7 grid.

Investigate the number of grey and white squares needed for any size of square grid.

Possible solution

In the pattern there are 17 grey squares and 32 white squares.

To solve the problem, I have decided that I will have to draw some more square grids and shade them in. I will draw some easy grids first.

Pattern 1   Pattern 2

Pattern 3

Pattern 4

Pattern 5

i	ii	iii	Notes
3			The examples show that the necessary information has been obtained.
4			The problem has been broken down into easy stages to make the counting easier.

i	ii	iii	Notes
		3	The results from the diagrams have been organised into a table.
		3	Correct patterns have been explained.
	4		A further example is given to show that the pattern works.
4			Tables and diagrams are linked by a clear explanation. The use of symbols has added variety to the presentation.

To look for a pattern for the number of squares needed, I will first draw a table to show my results.

In my table, I will show the number of grey and white squares for each pattern that I have drawn, and I will also show the total number of squares needed for each pattern.

Pattern no.	Size of grid	No. of grey squares	No. of white squares	Total no. of squares used
1	1 by 1	1	0	1
2	3 by 3	1	8	9
3	5 by 5	17	8	25
4	7 by 7	17	32	49
5	9 by 9	49	32	81

From my table, I can see that the total number of squares is always a square number and that the number of grey and white squares go down in pairs.

I think I can now predict the next pattern.

It will have 121 squares and there will be 49 grey ones. I can find the number of white ones by doing $121 - 49 = 72$.

I will now draw Pattern 6.

Pattern 6

My prediction was correct.

I can now extend my table, but I will make it clearer by using letters for the columns.

P = Pattern number G = No. of grey squares
W = No. of white squares T = Total no. of squares

P	G	W	T
1	1	0	1
2	1	8	9
3	17	8	25
4	17	32	49
5	49	32	81
6	49	72	121
7	97	72	169
8	97	128	225

I am now going to show these results on a graph.

I have decided to use a bar graph, as I think this will be easier to understand and will show my results more clearly.

To do this, I am going to use a computer spreadsheet to graph G and W, since this will show me how they are connected.

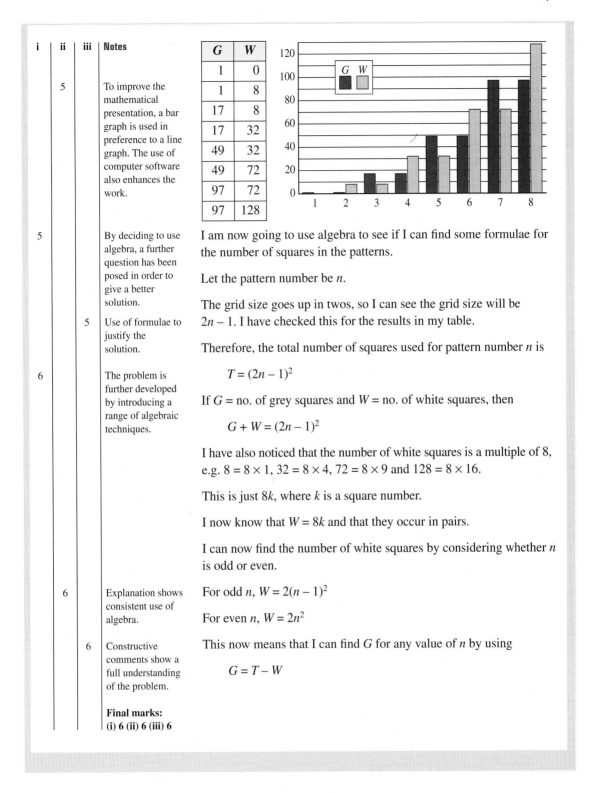

i	ii	iii	Notes

<table>
<tr><td></td><td>5</td><td></td><td>To improve the mathematical presentation, a bar graph is used in preference to a line graph. The use of computer software also enhances the work.</td></tr>
</table>

G	W
1	0
1	8
17	8
17	32
49	32
49	72
97	72
97	128

5 — By deciding to use algebra, a further question has been posed in order to give a better solution.

5 (iii) Use of formulae to justify the solution.

6 — The problem is further developed by introducing a range of algebraic techniques.

6 Explanation shows consistent use of algebra.

6 Constructive comments show a full understanding of the problem.

Final marks:
(i) 6 (ii) 6 (iii) 6

I am now going to use algebra to see if I can find some formulae for the number of squares in the patterns.

Let the pattern number be n.

The grid size goes up in twos, so I can see the grid size will be $2n - 1$. I have checked this for the results in my table.

Therefore, the total number of squares used for pattern number n is

$$T = (2n - 1)^2$$

If G = no. of grey squares and W = no. of white squares, then

$$G + W = (2n - 1)^2$$

I have also noticed that the number of white squares is a multiple of 8, e.g. $8 = 8 \times 1$, $32 = 8 \times 4$, $72 = 8 \times 9$ and $128 = 8 \times 16$.

This is just $8k$, where k is a square number.

I now know that $W = 8k$ and that they occur in pairs.

I can now find the number of white squares by considering whether n is odd or even.

For odd n, $W = 2(n - 1)^2$

For even n, $W = 2n^2$

This now means that I can find G for any value of n by using

$$G = T - W$$

12 Algebra 2

This chapter is going to ...

show you how to solve a pair of simultaneous equations, how to solve inequalities, and how to represent inequalities on the number line.

What you should already know

✔ How to solve simple linear equations (pages 101–2).
✔ The inequality signs

< is less than	≤ is less than or equal to
> is greater than	≥ is greater than or equal to

Simultaneous equations

A pair of simultaneous equations is exactly that – two equations (usually linear) for which we want the same solution, and which we therefore **solve together**. For example, $x + y = 10$ has many solutions:

$$x = 2, y = 8 \qquad x = 4, y = 6 \qquad x = 5, y = 5 \quad \ldots$$

and $2x + y = 14$ has many solutions:

$$x = 2, y = 10 \qquad x = 3, y = 8 \qquad x = 4, y = 6 \quad \ldots$$

But only **one** solution, $x = 4$ and $y = 6$, satisfies both equations at the **same time**.

Elimination method

In this book, we solve simultaneous equations by the elimination method only. Follow through Examples 1 to 3 to see how this works.

Example 1 Solve $6x + y = 15$
$\qquad\qquad\qquad 4x + y = 11$

Since the y-term in both equations is the same, we can subtract one equation from the other to give

$$2x = 4$$
$$\Rightarrow \quad x = 2$$

We now substitute $x = 2$ into one of the original equations (usually the one with smallest numbers involved).

So substitute into $\quad 4x + y = 11$

which gives $\qquad 8 + y = 11$

$\Rightarrow \quad y = 11 - 8$

$y = 3$

We should test our solution in the other original equation. So substitute $x = 2$ and $y = 3$ into $6x + y$, which gives $12 + 3 = 15$. This is correct, so we can confidently say the solution is $x = 2$ and $y = 3$.

Example 2 Solve $5x + y = 22$

$2x - y = 6$

Since both equations have the same y-term but **different** signs, we **add** the two equations, which gives

$$7x = 28$$
$$\Rightarrow \quad x = 4$$

We now substitute $x = 4$ into one of the original equations.

So substitute into $\quad 5x + y = 22$

which gives $\qquad 20 + y = 22$

$\Rightarrow \quad y = 2$

We test our solution by putting $x = 4$ and $y = 2$ into the other equation $2x - y$, which gives $8 - 2 = 6$. This is correct, so our solution is $x = 4$ and $y = 2$.

Example 3 Solve $4x - 2y = 14$

$2x - 2y = 4$

Since the term $-2y$ is in both equations, we can subtract one equation from the other to get

$$2x = 10$$
$$\Rightarrow \quad x = 5$$

We now substitute $x = 5$ into $2x - 2y = 4$ to get

$$2 \times 5 - 2y = 4$$
$$10 - 2y = 4$$
$$\Rightarrow \quad -2y = 4 - 10 = -6$$
$$\Rightarrow \quad y = -6 \div -2$$
$$\Rightarrow \quad y = 3$$

The solution $x = 5$ and $y = 3$ can be checked in the top equation to give

$$4 \times 5 - 2 \times 3 = 20 - 6 = 14$$

This is correct, so our solution is $x = 5$ and $y = 3$.

EXERCISE 12A

Solve the following simultaneous equations by
- subtracting the equations when the identical terms have the same sign
- adding the equations when the identical terms have opposite signs.

1 $4x + y = 17$
  $2x + y = 9$

2 $5x + 2y = 13$
  $x + 2y = 9$

3 $2x + y = 7$
  $5x - y = 14$

4 $3x + 2y = 19$
  $2x - 2y = 6$

5 $3x - 4y = 17$
  $x - 4y = 3$

6 $3x + 2y = 16$
  $x - 2y = 4$

7 $x + 3y = 10$
  $x + y = 6$

8 $2x + 5y = 24$
  $2x + 3y = 16$

9 $3x - y = 4$
  $2x + y = 11$

10 $2x + 5y = 37$
  $2x + y = 11$

11 $4x - 3y = 7$
  $x + 3y = 13$

12 $4x - y = 17$
  $x - y = 2$

You were able to work out all the pairs of equations in Exercise 12A simply by adding or subtracting the equations in each pair. This does not always happen. So follow through the next two worked examples to see what to do when there are no identical terms to begin with.

Example 4 Solve $3x + 2y = 18$
  $2x - y = 5$

Here we do not have any identical terms, so we have to make them because that is the only way we can solve such simultaneous equations by the elimination method. So multiply the second equation right through by 2 to match the y-terms:

$(2x - y = 5) \times 2 \quad \Rightarrow \quad 4x - 2y = 10$

Our pair of simultaneous equations is now

$3x + 2y = 18$
$4x - 2y = 10$

which can be solved by the method in Example 1.

Example 5 Solve $2x + 3y = 21$
  $6x + 2y = 28$

Again, there are no identical terms, but we can see that by multiplying the first equation through by 3 the terms in x become equal:

$(2x + 3y = 21) \times 3 \quad \Rightarrow \quad 6x + 9y = 63$

Our pair of simultaneous equations is now

$6x + 9y = 63$
$6x + 2y = 28$

which can be solved by the method in Example 1.

EXERCISE 12B

Solve the following pairs of simultaneous equations by first changing one of the equations in each pair to obtain identical terms, and then adding or subtracting the equations to eliminate those terms.

1 $3x + 2y = 12$
$4x - y = 5$

2 $4x + 3y = 37$
$2x + y = 17$

3 $x + 3y = 7$
$2x - y = 7$

4 $2x + 3y = 19$
$6x + 2y = 22$

5 $5x - 2y = 14$
$3x - y = 9$

6 $10x - y = 3$
$3x + 2y = 17$

7 $2x + 5y = 9$
$x + 2y = 4$

8 $3x + 4y = 29$
$4x - 2y = 2$

9 $5x - 2y = 24$
$3x + y = 21$

10 $5x - 2y = 36$
$2x - 6y = 4$

11 $2x + 3y = 17$
$4x + 7y = 39$

12 $3x - 2y = 6$
$5x + 6y = 38$

There are also cases where both equations have to be changed to obtain identical terms. Follow through the next two examples to see how this is done.

Example 6   Solve $4x + 5y = 33$
$3x + 2y = 16$

Note that we cannot obtain identical terms simply by multiplying only one of these equations by a whole number. So we have to multiply **both** equations.

We can choose to make either the x-terms or the y-terms the same. Sometimes there is an obvious choice, sometimes it doesn't matter. In this example, there is no great advantage in choosing either.

Let's take the terms in x, and multiply the first equation through by 3, and the second equation through by 4. This gives

and $(4x + 5y = 33) \times 3 \quad \Rightarrow \quad 12x + 15y = 99$
and $(3x + 2y = 16) \times 4 \quad \Rightarrow \quad 12x + 8y = 64$

These are solved in the same way as in Example 1.

Example 7   Solve $4x + 3y = 27$
$5x - 2y = 5$

Both equations have to be changed to obtain identical terms in either x or y. However, we can see that if we make the y-terms the same, we also eliminate the negative situation so this is obviously the better choice. We do this by multiplying the first equation by 2 and the second equation by 3, to give

and $(4x + 3y = 27) \times 2 \quad \Rightarrow \quad 8x + 6y = 54$
and $(5x - 2y = 5) \times 3 \quad \Rightarrow \quad 15x - 6y = 15$

These are solved in the same way as in Example 1.

EXERCISE 12C

Solve the following simultaneous equations.

1	$5x + 2y = 20$	**2**	$3x + 4y = 25$	**3**	$10x - 2y = 2$
	$4x + 3y = 23$		$2x + 3y = 18$		$4x + 3y = 16$
4	$3x + 2y = 22$	**5**	$3x + 2y = 27$	**6**	$5x - 3y = 11$
	$4x - 3y = 18$		$4x + 5y = 43$		$2x + 4y = 20$
7	$2x + 5y = 15$	**8**	$2x + 3y = 30$	**9**	$2x - 3y = 15$
	$3x - 2y = 13$		$5x + 7y = 71$		$5x + 7y = 52$
10	$3x - 2y = 15$	**11**	$5x - 3y = 14$	**12**	$3x + 2y = 28$
	$2x - 3y = 5$		$4x - 5y = 6$		$2x + 7y = 47$

So far, all the simultaneous equations you have met in this chapter have had positive whole numbers as their solutions. But you do need to be prepared to meet simultaneous equations that have negative and decimal solutions.

The next exercise is a selection of simultaneous equations whose solutions are negative or decimal or both.

EXERCISE 12D

Solve the following simultaneous equations.

1	$2x + y = 4$	**2**	$5x + 2y = 11$	**3**	$5x + 4y = 11$
	$x - y = 5$		$3x + 4y = 8$		$2x + 3y = 9$
4	$4x + 2y = 14$	**5**	$3x - 4y = 4.5$	**6**	$x - 2y = 4$
	$2x + 3y = 15$		$2x + 2y = 10$		$3x - y = -3$
7	$3x + 2y = 2$	**8**	$2x - 5y = 4$	**9**	$6x + 2y = 14$
	$2x + 6y = 13$		$x - 4y = 5$		$3x - 5y = 10$
10	$2x + 4y = 15$	**11**	$x - 5y = 15$	**12**	$3x - y = 5$
	$x + 5y = 21$		$3x - 7y = 17$		$x + 3y = -20$

Problems solved by simultaneous equations

We are now going to meet a type of problem which has to be expressed as a pair of simultaneous equations so that it can be solved. The next example shows you how to tackle such a problem.

Problem On holiday last year, I was talking over breakfast to two families about how much it cost them to go to the theatre. They couldn't remember how much was charged for each adult or each child, but they could both remember what they had paid altogether.

The Advani family, consisting of Mr and Mrs Advani with their daughter Rupa, paid £23.

The Shaw family, consisting of Mrs Shaw with her two children, Len and Sue, paid £17.50.

How much would I have to pay for my wife, my four children and me?

Solution We make a pair of simultaneous equations from the situation as follows.

Let x be the cost of an adult ticket, and y be the cost of a child's ticket. Then

and $2x + y = 23$ for the Advani family
and $x + 2y = 17.5$ for the Shaw family

We solve these equations just as we have done in the previous examples, to obtain $x = £9.50$ and $y = £4$. I can now find my cost, which will be

$$(2 \times £9.50) + (4 \times £4) = £35$$

EXERCISE 12E

Read each situation carefully, then make a pair of simultaneous equations in order to solve the problem.

1 Amul and Kim have £10.70 between them. Amul has £3.70 more than Kim. How much does each have?

2 The two people in front of me were both buying stamps. One bought 10 second-class and five first-class stamps at a total cost of £3.05. The other bought 8 second-class and 10 first-class stamps at a total cost of £3.82. How much did I pay for 3 second-class and 4 first-class stamps?

3 At a local tea room I couldn't help noticing that at one table, where the customers had eaten 6 buns and had 3 teas, it had cost them £1.65. At another table, the customers had eaten 11 buns and had 7 teas at a total cost of £3.40. My family and I had 5 buns and 6 teas. What did it cost us?

4 Three chews and four bubblies cost 72p. Five chews and two bubblies cost 64p. What would three chews and five bubblies cost?

5 On a nut-and-bolt production line, all the nuts weighed the same and all the bolts weighed the same. An order of 50 nuts and 60 bolts weighed 10.6 kg. An order of 40 nuts and 30 bolts weighed 6.5 kg. What should an order of 60 nuts and 50 bolts weigh?

6 A taxi firm charges a fixed amount plus so much per mile. A journey of 6 miles costs £3.70. A journey of 10 miles costs £5.10. What would be the cost of a journey of 8 miles?

7 Two members of the same church went to the same shop to buy material to make Christingles. One bought 200 oranges and 220 candles at a cost of £65.60. The other bought 210 oranges and 200 candles at a cost of £63.30. They only needed 200 of each. How much should it have cost them?

8 Three tins of soup and four packets of crisps cost £1.29. Five tins of soup and two packets of crisps cost £1.45. What would be the cost of two tins of soup and five packets of crisps?

9 When you book Bingham Hall for a conference, you pay a fixed booking fee plus a charge for each delegate at the conference. The total charge for a conference with 65 delegates was £192.50. The total charge for a conference with 40 delegates was £180. What will be the charge for a conference with 70 delegates?

10 My mother-in-law uses this formula to cook turkey:

$T = a + bW$

where T is the cooking time (minutes), W is the weight of the turkey (kg), and a and b are constants. She says it takes 4 hours 30 minutes to cook a 12 kg turkey, and 3 hours 10 minutes to cook an 8 kg turkey. How long will it take to cook a 5 kg turkey?

Inequalities

Inequalities behave similarly to equations which you have already met. In the case of linear inequalities, we use the same rules to solve them as we use for linear equations, as the following two examples show.

Example 1 Solve $\dfrac{3x + 7}{2} < 14$.

This is rewritten as

$$3x + 7 < 14 \times 2$$

that is $\quad 3x + 7 < 28$

$$\Rightarrow \quad 3x < 28 - 7$$

$$\Rightarrow \quad 3x < 21$$
$$\Rightarrow \quad x < 21 \div 3$$
$$\Rightarrow \quad x < 7$$

Note: the inequality sign given in the problem, is the sign to give in the answer.

Example 2 Solve $1 < 3x + 4 \le 13$.

Divide the inequality into two parts, and treat each separately.

$$
\begin{array}{ll}
1 < 3x + 4 & 3x + 4 \le 13 \\
\Rightarrow\ 1 - 4 < 3x & \Rightarrow\ 3x \le 13 - 4 \\
\Rightarrow\ -3 < 3x & \Rightarrow\ 3x \le 9 \\
\Rightarrow\ -\dfrac{3}{3} < x & \Rightarrow\ x \le \dfrac{9}{3} \\
\Rightarrow\ -1 < x & \Rightarrow\ x \le 3
\end{array}
$$

Hence, $-1 < x \le 3$.

EXERCISE 12F

1 Solve the following linear inequalities.

a $x + 4 < 7$ b $t - 3 > 5$ c $p + 2 \geq 12$

d $2x - 3 < 7$ e $4y + 5 \leq 17$ f $3t - 4 > 11$

g $\frac{x}{2} + 4 < 7$ h $\frac{y}{5} + 3 \leq 6$ i $\frac{t}{3} - 2 \geq 4$

j $3(x - 2) < 15$ k $5(2x + 1) \leq 35$ l $2(4t - 3) \geq 34$

m $4x + 1 \geq 3x - 5$ n $5t - 3 \leq 2t + 5$ o $3y - 12 \leq y - 4$

p $2x + 3 \geq x + 1$ q $5w - 7 \leq 3w + 4$ r $2(4x - 1) \leq 3(x + 4)$

2 Write down the value of x that satisfies each of the following.

a $x - 3 \leq 5$, where x is a positive integer.

b $x + 2 < 9$, where x is a positive, even integer.

c $3x - 11 < 36$, where x is a square number.

d $5x - 8 \leq 15$, where x is a positive, odd number.

e $2x + 1 < 19$, where x is a positive, prime number.

3 Solve the following linear inequalities.

a $\dfrac{x + 4}{2} \leq 3$ b $\dfrac{x - 3}{5} > 7$ c $\dfrac{2x + 5}{3} < 6$ d $\dfrac{4x - 3}{5} \geq 5$

e $\dfrac{3t - 2}{7} > 4$ f $\dfrac{5y + 3}{5} \leq 2$ g $\dfrac{4t - 3}{5} < 8$ h $\dfrac{2x - 13}{3} > 7$

4 Solve the following linear inequalities.

a $7 < 2x + 1 < 13$ b $5 < 3x - 1 < 14$ c $-1 < 5x + 4 \leq 19$

d $1 \leq 4x - 3 < 13$ e $11 \leq 3x + 5 < 17$ f $-3 \leq 2x - 3 \leq 7$

g $4 \leq 5x - 6 \leq 14$ h $9 \leq 4x + 5 < 29$

The number line

The solution to a linear inequality can be shown on the number line by using the following conventions.

 $x \leq$  $x \geq$

 $x <$ $x >$

Below are five examples.

represents $x < 3$

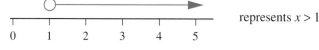

represents $x > 1$

represents $x \leq -2$

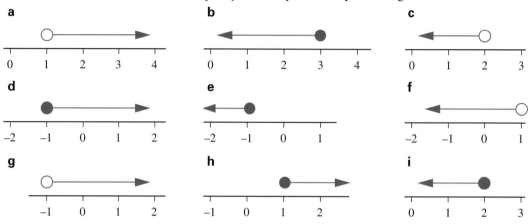

represents $x \geq 4$

represents $-1 \leq x < 2$

EXERCISE 12G

1 Write down the inequality that is represented by each diagram below.

a

b

c

d

e

f

g

h

i

2 Draw diagrams to illustrate the following.

    a $x \leq 3$ **b** $x > -2$ **c** $x \geq 0$ **d** $x < 5$

    e $x \geq -1$ **f** $2 < x \leq 5$ **g** $-1 \leq x \leq 3$ **h** $-3 < x < 4$

    i $-4 \leq x \leq 4$ **j** $3 \leq x < 7$

3 Solve the following inequalities and illustrate their solutions on number lines.

    a $x + 4 \geq 8$ **b** $x + 5 < 3$ **c** $x - 1 \leq 2$ **d** $x - 4 > -1$

    e $2x + 3 \leq 7$ **f** $4x - 2 \geq 12$ **g** $3x - 1 > 14$ **h** $2x + 5 < 3$

    i $2(4x + 3) < 18$ **j** $\frac{x}{2} + 3 \leq 2$ **k** $\frac{x}{5} - 2 > 8$ **l** $\frac{x}{3} + 5 \geq 3$

4 Solve the following inequalities and illustrate their solutions on number lines.

    a $\frac{2x + 5}{3} > 3$ **b** $\frac{4x - 3}{5} \leq 1$ **c** $\frac{3x + 4}{2} \geq 11$ **d** $\frac{5x - 2}{4} < 2$

    e $\frac{2x + 8}{3} \leq 2$ **f** $\frac{3x + 7}{5} > -1$ **g** $\frac{2x - 1}{3} \geq -3$ **h** $\frac{2x + 7}{3} \leq -1$

Inequalities involving x^2

When we have an inequality such as $x^2 < 9$, we have to think very carefully because there are two possible solutions to $x^2 = 9$. They are $x = 3$ and $x = -3$.

The solution $x = 3$ to the equation $x^2 = 9$ might suggest the condition $x < 3$, yet clearly $x < 3$ does satisfy the inequality $x^2 < 9$. Also, the condition to be obtained from the solution $x = -3$ cannot be $x < -3$. So it must be $x > -3$. That is, the inequality sign is changed. For convenience, $x > -3$ can be turned to give $-3 < x$.

Put this situation on the number line and the solution becomes clear.

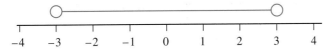

Namely, $-3 < x < 3$.

Example   Solve the inequality $x^2 > 16$ and show your solution on the number line.

The solution to $x^2 > 16$ will be $x > 4$ and $x < -4$, which is represented as

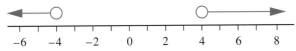

Notice the difference between inequalities of the type $x^2 < a^2$ and those of the type $x^2 > a^2$.

EXERCISE 12H

Solve the following inequalities, showing their solutions on number lines.

1 $x^2 \leq 4$	**2** $x^2 > 25$	**3** $x^2 < 49$	**4** $x^2 \geq 1$
5 $x^2 \geq 9$	**6** $x^2 - 1 > 8$	**7** $x^2 + 2 \leq 6$	**8** $x^2 - 3 < 13$
9 $x^2 + 5 > 6$	**10** $x^2 - 4 \geq 5$	**11** $2x^2 - 1 > 7$	**12** $3x^2 - 5 < 22$
13 $5x^2 + 3 \leq 8$	**14** $2x^2 - 4 < 28$	**15** $3x^2 - 9 \geq 66$	**16** $x^2 \geq 100$
17 $x^2 < 2.25$	**18** $x^2 \geq 0.25$	**19** $x^2 - 5 \leq 76$	**20** $x^2 > 0$

Possible coursework tasks

What difference does it make anyway?

a   The sum of two numbers is 20 and their difference is 2. What are the numbers?

b   What would the two numbers be if the difference were 3?

c   What would the two numbers be if the difference were 4.6?

d   Investigate for other differences.

Equal expressions

What values of x and y would you choose to make the three expressions below equal in value?

   $x + 2y + 2$ $2x + y + 4$ $x + 2y + 8$

Magic squares

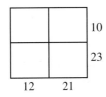

Find a number for each cell to make the rows and columns add up to the totals given. What do you notice?

Investigate for other magic squares.

Examination questions

1. Greg sold 40 tickets for a concert. He sold x tickets at £2 each and y tickets at £3.50 each. He collected £92.

   i   Write down two equations connecting x and y.

   ii Solve these simultaneous equations to find how many of each kind of ticket he sold.

   NEAB, Question 13, Specimen Paper 1, 1996

2. Solve the simultaneous equations $5x + 4y = 13$

   $3x + 8y = 5$

   OCR, Question 13, Intermediate (A) Paper 4, June 2000

3. Solve the simultaneous equations $2x + 6y = 17$

   $3x - 2y = 20$

   EDEXCEL, Question 14, Intermediate Paper 3, June 1999

4. Solve the inequality $x^2 < 9$.

   NEAB, Question 23, Paper 1Q, November 1995

5. Show on a number line the integers, n, that satisfy $3n + 7 < 1$.

   NICC, Question 15b, Paper 3, 1995

6. Solve the inequality $7x + 3 > 2x - 15$.

   SEG, Question 18b, Specimen Paper 10, 1996

7. Solve the simultaneous equations $2 = a + b$

   $7 = 4a + 2b$

   NEAB, Question 7ci, Paper 2Q, November 1994

8. Solve the simultaneous equations algebraically. Show your method clearly.

   $4x + 3y = 6$

   $3x - 2y = 13$

   OCR, Question 16, Intermediate (B) Paper 4, June 2000

9. Solve the inequalities

   a $3x - 7 > x - 3$ b $x^2 > 16$

   AQA (North), Question 14, Intermediate Paper 1, June 2000

10. a   The inequality $7 - 3n < 12 - 5n$ can be rearranged into one of the following forms:

   EITHER the form $n <$ a number

   OR   the form $n >$ a number

   Rearrange the inequality into whichever form is correct.

   Write down the least or the greatest whole number value of n which satisfies your inequality. State whether it is the least or the greatest.

   WJEC, Question 24, Intermediate Paper 2, June 1999

Summary

How well do you grade yourself?

To gain a grade **D**, you need to understand the difference between the inequality signs.

To gain a grade **C**, you need to be able to represent inequalities on the number line and to solve simple linear inequalities. You also need to be able to solve straightforward simultaneous equations where you only need to affect one equation in order to eliminate a variable.

To gain a grade **B**, you need to be able to find a full solution to inequalities of the types $x^2 < a^2$ and $x^2 > a^2$, and be able to solve any simultaneous linear equations, including those used in problems.

What you should know after you have worked through Chapter 12

- How to solve a variety of simultaneous linear equations.

- How to solve linear inequalities and represent their solutions on the number line.

- How to solve inequalities of the types $x^2 < a^2$ and $x^2 > a^2$.

13 Statistics 1

This chapter is going to ...

remind you of the three different types of average you need to be able
to find. It will then introduce you to frequency tables, from which you
can create pie charts, frequency polygons, bar charts and histograms,
and find averages.

What you should already know

✔ The mode is the item of data that occurs the most.
✔ The median is the item of data in the middle once all the items
   have been put in order of size, from lowest to highest.
✔ The mean is the sum total of all the items of data divided by the
   number of items. The mean is usually written as $\bar{x}$.
✔ The range is the difference between the highest item of data and
   the lowest.

For example, from

$$2, 2, 3, 3, 3, 3, 3, 4, 5, 6, 7, 7, 9, 9, 11, 17, 18, 19, 22$$

The mode is 3, since this occurs five times (more than any other).

The median is 6, since this is the middle item of data (in 10th place).

The mean is 8.1, since the sum total divided by the number of items is
$53 \div 19 = 8.1$ (rounded to 1 decimal place).

The range is 20, since the largest number, 22, minus the smallest
number, 2, is 20.

More about averages

The median

When you have a set of data and you need to find the median, you have to consider how
many items of data you have.

When the number of items is **odd**, say N, simply add 1 to N and divide by 2 to find how
many items of data to count off in order to get to the middle one. For example, if there are
19 items of data (see example above), we calculate $(19 + 1) \div 2 = 10$. That is, we count
off 10 items to arrive at the median (which is 6 in the example above).

When the number of items is **even**, there is no middle item. So we find instead the 'middle' of the middle two numbers. First, we have to find where the middle is, using $(N + 1) \div 2$. Then we find the 'middle' of the two middle numbers – in other words, their mean value. For example, find the median of

$3, 3, 4, 7, 7, 8, 9, 11, 14, 16, 19, 23, 27, 30$

There are 14 items of data, so $(N + 1) \div 2 = (14 + 1) \div 2 = 7.5$.

The median is therefore between the 7th and 8th numbers, which are 9 and 11. Halfway between them is 10, so the median is 10.

The mean

If your calculator has a statistical mode, the mean of a set of numbers can be found by simply entering the numbers and then pressing the $\bar{x}$ key. On some calculators, the statistical mode is represented by **SD**.

Try this example. Find the mean of 2, 3, 7, 8 and 10.

First put your calculator into statistical mode. Then press the following keys:

2 DATA **3** DATA **7** DATA **8** DATA **1** **0** DATA $\bar{x}$

You should find the mean $\bar{x} = 6$.

You can also find the number of data points by pressing the n key.

EXERCISE 13A

1 For each list **a** to **f** find
  i the mode **ii** the median **iii** the mean **iv** the range
  a 1, 1, 2, 3, 4 **b** 7, 9, 10, 11, 11
  c 4, 4, 9, 11, 15 **d** 2, 3, 3, 3, 4, 5, 6, 8, 11
  e 7, 7, 8, 9, 11, 15, 15, 15, 21 **f** 22, 23, 23, 23, 24, 25, 26, 28, 31

2 For each list **a** to **f** find
  i the mode **ii** the mean (rounded to 1 dp where necessary)
  a 1, 1, 2, 3, 4, 4, 4, 5, 5, 6, 7, 9, 9, 10, 11
  b 4, 5, 6, 5, 8, 3, 4, 3, 8, 9, 7, 7, 8, 8, 6
  c 11, 13, 13, 14, 16, 16, 17, 13, 12, 13, 13
  d 5, 4, 3, 5, 6, 7, 5, 9, 8, 5, 11
  e 4, 4, 4, 4, 4, 6, 7, 8, 9, 9, 9, 7, 6
  f 23, 23, 25, 23, 26, 23, 23, 27, 28, 29, 33

3 For each list **a** to **f** find
  i the median **ii** the mean (rounded to 1 dp where necessary)
  a 5, 6, 4, 3, 7, 8, 9 **b** 1, 1, 4, 7, 3, 5, 8, 2, 5
  c 8, 3, 4, 2, 8, 7, 9, 5 **d** 3, 7, 2, 4, 4, 8, 9, 7, 8, 1, 2
  e 2, 7, 5, 6, 7, 7, 8, 3, 2, 0, 5, 0, 2 **f** 3, 1, 6, 7
  g 2, 7, 4, 3, 9, 1 **h** 2, 1, 3, 4, 4, 7, 9, 0, 9, 3, 9, 2

4 A pack of matches consisted of 12 boxes. The contents of each box were counted as
34, 31, 29, 35, 33, 30, 31, 28, 29, 35, 32, 31
On the box it stated 'Average contents 32 matches'. Is this correct?

5 The ages of the members of a hockey team were
29, 26, 21, 24, 26, 28, 35, 23, 29, 28, 29
What is
   a the modal age **b** the median age **c** the mean age?
   d What is the range of the ages?

6 The mean age of a group of 10 young people was 15.
   a What do all their ages add up to?
   b What will be their mean age in 5 years time?

7 A firm showed the annual salaries for its employees as:

Chairman	£43 000
Managing director	£37 000
Floor manager	£25 000
Skilled worker 1	£24 000
Skilled worker 2	£24 000
Machinist	£18 000
Computer engineer	£18 000
Secretary	£18 000
Office junior	£7 000

   a What is
   i the modal salary **ii** the median salary **iii** the mean salary?
   b The management suggested a pay rise for all of 6%. The shopfloor workers
   suggested a pay rise for all of £1500.
   i One of the suggestions would cause problems for the firm. Which one is
   that and why?
   ii What difference to the average salary would each suggestion make?

8 Mr Brennan, a caring maths teacher, told each pupil his/her test result and only
gave the exam statistics to the whole class. He gave the class the modal score, the
median score and the mean.
   a Which average would tell a pupil whether he/she was in the top half or the
   bottom half?
   b Which average tells the pupils nothing really?
   c Which average allows a pupil to really gauge how he/she has done compared
   with everyone else?

9 a Find the median of each list below.
   i 2, 4, 6, 7, 9
   ii 12, 14, 16, 17, 19
   iii 22, 24, 26, 27, 29
   iv 52, 54, 56, 57, 59
   v 92, 94, 96, 97, 99
   b What do you notice about the lists and your answers?

    c   Use your answer above to help find the medians of the following lists.

        i   132, 134, 136, 137, 139

       ii   577, 576, 572, 574, 579

      iii   431, 438, 439, 432, 435

      iv   855, 859, 856, 851, 857

10   Find the mean of each list in question **9**.

11   A list of 9 numbers has a mean of 7.6. What number must be added to the list to give a new mean of 8?

12   A dance group of 17 teenagers had a mean weight of 44.5 kg. To enter a competition there needed to be 18 with an average weight of 44.4 kg or less. What is the maximum weight that the eighteenth person must be?

Frequency tables

When a lot of information has been gathered, it is often convenient to put it together in a frequency table. From this table you can then find the values of the four averages. For example, a survey was done on the number of people in each car leaving the Meadowhall Shopping Centre, in Sheffield. The results are summarised in the table below.

Number of people in each car	1	2	3	4	5	6
Frequency	45	198	121	76	52	13

- The modal number of people in a car is easy to spot. It is the number with the largest frequency of 198. Hence, the modal number is 2.

- The median number of people in a car is found by working out where the middle of the set of numbers is located. First, we add up frequencies to get the total number of cars surveyed, which comes to 505. Next, we calculate the middle position:

$(505 + 1) \div 2 = 253$

We now need to count the frequencies across the table to find which group contains the 253rd item. The 243rd item is the end of the group with 2 in a car. Therefore, the 253rd item must be in the group with 3 in a car. Hence, the median number in a car is 3.

- The mean number of people in a car is found by adding together all the people and then dividing this total by the number of cars surveyed.

Number in a car	Frequency	Number in these cars
1	45	$1 \times 45 = 45$
2	198	$2 \times 198 = 396$
3	121	$3 \times 121 = 363$
4	76	$4 \times 76 = 304$
5	52	$5 \times 52 = 260$
6	13	$6 \times 13 = 78$
Totals	505	1446

Hence, the mean number of people in a car is $1446 \div 505 = 2.9$.

Using your calculator

The previous example can also be done by using the statistical mode which is available on some calculators. However, not all calculators are the same, so you will have to either read your instruction manual or experiment with the statistical keys on your calculator. You may find one labelled

DATA or **M+** or **Σ+** or **x̄** where $\bar{x}$ is printed in blue.

Try the following key strokes.

1 **×** **4** **5** **DATA**   **2** **×** **1** **9** **8** **DATA**   …

6 **×** **1** **3** **DATA** **x̄**

EXERCISE 13B

1 Find **i** the mode, **ii** the median and **iii** the mean from each frequency table below.

a A survey of the shoe sizes of all the Y10 boys in a school gave these results.

Shoe size	4	5	6	7	8	9	10
Number of pupils	12	30	34	35	23	8	3

b A survey of the number of eggs laid by hens over a period of one week gave these results.

Number of eggs	0	1	2	3	4	5	6
Frequency	6	8	15	35	48	37	12

c This is a record of the number of babies born each week over one year in a small maternity unit.

Number of babies	0	1	2	3	4	5	6	7	8	9	10	11	12	13	14
Frequency	1	1	1	2	2	2	3	5	9	8	6	4	5	2	1

d A school did a survey on how many times in a week pupils arrived late at school. These are the findings.

Number of times late	0	1	2	3	4	5
Frequency	481	34	23	15	3	4

2 A survey of the number of children in each family of a school's intake gave these results.

Number of children	1	2	3	4	5
Frequency	214	328	97	26	3

a Assuming each child at the school is shown in the data, how many children are at the school?

b Calculate the mean number of children in a family.

c How many families have this mean number of children?

d How many families would consider themselves average from this survey?

3 A dentist kept records of how many teeth he extracted from his patients.

In 1970 he extracted 598 teeth from 271 patients.
In 1980 he extracted 332 teeth from 196 patients.
In 1990 he extracted 374 teeth from 288 patients.
  a Calculate the average number of teeth taken from each patient in each year.
  b Explain why you think the average number of teeth extracted falls each year.

4 100 cases of apples delivered to a supermarket were inspected and the number of bad apples counted.

Bad apples	0	1	2	3	4	5	6	7	8	9
Frequency	52	29	9	3	2	1	3	0	0	1

What is
  a the modal number of bad apples per case
  b the mean number of bad apples per case?

5 Two dice are thrown together 60 times. The sum of the scores is shown below.

Score	2	3	4	5	6	7	8	9	10	11	12
Frequency	1	2	6	9	12	15	6	5	2	1	1

Find **a** the modal score, **b** the median score and **c** the mean score.

6 During a 1 month period, the number of days off by 100 workers in a factory were noted as follows.

Number of days off	0	1	2	3	4
Number of workers	35	42	16	4	3

Calculate
  a the modal number of days off
  b the median number of days off
  c the mean number of days off.

7 Two friends often played golf together. They recorded their scores for each hole over the last five games to compare who was more consistent and who was the better player. Their results were summarised in the following table.

No. of shots to hole ball	1	2	3	4	5	6	7	8	9
Roger	0	0	0	14	37	27	12	0	0
Brian	5	12	15	18	14	8	8	8	2

  a What is the modal score for each player?
  b What is the range of scores for each player?
  c What is the median score for each player?
  d What is the mean score for each player?
  e Which player is the more consistent and explain why?
  f Who would you say is the better player and state why?

8 The table below shows the number of passengers in each of 100 taxis leaving a London airport one day.

No. of passengers in a taxi	1	2	3	4
No. of taxis	x	40	y	26

a Find the value of $x + y$.

b If the mean number of passengers per taxi is 2.66, show that $x + 3y = 82$.

c Find the values of x and y by solving appropriate equations.

d State the median of the number of passengers per taxi.

Grouped data

Sometimes the information we are given is grouped in some way, as in the table below, which shows the range of pocket money given to Y10 students in a particular class.

Pocket money (£)	0.00–1.00	1.01–2.00	2.01–3.00	3.01–4.00	4.01–5.00
No. of students	2	5	5	9	15

The modal group is still easy to pick out, since it is simply the one with the largest frequency. Here the modal group is £4.01–£5.00.

The median will be in the middle of a group, and the way to find it is to draw a particular type of graph called a cumulative frequency curve, which you will meet on pages 426–9.

The mean can only be estimated, since we do not have all the information. To estimate the mean, we simply assume that each person in each group has the 'mid-way' amount, then we proceed to build up the following table.

Note how we find the mid-way value. The two end values are added together and then divided by two. The result could be rounded off to the nearest penny if we wished, since it is only an estimate, but it is usual not to round off until the final calculation is complete.

Pocket money (£)	Frequency (f)	Mid-way (m)	$f \times m$
0.00–1.00	2	0.50	$2 \times 0.50 = 1.00$
1.01–2.00	5	1.505	$5 \times 1.505 = 7.525$
2.01–3.00	5	2.505	$5 \times 2.505 = 12.525$
3.01–4.00	9	3.505	$9 \times 3.505 = 31.545$
4.01–5.00	15	4.505	$15 \times 4.505 = 67.575$
Totals	36		120.170

The estimated mean will be £120.17 ÷ 36 = £3.34 (rounded off).

There are several different ways of giving the groups in a grouped-frequency table. For example, the group headings in the first table could have been given as:

Pocket money £p $0 \le p \le 1$ $1 < p \le 2$ $2 < p \le 3$ $3 < p \le 4$ $4 < p \le 5$

where, for instance, $2 < p \le 3$ means 'the pocket money is more than £2 but less than or equal to £3'.

You will meet different ways of using inequalities in this type of table. Usually, it will make little difference to the middle value but could make it simpler to find the middle.

EXERCISE 13C

1   Find for each table of values given below
   i   the modal group
   ii   an estimate for the mean.

a

Score	0–10	11–20	21–30	31–40	41–50
Frequency	4	6	11	17	9

b

Records	0–100	101–200	201–300	301–400	401–500	501–600
Frequency	95	56	32	21	9	3

c

Cost (£)	0.00–5.00	5.01–10.00	10.01–15.00	15.01–20.00
Frequency	16	27	19	13

d

Weeks	0–3	4–6	7–9	10–12	13–15
Frequency	5	8	14	10	7

2   Jason brought 100 pebbles back from the beach and weighed them all to the nearest gram. His results are summarised in the table below.

Weight (grams)	40–60	61–70	71–80	81–90	91–100	101–140
Frequency	5	9	22	27	26	11

Find
   a   the modal weight of the pebbles
   b   an estimate of the total weight of all the pebbles
   c   an estimate of the mean weight of the pebbles.

3   A gardener measured the heights of all his daffodils to the nearest centimetre and summarised his results as follows.

Height (cm)	10–14	15–18	19–22	23–26	27–40
Frequency	21	57	65	52	12

   a   How many daffodils did the gardener have?
   b   What is the modal height of the daffodils?
   c   What is the estimated mean height of the daffodils?

4 In the Y10 end-of-year exams the results were grouped for easy comparison.

Marks	0–10	11–20	21–30	31–40	41–50	51–60	61–70	71–80	81–90	91–100
Frequency	3	5	11	19	34	26	18	10	6	2

Find

a the modal mark

b the estimated mean mark.

c What percentage of marks were over 70?

5 A survey was made to see how quickly the AA attended calls which were not on a motorway. The following table summarises the results.

Time (min)	0–15	16–30	31–45	46–60	61–75	76–90	91–105
Frequency	2	23	48	31	27	18	11

a How many calls were used in the survey?

b Estimate the mean time taken per call.

c Which average would the AA use for the average call-out time?

d What percentage of calls do the AA get to within the hour?

6 A certain London train was notorious for arriving late. So a survey was carried out over a month to see just how bad the problem was. The table summarises the results.

Minutes late	0–2	3–4	5–6	7–8	9–10	11–12
Frequency	9	6	5	4	4	2

a Estimate the mean number of minutes late.

b Which average would the rail company use?

c Do you think the criticism of the railway is justified by these results? Fully explain your reasons.

7 One hundred light bulbs were tested by their manufacturer to see whether the average life span of the manufacturer's bulbs was over 200 hours. The following table summarises the results.

Life span (h)	150–175	176–200	201–225	226–250	251–275
Frequency	24	45	18	10	3

a What is the modal length of time a bulb lasts?

b What percentage of bulbs last longer than 200 hours?

c Estimate the mean life span of the light bulbs.

d Do you think the test shows that the average life span is over 200 hours? Fully explain your answers.

8 Three supermarkets each claimed to have the lowest average price increase over the year. The following table summarises their average price increases.

Price increase (p)	0–5	6–10	11–15	16–20	21–25	26–30	31–35
Soundbuy	4	10	14	23	19	8	2
Springfields	5	11	12	19	25	9	6
Setco	3	8	15	31	21	7	3

Using their average price increases, make a comparison of the supermarkets and write a report on which supermarket, in your opinion, has the lowest price increases over the year. Don't forget to justify your answers.

Discrete and continuous data

You will need to be able to recognise the important difference between discrete data and continuous data.

Discrete data

This is data which consists of a set of separate numbers. For example, goals scored, marks in a test, number of children, shoe sizes.

Continuous data

This is data which can have an infinite number of different values. It is always rounded-off information. For example, height, weight, time, area, capacity. When representing continuous data on an axis in a chart you need to be careful how you represent it, and be clear about what rounding off has taken place in obtaining the data.

Charts

To help people understand it, statistical information is often presented in pictorial or diagrammatic form, which includes the pie chart, the frequency polygon, the bar chart and the histogram.

Frequency polygons

Frequency polygons can be used to represent both ungrouped data and grouped data, as shown in Example 1 and Example 2 respectively.

Example 1

No. of children	0	1	2	3	4	5
Frequency	12	23	36	28	16	11

This is the frequency polygon for the **ungrouped data** in the table.

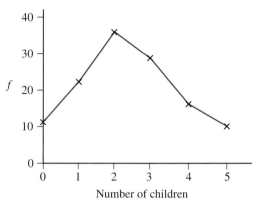

Notice the following:

- We simply plot the co-ordinates from each ordered pair in the table.

- We complete the polygon by joining up the plotted points with straight lines.

Example 2

Score	1–5	6–10	11–15	16–20	21–25	26–30
Frequency	4	13	25	32	17	9

This is the frequency polygon for the **grouped data** in the table.

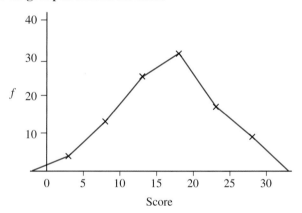

Notice the following:

- We use the mid-point of each group, just as we did in estimating the mean.

- We plot the ordered pairs of mid-points with frequency, namely,

    $(3, 4)$, $(8, 13)$, $(13, 25)$, $(18, 32)$, $(23, 17)$, $(28, 9)$

- We complete the polygon by joining up the plotted points with straight lines and bringing it down to 0 on the frequency axis to intercept the score axis 5 units back from the first plotted point $(3, 4)$ and 5 units on from the last plotted point $(28, 9)$.

Bar charts and histograms

You should already be familiar with the bar chart in which the vertical axis represents frequency, and the horizontal axis represents the type of data. (Sometimes it is more convenient to label the axes the other way.)

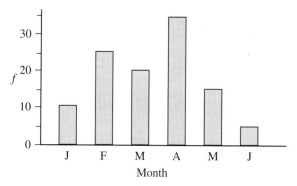

A histogram looks similar to a bar chart but there are three fundamental differences.

- There are no gaps between the bars.

- The horizontal axis has a continuous scale since it represents mainly continuous data, such as time, weight or length.

- The area of each bar represents the frequency.

All the histograms you will meet at the intermediate level of GCSE will be concerned only with continuous data. Also, they will always have bars of equal width, hence the heights of the bars will represent frequencies.

When the data is not continuous, a simple bar chart is used. For example, the runs scored in a test match or the goals scored by a hockey team.

Look at the histogram below, which has been drawn from this table of times taken by people to walk to work, measured to the nearest minute.

Time (min)	1–4	5–8	9–12	13–16
Frequency	8	12	10	7

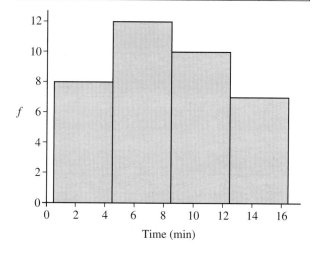

Notice that each histogram bar starts at the **least possible** time and finishes at the **greatest possible** time for its group. For example, in the time interval 5–8 minutes,

the least possible time is $4\frac{1}{2}$ minutes

the greatest possible time is $8\frac{1}{2}$ minutes

In the same way, the bar for 9–12 minutes starts at $8\frac{1}{2}$ minutes and finishes at $12\frac{1}{2}$ minutes.

Because all widths are the same, the heights can be used to represent the frequencies.

Using your calculator

Histograms can also be drawn on graphics calculators or by using computer software packages. If you have access to either of these, try to use them.

EXERCISE 13D

1 The table shows the range of heights of the girls in Y11 at a London school.

Height (cm)	121–130	131–140	141–150	151–160	161–170
Frequency	15	37	25	13	5

    i Draw a frequency polygon from this data.

    ii Draw a histogram from this data.

    iii Estimate the mean height of the girls.

2 After a spelling test, all the results were collated for girls and boys as below.

Number correct	1–4	5–8	9–12	13–16	17–20
Boys	3	7	21	26	15
Girls	4	8	17	23	20

    i Draw frequency polygons to illustrate the differences between the boys' scores and the girls' scores.

    ii Estimate the mean score for boys and girls separately, and comment on the results.

3 The following table shows how many students were absent from one particular class throughout the year.

Students absent	0–1	2–3	4–5	6–7	8–9
Frequency	48	32	12	3	1

    i Draw a frequency polygon to illustrate the data.

    ii Estimate the mean number of absences each lesson.

    iii Why is a histogram not a particularly useful chart to draw for this information?

4 The table below shows the number of goals scored by a hockey team in one season.

Goals	0–1	2–4	5–8	9–13	14–19
Frequency	3	9	7	5	2

    i Draw the frequency polygon for this data.

    ii Estimate the mean number of goals scored per game this season.

5 A doctor was concerned at the length of time her patients had to wait to see her when they came to the morning surgery. The survey she did gave her the following results.

Time (min)	1–10	11–20	21–30	31–40	41–50	51–60
Monday	5	8	17	9	7	4
Wednesday	9	8	16	3	2	1
Friday	7	6	18	2	1	1

    i Draw a frequency polygon for each day on the same pair of axes.

    ii What is the average amount of time spent waiting each day?

    iii Why might the average time for each day be different?

6 At a maternity clinic, the following data was collected one month on the weights at birth of the babies born in that month. The weights were recorded to the nearest kg.

Weight (kg)	3	4	5	6	7	8
Boys	4	26	11	8	4	3
Girls	5	28	14	5	2	1

    i Were more girls or boys born that month?

    ii How many babies were born at the unit that month?

    iii Draw a frequency polygon for each sex on the same pair of axes.

    iv Draw a histogram for the combined weights of the babies.

    v What was the average weight of each sex? Comment on your results.

7 In a survey of over 200 families about the number of children in a family, the following results were obtained.

Number of children	1	2	3	4
Frequency	69	134	19	7

    i What is the mean number of children per family?

    ii Why is the data not particularly suitable for a frequency polygon or a histogram to be drawn?

8 The wages paid to Saturday workers in a market were found to be:

Wages (£)	6–10	11–15	16–20	21–25	26–30
Age 16–17	12	9	8	3	0
Age 18–20	6	15	11	8	2

    i What are the average Saturday wages paid to each age group?

    ii Illustrate the difference between each age group on a frequency polygon.

9 The speeds achieved by computer secretaries are given in this table.

Speed (words/min)	21–30	31–40	41–50	51–60	61–70
Frequency	3	7	12	8	3

    i Draw a histogram to illustrate the data.

    ii Estimate the mean speed of the secretaries.

    iii What percentage have a speed over 50 words per minute?

10 The number of passengers in each taxi leaving a night-club one night were:

Passengers	1	2	3	4	5	6
Frequency	8	15	23	9	6	2

    i   How many taxis were in the survey?

    ii   What is the mean number of passengers in each taxi?

    iii Draw a frequency polygon from the given data.

Pie charts

In the last exercise, you saw some situations where it was not appropriate to draw a frequency polygon or a histogram to illustrate the data. This was mainly because of the huge differences between some of the frequencies.

A pie chart is ideal for showing this sort of information, as the whole diagram is contained within a circle.

However, when there is much information to illustrate, a pie chart is not as good as a histogram or a frequency polygon.

Example   Draw a pie chart to illustrate the following information.

Type of transport	Train	Coach	Car	Ship	Plane
Frequency	48	28	125	22	27

We need to find the fraction of 360° which represents each type of transport. This is usually done in a table such as that presented below.

Type of transport	Frequency	Calculation	Angle
Train	48	$\frac{48}{250} \times 360 = 69.12°$	$\approx 69°$
Coach	28	$\frac{28}{250} \times 360 = 40.32°$	$\approx 40°$
Car	125	$\frac{125}{250} \times 360 = 180°$	$180°$
Ship	22	$\frac{22}{250} \times 360 = 31.68°$	$\approx 32°$
Plane	27	$\frac{27}{250} \times 360 = 38.88°$	$\approx 39°$
Totals	250		$360°$

Notice

- We use the total of 250 to calculate each fraction.

- We round off each angle to the nearest degree.

- We check that the sum of all the angles is 360°.

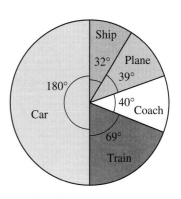

The pie chart can now be drawn. Remember, it is always good practice to draw the smallest angle first, then the next smallest and so on, until the last angle will automatically be the largest. This reduces the effect that the successive additions of error have on the accuracy of the last angle drawn.

EXERCISE 13E

1 Draw pie charts to represent the following sets of data.

a

Month	May	June	July	August	September
Number	35	12	51	85	17

b

Holiday place	England	Scotland	Wales	Ireland
Number	132	68	95	43

c

Types of crisp	Plain	Salt and vinegar	Cheese and onion	Barbecue	Chicken
Number	145	126	83	15	8

2 All the Y9s in a Lancashire school were asked to name their favourite fruit. The results are shown in this table.

Fruit	Apple	Orange	Pear	Banana	Pineapple
Number	42	35	14	21	28

Illustrate this information on a pie chart.

3 The sales of the *Star* newspaper over a period of five years were recorded as:

Year	1991	1992	1993	1994	1995
Copies	62 000	58 000	51 000	55 000	63 000

a Illustrate this information on a pie chart.
b Illustrate this information with a frequency polygon.
c Illustrate this information with a bar chart.
d Which diagram best illustrates the data?

4 An investigation into how healthy some fast foods are gave the following results.

Food	Beefburger	Hot dog	Chips	Pizza	Meat pie
Calories per 100 g	115	95	73	32	81
Fat per 100 g	40 g	35 g	25 g	8 g	11 g
Carbohydrates per 100 g	44 g	41 g	56 g	65 g	31 g

    a Use a pie chart to illustrate the calorie content of each fast food.

    b Use a bar chart to illustrate the carbohydrate content of each fast food.

    c What is the mean amount of fat in these foods?

    d Which of these fast foods looks the healthiest and which looks the least healthy? Give clear reasons to support your answers.

5 This pie chart illustrates the favourite lessons of the 120 pupils in Y10 in a Cornish school.

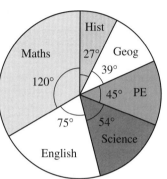

    a How many pupils had as their favourite lesson

        i Mathematics

        ii PE

        iii English?

    b What percentage of pupils chose science as their favourite lesson?

6 This pie chart shows the proportions of the different shoe sizes worn by 144 pupils in Y11 in a London school.

    a What is the angle of the sector representing shoe sizes 11 and 12?

    b How many pupils had a shoe size of 11 or 12?

    c What percentage of pupils wore the modal size?

7 A milkman delivers his milk to his regular customers in the following amounts:

    Gold Top   24 pints

    Red Top   59 pints

    Silver Top   1240 pints

    Blue Top   18 pints

    a If this information were put into a pie chart, what would be the angle for

        i Silver Top   **ii** Blue Top?

    b Why is the information totally unsuitable for either a bar chart or a histogram?

8 The following information was found out about the range of pocket money given to 12-year-olds.

Pocket money (£)	0.00–1.00	1.01–2.00	2.01–3.00	3.01–4.00	4.01–5.00
Girls	8	15	22	11	4
Boys	6	11	25	12	6

    a Represent the information about the girls on a pie chart.

    b Represent the information about the boys on a histogram.

    c Represent both sets of data with a frequency polygon, using the same pair of axes.

    d What is the mean amount of pocket money given to each sex? Comment on your answer.

Surveys

A survey is an organised way of asking a lot of people a few well-constructed questions, or of making a lot of observations in an experiment, in order to reach a conclusion about something.

We use surveys to test out people's opinions or to test a hypothesis.

Simple data collection sheet

If you need just to collect some data to analyse, you will have to design a simple data capture sheet. For example: 'Where do you want to go to for the Y10 trip at the end of term – Blackpool, Alton Towers, the Great Western Show or London?'

You would put this question one day to a lot of Y10s, and enter their answers straight onto a data capture sheet, as below.

Place	Tally	f
Blackpool	ⅢⅢ ⅢⅢ ⅢⅢ ⅢⅢ III	
Alton Towers	ⅢⅢ ⅢⅢ ⅢⅢ ⅢⅢ ⅢⅢ ⅢⅢ ⅢⅢ ⅢⅢ ⅢⅢ I	
The Great Western Show	ⅢⅢ ⅢⅢ IIII	
London	ⅢⅢ ⅢⅢ ⅢⅢ ⅢⅢ II	

Notice how plenty of space is made for the tally marks, and how the tallies are 'gated' in groups of five to make counting easier when the survey is complete.

This is a good, simple data collection sheet because

● only one question ('Where do you want to go?') has to be asked

● all the possible venues are listed

● the answer from each interviewee can be easily and quickly tallied, then on to the next interviewee.

Notice, too, that since the question listed specific places, they must appear on the data collection sheet. You would lose many marks in an examination if you just asked the open question: 'Where do you want to go?'

Using your computer

Once the data has been collected for your survey, it can be put into a computer database. This allows the data to be stored and amended or updated at a later date if necessary.

From the database, suitable diagrams can easily be drawn within the software and averages calculated for you. Your results can then be published in, for example, the school magazine.

EXERCISE 13F

1   'People like the supermarket to open on Sundays.'

   a   To see whether this statement is true, design a data collection sheet which will allow you to capture data while standing outside a supermarket.

   b   Does it matter on which day you collect data outside the supermarket?

2   The school tuck shop wanted to know which types of chocolate it should get in to sell – plain, milk, fruit and nut, wholenut or white chocolate.

   a   Design a data collection sheet which you could use to ask the pupils in your school which of these chocolate types is their favourite.

   b   Invent the first 30 entries on the chart.

3   When you throw two dice together, what numbers are you most likely to get?

   a   Design a data collection sheet on which you can record the data from an experiment in which two dice are thrown together and note the sum of the two numbers shown on the dice.

   b   Carry out this experiment for at least 100 throws.

   c   Which numbers are most likely to occur?

   d   Illustrate your results on a frequency polygon.

4   Which letters of the alphabet do printers use the most?

   a   Design a data collection sheet to record the frequency of each letter used on any page in this book.

   b   Carry out the experiment on any page you choose.

   c   Which letters are used the most?

5   What kind of vehicles pass your school each day? Design a data collection sheet to record the data necessary for a survey which will answer this question.

6   What types of television programme do your age group watch the most? Is it crime, romance, comedy, documentary, sport or something else? Design a data collection sheet to be used in a survey of your age group.

7   What do people of your age tend to spend their money on? Is it sport, magazines, clubs, cinema, sweets, clothes or something else? Design a data collection sheet to be used in a survey of your age group.

8   Who uses the buses the most in the mornings? Is it pensioners, mums, school children, the unemployed or some other group? Design a data collection sheet to be used in a survey of who uses the buses.

9   Who in your house gets up first most mornings? Is it mum, dad, a big brother, a little sister, you or who? Design a data collection sheet to be used in a survey of who gets up first.

10 Design a data collection sheet to be used in a survey of the usual time Y10s get up in the morning to go to school.

Questionnaires

When you are putting together a questionnaire, you must think very carefully about the sorts of question you are going to ask. Here are four rules that you should always follow.

● Never ask a leading question designed to get a particular response.

● Never ask a personal, irrelevant question.

● Keep each question as simple as possible.

● Include a question that will get a response from whomever is asked.

The following types of question are **badly constructed** and should never appear in any questionnaire.

What is your age? This is personal. Many people will not want to answer.

Slaughtering animals for food is cruel to the poor defenceless animals. Don't you agree? This is a leading question, designed to get a 'yes'.

Do you go to discos when abroad? This can be answered only by those who have been abroad.

When you first get up in a morning and decide to have some sort of breakfast that might be made by somebody else, do you feel obliged to eat it all or not? This question is too complicated.

The following types of question are **well constructed**.

Which age group are you in? 0–20 21–30 31–50 over 50

Do you think it is cruel to kill animals for meat to feed humans?

If you went abroad would you consider going to a disco?

Do you eat all your breakfast?

A questionnaire is usually put together to test a hypothesis or a statement. For example: 'People buy cheaper milk from the supermarket and they don't mind not getting it on their doorstep. They'd rather go out and buy it.'

A questionnaire designed to test whether this statement is true or not should include these questions:

'Do you have milk delivered to your doorstep?'
'Do you buy cheaper milk from the supermarket?'
'Would you buy your milk only from the supermarket?'

Once these questions have been answered, they can be looked at to see whether or not the majority of people hold views that agree with the statement.

EXERCISE 13G

1   Design a questionnaire to see whether or not the following statement is true in your area.

   'Tall men marry tall women, and short men marry short women.'

2   Design a questionnaire to test the following statement.

   'People under 16 do not know what is meant by all the jargon used in the business news on TV, but the over-twenties do.'

3   'Women think that men are bad drivers, while men think that women are slow drivers and that nobody drives as well as they do.'
   Design a questionnaire to test this statement.

4   'Woodlice will only live in cold, damp places.'
   Design an experiment to test whether this hypothesis is true or not.

5   'The under-twenties feel quite at ease with computers, while the over-forties would rather not bother with them. The 20–40s always try to look good with computers.'
   Design a questionnaire to test this statement.

6   'Most school children arrive at school having had a good breakfast of either bread or cereal and a warm drink.'
   I don't think this statement is true, do you? Design a questionnaire to be used to test the statement to see whether it is false or not.

7   Design a questionnaire to test the following hypothesis.

   'The older you get, the less sleep you need.'

8   'People leave football matches early because their team is either losing or playing badly. They never come out early to avoid traffic queues or to get home quickly for tea.'
   Design a questionnaire to test this statement for any truth.

9   Design a questionnaire to test this statement.

   'Everybody has played with a piano, but unless you learn to play before you are 12, you will not play the piano well.'

10 A head teacher wanted to find out if his pupils thought they had too much, too little or just the right amount of homework. She also wanted to know the parents' views about homework.
   Design a questionnaire that could be used to find the data the head teacher needs to look at.

Possible coursework tasks

If available, you could use a computer software package for these tasks.

School dinners

'School dinners are good value.'

Investigate the opinions of different people.

Brightly coloured cars

'The tendency nowadays is to own a red car.'

Investigate whether or not this statement is true, and for whom?

Advertisements

'There is too much time devoted to adverts on TV.'

Investigate who thinks this is true.

Win the pools

'There are more draws in the Premier Division than there are in Division Three.'

Investigate whether this is true or not.

Win the National Lottery

One week, the six main balls drawn out in the National Lottery were
21, 29, 31, 32, 34, 48
Is the average of these numbers higher than usual? What is the usual average of the Lottery numbers.

Examination questions: coursework type

1 Class 11B is doing a survey about pocket money. Each pupil says how much he or she has each week. These are the results.

£5	£4	£5	0	£5	£5	£7.50	£3	0	£6
£3	£2.50	0	£4	£4	£2	£5	0	£1	£7
£6	£5	£5	£4	£5	£5	0	£10	0	£2

a Ceri is a pupil in class 11B. She has £2 pocket money a week. She thinks she should get more. Use the survey data to help her argue for more pocket money.

b Tom is in class 11C. Class 11C is also doing a survey about pocket money. Tom compares the data for the two classes. This is what he writes.

90% of class 11C get pocket money. Only $\frac{4}{5}$ of class 11B get pocket money. The graphs show how much pocket money the pupils in each class get.

Class 11B

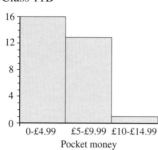

Class 11C

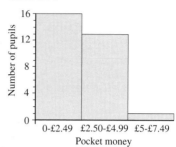

The modal class for 11B is 0 to £4.99.   The modal class for 11C is £5 to £7.49.

My work shows 11C pupils have more money to spend than 11B pupils.

Criticise Tom's work.   *NEAB, Question 4, Paper 3Q, June 1995*

2   'Which washing powder or liquid do people buy and why?'

   a   Lee is asked to investigate this question and present his work to his class. Write an outline plan for Lee to follow when carrying out this task.

   b   A washing powder survey is carried out by asking five 10- to 12-year-old children questions. Do you think the results would be useful? Give **two** reasons for your answer.

                              WJEC, Question 4, Specimen Paper 3, 1998

Examination questions

1   A small village in Africa recorded the number of days of sunshine it had each year for 20 years. The results are listed below.

   285 , 277 , 264 , 288 , 291 , 281 , 288 , 286 , 279 , 272,
   284 , 285 , 295 , 273 , 287 , 274 , 281 , 289 , 272 , 286

   a   Work out the range of these values.

   b   Copy and complete the frequency table below.

Number of days		Number of years
261 to 270		
271 to 280		
281 to 290		
291 to 300		

   c   Write down the modal class.

   d   Draw and label a pie chart to show the information in the frequency table.

                  OCR, Question 2, Intermediate (A) Paper 3, June 2000

2 a Ian and Alex decide to conduct a survey on the use of computers. They want to know whether boys and girls use a computer in their coursework for word processing, spreadsheets or both.
Design an observation sheet to collect information from a group of boys and girls.

b Alex used the spell-check on her computer to find spelling mistakes in some coursework. The table below shows the distribution of spelling mistakes.

Number of spelling mistakes on the page	0	1	2	3	4
Number of pages	10	6	1	1	2

Calculate the mean number of spelling mistakes per page.

OCR, Question 9, Intermediate (A) Paper 4, June 2000

3 Julia plays in her school netball team. She will be selected to play for her county team next season if her mean score of goals for the school team is at least 12 per game over seven games. After 6 games her mean score per game is 11.5 goals.

a What is the total number of goals that Julia has scored in these 6 games?

b What is the least number of goals she must score in the next game in order to be chosen for the county team?

c In the 7th game she scored 13 goals. Does her mean score increase or decrease?

You must show all your working.

NEAB, Question 8, Specimen Paper 2, 1998

4 At Murrey's rental shop the number of items rented out in one week were:

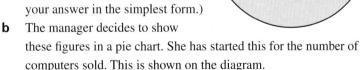

Televisions   68
Computers   24
Videos   36
Other equipment 16

a Write the number of videos as a fraction of the total sales. (Give your answer in the simplest form.)

b The manager decides to show these figures in a pie chart. She has started this for the number of computers sold. This is shown on the diagram.

   i Calculate the angle which represents the number of televisions sold.

   ii Complete the pie chart for all the week's rentals.

NEAB, Question 1, Specimen Paper 1, 1998

5 Mrs Wilson wants to sell her herd of dairy cows. A buyer will need to know the herd's average daily yield of milk. The daily milk yield, p litres, is monitored over 5 weeks. The table below shows the results of this survey.

Milk yield, p litres	Frequency
$140 \le p < 145$	3
$145 \le p < 150$	5
$150 \le p < 155$	9
$155 \le p < 160$	6
$160 \le p < 165$	8
$165 \le p < 170$	4
Total	35

a Mrs Wilson finds the modal class for the daily average. What is this value?

b Calculate an estimated mean daily milk yield.

c Which is the more suitable average for the buyer to use? Give a reason for your answer.

NEAB, Question 16, Specimen Paper 1, 1998

6 a A headline in a newspaper this year stated:

Students Skip Breakfast

Our survey shows that few students
are eating cereals, fruit, or bread for breakfast.

In fact they eat nothing at all!

You are asked to conduct a survey to find out what students eat for breakfast. Design an observation sheet to collect the data you need. Invent the first 20 entries on your data sheet.

b The newspaper made the following statement about the eating habits of teenagers.

Only one in a hundred teenagers eat fruit and vegetables each day. Over half eat no vegetables other than chips.

You are asked to find out whether this statement is true in your area. Give three questions you could ask teenagers to see if what the article says is true in your area.

NEAB, Question 13, Paper 1, June 1995

7 Sybil weighed some pieces of cheese.
The table gives information about her results.

Weight (w) grams	Frequency
$90 < w \le 94$	1
$94 < w \le 98$	2
$98 < w \le 102$	6
$102 < w \le 106$	1

Work out an estimate of the mean weight.

EDEXCEL, Question 18, Intermediate Paper 3, June 2000

8   A forester measures the heights of 100 trees, correct to the nearest metre. This table shows her results.

Height to nearest metre	1 to 5	6 to 10	11 to 15	16 to 20	21 to 25
Frequency	12	23	33	26	6

  a   Calculate an estimate of the mean height of the trees in the sample.

  b   Draw a frequency polygon to show the forester's results.

  c   The forester also measures the heights of 100 trees in a different wood. This frequency polygon shows these results. The mean of this set of data is 13.2 m. How does this second set of 100 trees compare with the first set?

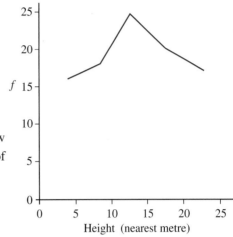

WJEC, Question 10, Specimen Paper 2, 1998

9   This graph shows the number of people attending a holiday camp each month from March 1992 to February 1993.

  a   How many people attended the holiday camp in April?

  b   Which was the modal month?

  c   What is the range of this data?

  d   Calculate the mean number of visitors per month.

  e   The holiday camp owners call March, April and May 'Spring'; June, July and August 'Summer'; September, October and November 'Autumn'; and December, January and February 'Winter'. Complete the table below to show the number of visitors by seasons.

Spring	Summer	Autumn	Winter

  f   Draw and label a pie chart to show the distribution of visitors by seasons. You must show how you calculated the angles of your pie chart.   *WJEC, Question 3, Specimen Paper 2, 1998*

10 This statement is made on a television programme about health.

'Three in every eight pupils do not take any exercise outside school.'

a Clare says, 'I go to the gym twice a week after school'.

She decides to do a survey to investigate what exercise other pupils do outside school.

Write down **two** questions that she could ask.

b Matthew decides to do a survey in his school about the benefits of exercise. He decides to ask the girls netball team for their opinion.

Give **two** reasons why this is not a suitable sample to take.

c This is part of Matthew's questionnaire.

> **Question** *Don't you agree that adults who were sportsmen when they were younger suffer more from injuries as they get older?*
>
> **Response** *Tick one box*
>
> ☐ *Yes*   ☐ *Usually*   ☐ *Sometimes*   ☐ *Occasionally*

i Write down one criticism of Matthew's question.

ii Write down one criticism of Matthew's response section.

AQA (North), Question 9, Intermediate Paper 1, June 2000

11 The South Mappin Philharmonic Choir has both men and women members.

This is the distribution of the men's ages.

Age in years	Frequency	
0 – 9	0	
10 – 19	4	
20 – 29	12	
30 – 39	14	
40 – 49	16	
50 – 59	10	
60 – 69	6	
70 – 79	2	
80 – 89	0	
	64	

a Explain why the midpoint of the age group 40 – 49 is 45.

b Calculate an estimate of the mean age of the men.

This frequency polygon shows the grouped distribution of the ages of the women in the choir.

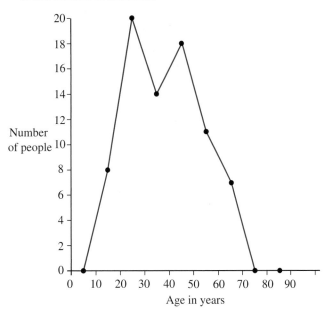

c What is the modal group for the women?

d Draw a frequency polygon for the men on a copy of the above diagram.

The mean age of the women is 38.2 and the range of their ages is 53.

e Compare the two distributions. Make at least two comments.

OCR, Question 13, Intermediate (B) Paper 4, June 2000

Summary

How well do you grade yourself?

To gain a grade **E**, you need to be able to find the mode and median from a simple list of data, and to calculate the mean from a list of data. You also need to be able to read a variety of statistical diagrams, such as a bar chart and a pie chart, and to compare two different distributions by using the range and the mean of each.

To gain a grade **C**, you need to be able to construct and interpret frequency diagrams, such as frequency polygons and pie charts, to test a hypothesis, to find the modal group and to estimate the mean of a set of grouped data, choosing the type of average most appropriate to the enquiry. You also need to be able to use the measures of average and range with frequency polygons to compare distributions.

To gain a grade **B**, you need to be able to read and construct a histogram. You also need to be able to criticise and to create questionnaires to test a hypothesis.

What you should know after you have worked through Chapter 13

- How to find the three averages – mode, median and mean.
- How to interpret frequency tables and find averages from frequency tables of both ungrouped and grouped data.
- How to create frequency polygons and histograms.
- How to read and create pie charts.
- How to create a data collection sheet.
- How to create a questionnaire to test a hypothesis.

14 Algebra 3

This chapter is going to ...

show you how to expand algebraic expressions involving brackets, how to factorise an expression back into a single pair of brackets, and how to transpose formulae. It will also show you how to create a quadratic expression, and how to factorise and solve quadratic equations.

What you should already know

✔ How to combine algebraic expressions. For example,

$$2 \times t = 2t$$
$$m \times t = mt$$
$$2t \times 5 = 10t$$
$$3y \times 2m = 6my$$

✔ The convention that states: always put the letters in alphabetical order. In other words, do not write $2ba$, but $2ab$.

✔ How to multiply together similar terms. Remember: the indices are added together. For example,

$$t \times t = t^2 \quad \text{(Also remember: } t = t^1\text{)}$$
$$3t \times 2t = 6t^2$$
$$3t^2 \times 4t = 12t^3$$
$$2t^3 \times 4t^2 = 8t^5$$

EXERCISE 14A

Evaluate these expressions, writing them as simply as possible.

1 $2 \times 3t$	**2** $3 \times 4y$	**3** $5y \times 3$	**4** $2w \times 4$
5 $3t \times t$	**6** $5b \times b$	**7** $2w \times w$	**8** $5y \times 3y$
9 $4p \times 2p$	**10** $3t \times 2t$	**11** $4m \times 3m$	**12** $5t \times 3t$
13 $m \times 2t$	**14** $3y \times w$	**15** $5t \times q$	**16** $n \times 6m$
17 $3t \times 2q$	**18** $4f \times 3g$	**19** $5h \times 2k$	**20** $3p \times 7r$
21 $y^2 \times y$	**22** $t \times t^2$	**23** $3m \times m^2$	**24** $4t^2 \times t$
25 $3n \times 2n^2$	**26** $4r^2 \times 5r$	**27** $t^2 \times t^2$	**28** $h^3 \times h^2$
29 $3n^2 \times 4n^3$	**30** $5t^3 \times 2t^4$	**31** $3a^4 \times 2a^3$	**32** $k^5 \times 4k^2$
33 $-t^2 \times -t$	**34** $-2y \times -3y$	**35** $-4d^2 \times -3d$	**36** $-3p^4 \times -5p^2$
37 $3mp \times p$	**38** $2ty \times 3t$	**39** $3mn \times 2m$	**40** $4mp \times 2mp$

Expansion

In mathematics, the term 'expand' usually means 'multiply out'. For example, expressions such as $3(y + 2)$ and $4y^2(2y + 3)$ can be expanded by multiplying out.

You need to remember that there is an invisible multiplication sign between the outside number and the bracket. So that $3(y + 2)$ is really $3 \times (y + 2)$, and $4y^2(2y + 3)$ is really $4y^2 \times (2y + 3)$.

We expand by multiplying **everything inside** the bracket by what is outside the bracket. So in the case of these two examples,

$$3(y + 2) = 3 \times (y + 2) = 3y + 6$$

$$4y^2(2y + 3) = 4y^2 \times (2y + 3) = 8y^3 + 12y^2$$

Look at these next examples of expansion, which show clearly how the term outside the bracket has been multiplied to the terms inside it.

$2(m + 3) = 2m + 6$ $y(y^2 - 4x) = y^3 - 4xy$

$3(2t + 5) = 6t + 15$ $3x^2(4x + 5) = 12x^3 + 15x^2$

$m(p + 7) = mp + 7m$ $-3(2 + 3x) = -6 - 9x$

$x(x - 6) = x^2 - 6x$ $-2x(3 - 4x) = -6x + 8x^2$

$4t(t + 2) = 4t^2 + 8t$ $3t(2 + 5t - p) = 6t + 15t^2 - 3pt$

EXERCISE 14B

Expand these expressions.

1 $2(3 + m)$	**2** $5(2 + l)$	**3** $3(4 - y)$	**4** $4(5 + 2k)$
5 $3(2 - 4f)$	**6** $2(5 - 3w)$	**7** $3(g + h)$	**8** $5(2k + 3m)$
9 $4(3d - 2n)$	**10** $t(t + 3)$	**11** $m(m + 5)$	**12** $k(k - 3)$
13 $g(3g + 2)$	**14** $y(5y - 1)$	**15** $p(5 - 3p)$	**16** $3m(m + 4)$
17 $4t(t - 1)$	**18** $2k(4 - k)$	**19** $4g(2g + 5)$	**20** $5h(3h - 2)$
21 $3t(5 - 4t)$	**22** $3d(2d + 4e)$	**23** $2y(3y + 4k)$	**24** $5m(3m - 2p)$
25 $y(y^2 + 5)$	**26** $h(h^3 + 7)$	**27** $k(k^2 - 5)$	**28** $3t(t^2 + 4)$
29 $4h(h^3 - 1)$	**30** $5g(g^3 - 2)$	**31** $4m(3m^2 + m)$	**32** $5k(2k^3 + k^2)$
33 $3d(5d^2 - d^3)$	**34** $3w(2w^2 + t)$	**35** $5a(3a^2 - 2b)$	**36** $3p(4p^3 - 5m)$
37 $m^2(5 + 4m)$	**38** $t^3(t + 2t)$	**39** $g^2(5t - 4g^2)$	**40** $3t^2(5t + m)$
41 $4h^2(3h + 2g)$	**42** $2m^2(4m + m^2)$		

Simplification

Simplification is the process whereby an expression is written down as simply as possible, any like terms being combined. Like terms are terms which have the same letter(s) raised to the same power and can differ only in their numerical coefficients (numbers in front). For example,

m, $3m$, $4m$, $-m$ and $76m$ are all like terms in m

t^2, $4t^2$, $7t^2$, $-t^2$, $-3t^2$ and $98t^2$ are all like terms in t^2

pt, $5pt$, $-2pt$, $7pt$, $-3pt$ and $103pt$ are all like terms in pt

Note also that all the terms in tp are also like terms to all the terms in pt.

In simplifying an expression, only like terms can be added or subtracted. For example,

$4m + 3m = 7m$ $\qquad$ $3y + 4y + 3 = 7y + 3$ $\qquad$ $4h - h = 3h$

$2t^2 + 5t^2 = 7t^2$ $\qquad$ $2m + 6 + 3m = 5m + 6$ $\qquad$ $7t + 8 - 2t = 5t + 8$

$3ab + 2ab = 5ab$ $\qquad$ $5k - 2k = 3k$ $\qquad$ $10g - 4 - 3g = 7g - 4$

Expand and simplify

This process often occurs in mathematics and is illustrated by Examples 1 to 3.

1 $\quad 3(4 + m) + 2(5 + 2m)$

$\quad = 12 + 3m + 10 + 4m = 22 + 7m$

2 $\quad 3t(5t + 4) - 2t(3t - 5)$

$\quad = 15t^2 + 12t - 6t^2 + 10t = 9t^2 + 22t$

3 $\quad 4a(2b - 3f) - 3b(a + 2f)$

$\quad = 8ab - 12af - 3ab - 6bf = 5ab - 12af - 6bf$

EXERCISE 14C

1 Simplify these expressions.

    a $4t + 3t$ **b** $5m + 4m$ **c** $2y + y$ **d** $3d + 2d + 4d$

    e $5e - 2e$ **f** $7g - 5g$ **g** $4p - p$ **h** $3t - t$

    i $2t^2 + 3t^2$ **j** $6y^2 - 2y^2$ **k** $3ab + 2ab$ **l** $7a^2d - 4a^2d$

2 Expand and simplify.

    a $3(4 + t) + 2(5 + t)$ **b** $5(3 + 2k) + 3(2 + 3k)$ **c** $4(1 + 3m) + 2(3 + 2m)$

    d $2(5 + 4y) + 3(2 + 3y)$ **e** $4(3 + 2f) + 2(5 - 3f)$ **f** $5(1 + 3g) + 3(3 - 4g)$

    g $3(2 + 5t) + 4(1 - t)$ **h** $4(3 + 3w) + 2(5 - 4w)$

3 Expand and simplify.

    a $4(3 + 2h) - 2(5 + 3h)$ **b** $5(3g + 4) - 3(2g + 5)$ **c** $3(4y + 5) - 2(3y + 2)$

    d $3(5t + 2) - 2(4t + 5)$ **e** $5(5k + 2) - 2(4k - 3)$ **f** $4(4e + 3) - 2(5e - 4)$

    g $3(5m - 2) - 2(4m - 5)$ **h** $2(6t - 1) - 3(3t - 4)$

4 Expand and simplify.

a $m(4 + p) + p(3 + m)$ **b** $k(3 + 2h) + h(4 + 3k)$ **c** $t(2 + 3n) + n(3 + 4t)$

d $p(2q + 3) + q(4p + 7)$ **e** $3h(2 + 3j) + 2j(2h + 3)$ **f** $2y(3t + 4) + 3t(2 + 5y)$

g $4r(3 + 4p) + 3p(8 - r)$ **h** $5k(3m + 4) - 2m(3 - 2k)$

5 Expand and simplify.

a $t(3t + 4) + 3t(3 + 2t)$ **b** $2y(3 + 4y) + y(5y - 1)$

c $4w(2w + 3) + 3w(2 - w)$ **d** $5p(3p + 4) - 2p(3 - 4p)$

e $3m(2m - 1) + 2m(5 - m)$ **f** $6d(4 - 2d) + d(3d - 2)$

g $4e(3e - 5) - 2e(e - 7)$ **h** $3k(2k + p) - 2k(3p - 4k)$

6 Expand and simplify.

a $4a(2b + 3c) + 3b(3a + 2c)$ **b** $3y(4w + 2t) + 2w(3y - 4t)$

c $2g(3h - k) + 5h(2g - 2k)$ **d** $3h(2t - p) + 4t(h - 3p)$

e $a(3b - 2c) - 2b(a - 3c)$ **f** $4p(3q - 2w) - 2w(p - q)$

g $5m(2n - 3p) - 2n(3p - 2m)$ **h** $2r(3r + r^2) - 3r^2(4 - 2r)$

Factorisation

Factorisation is the opposite of expansion. It puts an expression back into the brackets it may have come from.

In factorisation, we have to look for the common factors in every term of the expression. Follow through the examples below to see how this works.

$$6t + 9m = 3(2t + 3m)$$
$$6my + 4py = 2y(3m + 2p)$$
$$5k^2 - 25k = 5k(k - 5)$$
$$8kp + 4kt - 12km = 4k(2p + t - 3m)$$

Notice that if you multiply out each answer you will get the expressions you started with.

This diagram may help you to see the difference and the connection between expansion and factorisation.

Expanding

$$3 (2t + 3m) = 6t + 9m$$

Factorising

EXERCISE 14D

Factorise the following expressions.

1 $6m + 12t$	**2** $9t + 3p$	**3** $8m + 12k$	**4** $4r + 8t$
5 $mn + 3m$	**6** $5g^2 + 3g$	**7** $4w - 6t$	**8** $8p - 6k$
9 $16h - 10k$	**10** $2mp + 2mk$	**11** $4bc + 2bk$	**12** $6ab + 4ac$
13 $3y^2 + 2y$	**14** $4t^2 - 3t$	**15** $4d^2 - 2d$	**16** $3m^2 - 3mp$
17 $6p^2 + 9pt$	**18** $8pt + 6mp$	**19** $8ab - 4bc$	**20** $12a^2 - 8ab$
21 $9mt - 6pt$	**22** $16at^2 + 12at$	**23** $5b^2c - 10bc$	**24** $8abc + 6bed$
25 $4a^2 + 6a + 8$	**26** $6ab + 9bc + 3bd$	**27** $5t^2 + 4t + at$	
28 $6mt^2 - 3mt + 9m^2t$	**29** $8ab^2 + 2ab - 4a^2b$	**30** $10pt^2 + 15pt + 5p^2t$	

Factorise the following expressions where possible. List those which cannot factorise.

31 $7m - 6t$ **32** $5m + 2mp$ **33** $t^2 - 7t$ **34** $8pt + 5ab$

35 $4m^2 - 6mp$ **36** $a^2 + b$ **37** $4a^2 - 5ab$ **38** $3ab + 4cd$

39 $5ab - 3b^2c$

Quadratic expansion and factorisation

A quadratic expression is one in which the highest power of its terms is 2. For example,

$$y^2 \qquad 3t^2 + 5t \qquad 5m^2 + 3m + 8$$

An expression such as $(3y + 2)(4y - 5)$ can be expanded to give a quadratic expression. This multiplying out of such pairs of brackets is usually called **quadratic expansion**.

The rule for expanding such expressions as $(t + 5)(3t - 4)$ is similar to that for expanding single brackets: multiply everything in one bracket by everything in the other bracket.

Follow through Examples 1 to 4 below to see how a pair of brackets can be expanded. Notice how we split up the first bracket and make each of its terms multiply the second bracket. We then simplify the outcome.

Example 1   Expand $(x + 3)(x + 4)$.

$(x + 3)(x + 4) = x(x + 4) + 3(x + 4)$
$= x^2 + 4x + 3x + 12$
$= x^2 + 7x + 12$

Example 2   Expand $(t + 5)(t - 2)$.

$(t + 5)(t - 2) = t(t - 2) + 5(t - 2)$
$= t^2 - 2t + 5t - 10$
$= t^2 + 3t - 10$

Example 3   Expand $(m - 3)(m + 1)$.

$(m - 3)(m + 1) = m(m + 1) - 3(m + 1)$
$= m^2 + m - 3m - 3$
$= m^2 - 2m - 3$

Example 4   Expand $(k - 3)(k - 2)$.

$(k - 3)(k - 2) = k(k - 2) - 3(k - 2)$
$= k^2 - 2k - 3k + 6$
$= k^2 - 5k + 6$

Warning   Be careful with the signs, since this is the main place where marks are lost in examination questions involving the expansion of brackets.

EXERCISE 14E

Expand the following expressions.

1 $(x + 3)(x + 2)$ **2** $(t + 4)(t + 3)$ **3** $(w + 1)(w + 3)$ **4** $(m + 5)(m + 1)$

5 $(k + 3)(k + 5)$ **6** $(a + 4)(a + 1)$ **7** $(x + 4)(x - 2)$ **8** $(t + 5)(t - 3)$

9 $(w + 3)(w - 1)$ **10** $(f + 2)(f - 3)$ **11** $(g + 1)(g - 4)$ **12** $(y + 4)(y - 3)$

13 $(x - 3)(x + 4)$ **14** $(p - 2)(p + 1)$ **15** $(k - 4)(k + 2)$ **16** $(y - 2)(y + 5)$

17 $(a - 1)(a + 3)$ **18** $(t - 3)(t + 4)$ **19** $(x - 4)(x - 1)$ **20** $(r - 3)(r - 2)$

21 $(m - 3)(m - 1)$ **22** $(g - 4)(g - 2)$ **23** $(h - 5)(h - 3)$ **24** $(n - 1)(n - 4)$

25 $(5 + x)(4 + x)$ **26** $(6 + t)(3 - t)$ **27** $(3 - b)(5 + b)$ **28** $(5 - y)(1 - y)$

29 $(2 + p)(p - 3)$ **30** $(5 - k)(k - 2)$

The expansions of the expressions below follow a pattern. Work out the first few and try to spot the pattern that will allow you immediately to write down the answers to the rest.

31 $(x + 3)(x - 3)$ **32** $(t + 5)(t - 5)$ **33** $(m + 4)(m - 4)$ **34** $(t + 2)(t - 2)$

35 $(y + 8)(y - 8)$ **36** $(p + 1)(p - 1)$ **37** $(5 + x)(5 - x)$ **38** $(7 + g)(7 - g)$

39 $(x - 6)(x + 6)$

All the algebraic terms in Exercise 14E have a coefficient of 1 or −1. The next two examples show you what to do if you have to expand brackets containing algebraic terms whose coefficients are not 1 or −1.

Example 1   Expand $(2t + 3)(3t + 1)$.

$$(2t + 3)(3t + 1) = 2t(3t + 1) + 3(3t + 1)$$
$$= 6t^2 + 2t + 9t + 3$$
$$= 6t^2 + 11t + 3$$

Example 2   Expand $(4x - 1)(3x - 5)$.

$$(4x - 1)(3x - 5) = 4x(3x - 5) - (3x - 5) \text{ [Note: } (3x - 5) \text{ is the same as } 1(3x - 5).]$$
$$= 12x^2 - 20x - 3x + 5$$
$$= 12x^2 - 23x + 5$$

EXERCISE 14F

Expand the following expressions.

1 $(2x + 3)(3x + 1)$ **2** $(3y + 2)(4y + 3)$ **3** $(3t + 1)(2t + 5)$

4 $(4t + 3)(2t - 1)$ **5** $(5m + 2)(2m - 3)$ **6** $(4k + 3)(3k - 5)$

7 $(3p - 2)(2p + 5)$ **8** $(5w + 2)(2w + 3)$ **9** $(2a - 3)(3a + 1)$

10 $(4r - 3)(2r - 1)$ **11** $(3g - 2)(5g - 2)$ **12** $(4d - 1)(3d + 2)$

13 $(5 + 2p)(3 + 4p)$ **14** $(2 + 3t)(1 + 2t)$ **15** $(4 + 3p)(2p + 1)$

16 $(6 + 5t)(1 - 2t)$ **17** $(4 + 3n)(3 - 2n)$ **18** $(2 + 3f)(2f - 3)$

19 $(3 - 2q)(4 + 5q)$ **20** $(1 - 3p)(3 + 2p)$ **21** $(4 - 2t)(3t + 1)$

22 $(3 - 4r)(1 - 2r)$ **23** $(5 - 2x)(1 - 4x)$ **24** $(3 - 4m)(3m - 2)$

Try to spot the pattern in the following expressions so that you can immediately write down their expansions.

25 $(2x + 1)(2x - 1)$ **26** $(3t + 2)(3t - 2)$ **27** $(5y + 3)(5y - 3)$

28 $(4m + 3)(4m - 3)$ **29** $(2k - 3)(2k + 3)$ **30** $(4h - 1)(4h + 1)$

31 $(2 + 3x)(2 - 3x)$ **32** $(5 + 2t)(5 - 2t)$ **33** $(6 - 5y)(6 + 5y)$

Expanding squares

Example 1 Expand $(x + 3)^2$.

$$(x + 3)^2 = (x + 3)(x + 3)$$
$$= x(x + 3) + 3(x + 3)$$
$$= x^2 + 3x + 3x + 9$$
$$= x^2 + 6x + 9$$

Example 2 Expand $(3x - 2)^2$.

$$(3x - 2)^2 = (3x - 2)(3x - 2)$$
$$= 3x(3x - 2) - 2(3x - 2)$$
$$= 9x^2 - 6x - 6x + 4$$
$$= 9x^2 - 12x + 4$$

EXERCISE 14G

Expand the following squares.

1 $(x + 5)^2$ **2** $(m + 4)^2$ **3** $(6 + t)^2$ **4** $(3 + p)^2$

5 $(m - 3)^2$ **6** $(t - 5)^2$ **7** $(4 - m)^2$ **8** $(7 - k)^2$

9 $(3x + 1)^2$ **10** $(4t + 3)^2$ **11** $(2 + 5y)^2$ **12** $(3 + 2m)^2$

13 $(4t - 3)^2$ **14** $(3x - 2)^2$ **15** $(2 - 5t)^2$ **16** $(6 - 5r)^2$

17 $(x + y)^2$ **18** $(m - n)^2$ **19** $(2t + y)^2$ **20** $(m - 3n)^2$

Quadratic factorisation

This is putting a quadratic expression back into its brackets (if possible). For the intermediate level in GCSE, you need to be able to factorise only one type of quadratic expression:

$$x^2 + ax + b$$

where a and b are integers.

Sometimes it is easy to put a quadratic expression back into its brackets, other times it seems hard. However, there are three simple rules that will help you to factorise.

- The signs start off the brackets.

  $x^2 + ax + b = (x + ?)(x + ?)$ since everything is positive.

  $x^2 - ax + b = (x - ?)(x - ?)$ since $-$ve $\times$ $-$ve $= +$ve.

  ○ When the **second** sign in the expression is a *plus*, both bracket signs are the **same** as the **first** sign.

  ○ When the **second** sign is a *minus*, the bracket signs are **different**.

  $x^2 + ax - b = (x + ?)(x - ?)$ since $+$ve $\times$ $-$ve $= -$ve.

  $x^2 - ax - b = (x + ?)(x - ?)$

- Next, look at the **last** number, b, in the expression. When multiplied together, the two numbers in the brackets must give b.

- Finally, look at the **middle** number, a.

  - When the bracket signs are the **same**, the **sum** of the numbers in the brackets must be a.

  - When the bracket signs are **different**, the **difference** between the numbers in the brackets must be a.

Follow through Examples 1 to 5 below to see how easy it is to apply these rules.

Example 1   Factorise $x^2 + 7x + 12$.

- We note that both brackets must start with an x: $(x\quad)(x\quad)$

- We see that the second sign is +, hence both bracket signs must be the same as the first sign, which is +. So the brackets become

  $$(x +\quad)(x +\quad)$$

- We note that the bracket numbers when multiplied together must give 12. That is, we have three choices: 1, 12 or 2, 6 or 3, 4.

- As the bracket signs are the same, we know that the bracket numbers must add up to 7. Hence, we must choose 3, 4.

- So the brackets finally become

  $$(x + 3)(x + 4)$$

To prove that the method has worked, just multiply out this expression.

Example 2   Factorise $x^2 - 16x + 15$.

- We note that both brackets must start with an x: $(x\quad)(x\quad)$

- We see that the second sign is +, so both bracket signs must be the same as the first sign, which is −. So the brackets become

  $$(x -\quad)(x -\quad)$$

- We note that the bracket numbers when multiplied together must give 15. That is, we have two choices: 1, 15 or 3, 5.

- As the bracket signs are the same, we know that the bracket numbers must add up to 16. Hence, we must choose 1, 15.

- So the brackets finally become

  $$(x - 1)(x - 15)$$

To prove that the method has worked, just multiply out this expression.

Example 3 Factorise $t^2 + 2t - 8$.

- We note both brackets must start with a t: $(t\quad)(t\quad)$

- We see that the second sign is $-$, hence the bracket signs must be different. So the brackets become

    $(t+\quad)(t-\quad)$

- We note the bracket numbers when multiplied together must give 8. That is, we have two choices: $1, 8$ or $2, 4$.

- As the bracket signs are different, we know that we must use the difference between the bracket numbers, which is 2. Hence, we must choose $2, 4$.

- We now have to decide which number goes with $-$ and which with $+$. Since the middle term, $2t$, is positive, we need the positive value of t to be greater than its negative value. Hence, the larger number goes with $+$.

- So the brackets finally become

    $(t+4)(t-2)$

To prove that the method has worked, just multiply out $-$ as in the previous examples.

Example 4 Factorise $x^2 - 2x - 24$.

- We note both brackets must start with an x: $(x\quad)(x\quad)$

- We see that the second sign is $-$, hence both bracket signs must be different. So the brackets become

    $(x+\quad)(x-\quad)$

- We note the bracket numbers when multiplied together must give 24. That is, we have four choices: $1, 24$ or $2, 12$ or $3, 8$ or $4, 6$.

- As the signs in the brackets are different, we know that we must use the difference between the bracket numbers, which is 2. Hence, we must choose $4, 6$.

- We now have to decide which number goes with $-$ and which with $+$. Since the middle term, $2x$, is negative, we need the negative value of x to be greater than its positive value. Hence, the larger number goes with $-$.

- So the brackets finally become

    $(x+4)(x-6)$

As in the previous examples, multiply out to prove that the factorisation is correct.

Example 5   Factorise $x^2 - 36$ (the difference of two squares).

- If we write this as $x^2 + 0x - 36$, it will help us to see a pattern.

- We note that the brackets must start with an x: $(x \quad)(x \quad)$

- We see the second sign is $-$, hence the bracket signs must be different. So the brackets become

$$(x + \quad)(x - \quad)$$

- As the difference between the bracket numbers is 0, they must be the same.

- The product of the bracket numbers must be 36. So both must be 6.

- So the brackets finally become

$$(x + 6)(x - 6)$$

Difference of two squares

This last example shows a pattern of factorisation that will always work for the difference of two squares such as

$$x^2 - 9 \qquad x^2 - 25 \qquad x^2 - 4 \qquad x^2 - 100$$

- The pattern is x^2 minus a square number (n^2).

- Its factors are $(x + n)(x - n)$.

Expanding these brackets shows that they come from the original expression.

EXERCISE 14H

Factorise the following.

1 $x^2 + 5x + 6$	**2** $t^2 + 5t + 4$	**3** $m^2 + 7m + 10$	**4** $k^2 + 10k + 24$
5 $p^2 + 14p + 24$	**6** $r^2 + 9r + 18$	**7** $w^2 + 11w + 18$	**8** $x^2 + 7x + 12$
9 $a^2 + 8a + 12$	**10** $k^2 + 10k + 21$	**11** $f^2 + 22f + 21$	**12** $b^2 + 20b + 96$
13 $t^2 - 5t + 6$	**14** $d^2 - 5d + 4$	**15** $g^2 - 7g + 10$	**16** $x^2 - 15x + 36$
17 $c^2 - 18c + 32$	**18** $t^2 - 13t + 36$	**19** $y^2 - 16y + 48$	**20** $j^2 - 14j + 48$
21 $p^2 - 8p + 15$	**22** $y^2 + 5y - 6$	**23** $t^2 + 2t - 8$	**24** $x^2 + 3x - 10$
25 $m^2 - 4m - 12$	**26** $r^2 - 6r - 7$	**27** $n^2 - 3n - 18$	**28** $m^2 - 7m - 44$
29 $w^2 - 2w - 24$	**30** $t^2 - t - 90$	**31** $h^2 - h - 72$	**32** $t^2 - 2t - 63$
33 $d^2 + 2d + 1$	**34** $y^2 + 20y + 100$	**35** $t^2 - 8t + 16$	**36** $m^2 - 18m + 81$
37 $x^2 - 24x + 144$	**38** $d^2 - d - 12$	**39** $t^2 - t - 20$	**40** $q^2 - q - 56$
41 $p^2 + p - 2$	**42** $v^2 + 2v - 35$	**43** $t^2 + 4t + 3$	**44** $m^2 - 3m - 4$
45 $x^2 - x - 6$			

All the following are the difference of two squares. Factorise them.

46 $x^2 - 9$	**47** $t^2 - 25$	**48** $m^2 - 16$	**49** $9 - x^2$
50 $49 - t^2$	**51** $k^2 - 100$		

Solving the quadratic equation $x^2 + ax + b = 0$

To solve a quadratic equation such as $x^2 - 2x - 3 = 0$, you first have to be able to factorise it. Follow through Examples 1 to 3 below to see how this is done.

Example 1 Solve $x^2 + 6x + 5 = 0$.

This factorises into $(x + 5)(x + 1) = 0$

The only way this expression can ever equal 0 is if the value of one of the brackets is 0. Hence

$$\text{either} \quad (x + 5) = 0 \quad \text{or} \quad (x + 1) = 0$$
$$\Rightarrow \quad x + 5 = 0 \quad \text{or} \quad x + 1 = 0$$
$$\Rightarrow \quad x = -5 \quad \text{or} \quad x = -1$$

So the solution is $x = -5$ and $x = -1$.

Example 2 Solve $x^2 + 3x - 10 = 0$.

This factorises into $(x + 5)(x - 2) = 0$

$$\text{Hence} \quad x + 5 = 0 \quad \text{or} \quad x - 2 = 0$$
$$\Rightarrow \quad x = -5 \quad \text{or} \quad x = 2$$

So the solution is $x = -5$ and $x = 2$.

Example 3 Solve $x^2 - x = 7$.

We first have to rewrite the equation so that it equals 0. To do this, move the 7 across to the left-hand side:

$$x^2 - x - 7 = 0$$

Now factorise into $(x + 3)(x - 4) = 0$

$$\text{Hence} \quad x + 3 = 0 \quad \text{or} \quad x - 4 = 0$$
$$\Rightarrow \quad x = -3 \quad \text{or} \quad x = 4$$

So the solution is $x = -3$ and $x = 4$.

EXERCISE 14I

Solve these equations.

1 $(x + 2)(x + 5) = 0$	**2** $(t + 3)(t + 1) = 0$	**3** $(a + 6)(a + 4) = 0$
4 $(x + 3)(x - 2) = 0$	**5** $(x + 1)(x - 3) = 0$	**6** $(t + 4)(t - 5) = 0$
7 $(x - 1)(x + 2) = 0$	**8** $(x - 2)(x + 5) = 0$	**9** $(a - 7)(a + 4) = 0$
10 $(x - 3)(x - 2) = 0$	**11** $(x - 1)(x - 5) = 0$	**12** $(a - 4)(a - 3) = 0$

First factorise, then solve these equations.

13 $x^2 + 5x + 4 = 0$	**14** $x^2 + 11x + 18 = 0$	**15** $x^2 - 6x + 8 = 0$
16 $x^2 - 8x + 15 = 0$	**17** $x^2 - 3x - 10 = 0$	**18** $x^2 - 2x - 15 = 0$
19 $t^2 + 4t - 12 = 0$	**20** $t^2 + 3t - 18 = 0$	**21** $x^2 - x - 2 = 0$

First rearrange these equations, then solve them.

22 $x^2 + 10x = -24$ **23** $x^2 - 18x = -32$ **24** $x^2 + 2x = 24$ **25** $x^2 + 3x = 54$

26 $t^2 + 7t = 30$ **27** $x^2 - 7x = 44$ **28** $t^2 - t = 72$ **29** $x^2 = 17x - 72$

30 $x^2 + 1 = 2x$

Transposition of formulae

The subject of a formula is the variable (letter) in the formula which stands on its own, usually on the left-hand side of the 'equals' sign. For example, x is the subject of each of the following:

$$x = 5t + 4 \qquad x = 4(2y - 7) \qquad x = \frac{1}{t}$$

If we wish to change the existing subject to a different variable, we have to rearrange (transpose) the formula to get that variable on the left-hand side.

We do this by using the same rule as that for solving equations: move the terms concerned from one side of the 'equals' sign to the other.

Follow through Examples 1 to 3 below to see how the process works.

Example 1   Make m the subject of $T = 5m - 3$.

Move the 3 away from the $5m$: $T + 3 = 5m$

Move the 5 away from the m: $\dfrac{T + 3}{5} = m$

Change to opposite sides and the transposed formula becomes $m = \dfrac{T + 3}{5}$

Example 2   From the formula $P = 3(4t + 1)$, express t in terms of P.
[This is another common way of asking you to make t the subject.]

Expand the bracket: $P = 12t + 3$

Move the 3 away from the $12t$: $P - 3 = 12t$

Move the 12 away from the t: $\dfrac{P - 3}{12} = t$

Change to opposite sides and the transposed formula becomes $t = \dfrac{P - 3}{12}$

Example 3   From the formula $C = m^2 - t$, **i** make m the subject, **ii** make t the subject.

i   Make m the subject.

Move the t away from the m^2: $C + t = m^2$

Take the square root of both sides: $\sqrt{(C + t)} = m$

Change to opposite sides and the transformed formula becomes $m = \sqrt{(C + t)}$

ii   Make t the subject.

Take over t to make it positive: $C + t = m^2$

Move the C away from the t: $t = m^2 - C$

The transformed formula is $t = m^2 - C$

EXERCISE 14J

1. $T = 3k - 2$ Make k the subject.
2. $P = 2m + 7$ Make m the subject.
3. $X = 5y - 1$ Express y in terms of X.
4. $Q = 8p + 3$ Express p in terms of Q.
5. $A = 4r - 9$ Make r the subject.
6. $W = 3n + t$ **i** Make n the subject.   **ii** Express t in terms of n and W.
7. $x = 5y - w$ **i** Make y the subject.   **ii** Express w in terms of x and y.
8. $p = 7m + t$ **i** Make m the subject.   **ii** Make t the subject.
9. $t = 2k - f$ **i** Express k in terms of f and t.   **ii** Make f the subject.
10. $g = 6m + v$ **i** Express m in terms of v and g.   **ii** Make v the subject.
11. $t = m^2$ Make m the subject.
12. $k = p^2$ Make p the subject.
13. $a = b^2 + 3$ Make b the subject.
14. $w = h^2 - 5$ Express h in terms of w.
15. $m = p^2 + 2$ Make p the subject.
16. $v = u^2 - t$ **i** Make t the subject.   **ii** Make u the subject.
17. $k = m + n^2$ **i** Make m the subject.   **ii** Make n the subject.
18. $T = 5r^2$ Make r the subject.
19. $P = 3t^2$ Make t the subject.
20. $K = 5n^2 + w$ **i** Make w the subject.   **ii** Make n the subject.

Possible coursework tasks

Handshakes

At an annual dinner, all 500 guests were asked to introduce themselves to each other and shake hands.

a How many handshakes will there be that evening?

b How many handshakes would there be if, halfway through the evening, N number of guests suddenly left and shook no more hands? (Assume 'halfway' means that only half the people were introduced by that time.)

Sums and products

Solve $x^2 - 5x + 6 = 0$.

a What is the sum of both solutions?

b What is the product of both solutions?

c Investigate this for other quadratic equations.

Examination questions

1   A rocket is fired vertically upwards with a velocity u metres per second. After t seconds, the rocket's velocity, v metres per second, is given by the formula

$v = u + gt$ (where g is a constant)

   a   Calculate v when $u = 100$, $g = -9.8$ and $t = 5$.

   b   Rearrange the formula to express t in terms of v, u and g.

   c   Calculate t when $u = 93.5$, $g = -9.8$ and $v = 20$.

NEAB, Question 17, Specimen Paper 11, 1998

2   The length of a man's forearm (f cm) and his height (h cm) are approximately related by the formula $h = 3f + 90$.

   a   Part of a skeleton is found and the forearm is 20 cm long. Use the formula to estimate the man's height.

   b   Use the formula to find an expression for f in terms of h.

MEG, Question 7, Specimen Paper 4, 1998

3   Make x the subject of the formula $y = \dfrac{x^2 + 4}{5}$

EDEXCEL, Question 24, Intermediate Paper 3, June 2000

4   Make p the subject of the formula $\dfrac{4(p + 3)}{7} = r$

AQA (North), Question 17, Intermediate Paper 1, June 2000

5   **a**   Expand and simplify $(x + 5)(x - 3)$

   b   Factorise completely $6a^2 - 9ab$

EDEXCEL, Question 20, Intermediate Paper 4, June 2000

6   **a**   Factorise completely $6x^2 - 9xy$

   b   **i**   Factorise $x^2 - 8x + 12$

      ii   Hence solve $x^2 - 8x + 12 = 0$

OCR, Question 15, Intermediate (A) Paper 4, June 2000

7   **a**   Factorise $2ab - a$.

   b   Solve the equations

      i $3(x - 1) = 15$ **ii** $x^2 - 5x + 6 = 0$

SEG, Question 18, Specimen Paper 13, 1998

8   **a**   Expand the following expression, simplifying your answer as far as possible. $(3x - 4)(2x + 3)$

   b   Make c the subject of the equation $\dfrac{bc^2}{d} = 6$

WJEC, Question 23, Intermediate Paper 2, June 1999

9   A rectangle has a length of $(x + 5)$ cm and a width of $(x - 2)$ cm.

   a   If the perimeter of the rectangle is 24 cm, what is the value of x?

   b   **i**   If the area of the rectangle is 60 cm^2, show that $x^2 + 3x - 70 = 0$.

      ii   Find the value of x when the area of the rectangle is 60 cm^2.

NEAB, Question 23, Specimen Paper 21, 1998

10 a Simplify $3x - 2xy + 7y + 4x + yx$.

    b Factorise completely $6p^2 - 8p$.

    c Expand and simplify $(2x - 3)(x + 5)$.

MEG, Question 16, Specimen Paper 3, 1998

Summary

How well do you grade yourself?

To gain a grade **E**, you need to be able to expand a simple expression.

To gain a grade **D**, you need to be able to use and change the subject of simple formulae.

To gain a grade **C**, you need to be able to manipulate simple formulae, equations and expressions. You also need to be able to expand a two-bracket expression.

To gain a grade **B**, you need to be able to factorise quadratic expressions and to solve quadratic equations by factorising.

What you should know after you have worked through Chapter 14

- How to expand expressions such as $5m(2m - t)$.

- How to expand expressions such as $(3x - 2)(4x + 5)$.

- How to factorise into either one or two brackets.

- How to factorise a simple quadratic expression such as $x^2 - 2x - 3$.

- How to solve a quadratic equation such as $x^2 - 2x - 3 = 0$.

- How to transpose a formula to change its subject.

Revision paper for Chapters 1 to 14

Answer **all** questions, showing your methods of solution.

1 Evaluate
    a $-3 - 7$ **b** -3×-6 **c** $-20 \div 4$ **d** $-3 + 7$

2 Water evaporates one day at the rate of 15% per hour. A garden pool started the day, at 9.00 am, full with 65 litres of water. How much water is still in the pool at
    i 10 am   **ii** 12 noon?

3 **a** It took me 3 hours 20 minutes to travel 250 miles. What was my average speed?
    b How long will it take me to travel 130 miles at an average speed of 50 mph?
    c I travelled along a motorway for four and a half hours at an average speed of 70 mph. How far had I travelled?

4 Calculate the perimeter and the area of each of these shapes.

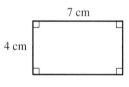
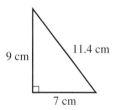
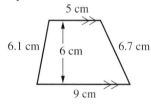

5 A block of metal, measuring 2 cm by 3 cm by 1 metre, is rolled into wire of radius 1 mm. How long is the wire?

6 **a** Solve these equations.
    i $4x + 3 = 17$ **ii** $\dfrac{5x - 2}{4} = 3$
    b Solve $x^3 + x = 100$, correct to 1 decimal place.

7 **a** What is the size of an exterior angle of a regular decagon?
    b How many sides has a regular polygon that has an interior angle of 165°?

8 **a** Draw the triangle ABC with co-ordinates A(2, 1), B(4, 1), C(4, 2).
    b Reflect ABC in the y-axis and label the image (i).
    c Rotate ABC about the origin 90° clockwise and label the new position (ii).
    d Describe clearly the single operation that would transform shape (i) into shape (ii).

9 **a** Construct an equilateral triangle ABC of side 6 cm.
    b Bisect angle B, showing clearly your method.
    c Bisect side BC, showing clearly your method.
    d Use the point of intersection of your two bisectors as the centre of a circle, and draw the circle passing through point A.

10 Draw a diagram to illustrate a tessellation of a hexagon.

11 $a = 3.7 \times 10^8$ $\qquad b = 1.9 \times 10^{-5}$

Evaluate the following, leaving your answers in standard form.

i $\quad ab$ $\qquad$ **ii** $a \div b$ $\qquad$ **iii** $\sqrt{a}$ $\qquad$ **iv** b^2

12 Solve the simultaneous equations

$$6x + 5y = 67$$
$$2x - y = 17$$

13 The following results were obtained by Y10 in their maths exams.
Calculate an estimate of the mean mark.

Mark x	$0 < x \le 25$	$25 < x \le 50$	$50 < x \le 75$	$75 < x \le 100$
Frequency	4	39	53	26

14 **a** Expand and simplify $(x + 3)(x - 5)$.

b Solve $x^2 + 5x + 6 = 0$.

15 Graphs 1

This chapter is going to ...

remind you about conversion graphs and travel graphs. It will also introduce you to the idea of the gradient of a straight line.

What you should already know

✔ Be familiar with conversion graphs and be able to read information from them.

✔ Be able to read information from travel graphs.

Look at these two examples and make sure that you follow through the conversions

Example 1   This is a conversion graph between litres and gallons.

From the graph we can see that:

   5 gallons are approximately equivalent to 23 litres

   15 litres are approximately equivalent to $3\frac{1}{4}$ gallons

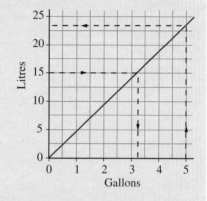

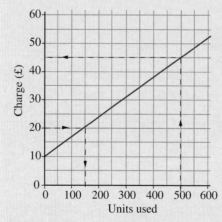

Example 2   A graph of the charges made in 1996 for units of electricity used in the home is shown here.

From the graph we can see that:

   If a customer uses 500 units of electricity, that customer will be charged £45.

   If a customer is charged £20, that customer will have used about 150 units.

You need to be able to read these types of graph by finding a value on one axis and following it through to the other axis, as shown in Examples 1 and 2.

EXERCISE 15A

1 The following is a conversion graph between kilograms (kg) and pounds (lb).

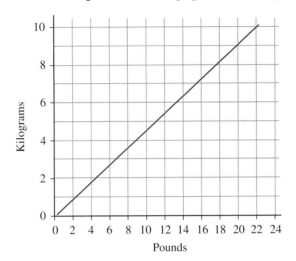

a Use the graph to approximately convert:
  i 18 lb to kilograms
  ii 5 lb to kilograms
  iii 4 kg to pounds
  iv 10 kg to pounds.
b Approximately how many pounds are equivalent to 1 kg?

2 The following is a conversion graph between inches (in) and centimetres (cm).

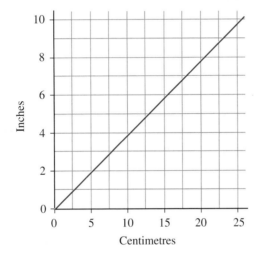

a Use the graph to approximately convert:
  i 4 in to centimetres
  ii 9 in to centimetres
  iii 5 cm to inches
  iv 22 cm to inches.
b Approximately how many centimetres are equivalent to 1 inch?

3 The following graph was produced to show the approximate equivalence of the British £ to the Singapore $ during the summer of 1995.

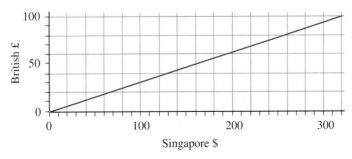

a Use the graph to approximately convert
  i £100 to Singapore $
  ii £30 to Singapore $
  iii $150 to British £
  iv $250 to British £
b Approximately how many Singapore $ are equivalent to £1?

263

4 A hire firm hired out industrial blow heaters. They used this graph to approximate what the charges would be.

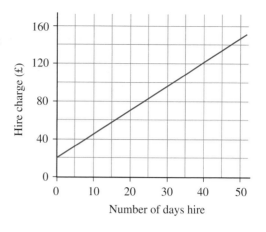

a Use the graph to find the approximate charge for hiring a heater for

   i 40 days   **ii** 25 days

b Use the graph to find out how many days hire you would get for a cost of

   i £100   **ii** £150

c Why does the graph show that you appear to pay £20 for hiring a heater for no days at all?

5 A conference centre had this chart on the office wall so that the staff could see the approximate cost of a conference based on the number of people attending it.

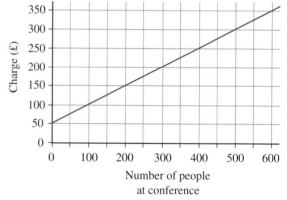

a Use the graph to find the approximate charge for

   i 100 people

   ii 550 people

b Use the graph to estimate how many people can attend a conference at the centre for a cost of

   i £300   **ii** £175

c Why does the centre appear to charge £50 even if nobody uses the conference centre?

6 At a small shop, the manager priced all goods at the pre-VAT prices and the sales assistant had to use the following chart to convert these prices to selling prices.

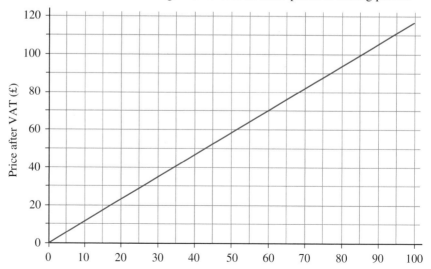

a Use the chart to find the selling price of goods marked **i** £60 **ii** £25.

b What was the marked price if you bought something for **i** £100 **ii** £45?

7 Amanda did an experiment at school. She put a series of different weights on the end of a spring, measuring its length after putting on each weight. She then drew this graph from her results.

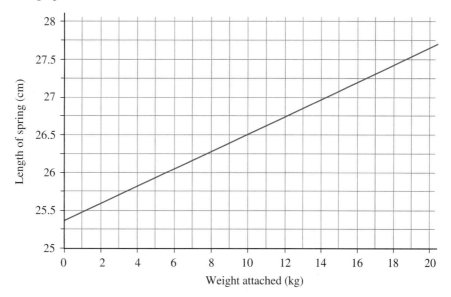

a Use the graph to find the length of the spring with the following weights on its end:

i 10 kg **ii** 19 kg

b What weights were on the end of the spring when its length was

i 26 cm **ii** 27.25 cm?

c What is the length of the spring when no weight is on its end?

8 When Leon travelled abroad in his car he always took this conversion graph. It helped him to convert between miles and kilometres.

a Use the graph to approximately convert

i 25 miles to kilometres

ii 10 miles to kilometres

iii 40 km to miles

iv 15 km to miles

b Approximately how many kilometres are equivalent to 5 miles?

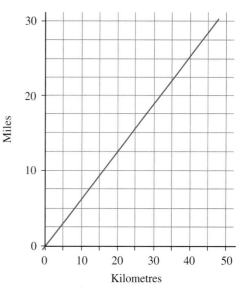

9 Granny McAllister still finds it hard to think in degrees Celsius. So she always uses the following conversion graph to help her to understand the weather forecast.

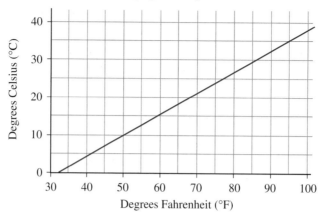

a Use the graph to approximately convert

    i 35 °C to Fahrenheit

    ii 20 °C to Fahrenheit

    iii 50 °F to Celsius

    iv 90 °F to Celsius

b Water freezes at 0 °C, what temperature is this in Fahrenheit?

10 Concrete was sold in cubic yards for many years. In 1995 Mr Hutchinson was told that he now had to sell it in cubic metres (m³). He made himself the following conversion graph to help him get to grips with the new measure.

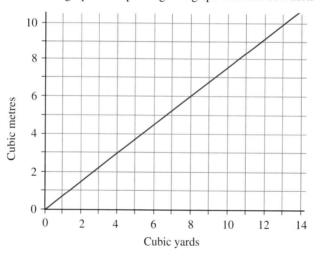

a Use the graph to approximately convert

    i 4 cubic yards to m³   **ii** 11 cubic yards to m³

    iii 10 m³ to cubic yards   **iv** 5 m³ to cubic yards

b Approximately how big in cubic yards is 1 m³?

11 Tea is sold at a school fete between 1.00 pm and 3.30 pm. The numbers of cups of tea that had been sold were noted at half-hour intervals.

Time	1.00	1.30	2.00	2.30	3.00	3.30
No. of cups of tea sold	0	24	48	72	96	120

    a Draw a graph to illustrate this information.

    b Use your graph to estimate when the 60th cup of tea was sold.

12 I lost my fuel bill, but while talking to my friends I found out that

> Bill who had used 850 units was charged £57.50
> Wendy who had used 320 units was charged £31
> Rhanni who had used 540 units was charged £42

    a Plot the given information and draw a straight-line graph.

    b Use your graph to find what I will be charged for using 700 units.

Travel graphs

As the name suggest, a travel graph gives information about how far someone or something has travelled. It is also called a 'distance–time' graph. A travel graph is read in a similar way to the conversion graphs you have just done. But you can also find the average speed from a distance–time graph by using the formula

$$\text{Average speed} = \frac{\text{Total distance travelled}}{\text{Time taken}}$$

Remember the helpful diagram on page 51. You can use it again here to recall the relationships between speed, time and distance.

Example The distance–time graph below represents a car journey from Barnsley to Nottingham, a distance of 50 km, and back again.

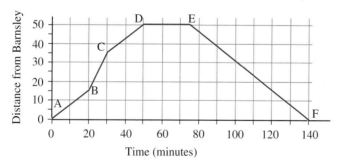

From the graph, we can read the following information.

> After 10 minutes the car was 8 km away from Barnsley.
> After 50 minutes the car was 50 km away from Barnsley, at Nottingham.
> The car stayed at Nottingham for 25 minutes, and took 65 minutes for the return journey.

The average speeds over the four stages of the journey are worked out as follows.

A to B represents 16 km in 20 minutes.

Multiplying both numbers by 3 gives 48 km in 60 minutes, which is 48 km/h.

B to C represents 19 km in 10 minutes.

Multiplying both numbers by 6 gives 114 km in 60 minutes, which is 114 km/h.

D to E represents a stop, where no further distance had been travelled.

E to F represents the return journey of 50 km in 65 minutes.

Divide 50 by 65 to give km per minute, then multiply by 60 to find km per hour. Hence

$$(50 \div 65) \times 60 = 46.2$$

The return journey was at an average speed of 46.2 km/h.

Changing units

Remember: to change a speed given in one set of units to its value in another set of units, you need to change the units stage by stage.

Work through Examples 1 and 2 below to remind yourself of the process.

Example 1   Change 15 metres per second to kilometres per hour.

15 m/s = 15 × 60 × 60 metres per hour = 54 000 m/h
54 000 m/h = 54 000 ÷ 1000 km/h = 54 km/h

Example 2   Change 24 kilometres per hour to metres per minute.

24 km/h = 24 × 1000 m/h = 24 000 m/h
24 000 m/h = 24 000 ÷ 60 m/min = 400 m/min

EXERCISE 15B

1   Paul was travelling in his car to a meeting. He set off from home at 7.00 am, and stopped on the way for a break. This distance–time graph illustrates his journey.

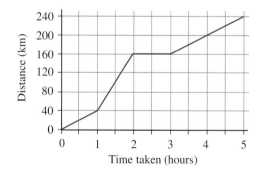

a At what time did he

   i stop for his break

   ii set off after his break

   iii get to his meeting place?

b At what average speed was he travelling

   i over the first hour

   ii over the second hour

   iii for the last part of his journey?

2 James was travelling to Cornwall on his holidays. This distance–time graph illustrates his journey.

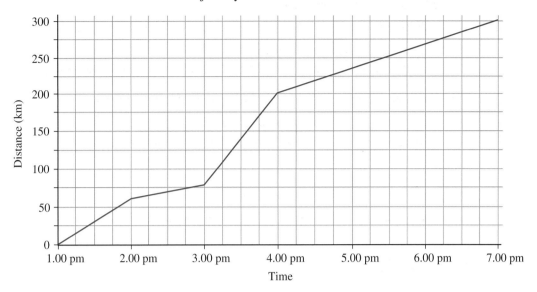

a His fastest speed was on the motorway.

  i How much motorway did he use?

  ii What was his average speed on the motorway.

b **i** When did he travel the slowest?

  ii What was his slowest average speed?

3 A small bus set off from Leeds to pick up Mike and his family. It then went on to pick up Mike's parents and grandparents, dropping them all off at a hotel. The bus then went on a further 10 km to pick up another party and took them back to Leeds. This distance–time graph illustrates the journey.

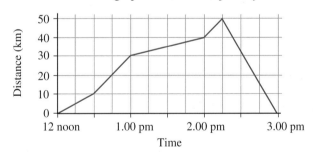

a How far from Leeds did Mike's parents and grandparents live?

b How far from Leeds is the hotel at which they all stayed?

c What was the average speed of the bus while returning the second party to Leeds?

4 Richard and Paul had a race. The distance covered is illustrated below.

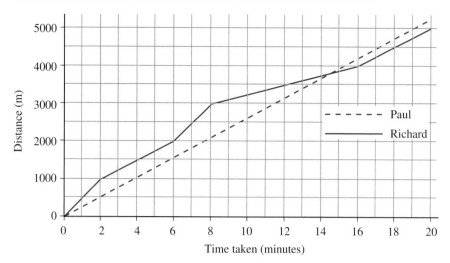

a Paul ran a steady race. What is his average speed in
  i metres per minute   **ii** km/h?
b Richard ran in spurts. What was his quickest average speed?
c Who won the race and by how much?

5 Azam and Jafar were having a race. The distance–time graph below illustrates the distances covered.

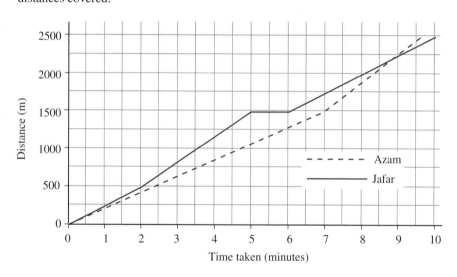

a Jafar stopped in the middle of the race. Why might this have happened?
b Write a description of this race, but do not include actual speeds.
c What was the fastest average speed that was run by
  i Azam in metres per minute
  ii Jafar in kilometres per hour?

6 Three school friends all set off from school at the same time, 3.45 pm. They all lived 12 km away from the school. The distance–time graph below illustrates their journeys.

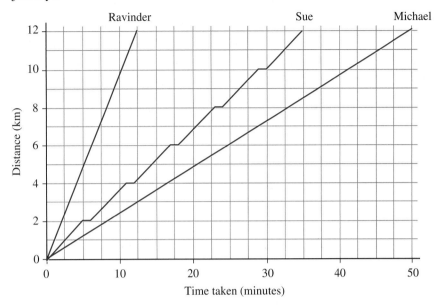

One of the friends went by bus, one cycled and one was taken by car.

a Who used which transport?

b At what time did each friend get home?

c When the bus was moving, what was its average speed in km/min?

d What was Michael's average speed on the journey home? Give your answer in km/h.

7 Dad took the family out in his car for a picnic. Billy followed on his bike. Dad waited at the agreed picnic site for Billy but he didn't turn up, so Dad drove to another site, where the family (apart from Billy) had a picnic. They then set off for home. Billy, meanwhile, rode to only the first picnic site, saw nobody there and so decided to go straight home. Part of the distance–time graph is shown below.

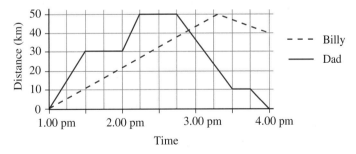

a How long did Dad spend at each site?

b What was Dad's fastest average speed?

c What was Billy's average speed on his way to the picnic site?

d i What average speed was Billy doing on his journey home?

    ii If he had continued at that speed, at what time would he have got home?

8 Three friends, Patrick, Araf and Sean, ran a 1000 metres race. The race is illustrated on the distance–time graph below.

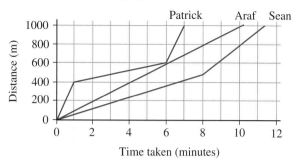

a Describe the race of each friend.

b **i** What is the average speed of Araf in m/s?

    ii What is this speed in km/h?

Rules from graphs

Many of the graphs we have already met represent simple rules or relationships. To help us understand these, we will look at two properties of straight-line graphs.

The gradient

The gradient of a straight line is a measure of its slope.

The gradient of the line shown below can be found by constructing a right-angled triangle whose hypotenuse (sloping side) is on the line. The gradient is then given by

$$\text{Gradient} = \frac{\text{Distance measured vertically}}{\text{Distance measured horizontally}} = \frac{6}{4} = 1.5$$

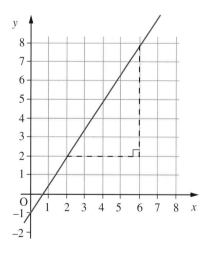

Look at the following examples of straight lines and their gradients.

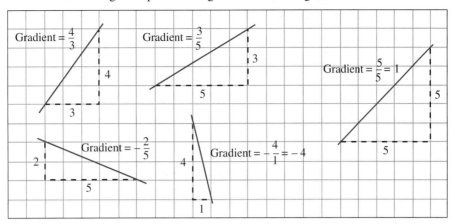

Notice Lines which slope downwards from left to right have **negative gradients**.

In the case of a straight-line graph between two quantities, its gradient is found using the **scales** on its axes, **not** the actual number of grid squares. It usually represents a third quantity whose value we want to know. For example, look at these four graphs.

The gradient on this distance–time graph represents average speed.

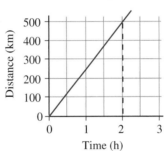

Gradient $= \dfrac{500}{2} = 250$ km/h

The gradient on this graph represents the price per unit.

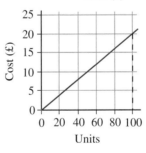

Gradient $= \dfrac{20}{100} = £0.20\,/\,\text{unit}$

The gradient on this graph represents the exchange rate between British pounds and French francs.

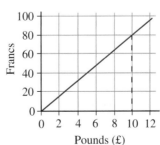

Gradient $= \dfrac{80}{10} = 8$ Fr/£

273

The gradient on this graph of a spring being stretched represents the extension per kilogram.

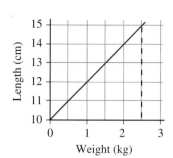

Gradient = $\frac{5}{2.5}$ = 2 cm/kg

In your GCSE examination, you will be expected to know that the gradient of a distance–time graph is speed, and to be able to work out what the gradient of a conversion graph represents. Here is a typical question you could be asked.

The following graph is a conversion graph between pounds (lb) and kilograms (kg).

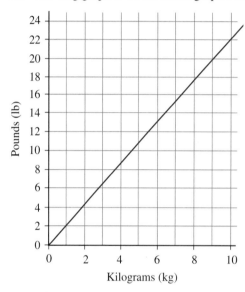

a Calculate the gradient of the line in the graph.

b Use the gradient to tell you how many pounds are equivalent to 1 kilogram.

Solution

a This is the largest right-angled triangle you can draw.

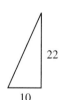

This gives a gradient = $\frac{22}{10}$ = 2.2

b Hence 1 kilogram = 2.2 lb.

EXERCISE 15C

1 Calculate the gradient of each line.

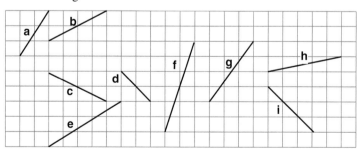

2 Calculate the gradient of each line, using the scales on the axes.

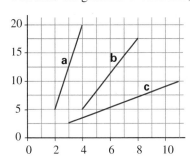
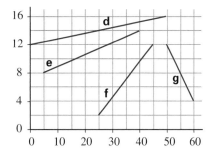

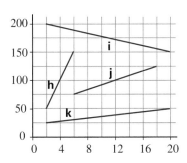
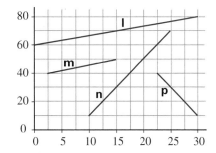

3 This graph gives the price of goods after VAT is added and their price before.

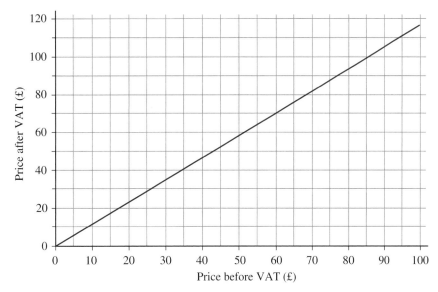

a Calculate the gradient of the line.

b How can you use this gradient to estimate the price of goods after VAT is added?

275

4   This is a conversion graph between inches and centimetres.

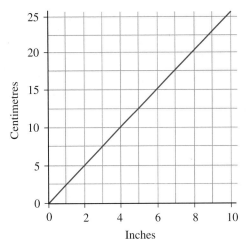

a   Calculate the gradient of the line.

b   Use the gradient of the line to find the number of centimetres equivalent to 1 inch.

5   This is a conversion graph between the British pound and the Singapore dollar.

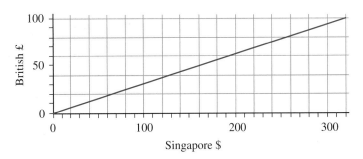

a   Calculate the gradient of the line.

b   Use the gradient of the line to find how much British money you will get for one Singapore dollar.

6   This is a conversion graph between miles and kilometres.

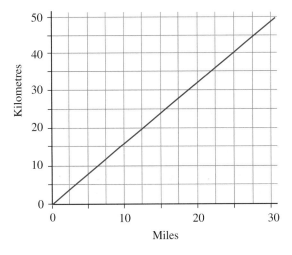

a   Calculate the gradient of the line.

b   Use the graph to find the number of kilometres equivalent to 1 mile.

7 This is a conversion graph between cubic metres and cubic feet

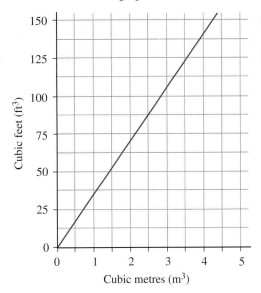

a Calculate the gradient of the line.

b Use the graph to find the number of cubic feet equivalent to 1 cubic metre.

8 This is a conversion graph between gallons and litres.

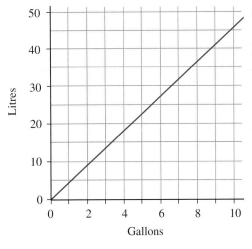

a Calculate the gradient of the line.

b Use the graph to find the number of litres equivalent to 1 gallon.

The constant

In all the graphs in Exercise 15C, the straight line passed through the origin. But in some cases the line doesn't pass through the origin, so the rule has to include a constant. Follow through this next example to see what to do.

Example A taxi fare will cost you more the further you go. The graph at the top of the next page illustrates the fares in one part of England.

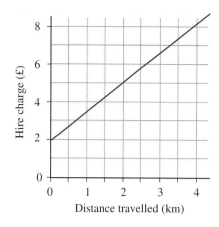

The taxi company charges a basic hire fee to start with of £2.00. This is shown on the graph as the point where the line cuts through the hire-charge axis (when distance travelled is 0).

The gradient of the line is

$$\frac{8-2}{4} = \frac{6}{4} = 1.5$$

This represents the hire charge per kilometre travelled.

So the total hire charge is made up of two parts: a basic hire charge of £2.00 and an additional charge of £1.50 per kilometre travelled. This can be put in a formula as

Hire charge = £2.00 + £1.50 per kilometre.

In this example, £2.00 is the constant in the rule.

EXERCISE 15D

1 This graph is a conversion graph between °C and °F.

a How many °F are equivalent to 0 °C?

b What is the gradient of the line?

c From your answers to parts **a** and **b**, write down a rule which can be used to convert °C to °F.

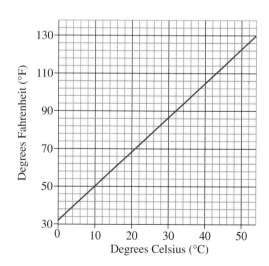

2 Each of the graphs represents a different taxi firm in a different part of Britain. In each case, find the basic hire charge by looking at the charge for a distance of 0, and the rate per kilometre by looking at the gradient. Then give the total hire charge as the sum of the two.

a

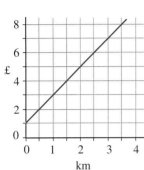

b

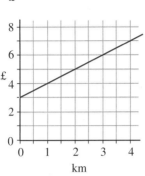

c

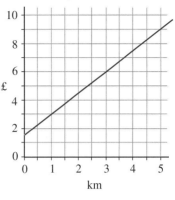

3 The following graph illustrates the charges for fuel.

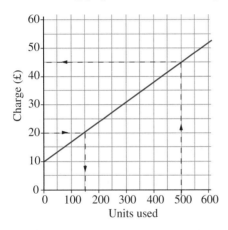

a What is the gradient of the line?

b The standing charge is the basic charge before the cost per unit is added. What is the standing charge?

c Write down the rule used to work out the total charge for different amounts of units used.

4 This graph shows the hire charge for heaters over so many days.

a Calculate the gradient of the line.

b What is the basic charge before the daily hire charge is added on?

c Write down the rule used to work out the total hire charge.

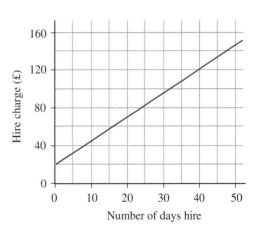

5 This graph shows the hire charge for a conference centre depending on the number of people at the conference.

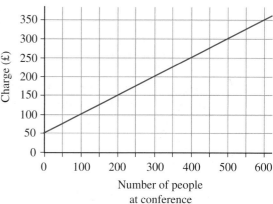

  a Calculate the gradient of the line.

  b What is the basic fee for hiring the conference centre?

  c Write down the rule used to work out the total hire charge for the centre.

6 This graph shows the length of a spring for different weights attached to it.

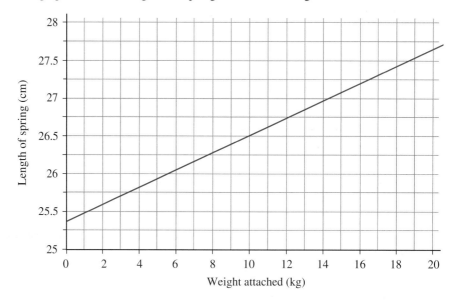

  a Calculate the gradient of the line.
  b How long is the spring when no weight is attached to it?
  c By how much does the spring extend per kilogram?
  d Write down the rule for finding the length of the spring for different weights.

Possible coursework tasks

Steep hill ahead

The road sign states that the hill ahead has a gradient of 15%. Investigate different ways of expressing gradients.

Gradients from co-ordinates

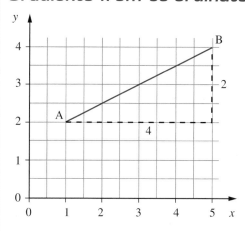

The line joining A(1, 2) to B(5, 4) has a gradient of

$$\frac{2}{4} = \frac{1}{2}$$

Can you find a way of calculating the gradient of a line joining two points just using their co-ordinates?

Money matters

Look up the Tourist Rates for different currencies in a newspaper. Choose a number of them and draw your own conversion graphs. Make a display that could be used in a local travel agency. (Your presentation could be improved if you use a computer graph plotter.)

Swimming pools

A swimming pool is being filled at the local sports centre.

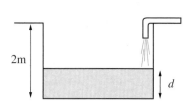

The hosepipe delivers water at a constant rate and it takes 30 minutes to fill the pool.

a Draw a graph to show how the depth of water (*d*) varies with time (*t*) as the pool fills with water.

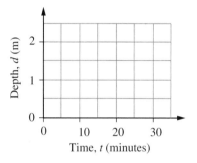

b Draw graphs as in part **a** for the two pools whose regular cross-sections are shown below. Each pool takes 30 minutes to fill.

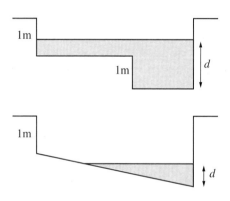

c Draw your own pools and comment on anything you notice for each one.

Examination questions

1   The distance–time graph shows the journeys made by a van and a car starting from Oxford, travelling to Luton, and returning to Oxford.

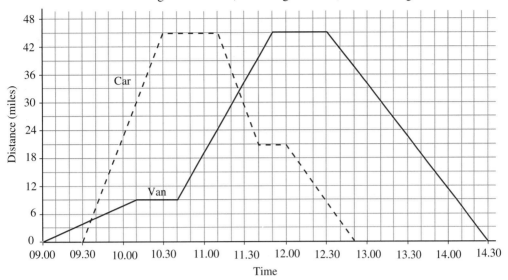

a   How far had the car travelled when it met the van for the second time?

b   Calculate, in miles per hour, the average speed of the car between 09.59 and 10.00.

c   During which period of time was the van travelling at its greatest average speed?

SEG, Question 9, Specimen Paper 14, 1998

2   The table shows the charge for using different numbers of units of electricity.

Units	0	200	500	700	900	1000
Charge £	10	34	70	94	118	130

a   Plot these points on a grid.

b   Use your graph to find
   i   the charge for using 600 units of electricity
   ii   how many units of electricity you have used if you are charged £50.

NEAB, Question 4, Specimen Paper 2, 1995

3   Elizabeth went for a cycle ride. The distance–time graph shows her ride.

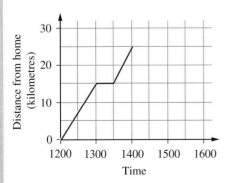

She set off from home at 1200 and had a flat tyre at 1400. During her ride, she stopped for a rest.

a   i   At what time did she stop for a rest?
   ii   At what speed did she travel after her rest?

It took Elizabeth 15 minutes to repair the flat tyre. She then cycled home at 25 kilometres per hour.

b   Copy and complete the distance–time graph to show this information.

EDEXCEL, Question 8, Intermediate Paper 4, June 2000

4 **a** Complete the table of values below for the equation $y = 120/x$.

x	10	15	20	30	40	50	60
y						2.4	

b Hence, on a grid with y from 0 to 12 and x from 0 to 60, draw the graph of $y = 120/x$.

c Use your graph to find the time to travel 120 km at a speed of 37 km/h.

d Given that 1 gallon is equivalent to 4.5 litres, use your graph to find the number of gallons in 120 litres.

OCR, Question 18, Intermediate (A) Paper 3, June 2000

5 The table shows the largest quantity of salt, w grams, which can be dissolved in a beaker of water at temperature t °C.

t °C	10	20	25	30	40	50	60
w **grams**	54	58	60	62	66	70	74

a On a grid plot the points and draw a graph to illustrate this information.

b Use your graph to find
  i the lowest temperature at which 63 g of salt will dissolve in water
  ii the largest amount of salt that will dissolve in the water at 44 °C.

c **i** The equation of the graph is of the form $w = at + b$. Use your graph to estimate the values of the constants a and b.
  ii Use the equation to calculate the largest amount of salt which will dissolve in the water at 95 °C.

NEAB, Question 19, Paper 1, June 1995

6 The graph below represents the journey of a train that travels from Shrewsbury to Hereford and then on to Newport.

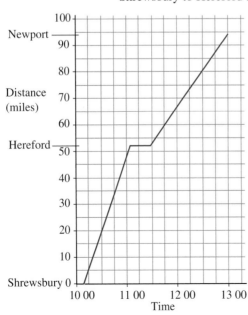

a Draw a copy of the graph.

b What was the average speed of the train from Shrewsbury to Hereford?

c How long did the train wait at Hereford?

d Without calculating another average speed, show how the graph can tell whether or not the average speed of the train from Hereford to Newport was more than its average speed from Shrewsbury to Hereford.

e Another train starts from Newport at 11.15 and travels non-stop to Shrewsbury at an average speed of 60 mph. Draw the graph of its journey on your graph.

f Write down how far from Hereford the trains were when they passed each other.

WJEC, Question 11, Specimen Paper 1, 1998

Summary

How well do you grade yourself?

To gain a grade **E**, you need to be able to use conversion graphs and interpret travel graphs.

To gain a grade **D**, you need to be able to draw a distance–time graph from information given.

To gain a grade **C**, you need to be able to calculate the gradient of a straight-line graph, as well as find the speed from a distance–time graph.

To gain a grade **B**, you need to be able to interpret the gradient on a straight-line graph and write down a rule or equation from a graph that illustrates two connected variables with a straight line.

What you should know after you have worked through Chapter 15

- How to use a conversion graph.

- How to draw and interpret distance–time graphs.

- How to find the gradient of a straight line.

- The relevance of the gradient of a straight-line graph.

- How to find a rule or equation from a straight-line graph.

16 Similarity

This chapter is going to ...

introduce you to similar triangles. It will also show you how to work out the scale factor between similar figures, and how to use this to calculate unknown sides in such figures.

What you should already know

✔ What congruency is.
✔ How to calculate a ratio.
✔ How to work out the square and cube of numbers.
✔ How to solve equations of the form $\frac{x}{9} = \frac{2}{3}$.

Discovery activity

Investigate similarity among these triangles.

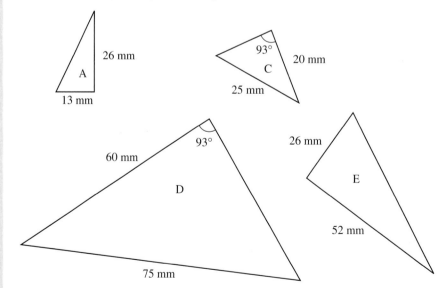

Triangle A goes with triangle E.

Triangle C goes with triangle D.

This is because each pair of triangles is **similar**.

Let's take a closer look at each pair of triangles.

Measure the sides and angles of triangle A.
Measure the sides and angles of triangle E.
You should find that the angles are the same and that the lengths of the sides of triangle E are twice those of the corresponding sides of triangle A.
This means that triangles A and E are **similar** because their corresponding angles are the same and their corresponding sides are in the ratio 1:2.
The enlargement from the smaller triangle to the larger is by a scale factor of 2.

Measure the sides of triangles C and D. You should find that the angles are the same and that the lengths of the sides of triangle D are three times those of triangle C. The triangles are similar and the scale factor is 3.

Similar triangles

Triangles are similar if their corresponding angles are equal. Their corresponding sides are then in the same ratio.

Example The triangles ABC and PQR are similar. Find the length of the side PR.

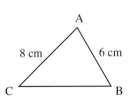
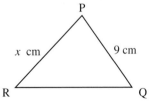

Take two pairs of corresponding sides, one pair of which must contain the unknown x. Form each pair into a fraction, so that x is on top. Since these fractions must be equal,

$$\frac{PQ}{AB} = \frac{PR}{AC}$$

$$\frac{9}{6} = \frac{x}{8}$$

To find x:

$$\frac{9 \times 8}{6} = x \quad \Rightarrow \quad x = \frac{72}{6} = 12 \, cm$$

EXERCISE 16A

1 These diagrams are drawn to scale. What is the scale factor of the enlargement in each case?

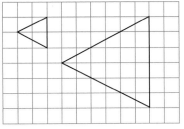

2 Are the following pairs of shapes similar? If so, give the scale factor. If not, give a reason.

5 cm
3 cm

20 cm
12 cm

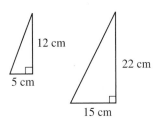

12 cm
5 cm

22 cm
15 cm

3 **a** Explain why these shapes are similar.
   b Give the ratio of the sides.
   c Which angle corresponds to angle C?
   d Which side corresponds to side QP?

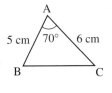

5 cm 70° 6 cm
A
B   C

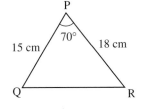

P
15 cm 70° 18 cm
Q   R

4 **a** Explain why these shapes are similar.
   b What is the ratio of the corresponding sides?
   c Which angle corresponds to angle B?

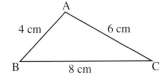

A
4 cm   6 cm
B   8 cm   C

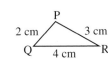

P
2 cm   3 cm
Q 4 cm R

5 **a** Explain why these shapes are similar.
   b Which angle corresponds to angle A?
   c Which side corresponds to side AC?

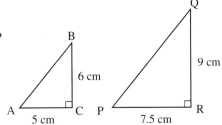

B
6 cm
A   C
5 cm

Q
9 cm
P   R
7.5 cm

6 **a** Explain why triangle ABC is similar to triangle AQR.

b Which angle corresponds to the angle at B?

c Which side of triangle AQR corresponds to side AC of triangle ABC? Your answers to question **5** may help you.

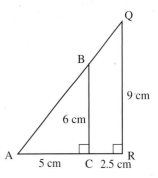

7 In the diagrams **a** to **h** below, find the lengths of the sides as requested. Each pair of shapes are similar but not drawn to scale.

a Find x.

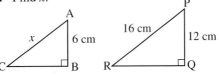

b Find PQ.

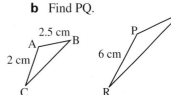

c Find x.

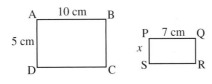

d Find x and y.

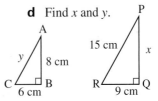

e Find x and y.

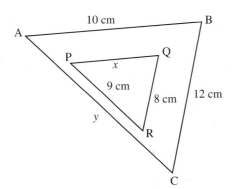

f Find x and y.

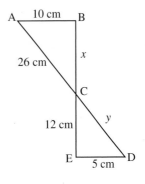

g Find AB and PQ.

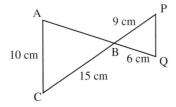

h Find QR.

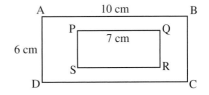

8 a Explain why these two triangles are similar.

b What is the ratio of their sides?

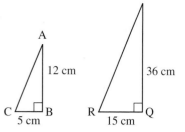

9 A model railway is made to a scale of 1:40. If the model bridge is 12 cm high, how high would a real railway bridge be? Give your answer in metres.

Special cases of similar triangles

Example 1 Find the sides marked x and y in these triangles (not drawn to scale).

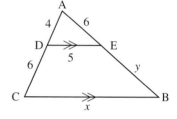

Triangles AED and ABC are similar. So using the corresponding sides CB, DE with AC, AD gives

$$\frac{x}{5} = \frac{10}{4}$$

$$\Rightarrow \quad x = \frac{10 \times 5}{4} = 12.5$$

Using the corresponding sides AE, AB with AD, AC gives

$$\frac{y+6}{6} = \frac{10}{4}$$

$$\Rightarrow \quad y = \frac{60}{4} - 6 = 15 - 6 = 9$$

Example 2 Ahmed wants to work out the height of a tall building. He walks 100 paces from the building and sticks a pole, 6 feet long, vertically into the ground. He then walks another 10 paces on the same line and notices that when he looks from ground level, the top of the pole and the top of the building are in line. How tall is the building?

First, draw a diagram of the situation and label it.

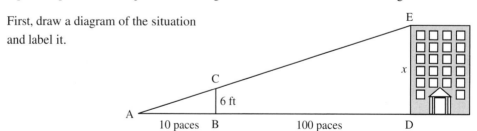

Using corresponding sides ED, CB with AD, AB gives

$$\frac{x}{6} = \frac{110}{10}$$

$$\Rightarrow \quad x = \frac{110 \times 6}{10} = 66$$

Hence the building is 66 feet high.

EXERCISE 16B

1 In each of the cases below, state a pair of similar triangles and find the length marked x. Separate the similar triangles if it makes it easier for you.

a

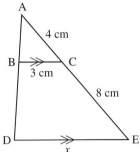

b

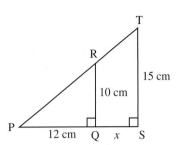

2 In the diagrams **a** to **h** below, find the lengths of the sides as requested.

a Find x.

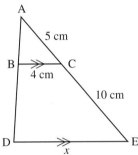

b Find x.

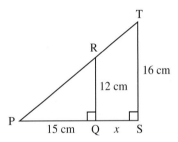

c Find x.

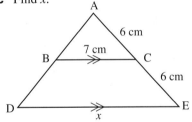

d Find CE.

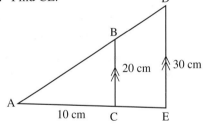

e Find x and y.

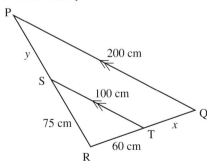

f Find PQ and PS.

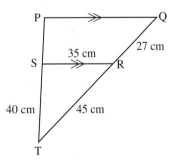

g Find x and y.

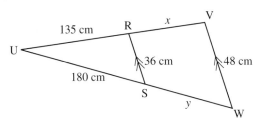

h Find DC and EB.

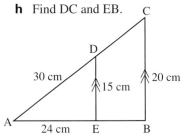

3 This diagram shows a method of working out the height of a tower.

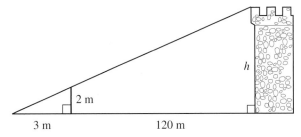

A stick, 2 metres long, is placed vertically 120 metres from the base of a tower so that the top of the tower and the top of the stick are in line with a point on the ground 3 metres from the base of the stick. How high is the tower?

4 It is known that a factory chimney is 330 feet high. Patrick paces out distances as shown in the diagram, so that the top of the chimney and the top of the flag pole are in line with each other. How high is the flag pole?

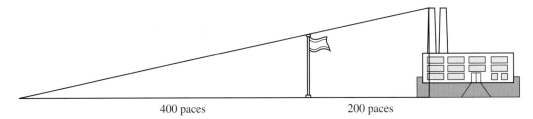

5 The shadow of a tree and the shadow of a golf flag coincide, as shown in the diagram. How high is the tree?

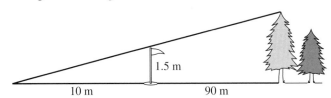

6 Find the lengths DE, FG and HJ.

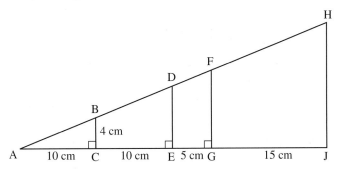

7 Find the height of a pole which casts a shadow of 1.5 metres when at the same time a man of height 165 cm casts a shadow of 80 cm.

8 Andrew, who is about 120 cm tall, notices that when he stands at the bottom of his garden, which is 20 metres away from his house, his dad, who is about 180 cm tall, looks as big as the house when he is about 2.5 metres away. (See diagram.) How high is the house?

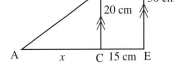

More complicated problems

The information given in a similar triangle situation can be more complicated than anything you have so far met, and you will need to have good algebraic skills to deal with it. The example given here is typical of the more complicated problems you may be asked to solve, so follow it through carefully.

Example   Find the value of x in this triangle.

We know that triangle ABC is similar to triangle ADE.

Splitting the triangles up may help us to see what will be awkward (and often missed).

So our equation will be $\dfrac{x+15}{x} = \dfrac{30}{20}$

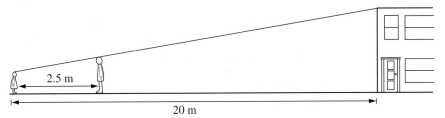

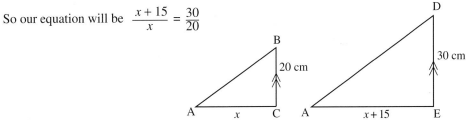

Cross-multiplying (moving each of the two bottom terms to the opposite side and multiplying) gives

$$20x + 300 = 30x$$
$$\Rightarrow\quad 300 = 10x \quad\Rightarrow\quad x = 30\,\text{cm}$$

EXERCISE 16C

Find the lengths x and y in the diagrams **1** to **8**.

1
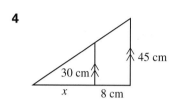
x

3 cm

10 cm

9 cm

2
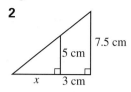
7.5 cm

5 cm

x 3 cm

3
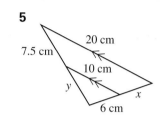
x

5 cm   6 cm

8 cm

4
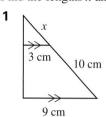
45 cm

30 cm

x 8 cm

5
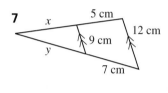
20 cm

7.5 cm

10 cm

y

x

6 cm

6
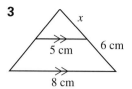
y

4.8 cm   5.4 cm

7 cm

x 9 cm

7
5 cm

x 9 cm   12 cm

y

7 cm

8
1 cm

x

1.5 cm   2 cm

y 0.8 cm

Possible coursework tasks

Similar co-ordinates

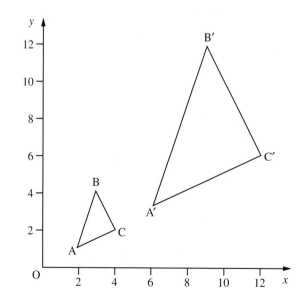

Triangle ABC is similar to triangle A′B′C′.

Investigate the relationship between the co-ordinates of any two similar triangles.

Similar shapes and area

The two right-angled triangles are
similar.
Find the ratio of the areas of these
triangles.
What do you notice?
Can you find a relationship
between the ratio of the sides and
the ratio of the areas for any pair of similar triangles?

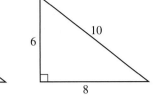

Don't be a square

What have all squares got in common? Investigate for other shapes.

Keep your distance

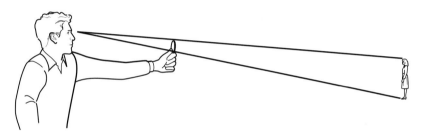

Hold a coin at arm's length so that you can just cover a person standing in the
distance. Can you use this method to find approximately how far away the
person is?

Examination questions

1 The diagram shows two similar
triangles ABC and DEC.
The lines AB and DE are parallel.
AB is 10 cm, DE is 8 cm, DC is 5 cm
and EC is 6 cm.
Calculate the length of the side BC.

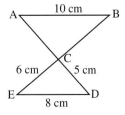

WJEC, Question 19, Intermediate Paper 2, June 1999

2 The diagram shows a kite ABCD with measurements in metres.

PQRS is similar to ABCD.

PR is of length 1 metre.

Calculate the length of the side PS.

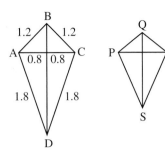

OCR, Question 16, Intermediate (A) Paper 4, June 2000

3 The model of a cross-section of a roof is illustrated below.

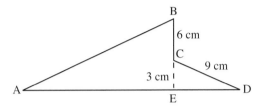

BC = 6 cm, CE = 3 cm and CD = 9 cm. Triangles ABE and DCE are similar triangles with angle BAE = angle CDE. Calculate the length of AB.

SEG, Question 10, Specimen Paper 14, 1998

4 I stood 420 m away from the OUB Centre, the tallest building in Singapore. I held a piece of wood 40 cm long at arm's length, 60 cm away from my eye. The piece of wood, held vertically, just blocked the building from my view. Use similar triangles to calculate the height, *h* metres, of the building.

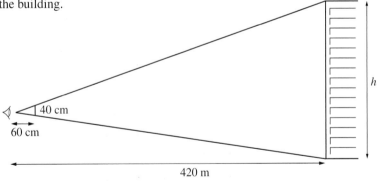

NEAB, Question 20, Paper 1, June 1995

5 BC is parallel to DE.

AB is twice as long as BD.

  a Work out the length of AB.

  b Work out the length of AE.

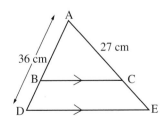

EDEXCEL, Question 28, Intermediate Paper 3, June 2000

6 In the diagram CD = 4 metres, CE = 3 metres and BC = 5 metres. AB is parallel to DE. ACE and BCD are straight lines.

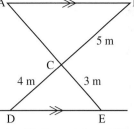

    a Explain why triangle ABC is similar to triangle EDC.

    b Calculate the length of AC.

ULEAC, Question 23, Paper 4, June 1995

7 Find the height of a tree which casts a shadow of 1.2 metres, when at the same moment in the same place a woman of height 140 cm casts a shadow of 60 cm.

8 **a** State which two triangles are similar.

    b Calculate the lengths of

        i x **ii** y

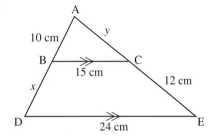

Summary

How well do you grade yourself?

To gain a grade **D**, you need to be able to recognise that two simple shapes, such as a pair of rectangles, have sides in a simple ratio, such as 1:2, and be able to use this to work out an unknown side.

To gain a grade **C**, you need to know what makes two shapes similar. You also need to be able to work out unknown sides using ratios. You should be able to solve simple problems using linear scale factors between two similar shapes.

To gain a grade **B**, you need to be able to work out the unknown side in one of two similar shapes, using an equation.

What you should know after you have worked through Chapter 16

- How to work out the ratio between two similar shapes.

- How to work out the unknown side in a shape when the corresponding side of a similar shape is known.

- How to solve practical problems using similar shapes.

17 Pythagoras

This chapter is going to ...

introduce you to the theorem of Pythagoras. By the end of the chapter, you should understand the theorem and be able to apply it when solving 2-D problems.

What you should already know

✔ Squares: for example,

$$3^2 = 3 \times 3 = 9 \qquad 2.7^2 = 2.7 \times 2.7 = 7.29$$

You can use your calculator if it has an $\boxed{x^2}$ key. For example, to work out 8.3^2, press the key sequence

$\boxed{8}$ $\boxed{\cdot}$ $\boxed{3}$ $\boxed{x^2}$ $\boxed{=}$

to get the answer 68.89.

Check that you can use your calculator to work out the squares

$$3.5^2 = 12.25 \qquad 9.1^2 = 82.81 \qquad 0.8^2 = 0.64$$

✔ Square root: for example, the square root of 81 is 9 (because $9 \times 9 = 81$) or written mathematically

$$\sqrt{81} = 9$$

The square-root key on your calculator looks like this: $\boxed{\sqrt{}}$

Use your calculator to check that

$$\sqrt{121} = 11 \qquad \sqrt{2.89} = 1.7 \qquad \sqrt{9.61} = 3.1$$

Usually the square root of a number does not work out exactly and we need to round off our calculator display to a suitable degree of accuracy. (See pages 1–24.)

Check that you can evaluate the square root of each number below and round off your answer to 1 decimal place.

$$\sqrt{10} = 3.2 \qquad \sqrt{27} = 5.2 \qquad \sqrt{60} = 7.7$$

Pythagoras's theorem

Pythagoras, who was a philosopher as well as a mathematician, was born in 580 BC, on the island of Samos, Greece. He later moved to Crotona (Italy), where he established the Pythagorean Brotherhood, which was a secret society devoted to politics, mathematics and astronomy. It is said that when he discovered his famous theorem, he was so full of joy that he showed his gratitude to the gods by sacrificing a hundred oxen. Others say that he sacrificed only one ox since he wasn't keen on killing animals.

The following activity will help you to discover for yourself this most famous and useful theorem.

Discovery activity

1 Draw a right-angled triangle with sides of 3 cm and 4 cm, as shown.

2 Measure accurately the long side of the triangle (the hypotenuse).

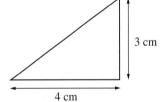

3 Draw four more right-angled triangles, choosing your own lengths for the short sides.

4 When you have done this, measure the hypotenuse for each triangle.

5 Copy and complete the table below for your triangles.

Short side	Short side	Hypotenuse			
a	b	c	a^2	b^2	c^2
3	4	5	9	16	25

Is there a pattern in your results? Can you see that a^2, b^2 and c^2 are related in some way?

You should spot that the value of a^2 added to that of b^2 is very close to the value of c^2. (Why don't the values add up exactly?)

You have 'rediscovered' Pythagoras's theorem. His theorem can be expressed in several ways, two of which are given on the next page.

Consider squares being drawn on each side of a right-angled triangle.

Pythagoras's theorem can then be stated as follows:

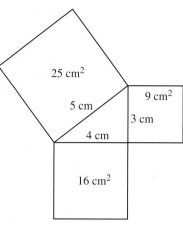

For any right-angled triangle, the area of the square drawn on the hypotenuse is equal to the sum of the areas of the squares drawn on the other two sides.

The form in which most of your parents would have learnt the theorem when they were at school – and which is still in use today – is as follows:

In any right-angled triangle, the square of the hypotenuse is equal to the sum of the squares of the other two sides.

Ask your parents whether they remember it. They may well remember Pythagoras's theorem given as

$a^2 + b^2 = c^2.$

EXERCISE 17A

This exercise will test both your drawing accuracy and your understanding of Pythagoras's theorem.

1   Draw as accurately as you can a right-angled triangle with short sides of 6 cm and 5 cm. Then follow through the process below.

What you should do	What you should find	
Measure the hypotenuse	7.8 cm	[Do you agree?]
Apply Pythagoras		
square one short side	25	[From 5×5]
square other short side	36	[From 6×6]
add together the squares	61	[From $25 + 36$]
Square hypotenuse measurement	60.84	[From 7.8×7.8]
Find the difference between last two	0.16	[From $61 - 60.84$]
How accurate were you?		

2 Draw as accurately as you can a right-angled triangle with short sides of 2 cm and 7 cm. Copy and complete the routine below.

What you should do	**What you should find**
Measure the hypotenuse	

Apply Pythagoras
  square one short side
  square other short side
  add together the squares
Square hypotenuse measurement
Find the difference between last two
How accurate were you?

3 Do exactly the same as in questions **1** and **2** for the following right-angled triangles.
  a Short sides 3 cm and 6 cm **b** Short sides 5 cm and 7 cm
  c Short sides 4 cm and 7 cm **d** Short sides 3 cm and 8 cm

4 Do exactly the same for the following isosceles, right-angled triangles.
  a Short sides 5 cm **b** Short sides 3 cm
  c Short sides 4 cm **d** Short sides 6 cm

5 Without doing any drawing, find the value of the square of the hypotenuse (marked x), i.e. find the value of x^2.

a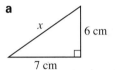
6 cm
7 cm

b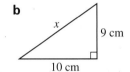
9 cm
10 cm

c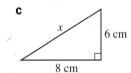
6 cm
8 cm

d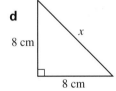
8 cm
x
8 cm

e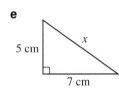
5 cm
x
7 cm

f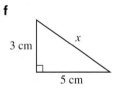
3 cm
x
5 cm

6 Without doing any drawing, find the value of the square of the unknown short side (marked x), i.e. find the value of x^2.

a
9 cm
x
7 cm

b
11 cm
x
9 cm

c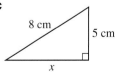
8 cm
5 cm
x

d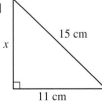
15 cm
x
11 cm

e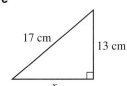
17 cm
13 cm
x

f
14 cm
x
11 cm

7 Without doing any drawing, find the value of the square of the unknown side (marked x), i.e. find the value of x^2.

a

9 cm

x

7 cm

b

17 cm

x

13 cm

c

9 cm

13 cm

x

d

5 cm

4.5 cm

x

e

7 cm

12 cm

x

f

15 cm

13 cm

x

8 The length of the hypotenuse of a right-angled triangle is 13 cm, and one of its short sides is 5 cm. Describe how you would find the square of the other short side **without** drawing the triangle and measuring it.

Using Pythagoras's theorem to find a length

Now that you are familiar with Pythagoras's theorem, you will be able to find the length of any side of a right-angled triangle when you know the lengths of the other two sides.

Finding the hypotenuse

Example   Find the length x.

Using Pythagoras's theorem gives

$$x^2 = 8^2 + 5.2^2$$
$$= 64 + 27.04$$
$$= 91.04$$
$$\Rightarrow \quad x = \sqrt{91.04} = 9.54\,\text{cm}$$

8 cm

x

5.2 cm

EXERCISE 17B

In each of the following triangles, find the hypotenuse, rounding off to a suitable degree of accuracy.

1

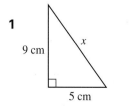

9 cm

x

5 cm

2

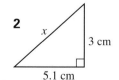

x

3 cm

5.1 cm

3

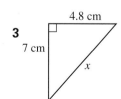

4.8 cm

7 cm

x

4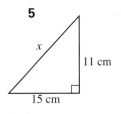

5

6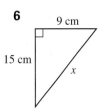

16 cm

13 cm

x

5
x

15 cm

11 cm

6
9 cm

15 cm

x

7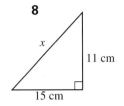

8

9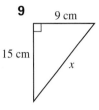

16 cm

13 cm

x

8
x

15 cm

11 cm

9
9 cm

15 cm

x

10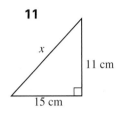

11

12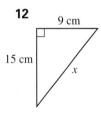

16 cm

13 cm

x

11
x

15 cm

11 cm

12
9 cm

15 cm

x

Finding a short side

Example   Find the length x.

Using Pythagoras's theorem gives

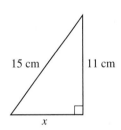

15 cm   11 cm

x

$$x^2 + 11^2 = 15^2$$
$$x^2 = 15^2 - 11^2$$
$$= 225 - 121$$
$$= 104$$
$$\Rightarrow \quad x = \sqrt{104} = 10.2\,\text{cm}$$

EXERCISE 17C

1   In each of the following triangles, find the length x to a suitable degree of accuracy.

a
x
17 cm
8 cm

b
24 cm
x
19 cm

c
6.4 cm
x
9 cm

d
31 cm
25 cm
x

e
x
7.2 cm
9 cm

f
500 m
x
450 m

g
x
1 cm
0.9 cm

h
17 m
x
15 m

2 In each of the following triangles, find the length *x* to a suitable degree of accuracy.

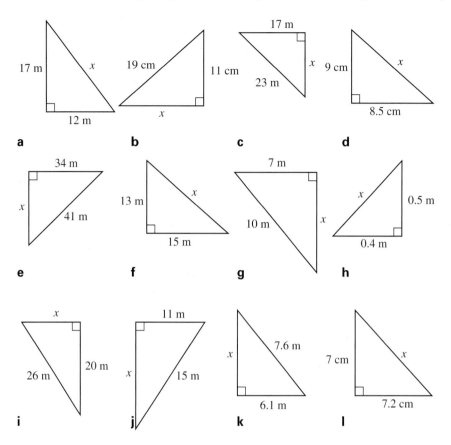

a b c d

e f g h

i j k l

Discovery activity

1 This right-angled triangle of sides 3, 4 and 5 units has been met before.

It is one of a number of right-angled triangles that have integer side lengths.

If we enlarge the triangle by scale factor 2, we get the second figure.

This is also a right-angled triangle. (Check it out and see.)

a Choose any enlargement scale factor and enlarge the 3, 4, 5 triangle.

b Does Pythagoras's theorem hold for your triangle?

c Sketch 5 more similar right-angled triangles which are enlargements of the 3, 4, 5 triangle and see if Pythagoras's theorem holds for them all.

d Write down a further 5 more right-angled triangles that are simple enlargements of the 3, 4, 5 triangle.

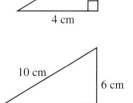

> **2** Check that the triangle with sides 5, 12 and 13 units is a another right-angled triangle with integer side lengths.
> Repeat the above investigation from **a** to **d** with this triangle.
>
> **3** Repeat the above for the triangles with sides **i** 8, 15 and 17 **ii** 7, 24 and 25

Pythagorean triples

The numbers 3, 4, 5 are called a Pythagorean triple because they are the integer side lengths of a right-angled triangle and hence $3^2 + 4^2 = 5^2$.

Any three (positive) whole numbers a, b and c such that $a^2 + b^2 = c^2$ are said to form a Pythagorean triple. If you have done the above investigation you will have found many more Pythagorean triples.

You ought to recognise the two simplest Pythagorean triples, which are

   3, 4, 5   and   5, 12, 13

It is also helpful to be aware of the next two simplest, which are

   8, 15, 17   and   7, 24, 25

You also need to know that any multiple of a Pythagorean triple is also a Pythagorean triple.

Pythagoras problems without a calculator

If you are given a Pythagoras-type problem to solve without a calculator, it is most likely to be dependent on one of the Pythagorean triples.

You would need to find out which triple the problem was based on, find the scale factor and hence solve the problem.

For example
Without using a calculator, find the value of x
- Recognise that both sides 15 and 36 are multiples of 3, so the triangle can be seen as an enlargement scale

   factor 3 of   where $y = \frac{x}{3}$

- We recognise that 5 and 12 are part of the triple 5, 12, 13 so $y = 13$ and hence
   $x = 3 \times 13 = 39\,\text{cm}$

EXERCISE 17D

Without using your calculator find the value of *x* in each of the triangles below.

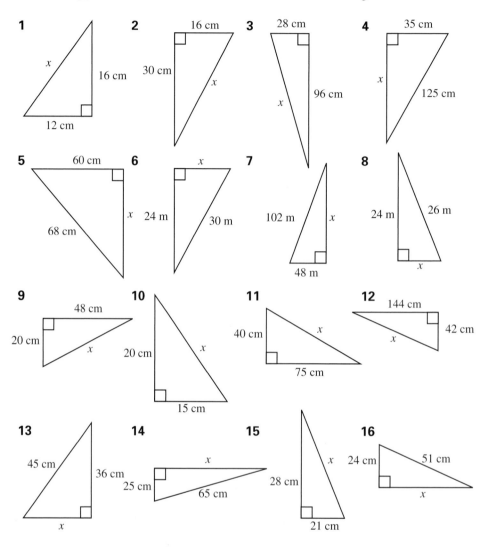

Pythagoras and real problems

Pythagoras's theorem can be used to solve certain practical problems. When a problem involves two lengths only:

- Draw a diagram from the problem that includes a right-angled triangle.
- Look at the diagram and decide which side has to be found: the hypotenuse or one of the other sides.
- If it's the hypotenuse, then square both numbers, add the squares and take the square root of the sum.
- If it's one of the other sides, then square both numbers, subtract the squares and take the square root of the difference.
- Finally, round off the answer.

Follow through the next two examples.

Example 1   A plane leaves Manchester airport heading due east. It flies 160 km before turning due north. It then flies a further 280 km and lands.
How far will the return flight be if the plane flies straight back to Manchester?

First, sketch the situation.

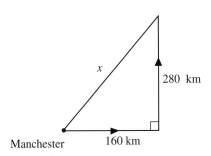

Using Pythagoras's theorem gives

$$x^2 = 160^2 + 280^2$$

$$= 25\,600 + 78\,400$$

$$= 104\,000$$

$$\Rightarrow \quad x = \sqrt{104\,000} = 322 \text{ km}$$

Example 2   How far up a wall will a 5-metre ladder reach when the foot of the ladder is 1.1 metres away from the wall?

First, sketch the situation.

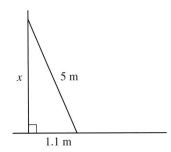

Using Pythagoras's theorem gives

$$x^2 + 1.1^2 = 5^2$$

$$x^2 = 5^2 - 1.1^2$$

$$= 25 - 1.21$$

$$= 23.79$$

$$\Rightarrow \quad x = \sqrt{2.79} = 4.88 \text{ m}.$$

Remember the following tips when solving problems.
- Always sketch the right-angled triangle you need. Sometimes, the triangle is already drawn for you but some problems involve other lines and triangles that may confuse you. So identify which right-angled triangle you need and sketch it separately.
- Label the triangle with necessary information, such as the lengths of its sides, from the question. Label the side which is being found with an x.
- Set out your solution as we have above. Try to avoid short cuts, since they often cause errors. You gain marks in your examination for clearly showing how you are applying Pythagoras's theorem to the problem.
- Round off to a suitable degree of accuracy.

EXERCISE 17E

1   A ladder, 12 metres long, leans against a wall. The ladder reaches 10 metres up the wall. How far away from the foot of the wall is the foot of the ladder?

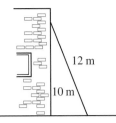

12 m
10 m

2   A model football pitch is 2 metres long and 0.5 metres wide. How long is the diagonal?

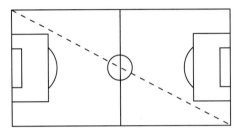

3   How long is the diagonal of a rectangle 6 metres long and 9 metres wide?

4   How long is the diagonal of a square with a side of 8 metres?

5   In a hockey game, a pass is made that leaves the ball 7 metres up the field and 6 metres across the field. How long was the actual pass?

6   A ship going from a port to a lighthouse steams 15 km east and 12 km north. How far is the lighthouse from the port?

7   A plane flies from London due north for 120 km before turning due west and flying for a further 85 km and landing at a secret location. How far from London is the secret location?

8   At the moment, three towns, A, B and C, are joined by two roads, as in the diagram. The council wants to make a road which runs directly from A to C. How much distance will the new road save?

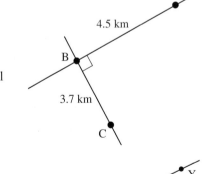

A
4.5 km
B
3.7 km
C

9   Some pedestrians want to get from point X on one road to point Y on another. The two roads meet at right angles.

    a   If they follow the roads, how far will they walk?

    b   Instead of walking along the road, they take the shortcut, XY. Find the length of the shortcut.

    c   How much distance do they save?

X
33 m
94 m
Y

10   A mast on a sailboat is strengthened by a wire (called a stay), as shown on the diagram. The mast is 35 feet tall. The stay is 37 feet long. How far from the base of the mast does the stay reach?

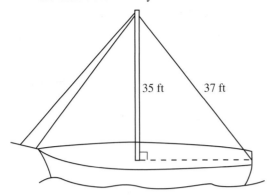

11   A 4-metre ladder is put up against a wall.
      a   How far up the wall will it reach when the foot of the ladder is 1 m away from the wall?
      b   When it reaches 3.6 m up the wall, how far is the foot of the ladder away from the wall?

12   A pole, 8 m high, is supported by metal wires, each 8.6 m long, attached to the top of the pole. How far from the foot of the pole are the wires fixed to the ground?

13   How long is the line that joins the two points A(2, 6) and B(1, 1)?

14   The regulation for safe use of ladders states that for a 5 m ladder: the foot of the ladder must be placed between 1.6 m and 2.1 m from the foot of the wall.
      a   What is the maximum height the ladder can safely reach up the wall?
      b   What is the minimum height the ladder can safely reach up the wall?

15   A rectangle is 4.5 cm long. The length of its diagonal is 5.8 cm. What is the area of the rectangle?

16   A boat sails from port 31 km due north, then 27 km due east, then 21 km due north again. How far is it now from the port?

17   A plane leaves an airport and heads due west for 90 km before turning due south for 170 km and landing. How far is the plane now from the airport?

18   Two large trees, 5.5 m and 6.8 m tall, stand 120 m apart. A bird flies directly from the top of one tree to the top of the other. How far has the bird flown?

19   Is the triangle with sides 7 cm, 24 cm and 25 cm a right-angled triangle?

20   How long is the line that joins the two points A(−2, 3) and B(4, −1).

Pythagoras in isosceles triangles

Every isosceles triangle has a line of symmetry that divides the triangle into two congruent right-angled triangles. So when you are faced with a problem involving an isosceles triangle, be aware that you are quite likely to have to split that triangle down the middle to create a right-angled triangle which will help you to solve the problem.

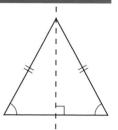

For example, suppose we have to find the area of this triangle.

It is an isosceles triangle and we need to know its height to find its area. Splitting the triangle into two right-angled triangles will help us to find its height.

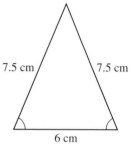

Call the height x. Then, using Pythagoras's theorem, we get

$$x^2 + 3^2 = 7.5^2$$

$$\Rightarrow \quad x^2 = 7.5^2 - 3^2$$

$$= 56.25 - 9$$

$$= 47.25$$

$$\Rightarrow \quad x = \sqrt{47.25}$$

$$x = 6.87$$

Keep the accurate figure in the calculator memory.

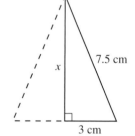

The area of the triangle is $\frac{1}{2} \times 6 \times 6.87$ (from the calculator memory), which is $20.6\,\text{cm}^2$.

EXERCISE 17F

1 Calculate the area of these isosceles triangles.

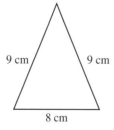 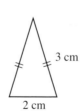 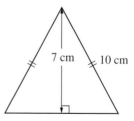

2 Calculate the area of an isosceles triangle whose sides are 8 cm, 8 cm and 6 cm.

3 Calculate the area of an equilateral triangle of side 6 cm.

4 Calculate the area of an equilateral triangle of side 8 cm.

5 An isosceles triangle has sides of 5 cm and 6 cm.

    a Sketch the two different isosceles triangles that fit this data.

    b Which of the two triangles has the greater area?

6 **a** Sketch a regular hexagon, showing all its lines of symmetry.

    b Calculate the area of the hexagon if its side is 8 cm.

7 Calculate the area of a hexagon of side 10 cm.

8 Calculate the lengths marked x in these isosceles triangles.

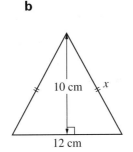 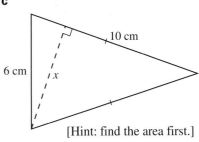

a   8 cm   9 cm x

b   10 cm x 12 cm

c   6 cm x 10 cm

[Hint: find the area first.]

Possible coursework tasks

Always right

- Choose any two integers, x and y, so that x is greater than y.
- Let $a = x^2 + y^2$ $b = x^2 - y^2$ $c = 2xy$

Is the triangle with sides of lengths a, b and c always right-angled?

Pythagorean triples

We know Pythagoras discovered that for any right-angled triangle

$$a^2 + b^2 = c^2$$

Any set of three numbers a, b and c for which this rule works are called Pythagorean triples. For example,

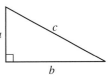

    3, 4 and 5   since $3^2 + 4^2 = 5^2$

    5, 12 and 13   since $5^2 + 12^2 = 13^2$

He also found the following interesting way of finding sets of whole numbers that fit the $a^2 + b^2 = c^2$ rule.

Choose any odd number greater than 1, say 7.

Square it: $7 \times 7 = 49$

Divide the square by 2: $49 \div 2 = 24.5$

Take the whole numbers just below and just above the answer:
24 and 25

Then the three numbers 7, 24 and 25 form a Pythagorean triple, because
$7^2 + 24^2 = 25^2$.

a Find out whether this routine works for three more odd numbers.

b Will it work for every odd number? Explain your answer.

c Can you find a similar rule that works for even numbers?

Rotating Pythagoras

The diagram below is made up of a shaded triangle with base length of 3 cm and a height of 1 cm.

a Find the length of a_1.

A second triangle is built on top of the shaded one, with a base length of a_1 and a height of 1 cm.

b Find the length of a_2.

The sequence of triangles continues.

c Find the lengths a_3, a_4 and a_5.

a Calculate the length of the twelfth line a_{12}.

e Continue drawing the shapes as far as you can. What stops you?

Equilateral Pythagoras

Equilateral triangles can be drawn on each side of a right-angled triangle.

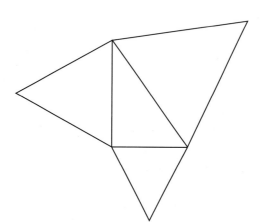

Is it true to say: the sum of the areas of the two smaller equilateral triangles is equal to the area of the larger one?

Examination questions

1 The diagram shows the end view of the framework for a sports arena stand.

Calculate the length AB.

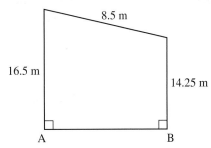

NEAB, Question 22, Specimen Paper 1, 1998

2 The diagram shows the positions of three airports:
E (East Midlands), M (Manchester) and L (Leeds).

  a Calculate, correct to three significant figures, the distance LE.

  b An aircraft leaves M at 10.45 am and flies direct to E, arriving at 11.03 am. Calculate the average speed of the aircraft in km/hour, giving your answer correct to an appropriate number of significant figures.

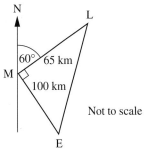

Not to scale

MEG, Question 11, Specimen Paper 4, 1998

3 Hotten is 8 miles due north of Kirrin. Budle is 14 miles due east of Hotten.

  a Draw a sketch to show the relative positions of Hotten, Kirrin and Budle.

  b Write down the three-figure bearing of Hotten from Budle.

  c Calculate the direct distance from Kirrin to Budle.

NEAB, Question 6, Paper 1, June 1995

4 The diagram represents Nelson's voyage from Great Yarmouth to position B. Nelson's boat sails due east from Great Yarmouth for 14 km to position A. The boat then changes course and sails for 20 km to position B. On a map, the distance between G and A is 56 cm.

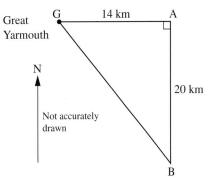

Not accurately drawn

  a Work out the scale of the map.

  a Calculate the distance, in km, of B from Great Yarmouth.

ULEAC, Question 14, Specimen Paper 3, 1998

5 The diagram shows a sketch of a triangle.
  a Work out the area of the triangle.
  b Work out the perimeter of the triangle.

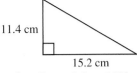

EDEXCEL, Question 5, Intermediate Paper 4, June 2000

6 A moving walkway runs between the ground floor and the first floor in a department store.

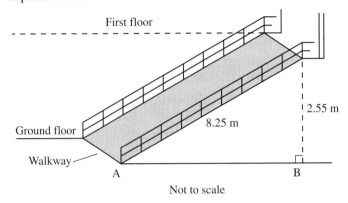

Not to scale

The walkway is 8.25 m in length and rises 2.55 m. Calculate the distance AB.

SEG, Question 20, Specimen Paper 10, 1998

7 The diagram shows the position of points A, B and C.

A is due North of C. B is due West of C. Calculate the distance BC.

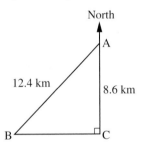

OCR, Question 14, Intermediate (A) Paper 4, June 2000

8 This diagram is not drawn to scale. It shows the cross-section of a swimming pool 50 m long. It is 3 m deep at the deep end. The deepest part of the pool is 12 m long.
  a Calculate the length of the sloping bottom of the pool AB.
  b The pool is 7.5 m wide. What is its volume?

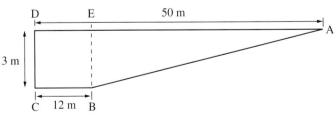

9 The diagram shows the layout of five paths in a garden.

AB is 8.3 m long. BC is 6.1 m long.

BD is 5.0 m long.

$A\hat{B}C$ and $B\hat{D}A$ are both right angles.

a Calculate the length of the path AC, giving your answer to a suitable degree of accuracy.

b Calculate the length of the path AD, giving your answer to a suitable degree of accuracy.

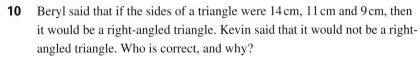

WJEC, Question 13, Intermediate Paper 2, June 1999

10 Beryl said that if the sides of a triangle were 14 cm, 11 cm and 9 cm, then it would be a right-angled triangle. Kevin said that it would not be a right-angled triangle. Who is correct, and why?

NEAB, Question 5, Paper 1I, June 1995

Summary

How well do you grade yourself?

To gain a grade **E**, you need to be able to make a start on the Pythagoras questions, by substituting the correct values into the given formula.

To gain a grade **C**, you need to be able to show that you understand and can use Pythagoras's theorem.

To gain a grade **B**, you need to be able to draw out of a complicated situation the need to use Pythagoras's theorem and apply it.

What you should know after you have worked through Chapter 17

- Pythagoras's theorem.
- How to show that you know when to use Pythagoras's theorem.
- How to use Pythagoras's theorem to find the hypotenuse or a short side of a right-angled triangle, given the two other sides.
- How to draw out a right-angled triangle from a problem and label it with necessary information.

Coursework example 3

Tilt vectors

Refer to the Appendix for a summary of coursework marks.

Problem statement

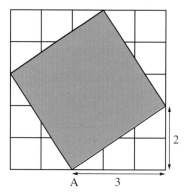

The square has been tilted about the point A.

The tilt is described by using the vector $\begin{pmatrix} 3 \\ 2 \end{pmatrix}$ as shown in the diagram.

Find the area of the square.

Investigate the area of squares described by using different 'tilt vectors'.

Possible solution

i	ii	iii	Notes
3			Necessary information found in order to solve the problem.
4			Problem broken down into easy stages.

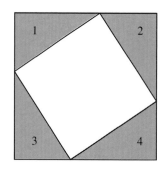

The 4 triangles I have shaded are congruent. The area of the square will be the area of the large surrounding square minus the 4 triangles.

Area of large square is $5 \times 5 = 25$.
Area of triangle 1 is $\frac{1}{2}(3 \times 2) = 3$.
Area of 4 triangles is 12.
So the area of the square with tilt vector $\begin{pmatrix} 3 \\ 2 \end{pmatrix}$ is 13.

I am now going to draw some more diagrams to show tilt vectors. I will start by looking at easy examples.

Tilt vector $\begin{pmatrix} 1 \\ 1 \end{pmatrix}$

Area of square: $4 - (4 \times \frac{1}{2}) = 2$

i   ii   iii   **Notes**

Tilt vector $\begin{pmatrix} 2 \\ 1 \end{pmatrix}$

Area of square: $9 - (4 \times 1) = 5$

Tilt vector $\begin{pmatrix} 3 \\ 1 \end{pmatrix}$

Area of square: $16 - (4 \times \frac{3}{2}) = 10$

Tilt vector $\begin{pmatrix} 4 \\ 2 \end{pmatrix}$

Area of square:
$36 - (4 \times 4) = 20$

Tilt vector $\begin{pmatrix} 3 \\ 3 \end{pmatrix}$

Area of square:
$36 - (4 \times 4\frac{1}{2}) = 18$

Tilt vector $\begin{pmatrix} 4 \\ 3 \end{pmatrix}$

Area of square:
$49 - (4 \times 6) = 25$

i	ii	iii	Notes
	3		Results shown on diagrams and in a table
	4		Explanation links the diagrams and the table of results.
		3	Correct rule found.
		4	A further example has shown that the rule has been tested.
5			The introduction of Pythagoras's theorem extends the problem.

To help me look for a pattern, so that I can find the area of the square without drawing the tilt vectors, I will first put all my results in a table.

I have tried adding together the 2 numbers in the vector and then multiplying this sum by different numbers. This idea doesn't work.

Tilt vector	Area
$\begin{pmatrix} 1 \\ 1 \end{pmatrix}$	2
$\begin{pmatrix} 2 \\ 1 \end{pmatrix}$	5
$\begin{pmatrix} 3 \\ 1 \end{pmatrix}$	10
$\begin{pmatrix} 4 \\ 2 \end{pmatrix}$	20
$\begin{pmatrix} 3 \\ 3 \end{pmatrix}$	18
$\begin{pmatrix} 4 \\ 3 \end{pmatrix}$	25

I then noticed that for the first 3 examples:

$$1 + 1 = 2 \qquad 4 + 1 = 5 \qquad 9 + 1 = 10$$

The first number is a square number. This gave me the idea of squaring the numbers in the vector and adding them together. I tried this for the next example:

$$4^2 + 2^2 = 20$$

When I tried this for the other examples, I found that it worked.

So my rule for finding the area of the square is:

Square the numbers in the vector and add them together.

To see if my rule is correct, I am going to predict that the tilt vector $\begin{pmatrix} 5 \\ 2 \end{pmatrix}$ will give the square an area of 29.

Tilt vector $\begin{pmatrix} 5 \\ 2 \end{pmatrix}$

Area of square:
$49 - (4 \times 5) = 29$

My prediction was correct.

I think I can see another way of finding the area of the square by using Pythagoras's theorem.

i	ii	iii	Notes
	5		Presentation improved by use of algebra.
		5	Rule justified by use of Pythagoras's theorem.
6			Problem follows an alternative approach using algebra.
	6		Solution shows a consistent use of algebraic notation.
		6	Correct formula obtained with clear reasoning shown throughout.

Final marks:
(i) 6 (ii) 6 (iii) 6

In my example, I will let the side of the square be x. Using algebra will help me to find a formula.

By Pythagoras's theorem:

$$x^2 = 5^2 + 2^2 = 29$$

But the area of the square is also x^2. Therefore, the area of the square is also 29.

I can now find a formula for any tilt vector.

Let the tilt vector be $\begin{pmatrix} a \\ b \end{pmatrix}$.

By Pythagoras's theorem: $x^2 = a^2 + b^2$.

Since the area of the square is x^2, then the area of the square is also $a^2 + b^2$.

I have discovered the following by doing this investigation.

If I have a tilt vector $\begin{pmatrix} a \\ b \end{pmatrix}$, then the area A of the square formed by the tilt vector is given by

$$A = a^2 + b^2$$

Trigonometry

This chapter is going to ...

show you how to find the lengths and angles in right-angled triangles.
It will lead you through some simple exercises and introduce you to
the three basic trigonometric ratios. It will also show you how to
recognise which of the ratios to use when given certain information,
and how to interpret practical problems and solve them using
trigonometry.

What you should already know

✔ The angles in a triangle add up to 180°.
✔ How to draw a triangle using a ruler and a protractor.
✔ How to round off numbers to decimal places and significant figures.
✔ Pythagoras's theorem.

You should also have a scientific calculator with sin, cos and tan keys.

Discovery activity

1 Choose any angle
   between 10° and
   80°, except 44°,
   45°, 46° and the
   angle used in the
   example below.

2 Draw five different-
   sized right-angled
   triangles which
   contain the angle
   you have chosen.
   For example, all
   these triangles
   include the chosen
   angle of 53°.

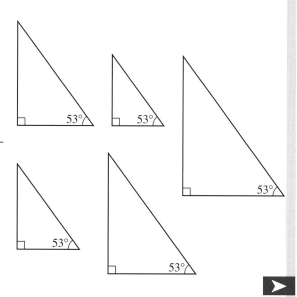

3 Label your right angle and your chosen angle as shown.

4 Label the sides of each triangle as below.
The longest side is called the **hypotenuse**.
The side opposite your chosen angle is
called the **opposite**.
The side next to both the right angle and
your chosen angle is called the **adjacent**.

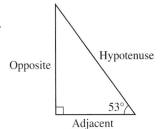

5 Measure as accurately as you can all the
sides of each triangle.

6 Complete the following table with your measurements. Then work out
each fraction as a decimal number correct to 2 decimal places.

Triangle	Opposite O	Adjacent A	Hypotenuse H	$\dfrac{O}{H}$	$\dfrac{A}{H}$
1					
2					
3					
4					
5					

7 Look at the results in your table and make some comments.

8 Comment on the class results.

9 Can you find any link between your results, your chosen angle, and the
keys **sin** and **cos** on your scientific calculator?

Trigonometric ratios

You have just discovered some important facts about the trigonometric ratios sine
and cosine.

- The sine and cosine of angles between 0° and 90° have values between 0 and 1.

- $\text{sine } \theta = \dfrac{\text{Opposite}}{\text{Hypotenuse}}$ $\qquad \text{cosine } \theta = \dfrac{\text{Adjacent}}{\text{Hypotenuse}}$

- You can use your calculator to find the sine and the cosine of **any** angle.

   To find the sine, press the key labelled **sin** (short for sine)
   To find the cosine, press the key labelled **cos** (short for cosine).

Make sure you can find sine and cosine on your calculator.

Important   Make sure your calculator is working in **degrees**. When it is, D or DEG
appears in the display.

Depending on your type of calculator, you need to be able to put it into 'degree mode' before you start working on sines and cosines. This can be done either

- by pressing the keys `MODE` `4`

- or by pressing the key `DEG` until DEG is on display.

Try this **now** to make sure you can do it.

Example 1 Use your calculator to find the sine of 27° (written as sin 27°).

If you have an ordinary scientific calculator, the function is keyed in 'numbers first':

`2` `7` `sin`

The display should read 0.4539905. (You may have more or less digits depending on your calculator.) This is 0.454 to 3 sf.

If you have a graphics calculator or a certain type of 'algebraic logic' (DAL) calculator, you key in the function as it reads:

`sin` `2` `7` `EXE`   (EXE or ENTER may be = on your calculator.)

You should get the same value as above. If you don't then consult your calculator manual or your teacher.

Example 2 Use your calculator to find the cosine of 56° (written as cos 56°).

cos 56° = 0.5591929035 = 0.559 to 3 sf

Check that you agree with this, using as many digits as your calculator allows.

Example 3 Use your calculator to work out 3 × cos 57° (written as 3 cos 57°).

Depending on your type of calculator, key in either

`3` `×` `5` `7` `cos` `=`   or   `3` `×` `cos` `5` `7` `=`

Check that you get an answer of 1.634 to 3 decimal places (actual 1.633917105).

EXERCISE 18A

Find these values, rounding off your answers to 3 sf.

1	**a** sin 43°	**b** sin 56°	**c** sin 67.2°	**d** sin 90°
	e sin 45°	**f** sin 20°	**g** sin 22°	**h** sin 0°
	i sin 35°	**j** sin 75°	**k** sin 89°	**l** sin 71°

2	**a** cos 43°	**b** cos 56°	**c** cos 67.2°	**d** cos 90°
	e cos 45°	**f** cos 20°	**g** cos 22°	**h** cos 0°
	i cos 35°	**j** cos 75°	**k** cos 89°	**l** cos 71°

3 From your answers to questions **1** and **2**, what angle has the same value for sine and cosine?

4 **a** **i**   What is sin 35°?   **ii**   What is cos 55°?
    b **i**   What is sin 12°?   **ii**   What is cos 78°?
    c **i**   What is cos 67°?   **ii**   What is sin 23°?
    d   What connects the values in parts **a**, **b** and **c**?
    e   Copy and complete these sentences.
        i   sin 15° is the same as cos …
        ii   cos 82° is the same as sin …
        iii sin x is the same as cos …

5   Use your calculator to work out the value of
    a   5 sin 65°   **b**   6 cos 42°   **c**   12 sin 17°   **d**   3 cos 78°
    e   6 sin 90°   **f**   5 sin 0°   **g**   12 cos 73°   **h**   9 sin 12°

6   Use your calculator to work out the value of
    a $\dfrac{5}{\sin 63°}$ **b** $\dfrac{6}{\cos 32°}$ **c** $\dfrac{12}{\sin 37°}$ **d** $\dfrac{3}{\cos 48°}$

    e $\dfrac{6}{\sin 90°}$ **f** $\dfrac{5}{\sin 30°}$ **g** $\dfrac{12}{\sin 73°}$ **h** $\dfrac{9}{\sin 12°}$

7   Use your calculator to work out the value of
    a   8 sin 75°   **b** $\dfrac{19}{\sin 23°}$ **c**   7 cos 71°   **d** $\dfrac{15}{\sin 81°}$

    e $\dfrac{23}{\sin 54°}$ **f**   23 sin 17°   **g** $\dfrac{12}{\sin 34°}$ **h**   17 sin 85°

Working backwards: inverse functions

The sine of 54° is 0.809 016 9944 (to 10 dp).
The sine of 55° is 0.819 152 0443 (to 10 dp).

What angle has a sine of 0.815?

Obviously, it is between 54° and 55°, so we could probably use a trial-and-improvement method to find it. But there is an easier way which uses the **inverse functions** of your calculator.

An inverse function can be accessed in several different ways. For example, that for sine may be any of these:

The inverse function printed above the sine key is usually given in either of the following ways:

sin⁻¹   arcsin
sin   or   **sin**

You will need to find out how your calculator deals with inverse functions.

When you do the inverse sine of 0.815, you should get 54.58736189°.

It is usually acceptable in trigonometry to round off angles to 1 decimal place, so the angle with a sine of 0.815 is 54.6° (to 1 dp).

Try these two examples.

1 Find the angle with a cosine of 0.654. Then check that your calculator gives an answer of 49.15613192 = 49.2° (1 dp).

2 Find the angle with a sine of 3 ÷ 4. How you solve this will depend on your type of calculator. So key in either

Check that you get an answer of 48.6° to 1 dp (actual 48.59037789).

EXERCISE 18B

Use your calculator to find the answers to the following. Give your answers to 1 dp.

1 What angles have sines of
a 0.5	**b** 0.785	**c** 0.64	**d** 0.877
e 0.999	**f** 0.707	**g** 0.102	**h** 0.722
i 0.888	**j** 0.2	**k** 0.7	**l** 0.75

2 What angles have cosines of
a 0.5	**b** 0.785	**c** 0.64	**d** 0.877
e 0.999	**f** 0.707	**g** 0.102	**h** 0.722
i 0.888	**j** 0.2	**k** 0.7	**l** 0.75

3 What angles have sines of
a 4 ÷ 5	**b** 2 ÷ 3	**c** 7 ÷ 10	**d** 5 ÷ 6
e 1 ÷ 24	**f** 5 ÷ 13	**g** 24 ÷ 25	**h** 1 ÷ 4

4 What angles have cosines of
a 4 ÷ 5	**b** 2 ÷ 3	**c** 7 ÷ 10	**d** 5 ÷ 6
e 1 ÷ 24	**f** 5 ÷ 13	**g** 24 ÷ 25	**h** 1 ÷ 4

5 What happens when you try to find the angle with a sine of 1.2? What is the largest value of sine you can put into your calculator without getting an error when you ask for the inverse sine? What is the smallest?

6 **a** **i** What angle has a sine of 0.3? (Keep the answer in your calculator memory.)
      ii What angle has a cosine of 0.3?
      iii Add the two accurate answers of **i** and **ii** together.
  b Will you always get the same answer to the above no matter what number you start with?

Tangent

In addition to sine and cosine, there is a third trigonometric ratio called 'tangent'. The following brief exercise introduces tangent in a practical way. If you want to move on to the next section, it is not necessary to do Exercise 18C.

EXERCISE 18C

1   Draw five right-angled triangles with different side lengths but each with an angle on the base of 20°, as shown below.

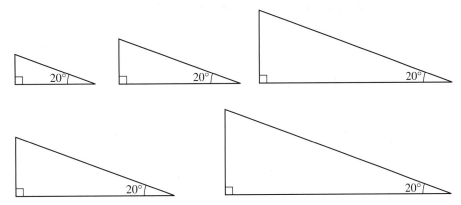

2   Measure the sides. Then label the side facing the 20° as 'Opposite', and the side next to both the right angle and the 20°, as 'Adjacent'.

3   For each triangle, calculate to 2 decimal places the value of $\dfrac{\text{Opposite}}{\text{Adjacent}}$.

4   Use your calculator to find tan 20°. (Should be 0.364 to 3 sf.)

5   What do you notice? You should have found out that

$$\tan \theta = \frac{\text{Opposite}}{\text{Adjacent}}$$

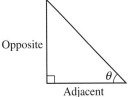

6   **a**   What happens when you find tan 90°?
   b   Explain why this might happen.

EXERCISE 18D

Find these values, rounding off your answers to 3 dp.

1   **a**   tan 43°   **b**   tan 56°   **c**   tan 67.2°   **d**   tan 90°
   e   tan 45°   **f**   tan 20°   **g**   tan 22°   **h**   tan 0°
   i   tan 35°   **j**   tan 75°   **k**   tan 89°   **l**   tan 71°

2   **a**   sin 73°   **b**   cos 26°   **c**   tan 65.2°   **d**   sin 88°
   e   cos 35°   **f**   tan 30°   **g**   sin 28°   **h**   cos 5°
   i   tan 37°   **j**   sin 73°   **k**   cos 79°   **l**   tan 79°

3   In what way is tan very different from both sin and cos?

4   Use your calculator to work out the value of
   a   5 tan 65°   **b**   6 tan 42°   **c**   12 tan 17°   **d**   3 tan 78°
   e   6 tan 90°   **f**   5 tan 0°   **g**   12 tan 73°   **h**   9 tan 12°

5 Use your calculator to work out the value of

a $\dfrac{3}{\tan 64°}$ **b** $\dfrac{7}{\tan 42°}$ **c** $\dfrac{13}{\tan 36°}$ **d** $\dfrac{23}{\tan 58°}$

e $\dfrac{5}{\tan 89°}$ **f** $\dfrac{6}{\tan 40°}$ **g** $\dfrac{16}{\tan 63°}$ **h** $\dfrac{8}{\tan 22°}$

6 Use your calculator to work out the value of

a $8 \tan 75°$ **b** $\dfrac{19}{\tan 23°}$ **c** $7 \tan 71°$ **d** $\dfrac{15}{\tan 81°}$

e $\dfrac{23}{\tan 54°}$ **f** $23 \tan 17°$ **g** $\dfrac{12}{\tan 34°}$ **h** $17 \tan 85°$

7 Use your calculator to work out the value of

a $4 \sin 63°$ **b** $7 \tan 52°$ **c** $18 \cos 37°$ **d** $4 \tan 68°$

e $5 \tan 80°$ **f** $9 \cos 8°$ **g** $19 \tan 74°$ **h** $7 \sin 22°$

8 Use your calculator to work out the value of

a $\dfrac{6}{\sin 66°}$ **b** $\dfrac{8}{\tan 32°}$ **c** $\dfrac{14}{\cos 76°}$ **d** $\dfrac{24}{\tan 68°}$

e $\dfrac{8}{\tan 79°}$ **f** $\dfrac{5}{\cos 50°}$ **g** $\dfrac{17}{\tan 65°}$ **h** $\dfrac{9}{\sin 32°}$

9 Use your calculator to work out the value of

a $7 \sin 85°$ **b** $\dfrac{12}{\cos 53°}$ **c** $8 \tan 61°$ **d** $\dfrac{35}{\tan 71°}$

e $\dfrac{13}{\cos 34°}$ **f** $27 \tan 47°$ **g** $\dfrac{19}{\sin 64°}$ **h** $18 \cos 75°$

A closer look at the trigonometric ratios

Sine

Remember

$$\text{sine } \theta = \frac{\text{Opposite}}{\text{Hypotenuse}}$$

Example 1   Find the angle θ, given that the opposite side is $7\,\text{cm}$ and the hypotenuse is $10\,\text{cm}$.

Draw a diagram. [This is an **essential step**.]

From the information given, we cannot directly find the angle and so we use the sine of the angle.

$$\sin \theta = \frac{\text{Opposite}}{\text{Hypotenuse}} = \frac{7}{10} = 0.7$$

What angle has a sine of 0.7? To find out, use the inverse sine function on your calculator.

Check that you get $44.4°$ to 1 dp.

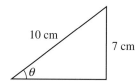

Example 2 Find the length of the side marked *a* in this triangle.

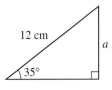

Side *a* is the opposite, so we use sin 35°.

$$\sin 35° = \frac{\text{Opposite}}{\text{Hypotenuse}} = \frac{\text{Opposite}}{12}$$

⟹ Opposite = Hypotenuse × sin 35°

⟹ $a = 12 \times \sin 35° = 6.9$ cm

Example 3 Find the hypotenuse of this triangle.

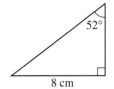

Note that although the angle is in the other 'corner', the opposite (8 cm) is again given. So we use

$$\sin 52° = \frac{8}{\text{Hypotenuse}}$$

⟹ Hypotenuse × sin 52° = 8

⟹ Hypotenuse $= \dfrac{8}{\sin 52°} = 10.2$ cm

EXERCISE 18E

1 Find the angle marked *x* in each of these triangles.

a   **b**   **c**

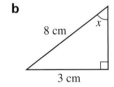

2 Find the side marked *x* in each of these triangles.

a   **b**   **c**

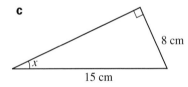

3 Find the side marked *x* in each of these triangles.

a   **b**   **c**

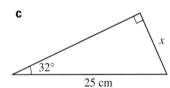

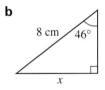

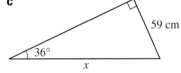

4 Find the side marked x in each of these triangles.

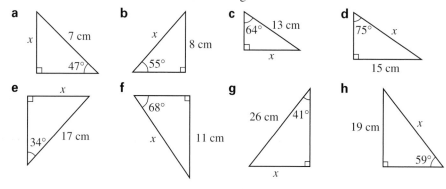

5 Find the value of x in each of these triangles.

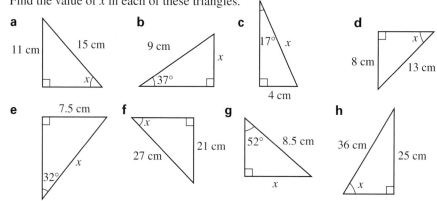

Cosine

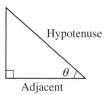

Remember

$$\text{cosine } \theta = \frac{\text{Adjacent}}{\text{Hypotenuse}}$$

Example 1 Find the angle θ, given that the adjacent side is 5 cm and the hypotenuse is 12 cm.

Draw a diagram. [This is an **essential step**.]

From the information given, we cannot directly find the angle and so we use the cosine of the angle.

$$\cos \theta = \frac{\text{Adjacent}}{\text{Hypotenuse}} = \frac{5}{12} = 0.416\,6667$$

What angle has a cosine of 0.416 6667? To find out, use the inverse cosine function on your calculator.

Check that you get 65.4° to 1 dp.

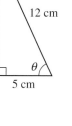

Example 2 Find the side marked a in this triangle.

Side a is the adjacent, so we use cos 47°.

$$\cos 47° = \frac{\text{Adjacent}}{\text{Hypotenuse}} = \frac{a}{9}$$

$$\Rightarrow \quad a = 9 \times \cos 47° = 6.14\,\text{cm}$$

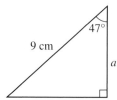

Example 3 Find the hypotenuse of this triangle.

Side 20 cm is the adjacent, so we use cos 40°.

$$\cos 40° = \frac{20}{\text{Hypotenuse}}$$

$$\Rightarrow \quad \text{Hypotenuse} = \frac{20}{\cos 40°} = 26.1 \text{ cm}$$

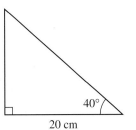

EXERCISE 18F

1 Find the angle marked x in each of these triangles.

 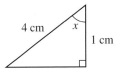 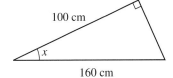

2 Find the side marked x in each of these triangles.

  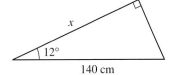

3 Find the side marked x in each of these triangles.

a   **b**   **c**   **d**

  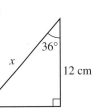

e   **f**   **g**   **h**

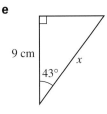 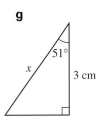 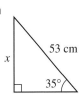

4 Find the side marked x in each of these triangles.

 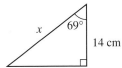

5   Find the value of x in each of these triangles.

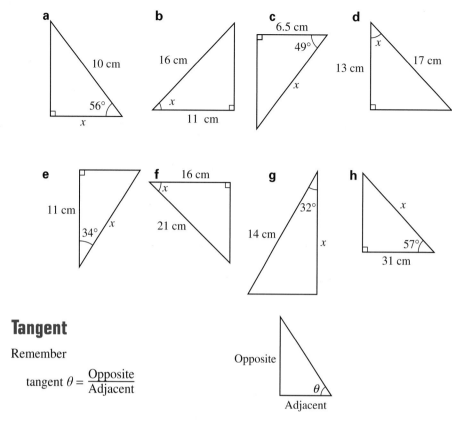

Tangent

Remember

$$\text{tangent } \theta = \frac{\text{Opposite}}{\text{Adjacent}}$$

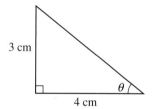

Example 1   Find the angle θ, given that the opposite side is 3 cm and the adjacent side is 4 cm.

Draw a diagram. [This is an **essential step**.]

From the information given, we cannot directly find the angle and so we use the tangent of the angle.

$$\tan \theta = \frac{\text{Opposite}}{\text{Adjacent}} = \frac{3}{4} = 0.75$$

What angle has a tangent of 0.75? To find out, use the inverse tangent function on your calculator.

Check that you get 36.9° to 1 dp.

Example 2   Find the side marked x in this triangle.

Note that the angle is in the other 'corner', so side x is the opposite and tan 62° is given by

$$\tan 62° = \frac{\text{Opposite}}{9} = \frac{x}{9}$$

$$\Rightarrow \quad = 9 \times \tan 62° = 16.9 \, \text{cm}$$

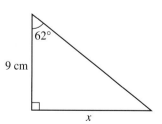

Example 3 Find the side marked a in this triangle.

Side a is the adjacent, so tan 35° is given by

$$\tan 35° = \frac{6}{a}$$

$$\Rightarrow \quad a = \frac{6}{\tan 35°} = 8.6\,\text{cm}$$

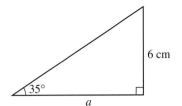

EXERCISE 18G

1 Find the angle marked x in each of these triangles.

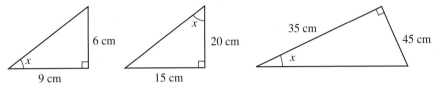

2 Find the side marked x in each of these triangles.

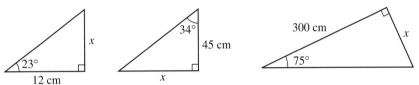

3 Find the side marked x in each of these triangles.

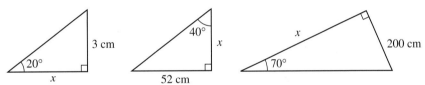

4 Find the side marked x in each of these triangles.

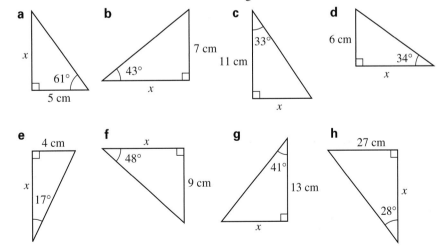

5 Find the value x in each of these triangles.

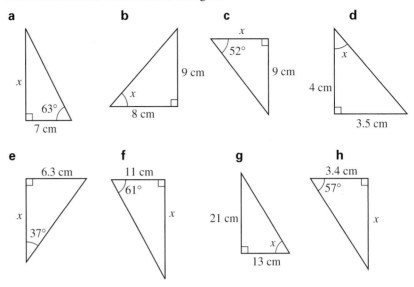

Which ratio do I use?

The examples just given cover every possible situation you will be asked to solve.

The difficulty with any trigonometric problem is knowing which ratio to use to solve it.

Examples 1 to 4 will show you how to determine which ratio you need in any given situation.

Example 1 Find the side marked x in this triangle.

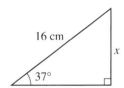

Step 1 Identify what information is given and what needs to be found. Namely, x is **opposite** the angle and 16 cm is the **hypotenuse**

Step 2 Decide which ratio to use. Only one ratio uses opposite and hypotenuse: **sine**.

Step 3 Remember: $\sin \theta = \dfrac{\text{Opposite}}{\text{Hypotenuse}}$

Step 4 Put in the numbers and letters: $\sin 37° = \dfrac{x}{16}$

Step 5 Rearrange the expression and work out the answer: $x = 16 \sin 37° = 9.6290404$

Step 6 Give the answer to an appropriate degree of accuracy: $x = 9.63$ (3 sf)

The answer has been given to 3 sf because the 16 cm was to 2 sf. We have gone to one more figure, as discussed on page 24.

In reality, you do not write down every step as above. Step 1 can be done by marking the triangle. Step 2 is done in your head. Steps 3–6 are what you write down.

Remember that examiners will want to see evidence of working. Any reasonable attempt at identifying the sides and using a ratio will probably get you some method marks – but only if the fraction is the right way up.

The following example is set out in a way that requires the **minimum** amount of working but gets **maximum** marks.

Example 2   Find the side marked x in this triangle.

Mark on the triangle the sides we know and want to know (O, A or H).

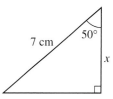

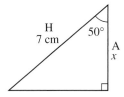

Recognise it is a cosine problem because we have A and H. So

$$\cos 50° = \frac{x}{7}$$

$$\Rightarrow \quad x = 7\cos 50° = 4.5\,\text{cm}$$

Example 3   Find the angle marked x in this triangle.

Mark on the triangle what we know and want to know.

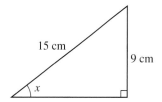

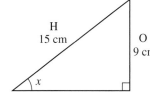

Recognise it is a sine problem because we have O and H. So

$$\sin x = \frac{9}{15} = 0.6$$

$$\Rightarrow \quad x = 36.9°$$

Example 4   Find the angle marked x in this triangle.

This triangle is not oriented in the usual way. So be careful when deciding which sides are which. If you are unsure, redraw the triangle so that it is oriented in a way that makes more sense. (This is the same as turning the page round to look at the triangle a different way.)

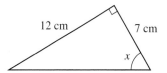

Mark on the triangle what we know and want to know.

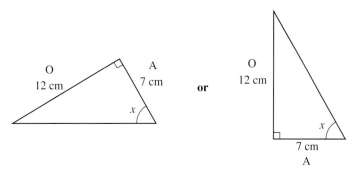

Recognise it is a tangent problem because we have O and A. So

$$\tan x = \frac{12}{7} = 1.714$$

$$\Rightarrow \quad x = 59.7°$$

EXERCISE 18H°

1 Find the length marked x in each of these triangles.

a
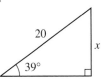

b
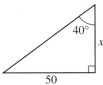

c

d

e
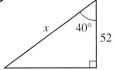

f
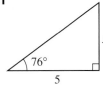

g

h
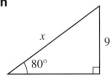

i

2 Find the angle marked x in each of these triangles.

a

b

c

d

e
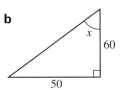

f

g
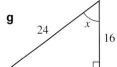

h

i
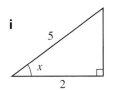

3 Find the angle or length marked x in each of these triangles.

a

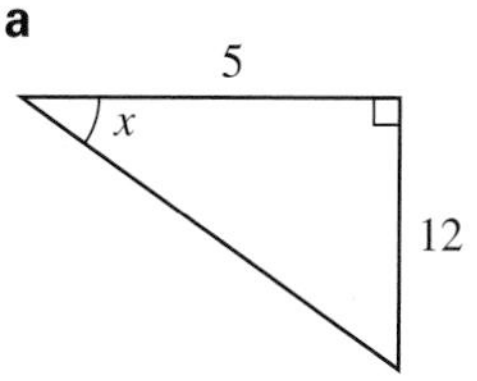

5

x

12

b

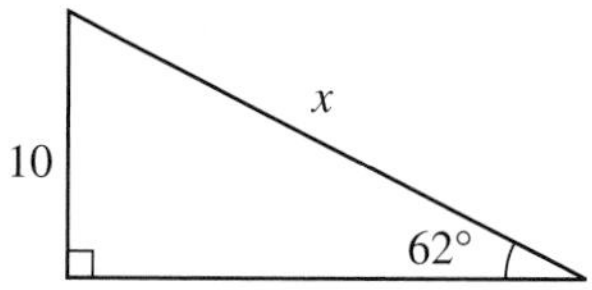

10

x

62°

c

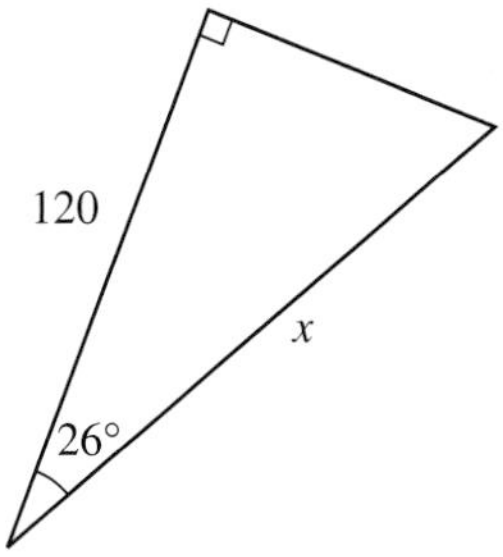

120

x

26°

d

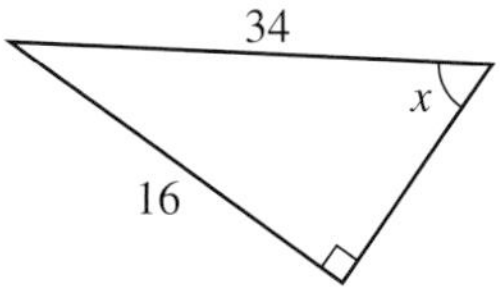

34

x

16

e

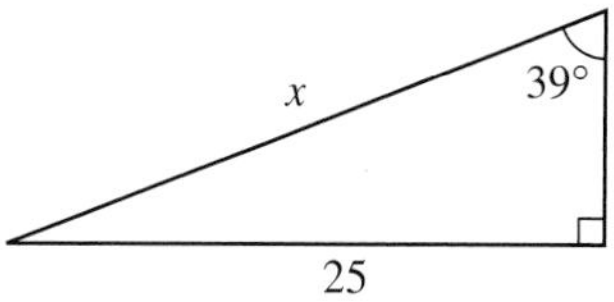

x

39°

25

f

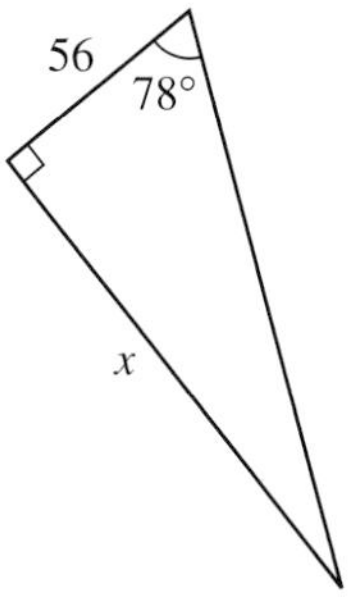

56

78°

x

g

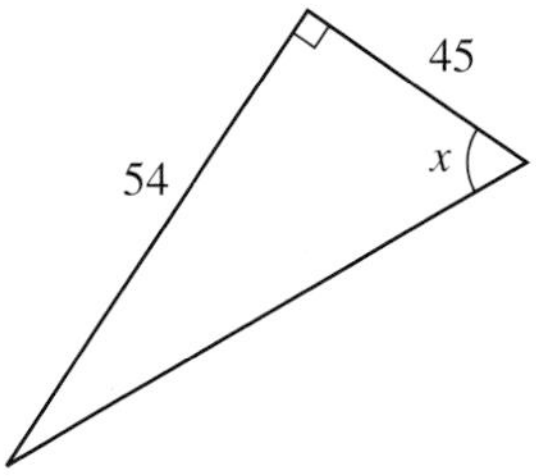

45

54

x

h

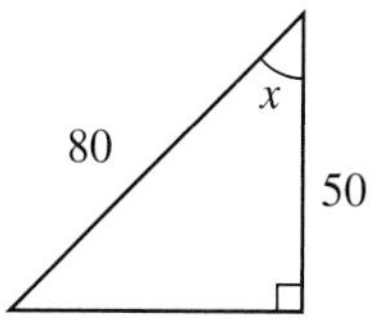

80

x

50

i

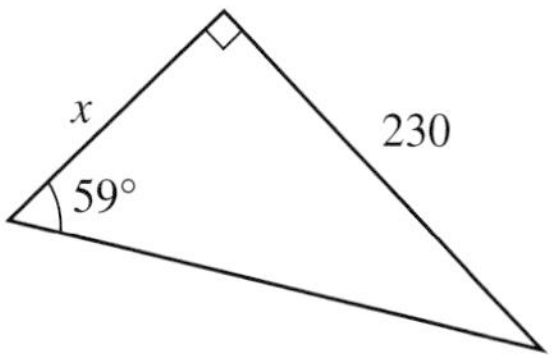

x

230

59°

j

x

23

82°

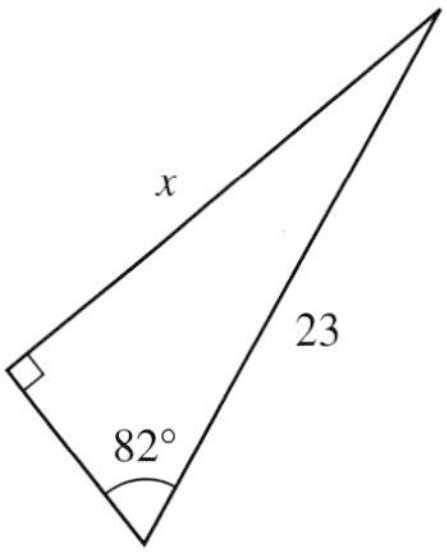

In the real world

Most trigonometry problems in GCSE examinations do not come as a straightforward triangle. Usually, solving a triangle is part of solving a practical problem. In this case, you **must draw** the triangle. Sometimes, the triangle is a section of the diagram that accompanies the problem. Even in this case, **redraw** the triangle. This will avoid any confusion and help you not only correctly to identify the sides but also to choose the correct ratio.

Example   A window cleaner has a ladder which is 7 m long. He leans it against a wall so that the foot of the ladder is 3 m from the wall. What angle does the ladder make with the wall?

Draw the situation as a right-angled triangle.

Then mark the sides and angle.

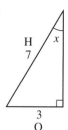

Recognise it is a sine problem because we have O and H. So

$$\sin x = \frac{3}{7} = 0.428$$

$$\Rightarrow x = 25.4°$$

EXERCISE 18I

In questions **1** to **7**:

- Draw the triangle required.

- Put on the information given (angles and/or sides).

- Put on x for the unknown angle or side.

- Mark on two of O, A or H as appropriate.

- Choose the ratio to use.

- Write out the ratio with the numbers in.

- Rearrange if necessary, then work out the answer.

1   A ladder 6 m long rests against a wall. The foot of the ladder is 2.5 m from the base of the wall. What angle does the ladder make with the ground?

2   The ladder in question **1** has a 'safe angle' with the ground of between 60° and 70°. What are the safe limits for the distance of the foot of the ladder from the wall?

3   Another ladder of length 10 m is placed so that it reaches 7 m up the wall. What angle does it make with the ground?

4   Yet another ladder is placed so that it makes an angle of 76° with the ground. When the foot of the ladder is 1.7 m from the foot of the wall, how high up the wall does the ladder reach?

5   Use trigonometry to calculate the length of the ladder in question **4**.

6   Use trigonometry to calculate the angle that the diagonal makes with the long side of a rectangle 10 cm by 6 cm.

7   Use trigonometry to calculate the length of the diagonal of a square with side 4 cm.

8   The diagram on the right shows a frame for a bookcase. What angle does the diagonal strut make with the long side? Use trigonometry to calculate the length of the strut.

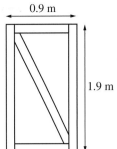

9   The diagram below shows a roof truss. What angle will the roof make with the horizontal? Use trigonometry to calculate the length of the sloping strut.

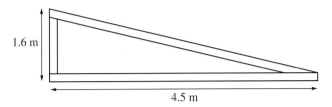

10   Building regulations state that the angle of a roof must be at least 25° to the horizontal. If the width of the roof truss in question **9** cannot be decreased, by how much does the vertical strut need to be increased so that the truss meets the regulations?

11   Alicia paces out 100 m from the base of a church. She then measures the angle to the top of the spire as 23°. How high is the church spire?

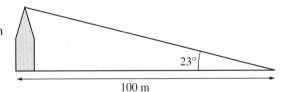

12   A girl is flying a kite on a string 32 m long. The string which is being held at 1 m above the ground, makes an angle of 39° with the horizontal. How high is the kite?

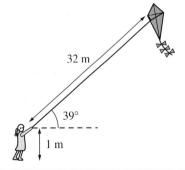

Special situations

A variety of special situations occur in trigonometry problems. These are commonly used in GCSE examinations because they give examiners opportunities to ask questions related to everyday experiences.

Angle of elevation and angle of depression

When you look **up** at an aircraft in the sky, the angle through which your line of sight turns from looking straight ahead (the horizontal) is called the **angle of elevation**.

When you are standing on a high point and look **down** at an object, the angle through which your line of sight turns from looking straight ahead (the horizontal) is called the **angle of depression**.

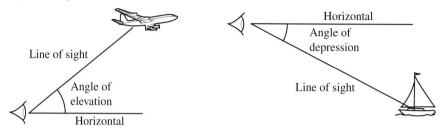

Example   From the top of a vertical cliff, 100 m high, Andrew sees a boat out at sea. The angle of depression from Andrew to the boat is 42°. How far from the base of the cliff is the boat?

The diagram of the situation is shown in figure **i**.

From this, we get the triangle shown in figure **ii**.

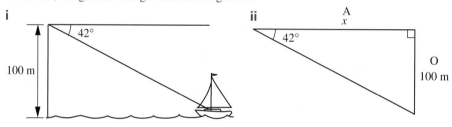

From figure **ii**, we see that this is a tangent problem. So

$$\tan 42° = \frac{100}{x}$$

$$\Rightarrow \quad x = \frac{100}{\tan 42°} = 111 \, \text{m} \quad (3 \, \text{sf})$$

EXERCISE 18J

1   Eric sees an aircraft in the sky. The aircraft is at a horizontal distance of 25 km from Eric. The angle of elevation is 22°. How high is the aircraft?

2   A passenger in the same aircraft hears the pilot say that they are flying at an altitude of 4000 m and are 10 km from the airport. If the passenger can see the airport, what is the angle of depression?

3   A man standing 200 m from the base of a television transmitter looks at the top of it and notices that the angle of elevation of the top is 65°. How high is the tower?

4   From the top of a vertical cliff, 200 m high, a boat has an angle of depression of 52°. How far from the base of the cliff is the boat?

5   From a boat, the angle of elevation of the foot of a lighthouse on the edge of a cliff is 34°. If the cliff is 150 m high, how far from the base of the cliff is the boat? If the lighthouse is 50 m high, what would the angle of elevation of the top of the lighthouse from the boat be?

6   A bird flies from the top of a 12 m tall tree, at an angle of depression of 34°, to catch a worm on the ground.
   a   How far does the bird actually fly?
   b   How far was the worm from the base of the tree?

7   I stand about 50 m away from a building. The angle of elevation from me to the top of the building is about 15°. How tall is the building?

8   The top of a ski run is 100 m above the finishing line. The run is 300 m long. What is the angle of depression of the ski run?

Bearings and trigonometry

A bearing is the direction of one place from another. The usual way of giving a bearing is as an angle measured from north in a clockwise direction (see pages 149–50). This is how a navigational compass and a surveyor's compass measure bearings.

A bearing is always written as a three-digit number. The diagram shows how this works, using the main compass points as examples.

When working with bearings, these three rules must be followed:

- Always start from **north**.

- Always measure **clockwise**.

- Always give a bearing (in degrees) as a **three-digit number**.

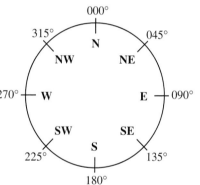

The difficulty with trigonometric problems involving bearings is dealing with those angles greater than 90° whose trigonometric ratios have negative values. To avoid this, we have to find a right-angled triangle that we can use.

Example 1   A ship sails on a bearing of 120° for 50 km. How far east has it travelled?

The diagram of the situation is shown in figure **i**. From this, we get the acute-angled triangle shown in figure **ii**.

From figure **ii**, we see that this is a cosine problem. So

$$\cos 30° = \frac{x}{50}$$

$$\Rightarrow \quad x = 50 \cos 30° = 43.301 = 43.3 \quad (3\text{ sf})$$

Example 2 A walker takes a bearing on a mountain top and finds that it is 233°. He knows he is 5 km east of the peak. How far will he have to walk to get to the peak?

The diagram of the situation is shown in figure **i**. From this, we can get the triangle shown in figure **ii**.

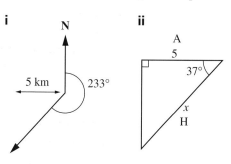

From figure **ii**, we see that this is a cosine problem. So

$$\cos 37° = \frac{5}{x}$$

$$\Rightarrow \quad x = \frac{5}{\cos 37°} = 6.26067\ldots = 6.26 \text{ km} \quad \text{(3 sf)}$$

EXERCISE 18K

1 **a** A ship sails for 75 km on a bearing of 078°. How far east has it travelled?
  b How far north has the ship sailed?

2 Lopham is 17 miles from Wath on a bearing of 210°.
  a How far south of Wath is Lopham?
  b How far east of Lopham is Wath?

3 A plane sets off from an airport and flies due east for 120 km, then turns to fly due south for 70 km before landing at Seddeth. What is the bearing of Seddeth from the airport?

4 A helicopter leaves an army base and flies 60 km on a bearing of 078°.
  a How far east has the helicopter flown?
  b How far north has the helicopter flown?

5 A ship sails from a port on a bearing of 117° for 35 km before heading due north for 40 km and docking at Angle Bay.
  a How far south had the ship sailed before turning?
  b How far north had the ship sailed from the port to Angle Bay?
  c How far east is Angle Bay from the port?
  d What is the bearing from the port to Angle Bay?

6 Mountain A is due west of a walker. Mountain B is due north of the walker. The guidebook says that mountain B is 4.3 km from mountain A, on a bearing of 58°. How far is the walker from mountain B?

7 The diagram shows the relative distances and bearings of three ships A, B and C.

  a How far north of A is B? (Distance x on diagram.)

  b How far north of B is C? (Distance y on diagram.)

  c How far west of A is C? (Distance z on diagram.)

  d What is the bearing of A from C? (Angle $w°$ on diagram.)

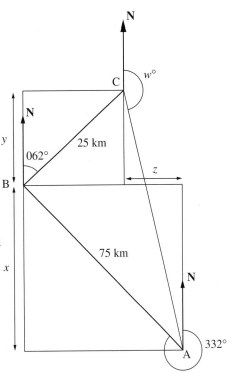

8 A ship sails from port A for 42 km on a bearing of 130° to point B. It then changes course and sails for 24 km on a bearing of 040° to point C, where it breaks down and anchors. What distance and on what bearing will a helicopter have to fly from port A to go directly to the ship at C?

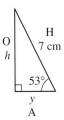

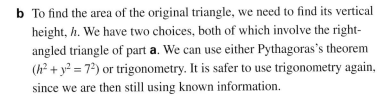

Isosceles triangles

Isosceles triangles often feature in trigonometry problems because such a triangle can be split into two right-angled triangles that are congruent.

Example   a Find the length x in this triangle.   **b** Calculate the area of the triangle.

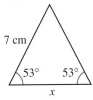

We look for a right-angled triangle. So draw a perpendicular from the apex of the triangle to its base, splitting the triangle into two congruent, right-angled triangles.

a To find the length $y \; (= \frac{1}{2}x)$, use the cosine of 53°, which gives

$$\cos 53° = \frac{y}{7}$$

$$\Rightarrow \quad y = 7 \cos 53° = 4.2 \, \text{cm}$$

So the length $x = 2y = 8.4 \, \text{cm}$.

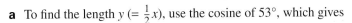

b To find the area of the original triangle, we need to find its vertical height, h. We have two choices, both of which involve the right-angled triangle of part **a**. We can use either Pythagoras's theorem ($h^2 + y^2 = 7^2$) or trigonometry. It is safer to use trigonometry again, since we are then still using known information.

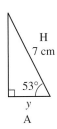

This is a sine problem, so

$$\sin 53° = \frac{h}{7}$$

$\Rightarrow \quad h = 7 \sin 53° = 5.6\,\text{cm}$ (Keep the accurate figure in the calculator.)

The area of the triangle $= \frac{1}{2} \times$ base $\times$ height. (We should use the most accurate figures we have for this calculation.)

$$\text{Area} = \frac{1}{2} \times 8.425\,4103 \times 5.590\,4486$$

$$= 23.55\,\text{cm}^2$$

You are not expected to write down these 8-figure numbers, just to use them.

Notice that if we used the rounded-off answers to calculate the area, the answer would be 23.52, which is significantly different from the one calculated using the most accurate data. So **never** use rounded-off data when you can use accurate data – unless you are just estimating.

EXERCISE 18L

In questions **1** to **4** find the side or angle marked x.

1

2

3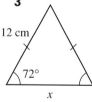

4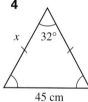

5 This diagram below shows a roof truss. Approximately how wide is the roof?

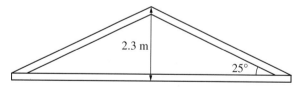

6 Calculate the area of each of these triangles.

a

b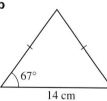

c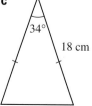

d

Possible coursework

Trig squared

   a   Calculate **i** $\sin 73°$ **ii** $\cos 73°$

   b   Calculate **i** $(\sin 73°)^2$ **ii** $(\cos 73°)^2$

   c   Calculate $(\sin 73°)^2 + (\cos 73°)^2$

   d   What do you notice?

   e   Investigate for other angles.

Special trig ratios

Use the diagram to find $\cos 60°$ without using a calculator.

What about $\sin 60°$ and $\tan 60°$?

What about $\sin 30°$, $\cos 30°$ and $\tan 30°$?

Draw another triangle to find $\cos 45°$ without using a calculator.

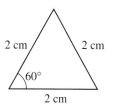

Rectangle in a semicircle

A rectangle can be drawn inside a
semicircle as shown in the diagram.
Investigate the area for different rectangles
that can be drawn inside the semicircle.

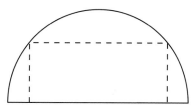

Examination questions

1   The sensor for a security light is fixed to
a house wall 2.5 m above the ground.
It can detect movement on the ground up
to 12.0 m away from the house.

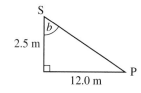

P is the furthest point where the sensor, S, can detect movement.

   a   Calculate the distance SP.   **b**   Calculate the size of angle b.

      OCR, Question 15, Intermediate (B) Paper 4, June 2000

2   A boat B is moored 40 m from the foot of
a vertical cliff. The angle of depression of
the boat from the top of the cliff is 42°.

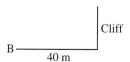

   a   Calculate the height of the cliff.

   b   The boat is released from its mooring
and it drifts 250 m directly away from the cliff. Calculate the angle
of elevation of the top of the cliff from the boat.

      WJEC, Question 19, Intermediate Paper 1, June 1999

3 The diagram shows two right-angled triangles ADC and BAC.
AB = 5 cm, DA = 15 cm and $\hat{ADC}$ = 65°

a Calculate the length of AC.

b Calculate the length of BC.

c Calculate $A\hat{B}C$.

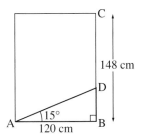

WJEC, Question 17, Intermediate Paper 2, November 1999

4 AB and BC are two sides of a rectangle.
AB = 120 cm and BC = 148 cm.
D is a point on BC.
Angle BAD = 15°.

Work out the length of CD.
Give your answer correct to the nearest centimetre.

EDEXCEL, Question 22, Intermediate Paper 4, June 2000

5 Dr Spooner was asked to use his calculator to work out the value of the expression 80 sin 30°. He made a mistake and actually found the value of 30 sin 80°.

a What value did Dr Spooner get?

b **i** What is the correct value of 80 sin 30°?

ii Calculate the percentage error in Dr Spooner's incorrect value.

MEG, Question 15, Specimen Paper 3, 1998

6 A top of a vertical cliff is 60 m above sea level. At 23.45 on Thursday, a life raft is 1800 m from the base of the cliff.

a Calculate the angle of elevation of the top of the cliff from the life raft.

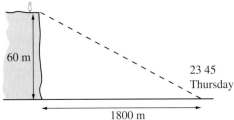

b At 01.15 on Friday, the angle of elevation of the top of the cliff from the life raft is 7.6°.
How far from the foot of the cliff is the life raft?

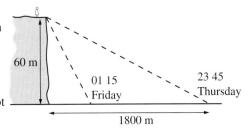

c At what speed is the life raft drifting towards the cliff?

WJEC, Question 14, Specimen Paper 2, 1998

7 In the diagram, ABCD is a parallelogram.

a Calculate the height, DN, of the parallelogram.

b Calculate the area of the parallelogram.

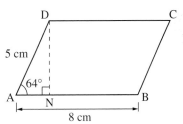

MEG, Question 14, Specimen Paper 3, 1998

8 The diagram shows the positions of three airports E (East Midlands), M (Manchester), and L (Leeds).

The distance from M to L is 65 km on a bearing of 060°. Angle LME = 90° and ME = 100 km.

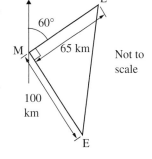

a Calculate, correct to three significant figures, the distance LE.

b Calculate, correct to the nearest degree, the size of angle MEL.

c An aircraft leaves M at 10.45 am and flies direct to E, arriving at 11.03 am. Calculate, correct to three significant figures, the average speed of the aircraft in kilometres per hour.

MEG, Question 11, Specimen Paper 4, 1998

9 A moving walkway runs between the ground floor and the first floor in a department store. The walkway is 8.25 m in length and rises 2.55 m.

a Calculate the distance AB.

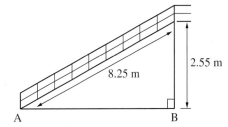

b Calculate the angle that the walkway slopes to the horizontal.

SEG, Question 20, Specimen Paper 13, 1998

10 The diagram shows a kite with measurements in metres.

BD bisects AC at right angles.

Calculate the angle ABC.

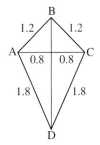

OCR, Question 16, Intermediate (A) Paper 4, June 2000

Summary

How well do you grade yourself?

To gain a grade **E**, you need to be able to solve triangle problems by scale drawing.

To gain a grade **C**, you need to be able to use sine, cosine and tangent in right-angled triangles when solving problems in two dimensions. These problems will usually be restricted to finding angles and short sides.

To gain a grade **B**, you need to be able to use sine, cosine and tangent in right-angled triangles when solving problems in two dimensions. These problems may include finding the hypotenuse, for example. They may also involve angles of depression and elevation, and bearings. Generally, questions for grade B will require you to interpret a practical situation before solving the trigonometry problem.

What you should know after you have worked through Chapter 18

- The three basic trigonometric ratios:

$$\text{sine } \theta = \frac{\text{Opposite}}{\text{Hypotenuse}} \qquad \text{cosine } \theta = \frac{\text{Adjacent}}{\text{Hypotenuse}} \qquad \text{tangent} = \frac{\text{Opposite}}{\text{Adjacent}}$$

  where the opposite, adjacent and hypotenuse are the three sides of a right-angled triangle such that:

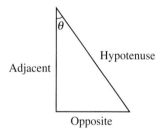

  Opposite is the side opposite to the angle being used.
  Adjacent is the side next to both that angle and the right angle.
  Hypotenuse is the side opposite to the right angle.

- In a right-angled triangle:

  ○ Given one side and one angle (other than the right angle), calculate the length of the other two sides.
  ○ Given two sides, calculate the two angles (other than the right angle).

- Interpret a practical situation to obtain a right-angled triangle which can be used to solve the problem.

19 Units

This chapter is going to ...

show you how to convert one metric unit to another and one imperial unit to another, and how to change between metric and imperial units. It will also show you how to use foreign currency exchange rates. You will be introduced to the idea of 'best buy' and some methods for deciding which are best buys.

What you should already know

✔ How to estimate a reasonable length or distance in metric units. For example, you ought to be able to make a good estimate in metric units for the following quantities, and know which is the best unit to use for each.

Your own height   centimetres
The length of your pen   centimetres
The thickness of your book   millimetres
The length of your classroom   metres
The distance from home to school   kilometres

✔ Have an understanding of weight and the difference between a gram, a kilogram and a tonne. You should know which unit is used when

Finding your own weight   kilograms
Finding the weight of a coin   grams
Finding the weight of a bus   tonnes

✔ Know when you are most likely to see the use of millilitres, centilitres and litres.

Bottles of pop   litres
Medicines   millilitres
Cans of pop   millilitres
Bottles of wine   centilitres
Cartons of cream   millilitres

EXERCISE 19A

Decide in which metric unit you would most likely measure each of the following amounts.

1   The height of your classroom.

2   The distance from London to Barnsley.

3   The thickness of your little finger.

4   The weight of this book.

5   The amount of water in a fish tank.

6   The weight of water in a fish tank.

7   The weight of an aircraft.

8   The amount of medicine you get on one spoon.

9   The amount of wine in a standard bottle.

10   The length of a football pitch.

11   The weight of your head teacher.

12   The amount of water in a bath.

13   The weight of a mouse.

14   The amount of tea in a teapot.

15   The thickness of a piece of wire.

Estimate the approximate metric length, weight or capacity of each of the following.

16   This book (both length and weight).

17   The length of your school hall. (You do **not** need to look at it.)

18   The capacity of a milk bottle (metric measure).

19   A brick (length, width and weight).

20   The diameter of a 10p coin, and its weight.

21   The distance from your school to Manchester city centre.

22   The weight of a cat.

23   The amount of water in one raindrop.

24   The dimensions of the room you are in.

25   Your own height and weight. (You can check this later and keep it to yourself.)

Metric and imperial units

Metric relationships

You should already know the relationships between the metric units.

Length   10 millimetres = 1 centimetre

1000 millimetres = 100 centimetres = 1 metre

1000 metres = 1 kilometre

Weight   1000 grams = 1 kilogram

1000 kilograms = 1 tonne

Capacity   10 millilitres = 1 centilitre

1000 millilitres = 100 centilitres = 1 litre

Volume 1000 litres = 1 metre^3

1 millilitre = 1 centimetre^3

You need to be able, with confidence, to convert from one unit to another. Since the metric system is based on powers of 10, you should be able easily to multiply or divide to change units. Follow through these examples.

To change **small** units to **larger** units, always **divide**.

Change

a   732 cm to metres $\rightarrow 732 \div 100 = 7.32$ m

b   410 mm to centimetres $\rightarrow 410 \div 10 = 41$ cm

c   840 mm to metres $\rightarrow 840 \div 1000 = 0.84$ m

d   5300 m to kilometres $\rightarrow 5300 \div 1000 = 5.3$ km

e   650 g to kilograms $\rightarrow 650 \div 1000 = 0.65$ kg

f   75 kg to tonnes $\rightarrow 75 \div 1000 = 0.075$ t

g   85 ml to centilitres $\rightarrow 85 \div 10 = 8.5$ cl

h   3250 ml to litres $\rightarrow 3250 \div 1000 = 3.25$ l

i   450 cl to litres $\rightarrow 450 \div 100 = 4.5$ l

j   7150 l to metres^3 $\rightarrow 7150 \div 1000 = 7.15$ m^3

To change **large** units to **smaller** units, always **multiply**.

Change

a   1.2 m to centimetres $\rightarrow 1.2 \times 100 = 120$ cm

b   0.62 cm to millimetres $\rightarrow 0.62 \times 10 = 6.2$ mm

c   3 m to millimetres $\rightarrow 3 \times 1000 = 3000$ mm

d   2.75 km to metres $\rightarrow 2.75 \times 1000 = 2750$ m

e   5.1 kg to grams $\rightarrow 5.1 \times 1000 = 5100$ g

f   7.02 t to kilograms $\rightarrow 7.02 \times 1000 = 7020$ kg

g   75 cl to millilitres $\rightarrow 75 \times 10 = 750$ ml

h   0.85 l to millilitres $\rightarrow 0.85 \times 1000 = 850$ ml

i   1.2 l to centilitres $\rightarrow 1.2 \times 100 = 120$ cl

j   20 000 m^3 to litres $\rightarrow 20\,000 \times 1000 = 20\,000\,000$ l

EXERCISE 19B

Complete the gaps using the conversion factors given on these two pages.

1	125 cm = m	**2**	82 mm = cm	**3**	550 mm = m
4	2100 m = km	**5**	208 cm = m	**6**	1240 mm = m
7	142 mm = cm	**8**	3560 m = km	**9**	3550 mm = m
10	94 cm = m	**11**	650 m = km	**12**	45 mm = m
13	805 mm = cm	**14**	1250 cm = m	**15**	2060 m = km
16	4200 g = kg	**17**	5750 kg = t	**18**	85 ml = cl
19	2580 ml = l	**20**	340 cl = l	**21**	600 kg = t
22	755 g = kg	**23**	800 ml = l	**24**	200 cl = l
25	630 ml = cl	**26**	1020 kg = t	**27**	4500 ml = l
28	2040 g = kg	**29**	450 cl = l	**30**	55 ml = l
31	8400 l = m^3	**32**	35 ml = cm^3	**33**	1035 l = m^3
34	530 l = m^3	**35**	5.3 m = cm	**36**	34 km = m
37	3.4 m = mm	**38**	13.5 cm = mm	**39**	0.67 m = cm
40	7.03 km = m	**41**	0.72 cm = mm	**42**	0.25 m = cm
43	0.05 m = cm	**44**	0.64 km = m	**45**	0.11 m = mm
46	2.4 l = ml	**47**	5.9 l = cl	**48**	8.4 cl = ml
49	5.2 m^3 = l	**50**	0.58 kg = g	**51**	3.75 t = kg
52	0.74 l = cl	**53**	0.94 cm^3 = l	**54**	45.8 kg = g
55	12.5 l = ml	**56**	21.6 l = cl	**57**	15.2 kg = g
58	14 m^3 = l	**59**	1.56 t = kg	**60**	0.19 cm^3 = ml

Imperial units

You need to be familiar with imperial units which are still in daily use.
The main ones are:

Length
12 inches = 1 foot
3 feet = 1 yard
1760 yards = 1 mile

Weight
16 ounces = 1 pound
14 pounds = 1 stone
2240 pounds = 1 ton

Capacity   8 pints = 1 gallon

- To change **large** units to **smaller** units, always **multiply**.

- To change **small** units to **larger** units, always **divide**.

EXERCISE 19C

Complete the gaps using the above information.

1 2 feet = inches   **2** 4 yards = feet

3 2 miles = yards   **4** 5 pounds = ounces

5 4 stone = pounds   **6** 3 tons = pounds

7 5 gallons = pints   **8** 4 feet = inches

9 1 yard = inches   **10** 10 yards = feet

11 4 pounds = ounces   **12** 60 inches = feet

13 5 stone = pounds   **14** 36 feet = yards

15 1 stone = ounces   **16** 8800 yards = miles

17 15 gallons = pints   **18** 1 mile = feet

19 96 inches = feet   **20** 98 pounds = stone

21 56 pints = gallons   **22** 32 ounces = pounds

23 15 feet = yards   **24** 11 200 pounds = tons

25 1 mile = inches   **26** 128 ounces = pounds

27 72 pints = gallons   **28** 140 pounds = stone

29 15 840 feet = miles   **30** 1 ton = ounces

Examples of the everyday use of imperial measures are:

> miles for distances by road
>
> pints for milk
>
> gallons of petrol (in conversation)
>
> pounds for the weight of babies (in conversation)
>
> feet for people's heights

Conversion factors

Several imperial measures are still widely used and it will take many years before they disappear from our thinking. So you do need to know the relationships between certain metric and imperial units.

The conversion factors you should be familiar with are given below (the symbol ≈ means 'is approximately equal to'). Those you need to know for use in your examinations are in bold type.

Length	**1 inch ≈ 2.5 centimetres**
	1 mile ≈ 1.61 kilometres or **5 miles ≈ 8 kilometres**
Weight	1 pound ≈ 450 grams or **2.2 pounds ≈ 1 kilogram**
Capacity	1 pint ≈ 570 millilitres or **1 gallon ≈ 4.5 litres**

Remember To convert between these units:

- **Multiply** when changing **large** units to **smaller** units

- **Divide** when changing **small** units to **larger** units.

Follow through these examples.

Change

    a   5 gallons to litres $\rightarrow 5 \times 4.5 = 23$ litres (rounded)

    b   36 litres to gallons $\rightarrow 36 \div 4.5 = 8$ gallons

    c   45 miles to kilometres $\rightarrow 45 \times 1.61 = 72.5$ kilometres (rounded)

    d   150 kilometres to miles $\rightarrow 150 \div 1.61 = 93$ miles (rounded)

    e   25 kilograms to pounds $\rightarrow 25 \times 2.2 = 55$ pounds

    f   5 pounds to kilograms $\rightarrow 5 \div 2.2 = 2.3$ kilograms (rounded)

Notice that it is most appropriate to round off your answers, since the original information is only an approximation.

EXERCISE 19D

In questions **1** to **30**, complete the gaps using the conversion factors on page 351.

1 8 inches = cm   **2** 6 kg = pounds   **3** 30 miles = km

4 15 gallons = litres   **5** 5 pints = ml **6** 45 litres = gallons

7 30 cm = inches   **8** 50 km = miles   **9** 12 pounds = kg

10 1750 ml = pints   **11** 100 miles = km   **12** 60 inches = cm

13 56 kg = pounds   **14** 40 gallons = litres   **15** 2 pints = ml

16 150 km = miles   **17** 200 pounds = kg   **18** 100 cm = inches

19 2300 ml = pints   **20** 100 litres = gallons   **21** 1 gallon = ml

22 1 km = yards   **23** 1 foot = cm   **24** 1 stone = kg

25 5 litres = pints   **26** 1 tonne = pounds   **27** 1 yard = cm

28 2000 feet = km   **29** 1 ton = kg   **30** 1 yard = m

31 Which is heavier, a tonne or a ton? Show your working clearly.

32 Which is longer, a metre or a yard? Show your working clearly.

33 1 cm^3 of water weighs about 1 gram.

    a What is the weight of 1 litre of water

        i in grams   **ii** in kilograms   **iii** in ounces?

    b What is the weight of 1 gallon of water

        i in grams   **ii** in kilograms   **iii** in ounces?

34 What is the largest amount of water you will be able to put into the following containers:

    a a cuboid measuring 30 cm by 18 cm by 12 cm

    b a cylinder with radius of 10 cm and a height of 8 cm

    c a drum measuring 2 feet in diameter and with a height of 36 inches?

35 While on holiday in France, I saw a sign that said: 'Paris 210 km'. I was travelling on a road that had a speed limit of 80 km/h.

    a How many miles was I from Paris?

    b What was the speed limit in miles per hour?

    c If I travelled at the top speed all the way, how long would it take me to get to Paris?

Foreign currency

Each country has developed its own currency with which goods can be bought and sold in that country. But when someone wants to buy goods from another country, a problem arises because its currency is different. This is overcome by having **exchange rates** between currencies.

So, for example, when a British company wants to buy goods from a Jamaican company, the British company has to exchange pounds sterling for Jamaican dollars.

We exchange our currency when we go abroad for holidays or business, so that we can buy goods and pay for trips and entertainment.

Official exchange rates exist between the world's major currencies. They change frequently and so are given daily in newspapers and displayed in banks and other places where money is exchanged.

For example, the exchange rate of the British £ to the US $ was recently £1 = $1.82. So a British visitor to New York at that time, with £1000 to spend, would have exchanged her money for

$1.82 \times 1000 = $1820

That is, the visitor would have had $1820 to spend in New York.

If she had returned to Britain with $250, she would have converted this back to British currency and received $250 \div 1.82 = £137.36.

Warning   Money-changers always make a charge (called a commission) for exchanging currency, so the amount you will receive in exchange for your foreign currency is less than what you would expect from the exchange rate. But, fortunately, all your examination questions will assume that money exchange costs nothing unless you are told otherwise.

You need to be careful when finding and using exchange rates to make sure you multiply or divide by the correct amount for the time of the exchange.

Look at Examples 1 to 4. For these, we assume exchange rates of £1 to 10.77 Swedish kronor and of US $1 to 1.39 Swiss francs.

Example 1   Exchange £150 to Swedish kronor: $150 \times 10.77 = 1615.50$ kronor
Example 2   Exchange 250 Swedish kronor to £s: $250 \div 10.77 = £23.21$
Example 3   Exchange US $200 to Swiss francs: $200 \times 1.39 = 278$ francs
Example 4   Exchange 500 Swiss francs to US $s: $500 \div 1.39 = 359.71

To summarise: when the exchange rate is £1 = …

- to change **from £s**, **multiply** by …

- to change back **to £s**, **divide** by …

EXERCISE 19E

In answering all of these questions, use this exchange rate table.

Currency	Exchange rates for £1
US dollar	$1.389
German deutschmark	DM 3.1155
Japanese yen	¥160.7
Swiss franc	SFr 2.4165
French franc	FFr 10.43
Belgian franc	BFr 64.01
Euro	€1.2153
Italian lira	L 3074
Swedish krona	SKr 12.09

1 £50 to $ **2** £80 to DM   **3** £100 to euros   **4** £120 to BFr

5 £150 to SKr   **6** £250 to ¥   **7** £560 to SFr   **8** £1700 to L

9 DM 96 to £   **10** SFr 340 to £   **11** BFr 640 to £   **12** ¥360 to £

13 L 50 000 to £   **14** SKr 175 to £   **15** €150 to £   **16** FFr 430 to £

17 £170 to $ **18** £71 to L   **19** £490 to BFr   **20** L 1 million to £

21 $328 to £   **22** ¥395 to £   **23** £65 to SKr   **24** 87 euros to £

25 £900 to SFr   **26** £500 to DM   **27** SFr 600 to £   **28** £410 to euros

29 Joseph went on a trip around Europe, starting out with £50. He first went to France, where he earned 540 francs and spent 112 francs. Then he moved on to Belgium, where he earned 2300 francs and spent 870 francs. Next, he stayed in Italy, where he earned 145 000 lire and spent 30 000 lire. He then stayed in Sweden, earning nothing but spending 1500 kronor. After Sweden, Joseph returned to Britain and changed all his money back into £s. How much did he have in £s when he came back home?

30 At a world conference of geologists, the following figures were quoted as being the average annual salaries of geologists in these countries.

Britain	£27 500	Japan	3.5 million yen
France	193 500 francs	Germany	72 200 DM
Italy	45 million lire		

Compare their earnings and rank them in order, the highest at the top of the list.

31 Paul was travelling from the USA to France, but he forgot to exchange his $2500 before he left the States. His plane stopped in England to refuel, giving him the chance to exchange his money at the airport. The money-changer he went to said: 'I can only change your money to pounds, then change that to French francs. I charge 2% commission on each exchange.' Paul was desperate to get French francs, so he agreed.

a How many French francs would Paul get?

b How much did the money-changer make on the deal?

Best buys

When you wander around a supermarket and see all the different prices for the many different-sized packets, it is rarely obvious which are the 'best buys'. However, with a calculator you can quite easily compare value for money by finding either

the price per gram (or 100 grams etc.)   or   the weight per 1p (or £1 etc.)

To find:

- **cost per unit weight**, divide **cost by weight**

- **weight per unit cost**, divide **weight by cost**.

The next two examples show you how to find the above quantities.

Example 1   A 250 g tin of cocoa costs £1.13.

First, change the cost to pence. Then divide to get

cost per unit weight $113 \div 250 = 0.452$ p per gram
weight per unit cost $250 \div 113 = 2.21$ g per penny

Example 2   A 205 g tin of beans costs 14 p.

First, change the cost to pence. Then divide to get

cost per unit weight $14 \div 205 = 0.068$ p per gram
weight per unit cost $205 \div 14 = 14.6$ g per penny

To compare the value of two commodities, we need to find for both

either   the cost per unit weight and take the **smaller value**
or   the weight per unit cost and take the **larger value**.

Example 3   There are two different-sized packets of Whito soap powder at a supermarket. The medium size contains 780 g at a cost of £1.85, and the large size contains 2.5 kg at a cost of £5.85. Which is the better buy?

We find weight per cost: Medium $780 \div 185 = 4.216$ g per penny
                           Large $2500 \div 585 = 4.27$ g per penny

From these we see that there is more weight per penny with the large size, so the large size is the better buy.

Mixture of metric and imperial

Sometimes we need to compare the prices of two commodities where the weight of one is in metric units and the weight of the other in imperial units. In such a case, we must convert one set of units to the other in order to be able to make a comparison.

Example A pint of milk costs 36p from the milkman, and a 2-litre packet costs 99p from the supermarket. Which is the better buy?

We need to convert either pints to litres, or litres to pints. As we already know 1 pint ≈ 570 millilitres, for the bottle of milk

570 ml costs 36p, so capacity per penny = 570 ÷ 36 = 15.833 ml per penny

For the 2-litre packet

2000 ml costs 99p, so capacity per penny = 2000 ÷ 90 = 20.2 ml per penny

So the 2-litre packet is the better buy.

EXERCISE 19F

1   Compare the following pairs of product and state which is the better buy and why.
   a   Coffee: a medium jar which is 140 g for £1.10 or a large jar which is 300 g for £2.18.
   b   Beans: a 125 g tin at 16p or a 600 g tin at 59p.
   c   Flour: a 3 kg bag at 75p or a 5 kg bag at £1.20.
   d   Toothpaste: a large tube which is 110 ml for £1.79 or a medium tube which is 75 ml for £1.15.
   e   Frosties: a large box which is 750 g for £1.64 or a medium box which is 500 g for £1.10.
   f   Rice Crispies: a medium box which is 440 g for £1.64 or a large box which is 600 g for £2.13.
   g   Hair shampoo: a bottle containing 400 ml for £1.15 or a bottle containing 550 ml for £1.60.

2   Compare the following pairs of product and state which is the better buy and why.
   a   Sugar: a 1 kg packet costing 75p or a 2 pound (weight) bag costing 68p
   b   Rice: a 1.5 kg packet costing 38p or a 5 pound (weight) packet costing 55p
   c   Marmalade: a 1 pound (weight) jar costing 57p or a 500 g jar costing 63p
   d   Orange juice: a litre carton costing 49p or a pint bottle costing 29p

3   Julie wants to respray her car with yellow paint. In the local automart she sees the following tins:

   small tin   350 ml at a cost of £1.79
   medium tin 500 ml at a cost of £2.40
   large tin   1.5 litres at a cost of £6.70

   a   Which tin is offered at the cheapest cost per litre?
      Each of the tins states: 'Used correctly this paint will cover 1 m² per 200 ml of paint'.
   b   Julie needs just enough paint to cover 11 m². What is the cheapest way in which this can be done?

Possible coursework tasks

An easy job

Design a bookcase for your school library that will hold 500 paperback books.

Breakfast buys

Find out which are the most popular
breakfast cereals.
Which cereals give the best value for money?

Examination questions

1 Ivy needs 150 pounds of Christmas pudding for the canteen. She can
   only order the puddings in kilogram packets.

   a About how many kilograms are equivalent to 150 pounds?

   b Ivy knows that each serving of Christmas pudding should be about 5
       ounces (16 ounces = 1 pound). How many servings of Christmas
       pudding can be obtained from 150 pounds?

   c Ivy wanted about 60% of the servings of Christmas pudding to have
       a sprig of holly on the top. Approximately how many sprigs of holly
       should she buy?   *NEAB, Question 15, Paper 1, November 1995*

2 Sarah's father sends her to the shops to buy 5 pounds of potatoes and
   2 pints of milk. She buys a 3 kilogram bag of potatoes and a litre carton
   of milk. Does she buy enough potatoes and milk?

                                WJEC, Question 2, Specimen Paper 2, 1998

3 Costsave and Pricewell supermarkets
   have corn flakes on special offer.
   Which supermarket has the better offer?
   Show clear working to explain your
   answer.

   COSTSAVE   **PRICEWELL**

   BUY 2, get another   *BUY 1, get another*
   FREE!   ***FREE!***

       OCR, Question 1, Intermediate (A) Paper 4, June 2000

4 A French supermarket buys coffee for 25.80 francs per kilogram.

   a The supermarket sells the coffee to make a profit of 60%.
       Calculate the selling price of one kilogram of coffee.

   b A British importer also buys the coffee at 25.80 francs per kilogram.
       The exchange rate is £1 = 9.63 francs.
       Calculate the cost of one kilogram of coffee in British money.
       Give your answer to an appropriate degree of accuracy.

       OCR, Question 3, Intermediate (A) Paper 4, June 2000

5 **a** Susan changed £500 into South African Rand, when the rate of exchange was £1 = 9.90 Rand. How many Rand did she get?

b During her holiday Susan spent 4005 Rand.

  i How many Rand did she have left?

  ii She changed her remaining Rand into pounds, when the exchange rate was £1 = 10.50 Rand.

  How many pounds did she get?

WJEC, Question 6, Intermediate Paper 1, June 1999

6 Mary went to Heidelberg for her holiday.

The rate of exchange was £1 = 2.83 DM (Deutschmarks).

a She changed £250 into Deutschmarks.

How many Deutschmarks did she receive?

b In Heidelberg she bought a new camera. The price was 130 DM.

How much was this in £?

c Mary drove 135 miles home from the airport in $2\frac{1}{2}$ hours.

What was her average speed?

OCR, Question 2, Intermediate (B) Paper 4, June 2000

7 A rectangular tank has length 60 cm, breadth 40 cm and height 36 cm. It is placed on a horizontal table. Water is poured into the tank until it is three-quarters full.

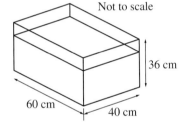

Not to scale

36 cm

60 cm

40 cm

a Calculate the depth of the water in the tank.

b Calculate the volume, in cubic centimetres, of water in the tank.

c Express your answer to part **b** in litres.

MEG, Question 2, Specimen Paper 3, 1998

8 Kylie went to Paris. She changed £200 into French francs.

The exchange rate was £1 = 9.60 French francs.

a Work out the number of French francs Kylie got.

Kylie brought 25 French francs back from Paris.

The exchange rate was now £1 = 10 French francs.

b Work out how much Kylie got in pounds.

EDEXCEL, Question 10, Intermediate Paper 3, June 2000

9 This camera was for sale at a shop in Singapore. The rate of exchange was £1 = $2.73. Calculate the cost of the camera in British money, correct to the nearest penny.

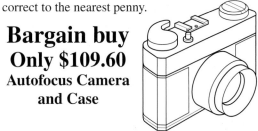

Bargain buy
Only $109.60
Autofocus Camera
and Case

MEG, Question 10, Paper 2, June 1998

10 Susan is driving through a French town.
The speed limit in the French town is 50 kilometres per hour.
Her speed is 35 miles per hour. Is she breaking the speed limit?
You must show all your working.

AQA (North), Question 8, Intermediate Paper 1, June 2000

Summary

How well do you grade yourself?

To gain a grade **E**, you need to know the approximate metric equivalents of the imperial units still in daily use and be able to convert one metric unit to another. You should also be able to make sensible estimates of lengths and weights of everyday objects.

To gain a grade **C**, you need to be able to compare prices between a metric measure and an imperial measure.

To gain a grade **B**, you have to be able to recognise the need to change units within a problem when comparing two different types of unit, and be able to change from one unit to the other.

What you should know after you have worked through Chapter 19

- How to convert from one metric unit to another.

- How to convert between some imperial units.

- How to convert between metric and imperial units.

- How to use exchange rates in dealing with foreign currencies.

- How to compare the prices of different units of goods.

20 Loci and angles in a circle

This chapter is going to ...

introduce you to the idea of a locus, and to some of the more common loci (plural of locus). It will then show you how to use these loci in practical situations. It will also show you a number of facts about angles in a circle.

What you should already know

✔ How to use a pair of compasses to draw circles accurately.
✔ How to use a ruler accurately to measure distances and to draw straight lines.
✔ Understand the idea of a scale when it applies to maps.
✔ A plan view of a situation is what you see when looking down on it.
✔ How to draw the line that bisects the distance between two points (known as the perpendicular bisector).
✔ How to draw the line that bisects an angle.

If you feel the need to revise some of these items, you should turn to Chapter 9, pages 149–159.

What is a locus?

A locus (plural loci) is the movement of a point according to a rule.

For example, a point that moves so that it is always at a distance of 5 cm from a fixed point A will have a locus that is a circle of radius 5 cm.

To express this mathematically, we say:

The locus of the point P is such that AP = 5 cm

Another point moves so that it is always the same distance from two fixed points A and B.

To express this mathematically, we say:

The locus of the point P is such that AP = BP

Another point moves so that it is always 5 cm from a line AB; we would give the locus of the point P as a 'racetrack' shape. This is difficult to express mathematically.

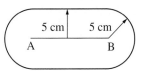

The three examples of loci just given occur frequently.

Imagine a grassy, flat field in which a horse is tethered to a stake by a rope that is 10 m long. What is the shape of the area that the horse can graze?

In reality, the horse may not be able to reach the full 10 m if the rope is tied round its neck but we ignore fine details like that. We 'model' the situation by saying that the horse can move around in a 10 m circle and graze all the grass within that circle.

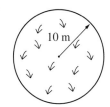

In this example, the locus is the whole of the area inside the circle. We express this mathematically as

The locus of the point P is such that AP ≤ 10 m

EXERCISE 20A

1   A is a fixed point. Sketch the locus of the point P when
    a   AP = 2 cm   **b**   AP = 4 cm   **c**   AP = 5 cm

2   A and B are two fixed points 5 cm apart. Sketch the locus of the point P for the following situations:
    a   AP = BP   **b**   AP = 4 cm and BP = 4 cm
    c   P is always within 2 cm of the line AB.

3   A horse is tethered in a field on a rope 4 m long. Describe or sketch the area that the horse can graze.

4   The same horse is still tethered by the same rope but there is now a long, straight fence running 2 m from the stake. Sketch the area that the horse can now graze.

5   ABCD is a square of side 4 cm. In each of the following loci, the point P moves only inside the square. Sketch the locus in each case.
    a   AP = BP   **b**   AP < BP
    c   AP = CP   **d**   CP < 4 cm
    e   CP > 2 cm   **f**   CP > 5 cm

6   One of the following diagrams is the locus of a point on the rim of a bicycle wheel as it moves along a flat road. Which is it?

    a   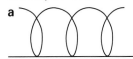   **b**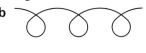

    c      **d**

7   Draw the locus of the centre of the wheel for the bicycle in question **6**.

Practical problems

Most of the loci problems in your GCSE examination will be of a practical nature, as in the next three examples.

Example 1   Imagine that a radio company wants to find a site for a transmitter. The transmitter must be the same distance from Doncaster and Leeds and within 20 miles of Sheffield.

In mathematical terms, this means we are concerned with the perpendicular bisector between Leeds and Doncaster and the area within a circle of radius 20 miles from Sheffield.

The map, drawn to a scale of 1 cm ≡ 10 miles, illustrates the situation and shows that the transmitter can be built anywhere along the thick black line.

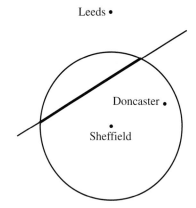

Example 2   A radar station in Birmingham has a range of 150 km (i.e. it can pick up any aircraft within a radius of 150 km). Another radar station in Norwich has a range of 100 km. Can an aircraft be picked up by both radar stations at the same time?

The situation is represented by a circle of radius 150 km around Birmingham and another circle of radius 100 km around Norwich. Because the two circles overlap, then an aircraft could be picked up by both radar stations in the overlap.

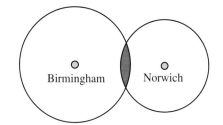

Example 3   A dog is tethered by a rope, 3 m long, to the corner of a shed, 4 m by 2 m. What is the area that the dog can guard effectively?

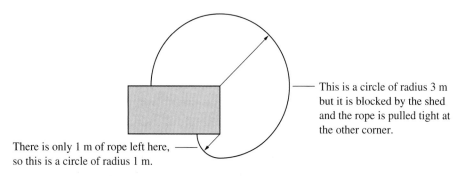

This is a circle of radius 3 m but it is blocked by the shed and the rope is pulled tight at the other corner.

There is only 1 m of rope left here, so this is a circle of radius 1 m.

EXERCISE 20B

For questions **1** to **7**, you should start by sketching the picture given in each question on a 6 × 6 grid, each square of which is 2 cm by 2 cm. The scale for each question is given.

1   A goat is tethered by a rope, 7 m long, in a corner of a field with a fence at each side. What is the locus of the area that the goat can graze? Use a scale of 1 cm ≡ 1 m.

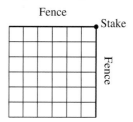

2   A horse in a field is tethered to a stake by a rope 6 m long. What is the locus of the area that the horse can graze? Use a scale of 1 cm ≡ 1 m.

3   A cow is tethered to a rail at the top of a fence 6 m long. The rope is 3 m long. Sketch the area that the cow can graze. Use a scale of 1 cm ≡ 1 m.

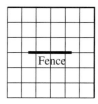

4   A horse is tethered to a stake near a corner of a fenced field, at a point 4 m from each fence. The rope is 6 m long. Sketch the area that the horse can graze. Use a scale of 1 cm ≡ 1 m.

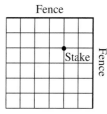

5   A horse is tethered to a corner of a shed, 2 m by 1 m. The rope is 2 m long. Sketch the area that the horse can graze. Use a scale of 2 cm ≡ 1 m.

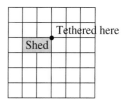

6   A goat is tethered by a 4 m rope to a stake at one corner of a pen, 4 m by 3 m. Sketch the area of the pen on which the goat cannot graze. Use a scale of 2 cm ≡ 1 m.

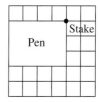

7   A puppy is tethered to a stake by a rope, 3 m long, on a flat lawn on which are two raised brick flower beds. The stake is situated at one corner of a bed, as shown. Sketch the area that the puppy is free to roam in. Use a scale of 1 cm ≡ 1 m.

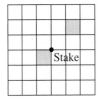

For questions **8** to **15**, you should use a copy of the map on page 364. For each question trace the map and mark on those points that are relevant to that question.

8   A radio station broadcasts from London on a frequency of 1000 kHz with a range of 300 km. Another radio station broadcasts from Glasgow on the same frequency with a range of 200 km.

    a   Sketch the area to which each station can broadcast.

    b   Will they interfere with each other?

    c   If the Glasgow station increases its range to 400 km, will they then interfere with each other?

9   The radar at Leeds airport has a range of 200 km. The radar at Exeter airport has a range of 200 km.

    a   Will a plane flying over Glasgow be detected by the Leeds radar?

    b   Sketch the area where a plane can be picked up by both radars at the same time.

10   A radio transmitter is to be built according to the following rules.

    i   It has to be the same distance from York and Birmingham.

    ii   It must be within 350 km of Glasgow.

    iii   It must be within 250 km of London.

    a   Sketch the line that is the same distance from York and Birmingham.

    b   Sketch the area that is within 350 km of Glasgow and 250 km of London.

    c   Show clearly the possible places at which the transmitter could be built.

11   A radio transmitter centred at Birmingham is designed to give good reception in an area greater than 150 km and less than 250 km from the transmitter. Sketch the area of good reception.

12   Three radio stations pick up a distress call from a boat in the Irish Sea. The station at Glasgow can tell from the strength of the signal that the boat is within 300 km of the station. The station at York can tell that the boat is between 200 km and 300 km from York. The station at London can tell that it is less than 400 km from London. Sketch the area where the boat could be.

13   Sketch the area that is between 200 km and 300 km from Newcastle upon Tyne, and between 150 km and 250 km from Bristol.

14   An oil rig is situated in the North Sea in such a position that it is the same distance from Newcastle upon Tyne and Manchester. It is also the same distance from Sheffield and Norwich. Draw the line that shows all the points that are the same distance from Newcastle upon Tyne and Manchester. Repeat for the points that are the same distance from Sheffield and Norwich and find out where the oil rig is located.

15   Whilst looking at a map, Fred notices that his house is the same distance from Glasgow, Norwich and Exeter. Where is it?

16 Wathsea Harbour is as shown in the diagram. A boat sets off from point A and steers so that it keeps the same distance from the sea-wall and the West Pier. Another boat sets off from B and steers so that it keeps the same distance from the East Pier and the sea-wall. Copy the diagram below, and on your diagram show accurately the path of each boat.

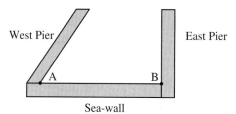

West Pier   East Pier

A   B

Sea-wall

Circles and angles

Angles in a circle

Here are three theorems you need to know. Try proving them for yourself.

- An angle at the centre of a circle is twice any angle at the circumference subtended by the same arc.

  $\angle AOB = 2 \times \angle ACB$

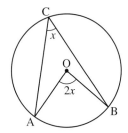

- Every angle at the circumference of a semicircle that is subtended by the diameter of the semicircle is a right angle.

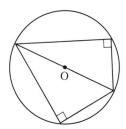

- Angles at the circumference in the same segment of a circle are equal. (That is, they are subtended by the same arc.)

  $\angle AC_1B = \angle AC_2B = \angle AC_3B = \angle AC_4B$

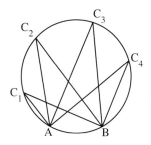

Follow through Examples 1 to 3 to see how these theorems are applied.

Example 1 O is the centre of each circle. Find the angles marked *a* and *b* in each circle.

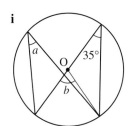

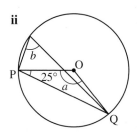

i $a = 35°$ (Angles in same segment)

  $b = 2 \times 35°$ (Angle at centre = Twice angle at circumference)

   $= 70°$

ii With OP = OQ, triangle OPQ is isosceles. So the sum of the angles in this triangle is given by

$$a + (2 \times 25°) = 180°$$
$$\Rightarrow \quad a = 180° - (2 \times 25°)$$
$$= 130°$$

$$b = \frac{1}{2} \times 130° \quad \text{(Angle at circumference)}$$
$$= 65°$$

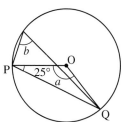

Example 2 O is the centre of the circle. PQR is a straight line. Find the angle labelled *a*.

$$\angle PQT = 180° - 72°$$
$$= 108°$$
$$\text{(Reflex) } \angle POT = 2 \times 108° \quad \text{(Angle at centre)}$$
$$= 216°$$

$$a + 216° = 360° \quad \text{(Sum of angles around a point)}$$
$$\Rightarrow \quad a = 360° - 216°$$
$$= 144°$$

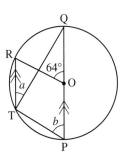

Example 3 O is the centre of the circle. POQ is parallel to TR. Find the angles labelled *a* and *b*.

$$a = \frac{1}{2} \times 64° \quad \text{(Angle at circumference)}$$
$$= 32°$$
$$\angle TQP = a \quad \text{(Alternate angles)}$$
$$= 32°$$
$$\angle PTQ = 90° \quad \text{(Angle in a semicircle)}$$
$$b + 90° + 32° = 180° \quad \text{(Sum of angles in } \Delta PQT)$$
$$\Rightarrow \quad b = 180° - 122° = 58°$$

EXERCISE 20C

1 Find the value of *x* in each of these circles with centre O.

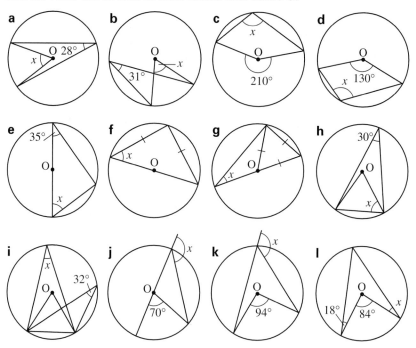

2 Find the value of *x* in each of these circles with centre O.

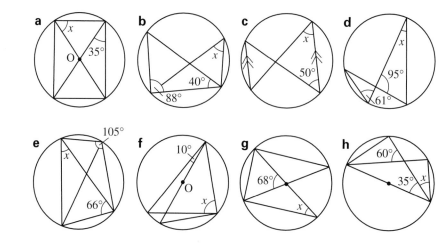

3 In the diagram, O is the centre of the circle. Find

   a ∠ADB

   b ∠DBA

   c ∠CAD

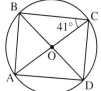

4 In the diagram, O is the centre of the circle. Find *x*.

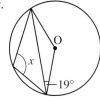

5 In the diagram, O is the centre of the circle. Find

a ∠EDF

b ∠DEG

c ∠EGF

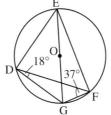

6 In the diagram, O is the centre, AD a diameter of the circle. Find *x*.

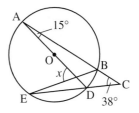

7 Find the values of *x* and *y* in each of these circles with centre O.

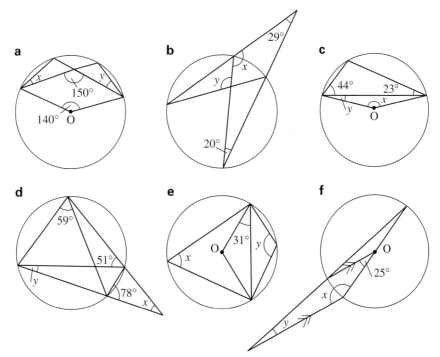

Cyclic quadrilaterals

A quadrilateral whose four vertices lie on the circumference of a circle is called a **cyclic quadrilateral**.

The sum of the opposite angles of a cyclic quadrilateral is 180°. (See the example on the right.)

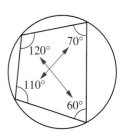

EXERCISE 20D

1 Find the size of the lettered angles in each of these circles.

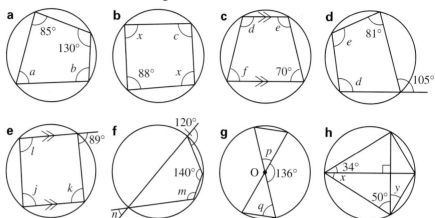

2 Find the values of *x* and *y* in each of these circles, centre O.

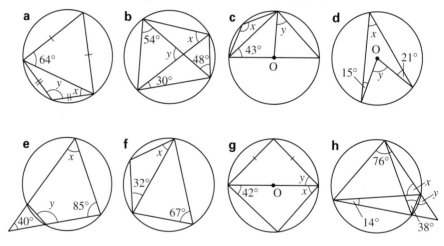

3 Find the values of *x* and *y* in each of these circles, centre O.

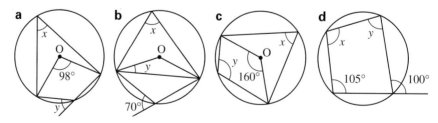

4 Find the values of *x* and *y* in each of these circles.

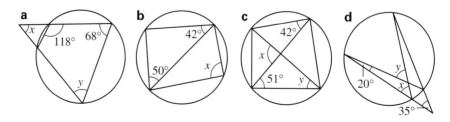

5 Find the values of *x* and *y* in each of these circles, centre O.

a

42° *x* *y* 85°
O

b

O
x
y
76°

c

O
x
y
16°

d

x
38°
O

6 The cyclic quadrilateral PQRT has ∠ROQ equal to 38°. POT is a diameter of a circle, centre O and parallel to QR. Calculate

a ∠ROT   **b** ∠QRT

Tangents to a circle

A tangent is a straight line that **touches** a circle **at one point only**. This point is called the **point of contact**.

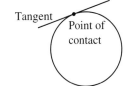

Tangent
Point of contact

There are three other important properties of tangents which you need to know.

- A tangent to a circle is perpendicular to the radius drawn to the point of contact.

- The tangents to a circle from an external point are equal in length from that external point to the points of contact.

- The line joining the external point to the centre of the circle bisects the angle between the tangents.

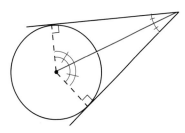

EXERCISE 20E

1 In each diagram, TP and TQ are tangents to a circle, centre O. Find each value of *x*.

a

x T
52°
O

b

P
70° T
x
O
Q

c

O
5*x*
x
P   T

d

O
P
3*x*
Q
x
T

2 Each diagram shows a tangent to a circle, centre O. Find each value of *y*.

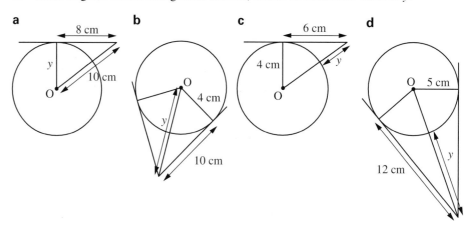

a 8 cm · *y* · 10 cm · O

b O · 4 cm · *y* · 10 cm

c 6 cm · 4 cm · *y* · O

d O · 5 cm · 12 cm · *y*

3 Each diagram shows a tangent to a circle, centre O. Find *x* and *y* in each case.

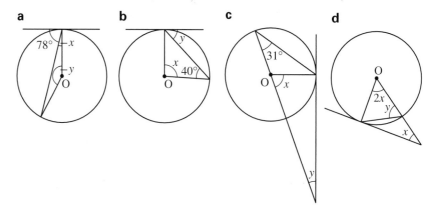

a 78° · *x* · *y* · O

b *y* · *x* · 40° · O

c 31° · O · *x* · *y*

d O · 2*x* · *y* · *x*

4 In each of the diagrams, TP and TQ are tangents to the circle, centre O. Find each value of *x*.

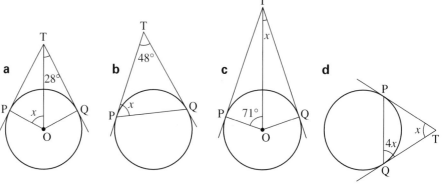

a T · 28° · P · *x* · Q · O

b T · 48° · P · *x* · Q

c T · *x* · P · 71° · Q · O

d P · *x* · 4*x* · T · Q

5 Three circles are drawn so that they just touch each other on the outside. Their centres form a triangle with sides 10 cm, 9 cm and 7 cm. What is the total area of the three circles?

6 A point P is 8.5 cm from the centre of a circle. A tangent from P to the circle is 7.2 cm long. What is the area of the circle?

7 Two circles with the same centre have radii of 7 cm and 12 cm respectively. A tangent to the inner circle cuts the outer circle at A and B. Find the length of AB.

Possible coursework tasks

Dangerous ladders

A window cleaner is climbing a ladder when, unfortunately, the ladder slips down the wall. If he is halfway up the ladder when this happens, draw diagrams to show the locus of his path as he clings to the ladder.

Investigate the locus of his path for different positions on the ladder.

Toppling boxes

A square box is rolled along the ground. The box will rotate about D to end up in the position shown on the diagram. The locus of A as it moves is also shown.

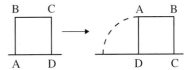

Complete the locus of A until A is on the ground again.
What is the locus of A if the box is a cuboid?
Investigate for different-shaped boxes.

A practical locus

Cut out a number of circles from paper. Mark a point A inside one circle. Fold the paper so that the circumference of the circle touches A.

Repeat as many times as you can, making sure that the fold lines are very clear.
Explain what you find.

Investigate for different positions of A.

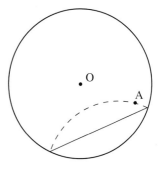

The conchoid

XY is a fixed line and O is a fixed point. Lines OP are drawn such that PQ is a fixed distance. Three positions for P are shown on the diagram.

By plotting other points, show the locus of P. Investigate other possible loci in this situation.

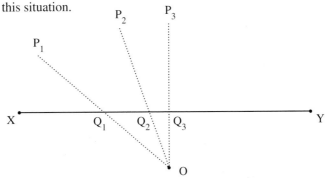

Examination questions: coursework type

Fred has a goat called Billy. Billy grazes in a square field, 60 ft by 60 ft which has a footpath running diagonally across it from B to D. Fred has lots of rope and he wants Billy to have the maximum amount of grass to eat, but Billy must not be able to cross over the footpath. Fred has worked out that the best place to tether Billy is to a post in one of the corners, A or C, as shown in the diagram.

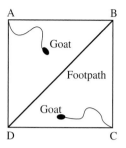

Fred also has a rectangular field which measures 60 ft by 180 ft. This field also has a footpath running diagonally across it. Sometimes he wants Billy to graze in this rectangular field without being able to cross over the footpath. He thinks the best places to tether Billy are the corners, as shown in the diagram.

Is Fred correct? Can you find any better places?

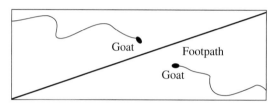

You may use any combination of accurate drawing, measurement and calculation. Explain your method and reasons fully. (You will need to draw scale diagrams.)

NEAB, Question 4, Paper 3, June 1995

Examination questions

1   A ⊢————————————————⊣ B

The line AB is 7.5 cm long. Copy AB and draw the locus of all the points which are 3 cm away from your line AB.

EDEXCEL, Question 12, Intermediate Paper 3, June 2000

2   The rectangle is 4.7 cm by 6.6 cm.
On a copy of the rectangle drawn the correct size, draw the locus of the points, **outside the rectangle**, that are 3 cm from the edge of the rectangle.

EDEXCEL, Question 23, Intermediate Paper 3, June 2000

3 The scale diagram below shows a plan of a room.
The dimensions of the room are 9 m by 7 m.

Two plug sockets are fitted along the walls.

One is at the point marked A, 1 m from the corner.
The other is at the point marked B,
2 m from the corner.
A third plug socket is to be fitted along a wall.
It must be equidistant from A and B.

On a scale drawing of your own, use ruler and compasses to find the
position of the new socket. Label it C.

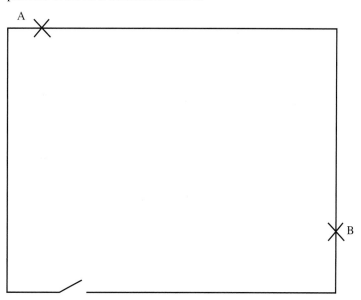

AQA (North), Question 11, Intermediate Paper 1, June 2000

4 The diagram overleaf shows a vertical cross view of a garage and drive.
It is drawn to a scale of 2 cm to represent 1 m. There is a security light at
L. The light has a sensor which switches on the light when anything
moves into its range. Its range is 2 m.

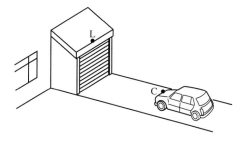

a On the diagram below draw the boundary of the sensor's range.

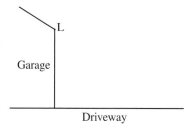

The top of the front of the car C (see the sketch at the top of this question) is 1 m above the ground.

b Draw the locus of the point C as the car is driven towards the garage.

c How far is the front of the car from the garage door when it switches on the light?

NEAB, Question 21, Specimen Paper 2I, 1998

5 The diagram here shows a scale drawing of a stage 9 m by 15 m. It shows a rectangular stage ABCD. A light has to be placed so that it is closer to C than A, it is more than 5 m from AB and it is less than 10 m from B. Indicate clearly on a diagram the area where the light can be placed.

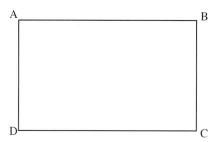

WJEC, Question 9, Intermediate Paper 2, November 1999

Summary

How well do you grade yourself?

To gain a grade **E**, you need to be able to draw a simple given locus, measuring lines and angles accurately.

To gain a grade **D**, you need to be able to interpret a simple practical problem with only a single condition and draw the locus that describes it.

To gain a grade **C**, you need to be able to express a problem in terms of a locus and have a good idea of which locus is wanted.

To gain a grade **B**, you need to be able to sketch and interpret complicated loci with more than one condition. You need also to know the circle theorems: angle at the centre, angles in the same segment, angles in a semicircle and angles in a cyclic quadrilateral.

What you should know after you have worked through Chapter 20

- Understand what is meant by a locus.

- How to draw a locus round a point, line or plane shape.

- How to draw a locus that depends on the bisecting of lines or angles or both.

- Be able to recognise when a locus is being asked for.

- An angle at the centre of a circle is twice any angle at the circumference subtended by the same arc.

- Every angle at the circumference of a semicircle that is subtended by a diameter of the semicircle is a right angle.

- Angles at the circumference in the same segment of a circle are equal.

- The sum of the opposite angles of a cyclic quadrilateral is $180°$.

- A tangent is a straight line that touches a circle at one point only. This point is called the point of contact.

- A tangent is perpendicular to the radius at the point of contact.

Revision paper for Chapters 1 to 20

Answer **all** questions, showing your methods of solution.

1 Evaluate: **a** $-5 - 7$ **b** $-9 \div -8$ **c** $-1.54 + 7.2$

2 **a** Increase £432 by 12%.

 b What % is £4 out of £32?

 c I put £250 into a savings account that adds 8% interest every year. How much will I have in this account if I leave my money in for 3 years?

3 A length of wire, 2 mm thick and 10 m in length, weighs 280 grams. What is the density of the metal used in the wire?

4 A circle has a circumference of 50 cm. What is its area?

5 What is the volume of the following prisms?

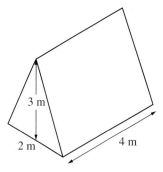
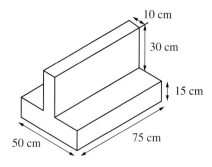

6 **a** Calculate the value of F, where $F = 3m^2 - \dfrac{4}{t}$ and $m = 3.75$, $t = -0.35$.

 b Solve by trial and improvement the equation $x^2 + 5x = 10$, correct to 2 decimal places.

7 State the size of the lettered angles.

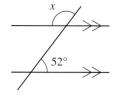
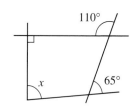

8 **a** Draw a triangle ABC with the co-ordinates A(1, 1), B(3, 2), C(4, 0).

   b Enlarge triangle ABC with a scale factor of 2 from the centre of enlargement (5, 3).

9 Using ruler and compasses only, construct the triangle ABC, where the side AB is 8 cm, the angle CAB is 30° and the angle CBA is 45°.

10 **a** Draw a shape that has two lines of symmetry and order of rotational symmetry 1.

   b Draw a shape that has rotational symmetry of order 2 and no lines of symmetry.

11 **a** What is the square root of 4.5×10^7?

   b What is the smallest integer value of n that satisfies the inequality $7^n > 7000$?

12 Train A leaves station A at 8.00 am, travelling towards station B at an average speed of 40 mph. Train B leaves station B at 8.30 am, travelling towards station A at an average speed of 50 mph. The two stations are 100 miles apart. At what time do the trains pass each other and where?

13 A schoolteacher's 15-day holiday is usually spent as:

   Rest   3 days

   Schoolwork   2 days

   Jobs on the house   4 days

   Gardening   6 days

Draw a pie chart to illustrate this data.

14 A formula used to calculate the charge, £C, for cleaning N windows is given by

   $$C = 3 + \frac{N}{4}$$

   a Calculate the charge for cleaning the windows of a house with 12 windows.

   b **i** Transform the formula to make N the subject.

   ii Mr Brown was charged £8 for his windows to be cleaned. How many windows did he have?

15 Calculate the gradients of the lines joining the following points.

   a (1, 3) to (5, 7)   **b** (1, 8) to (3, 5)

16 The lines AE and BD are parallel.

   a Which are the two similar triangles in the diagram?

   b Calculate the lengths of

   i CD   **ii** AB

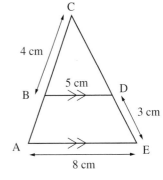

17 **a** Calculate the length of BD to
1 decimal place.
   b Calculate the length of BC correct to
4 significant figures.
   c Is the triangle ADC a right-angled
triangle? Give your reasons.

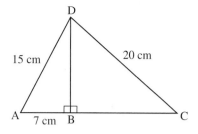

18 From the diagram calculate
   a the length x
   b the length y
   c the size of the angle z.

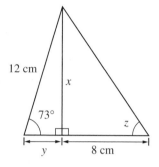

19 Which of the following represents the better buy and why?
Large packet of Sudso soap powder   3.5 kg for £5.80
Medium packet of Sudso soap powder   2.7 kg for £4.50

20 **a** Draw an isosceles triangle whose base length is 8 cm, and whose other two
sides are 6 cm.
   b Draw the locus of all the points exactly 1 cm away from the perimeter of the
isosceles triangle.

21 Graphs 2

This chapter is going to ...

show you how to draw a straight-line graph from its equation, and how to find the equation of a given graph. It will also show you how to use graphs to solve simultaneous equations and to represent inequalities.

What you should already know

✔ How to read and plot co-ordinates.
✔ How to work out expressions using directed numbers.
✔ That letters can be used to represent numbers.
✔ How to substitute into simple algebraic formulae.

Flow diagrams

One way of drawing the graph of an equation is to obtain a set of co-ordinates from the equation by means of a flow diagram. These co-ordinates are then plotted and the graph is drawn.

In its simplest form, a flow diagram consists of a single box which may be thought of as containing a mathematical operation (called a **function**). A set of numbers fed into one side of the box is changed by the operation into another set which comes out from the opposite side of the box. For example, the box shown here represents the operation of multiplying by 3.

Input $-2, -1, 0, 1, 2$ $\longrightarrow$ $\boxed{\times 3}$ $\longrightarrow$ **Output** $-6, -3, 0, 3, 6$

Flow diagrams are sometimes called function diagrams. The numbers that are fed into a box are called **input values,** and the numbers that come out are called **output values.**

We can match the input and output values and arrange them as a table,

x	-2	-1	0	1	2
y	-6	-3	0	3	6

in which the input values are called x-values, and the output values are called y-values. We thus obtain a set of **co-ordinates** that can be **plotted on a graph**: in this case $(-2, -6)$, $(-1, -3)$, $(0, 0)$, $(1, 3)$ and $(2, 6)$.

Most functions consist of more than one operation, so most flow diagrams consist of more than one box. In such cases, we match the first input values to the last output values. The values produced in the middle operations are just working numbers and can be missed out.

$$-4, -2, -1, 0, 1 \xrightarrow{\quad} \boxed{\times 2} \xrightarrow{-8, -4, -2, 0, 2} \boxed{+3} \xrightarrow{-5, -1, 1, 3, 5}$$

So, for the two-box flow diagram the table is

x	-4	-2	-1	0	1
y	-5	-1	1	3	5

This gives us the co-ordinates $(-4, -5)$, $(-2, -1)$, $(-1, 1)$, $(0, 3)$ and $(1, 5)$.

The diagram on page 381 represents the equation (or function) $y = 3x$, and the diagram above represents the equation $y = 2x + 3$, as shown below.

$$x \xrightarrow{\quad} \boxed{\times 3} \xrightarrow{3x} \qquad\qquad x \xrightarrow{\quad} \boxed{\times 2} \xrightarrow{2x} \boxed{+3} \xrightarrow{2x+3}$$

$$y = 3x \qquad\qquad\qquad\qquad y = 2x + 3$$

It is now an easy step to plot the co-ordinate pairs for each equation on a set of axes, to produce the graphs of $y = 3x$ and $y = 2x + 3$, as shown below.

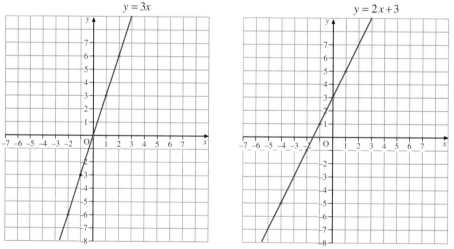

One of the practical problems in graph work is deciding the extent (range) of the axes. In examinations this is not usually a problem as the axes are either drawn for you or you are given a piece of graph paper and told how large to draw them. Throughout this chapter and Chapter 25, we will use diagrams like the one at the top of the next page to show you the range of your axes for each question. These diagrams are not necessarily drawn to scale.

This particular diagram means draw the *x*-axis (horizontal axis) from −10 to 10 and the *y*-axis (vertical axis) from −10 to 10. You can use any type of graph or squared paper to draw your axes.

But do note that the **scale** on each axis is **not always the same**.

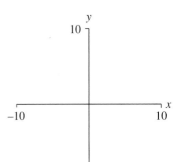

Example   For each of these flow diagrams:
  i   Work out the missing numbers.
  ii Complete the table of values.
  iii Write down the equation that each set of co-ordinate pairs represents.
  iv Use the co-ordinates from each table to plot points on a graph and hence draw the graph of the line given by each equation.

a

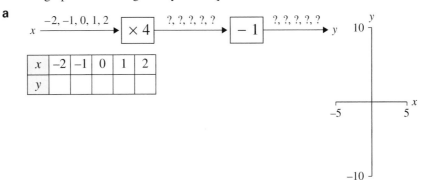

x	−2	−1	0	1	2
y					

b

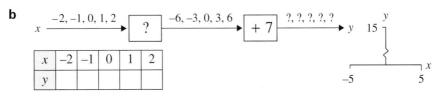

x	−2	−1	0	1	2
y					

c

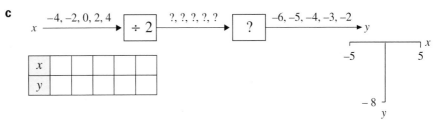

x					
y					

a The missing set of values is −8, −4, 0, 4 and 8. The table becomes

x	−2	−1	0	1	2
y	−9	−5	−1	3	7

The co-ordinate pairs are (−2, −9), (−1, −5), (0, −1), (1, 3), (2, 7).
The equation is $y = 4x − 1$.
The graph is shown on the right.

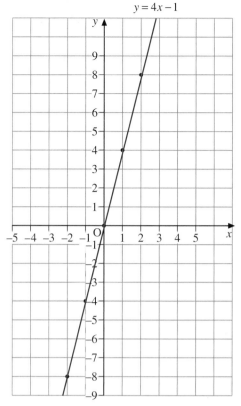

$y = 4x - 1$

b The missing function in the first box is × 3. The table becomes

x	−2	−1	0	1	2
y	1	4	7	10	13

The co-ordinate pairs are (−2, 1), (−1, 4), (0, 7), (1, 10), (2, 13).
The equation is $y = 3x + 7$.
The graph is shown on the right.

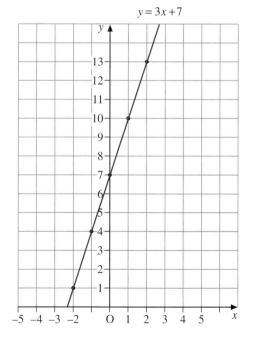

$y = 3x + 7$

c The input values have been carefully chosen in this example. Can you see why? This missing set of values are −2, −1, 0, 1 and 2. The missing function in the second box is −4. The table becomes

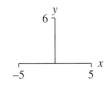

x	−4	−2	0	2	4
y	−6	−5	−4	−3	−2

The co-ordinate pairs are (−4, −6), (−2, −5), (0, −4), (2, −3), (4, −2).

The equation is $y = \frac{x}{2} - 4$.

The graph is shown on the right.

EXERCISE 21A

1 Draw the graph of $y = 2x$.

x	−2	−1	0	1	2
y					

2 Draw the graph of $y = x + 2$.

x	−4	−2	0	2	4
y					

3 Draw the graph of $y = 2x - 2$.

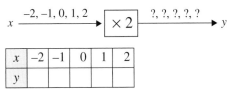

x	−2	−1	0	1	2
y					

4 Draw the graph of $y = \frac{x}{3} + 1$.

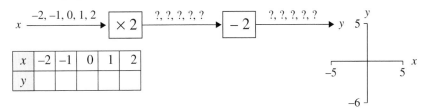

x	−6	−3	0	3	6
y					

5 Draw the graph of $y = \frac{x}{2} - 4$.

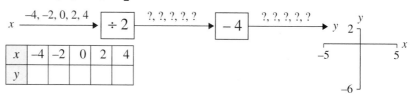

x	–4	–2	0	2	4
y					

6 a Draw the graphs of $y = x - 5$ and $y = 2x - 4$ on the same grid.

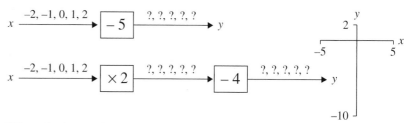

b Where do the graphs cross?

7 a Draw the graphs of $y = 2x$ and $y = x + 6$ on the same grid.

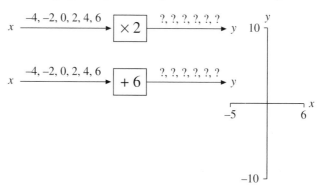

b Where do the graphs cross?

8 a Draw the graphs of $y = 3x - 1$ and $y = \frac{x}{2} + 4$ on the same grid.

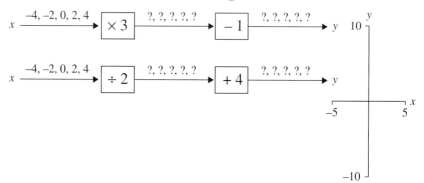

b Where do the graphs cross?

9 Draw the graph of $y = 5x - 1$. Choose your own inputs. Draw your own axes.

Linear graphs

This chapter is concerned with linear graphs. That is, graphs that give a straight line.

If any of the graphs you draw in working through this chapter are not straight lines, you have made a mistake.

A linear graph only has terms in x and/or y in its equation. Any equation that has terms which are powers of x and/or y (squares, cubes, etc.) gives a curved graph. (These will be dealt with in Chapter 25, pages 486–504.)

The minimum number of points needed to draw a straight line is two, but three or more is better because that gives at least one point to act as a check. In the graphs you drew in Exercise 21A, you plotted five points. There is no rule about how many points to plot but here are some tips.

- Use a sharp pencil and mark each point with a fine dot or an accurate cross.

- Do not plot two points that are very close together because it is extremely difficult to draw a line that passes **exactly** through two such points. More often than not, the line will be out by a couple of millimetres. Examiners usually work to a tolerance of 1 mm. The examples given here are exaggerated but do demonstrate what can happen.

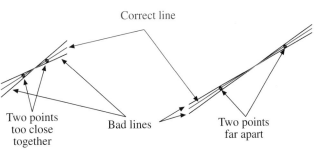

- When the points are far apart, it is easier to draw a line within the tolerance allowed – even if you have difficulty in drawing accurately.

- Get your eyes directly over the graph. If you look from the side, you will not be able to line up your ruler accurately.

Drawing graphs by finding points

This method is a bit quicker and does not need flow diagrams. However, if you prefer flow diagrams, use them.

Follow through the next example to see how this method works.

Example Draw the graph of $y = 4x - 5$ for values of x from -3 to 3 ($-3 \leq x \leq 3$).

Choose three values for x, not too close together, say -3, 0 and 3 (the limits given). Work out the y-values by substituting the x-values into the equation. Keep a record of your calculations in a table.

x	-3	0	3
y			

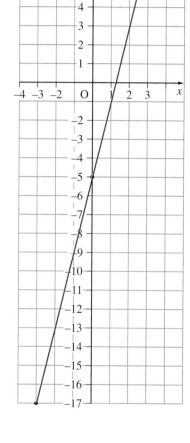

$y = 4x - 5$

When $x = -3$, $y = 4(-3) - 5 = -17$.
This gives the point $(-3, -17)$.

When $x = 0$, $y = 4(0) - 5 = -5$.
This gives the point $(0, -5)$.

When $x = 3$, $y = 4(3) - 5 = 7$.
This gives the point $(3, 7)$.

Hence your table is

x	-3	0	3
y	-17	-5	7

You now have to decide the extent (range) of the axes. You can find this out by looking at the co-ordinates that we have so far.

The smallest x-value is -3, the largest is 3. The smallest y-value is -17, the largest is 7.

Now draw the axes, plot the points and complete the graph, as shown above.

It is nearly always a good idea to choose 0 as one of the x-values. In an examination, the limits of x will be given and the axes already drawn, so you will not have to make too many decisions.

EXERCISE 21B

Draw the graph for each of the equations given. Where they are not given, you will have to choose your own x-values and decide how big to draw the axes.

Follow these hints and try to remember them.

- Don't pick silly numbers, such as 17 or -36, as x-values.

- Try to use the highest and smallest values of x given as your range.

- If the numbers you pick give very large y-values, choose others.

- Don't pick *x*-values that are too close together, e.g. 1 and 2. Try to space them out so that you can draw a more accurate graph.

- When the first part of the function is a division, pick *x*-values that divide exactly to avoid fractions.

- Try to use some negative numbers as input values. Examiners expect you to use negative values, so practise them now.

- Always label your graphs. This is particularly important when you are drawing two graphs on the same axes.

- If you want to use a flow diagram, use one.

- Create a table of values. You will often have to complete these in your examinations.

1 Draw the graph of $y = 3x + 4$ for *x*-values from -1 to 4 ($-1 \leq x \leq 4$).

2 Draw the graph of $y = 2x - 5$, $-3 \leq x \leq 3$.

3 Draw the graph of $y = \frac{x}{2} - 3$, $-2 \leq x \leq 10$.

4 Draw the graph of $y = 3x + 5$, $-2 \leq x \leq 2$.

5 Draw the graph of $y = \frac{x}{3} - 4$, $-1 \leq x \leq 6$.

6 **a** On the same axes, draw the graphs of $y = 3x + 2$ and $y = 2x + 1$, $-2 \leq x \leq 3$.
   b Where do the two graphs cross?

7 **a** On the same axes, draw the graphs of $y = 4x + 5$ and $y = 2x - 3$.
   b Where do the two graphs cross?

8 **a** On the same axes, draw the graphs of $y = \frac{x}{3} - 1$ and $y = \frac{x}{2} - 2$, $0 \leq x \leq 9$.
   b Where do the two graphs cross?

9 **a** On the same axes, draw the graphs of $y = 3x + 1$ and $y = 3x - 2$.
   b Do the graphs cross? If not, why not?

10 **a** On the same axes, draw the graphs of $y = x$, $y = 2x + 1$ and $y = \frac{x}{2} - \frac{1}{2}$, $-4 \leq x \leq 4$.
   b Where do all three graphs cross?
   c Describe any symmetry that the graphs may have.

Gradient

The slope of a line is called its gradient. The steeper the slope of the line, the larger the value of the gradient. (You met the idea of gradient on pages 272–274.)

The gradient of the line shown here can be measured by drawing, as large as possible, a right-angled triangle which has part of the line as its hypotenuse (sloping side). The gradient is then given by

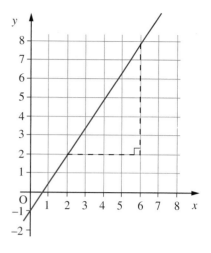

$$\text{Gradient} = \frac{\text{Distance measured up}}{\text{Distance measured along}}$$

$$= \frac{\text{Difference on } y\text{-axis}}{\text{Difference on } x\text{-axis}}$$

For example, to measure the steepness of the line in the next figure, you first draw a right-angled triangle whose hypotenuse is part of this line. It does not matter where you draw the triangle but it makes the calculations much easier if you choose a sensible place. This usually means using existing grid lines, so that you avoid fractional values. See the two diagrams below.

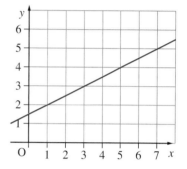

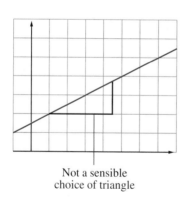

Not a sensible
choice of triangle

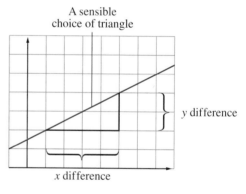

A sensible
choice of triangle

y difference

x difference

After you have drawn the triangle, you measure (or count) how many squares there are on the vertical side. This is the difference between your y-co-ordinates. In the case above, this is 2. You then measure (or count) how many squares there are on the horizontal side. This is the difference between your x-co-ordinates. In the case above, this is 4. To work out the gradient, you do the following calculation.

$$\text{Gradient} = \frac{\text{Difference of the } y\text{-co-ordinates}}{\text{Difference of the } x\text{-co-ordinates}}$$

$$= \frac{2}{4} = \frac{1}{2} \quad \text{or } 0.5$$

Note that the value of the gradient is not affected by where the triangle is drawn. As we are calculating the ratio of two sides of the triangle, the gradient will always be the same wherever we draw the triangle.

Remember When a line slopes down from left to right, the gradient is negative, so a minus sign must be placed in front of the calculated fraction.

Example Find the gradient of each of these lines.

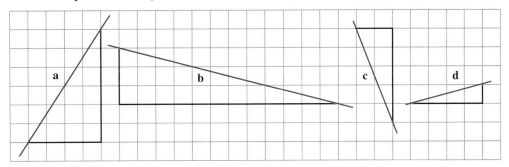

In each case, a sensible choice of triangle has already been made.

a y difference = 6, x difference = 4   Gradient = $6 \div 4 = \frac{3}{2} = 1.5$

b y difference = 3, x difference = 12   Line slopes down left to right,
  so Gradient = $-(3 \div 12) = -\frac{1}{4} = -0.25$

c y difference = 5, x difference = 2   Line slopes down from left to right,
  so Gradient = $-(5 \div 2) = -\frac{5}{2} = -2.5$

d y difference = 1, x difference = 4   Gradient = $1 \div 4 = \frac{1}{4} = 0.25$

Drawing a line with a certain gradient

To draw a line with a certain gradient, you 'reverse' the process described above. That is, first you draw the right-angled triangle using the given gradient. For example, take a gradient of 2.

Start at a convenient point (A in the diagrams below). A gradient of 2 means for an x-step of 1 the y-step must be 2 (because 2 is the fraction $\frac{2}{1}$). So, move 1 square across and 2 squares up, and mark a dot.

Repeat this as many times as you like and draw the line. You can also move 1 square back and 2 squares down, which gives the same gradient, as the third diagram shows.

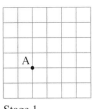

Stage 1   Stage 2   Stage 3

Example Draw lines with gradients of   **a** $\frac{1}{3}$ **b** -3 **c** $-\frac{1}{4}$

a This is a fractional gradient which has a y-step of 1 and an x-step of 3. Move 3 squares across and 1 square up every time.

b This is a negative gradient, so for every 1 square across, move 3 squares down.

c This is also a negative gradient and it is a fraction. So for every 4 squares across, move 1 square down.

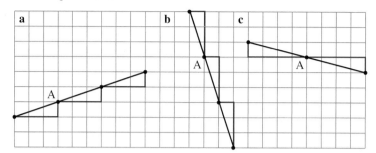

EXERCISE 21C

1 Find the gradient of each of these lines.

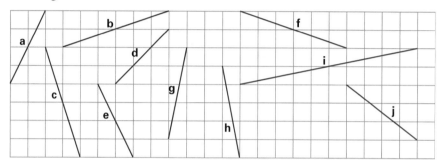

2 Draw lines with gradients of

a 4   **b** $\frac{2}{3}$ **c** −2   **d** $-\frac{4}{5}$ **e** 6   **f** −6

3 Find the gradient of each of these lines. What is special about these lines?

a $y = x$ **b**

4 The line on grid **e** is horizontal. The lines on grids **a** to **d** get nearer and nearer to the horizontal.

a   **b**   **c**   **d**   **e**

Measure the gradient of each line in grids **a** to **d**. By looking at the values you obtain, what do you think the gradient of a horizontal line is?

5   The line on grid **e** is vertical. The lines on grids **a** to **d** get nearer and nearer to the vertical.

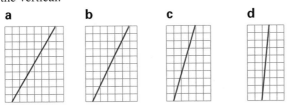

Measure the gradient of each line in grids **a** to **d**. By looking at the values you obtain, what do you think the gradient of a vertical line is?

Remember The gradient of a vertical line is **infinite**, the gradient of a horizontal line is **zero**.

Discovery activity

On the same grid (take *x* from −10 to 10 and *y* from −10 to 10) draw this 'family' of lines.

    a $y = 2x - 1$ **b** $y = 2x + 4$ **c** $y = 2x + 3$ **d** $y = 2x$

What do you notice about the equations?
What do you notice about the lines?

On another grid (take *x* from −10 to 10 and *y* from −10 to 10) draw this 'family' of lines.

    a $y = 3x + 1$ **b** $y = \dfrac{x}{2} + 1$ **c** $y = x + 1$ **d** $y = 4x + 1$

What do you notice about the equations?
What do you notice about the lines?

The number in front of *x* is called the **coefficient** of *x* and determines how steep the line is. In fact, the gradient of the line is the same as the coefficient of *x*.

The number on its own is called the **constant term** and determines where the graph crosses the *y*-axis. It is often referred to as the **y-axis intercept**.

Gradient–intercept method for drawing graphs

The ideas that you will have discovered in the last activity lead to another way of plotting lines, known as the **gradient–intercept** method or **y = mx + c**.

Example   Draw the graph of $y = 3x - 1$, using the gradient–intercept method.

• Because the constant term is −1, we know that the graph goes through the *y*-axis at −1. We mark this point with a dot or a cross (diagram **A**).

• Because the coefficient of *x* is 3, the gradient is 3. For an *x*-step of 1 unit, there is a *y*-step of 3. Starting at −1 on the *y*-axis, we move 1 square across and 3 squares up and mark this point with a dot or a cross (diagram **B**).

- Repeat this from every new point. We can also move 1 square back and 3 squares down. When enough points have been marked, we join the dots (or crosses) to make the graph (diagram **C**).

A

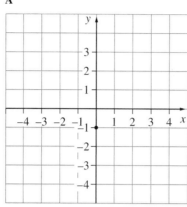

B

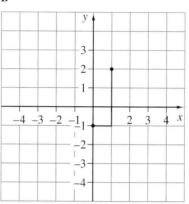

C

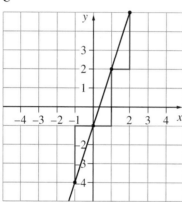

Note If the points are not in a straight line, a mistake has been made.

EXERCISE 21D

1 Draw these lines using the gradient–intercept method. Use the same grid, taking x from −10 to 10 and y from −10 to 10. If the grid gets too 'crowded', draw another one.

   a $y = 2x + 6$ **b** $y = 3x - 4$ **c** $y = \frac{1}{2}x + 5$ **d** $y = x + 7$

   e $y = 4x - 3$ **f** $y = 2x - 7$ **g** $y = \frac{1}{4}x - 3$ **h** $y = \frac{2}{3}x + 4$

   i $y = 6x - 5$ **j** $y = x + 8$ **k** $y = \frac{4}{5}x - 2$ **l** $y = 3x - 9$

   The axes for questions **2** to **4** are given alongside question **4**.

2 **a** Using the gradient–intercept method, draw the following lines on the same grid.
      i $y = 3x + 1$ **ii** $y = 2x + 3$
   b Where do the lines cross?

3 **a** Using the gradient–intercept method, draw the following lines on the same grid.

      i $y = \dfrac{x}{2} + 3$ **ii** $y = \dfrac{x}{4} + 2$

  b Where do the lines cross?

4 **a** Using the gradient–intercept method draw the following lines on the same grid.

      i $y = x + 3$ **ii** $y = 2x$

  b Where do the lines cross?

Finding the equation of a line from its graph

The equation $y = mx + c$

When a graph can be expressed in the form $y = mx + c$, the coefficient of x, m, is the gradient, and the constant term, c, is the intercept on the y-axis.

This means that if we know the gradient, m, of a line and its intercept, c, on the y-axis, we can write down the equation of the line immediately. For example, if $m = 3$ and $c = -5$, the equation of the line is $y = 3x - 5$.

All linear graphs are of the form $y = mx + c$.

This gives us a method of finding the equation of any line drawn on a pair of co-ordinate axes.

Example   Find the equation of the line shown in the diagram.

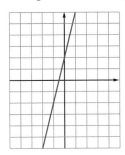

First, we find where the graph crosses the y-axis (diagram **A**). So $c = 2$.
Next, we measure the gradient of the line (diagram **B**). So $m = 4$.
Finally, we write down the equation of the line: $y = 4x + 2$.

A   **B**

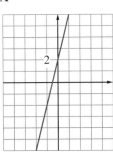 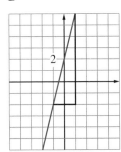

y-step = 8
x-step = 2
Gradient = $8 \div 2 = 4$

EXERCISE 21E

1   Give the equation of each of these lines, all of which have positive gradients.
    (Each square represents 1 unit.)

a   b   c

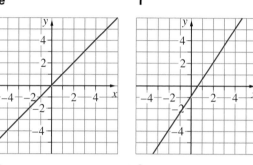

d   e   f

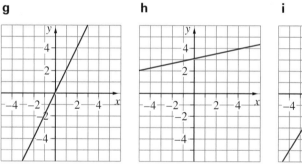

g   h   i

2   In each of these grids, there are two lines. (Each square represents 1 unit.)

a   b   c

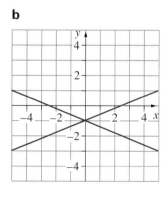
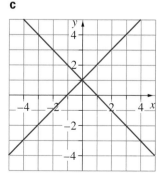

For each grid:
  i   Find the equation of each of the lines.
  ii Describe any symmetries that you can see.
  iii What connection is there between the gradients of each pair of lines?

3 Give the equation of each of these lines, all of which have negative gradients.
(Each square represents 1 unit.)

a
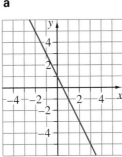

b
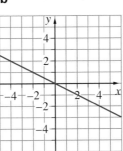

c
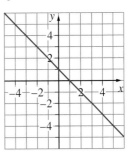

d
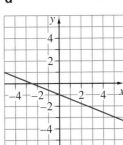

e
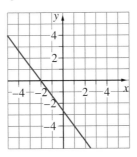

4 In each of these grids, there are three lines. One of them is $y = x$. (Each square represents one unit.)

a
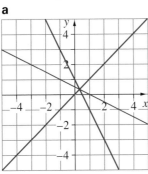

b
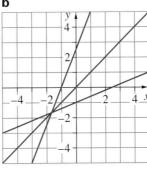

c
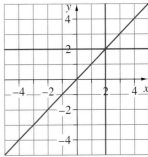

For each grid:
i Find the equation of each of the other two lines.
ii Describe any symmetries that you can see.
iii What connection is there between the gradients of each pair of lines?

Cover-up method for drawing graphs

The x-axis has the equation $y = 0$. This means that all points on that axis have a y-value of 0.

The y-axis has the equation $x = 0$. This means that all points on the y-axis have an x-value of 0.

We can use these facts to draw any line that has an equation of the form $ax + by = c$.

Example 1   Draw the graph of $4x + 5y = 20$.

Because the value of x is 0 on the y-axis, we can solve the equation for y:

$$4(0) + 5y = 20$$
$$5y = 20$$
$$\Rightarrow \quad y = 4$$

Hence, the line passes through the point $(0, 4)$ on the y-axis (diagram **A**).

Because the value of y is 0 on the x-axis, we can also solve the equation for x:

$$4x + 5(0) = 20$$
$$4x = 20$$
$$\Rightarrow \quad x = 5$$

Hence, the line passes through the point $(5, 0)$ on the x-axis (diagram **B**). We need only two points to draw a line. (Normally, we would like a third point but in this case we can accept two.) The graph is drawn by joining the points $(0, 4)$ and $(5, 0)$ (diagram **C**).

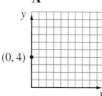
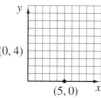
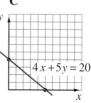

This type of equation can be drawn very easily, without much working at all, using the **cover-up** method.

Start with the equation $\qquad 4x + 5y = 20$

Cover up the x-term: $\qquad$ $+ 5y = 20$

Solve the equation: $\qquad\qquad\qquad y = 4$

Now cover up the y-term: $\quad 4x + \;\square\; = 20$

Solve the equation: $\qquad\qquad\qquad x = 5$

This gives the points 5 on the x-axis and 4 on the y-axis.

Example 2   Draw the graph of $2x - 3y = 12$.

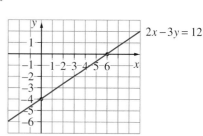

Start with the equation $\qquad 2x - 3y = 12$

Cover up the x-term: $\qquad\;\square\; - 3y = 12$

Solve the equation: $\qquad\quad y = -4$

Now cover up the y-term: $2x + \;\square\; = 12$

Solve the equation: $\qquad\quad x = 6$

This gives the points 6 on the x-axis and -4 on the y-axis.

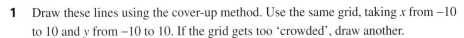

EXERCISE 21F

1 Draw these lines using the cover-up method. Use the same grid, taking x from -10 to 10 and y from -10 to 10. If the grid gets too 'crowded', draw another.

a $3x + 2y = 6$	**b** $4x + 3y = 12$	**c** $4x - 5y = 20$	**d** $x + y = 10$
e $3x - 2y = 18$	**f** $x - y = 4$	**g** $5x - 2y = 15$	**h** $2x - 3y = 15$
i $6x + 5y = 30$	**j** $x + y = -5$	**k** $x + y = 3$	**l** $x - y = -4$

The axes for questions **2** to **4** are given after question **4**.

2 **a** Using the cover-up method, draw the following lines on the same grid.

   i $2x + y = 4$ **ii** $x - 2y = 2$

   b Where do the lines cross?

3 **a** Using the cover-up method, draw the following lines on the same grid.

   i $x + 2y = 6$ **ii** $2x - y = 2$

   b Where do the lines cross?

4 **a** Using the cover-up method, draw the following lines on the same grid.

   i $x + y = 6$ **ii** $x - y = 2$

   b Where do the lines cross?

   Axes for questions **2** to **4**:

2   **3**   **4**

Uses of graphs

On pages 262–274, you met conversion graphs and other practical ways of using graphs to represent relationships. Two other uses of graphs we will now look at are solving simultaneous equations (also done algebraically on pages 204–209) and representing inequalities, which involves locating regions in the x–y plane.

Solving simultaneous equations

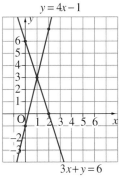

Example By drawing their graphs on the same grid, find the solution of the simultaneous equations

a $3x + y = 6$ **b** $y = 4x - 1$

a The first graph is drawn using the cover-up method. It crosses the x-axis at $(2, 0)$ and the y-axis at $(0, 6)$.

b This graph can be drawn by finding some points or by the gradient–intercept method. If we use the gradient–intercept method, the graph crosses the y-axis at -1 and has a gradient of 4.

The point where the graphs intersect is $(1, 3)$. So the solution to the simultaneous equations is $x = 1$, $y = 3$.

399

EXERCISE 21G

By drawing their graphs, find the solution of each of these pairs of simultaneous equations.

1 $x + 4y = 8$
   $x - y = 3$

2 $y = 2x - 1$
   $3x + 2y = 12$

3 $y = 2x + 4$
   $y = x + 7$

4 $y = x$
   $x + y = 10$

5 $y = 2x + 3$
   $5x + y = 10$

6 $y = 5x + 1$
   $y = 2x + 10$

7 $y = x + 8$
   $x + y = 4$

8 $y - 3x = 9$
   $y = x - 3$

9 $y = -x$
   $y = 4x - 5$

10 $3x + 2y = 18$
   $y = 3x$

11 $y = 3x + 2$
   $y + x = 10$

12 $y = \dfrac{x}{3} + 1$
   $x + y = 11$

Representing inequalities

A linear inequality can be plotted on a graph. The result is a **region** that lies on one side of a straight line or the other. You will recognise an inequality by the fact that it looks like an equation but instead of the equals sign it has an inequality sign: $<$, $>$, $\leq$, or $\geq$.

The following are examples of linear inequalities which can be represented on a graph.

$$y < 3 \qquad x > 7 \qquad -3 \leq y < 5 \qquad y \geq 2x + 3 \qquad 2x + 3y < 6 \qquad y \leq x$$

The method for graphing an inequality is to draw the boundary line that defines the inequality. This is found by replacing the inequality sign with an equals sign.

When a strict inequality is stated, i.e. $<$ or $>$ is used, the boundary line should be drawn as a **dashed** line to show that it is **not included** in the range of values. But when $\leq$ or $\geq$ is used to state the inequality, the boundary line should be drawn as a **solid** line to show that the boundary is **included**. If you can remember to do this, it is mathematically correct to do so, but you will not be penalised for drawing a solid line when it should be dashed.

After the boundary line has been drawn, **the required region is shaded**.

To confirm on which side of the line the region lies, choose any point that is not on the boundary line and test it in the inequality. If it satisfies the inequality, that is the side required. If it doesn't, the other side is required.

Example 1   Show each of the following inequalities on a graph.

$$y \leq 3 \qquad x > 7 \qquad -3 \leq y < 5 \qquad y \leq 2x + 3 \qquad 2x + 3y < 6 \qquad y \leq x$$

a   Draw the line $y = 3$. Since the inequality is stated as $\leq$, the line is **solid**. Test a point that is not on the line. The **origin** is always a good choice if possible, as 0 is easy to test. Putting 0 into the inequality gives $0 \leq 3$. The inequality is satisfied and so the region containing the origin is the side we want. Shade it in.

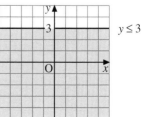

b Since the inequality is stated as >, the line is **dashed**. Draw the line $x = 7$. Test the origin $(0, 0)$, which gives $0 > 7$. This is not true, so we want the other side of the line from the origin. Shade it in.

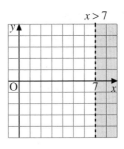

c Draw the lines $y = -3$ (solid for ≤) and $y = 5$ (dashed for <). Test a point that is not on either line, say $(0, 0)$. Zero is between −3 and 5, so the required region lies between the lines. Shade it in.

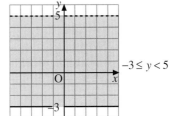

d Draw the line $y = 2x + 3$. Since the inequality is stated as ≤, the line is solid. Test a point that is not on the line, $(0, 0)$. Putting these x- and y-values in the inequality gives $0 \leq 2(0) + 3$, which is true. So the region that includes the origin is what we want. Shade it in.

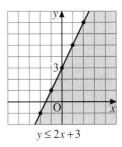

e Draw the line $2x + 3y = 6$. Since the inequality is stated as <, the line is dashed. Test a point that is not on the line, say $(0, 0)$. Is it true that $2(0) + 3(0) < 6$? The answer is yes, so the origin is in the region that we want. Shade it in.

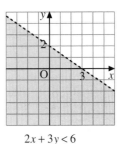

f Draw the line $y = x$. Since the inequality is stated as ≤, the line is solid. This time the origin is on the line, so pick any other point, say $(1, 3)$. Putting $x = 1$ and $y = 3$ in the inequality gives $3 \leq 1$. The answer is not true, so the point $(1, 3)$ is not in the region we want. Shade in the other side from $(1, 3)$.

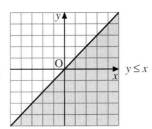

Example 2

a On the same grid, shade in the regions that represent the inequalities

   i $x > 2$ **ii** $y \geq x$ **iii** $x + y < 8$

b Are the points $(3, 4)$, $(2, 6)$ and $(3, 3)$ in the region that satisfies all three inequalities?

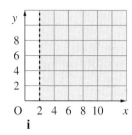
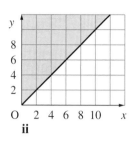
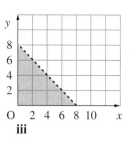

i   **ii**   **iii**

a   **i**   This region is shown in diagram **i**.

          The boundary line is $x = 2$ (dashed)

    ii   This region is shown in diagram **ii**.
          The boundary line is $y = x$ (solid)

   iii   This region is shown in diagram **iii**.
          The boundary line is $x + y = 8$ (dashed)

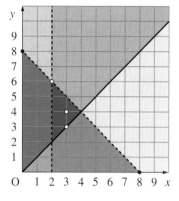

          The regions have first been drawn separately so
          that each may be clearly seen. The diagram on
          the right shows all three regions on the same
          grid – as required. The part of the diagram that
          is shaded three times (darkest tint) defines the
          region that satisfies all three inequalities.

b   **i**   The point (3, 4) is clearly within the region that satisfies all three inequalities.

    ii   The point (2, 6) is on the boundary lines $x = 2$ and $x + y = 8$. As these are dashed
          lines, they are not included in the region defined by all three inequalities. So, the
          point (2, 6) is also not in this region.

   iii   The point (3, 3) is on the boundary line $y = x$. As this is a solid line, it is included
          in the region defined by all three inequalities. So, the point (3, 3) is also included
          in this region.

EXERCISE 21H

For all of the axes in this exercise, take x from -10 to 10 and y from -10 to 10.

1   **a**   Draw the line $x = 2$ (as a solid line).
     b   Shade the region defined by $x \leq 2$

2   **a**   Draw the line $y = -3$ (as a dashed line).
     b   Shade the region defined by $y > -3$.

3   **a**   Draw the line $x = -2$ (as a solid line).
     b   Draw the line $x = 1$ (as a solid line) on the same grid.
     c   Shade the region defined by $-2 \leq x \leq 1$.

4   **a**   Draw the line $y = -1$ (as a dashed line).
     b   Draw the line $y = 4$ (as a solid line) on the same grid.
     c   Shade the region defined by $-1 < y \leq 4$.

5 **a** On the same grid, draw the regions defined by the inequalities
   i $-3 \le x \le 6$ **ii** $-4 < y \le 5$
 b Are the following points in the region defined by both inequalities?
   i $(2, 2)$ **ii** $(1, 5)$ **iii** $(-2, -4)$

6 **a** Draw the line $y = 2x - 1$ (as a dashed line).
 b Shade the region defined by $y < 2x - 1$.

7 **a** Draw the line $3x - 4y = 12$ (as a solid line).
 b Shade the region defined by $3x - 4y \le 12$.

8 **a** Draw the line $y = \frac{1}{2}x + 3$ (as a solid line).
 b Shade the region defined by $y \ge \frac{1}{2}x + 3$.

9 **a** Draw the line $y = -3$ (as a dashed line).
 b Shade the region defined by $y < -3$.

10 **a** Draw the line $y = 3x - 4$ (as a solid line).
 b Draw the line $x + y = 10$ (as a solid line) on the same diagram.
 c Shade the region defined by $y \ge 3x - 4$.
 d Shade the region defined by $x + y \le 10$.
 e Are the following points in the region defined by both inequalities?
   i $(2, 1)$ **ii** $(2, 2)$ **iii** $(2, 3)$

11 **a** Draw the line $y = x$ (as a solid line).
 b Draw the line $2x + 5y = 10$ (as a solid line) on the same diagram.
 c Draw the line $2x + y = 6$ (as a dashed line) on the same diagram.
 d Shade the region defined by $y \ge x$.
 e Shade the region defined by $2x + 5y \ge 10$.
 f Shade the region defined by $2x + y < 6$.
 g Are the following points in the region defined by these inequalities?
   i $(1, 1)$ **ii** $(2, 2)$ **iii** $(3, 3)$

12 **a** On the same grid, draw the regions defined by the following inequalities.
   i $y > x - 3$ **ii** $3y + 4x \le 24$ **iii** $x \ge 2$
 b Are the following points in the region defined by all three inequalities?
   i $(1, 1)$ **ii** $(2, 2)$ **iii** $(3, 3)$ **iv** $(4, 4)$

13 **a** On the same grid, draw the regions defined by the following inequalities.
   i $y \le 2x + 2$ **ii** $y > 4$ **iii** $x \le 4$
 b Are the following points in the region defined by all three inequalities?
   i $(3, 5)$ **ii** $(2, 4)$ **iii** $(4, 10)$

14 **a** On the same grid, draw the regions defined by the following inequalities.
   i $y \ge 0$ **ii** $x \ge 0$ **iii** $y \le 2x + 1$ **iv** $3x + 2y \le 12$
 b Are the following points in the region defined by all three inequalities?
   i $(3, 1)$ **ii** $(2, 2)$ **iii** $(3, 3)$ **iv** $(1, 4)$

Possible coursework tasks

Perpendicular lines

Draw the lines $y = 2x + 3$ and $y = -\frac{1}{2}x + 3$ on the same pair of axes.

What do you notice?

Investigate for other pairs of lines.

Equations from co-ordinates

A line passes through A (1, 5) and B (3, 11).

Can you find the equation of the line?

Can you find some rules for finding the equation of a line which goes through any two points?

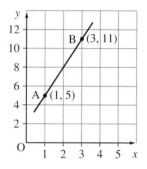

Division of lines

X (2, 4) and Y (6, 10) are the end points of the line segment XY. The points A, B, and C divide the line into four equal parts.

Find the co-ordinates of A, B and C.

Can you find the three co-ordinates by using only the co-ordinates of X and Y?

Investigate for different line segments.

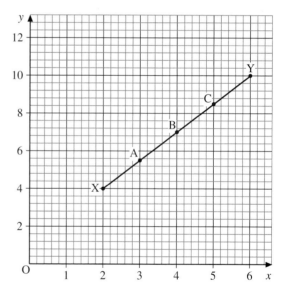

➤ *Lines and angles*

All linear graphs come from equations of the form $y = mx + c$.

If θ is the angle a line makes with the horizontal (see diagram), can you find θ when you know the equation of the line?

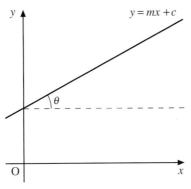

Examination questions

1 **a** On a pair of axes $0 \le x \le 5$ and $-5 \le y \le 15$, draw the graphs of

      i $y = 4x - 3$ **ii** $y = 6 - 2x$

  b Use the graphs to solve the simultaneous equations

    $y = 4x - 3$

    $y = 6 - 2x$

  c Indicate, on the graph, by suitable shading, the region containing points (x, y) which satisfy all the inequalities

    $y \ge 4x - 3$ $y \le 6 - 2x$ $x \ge 0$

NICCEA, Question 6, Paper 3. June 1995

2 Beth was asked to draw the graph of $y = 3x + 4$. She plotted the six points shown in the diagram.

  a **i** From the **shape** of the graph, how can you tell that one of the points is in the wrong place?

    ii Draw the graph of $y = 3x + 4$.

  b On your diagram, draw the graph of $y = 2 - x$.

  c Use the graphs to solve the simultaneous equations

    $y = 3x + 4$

    $y = 2 - x$

MEG, Question 10, Specimen Paper 3, 1998

3 The table shows the largest quantity of salt, w grams, which can be dissolved in a beaker of water at temperature $t°C$.

$t\,°C$	10	20	25	30	40	50	60
w **grams**	54	58	60	62	66	70	74

    a On a grid $0 \le t \le 60$ and $0 \le w \le 80$, plot the points and draw a graph to illustrate this information.

    b Use your graph to find

      i the lowest temperature at which 63 g of salt will dissolve in the water

      ii the largest amount of salt that will dissolve in the water at 44 °C.

    c **i** The equation of the graph is of the form $w = at + b$. Use your graph to estimate the constants a and b.

      ii Use the equation to calculate the largest amount of salt which will dissolve in the water at 95 °C.

NEAB, Question 19, Paper 1, June 1995

4 The diagram shows the graphs of $y = \frac{1}{2}x + 1$, $5x + 6y = 30$ and $x = 2$.

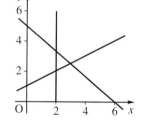

    a On the diagram, shade and label with the letter R, the region for which the points (x, y) satisfy the three inequalities

$$y \le \frac{1}{2}x + 1 \quad 5x + 6y \le 30 \quad x \ge 2$$

    b Solve the inequality $\frac{1}{2}x + 1 < 4$.

MEG, Question 20, Specimen Paper 3, 1998

5 The line $y + 4x = 14$ is shown on the right.

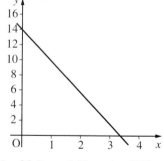

    a On a copy of the diagram draw the line $y = 2x - 1$.

    b Use your graph to solve the simultaneous equations

$$y + 4x = 14$$
$$y = 2x - 1$$

NEAB, Question 16, Paper 1, November 1995

6 The diagrams show axes with the lines $y = x + 3$ and $x + y = 6$ both drawn and labelled.

    a On copies of the diagrams:

      i shade the region $y < x + 3$

      ii shade the region $x + y > 6$.

    b Draw a similar grid as above, and on it shade the region $x < 3$.

NEAB, Question 22, Paper 1, November 1995

7   Jane buys 3 litres of oil and 40 litres of petrol for £30. Richard buys 2 litres of oil and 10 litres of petrol for £10. The cost of 1 litre of oil is £x. The cost of 1 litre of petrol is £y.

Therefore $3x + 40y = 30$

and $2x + 10y = 10$

a   Draw on a suitable pair of axes the two graphs of these equations.

b   What is the cost of 1 litre of petrol?

SEG, Question 9, Specimen Paper 13, 1998

Summary

How well do you grade yourself?

To gain a grade **E**, you need to be able to find the outputs from a given function or flow diagram and to plot co-ordinates to draw a straight-line graph.

To gain a grade **D**, you need to be able to plot any straight-line graph of the form $y = mx + c$, using any method.

To gain a grade **C**, you need to be able to draw any straight-line graph, measure its gradient and give its equation.

To gain a grade **B**, you need to be able to solve simultaneous equations using graphical methods and to find regions described by graphical inequalities.

What you should know after you have worked through Chapter 21

- How to find co-ordinates using flow diagrams, substitution of values, gradients and intercepts, and how to use these co-ordinates to draw graphs.

- How to draw the graphs of linear functions.

- How to solve two linear simultaneous equations using graphs.

- How graphically to find a region described by an inequality.

Scatter diagrams

A scatter diagram (also called a scattergraph, or scattergram) is a method of comparing two variables by plotting on a graph their corresponding values (usually taken from a table). In other words, treating them just like a set of (x, y) co-ordinates, as shown in this scatter diagram, in which the marks scored in an English test are plotted against the marks scored in a mathematics test.

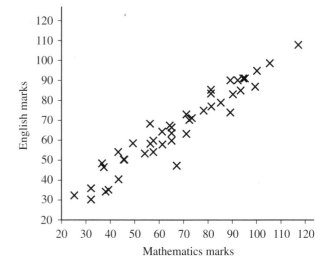

This graph shows **positive correlation**. This means that pupils who get high marks in mathematics tests also tend to get high marks in English tests.

Line of best fit

This is a straight line that goes through the middle of the data, passing as close to as many points as possible. A true line of best fit would go through a point that is the mean point of the data. For the scatter diagram below, this would be the point (66, 65) because its co-ordinates are the means of the mathematics and the English scores respectively. In your examinations, if you are guided to the mean marks you are expected to make sure your line of best fit goes through this mean point. If you are not given this point nor guided towards it then you are not expected to calculate it, but rather draw the line in by eye.

The line of best fit for the scattergraph on page 408 is shown below.

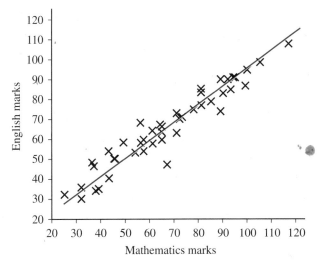

There will almost always be a follow-up question of the type: 'A girl took a mathematics test and scored 75 marks, but was ill and didn't take the English test. How many marks was she likely to have scored in English?'.

The answer to this is found by drawing a line up from 75 marks on the mathematics axis to the line of best fit and then going across to the English axis. This gives 74, which is the mark the girl is likely to have scored in the English test.

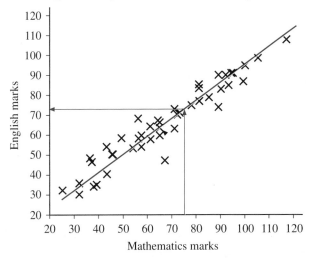

Correlation

Here are three statements that may or may not be true.

The taller people are, the wider their arm span is likely to be.

The older a car is, the lower its value will be.

The distance you live from your place of work will affect how much you earn.

These relationships could be tested by collecting data and plotting the data on a scatter diagram. For example, the first statement may give a scatter diagram like that on the right. This has a **positive correlation** because the data has a clear 'trend' and we can draw a line of best fit with a positive gradient that passes quite close to most of the points. From such a scatter diagram we could say that the taller someone is, the wider the arm span.

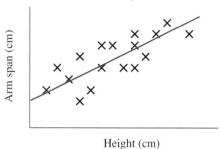

Testing the second statement may give a scatter diagram like that on the right. This has a **negative correlation** because the data has a clear 'trend' and we can draw a line of best fit with a negative gradient that passes quite close to most of the points. From such a scatter diagram we could say that as a car gets older, its value decreases.

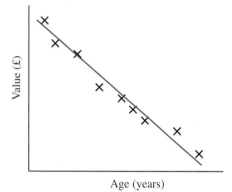

Testing the third statement may give a scatter diagram like that on the right. This scatter diagram has no correlation. It is not possible to draw a line of best fit. We could therefore say there is no relationship between the distance a person lives from his or her work and how much the person earns.

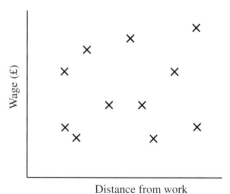

Example The graphs below show the relationship between the temperature and the amount of ice-cream sold, and that between the age of people and the amount of ice-cream they eat.

a Comment on the correlation of each graph.

b What does each graph tell you?

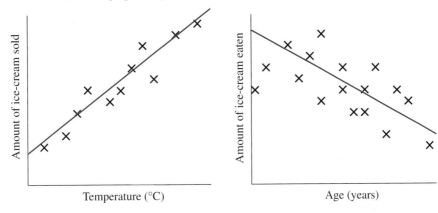

The first graph has positive correlation and tells us that as the temperature increases, the amount of ice-cream sold increases.

The second graph has negative correlation and tells us that as people get older, they eat less ice-cream.

EXERCISE 22A

1 Describe the correlation of each of these graphs.

a

b

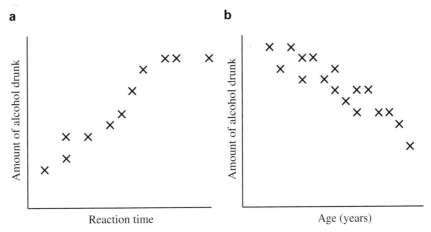

c   **d**

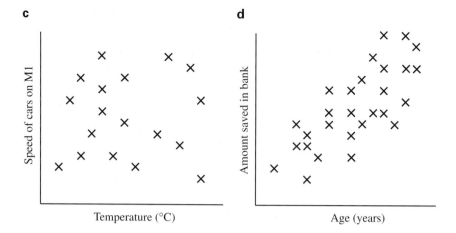

Temperature (°C)   Age (years)

2   Write in words what graph **1a** tells you.

3   Write in words what graph **1b** tells you.

4   Write in words what graph **1c** tells you.

5   Write in words what graph **1d** tells you.

6   The table below shows the results of a science experiment in which a ball is rolled along a desk top. The speed of the ball is measured at various points.

Distance from start (cm)	10	20	30	40	50	60	70	80
Speed (cm/s)	18	16	13	10	7	5	3	0

     a   Plot the data on a scatter diagram.   **b**   Draw the line of best fit.

     c   If the ball's speed had been measured at 5 cm from the start, what is it likely to have been?

     d   How far from the start was the ball when its speed was 12 cm/s?

7   The table below shows the marks for 10 pupils in their mathematics and geography examinations.

Pupil	Anna	Brodie	Cath	Dema	Emma	Fatima	Greta	Hannah	Imogen	Joy
Maths	57	65	34	87	42	35	59	61	25	35
Geog	45	61	30	78	41	36	35	57	23	34

     a   Plot the data on a scatter diagram and draw a line of best fit. Take the *x*-axis for the mathematics scores and mark it from 20 to 100. Take the *y*-axis for the geography scores and mark it from 20 to 100.

     b   One of the pupils was ill when she took the geography examination. Which pupil was it most likely to be?

     c   If another pupil, Kate, was absent for the geography examination but scored 75 in mathematics, what mark would you expect her to get in geography?

     d   If another pupil, Lynne, was absent for the mathematics examination but scored 65 in geography, what mark would you expect her to get in mathematics?

8 The heights, in centimetres, of 20 mothers and their 15-year-old daughters were measured. These are the results.

Mother	153	162	147	183	174	169	152	164	186	178
Daughter	145	155	142	167	167	151	145	152	163	168
Mother	175	173	158	168	181	173	166	162	180	156
Daughter	172	167	160	154	170	164	156	150	160	152

a Plot these results on a scatter diagram.
Take the x-axis for the mothers' heights from 140 to 200.
Take the y-axis for the daughters' heights from 140 to 200.

b Draw a line of best fit.

c Is it true that tall mothers have tall daughters?

9 The government wanted to see how much the prices of houses had risen over the last ten years in different areas of Britain. They surveyed 10 houses that had been sold 10 years ago and had them valued at today's prices.

This table shows the value of the houses (in thousands of pounds) ten years ago and today.

House	A	B	C	D	E	F	G	H	I	J
Value 10 years ago	32	54	89	25	43	58	38	47	95	39
Value today	43	61	94	34	56	67	46	56	105	48

a Plot the data on a scatter diagram.
Take the x-axis as the price 10 years ago and mark it from 20 to 100.
Take the y-axis as the price today and mark it from 20 to 110.

b Draw the line of best fit through the data.

c What would you expect a house worth £65 000 ten years ago to be worth today?

d Apart from inflation, what other factors could have affected the rise or fall in the value of a house?

e Would you say that there was a correlation between the value of a house 10 years ago and the value of the same house today?

10 A form teacher asked his class to say how many hours per week they spent playing sport and how many hours a week they spent watching TV. This table shows the results.

Pupil	1	2	3	4	5	6	7	8	9	10
Hours playing sport	12	3	5	15	11	0	9	7	6	12
Hours watching TV	18	26	24	16	19	27	12	13	17	14

Pupil	11	12	13	14	15	16	17	18	19	20
Hours playing sport	12	10	7	6	7	3	1	2	0	12
Hours watching TV	22	16	18	22	12	28	18	20	25	13

a Plot these results on a scatter diagram.

Take the *x*-axis as the number of hours playing sport and mark it from 0 to 20.

Take the *y*-axis as the number of hours watching TV and mark it from 0 to 30.

b Why can you not draw a line of best fit through the data?

c If you knew that another pupil from the form watched 8 hours of TV a week, would you be able to predict how long she or he spent playing sport?

11 Over a period of 10 years, a farmer kept a record of the number of days his crops had been without water before each harvest and their yield (in tons per acre) at each harvest. The results are in the table below.

Days without water before harvest	10	2	20	25	23	20	30	14	5	11
Crop yield (tons/acre)	25	28	18	16	18	20	14	21	27	23

a Plot the data on a scatter diagram.

Take the *x*-axis as the number of days without water and mark it from 0 to 30.

Take the *y*-axis as the crop yield and mark it from 0 to 30.

b Draw the line of best fit through the data.

c If in the following year there were 18 days without rain before the farmer harvested his crops, what yield would you expect him to get?

12 The table below shows the reaction times (in seconds) and the alcohol level in the blood (in millilitres per litre) of a volunteer in an experiment.

Level of alcohol	0	5	14	18	27	37	46	62	71	80
Reaction time	0.20	0.28	0.37	0.40	0.45	0.54	0.59	0.72	0.75	0.90

a Plot the data on a scatter diagram.

Take the *x*-axis as the level of alcohol and mark it from 0 to 80.

Take the *y*-axis as the reaction time and mark it from 0 to 1.0

b Draw the line of best fit through the data.

c Research has shown that people whose reaction time is greater than 0.65 seconds are likely to cause accidents when driving a car. The current legal level of alcohol for driving is 80 millilitres per litre of blood. What should it be set at if the risk of accidents is to be reduced?

Moving averages

A **moving average** gives a clear indication of the **trend** of a set of data. It smoothes out, for example, seasonal differences, monthly variations or daily differences.

Take the case of a van rental firm which keeps a record of how many vans were hired in each month of a year.

Month	Jan	Feb	Mar	Apr	May	Jun	Jul	Aug	Sep	Oct	Nov	Dec
Vans	9	24	37	16	15	24	45	10	13	27	48	15

We can graph this data.

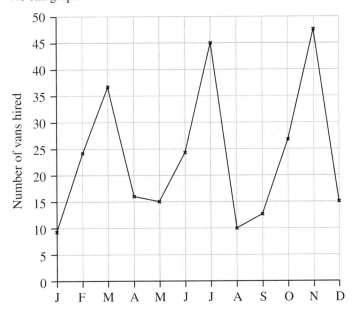

The resulting line graph shows a normal variation of business for the hire firm, but does not reveal the general trend of business. We can show the general trend by first calculating the mean for each four-month span, month on month, as below.

Mean for Jan, Feb, Mar and Apr	$(9 + 24 + 37 + 16) \div 4 = 21.5$
Mean for Feb, Mar, Apr and May	$(24 + 37 + 16 + 15) \div 4 = 23$
Mean for Mar, Apr, May and Jun	$(37 + 16 + 15 + 24) \div 4 = 23$
Mean for Apr, May, Jun and July	25
Mean for May, Jun, July and Aug	23.5
Mean for Jun, Jul, Aug and Sep	23
Mean for Jul, Aug, Sep and Oct	23.75
Mean for Aug, Sep, Oct and Nov	24.5
Mean for Sep, Oct, Nov and Dec	25.75

We then plot, on the first graph, each mean value at the mid-point of the corresponding four-month span. This produces a much smoother graph, which, in this case, shows a slight upward trend. In other words, business is improving.

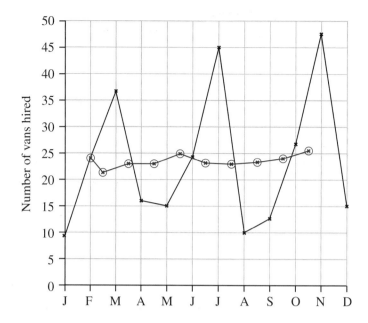

In this example, we used an interval of four months but there is nothing special about this interval. It could well have been five or six months, except that we would then have needed data for more months to give sufficient mean values to show a trend. The number of days, months, weeks, or even years used for moving averages depends on the likely variations of the data. We would not expect to use fewer than three more than 12 items of data at a time.

EXERCISE 22B

1   The following table shows the daily sales of milk at a corner shop

Sun	Mon	Tue	Wed	Thu	Fri	Sat
12	8	6	9	4	11	15
11	7	7	6	3	15	14
14	9	7	7	5	12	15
11	12	8	7	4	14	18

Make a table showing the moving average using a seven-day span, and draw a graph to show the trend of milk sales over the month.

2   A new play was opened at a West End theatre and ran for six weeks. The attendances are shown in the table.

	Mon	Tue	Wed	Thu	Fri	Sat
First week	243	268	407	384	348	489
Second week	445	501	623	621	527	684
Third week	602	625	800	763	728	800
Fourth week	800	800	800	800	800	800
Fifth week	721	785	800	800	800	800
Sixth week	647	664	683	642	608	726

    a   Plot a line graph from the above data.

    b   Calculate the six-days moving average for the data and plot this on the same graph.

    c   Comment on the weekly attendance.

3 **a**   Plot the line graph of the electricity bills shown in the table, and on the same axes plot a four-quarters moving average.

	1997	1998	1999	2000
First quarter	£123.39	£119.95	£127.39	£132.59
Second quarter	£108.56	£113.16	£117.76	£119.76
Third quarter	£87.98	£77.98	£102.58	£114.08
Fourth quarter	£112.47	£127.07	£126.27	£130.87

    b   Comment on the price of electricity over the four years.

4 The table shows how many units of gas a home used over three years.

    a   Plot a line graph of consumption, and also a four-quarters moving average

	1997	1998	1999
First quarter	83	77	83
Second quarter	33	39	21
Third quarter	18	30	42
Fourth quarter	71	59	58

    b   Comment on the trend in gas consumption over the three years.

5 The table shows the attendances at a cinema, to the nearest hundred, during one month.

	Mon	Tue	Wed	Thu	Fri	Sat	Sun
First week	5	10	15	16	19	21	15
Second week	5	6	13	12	15	21	14
Third week	4	6	12	13	15	19	14
Fourth week	4	7	12	10	14	20	13

    a   Plot a line graph of the attendances, and also plot a seven-days moving average.

    b   Comment on the trend in the attendances.

6 The table shows the telephone bills for a family over four years.

	1997	1998	1999	2000
First quarter	£82	£87	£98	£88
Second quarter	£87	£88	£95	£91
Third quarter	£67	£72	£87	£78
Fourth quarter	£84	£81	£97	£87

    a   Plot a line graph showing the amounts paid each month.

    b   Plot a four-quarters moving average.

    c   Comment on the trend shown and give a possible reason for it.

7 A factory making computer components has the following sales figures (in hundreds) for electric fans.

	Jan	Feb	Mar	Apr	May	Jun	Jul	Aug	Sep	Oct	Nov	Dec
1999	12	13	12	14	13	3	15	12	14	13	14	12
2000	13	14	12	14	13	14	13	13	15	15	11	14

a Plot a line graph of the sales, and a three-months moving average.

b Comment on the trend in the sales.

8 The table shows the amounts collected for a charity by students at Pope Pius School in the ten weeks leading up to Christmas.

Week	1	2	3	4	5	6	7	8	9	10
Amount (£)	42	45	44	47	33	40	45	51	42	45

a Plot a line graph of the amounts collected and a four-weeks moving average.

b Comment on the trend shown.

9 The table shows the total sales of video recorders and DVDs from 1995 to 2001 for an electrical store in the USA.

	1995	1996	1997	1998	1999	2000	2001
Video (thousands)	3.4	3.8	3.9	3.2	2.8	2.5	2.3
DVD (thousands)	0.2	0.8	0.9	1.5	1.9	2.8	3.7

a Plot a line graph showing the sales for each product over these years.

b On the same diagram, plot the three-years moving average of each product.

c Comment on the trends seen in the sales of video recorders and DVDs.

Cumulative frequency diagrams

This section will show you how to find a measure of dispersion – the **interquartile range** – using a graph. This method also enables you to find the median. The advantage of the interquartile range is that it eliminates extreme values and bases the measure of spread on the middle 50% of the data.

For example, the marks for the 50 pupils in the mathematics test (see page 408) could be put into a grouped table. A third column has been added into which the cumulative frequency can be placed. The cumulative frequency is found by adding each frequency to the sum of all preceding frequencies.

Mark	Number of pupils	Cumulative frequency
21 to 30	1	1
31 to 40	6	7
41 to 50	6	13
51 to 60	8	21
61 to 70	8	29
71 to 80	6	35
81 to 90	7	42
91 to 100	6	48
101 to 110	1	49
111 to 120	1	50

This data can then be used to plot a graph of the top point of the group against the cumulative frequency. That is, the points to be plotted are (30, 1), (40, 7), (50, 13), (60, 21) etc, which will give the graph shown below.

Note that the cumulative frequency is always the vertical (*y*) axis.

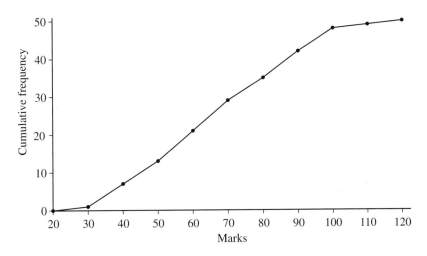

Also note that the scales on both axes are labelled at each graduation mark, in the usual way. **Do not** label the scales like this – it is **wrong**.

21–30	31– 40	41–50

The plotted points can be joined in two different ways:

- by straight lines, to give a **cumulative frequency polygon**

- by a freehand curve, to give a **cumulative frequency curve** or **ogive**.

They are both called cumulative frequency diagrams.

In an examination you are most likely to be asked to draw a cumulative frequency diagram, and the type (polygon or curve) is up to you. Both will give similar results.

The cumulative frequency diagram can be used in several ways, as you will now see.

The median

The median is the middle item (see pages 216–7). So, if we have n items of data plotted as a cumulative frequency diagram, the median can be found from the middle value of the cumulative frequency, that is the $\frac{n}{2}$th value.

But remember, if we want to find the median from a simple list of discrete data, we must use the $(\frac{n+1}{2})$th value. The reason for the difference is that the cumulative frequency diagram treats the data as continuous.

There are 50 values in the table on page 419. The middle value will be the 25th value. Draw a horizontal line from the 25th value to meet the graph, then go down to the horizontal axis. This will give an estimate of the median. In this example, the median is about 65.

The interquartile range

By dividing the cumulative frequency into four parts, we obtain **quartiles** and the **interquartile range**.

The **lower quartile** is the item one quarter of the way up the cumulative frequency axis and is found by looking at the $\frac{n}{4}$th value.

The **upper quartile** is the item three-quarters of the way up the cumulative frequency axis and is found by looking at the $\frac{3n}{4}$th value.

The **interquartile range** is the difference between the lower and upper quartiles.

These are illustrated on the graph below.

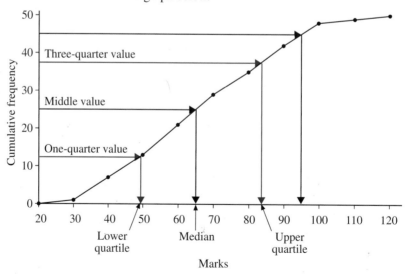

The quarter and three-quarter values out of 50 values are the 12.5th value and the 37.5th value. Draw lines across to the cumulative frequency curve from these values and down to the horizontal axis. These give the lower and upper quartiles. In this example, the lower quartile is 48, the upper quartile is 83, and the interquartile range is $83 - 48 = 35$.

Note that questions like these are often followed up with an extra question such as: 'The Head of Mathematics decides to give a special award to the top 10% of pupils. What would the cut-off mark be?'

The top 10% would be the top 5 pupils (10% of 50 is 5). Draw a line across from 45 pupils to the graph and down to the horizontal axis. This gives a cut-off mark of 96.

EXERCISE 22C

1 A class of 30 children were asked to estimate a minute. Their teacher recorded the times they actually said. This table shows the results.
   a Copy the table and complete a cumulative frequency column.
   b Draw a cumulative frequency diagram.
   c Use your diagram to estimate the median time and the interquartile range.

Time (seconds)	Number of pupils
$20 < x \le 30$	1
$30 < x \le 40$	3
$40 < x \le 50$	6
$50 < x \le 60$	12
$60 < x \le 70$	3
$70 < x \le 80$	3
$80 < x \le 90$	2

2 A group of 50 pensioners were given the same task as the children in question **1**. Their results are shown in the table.
   a Copy the table and complete a cumulative frequency column.
   b Draw a cumulative frequency diagram.
   c Use your diagram to estimate the median time and the interquartile range.
   d Which group, the children or the pensioners, would you say was better at estimating time? Give a reason for your answer.

Time (seconds)	Number of pensioners
$10 < x \le 20$	1
$20 < x \le 30$	2
$30 < x \le 40$	2
$40 < x \le 50$	9
$50 < x \le 60$	17
$60 < x \le 70$	13
$70 < x \le 80$	3
$80 < x \le 90$	2
$90 < x \le 100$	1

3 The temperature at a seaside resort was recorded over a period of 50 days. The table shows the results.
   a Copy the table and complete a cumulative frequency column.
   b Draw a cumulative frequency diagram.
   c Use your diagram to estimate the median temperature and the interquartile range.

Temperature (°F)	Number of days
41–45	2
46–50	3
51–55	5
56–60	6
61–65	6
66–70	9
71–75	8
76–80	6
81–85	5

4 The sizes of 360 secondary schools in South Yorkshire are recorded in the table.

Number of pupils	Number of schools
100–199	12
200–299	18
300–399	33
400–499	50
500–599	63
600–699	74
700–799	64
800–899	35
900–999	11

a Copy the table and complete a cumulative frequency column.

b Draw a cumulative frequency diagram.

c Use your diagram to estimate the median size of the schools and the interquartile range.

d Schools with less than 350 pupils are threatened with closure. About how many schools are these?

5 At the school charity fête, a game consists of throwing three darts and recording the total score. The results of the first 80 people to throw are recorded in the table.

Total score	Number of players
$1 \le x \le 20$	9
$21 \le x \le 40$	13
$41 \le x \le 60$	23
$61 \le x \le 80$	15
$81 \le x \le 100$	11
$101 \le x \le 120$	7
$121 \le x \le 140$	2

a Copy the table and complete a cumulative frequency column.

b Draw a cumulative frequency diagram.

c Use your diagram to estimate the median score and the interquartile range.

d People who score over 90 get a prize. About what percentage of the people get a prize?

6 One hundred pupils in a school were asked to say how much pocket money they each get in a week. The results are shown in the table.

Amount of pocket money (p)	Number of pupils
51–100	6
101–150	10
151–200	20
201–250	28
251–300	18
301–350	11
351–400	5
401–450	2

a Copy the table and complete a cumulative frequency column.

b Draw a cumulative frequency diagram.

c Use your diagram to estimate the median amount of pocket money and the interquartile range.

7 This list of numbers are the weights of 100 crows measured in grams.

963	1162	1053	1272	1205	1067	1112	1189	1269	1272
1212	1121	1237	1017	1130	1271	1157	1223	1143	1082
1107	1215	1226	1210	1167	1271	1206	1199	1031	1151
1270	1173	1067	1190	1379	1246	1137	1241	1301	1129
1115	1139	1119	1310	1289	1171	1281	1342	1076	1298
1159	1079	1232	1140	1024	1125	1235	1273	1337	1281
1155	1225	1262	1148	1173	1229	1180	1072	1173	1140
1091	1142	1070	1137	1121	1350	1043	1141	1180	1265
1263	1125	1399	1165	1257	1102	1255	1275	1325	1135
1187	1378	1190	1106	1390	1192	1379	1316	1093	1329

Copy and complete this table (the last group will be 1351–1400). Be careful counting the numbers. Use the tally column if this makes things easier.

Weight (grams)	Tally	Frequency	Cumulative frequency
951–1000			
1001–1050			

Use the table to draw a cumulative frequency diagram and use this to estimate the median and the interquartile range. Crows under a weight of 1075 grams are given a dose of vitamins. How many crows will get a vitamin dose?

Box plots

Another way of displaying data for comparison is by means of a **box and whisker plot** (or just **box plot**). This requires five pieces of data. These are the lowest value, the lower quartile (Q_1), the median (Q_2), the upper quartile ($Q3$) and the highest value. They are drawn in the following way.

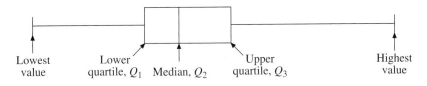

These data are always placed against a scale so that their values are accurately plotted.

The following diagrams show how the cumulative frequency curve, the frequency curve and the box plot are connected for three common types of distribution.

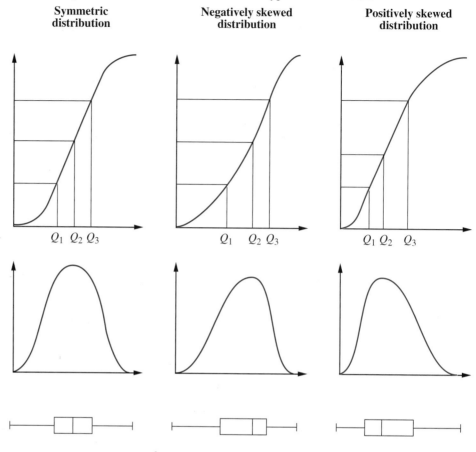

| Symmetric distribution | Negatively skewed distribution | Positively skewed distribution |

Example   The box plot for the girls' marks in last year's SATs is shown on the grid below.

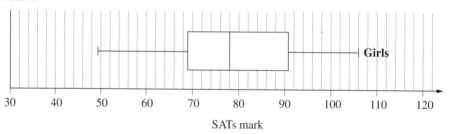

The boys' results for the same SATs are: lowest mark 39; lower quartile 65; median 78; upper quartile 87; highest mark 112.

a   On the same grid plot the box plot for the boys' marks.

b   Comment on the differences between the two distributions of marks.

a The data for boys and girls is plotted on the grid below

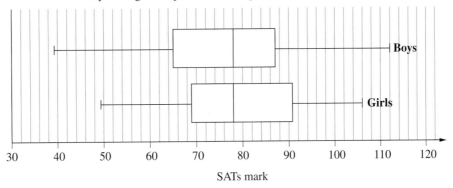

SATs mark

b The girls and boys have the same median mark but both the lower and upper quartiles for the girls are higher than those for the boys, and the girls' range is smaller than the boys'. These mean that the girls did better than the boys overall, even though a boy got the highest mark.

EXERCISE 22D

1 The box plot below shows the times taken for a group of pensioners to do a set of ten long-division calculations.

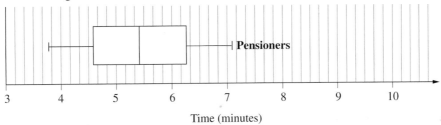

Time (minutes)

The same set of calculations were given to some students in Year 11. Their results are: shortest time 3 minutes 20 seconds; lower quartile 6 minutes 10 seconds; median 7 minutes; upper quartile 7 minutes 50 seconds; longest time 9 minutes 40 seconds.
a Copy the diagram and draw a box plot for the students' times.
b Comment on the differences between the two distributions.

2 The box plot below shows the sizes of secondary schools in Dorset.

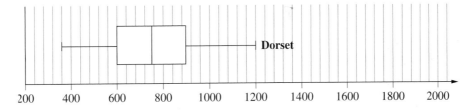

The data for schools in Rotherham is: smallest 400: lower quartile 1100; median 1400; upper quartile 1600; largest 1850.
a Copy the diagram and draw a box plot for the sizes of schools in Rotherham.
b Comment on the differences between the two distributions.

3 The box plots for the noon temperature at two resorts, recorded over a year, are shown on the grid below.

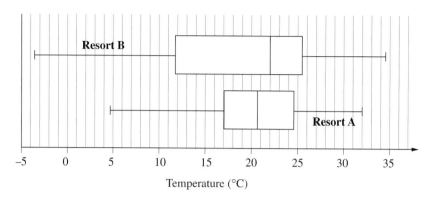

Temperature (°C)

a Comment on the differences in the two distributions.

b Mary wants to go on holiday in July. Which resort would you recommend and why?

4 The following table shows some data on the annual salaries for 100 men and 100 women.

	Lowest salary	Lowest quartile	Median salary	Upper quartile	Highest salary
Men	£6500	£16 000	£20 000	£22 000	£44 500
Women	£7000	£14 000	£16 000	£21 000	£33 500

a Draw box plots to compare the two sets of data.

b Comment on the differences between the distributions.

Possible coursework tasks

Adverts

How long? How often? Are there more adverts on TV at certain times of the day? What types of advert?

Investigate and draw up any conclusions that you make.

Who's a big head, then?

Investigate the circumference of a person's head and his/her height.

Watching TV is bad for your maths

'Young people today watch too much television. This is bound to affect their test results in mathematics.'

Draw up a suitable questionnaire to test the validity of this statement.

Gulliver's journey into mathematics

'... they measured my right thumb, and desired no more; for a mathematical computation that twice round my thumb is once round the wrist and so on to the neck and the waist ...'

Investigate this extract taken from Swift's *Gulliver's Travels*.

For these coursework tasks, you may find it helpful to design a questionnaire of your own using a computer. Statistical diagrams can also be drawn using computer databases. Their use will improve the presentation of your work.

Examination questions

1   The scatter graph shows information about eight countries.
    For each country, it shows the birth rate and the life expectancy, in years.

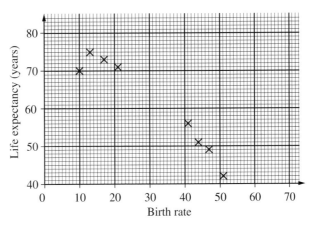

The table shows the birth rate and the life expectancy for six more countries.

Birth rate	25	28	30	31	34	38
Life expectancy (years)	68	65	62	61	65	61

a On a copy of the scatter graph, plot the information in the table.

b Describe the relationship between the birth rate and the life expectancy.

c Draw a line of best fit on the scatter graph.

EDEXCEL, Question 11, Intermediate Paper 4, June 2000

2 This table gives you the marks scored by pupils in a French test and in a German test.

French	15	35	34	23	35	27	36	34	23	24	30	40	25	35	20
German	20	37	35	25	33	30	39	36	27	20	33	35	27	32	28

a Work out the range of the pupils' marks in French.

b Draw a scattergraph of the marks scored in the French and German tests.

c Draw the line of best fit on the diagram.

d Use your line of best fit to estimate the mark of a pupil's test in French when their mark in German was 23.

e Describe the relationship between the marks scored in the two tests.

ULEAC, Question 8, Specimen Paper 4, 1998

3 A researcher asks people how many visits they have made to a city during the last three months and how far they live from the city. This table shows her results.

Visits to city	10	5	13	2	6	16	15	11		Mean	9.75
Distance (km)	5	8	3	9	7	1	3	4		Mean	5

a Draw a scatter diagram to show these results.

b Draw a line of best fit on your scatter diagram.

c Approximately how many visits would you expect a person who lives 2 km from the city to have made during the last three months?

WJEC, Question 8, Specimen Paper 2, 1998

4 Annie asked a group of teenagers to say how much time they spent doing homework one evening and how much time they spent watching TV. Here is a scatter diagram to show the results.

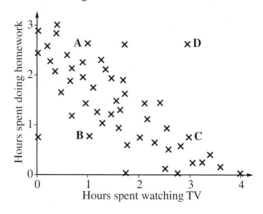

a Which of the four points A, B, C or D represents each of the statements shown below? Write one letter for each statement.

Amanda: 'I watched a lot of TV last night and I also did a lot of homework.'

Mark: 'I spent most of the evening doing homework. I only watched one programme on TV.'

Julie: 'I went out last night. I didn't do much homework or watch much TV.'

b Make up a statement that matches up the fourth point.

c What does the graph tell you about the relationship between time spent watching TV and time spent doing homework?

d Annie also drew scatter diagrams which showed that:

- Older students tend to spend more time doing homework than younger students.
- There is no correlation between the time students spend watching TV and the time students spend sleeping.

Use axes like those below to draw what Annie's scatter diagrams may have looked like.

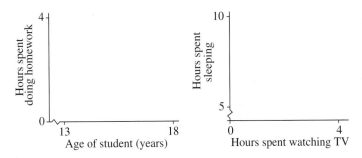

NEAB, Question 8, Specimen Paper 2, 1998

5 A scientist weighs some chicks. She records their weights in grams and their ages in days. The table below shows her results.

Age (days)	3	8	1	10	5	8	11	2
Weight (grams)	12	20	7	23	18	24	30	10

a On a grid draw a scatter diagram to show these results.

b The mean weight is 18 g. Calculate the mean age.

c Draw a line of best fit on your scatter diagram.

d Use your scatter diagram to estimate the weight of a chick 9 days old.

WJEC, Question 14, Intermediate Paper 2, November 1999

6 A psychologist asks some people how many times they have wired a plug. Each person is then asked to wire a plug and the time taken is recorded. The mean number of times people have wired a plug is 6. The mean time taken to wire a plug is 10 minutes.

The scatter diagram below shows the number of times a person has wired a plug and the time taken to wire a plug for each of 10 people.

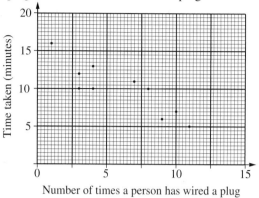

Number of times a person has wired a plug

a   Draw the line of best fit on the scatter diagram.

b   Jeremy had wired a plug 5 times. Estimate how long it will take him to wire one plug.

WJEC, Question 15, Intermediate Paper 1, November 1988

7   2400 people took an examination paper.

The maximum mark for this paper was 80.

The cumulative frequency graph below gives information about the marks.

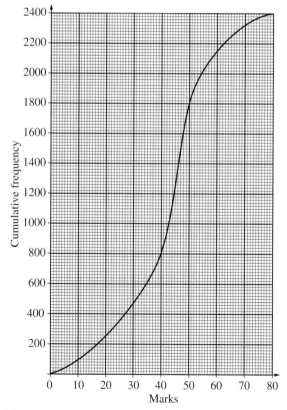

Marks

The pass mark was 44 marks.

a Use the cumulative frequency graph to estimate the number of people who did **not** pass this paper.

The same 2400 people took a second examination paper.

The table gives information about the marks for the second paper.

The maximum mark was 80.

Mark	Cumulative frequency
0 – 10	20
0 – 20	80
0 – 30	200
0 – 40	500
0 – 50	900
0 – 60	1800
0 – 70	2200
0 – 80	2400

b Draw the cumulative graph to show this information.

The same number of people did not pass this paper.

c Use your cumulative frequency graph to estimate the pass mark for the second paper.

EDEXCEL, Question 29, Intermediate Paper 3, June 2000

8 The table below illustrates the age distribution in a village of 360 people.

Age	0–	10–	20–	30–	40–	50–	60–	70–	80–100
Frequency	44	51	59	68	50	35	31	18	4

a Draw a cumulative frequency diagram to illustrate this data.

b Use your graph to estimate
- **i** the number of villagers who are more than 25 years old
- **ii** the median
- **iii** the interquartile range.

SEG, Question 17, Specimen Paper 14, 1998

9 This table shows the results for 160 pupils in a test.

Mark	0 to 19	20 to 39	40 to 49	50 to 59	60 to 69	70 to 99
Frequency	5	18	29	65	32	11

a Complete a cumulative frequency table and draw a cumulative frequency diagram to show these results.

b Copy and complete the table below to show the median and interquartile range for this distribution.

Median	Lower quartile	Upper quartile	Interquartile range

c The top 60% of pupils passed the test. What was the pass mark?

WJEC, Question 12, Specimen Paper 2, 1998

10 The table below shows the distribution of the ages, in complete years, of 60 people on a train.

Age (years)	0 to 19	20 to 29	30 to 39	40 to 49	50 to 59	60 to 69
Frequency	18	10	12	8	5	7

a Copy and complete the cumulative frequency table below.

Age (less than years)	20	30	40	50	60	70
Cumulative frequency						

b Draw a cumulative frequency diagram to show these results.

c Use your cumulative frequency diagram to find the interquartile range. You must show your working.

WJEC, Question 20, Intermediate Paper 2, June 1999

Summary

How well do you grade yourself?

To gain a grade **E**, you need to be able to plot points on a scatter diagram.

To gain a grade **D**, you need to be able to recognise a correlation from a scatter diagram and describe it in words.

To gain a grade **C**, you need to be able to use measures of average and range to compare distributions. You also need to be able to draw a line of best fit on a scatter diagram by inspection and interpret it, and have a knowledge of positive and negative correlation.

To gain a grade **B**, you need to be able to draw a cumulative frequency diagram and solve problems from it.

What you should know after you have worked through Chapter 22

- How to plot points on a scatter diagram.

- What correlation means and be able to distinguish between the different types.

- How to recognise positive and negative correlation when looking at scatter diagrams, and also be able to recognise 'no correlation'.

- How to draw an accurate line of best fit on a scatter diagram, and use it to predict.

- How to construct a cumulative frequency diagram.

- The difference between a cumulative frequency polygon and a cumulative frequency curve.

- How to find from a cumulative frequency diagram
  - the median using the $\frac{n}{2}$ th value
  - the lower quartile using the $\frac{n}{4}$ th value
  - the upper quartile using the $\frac{3n}{4}$ th value
  - the interquartile range.

**SOUTHALL AND WEST
LONDON COLLEGE
LEARNING CENTRE**

Coursework example **4**

Pulse rates

Refer to the Appendix for a summary of coursework marks.

Problem statement

An individual's pulse rate is affected by various factors. Suggest any likely factors and then investigate them by stating suitable hypotheses.

Possible solution

The aim of this investigation is to find out whether the resting pulse rate of a person is related to certain factors. I have decided to see if there is a connection between a person's pulse rate and their age, height and weight. To do this, I have designed a questionnaire using a computer database. So that my data is representative of the population and is reliable, I have taken a sample of 40 people of various ages. I have also tried to keep approximately the same number of males and females.

The hypotheses I propose are

1   Age does not affect a person's pulse rate.
2   Height is unlikely to affect a person's pulse rate.
3   Weight is likely to affect a person's pulse rate.

This is the questionnaire I designed. I then asked 40 people to complete it.

i	ii	iii	Notes
4			Overall plan meets the aims of the problem. Suitable sample size.

QUESTIONNAIRE FOR PULSE RATE

Please complete the following.

SEX   ☐ MALE
               ☐ FEMALE

AGE   ____ years

HEIGHT   ____ cm

WEIGHT   ____ kg

REST PULSE RATE ____

To find your rest pulse rate, take your wrist or neck pulse for 15 seconds and multiply by 4

i	ii	iii	Notes
6			Appropriate data collected with aims given in statistical terms. Report is well structured.
	4		Use of statistical concepts, words and diagrams. Information presented in a variety of forms and linked with relevant explanation.
		4	Summarise data and correctly interpret graphs.

I will now display the data from the 40 questionnaires in a table compiled by a computer database. To help me reach conclusions, the table will also include the means and ranges for the variables.

To show the data in a more convenient form and by using the computer database, I will draw bar graphs for the three variables I want to connect with pulse rate. This is a much clearer method for showing the data.

Sorted by: AGE

Sex	Age	Weight	Height	Pulse
STATISTICS:				
Range				
All sheets:	66.0	75.0	55.0	36.0
Mean				
All sheets:	37.9	68.5	168.3	75.3
MALE	11	33	140	66
FEMALE	11	32	140	72
FEMALE	12	39	147	80
FEMALE	12	41	142	80
FEMALE	12	44	157	64
FEMALE	13	51	157	76
MALE	14	41	154	72
FEMALE	14	60	168	68
FEMALE	14	50	163	84
MALE	15	66	178	76
MALE	17	76	183	76
MALE	24	83	178	80
MALE	24	105	195	100
FEMALE	25	58	175	76
MALE	27	70	191	76
MALE	28	101	182	80
MALE	30	77	188	64
MALE	32	76	185	86
MALE	35	107	190	92
MALE	35	76	185	80
FEMALE	36	63	147	64
MALE	37	100	173	80
FEMALE	37	66	172	68
MALE	45	82	178	76
MALE	45	69	172	66
FEMALE	46	69	170	84
FEMALE	47	66	160	72
MALE	49	78	175	68
FEMALE	52	65	157	76
MALE	53	79	175	80
FEMALE	54	72	157	72
FEMALE	56	76	174	72
MALE	62	96	190	84
FEMALE	62	63	155	64
FEMALE	64	77	154	80
FEMALE	71	51	150	76
MALE	72	69	165	72
FEMALE	73	72	159	68
MALE	74	72	178	64
MALE	77	69	173	80

i	ii	iii	Notes
		6	Use of more demanding statistical techniques. Appropriate diagrams used with reason given for the choice of presentation.

The bar graphs show me that I have taken a reasonable, representative sample of the population. This is important if my conclusions are to be valid. To see if there is any correlation between the three variables and pulse rate, I'm now going to represent the data by drawing scatter diagrams to connect the three variables with pulse rate. Once again, I am going to use the computer database to compile the diagrams.

From the work I have done in lessons, I know that the line of best fit drawn on the scatter diagrams will show me how well the data is correlated.

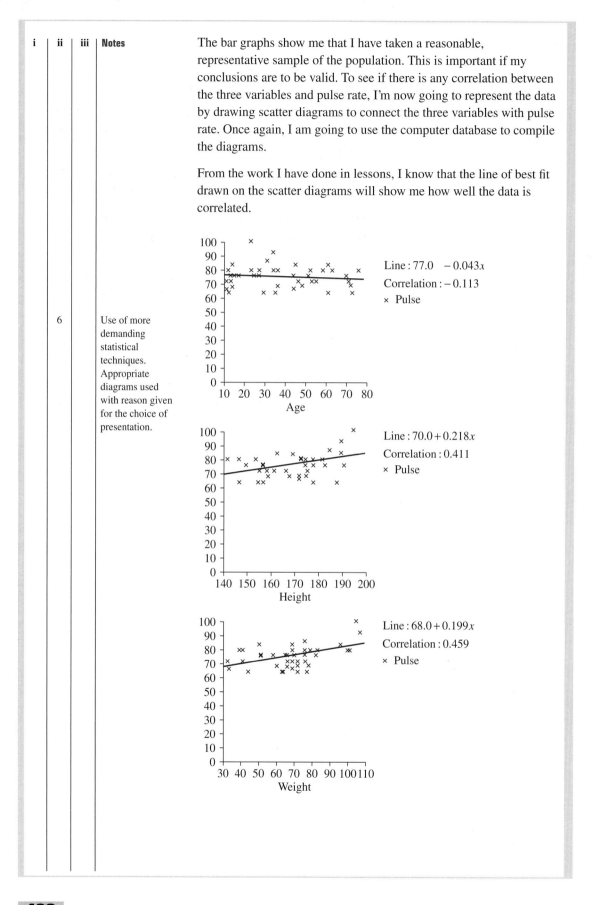

Line : $77.0 - 0.043x$

Correlation : -0.113

× Pulse

Line : $70.0 + 0.218x$

Correlation : 0.411

× Pulse

Line : $68.0 + 0.199x$

Correlation : 0.459

× Pulse

i	ii	iii	Notes

My conclusions

I can now see from my scatter diagrams how the three variables I have chosen are connected to pulse rate.

The correlation number given by the side of each scatter diagram shows how well the two variable correlate. The closer the number is to 1, the stronger the correlation.

Hypothesis 1 The line of best fit shows negative correlation and, since the correlation number is small, there is no correlation.

Hypothesis 2 The line of best fit shows positive correlation, and since the correlation number is fairly close to $\frac{1}{2}$, there is moderate correlation.

Hypothesis 3 The line of best fit shows positive correlation, and since the correlation number is nearly $\frac{1}{2}$, again there is moderate correlation.

In my investigation, I have found that for my sample, the average rest pulse rate is 75.3 and that my original hyptheses are just about true.

To take the investigation further, I could take a larger sample to back up my hypotheses. I could also find people's pulse rate after exercise and see how long it would take before they returned to their rest pulse rate.

6 | Summarise and correctly interpret graphs and calculations. Evaluate the overall strategy and draw relevant conclusions.

Final marks
(i) 6 (ii) 6 (iii) 6

23 Probability

This chapter is going to ...

remind you of the basic definition of probability. It will show you the difference between experimental probability and theoretical probability and how these quantities are related to each other. It will also show you how to deal with combined events by using a probability diagram, such as a tree diagram, or by considering all the outcomes of an experiment.

What you should already know

✔ Basic ideas of probability.
✔ The probability scale goes from 0 to 1.
✔ How to cancel, add, subtract and multiply fractions (using a calculator if necessary).

You have already met probability. The activity below is essentially revision and could be missed out if you are sure that you know what probability means.

Discovery activity

Toss a coin 10 times and record the results like this.

H	T	H	H	T	T	H	T	H	H

Record how many heads you obtained.

Now repeat the above so that altogether you toss the coin 50 times. Record your results and count how many heads you obtained. Now toss the coin another 50 times and once again record your results and count the heads.

It helps if you work with a partner. First, your partner records while you toss the coin. Then you swap over and record, while your partner tosses the coin. Add the number of heads you obtained to the number your partner obtained.

Now find three more people who have done the same activity and add together the number of heads that all five of you obtained.

Now find five more people and add their results to the previous total.

Combine as many results together as possible.

You should now be able to fill in a table like the one below. The first column is the number of times coins were tossed. The second column is the number of heads obtained. The third column is column 2 divided by column 1.

The results below are from a group who did the same experiment.

Number of tosses	Number of heads	Heads ÷ tosses
10	6	0.6
50	24	0.48
100	47	0.47
200	92	0.46
500	237	0.474
1000	488	0.488
2000	960	0.48
5000	2482	0.4964

If we drew a graph of these results, plotting the first column against the last column, it would look like this:

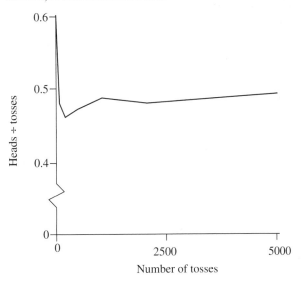

Your results should look very similar.

What happens to the value of heads ÷ tosses as the total number of tosses increases? You should find that it gets closer and closer to 0.5.

The value of heads ÷ tosses is an **experimental probability**. As the number of trials or experiments increases, the value of the experimental probability gets closer to the actual (theoretical) probability.

Experimental probability is also known as **relative frequency**. This is the frequency of an event divided by the total number of trials.

As a coin can land only two ways (head and tail) and we are interested in the number of heads, we can soon work out that the theoretical probability of getting a head is a half. (One way to get a head out of two ways in which the coin can land.)

We write this as

P(head) = $\frac{1}{2}$

This is read as: 'The probability of a head is a half'.

The topic of probability has its own special terminology which we will explain as it arises. For example, a **trial** is one go at performing something, such as throwing a dice or tossing a coin. So, if we throw a dice 10 times, we perform 10 trials.

Another probability term is **event**. This is anything whose probability we want to measure.

Note 'Dice' is used in this book in preference to 'die' for the singular form of the noun, as well as for the plural. This is in keeping with growing common usage, including in examination papers.

Finding probabilities

There are three ways in which the probability of an event can be found.

- **First method** If we can work out the theoretical probability of an event – for example, drawing a King from a pack of cards – this is called **using equally likely outcomes.**

- **Second method** Some events, such as buying a certain brand of dog food, cannot be calculated using equally likely outcomes. To find the probability of such an event, we can perform an experiment such as we already have or conduct a survey. This is called **collecting experimental data**. The more data we collect, the better the estimate is.

- **Third method** The probability of some events, such as an earthquake occurring in Japan, cannot be found by either of the above methods. One of the things we can do is to look at data collected over a long period of time and make an estimate (sometimes called a 'best guess') at the chance of the event happening. This is called **looking at historical data**.

Example Which method (A, B or C) would you use to estimate the probabilities of the events **a** to **e**?

    A: Use equally likely outcomes
    B: Conduct a survey/collect data
    C: Look at historical data.

a Someone in your class will go abroad for a holiday this year.
b You will win the National Lottery.
c Your bus home will be late.
d It will snow on Christmas Day.
e You will pick a red seven from a pack of cards.

a You would have to ask all the members of your class what they intended to do for their holidays this year. You would therefore conduct a survey, Method B.

b The odds on winning are about 14 million to 1, so this is an equally likely outcome, Method A.

c If you catch the bus every day, you can collect data over several weeks. This would be Method C.

d If you check whether it snowed on Christmas Day for the last few years you would be able to make a good estimate of the probability. This would be Method C.

e There are 2 red sevens out of 52 cards, so the probability of picking one can be calculated:

$$P(\text{red seven}) = \frac{2}{52} = \frac{1}{26}$$

This is Method A.

EXERCISE 23A

1 Naseer throws a dice and records the number of sixes that he gets after various numbers of throws. The table shows his results.

Number of throws	10	50	100	200	500	1000	2000
Number of sixes	2	4	10	21	74	163	329

    a Calculate the experimental probability of a six at each stage that Naseer recorded his results.

    b How many ways can a dice land?

    c How many of these ways give a six?

    d What is the theoretical probability of throwing a six with a dice?

    e If Naseer threw the dice a total of 6000 times, how many sixes would you expect him to get?

2 Marie made a five-sided spinner, like the one shown in the diagram She used it to play a board game with her friend Sarah. The girls thought that the spinner wasn't very fair as it seemed to land on some numbers more than others. They twirled the spinner 200 times and recorded the results. The results are shown in the table.

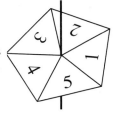

Side spinner lands on	1	2	3	4	5
Number of times	19	27	32	53	69

    a Work out the experimental probability of each number.

    b How many times would you expect each number to occur if the spinner is fair?

    c Do you think that the spinner is fair? Give a reason for your answer.

3 Sarah thought she could make a much more accurate spinner. After she had made it she tested it and recorded how many times she threw a 5. Her results were:

Number of throws	10	50	100	500
Number of fives	3	12	32	107

a   Sarah made a mistake in recording the number of fives. Which number in the second row above is wrong? Give a reason for your answer.

b   These are the full results for 500 throws.

Side spinner lands on	1	2	3	4	5
Number of times	96	112	87	98	107

Do you think the spinner is fair? Give a reason for your answer.

4   A sampling bottle contains 20 balls. The balls are either black or white. (A sampling bottle is a sealed bottle with a clear plastic tube at one end into which one of the balls can be tipped.) Kenny conducts an experiment to see how many black balls are in the bottle. He takes various numbers of samples and records how many of them showed a black ball. The results are shown in the table.

Number of samples	Number of black balls	Experimental probability
10	2	
100	25	
200	76	
500	210	
1000	385	
5000	1987	

a   Copy the table and calculate the experimental probability of getting a black ball at each stage.

b   Using this information, how many black balls do you think are in the bottle?

5   Another sampling bottle contains red, white and blue balls. It is known that there are 20 balls in the bottle altogether. Carrie performs an experiment to see how many of each colour are in the bottle. She starts off putting down a tally each time a colour shows in the clear plastic tube.

Red	White	Blue
JHT JHT JHT JHT II	JHT JHT JHT III	JHT JHT II

Unfortunately, she forgets to count how many times she performs the experiment, so every now and again she counts up the tallies and records them in a table (see below).

Red	White	Blue	Total
22	18	12	42
48	31	16	95
65	37	24	126
107	61	32	211
152	93	62	307
206	128	84	418

The experimental probability of the red balls is calculated by dividing the frequency of red by the total number of trials, so at each stage these are

0.524   0.505   0.516   0.507   0.495   0.493

These answers are rounded off to 3 significant figures.

a Calculate the experimental probabilities of the white balls at each stage to 3 sf.

b Calculate the experimental probabilities of the blue balls at each stage to 3 sf.

c Round off the final experimental probabilities for Carrie's 418 trials to 1 decimal place.

d What is the total of the answers in part **c**?

e How many of each colour do you think are in the bottle? Explain your answer.

6 Use a set of number cards from 1 to 10 (or make your own set) and work with a partner. Take it in turns to choose a card and keep a record each time of what card you get. Shuffle the cards each time and repeat the experiment 60 times. Put your results in a copy of this table.

Score	1	2	3	4	5	6	7	8	9	10
Total										

a How many times would you expect to get each number?

b Do you think you and your partner conducted this experiment fairly?

c Explain your answer to part **b**.

7 Which of these methods would you use to estimate or state the probability of each of the events **a** to **h**?

Method A: Equally likely outcomes

Method B: Survey or experiment

Method C: Look at historical data

a How people will vote in the next election.

b A drawing pin dropped on a desk will land point up.

c A Premier League team will win the FA Cup.

d You will win a school raffle.

e The next car to drive down the road will be red.

f You will throw a 'double six' with two dice.

g Someone in your class likes classical music.

h A person picked at random from your school will be a vegetarian.

8 A four-sided dice has faces numbered 1, 2, 3 and 4. The 'score' is the face on which it lands. Five pupils throw the dice to see if it is biased. They each throw it a different number of times. Their results are shown in the table.

Pupil	Total number of throws	Score 1	2	3	4
Alfred	20	7	6	3	4
Brian	50	19	16	8	7
Caryl	250	102	76	42	30
Deema	80	25	25	12	18
Emma	150	61	46	26	17

a   Which pupil will have the most reliable set of results? Why?

b   Add up all the score columns and work out the relative frequency of each score.

c   Is the dice biased? Explain your answer.

9   If you were about to choose a card from a pack of yellow cards numbered from 1 to 10, what would be the chance of each of the events **a** to **i** occurring? Copy and complete each of these statements with a word or phrase chosen from 'impossible', 'not likely', '50–50 chance', 'quite likely', or 'certain'.

a   The likelihood that the next card chosen will be a four is ......

b   The likelihood that the next card chosen will be pink is ......

c   The likelihood that the next card chosen will be a seven is ......

d   The likelihood that the next card chosen will be a number less than 11 is ......

e   The likelihood that the next card chosen will be a number bigger than 11 is ......

f   The likelihood that the next card chosen will be an even number is ......

g   The likelihood that the next card chosen will be a number more than 5 is ......

h   The likelihood that the next card chosen will be a multiple of 1 is ......

i   The likelihood that the next card chosen will be a prime number is ......

Definition of probability

Probability is defined as

$$P(event) = \frac{\text{Number of ways the event can happen}}{\text{Total number of all possible outcomes}}$$

This definition always leads to a fraction. Where possible, the fraction should be cancelled down to its simplest form.

This can be done with most scientific calculators. Make sure that you know how to cancel down fractions with or without a calculator. It is acceptable to give a probability as a decimal but fractions are better.

This definition can be used to work out the probability of events as the following examples show.

Example 1   A bag contains 5 red balls and 3 blue balls. A ball is taken out at random. What is the probability that it is

      a   red   **b**   blue   **c**   green?

a There are 5 red balls out of a total of 8, so P(red) = $\frac{5}{8}$

b There are 3 blue balls out of a total of 8, so P(blue) = $\frac{3}{8}$

c There are no green balls, so this event is impossible: P(green) = 0

Another probability term is **at random**. This means 'without looking' or 'not knowing what the outcome is in advance'.

Example 2 The spinner shown below right is spun and the score on the side on which it lands is recorded. What is the probability that the score is

      a   2   **b**   odd   **c**   less than 5?

a There are two 2s out of six sides, so P(2) = $\frac{2}{6}$ = $\frac{1}{3}$

b There are four odd numbers, so P(odd) = $\frac{4}{6}$ = $\frac{2}{3}$

c All of the numbers are less than 5, so this is a certain event: P(less than 5) = 1

EXERCISE 23B

1 What is the probability of each of the following?
    a Throwing a 2 with a dice.
    b Throwing a 6 with a dice.
    c Tossing a coin and getting a tail.
    d Drawing a Queen from a pack of cards.
    e Drawing a Heart from a pack of cards.
    f Drawing a black card from a pack of cards.
    g Throwing a 2 or a 6 with a dice.
    h Drawing a black Queen from a pack of cards.
    i Drawing an Ace from a pack of cards.
    j Throwing a 7 with a dice.

2 What is the probability of each of the following?
    a Throwing an even number with a dice.
    b Throwing a prime number with a dice.
    c Getting a Heart or a Club from a pack of cards.
    d Drawing the King of Hearts from a pack of cards.
    e Drawing a picture card or an Ace from a pack of cards.
    f Drawing the Seven of Diamonds from a pack of cards.

3 A bag contains only blue balls. If I take one out at random, what is the probability that
    a I get a black ball   **b** I get a blue ball?

4 The numbers 1 to 10 inclusive are placed in a hat. Bob takes a number out of the bag without looking. What is the probability that he draws
    a the number 7   **b** an even number   **c** a number greater than 6
    d a number less than 3   **e** a number between 3 and 8?

5 A bag contains 1 blue ball, 1 pink ball and 1 black ball. Joan takes a ball from the bag without looking. What is the probability that she takes out

    a   the blue ball   **b**   the pink ball   **c**   a ball that is not black?

6 A pencil case contains 6 red pens and 5 blue pens. Geoff takes a pen out without looking at what it is. What is the probability that he takes out

    a   a red pen   **b**   a blue pen   **c**   a pen that is not blue?

7 A bag contains 50 balls. Ten are green, 15 are red and the rest are white. Gemma takes a ball from the bag at random. What is the probability that she takes

    a   a green ball   **b**   a white ball   **c**   a ball that is not white

    d   a ball that is green or white?

8 A box contains 7 bags of cheese and onion crisps, 2 bags of beef crisps and 6 bags of plain crisps. Iklil takes a bag of crisps out at random. What is the probability that he gets

    a   a bag of cheese and onion crisps

    b   a bag of beef crisps

    c   a bag of crisps that are not cheese and onion

    d   a bag of prawn cracker crisps

    e   a bag of crisps that is either plain or beef?

9 In a Christmas raffle, 2500 tickets are sold. One family has 50 tickets. What is the probability that that family wins the first prize?

10 Arthur, Brenda, Charles, Doris and Eliza are in the same class. Their teacher wants two pupils to do a special job.

    a   Write down all the possible combinations of two people. For example, Arthur and Brenda, Arthur and Charles (there are 10 combinations altogether).

    b   How many pairs give two boys?

    c   What is the probability of choosing two boys?

    d   How many pairs give a boy and a girl?

    e   What is the probability of choosing a boy and a girl?

    f   What is the probability of choosing two girls?

11 A bag contains 10 chocolates. Six are soft-centred and the rest are hard-centred. I take out one chocolate and eat it.

    a   What is the probability that I get a hard-centred chocolate?

    b   If the first chocolate I get is hard-centred

        i   how many hard centres are left   **ii**   how many chocolates are left?

    c   After I have eaten the first chocolate, a hard centre, I pick another one. What is the probability that I pick

        i   a hard centre   **ii**   a soft centre?

12 An ordinary six-sided dice has 2 red faces, 1 blue face and 3 green faces. If this dice is thrown, what is the probability that the top face will be

    a   red   **b**   green   **c**   not blue

    d   black   **e**   red, green or blue?

13 Eight-sided dice are used in adventure games. They are marked with the numbers 1 to 8. The score is the uppermost face. If an eight-sided dice is thrown, what is the probability that the score will be

    a a number in the 3 times table   **b** a factor of 10

    c a square number   **d** a triangle number

    e a number that is not prime   **f** not a square number?

14 In a sale at the supermarket, there is a box of 10 unlabelled tins. On the side it says: 4 Tins of Creamed Rice and 6 Tins of Chicken Soup. Malcolm buys this box. When he gets home he wants to have a lunch of chicken soup followed by creamed rice.

    a What is the smallest number of tins he could open to get his lunch?

    b What is the largest number of tins he could open to get his lunch?

    c The first tin he opens is soup. What is the chance that the second tin he opens is

        i soup   **ii** rice?

15 What is the probability of each of the following?

    a Drawing a Jack from a pack of cards.

    b Drawing a 10 from a pack of cards.

    c Drawing a red card from a pack of cards.

    d Drawing a 10 or a Jack from a pack of cards.

    e Drawing a Jack or a red card from a pack of cards.

    f Drawing a red Jack from a pack of cards.

Mutually exclusive and exhaustive events

If a bag contains 3 black, 2 yellow and 5 white balls and only one ball is allowed to be taken at random from the bag, then by the basic definition of probability

$$P(\text{black ball}) = \frac{3}{10}$$

$$P(\text{yellow ball}) = \frac{2}{10} = \frac{1}{5}$$

$$P(\text{white ball}) = \frac{5}{10} = \frac{1}{2}$$

We can also say that the probability of choosing a black ball or a yellow ball is $\frac{5}{10} = \frac{1}{2}$.

The events 'picking a yellow ball' and 'picking a black ball' can never happen at the same time when only one ball is taken out. That is, a ball can be either black or yellow. Such events are called **mutually exclusive**. Other examples of mutually exclusive events are tossing a head or a tail with a coin, drawing a King or an Ace from a pack of cards and throwing an even or an odd number with a dice.

An example of events that are not mutually exclusive would be drawing a red card or a King from a pack of cards. There are two red Kings, so these events could be true at the same time.

Example 1   If an ordinary dice is thrown, what is the probability of throwing

    a an even number   **b** an odd number

    c What is the total of the answers to parts **a** and **b**?

    d Is it possible to get a score on a dice that is both odd and even?

a P(even) = $\frac{1}{2}$ **b** P(odd) = $\frac{1}{2}$ **c** $\frac{1}{2} + \frac{1}{2} = 1$ **d** No

Events such as those in Example 1 are mutually exclusive because they can never happen at the same time. Because there are no other possibilities, they are also called **exhaustive** events. The probabilities of exhaustive events **add up to 1**.

Any event is mutually exclusive and exhaustive to its complementary event. That is,

P(event A not happening) = 1 − P(event A happening)

So if the probability of getting a 4 from a pack of cards is $\frac{4}{52} = \frac{1}{13}$, the probability of not getting a 4 is $1 - \frac{1}{13} = \frac{12}{13}$.

Example 2 A bag contains only black and white balls. The probability of picking at random a black ball from the bag is $\frac{7}{10}$.

a What is the probability of picking a white ball from the bag?

b Can you say how many black and white balls are in the bag?

a As the event 'picking a white ball' and the event 'picking a black ball' are mutually exclusive and exhaustive then

P(white) = 1 − P(black) = $1 - \frac{7}{10} = \frac{3}{10}$

b We cannot say precisely what the number of balls is although we can say that there could be 7 black and 3 white, 14 black and 6 white, or any combination of black and white balls in the ratio 7:3.

EXERCISE 23C

1 Say whether these pairs of events are mutually exclusive or not.
  a Tossing a head with a coin/tossing a tail with a coin.
  b Throwing a number less than 3 with a dice/throwing a number greater than 3 with a dice.
  c Drawing a Spade from a pack of cards/drawing an Ace from a pack of cards.
  d Drawing a Spade from a pack of cards/drawing a red card from a pack of cards.
  e If two people are to be chosen from three girls and two boys: choosing two girls/choosing two boys.
  f Drawing a red card from a pack of cards/drawing a black card from a pack of cards.

2 Which of the pairs of mutually exclusive events in question **1** are also exhaustive?

3 Each morning I run to work or get a lift. The probability that I run to work is $\frac{2}{5}$. What is the probability that I get a lift?

4 A letter is to be chosen at random from this set of letter cards.

S T A T I S T I C S

a What is the probability the letter is

    i an S   **ii** a T   **iii** a vowel?

b Which of these pairs of events are mutually exclusive?

    i Picking an S / picking a T.   **ii** Picking an S / picking a vowel.

    iii Picking an S / picking a consonant.   **iv** Picking a vowel / picking a consonant.

c Which pair of mutually exclusive events in part **b** is also exhaustive?

5 Two people are to be chosen for a job from this set of five people.

    Jane   Dave   Anne   Jack   John

a List all of the possible pairs (there are 10 altogether).

b What is the probability that the pair of people chosen will be

    i both female   **ii** both male

    iii both have the same initial   **iv** have different initials?

c Which of these pairs of events are mutually exclusive?

    i Picking two women / picking two men.

    ii Picking two people of the same sex / picking two people of opposite sex.

    iii Picking two people with the same initial / picking two men.

    iv Picking two people with the same initial / picking two women.

d Which pair of mutually exclusive events in part **c** is also exhaustive?

6 A spinner consists of an outer ring of coloured sectors and an inner circle of numbered sectors, as shown.

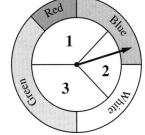

a The probability of getting 2 is $\frac{1}{4}$. The probabilities of getting 1 or 3 are equal. What is the probability of getting 3?

b The probability of getting blue is $\frac{1}{4}$. The probability of getting white is $\frac{1}{4}$. The probability of getting green is $\frac{3}{8}$. What is the probability of getting red?

c Which of these pairs of events are mutually exclusive?

    i Getting 3/getting 2.   **ii** Getting 3/getting green.

    iii Getting 3/getting blue.   **iv** Getting blue/getting red.

d Explain why it is not possible to get a colour that is mutually exclusive to the event 'getting an odd number'.

7 At the morning break, I have the choice of coffee, tea or hot chocolate. If the probability I choose coffee is $\frac{3}{8}$ and the probability I choose tea is $\frac{1}{4}$, what is the probability I choose hot chocolate?

8 Assemblies at school are always taken by the head, the deputy head or the senior teacher. If the head takes the assembly, the probability that he goes over time is $\frac{1}{2}$. If the deputy takes the assembly, the probability that he goes over time is $\frac{1}{4}$. Explain why it is not necessarily true to say that the probability that the senior teacher goes over time is $\frac{1}{4}$.

9 An electronic device chooses random numbers from 1 to 49. Here is a list of events.

> Event A: the number chosen is odd
> Event B: the number chosen is even
> Event C: the number chosen is a square number
> Event D: the number chosen is a multiple of 3
> Event E: the number chosen is a triangle number
> Event F: the number chosen is a multiple of 6
> Event G: the number chosen is a factor of 30

For each of the pairs of events **i** to **x**, say whether they are

a mutually exclusive   **b** exhaustive

c If they are not mutually exclusive, give an example of a number that fits both events.

i	Event A and Event B	**ii**	Event A and Event C
iii	Event B and Event D	**iv**	Event C and Event D
v	Event D and Event F	**vi**	Event C and Event G
vii	Event E and Event G	**viii**	Event A and event E
ix	Event A and Event F	**x**	Event B and Event F

Expectation

When we know the probability of an event, we can predict how many times we would expect that event to happen in a certain number of trials.

Note that this is what we **expect**. It is not what is going to happen. If what we expected always happened, life would be very dull and boring and the National Lottery would be a waste of time.

Example   A bag contains 20 balls, 9 of which are black, 6 white and 5 yellow. A ball is drawn at random from the bag, its colour noted and then it is put back in the bag. This is repeated 500 times.

a How many times would you expect a black ball to be drawn?
b How many times would you expect a yellow ball to be drawn?
c How many times would you expect a black or a yellow ball to be drawn?

a P(black ball) = $\frac{9}{20}$

Expected number of black balls = $\frac{9}{20} \times 500 = 225$

b P(yellow ball) = $\frac{5}{20} = \frac{1}{4}$

Expected number of yellow balls = $\frac{1}{4} \times 500 = 125$

c Expected number of black or yellow balls = 225 + 125 = 350

EXERCISE 23D

1 I throw an ordinary dice 150 times. How many times can I expect to get a score of 6?

2 I toss a coin 2000 times. How many times can I expect to get a head?

3 I draw a card from a pack of cards and replace it. I do this 520 times. How many times would I expect to get

    a a black card   **b** a King

    c a Heart   **d** the King of Hearts?

4 The ball in a roulette wheel can land on any number between 0 and 36. I always bet on the same number, 13. If I play all evening and there is a total of 185 spins of the wheel in that time, how many times could I expect to win?

5 I have 20 tickets for a raffle and I know that the probability of my winning the prize is 0.05. How many tickets were sold altogether in the raffle?

6 In a bag there are 30 balls, 15 of which are red, 5 yellow, 5 green, and 5 blue. A ball is taken out at random and then replaced. This is repeated 300 times. How many times would I expect to get

    a a red ball   **b** a yellow or blue ball

    c a ball that is not blue   **d** a pink ball?

7 The same experiment described in question **6** is carried out 1000 times. Approximately how many times would you expect to get

    a a green ball   **b** a ball that is not blue?

8 A sampling bottle (as described in question **4** of Exercise 23A) contains red and white balls. It is known that the probability of getting a red ball is 0.3 when 1500 samples are taken. How many of them would you expect to give a white ball?

9 Josie said: 'When I throw a dice, I expect to get a score of 3.5'.

    'Impossible', said Paul, 'you can't score 3.5 with a dice.'

    'Do this and I'll prove it', said Josie.

    a An ordinary dice is thrown 60 times. Fill in the table for the expected number of times each score will occur.

Score	1	2	3	4	5	6
Expected occurrences						

    b Now work out the average score that is expected over 60 throws.

    c There is an easy way to get an answer of 3.5 for the expected average score. Can you see what it is?

Addition rule for events

We have used this rule already but it has not yet been formally defined.

When two events are mutually exclusive, we can work out the probability of either of them occurring by **adding up the separate probabilities**.

Example   A bag contains 12 red balls, 8 green balls, 5 blue balls and 15 black balls. A ball is drawn at random. What is the probability that it is

a   red **b**   black **c**   red or black

d   not green **e**   neither green nor blue?

a $P(red) = \frac{12}{40} = \frac{3}{10}$ **b** $P(black) = \frac{15}{40} = \frac{3}{8}$

c $P(red\ or\ black) = P(red) + P(black) = \frac{3}{10} + \frac{3}{8} = \frac{27}{40}$

d $P(not\ green) = \frac{32}{40} = \frac{4}{5}$

e $P(neither\ green\ nor\ blue) = P(red\ or\ black) = \frac{27}{40}$

The last part is another example of how confusing probability can be. You might say

$P(neither\ green\ nor\ blue) = P(not\ green) + P(not\ blue) = \frac{32}{40} + \frac{35}{40} = \frac{67}{40}$

This cannot be correct, as $\frac{67}{40}$ is greater than 1. In fact, the events 'not green' and 'not blue' are not mutually exclusive, as there are lots of balls that fit both events.

EXERCISE 23E

1   Iqbal throws an ordinary dice. What is the probability that he throws
   a   2 **b**   5 **c**   2 or 5?

2   Jennifer draws a card from a pack of cards. What is the probability that she draws
   a   a Heart **b**   a Club **c**   a Heart or a Club?

3   A letter is chosen at random from the letters in the word PROBABILITY. What is the probability that the letter will be
   a   B **b**   a vowel **c**   B or a vowel?

4   A bag contains 10 white balls, 12 black balls and 8 red balls. A ball is drawn at random from the bag. What is the probability that it will be
   a   white **b**   black **c**   black or white
   d   not red **e**   not red or black?

5   At the local School Fayre the tombola stall gives out a prize if you draw from the drum a numbered ticket that ends in 0 or 5. There are 300 tickets in the drum altogether and the probability of getting a winning ticket is 0.4.
   a   What is the probability of getting a losing ticket?
   b   How many winning tickets are there in the drum?

6 John needs his calculator for his mathematics lesson. It is either in his pocket, bag or locker. The probability it is in his pocket is 0.35; the probability it is in his bag is 0.45. What is the probability that

    a   he will have the calculator for the lesson

    b   it is in his locker?

7 Debbie has 20 unlabelled pirate tapes, 12 of which are rock, 5 are pop and 3 are classical. She picks a tape at random. What is the probability that it will be

    a   rock or pop   **b**   pop or classical   **c**   not pop.

8 The probability that it rains on Monday is 0.5. The probability that it rains on Tuesday is 0.5 and the probability that it rains on Wednesday is 0.5. Kelly argues that it is certain to rain on Monday, Tuesday or Wednesday because 0.5 + 0.5 + 0.5 = 1.5, which is bigger than 1 so that it is a certain event. Explain why she is wrong.

Combined events

There are many situations where two or more events occur together. Some of the more common ones are demonstrated below.

Throwing two dice

Imagine that two dice, one red and one blue, are thrown. The red dice can land with any one of six scores: 1, 2, 3, 4, 5 or 6. The blue dice can also land with any one of six scores. This gives a total of 36 possible combinations. These are shown in the diagram below left, where each combination is given as (2, 3) etc., where the first number is the score on the blue dice and the second number is the score on the red dice.

The combination (2, 3) gives a total of 5. The total scores for all the combinations are shown in the diagram below right.

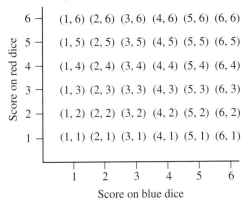

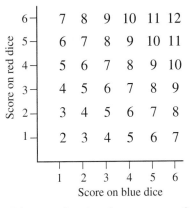

Diagram showing the outcomes of throwing two dice as 'co-ordinates'

Diagram showing the outcomes of throwing two dice as 'total scores'

From the diagram on the right, we can see that there are two ways to get a score of 3. This gives a probability of

$$P(3) = \frac{2}{36} = \frac{1}{18}$$

From the diagram on the left, we can see that there are six ways to get a 'double'. This gives a probability of

$$P(\text{double}) = \frac{6}{36} = \frac{1}{6}$$

Tossing coins

Tossing one coin

There are two equally likely outcomes, head or tail:

Tossing two coins together

There are four equally likely outcomes:

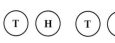

$$P(2 \text{ heads}) = \frac{1}{4}$$

$$P(\text{head or tail}) = 2 \text{ ways out of } 4 = \frac{2}{4} = \frac{1}{2}$$

Dice and coins

Throwing a dice and tossing a coin

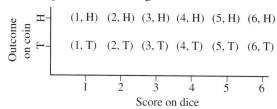

$$P(\text{head and an even number}) = 3 \text{ ways out of } 12 = \frac{3}{12} = \frac{1}{4}$$

EXERCISE 23F

1 To answer these questions, use the diagram on page 453 for the total scores when two dice are thrown together.

   a What is the most likely score?   **b** Which two scores are least likely?
   c Write down the probabilities of all scores from 2 to 12.
   d What is the probability of a score that is
      i bigger than 10   **ii** between 3 and 7   **iii** even
      iv a square number   **v** a prime number   **vi** a triangle number?

2 Using the diagram on page 453 that shows, as co-ordinates, the outcomes when two dice are thrown together, what is the probability that

   a the score is an even 'double'
   b at least one of the dice shows 2
   c the score on one dice is twice the score on the other dice
   d at least one of the dice shows a multiple of 3?

3 Using the diagram on page 453 that shows, as co-ordinates, the outcomes when two dice are thrown together, what is the probability that

a both dice show a 6

b at least one of the dice will show a 6

c exactly one dice shows a 6?

4 The diagram shows the score for the event 'the difference between the scores when two dice are thrown'. Copy and complete the diagram.

For the event described above, what is the probability of a difference of

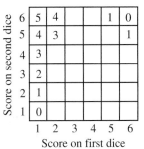

a 1   **b** 0   **c** 4

d 6   **e** an odd number?

5 When two coins are tossed together, what is the probability of

a 2 heads   **b** a head and a tail   **c** at least 1 tail   **d** no tails.

Use the diagram of the outcomes when two coins are tossed together, on page 453.

6 When three coins are tossed together, what is the probability of

a 3 heads   **b** 2 heads and 1 tail   **c** at least 1 tail   **d** no tails?

7 When one coin is tossed there are two outcomes. When two coins are tossed, there are four outcomes. When three coins are tossed, there are eight outcomes.

a How many outcomes will there be when four coins are tossed?

b How many outcomes will there be when five coins are tossed?

c How many outcomes will there be when ten coins are tossed?

d How many outcomes will there be when n coins are tossed?

8 If the outcomes of three coins being tossed together are written as a list across the page, they look like this:

HHH   HHT   HTH   HTT   THH   THT   TTH   TTT

a You should be able to see a pattern in the Hs and Ts. Describe any patterns that you see.

b This is part of the pattern for four coins. Copy and complete it.

HHHH   HHHT   HHTH   HHTT   HTHH   ....

c When four coins are tossed together, what is the probability of

i 4 heads   **ii** 3 heads and 1 tail

iii at least 1 tail   **iv** no tails?

9 When a dice and a coin are thrown together, what is the probability of each of the following outcomes?

a You get a head on the coin and a 6 on the dice.

b You get a tail on the coin and an even number on the dice.

c You get a head on the coin and a square number on the dice.

Use the diagram on page 454 that shows the outcomes when a dice and a coin are thrown together.

10 Two five-sided spinners are spun together and the total score of the faces that they land on is worked out. Copy and complete the probability space diagram below.

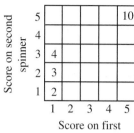

a What is the most likely score?

b When two five-sided spinners are spun together, what is the probability that

   i the total score is 5

   ii the total score is an even number

   iii the score is a 'double'

   iv the score is less than 7?

Tree diagrams

Example There are three red and five blue counters in a bag. A counter is drawn out at random, replaced and another counter is then drawn out. Draw a tree diagram to show the probabilities of all the possible outcomes and use your diagram to work out the probability of

a two red counters   **b** a red and a blue counter

c two of the same colour   **d** at least one blue

e What do the probabilities in parts **a** and **d** add up to? Can you explain why?

f What do the probabilities in parts **b** and **c** add up to? Can you explain why?

The complete tree diagram is

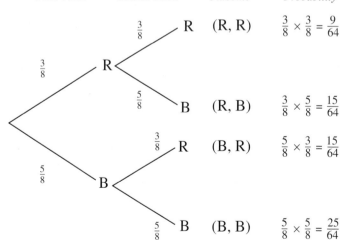

a $P(2 \text{ reds}) = \dfrac{9}{64}$

b $P(\text{red and blue}) = \dfrac{15}{64} + \dfrac{15}{64} = \dfrac{30}{64} = \dfrac{15}{32}$

c $P(2 \text{ same colour}) = \dfrac{9}{64} + \dfrac{25}{64} = \dfrac{34}{64} = \dfrac{17}{32}$

d P(at least 1 blue) = P(2 blues) + P(blue and red) + P(red and blue)

$$= \frac{25}{64} + \frac{15}{64} + \frac{15}{64} = \frac{55}{64}$$

e The probabilities in parts **a** and **d** add up to 1 because '2 reds' and 'at least 1 blue' take care of all the possibilities that there are. In fact, they are mutually exclusive.

f The probabilities in parts **b** and **c** add up to 1 because 'red and blue' and '2 of same colour' take care of all the possibilities that there are. In fact, they are also mutually exclusive.

EXERCISE 23G

1 A coin is tossed twice. Copy and complete the tree diagram below to show all the outcomes.

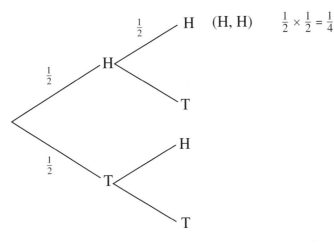

Use your tree diagram to work out the probability of

a getting two heads   **b** getting a head and a tail

c getting at least one tail

2 On my way to work, I drive through two sets of roadworks with traffic lights which only show green or red. I know that the probability of the first set being green is $\frac{1}{3}$ and the probability of the second set being green is $\frac{1}{2}$.

a What is the probability that the first set of lights will be red?

b What is the probability that the second set of lights will be red?

c Copy and complete the following tree diagram, showing the possible outcomes of passing through both sets of lights.

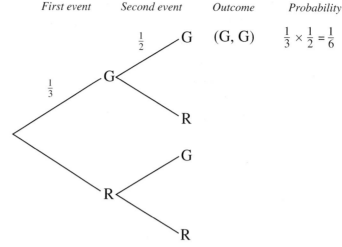

First event *Second event* *Outcome* *Probability*

$\frac{1}{2}$ G (G, G) $\frac{1}{3} \times \frac{1}{2} = \frac{1}{6}$

$\frac{1}{3}$ G

R

G

R

R

d Using the tree diagram, what is the probability of the following outcomes?

    i I do not get held up at either set of lights.

    ii I get held up at exactly one set of lights.

    iii I get held up at least once.

e Over a term I make 90 journeys to work. On how many days can I expect to get two green lights?

3 Six out of every 10 cars in Britain are foreign-made.

    a What is the probability that any car will be British-made?

    b Two cars can be seen approaching in the distance. Draw a tree diagram to work out the probability that

        i both cars will be British-made

        ii one car will be British and the other car will be foreign-made.

4 A card is drawn from a pack of cards. It is replaced, the pack is shuffled and another card is drawn.

    a What is the probability that either card was an Ace?

    b What is the probability that either card was not an Ace?

    c Draw a tree diagram to show the outcomes of two cards being drawn as described. Use the tree diagram to work out the probability that

        i both cards will be Aces   **ii** at least one of the cards will be an Ace.

5 A prison work party consists of five criminals. Two of them are robbers and the other three are fraudsters. Two of them are to be picked for a special job.

    a The first member of the special job detail is picked at random. What is the probability that he is

        i a robber   **ii** a fraudster?

    b If the first person chosen is a robber,

        i how many criminals are left to choose from

        ii how many of them are robbers?

    c If the first person chosen is a fraudster,

        i how many criminals are left to choose from

        ii how many of them are robbers?

d Copy and complete the tree diagram below.

e Use the tree diagram to work out the probability that

   i both criminals chosen are of the same type

   ii there is at least one robber chosen.

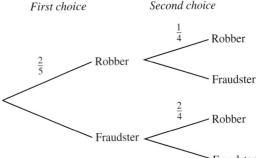

6 Three coins are tossed. Complete the tree diagram below and use it to answer the questions.

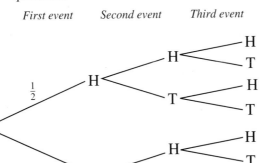

If a coin is tossed three times, what is the probability that you get

   a three heads   **b** two heads and a tail   **c** at least one tail?

7 Thomas has to take a three-part language examination paper. The first part is speaking. He has a 0.4 chance of passing this. The second is listening. He has a 0.5 chance of passing this. The third part is writing. He has a 0.7 chance of passing this. Draw a tree diagram covering three events where the first event is passing or failing the speaking part of the examination, the second event is passing or failing the listening part, and the third event is passing or failing the writing part.

   a If he passes all three parts, his father will give him £20. What is the probability that he gets the money?

   b If he passes two parts only, he can resit the third part. What is the chance he will have to resit?

   c If he fails all three parts, he will be thrown off the course. What is the chance he is thrown off the course?

8 In a group of ten girls, six like the pop group Smudge and four like the pop group Mirage. Two girls are to be chosen for a pop quiz.

   a What is the probability that the first girl chosen will be a Smudge fan?

   b Draw a tree diagram to show the outcomes of choosing two girls and which pop groups they like. (Remember: once a girl has been chosen the first time she cannot be chosen again.)

c Use your tree diagram to work out the probability that

   i both girls chosen will like Smudge

   ii both girls chosen will like the same group

   iii both girls chosen will like different groups.

9 There are three white eggs and one brown egg in an egg box. Sanjay decides to make a two-egg omelette. He takes each egg from the box without looking at its colour.

  a What is the probability that the first egg taken is brown?

  b If the first egg taken is brown, what is the probability that the second egg taken will also be brown?

  c Copy and complete this tree diagram.

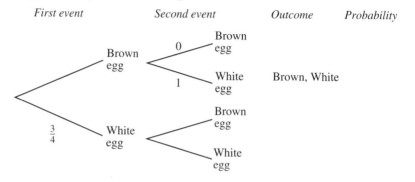

  d What is the probability that Sanjay gets an omelette made from

   i two white eggs **ii** one white and one brown egg **iii** two brown eggs?

10 Look at all the tree diagrams that have been drawn so far.

  a What do the probabilities across any set of branches (outlined in the diagram below) always add up to?

  b What do the final probabilities (outlined in the diagram below) always add up to?

  c You should now be able to fill in all of the missing values in the diagram.

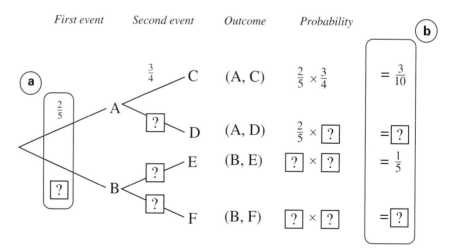

Using 'and' and 'or'. Independent events

If the outcome of event A does not effect the outcome of event B, then events A and B are called **independent events**. Most of the combined events we have looked at so far have been independent events.

It is possible to work out problems on combined events without using tree diagrams. The method explained in Examples 1 and 2 is basically the same as that of a tree diagram but uses the words **and** and **or**.

Example 1   The chance that Ashley hits a target with an arrow is $\frac{1}{4}$. He has two shots at the target. What is the probability that he

a hits the target both times

b hits the target once only

c hits the target at least once?

a P(hits **both** times) = P(first shot hits **and** second shot hits) $= \frac{1}{4} \times \frac{1}{4} = \frac{1}{16}$

b P(hits the target once only) = P(first hits **and** second misses **or** first misses **and** second hits) $= \left(\frac{1}{4} \times \frac{3}{4}\right) + \left(\frac{3}{4} \times \frac{1}{4}\right) = \frac{3}{8}$

c P(hits at least once) = P(both hit **or** one hits) $= \frac{1}{16} + \frac{3}{8} = \frac{7}{16}$

Example 2   There are 22 balls in a snooker set: 15 red, and 1 each of white, yellow, green, brown, blue, pink and black. The balls are kept in a bag. A ball is taken out, placed on the table and then another ball is taken out. What is the probability that

a both balls are red

b the balls will be red and black?

a We need to be careful here because the first ball is not replaced, so that alters the probabilities for the second event.

P(**both** are red) = P(first is red **and** second is red)
$$= \text{P(first is red)} \times \text{P(second is red)}$$
$$= \frac{15}{22} \times \frac{14}{21} = \frac{5}{11} = 0.455 \text{ (3dp)}$$

(A decimal would be acceptable in this case as some calculators, even with fraction buttons, could give a decimal answer.)

b To get one red and one black, we would have to have

P(first is red **and** second is black **or** first is black **and** second is red)
$$= \left(\frac{15}{22} \times \frac{1}{21}\right) + \left(\frac{1}{22} \times \frac{15}{21}\right)$$
$$= \frac{5}{77} = 0.065 \text{ (3dp)}$$

EXERCISE 23H

1 Alf tosses a coin twice. The coin is biased so it has a probability of landing a head of $\frac{2}{3}$. What is the probability that he gets
   a two heads   b a head and a tail (in any order)?

2 Bernice draws a card from a pack of cards, replaces it, shuffles the pack and then draws another card. What is the probability that the cards are
   a both Aces   b an Ace and a King (in any order)?

3 Charles draws a card from a pack of cards, does not replace it and then draws another card. What is the probability that the cards are
   a both Aces   b an Ace and a King (in any order)?

4 A dice is thrown twice. What is the probability that the scores are
   a both even   b one even and one odd (in any order)?

5 I throw a dice three times. What is the probability of getting three sixes?

6 A bag contains 15 white beads and 10 black beads. I take out a bead at random, replace it and take out another bead. What is the probability that
   a both beads are black   b one bead is black and the other white (in any order)?

7 A bag contains 15 white beads and 10 black beads. I take out a bead at random, do not replace it and take out another bead. What is the probability that
   a both beads are black   b one bead is black and the other white (in any order)?

8 The probability that I am late for work on Monday is 0.4. The probability that I am late on Tuesday is 0.2. What is the probability of each of the following outcomes?
   a I am late for work on Monday and Tuesday.
   b I am late for work on Monday and on time on Tuesday.
   c I am on time on both Monday and Tuesday.

9 Thomas has to take a three-part language examination paper. The first part is speaking. He has a 0.7 chance of passing this. The second part is listening. He has a 0.6 chance of passing this. The third part is writing. He has a 0.8 chance of passing this.
   a If he passes all three parts, his father will give him £20. What is the probability that he gets the money?
   b If he passes two parts only, he can resit the third part. What is the chance he will have to resit?
   c If he fails all three parts, he will be thrown off the course. What is the chance he is thrown off the course?

10 There are five white and one brown eggs in an egg box. Kate decides to make a two-egg omelette. She takes each egg from the box without looking at its colour.
   a What is the probability that the first egg taken is brown?
   b If the first egg taken is brown, what is the probability that the second egg taken will be brown?
   c What is the probability that Kate gets an omelette made from
      i two white eggs   ii one white and one brown egg   iii two brown eggs?

Possible coursework tasks

First to get a six

Investigate how many throws of a dice are needed before a six is first obtained.

Random digits

Most scientific calculators have a random digit key. It may be

| RAN # | or | RANDOM |

Press it and see what happens. If you get a number with decimal places, ignore the point. For example, after three successive presses the numbers may be 735, 313 and 907. These give a list of nine random digits: 7, 3, 5, 3, 1, 3, 9, 0, 7.

Find out how random these digits are. Use 'experimental probability' and 'theoretical probability' in your account.

Can you find other ways of obtaining lists of random digits?

The National Lottery

Find ways of drawing tree diagrams to help you find the probability of winning the jackpot on the National Lottery.

Examination questions

1   A bag contains five discs that are numbered 1, 2, 3, 4 and 5
    Rachel takes a disc at random from the bag. She notes the number and puts the disc back.
    She shakes the bag and picks again. She adds this number to the first number.

    a   Copy and complete the table to show all the possible totals.

		First number				
	+	1	2	3	4	5
	1	2				
Second number	2					
	3				7	
	4					
	5					

b Find the probability that Rachel's total is

   i 10   **ii** 1   **iii** 3 or 4

OCR, Question 2, Intermediate (A) Paper 4, June 2000

2 Chris is going to roll a biased dice.

The probability that he will get a six is 0.09

  a Work out the probability that he will **not** get a six

Chris is going to roll the dice 30 times.

  b Work out an estimate for the number of sixes he will get.

Tina is going to roll the same dice **twice**.

  c Work out the probability that she will get

    i **two** sixes   **ii** **exactly one** six

EDEXCEL, Question 18, Intermediate Paper 4, June 2000

3 The 500 children in a school each bought one ticket for the school prize draw. The 500 tickets, numbered 1 to 500, will be put into a barrel and the winning ticket drawn.

  a Ambrose has the ticket numbered 350. What is the probability that he will win the prize?

  b What is the probability that the winning ticket number will be greater than 350?

  c Melanie says, 'Either a boy or a girl must win, so the probability that a girl will win is $\frac{1}{2}$'. Explain why she might be wrong.

MEG, Question 7, Specimen Paper 3, 1998

4 When you drop a match box on to a table, there are three ways it can land. Jane has found that the probability of the match box landing 'on its end' is approximately 0.1 and the probability of it landing 'on its side' is approximately 0.6.

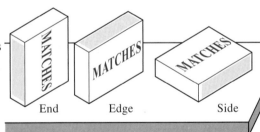

  End   Edge   Side

  a Jane drops two identical match boxes. What is the probability that both boxes will land 'on their edges'?

  b Jane and Sarah are playing a game.

I will drop two boxes.
If they land the same way up, I win.
If they don't land the same way up, you win.

Sarah   Jane

Who is more likely to win the game? Show all your working.

NEAB, Question 21, Specimen Paper 11, 1998

5 A car dealer kept a record of the cars he sold in September 1999.
One-fifth were black. Two-sevenths were made in the UK.
Assume that these are independent.

a Draw a tree diagram to illustrate this information.

b One of the cars is chosen at random. What is the probability that

   i it is black and made in the UK

   ii it is either a black car made abroad or a non-black car made in the UK.

OCR, Question 19, Intermediate (B) Paper 4, June 2000

6 There are two parts to a driving test. The first part is a theory test.
You must pass the theory test before you take the practical test.
Rob takes his driving test.
The probability that he passes the theory test is 0.8
The probability that he passes the practical test is 0.6

a The tree diagram shows the possible outcomes.
Copy and fill in the missing probabilities.

b **i** Calculate the probability that Rob passes both parts of the driving test.

   ii Calculate the probability that he fails the driving test.

AQA (North), Question 19, Intermediate Paper 1, June 2000

7 A bag contains a number of counters. Each counter is coloured red, blue, yellow or green. Each counter is numbered 1, 2 or 3. The table shows the probability of colour and number for these counters.

Number on counter	Colour of counter			
	Red	Blue	Yellow	Green
1	0.2	0	0.1	0
2	0.2	0.1	0.1	0
3	0.1	0.1	0	0.1

a A counter is taken from the bag at random.

   i What is the probability that it is red **and** numbered 2?

   ii What is the probability that it is green **or** numbered 2?

   iii What is the probability that it is red **or** numbered 2?

b There are two green counters in the bag. How many counters are in the bag altogether? *SEG, Question 15, Specimen Paper 14, 1998*

8 The diagram represents a fair dice and a fair spinner. The dice is a cube with faces labelled 1, 2, 3, 4, 5 and 6. The triangular spinner is labelled 1, 3 and 5. The score on the dice is 3. The score on the spinner is 5.

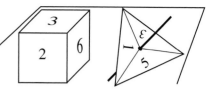

The dice is thrown and the spinner is spun. The two scores are added together.

a Calculate the probability that the total score will be 2.

b Calculate the probability that the total score will be 6.

ULEAC, Question 18, Specimen Paper 3, 1998

9 A bag contains 7 toffees and 5 mints.

a What is the probability that a sweet taken from the bag at random will be a toffee?

b Another bag contains 4 fruit drops and 6 mints. James takes one sweet from each bag without looking. Complete this tree diagram to show the possible outcomes and their probabilities.

c What is the probability that James takes

   i two mints

   ii exactly one mint?

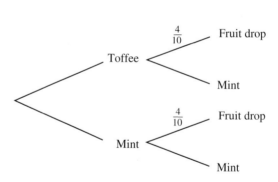

WJEC, Question 13, Specimen Paper 2, 1998

Summary

How well do you grade yourself?

To gain a grade **D**, you need to be able to understand and use the probability scale from 0 to 1. You also need to be able to make judgements about probabilities, using either experimental evidence or theoretical calculations. You should know that different outcomes may result from repeating an experiment.

To gain a grade **C**, you need to be able to understand relative frequency as an estimate of probability and be able to use this to compare outcomes of experiments. You also need to be able to calculate the probability of combined events using a probability diagram, such as a tree diagram. And you need to be able to work out the probability of an event not happening when you know the probability of the event happening, and to know what mutually exclusive events are.

To gain a grade **B**, you need to be able to work out the probabilities of combined events using theoretical considerations of all the likely outcomes, and to solve problems using the words *and* and *or*.

What you should know after you have worked through Chapter 23

- How to put events in order of likelihood.

- How approximately to place events on the probability scale from 0 to 1.

- How to calculate the experimental probability of an event from data supplied.

- How to calculate the theoretical probability of an event from considerations of all outcomes of the event.

- That as the number of trials of an event increases, the experimental probability of the event gets closer to its theoretical probability.

- How to use a probability diagram, such as a tree diagram, to calculate the probability of combined events.

- How to work out the probability of mutually exclusive events.

- How to use the words *and* and *or* to solve combined events problems.

> ## This chapter is going to ...
>
> show you how to recognise rules for sequences and how to express these rules in formulae. It will then show you what is meant by the *n*th term, and how to find it for simple sequences.
>
> ## What you should already know
>
> ✔ How to use the methods of algebra and indices.

Patterns in number

Look at these number patterns.

$$0 \times 9 + 1 = 1$$
$$1 \times 9 + 2 = 11$$
$$12 \times 9 + 3 = 111$$
$$123 \times 9 + 4 = 1111$$
$$1234 \times 9 + 5 = 11111$$

$$1 \times 8 + 1 = 9$$
$$12 \times 8 + 2 = 98$$
$$123 \times 8 + 3 = 987$$
$$1234 \times 8 + 4 = 9876$$
$$12345 \times 8 + 5 = 98765$$

$$1 \times 3 \times 37 = 111$$
$$2 \times 3 \times 37 = 222$$
$$3 \times 3 \times 37 = 333$$
$$4 \times 3 \times 37 = 444$$

$$7 \times 7 = 49$$
$$67 \times 67 = 4489$$
$$667 \times 667 = 444889$$
$$6667 \times 6667 = 44448889$$

Check that the patterns you see there are correct and then try to continue each pattern without using a calculator. Check them with a calculator afterwards.

Spotting patterns is an important part of mathematics. It helps us to see rules for making calculations.

EXERCISE 24A

Look for the pattern and then write the next two lines. Check your answers with a calculator afterwards.

1
$$1 \times 1 = 11$$
$$11 \times 11 = 121$$
$$111 \times 111 = 12321$$
$$1111 \times 1111 = 1234321$$

2
$$9 \times 9 = 81$$
$$99 \times 99 = 9801$$
$$999 \times 999 = 998001$$
$$9999 \times 9999 = 99980001$$

3
$$3 \times 4 = 3^2 + 3$$
$$4 \times 5 = 4^2 + 4$$
$$5 \times 6 = 5^2 + 5$$
$$6 \times 7 = 6^2 + 6$$

4
$$10 \times 11 = 110$$
$$20 \times 21 = 420$$
$$30 \times 31 = 930$$
$$40 \times 41 = 1640$$

5
$$1 = 1 = 1^2$$
$$1 + 2 + 1 = 4 = 2^2$$
$$1 + 2 + 3 + 2 + 1 = 9 = 3^2$$
$$1 + 2 + 3 + 4 + 3 + 2 + 1 = 16 = 4^2$$

6
$$1 = 1 = 1^3$$
$$3 + 5 = 8 = 2^3$$
$$7 + 9 + 11 = 27 = 3^3$$
$$13 + 15 + 17 + 19 = 64 = 4^3$$

7
$$1 = 1$$
$$1 + 1 = 2$$
$$1 + 2 + 1 = 4$$
$$1 + 3 + 3 + 1 = 8$$
$$1 + 4 + 6 + 4 + 1 = 16$$
$$1 + 5 + 10 + 10 + 5 + 1 = 32$$

8
$$12\,345\,679 \times 9 = 111\,111\,111$$
$$12\,345\,679 \times 18 = 222\,222\,222$$
$$12\,345\,679 \times 27 = 333\,333\,333$$
$$12\,345\,679 \times 36 = 444\,444\,444$$

9
$$1^3 = 1^2 = 1$$
$$1^3 + 2^3 = (1 + 2)^2 = 9$$
$$1^3 + 2^3 + 3^3 = (1 + 2 + 3)^2 = 36$$

10
$$3^2 + 4^2 = 5^2$$
$$10^2 + 11^2 + 12^2 = 13^2 + 14^2$$
$$21^2 + 22^2 + 23^2 + 24^2 = 25^2 + 26^2 + 27^2$$

$$\begin{bmatrix} \text{Hint: } 4 + 5 = 9 = 3^2 \\ \text{Hint: } 12 + 13 = 25 = 5^2 \\ \text{Hint: } 24 + 25 = 49 = 7^2 \end{bmatrix}$$

From your observations on the number patterns in questions **1** to **10**, answer questions **11** to **19** without using a calculator. (But check your answers with a calculator afterwards.)

11 $111\,111\,111 \times 111\,111\,111 =$

12 $999\,999\,999 \times 999\,999\,999 =$

13 $12 \times 13 =$

14 $90 \times 91 =$

15 $1 + 2 + 3 + 4 + 5 + 6 + 7 + 8 + 9 + 8 + 7 + 6 + 5 + 4 + 3 + 2 + 1 =$

16 $57 + 59 + 61 + 63 + 65 + 67 + 69 + 71 =$

17 $1 + 9 + 36 + 84 + 126 + 126 + 84 + 36 + 9 + 1 =$

18 $12\,345\,679 \times 81 =$

19 $1^3 + 2^3 + 3^3 + 4^3 + 5^3 + 6^3 + 7^3 + 8^3 + 9^3 =$

Number sequences

A number sequence is a set of numbers with a rule to find every number (term) in the sequence. This rule could be a simple addition or multiplication which takes you from one term to the next, but often it is more tricky than that. So you need to look most carefully at the pattern of a sequence.

Look at these sequences and their rules.

> 3, 6, 12, 24 … doubling the last term each time … 48, 96, …
>
> 2, 5, 8, 11, … adding 3 to the last term each time … 14, 17, …
>
> 1, 10, 100, 1000, … multiplying the last term by 10 each time … 10 000, 100 000
>
> 1, 8, 15, 22, … adding 7 to the last term each time … 29, 36, …

These are all quite straightforward once you have looked for the link from one term to the next (consecutive terms).

Differences

For some sequences we need to look at the differences between consecutive terms to determine the pattern.

Example   Find the next two terms of the sequence 1, 3, 6, 10, 15, …

Looking at the differences between each pair of consecutive terms, we notice

```
1    3    6    10    15
 ↑    ↑    ↑    ↑
 2    3    4    5
```

So we can continue the sequence as follows:

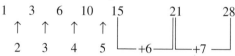

The differences usually form a number sequence of their own, so you need to find out the sequence of the differences before you can expand the original sequence.

EXERCISE 24B

1 Look at the following number sequences. Write down the next three terms in each and explain how each sequence is found.

a	1, 3, 5, 7, …	**b**	2, 4, 6, 8, …

a   1, 3, 5, 7, …   **b**   2, 4, 6, 8, …   **c**   5, 10, 20, 40, …

d   1, 3, 9, 27, …   **e**   4, 10, 16, 22, …   **f**   3, 8, 13, 18, …

g   2, 20, 200, 2000, …   **h**   7, 10, 13, 16, …   **i**   10, 19, 28, 37, …

j   5, 15, 45, 135, …   **k**   2, 6, 10, 14, …   **l**   1, 5, 25, 125, …

2 By considering the differences in the following sequences, write down the next two terms in each case.

a   1, 2, 4, 7, 11, …   **b**   1, 2, 5, 10, 17, …   **c**   1, 3, 7, 13, 21, …

d   1, 4, 10, 19, 31, …   **e**   1, 9, 25, 49, 81, …   **f**   1, 2, 7, 32, 157, …

g   1, 3, 23, 223, 2223, …   **h**   1, 2, 4, 5, 7, 8, 10, …   **i**   2, 3, 5, 9, 17, …

j   3, 8, 18, 33, 53, …

3 Look carefully at each number sequence below. Find the next two numbers in the sequence and try to explain the pattern.

a   1, 1, 2, 3, 5, 8, 13, …   **b**   1, 4, 9, 16, 25, 36, …   **c**   3, 4, 7, 11, 18, 29, …

4 Triangle numbers are found as follows.

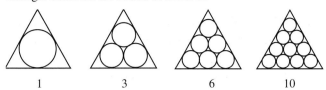

1   3   6   10

Find the next four triangle numbers.

5 Hexagon numbers are found as follows.

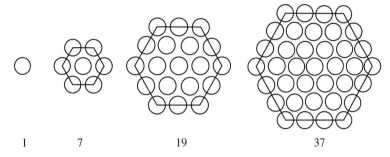

1   7   19   37

Find the next three hexagon numbers.

6 Look at the sequences below. Find the rule for each sequence and write down its next three terms.

a	3, 6, 12, 24, …	**b**	3, 9, 15, 21, 27, …	**c**	1, 3, 4, 7, 11, 18, …
d	50, 47, 44, 41, …	**e**	2, 5, 10, 17, 26, …	**f**	5, 6, 8, 11, 15, 20, …
g	5, 7, 8, 10, 11, 13, …	**h**	4, 7, 10, 13, 16, …	**i**	1, 3, 6, 10, 15, 21, …
j	1, 2, 3, 4, …	**k**	100, 20, 4, 0.8, …	**l**	1, 0.5, 0.25, 0.125, …

Generalising to find the rule

When using a number sequence, we sometimes need to know, say, its 50th term, or even a bigger number in the sequence. To do so, we need to find the generalised form of the rule which produces the sequence.

Let's first look at the problem backwards. That is, we'll take a rule and see how it produces a sequence.

Example 1   A sequence is formed by the rule $3n + 1$, where $n = 1, 2, 3, 4, 5, 6, …$. Write down the sequence.

Substituting $n = 1, 2, 3, 4, …$ in turn, we get

$$(3 \times 1 + 1), \quad (3 \times 2 + 1), \quad (3 \times 3 + 1), \quad (3 \times 4 + 1), \quad (3 \times 5 + 1), \quad …$$
$$4 \qquad\qquad 7 \qquad\qquad 10 \qquad\qquad 13 \qquad\qquad 16$$

So the sequence is 4, 7, 10, 13, 16, … .

Notice that the difference between each term and the next is always 3, which is the coefficient of n.

Example 2   The nth term of a sequence is $4n - 3$. Write down the sequence.

Taking n to be 1, 2, 3, 4, … in turn, we get

$$(4 \times 1 - 3), \quad (4 \times 2 - 3), \quad (4 \times 3 - 3), \quad (4 \times 4 - 3), \qquad \ldots$$
$$1 \qquad\qquad 5 \qquad\qquad 9 \qquad\qquad 13$$

So the sequence is 1, 5, 9, 13, … .

Notice again how the difference between each term and the next is the same as the coefficient of n.

EXERCISE 24C

1 Use each of the following rules to write down the first five terms of a sequence.

  a $2n + 1$ for $n = 1, 2, 3, 4, \ldots$ **b** $3n - 2$ for $n = 1, 2, 3, 4, \ldots$

  c $5n + 2$ for $n = 1, 2, 3, 4, \ldots$ **d** n^2 for $n = 1, 2, 3, 4, \ldots$

  e $n^2 + 3$ for $n = 1, 2, 3, 4, \ldots$

2 Write down the first five terms of the sequence which has its nth term as

  a $n + 3$ **b** $3n - 1$ **c** $5n - 2$ **d** $n^2 - 1$ **e** $4n + 5$

3 Write down the first six terms of the sequence of fractions $\dfrac{n-1}{n+1}$ for $n = 1, 2, 3, 4, \ldots$

4 A sequence is formed by the rule $\dfrac{1}{2} \times n \times (n+1)$ for $n = 1, 2, 3, 4, \ldots$

  a Write down the first six terms of this sequence.

  b This is a well-known sequence with a name you have met before. What is it?

5 $n!$ is a mathematical shorthand for $n \times (n-1) \times (n-2) \times (n-3) \times \ldots \times 2 \times 1$.

  a Calculate $n!$ for $n = 4, 5$ and 6.

  b Find the ! key on your calculator. What is the largest value of n that gives you an answer on the calculator?

Finding the nth term of a linear sequence

A linear sequence has the same difference between each term and the next.
For example,

  2, 5, 8, 11, 14, …   difference of 3
  5, 7, 9, 11, 13, …   difference of 2

The nth term of a linear sequence is **always** of the form $An + b$, where

- A, the coefficient of n, is the difference between each term and the next term (consecutive terms).
- b is the difference between the first term and A.

Example 1   Find the nth term of the sequence 5, 7, 9, 11, 13, …

The difference between consecutive terms is 2. So the first part of the nth term is $2n$.
Subtract the difference 2 from the first term 5, which gives $5 - 2 = 3$.
So the nth term is given by $2n + 3$.

(You can test it by substituting $n = 1, 2, 3, 4, \ldots$.)

Example 2 Find the *n*th term of a sequence 3, 7, 11, 15, 19, ...

The difference between consecutive terms is 4. So the first part of the *n*th term is 4*n*.
Subtract the difference 4 from the first term 3, which gives $3 - 4 = -1$.
So the *n*th term is given by $4n - 1$.

Example 3 From the sequence 5, 12, 19, 26, 33, ... find

a the *n*th term   **b** the 50th term   **c** the first term that is greater than 1000

a The difference between consecutive terms is 7. So the first part of the *n*th term
is 7*n*.
Subtract the difference 7 from the first term 5, which gives $5 - 7 = -2$.
So the *n*th term is given by $7n - 2$.

b The 50th term is found by substituting $n = 50$ into the rule, $7n - 2$. So

$$50\text{th term} = 7 \times 50 - 2 = 350 - 2$$
$$= 348$$

c The first term that is greater than 1000 is given by

$$7n - 2 > 1000$$
$$\Rightarrow 7n > 1000 + 2$$
$$\Rightarrow n > \frac{1002}{7}$$
$$n > 143.14$$

So the first term (which has to be a whole number) over 1000 is the 144th.

EXERCISE 24D

1 Find the *n*th term in each of these linear sequences.
   a 3, 5, 7, 9, 11, ...   **b** 5, 9, 13, 17, 21, ...   **c** 8, 13, 18, 23, 28, ...
   d 2, 8, 14, 20, 26, ...   **e** 5, 8, 11, 14, 17, ...   **f** 2, 9, 16, 23, 30, ...
   g 1, 5, 9, 13, 17, ...   **h** 3, 7, 11, 15, 19, ...   **i** 2, 5, 8, 11, 14, ...
   j 2, 12, 22, 32, ...   **k** 8, 12, 16, 20, ...   **l** 4, 9, 14, 19, 24, ...

2 Find the 50th term in each of these linear sequences.
   a 4, 7, 10, 13, 16, ...   **b** 7, 9, 11, 13, 15, ...   **c** 3, 8, 13, 18, 23, ...
   d 1, 5, 9, 13, 17, ...   **e** 2, 10, 18, 26, ...   **f** 5, 6, 7, 8, 9, ...
   g 6, 11, 16, 21, 26, ... **h** 3, 11, 19, 27, 35, ...   **i** 1, 4, 7, 10, 13, ...
   j 21, 24, 27, 30, 33, ... **k** 12, 19, 26, 33, 40, ...   **l** 1, 9, 17, 25, 33, ...

3 **a** Which term of the sequence 5, 8, 11, 14, 17, ... is the first one to be greater
        than 100?
     b Which term of the sequence 1, 8, 15, 22, 29, ... is the first one to be greater
        than 200?
     c Which term of the sequence 4, 9, 14, 19, 24, ... is the closest to 500?

4 For each sequence **a** to **j**, find

    i   the nth term   **ii**   the 100th term   **iii**   the term closest to 100

    a 5, 9, 13, 17, 21, …   **b** 3, 5, 7, 9, 11, 13, …   **c** 4, 7, 10, 13, 16, …

    d 8, 10, 12, 14, 16, …   **e** 9, 13, 17, 21, …   **f** 6, 11, 16, 21, …

    g 0, 3, 6, 9, 12, …   **h** 2, 8, 14, 20, 26, …   **i** 7, 15, 23, 31, …

    j 25, 27, 29, 31, …

5 A sequence of fractions is $\frac{3}{4}, \frac{5}{7}, \frac{7}{10}, \frac{9}{13}, \frac{11}{16}, \ldots$

    a Find the nth term in the sequence.

    b By changing each fraction to a decimal, can you see any pattern at all?

    c What, as a decimal, will be the value of the

        i 100th term   **ii** 1000th term?

    d Use your answers to part **c** to predict what the 10 000th term and the millionth term are. (Check these out on your calculator.)

6 Repeat the above set of questions for $\frac{3}{6}, \frac{7}{11}, \frac{11}{16}, \frac{15}{21}, \frac{19}{26}, \ldots$

General rules from given patterns

Many problem-solving situations that you are likely to meet involve number sequences. So you do need to be able to formulate general rules from given number patterns.

Example   The diagram shows a pattern of squares building up.

a How many squares will be on the base of the nth pattern?

b Which pattern has 99 squares in its base?

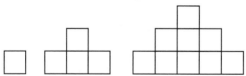

a Building up a table of results for the patterns, we see

Pattern number	1	2	3	4	5
Number of squares in base	1	3	5	7	9

Looking at the difference between consecutive patterns, we see it is always 2 squares. So, we use $2n$.

Subtract the difference 2 from the first number, which gives $1 - 2 = -1$.

So the number of squares in the nth pattern is $2n - 1$.

b We have to find n when $2n - 1 = 99$.

$$2n - 1 = 99$$
$$\Rightarrow 2n = 99 + 1 = 100$$
$$n = 100 \div 2 = 50$$

The pattern with 99 squares in its base is the 50th.

EXERCISE 24E

1   A pattern of squares is built up from matchsticks
    as shown.

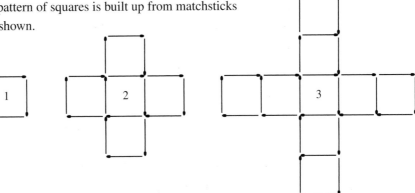

a   Draw the 4th diagram.
b   How many squares are in the *n*th diagram?
c   How many squares are in the 25th diagram?
d   With 200 squares, which is the biggest diagram that could be made?

2   A pattern of triangles is built up from matchsticks.

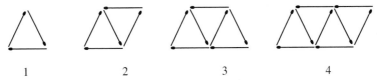

a   Draw the 5th set of triangles in this pattern.
b   How many matchsticks are needed for the *n*th set of triangles?
c   How many matchsticks are needed to make the 60th set of triangles?
d   If there are only 100 matchsticks, which is the largest set of triangles that could
    be made?

3   A conference centre had tables each of which could sit 6 people. When put
    together, the tables could seat people as shown.

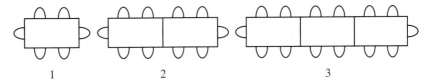

a   How many people could be seated at 4 tables?
b   How many people could be seated at *n* tables put together in this way?
c   A conference had 50 people who wished to use the tables in this way. How
    many tables would they need?

4 A pattern of squares is put together as shown.

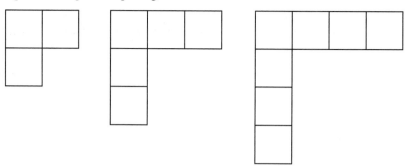

1   2   3

a Draw the 4th diagram.

b How many squares are in the *n*th diagram?

c How many squares are in the 50th diagram?

d With 300 squares, what is the biggest diagram that could be made?

5 Prepacked fencing units come in the shape shown on the right, made of 4 pieces of wood. When you put them together in stages to make a fence, you also need joining pieces, so the fence will start to build up as shown below.

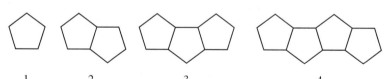

2   3

a How many pieces of wood would you have in a fence made up in
   i 5 stages   **ii** *n* stages   **iii** 45 stages?

b I made a fence out of 124 pieces of wood. How many stages did I use?

6 Regular pentagons of side length 1 cm are joined together to make a pattern as shown.

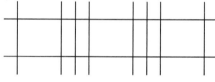

1   2   3   4

Copy this pattern and write down the perimeter of each shape.

a What is the perimeter of patterns like this made from
   i 6 pentagons   **ii** *n* pentagons   **iii** 50 pentagons?

b What is the largest number of pentagons that can be put together like this to have a perimeter less than 1000 cm?

7 A school dining hall had tables in the shape of a trapezium. Each table could seat 5 people, as shown on the right. When the tables were joined together as shown below, each table couldn't seat as many people.

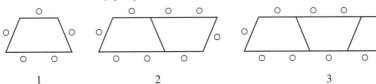

      1   2   3

  a In this arrangement, how many could be seated if they used
     i 4 tables   **ii** *n* tables   **iii** 13 tables?

  b For an outside charity event, up to 200 people had to be seated. How many tables like this did they need?

8 Lamp-posts are put at the end of every 100 m stretch of a motorway, as shown,

           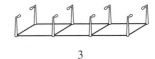

      1   2   3

  a How many lamp-posts are needed for
     i 900 m of this motorway   **ii** 8 km of this motorway?

  b The M99 is a motorway being built. The contractor has ordered 1598 lamp-posts. How long is this motorway?

9 A window can be split into small panes, as shown.

     1 strut   2 struts   3 struts

  a How many panes are there in a window with the following numbers of struts?
     i 4 struts   **ii** *n* struts   **iii** 9 struts

  b A window like this was made with 30 panes. How many struts did it have?

10 When setting out tins to make a display of a certain height, you need to know how many tins to start with at the bottom.

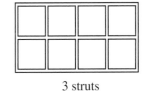

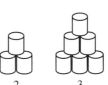

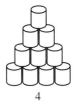

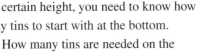

  a How many tins are needed on the bottom if you wish the display to be
     i 5 tins high
     ii *n* tins high
     iii 18 tins high?

                       2   3   4

  b I saw a shop assistant starting to build a display, and noticed he was starting with 20 tins on the bottom. How high was the display when it was finished?

Quadratic rules

Some problem-solving situations involve number sequences which are governed by a quadratic rule. You met some of these patterns in Exercise 24C, where we have, for example, n^2, $n^2 + 3$ and $n^2 - 1$.

You will recognise that a pattern is quadratic from the increasing difference between consecutive terms.

The simpler rules

These sequences will nearly always be based on n^2. So you do need to recognise the pattern 1, 4, 9, 16, 25, … .

The differences between consecutive terms of this pattern are the odd numbers 3, 5, 7, 9, … . So if you find that the differences form an odd-number sequence, you know the pattern is based on n^2.

Follow through the next two examples to see how sequences can be spotted when they are based on n^2.

Example 1 Find the nth term in the sequence 2, 5, 10, 17, 26, … .

The differences are the odd numbers 3, 5, 7, 9, … so we know the rule is based on n^2.

Next, we look for a link with the square numbers. We do this by subtracting from each term the corresponding square number:

$$\begin{array}{ccccc} 2 & 5 & 10 & 17 & 26 \\ -1 & -4 & -9 & -16 & -25 \\ \hline 1 & 1 & 1 & 1 & 1 \end{array}$$

Clearly, the link is +1, so the nth term is $n^2 + 1$.

(You should always quickly check the generalisation by substituting $n = 1, 2, 3, 4$ to see whether it does work.)

Example 2 Find the nth term in the sequence 1, 6, 13, 22, 33, … .

The differences are 5, 7, 9, 11, … so we know the pattern is based on n^2.

Next, we have to find the link. We notice that the first difference is 5 not 3, which means that the series of square numbers we use starts at 4, not at 1.

It follows that to obtain 4, 9, 16, 25, … from the original sequence we simply add 3 to each term of that sequence.

So to get from the square numbers to the sequence 1, 6, 13, 22, 33, … we have to use $(n + 1)^2$, since the sequence is based on 4, 9, 16, … .

The final step in finding the rule is to take away the 3, which gives the nth term as $(n + 1)^2 - 3$.

More complicated rules

Example 1   Find the *n*th term in the sequence 2, 6, 12, 20, 30, ...

Looking at the differences tells us that the sequence is not linear, and is not based on n^2. So we split each term into factors to see whether we can find a pattern which shows how the numbers have been formed. Constructing a table like the one below can help us to sort out which factors to use when we have a choice.

Term	2	6	12	20	30
Factors	1×2	2×3	3×4	4×5	5×6

We can further break down the factors to obtain

$$1 \times (1 + 1) \qquad 2 \times (2 + 1) \qquad 3 \times (3 + 1) \qquad 4 \times (4 + 1) \qquad 5 \times (5 + 1)$$

We can now see quite easily that the pattern is $n \times (n + 1)$. That is, the *n*th term is $n(n + 1)$.

Example 2   Find the *n*th term in the sequence of the triangle numbers 1, 3, 6, 10, 15, ...

Looking at the differences tells us that the sequence is not linear and is not based on n^2. So we split each term into factors and construct a table. (We have no problem with the choice of factors.)

Term	1	3	6	10	15
Factors	1×1	1×3	2×3	2×5	3×5

At this stage, we may not yet have spotted a pattern. So we investigate the effect of multiplying the smaller of each pair of factors by 2, and obtain an interesting pattern.

Term	1	3	6	10	15
Factors	1×1	1×3	2×3	2×5	3×5
Smaller $\times 2$	1×2	2×3	4×3	4×5	6×5

That is

$$1 \times 2 \qquad 2 \times 3 \qquad 3 \times 4 \qquad 4 \times 5 \qquad 5 \times 6$$

We can further break down this last set of numbers to obtain

$$1 \times (1 + 1) \qquad 2 \times (2 + 1) \qquad 3 \times (3 + 1) \qquad 4 \times (4 + 1) \qquad 5 \times (5 + 1)$$

the pattern of which is given by $n \times (n + 1)$.

This gives terms twice the size of those in the sequence 1, 3, 6, 10, 15, ... so we need to change the expression to $\frac{1}{2} \times n \times (n + 1)$.

So the *n*th term is $\frac{1}{2} n(n + 1)$.

Note   Questions with nasty *n*th terms like this will not be in your normal examination papers. They will only occur in coursework and the problem-solving papers.

EXERCISE 24F

1 For each of the sequences **a** to **e**
   i write down the next two terms   **ii** find the nth term.
   a   0, 3, 8, 15, 24, ...   **b**   3, 6, 11, 18, 27, ...   **c**   4, 7, 12, 19, 28, ...
   d   −1, 2, 7, 14, 23, ...   **e**   11, 14, 19, 26, ...

2 For each of the sequences **a** to **e**
   i write down the next two terms   **ii** find the nth term.
   a   5, 10, 17, 26, ...   **b**   3, 8, 15, 24, ...   **c**   9, 14, 21, 30, ...
   d   10, 17, 26, 37, ...   **e**   8, 15, 24, 35, ...

3 For each of the sequences **a** to **e**
   i write down the next two terms   **ii** find the nth term.
   a   0, 2, 6, 12, 20, ...   **b**   0, 4, 12, 24, 40, ...   **c**   6, 12, 20, 30, 42, ...
   d   0, 1, 3, 6, 10, ...   **e**   4, 10, 18, 28, 40, ...

4 Look at each of the following sequences to see whether the rule is linear, quadratic based on n^2 only or a difficult quadratic. Then
   i write down the nth term   **ii** write down the 50th term.
   a   5, 8, 13, 20, 29, ...   **b**   5, 8, 11, 14, 17, ...   **c**   3, 8, 15, 24, 35, ...
   d   5, 12, 21, 32, 45, ...   **e**   3, 6, 11, 18, 27, ...   **f**   1, 6, 11, 16, 21, ...

Possible coursework tasks

Fibonacci sequences

The Fibonacci sequence is 1, 1, 2, 3, 5, 8, ... Can you see the pattern?

Make up some other Fibonacci sequences starting with a different pair of numbers each time.

For Fibonacci sequences investigate the following:

a The ratio of successive terms.

b Take any three consecutive Fibonacci numbers, multiply the outside numbers and square the middle number.

c Take any four consecutive Fibonacci numbers, compare the product of the outside numbers with the product of the inside numbers.

d Invent different Fibonacci sequences of your own: for example, start with 1, 1, 1 and the next term is the sum of the previous three.

The above problems can be done on a computer spreadsheet. You may be able to find other patterns which perhaps haven't yet been discovered!

Squared numbers summed

$$1^2 + 2^2 = 5$$
$$1^2 + 2^2 + 3^2 = 14$$

Investigate $\quad 1^2 + 2^2 + 3^2 + \ldots + n^2 = ?$

Converging sequences

For the sequence 2, 9, 5.5, 7.25, ... each term is obtained by finding the mean of the previous two terms.

Investigate for different sequences. A computer spreadsheet will help.

A journey to infinity

Use your calculator or a computer spreadsheet to investigate these 'infinite' sequences.

a $\quad 1 + \dfrac{1}{2} + \dfrac{1}{4} + \dfrac{1}{8} + \ldots$

b $\quad \dfrac{1}{3} + \dfrac{1}{9} + \dfrac{1}{27} + \dfrac{1}{81} + \ldots$

c $\quad \dfrac{1}{2} - \dfrac{1}{4} + \dfrac{1}{8} - \dfrac{1}{16} + \ldots$

d $\quad \dfrac{1}{3} - \dfrac{1}{9} + \dfrac{1}{27} - \dfrac{1}{81} + \ldots$

Wallis sequence

Evaluate each line and investigate what happens when you continue the sequence.

$$2 \times \dfrac{2}{1} \times \dfrac{2}{3} =$$
$$2 \times \dfrac{2}{1} \times \dfrac{2}{3} \times \dfrac{4}{3} =$$
$$2 \times \dfrac{2}{1} \times \dfrac{2}{3} \times \dfrac{4}{3} \times \dfrac{4}{5} =$$
$$2 \times \dfrac{2}{1} \times \dfrac{2}{3} \times \dfrac{4}{3} \times \dfrac{4}{5} \times \dfrac{6}{5} =$$

Examination questions

1 **a** A number pattern begins 1, 1, 2, 3, 5, 8, ...

    i What is the next number in this pattern?

    ii The number pattern is continued. Explain how you would find the eighth number in the pattern.

  b Another number pattern begins 1, 4, 7, 10, 13, ... Write down, in terms of n, the nth term in this pattern.

SEG, Question 1, Specimen Paper 13, 1998

2 **a** Look at this sequence of numbers: 3, 8, 18, 38, ... The rule that has been used to get each number from the number before is

Add 1 and then multiply by 2

    i Write down the next number in this sequence.

    ii Using the same rule but a different starting number, the second number is 16. What is the starting number?

  b Look at this sequence of numbers: 5, 9, 13, 17, 21, ...

    i Write down, in words, the rule for getting each number from the one before it.

    ii Write down a formula, in terms of n, for the nth number of the sequence.

MEG, Question 3, Specimen Paper 4, 1998

3 **a** Write down the next two numbers in the number pattern 3, 7, 11, 15, 19, ...

  b Write down in words what you think the rule is for finding the next number in the pattern from the one before it.

  c Write down what you think the rule is for finding the nth number in the pattern.

WJEC, Question 6, Specimen Paper 1, 1998

4 Philipa makes some patterns by linking squares with rods.
Here are some of the patterns she makes.

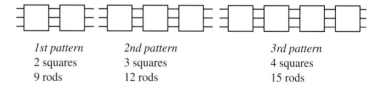

1st pattern	2nd pattern	3rd pattern
2 squares	3 squares	4 squares
9 rods	12 rods	15 rods

  a How many squares are in the 40th pattern?

  b How many squares are in the nth pattern?

  c How many rods are in the 40th pattern?

  d How many rods are in the nth pattern?

WJEC, Question 3, Intermediate Paper 2, June 1999

5 Find the *n*th term of each of the following sequences.

   a   3, 6, 9, 12, 15, …

   b   5, 9, 13, 17, 21, …

OCR, Question 5, Intermediate (A) Paper 3, June 2000

6 Here are the first five numbers of a simple sequence:

    2, 8, 14, 20, 26

Write down, in terms of *n*, an expression for the *n*th term of this sequence.

EDEXCEL, Question 6, Intermediate Paper 4, June 2000

7 There is a relationship between the terms in rows A, B and C.

Row A	1	2	3	4	5
Row B	1	4	9	16	25
Row C	2	6	12	20	30

   a   What is the formula for the *n*th term in row B?

   b   What is the formula for the *n*th term in row C?

NEAB, Question 20, Specimen Paper 2, 1998

8 Find an expression, in terms of *n*, for the *n*th term of each of the following sequences.

   a   12, 22, 32, 42, …   **b**   22, 32, 42, 52, …

WJEC, Question 17, Intermediate Paper 2, June 1999

9   **a**   What is the next number in this sequence?

        1, 3, 7, 15, …

   b   Find a formula, in terms of *n*, for the number of sticks in the *n*th shape in this sequence.

Shape 1   Shape 2   Shape 3

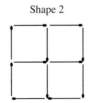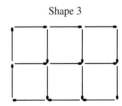

   c   Find a formula, in terms of *n*, for the *n*th term in this sequence.

        2, 6, 12, 20, 30, …

SEG, Question 13, Specimen Paper 14, 1998

10 The diagram shows part of a computer spreadsheet. The number 10 in column B is labelled B4. The rule for finding the numbers in column B is

B1 = 1

B2 = B1 + A2

B3 = B2 + A3

B4 = B3 + A4, and so on …

	COLUMN		
	A	B	C
1	1	1	1
2	2	3	4
3	3	6	9
ROW 4	4	10	16
5	5	15	
6	6		
7	7		

a Find the numbers B6 and B7.

b The numbers C2, C3, C4, … can be found from the numbers in column B.

Write down the rule for finding these numbers using column B.

c The pattern in column C is continued.

  i What number will be C20?

  ii Write down a formula for Cn, where n stands for any positive integer.

MEG, Question 9, Specimen Paper 4, 1998

Summary

How well do you grade yourself?

To gain a grade **E**, you need to be able to describe number patterns and to explain how a pattern works, writing down the next few terms.

To gain a grade **D**, you need to be able to write down the nth term of a linear sequence.

To gain a grade **C**, you need to be able to find the rules of a quadratic pattern and find the nth term in a quadratic sequence. You also need to be able to explain how you found the rule of a sequence.

To gain a grade **B**, you need to be able to find any nth term of any given sequence and also be able easily to recognise which are based on n^2 and which are more complicated to find, but be able to do so.

What you should know after you have worked through Chapter 24

- Be able to recognise a number pattern and explain how the pattern is made.

- Be able to recognise a linear sequence and find its nth term.

- Be able to recognise when a sequence is not linear and therefore look for a quadratic rule.

- Be able to recognise when a sequence is based on n^2.

- Start to look for the more complicated quadratic rules and be able to identify them.

Graphs 3

Discovery activity

The following activity makes an excellent piece of coursework.

Quadratic graphs

The general form of the quadratic equation is

$$y = ax^2 + bx + c$$

How does it affect the graph if the values of a, b and c change?

What effect do the values of a, b and c have on the points P, Q, S and V?

The techniques needed to draw nonlinear graphs are covered in this chapter, or you can use a graphics calculator.

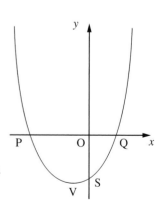

Quadratic graphs

A quadratic graph has a term in x^2 in its equation. All of the following are quadratic equations and each would produce a quadratic graph.

$$y = x^2 \qquad\qquad y = x^2 + 5 \qquad\qquad y = x^2 - 3x$$
$$y = x^2 + 5x + 6 \qquad\qquad y = 3x^2 - 5x + 4$$

Example 1   Draw the graph of $y = x^2 + 5x + 6$ for $-5 \le x \le 3$.

Make a table, as shown below. Work out each row (x^2, $5x$, 6) separately, adding them together to obtain the values of y. Then plot the points from the table.

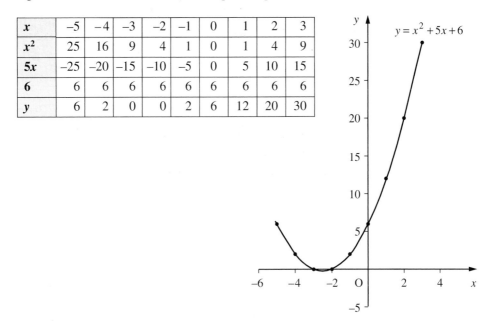

x	−5	−4	−3	−2	−1	0	1	2	3
x^2	25	16	9	4	1	0	1	4	9
$5x$	−25	−20	−15	−10	−5	0	5	10	15
6	6	6	6	6	6	6	6	6	6
y	6	2	0	0	2	6	12	20	30

Note that in an examination paper you may be given only the first and last rows, with some values filled in. For example,

x	−5	−4	−3	−2	−1	0	1	2	3
y	6		0		2				30

In this case, you would either construct your own table, or work out the remaining y-values with a calculator. Example 2 demonstrates this.

Example 2

a Complete the table for $y = 3x^2 - 5x + 4$ for $-1 \le x \le 3$, then draw the graph.

x	−1	−0.5	0	0.5	1	1.5	2	2.5	3
y	12			2.25	2			10.25	16

b Use your graph to find the value of y when $x = 2.2$.

c Use your graph to find the values of x that give a y-value of 9.

a The table gives only some values. So you either set up your own table with $3x^2$, $-5x$ and $+4$, or calculate each y-value. For example, on the majority of scientific calculators, the value for -0.5 will be worked out as

Check that you get an answer of 7.25.

If you want to make sure that you are doing the correct sums, try some value for x. For example, try $x = 0.5$, and see whether your answer is 2.25.

The complete table should be

x	−1	−0.5	0	0.5	1	1.5	2	2.5	3
y	12	7.25	4	2.25	2	3.25	6	10.25	16

The graph is shown on the right.

b To find the corresponding y-value for any value of x, you start on the x-axis at that x-value, go up to the curve, across to the y-axis and read off the y-value. This procedure is marked on the graph with arrows.

Always show these arrows because even if you make a mistake and misread the scales, you may still get a mark.

When $x = 2.2$, $y = 7.5$.

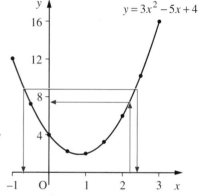

$$y = 3x^2 - 5x + 4$$

c This time start at 9 on the y-axis and read off the two x-values that correspond to a y-value of 9. Again, this procedure is marked on the graph with arrows.

When $y = 9$, $x = -0.7$ or $x = 2.4$.

Drawing accurate graphs

Note that although it is difficult to draw accurate curves, examiners work to a **tolerance of only 1 mm**.

Here are some of the more common ways in which marks are lost in an examination (see also diagrams).
- When the points are too far apart, a curve tends to 'wobble'.
- Drawing curves in small sections leads to 'feathering'.
- The place where a curve should turn sharply is drawn 'flat'.
- A line is drawn through a point which, clearly, has been incorrectly plotted.

A quadratic curve drawn correctly will always give a smooth curve.

Here are some tips which will make it easier for you to draw smooth, curved lines.

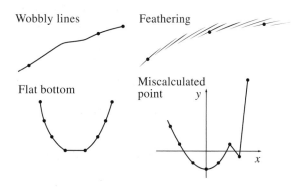

Wobbly lines   Feathering

Flat bottom   Miscalculated point

- If you are **right-handed**, turn your piece of paper or your exercise book round so that you draw from left to right. Your hand is steadier this way than trying to draw from right to left or away from your body. If you are **left-handed**, you should find drawing from right to left the more accurate way.
- Move your pencil over the points as a practice run without drawing the curve.
- Do one continuous curve and only stop at a plotted point.
- Use a **sharp** pencil and do not press too heavily, so that you may easily rub out mistakes.

Normally in an examination, grids are provided with the axes clearly marked. This is so that the examiner can place a transparent master over a graph and see immediately whether any lines are badly drawn or points are misplotted. Remember that a tolerance of 1 mm is all that you are allowed. In the exercises below, suitable ranges are suggested for the axes. You can use any type of graph paper to draw the graphs.

Also you do not need to work out all values in a table. If you use a calculator, you need only to work out the y-value. The other rows in the table are just working lines to break down the calculation.

EXERCISE 25A

1 a Copy and complete the table for the graph of $y = 3x^2$ for values of x from -3 to 3.

x	-3	-2	-1	0	1	2	3
y	27		3			12	

b Use your graph to find the value of y when $x = -1.5$.

c Use your graph to find the values of x that give a y-value of 10.

2 a Copy and complete the table for the graph of $y = x^2 + 2$ for values of x from -5 to 5.

x	-5	-4	-3	-2	-1	0	1	2	3	4	5
$y = x^2 + 2$	27		11					6			

b Use your graph to find the value of y when $x = -2.5$.

c Use your graph to find the values of x that give a y-value of 14.

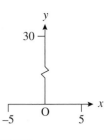

3 a Copy and complete the table for the graph of $y = x^2 - 3x$ for values of x from -5 to 5.

x	-5	-4	-3	-2	-1	0	1	2	3	4	5
x^2	25		9					4			
$-3x$	15							-6			
y	40							-2			

b Use your graph to find the value of y when $x = 3.5$.

c Use your graph to find the values of x that give a y-value of 5.

4 a Copy and complete the table for the graph of $y = x^2 - 2x - 8$ for values of x from -5 to 5.

x	-5	-4	-3	-2	-1	0	1	2	3	4	5
x^2	25		9					4			
$-2x$	10							-4			
-8	-8							-8			
y	27							-8			

b Use your graph to find the value of y when $x = 0.5$.

c Use your graph to find the values of x that give a y-value of -3.

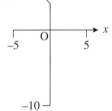

5 a Copy and complete the table for the graph of $y = x^2 - 5x + 4$ for values of x from -2 to 5.

x	-2	-1	0	1	2	3	4	5
y	18		4			-2		

b Use your graph to find the value of y when $x = -0.5$.

c Use your graph to find the values of x that give a y-value of 3.

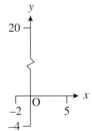

6 a Copy and complete the table for the graph of $y = x^2 + 2x - 1$ for values of x from -3 to 3.

x	-3	-2	-1	0	1	2	3
x^2	9				1	4	
$+2x$	-6		-2			4	
-1	-1	-1				-1	
y	2					7	

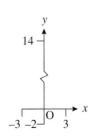

b Use your graph to find the y-value when $x = -2.5$.

c Use your graph to find the values of x that give a y-value of 1.

d On the same axes, draw the graph of $y = \dfrac{x}{2} + 2$.

e Where do the graphs $y = x^2 + 2x - 1$ and $y = \dfrac{x}{2} + 2$ cross?

7 a Copy and complete the table for the graph of $y = x^2 + 2x + 3$ for values of x from −3 to 3.

x	−3	−2	−1	0	1	2	3
x^2	9				1	4	
$-2x$	6					−4	
$+3$	+3					+3	
y	18					3	

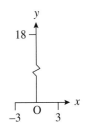

b Use your graph to find the y-value when $x = 1.5$.

c Use your graph to find the values of x that give a y-value of 4.

d On the same axes, draw the graph of $y = 2x + 8$.

e Where do the graphs $y = x^2 - 2x + 3$ and $y = 2x + 8$ cross?

8 a Copy and complete the table for the graph of $y = x^2 - x + 6$ for values of x from −3 to 3.

x	−3	−2	−1	0	1	2	3
x^2	9				1	4	
$-x$	3					−2	
$+6$	+6					+6	
y	18					8	

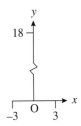

b Use your graph to find the y-value when $x = 2.5$.

c Use your graph to find the values of x that give a y-value of 8.

d Copy and complete the table to draw the graph of $y = x^2 + 5$ on the same axes.

x	−3	−2	−1	0	1	2	3
y	14		6				14

e Where do the graphs $y = x^2 - x + 6$ and $y = x^2 + 5$ cross?

9 a Copy and complete the table for the graph of $y = x^2 + 2x + 1$ for values of x from −3 to 3.

x	−3	−2	−1	0	1	2	3
x^2	9				1	4	
$+2x$	−6					4	
$+1$	+1					+1	
y	4						

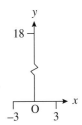

b Use your graph to find the y-value when $x = 1.7$.

c Use your graph to find the values of x that give a y-value of 2.

d On the same axes, draw the graph of $y = 2x + 2$.

e Where do the graphs $y = x^2 + 2x + 1$ and $y = 2x + 2$ cross?

10 a Copy and complete the table for the graph of $y = 2x^2 - 5x - 3$ for values of x from –2 to 4.

x	–2	–1.5	–1	–0.5	0	0.5	1	1.5	2	2.5	3	3.5	4
y	15	9			–3	–5				–3			9

b Where does the graph cross the x-axis?

The roots of a quadratic equation

If you look at your answer to question **10** in Exercise 25A, you will see that the graph crosses the x-axis at $x = -0.5$ and $x = 3$. Since the x-axis is the line $y = 0$, the y-value at any point on the axis is zero. So, you have found the answer to the equation

$$0 = 2x^2 - 5x - 3, \quad \text{that is} \quad 2x^2 - 5x - 3 = 0$$

You met equations of this type in Chapter 14. They are known as quadratic equations. You solved them by factorisation. That is, you found the values of x that made them true. Such values are called the **roots** of an equation. So in the case of the quadratic equation $2x^2 - 5x - 3 = 0$, its roots are –0.5 and 3.

Let's check these values:

For $x = 3.0$ $2(3)^2 - 5(3) - 3 = 18 - 15 - 3 = 0$
For $x = 0.5$ $2(-0.5)^2 - 5(-0.5) - 3 = 0.5 + 2.5 - 3 = 0$

We can find the roots of a quadratic equation by drawing its graph and finding where the graph crosses the x-axis.

Example

a Draw the graph of $y = x^2 - 3x - 4$ for $-2 \leq x \leq 5$.
b Use your graph to find the roots of the equation $x^2 - 3x - 4 = 0$

a Set up a table.

x	–2	–1	0	1	2	3	4	5
x^2	4	1	0	1	4	9	16	25
$-3x$	6	3	0	–3	–6	–9	–12	–15
-4	–4	–4	–4	–4	–4	–4	–4	–4
y	6	0	–4	–6	–6	–4	0	6

Draw the graph.

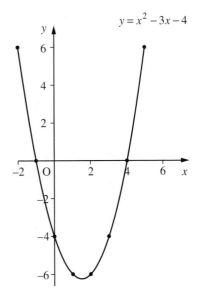

$y = x^2 - 3x - 4$

b The points where the graph crosses the
x-axis are −1 and 4.

So, the roots of $x^2 - 3x - 4 = 0$ are $x = -1$
and $x = 4$.

EXERCISE 25B

1 **a** Copy and complete the table to draw the graph of $y = x^2 - 4$ for values of *x*
from −4 to +4.

x	−4	−3	−2	−1	0	1	2	3	4
y	12			−3				5	

   b Use your graph to find the roots of $x^2 - 4 = 0$.

2 **a** Copy and complete the table to draw the graph of $y = x^2 - 9$ for the values of *x*
from −4 to +4.

x	−4	−3	−2	−1	0	1	2	3	4
y	7				−9			0	

   b Use your graph to find the roots of $x^2 - 9 = 0$.

3 **a** Look at the equations of the graphs you drew in questions **1** and **2**. Is there a
connection between the numbers in each equation and its roots?

   b Before you draw the graphs in parts **c** and **d**, try to predict what their roots will
be.

   c Copy and complete the table to draw the graph of $y = x^2 - 1$ for values of *x*
from −4 to 4.

x	−4	−3	−2	−1	0	1	2	3	4
y	15			−1				8	

   d Copy and complete the table to draw the graph of $y = x^2 - 5$ for values of *x*
from −4 to 4.

x	−4	−3	−2	−1	0	1	2	3	4
y	11		−1					4	

   e Were your predictions correct?

4 a Copy and complete the table to draw the graph of $y = x^2 + 4x$ for values of x from −5 to +2.

x	−5	−4	−3	−2	−1	0	1	2
x^2	25			4			1	
$+4x$	−20			−8			4	
y	5			−4			5	

b Use your graph to find the roots of the equation $x^2 + 4x = 0$.

5 a Copy and complete the table to draw the graph of $y = x^2 - 6x$ for values of x from −2 to +8

x	−2	−1	0	1	2	3	4	5	6
x^2	4			1			16		
$-6x$	12			−6			−24		
y	16			−5			−8		

b Use your graph to find the roots of the equation $x^2 - 6x = 0$.

6 a Copy and complete the table to draw the graph of $y = x^2 + 3x$ for values of x from −5 to +3.

x	−5	−4	−3	−2	−1	0	1	2	3
y	10			−2				10	

b Use your graph to find the roots of the equation $x^2 + 3x = 0$.

7 a Look at the equations of the graphs you drew in questions **4**, **5** and **6**. Is there a connection between the numbers in each equation and the roots?

b Before you draw the graphs in parts **c** and **d**, try to predict what their roots will be.

c Copy and complete the table to draw the graph of $y = x^2 - 3x$ for values of x from − 2 to 5.

x	−2	−1	0	1	2	3	4	5
y	10			−2				10

d Copy and complete the table to draw the graph of $y = x^2 + 5x$ for values of x from −6 to 2.

x	−6	−5	−4	−3	−2	−1	0	1	2
y	6			−6				6	

e Were your predictions correct?

8 a Copy and complete the table to draw the graph of $y = x^2 - 4x + 4$ for values of x from −1 to 3.

x	−1	0	1	2	3
y	9			0	

b Use your graph to find the roots of the equation $x^2 - 4x + 4 = 0$.

c What happens with the roots?

9 a Copy and complete the table to draw the graph of $y = x^2 - 6x + 3$ for values of x from -1 to $+7$.

x	-1	0	1	2	3	4	5	6	7
y	10			-5			-2		

b Use your graph to find the roots of the equation $x^2 - 6x + 3 = 0$.

Reciprocal graphs

A reciprocal equation is in the form $y = \dfrac{a}{x}$.

Examples of reciprocal equations or graphs are

$$y = \frac{1}{x} \qquad y = \frac{4}{x} \qquad y = -\frac{3}{x}$$

All reciprocal graphs have a similar shape and some symmetry properties.

Example Complete the table to draw the graph of $y = \dfrac{1}{x}$ for $1 \le x \le 8$.

x	1	1.5	2	2.5	3	3.5	4	4.5	5	5.5	6	6.5	7	7.5	8
y	1.00	0.67			0.33			0.22		0.18		0.15		0.13	

Values are rounded off to two decimal places, as it is unlikely that you could plot a value more accurately than this. The completed table is

x	1	1.5	2	2.5	3	3.5	4	4.5	5	5.5	6	6.5	7	7.5	8
y	1.00	0.67	0.50	0.40	0.33	0.29	0.25	0.22	0.20	0.18	0.17	0.15	0.14	0.13	0.13

The graph plotted from these values is shown in **A**. This is not much of a graph and does not show the properties of the reciprocal function. If we take x-values from 0.1 to 1.0 in steps of 0.1, we get this table:

x	0.1	0.2	0.3	0.4	0.5	0.6	0.7	0.8	0.9	1.0
y	10.0	5.00	3.33	2.50	2.00	1.67	1.43	1.25	1.11	1.00

Plotting these points as well gives the graph in **B**.

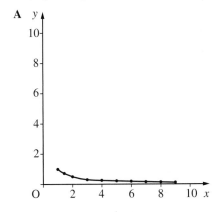

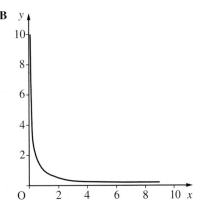

From the graph in **B**, the following properties can be seen.

- The line $y = x$ is a line of symmetry.
- The closer x gets to zero, the nearer the graph gets to the y-axis.
- As x increases, the graph gets closer to the x-axis.

The graph never actually touches the axes; it just gets closer and closer to them. A line to which a graph gets closer but never touches or crosses is called an **asymptote**.

These properties are true for **all reciprocal graphs**.

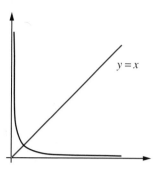

EXERCISE 25C

1 a Complete the table to draw the graph of $y = \dfrac{2}{x}$ for $-4 \le x \le 4$.

x	0.2	0.4	0.5	0.8	1	1.5	2	3	4
y	10.00		4.00	2.50			1.00		0.50

b Use your graph to find

    i the y-value when $x = 2.5$ **ii** the x-value when $y = -1.25$.

2 a Complete the table to draw the graph of $y = \dfrac{4}{x}$ for $-10 \le x \le 10$.

x	0.4	0.5	0.8	1	2	4	5	8	10
y	10.00		5.00				0.80		0.40

b Use your graph to find

    i the y-value when $x = 6$ **ii** the x-value when $y = -6$.

3 a Complete the table to draw the graph of $y = \dfrac{1}{x}$ for $-15 \le x \le 15$.

x	0.1	0.2	0.3	0.5	0.8	1	3	5	10	15
y	10.00		3.33			1.00			0.10	

b Use your graph to find

    i the y-value when $x = 8$ **ii** the x-value when $y = -4$.

4 a Complete the table to draw the graph of $y = \dfrac{100}{x}$ for $-400 \le x \le 400$.

x	10	20	40	50	80	100	200	300	400
y	10.00		2.5			1.00			0.25

b Use your graph to find

    i the y-value when $x = -150$ **ii** the x-value when $y = 4$.

5 a Complete the table to draw the graph of $y = \dfrac{1}{x}$ for $-5 \le x \le 5$.

x	0.1	0.2	0.4	0.5	1	2	2.5	4	5
y	10.00		2.5		1.00				0.2

b On the same axes, draw the line $x + y = 5$.

c Use your graph to find the x-values of the points where the graphs cross.

6 **a** Complete the table to draw the graph of $y = \dfrac{5}{x}$ for $0 \le x \le 20$.

x	0.2	0.4	0.5	1	2	5	10	15	20
y	25.00		10						0.25

b On the same axes, draw the line $y = x + 10$.

c Use your graph to find the x-value of the point where the graphs cross.

7 **a** Complete the table to draw the graph of $y = \dfrac{2}{x} + 1$ for $-4 \le x \le 4$.

x	-4	-2	-1.5	-1	-0.8	-0.5	-0.4	-0.2	0.2	0.4	0.5	0.8	1	1.5	2	4
y	0.5	0.0				-3.0			11		5.00	3.50			2.00	1.5

b Complete the table to draw the graph of $y = \dfrac{2}{x} - 3$ for $-4 \le x \le 4$. Use the same axes as for graph **a**.

x	-4	-2	-1.5	-1	-0.8	-0.5	-0.4	-0.2	0.2	0.4	0.5	0.8	1	1.5	2	4
y	-3.5	-4.0				-7.0			7.0		1.00	-0.5			-2.0	-2.5

c Compare your graphs to the one you drew in question **1**. Describe the differences.

Cubic graphs

A cubic function or graph is one which contains a term in x^3. The following are examples of cubic graphs:

$$y = x^3 \qquad y = x^3 - 2x^2 - 3x - 4 \qquad y = x^3 - x^2 - 4x + 4$$

The techniques used to draw them are exactly the same as those for quadratic and reciprocal graphs.

Example

a Complete the table to draw the graph of $y = x^3 - x^2 - 4x + 4$ for $-3 \le x \le 3$.

x	-3	-2.5	-2	-1.5	-1	-0.5	0	0.5	1	1.5	2	2.5	3
y	-20.00		0.00		6.00		4.00	1.88				3.38	10.00

b Use the graph to find the solution of the equation $x^3 - x^2 - 4x - 1 = 0$.

a The completed table (to two decimal places) is given below. The graph is on the next page.

x	-3	-2.5	-2	-1.5	-1	-0.5	0	0.5	1	1.5	2	2.5	3
y	-20.00	-7.88	0.00	4.38	6.00	5.63	4.00	1.88	0.00	-0.88	0.00	3.38	10.00

b We need to see the similarity between the equation of the graph, $y = x^3 - x^2 - 4x + 4$, and the equation to be solved, $x^3 - x^2 - 4x - 1 = 0$. So we rearrange the equation to be solved as

$$x^3 - x^2 - 4x + 4 = something$$

That is, we want to make the left-hand side of the equation to be solved the same as the right-hand side of the equation of the graph. We can do this by adding 5 to the -1 to make $+4$. So we add 5 to **both** sides of the equation to be solved, which gives

$$x^3 - x^2 - 4x - 1 + 5 = 0 + 5$$
$$x^3 - x^2 - 4x + 4 = 5$$

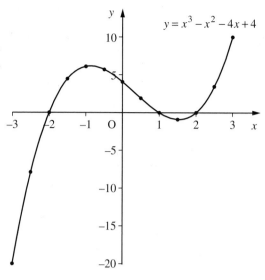

Hence, we simply need to draw the straight line $y = 5$ and find the x co-ordinates of the points where it crosses $y = x^3 - x^2 - 4x + 4$.

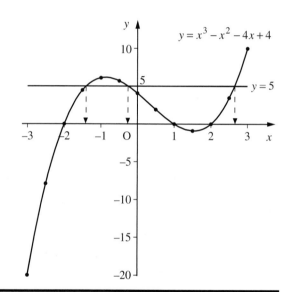

The solutions can now be read from the graph as $x = -1.4$, -0.3 and 2.7.

EXERCISE 25D

In this exercise, the ranges of the axes are shown after questions **5** and **10**.

1 a Complete the table to draw the graph of $y = x^3 + 3$ for $-3 \le x \le 3$.

x	-3	-2.5	-2	-1.5	-1	-0.5	0	0.5	1	1.5	2	2.5	3
y	-24.00	-12.63			2.00		3.00	3.13			11.00		30.00

b Use your graph to find the y-value for an x-value of 1.2.

2 a Complete the table to draw the graph of $y = 2x^3$ for $-3 \le x \le 3$.

x	-3	-2.5	-2	-1.5	-1	-0.5	0	0.5	1	1.5	2	2.5	3
y		-31.25		-6.75			0.00	0.25			16.00		

b Use your graph to find the y-value for an x-value of 2.7.

3 **a** Complete the table to draw the graph of $y = -x^3$ for $-3 \le x \le 3$.

x	-3	-2.5	-2	-1.5	-1	-0.5	0	0.5	1	1.5	2	2.5	3
y	27.00		8.00	3.38			0.00	-0.13			-8.00	-15.63	

b Use your graph to find the y-value for an x-value of -0.6.

4 **a** Complete the table to draw the graph of $y = x^3 + 3x$ for $-3 \le x \le 3$.

x	-3	-2.5	-2	-1.5	-1	-0.5	0	0.5	1	1.5	2	2.5	3
y	-36.00		-14.00	-7.88			0.00	1.63				23.13	

b Use your graph to find the x-value for a y-value of 2.

5 **a** Complete the table to draw the graph of $y = x^3 - 3x^2 - 3x$ for $-3 \le x \le 3$.

x	-3	-2.5	-2	-1.5	-1	-0.5	0	0.5	1	1.5	2	2.5	3
y	-45.00		-14.00	-5.63			0.00	-0.63				-10.63	

b Use your graph to find the y-value for an x-value of 1.8.

Axes for questions **1** to **5**:

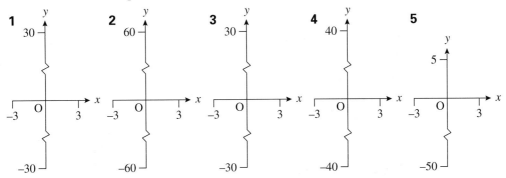

6 **a** Complete the table to draw the graph of $y = x^3 - 3x + 1$ for $-3 \le x \le 3$.

x	-3	-2.5	-2	-1.5	-1	-0.5	0	0.5	1	1.5	2	2.5	3
y	-17.00		-1.00	2.13			1.00	-0.38				9.13	

b Use your graph to find the roots of the equation $x^3 - 3x + 1 = 0$.

7 **a** Complete the table to draw the graph of $y = x^3 - 3x^2 + 1$ for $-2 \le x \le 4$.

x	-2	-1.5	-1	-0.5	0	0.5	1	1.5	2	2.5	3	3.5	4
y	-19.00		-3.00	0.13			-1.00	-2.38				7.13	

b Use your graph to solve the equation $x^3 - 3x^2 - 2 = 0$.

8 **a** Complete the table to draw the graph of $y = x^3 - 6x + 2$ for $-3 \le x \le 3$.

x	-3	-2.5	-2	-1.5	-1	-0.5	0	0.5	1	1.5	2	2.5	3
y	-7.00		6.00	7.63			2.00	-0.88				2.63	

b Use your graph to solve the equation $x^3 - 6x + 3 = 0$.

9 **a** Complete the table to draw the graph of $y = x^3 - 2x + 5$ for $-3 \le x \le 3$.

x	-3	-2.5	-2	-1.5	-1	-0.5	0	0.5	1	1.5	2	2.5	3
y	-16.00		1.00	4.63			5.00	4.13				15.63	

b On the same axes, draw the graph of $y = x + 6$.

c Use your graph to find the x-values of the points where the graphs cross.

10 **a** Complete the table to draw the graph of $y = x^3 - 2x + 1$ for $-3 \le x \le 3$.

x	-3	-2.5	-2	-1.5	-1	-0.5	0	0.5	1	1.5	2	2.5	3
y	-20.00		-3.00	0.63			1.00	0.13				11.63	

b On the same axes, draw the graph of $y = x$.

c Use your graph to find the x-values of the points where the graphs cross.

Axes for questions **6** to **10**:

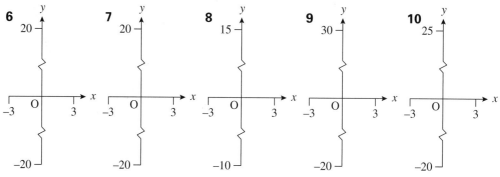

11 Sketch a copy of each of these graphs and label it as linear, quadratic, reciprocal, cubic or none of these.

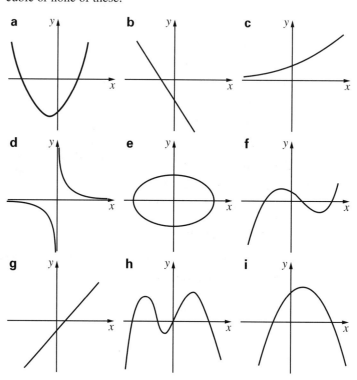

Possible coursework tasks

Quadratic graphs

The general form of a quadratic graph is

$$y = ax^2 + bx + c$$

Investigate what happens to the graph if the values of a, b and c change. (If you can use a graphics calculator for this investigation, it would help.)

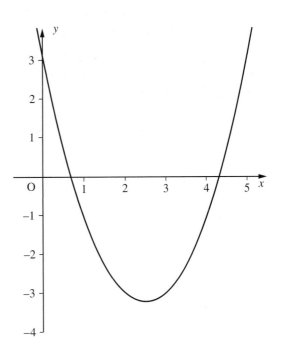

Getaway

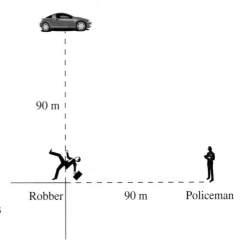

A robber has just been spotted by a police officer. They see each other at the same time. The police officer runs straight at the robber. The robber runs straight for the getaway car.

The diagram shows their positions when each spots the other. The robber runs at $10\,\text{m/s}$ and the police officer at $12\,\text{m/s}$.

a Will the robber get away?

b What are the various speeds that would allow the robber always to get away or the police officer always to catch him?

Examination questions

1 Given that $y = x^2 + 1$:

  a Complete the table below.

x	0	1	2	3	4	5	6	7
y				10			37	

  b Plot these points on a grid and hence draw the graph of $y = x^2 + 1$.
  c Use your graph to find the value of x when $y = 45$.

  NEAB, Question 9, Specimen Paper 11, 1998

2 **a** Complete the table, which gives the values of $y = x^2 - 3$ for x ranging from –2 to 4.

x	–2	–1	0	1	2	3	4
$y = x^2 - 3$	1			–2	1	6	13

  b Draw the graph of $y = x^2 - 3$ for values of x between –2 and 4.
  c Draw the line $y = 5$ on the same graph and write down the co-ordinates of the points where your two graphs intersect.

  WJEC, Question 12, Specimen Paper 1, 1998

3 The radius, r, and value, v, of gold coins were measured and recorded.

r (cm)	0.5	1	1.5	2	2.5
v (£)	250	1000	2250	4000	6250

  a Which of the following graphs represents the information shown in the table?

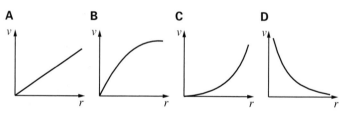

  b Which of these equations describes the information shown in the table?
  $$v = k\sqrt{r} \qquad v = kr \qquad v = kr^2 \qquad v = \frac{k}{r}$$
  where k is a constant.

  SEG, Question 13, Specimen Paper 13, 1998

4 **a** Alex is using 'trial and improvement' to solve the equation $x^2 - 3x = 1$. First he tries $x = 3$ and finds the value of $x^2 - 3x$ is 0. By trying other values of x, find a solution of the equation $x^2 - 3x = 1$, correct to one decimal place. You must show all your working.
  b **i** Draw the graph of $y = x^2 - 3x$, for values of x from –1 to 4.
   ii By drawing a suitable line on your graph, show that the equation $x^2 - 3x = 1$ has two solutions.

  SEG, Question 16, Specimen Paper 14, 1998

5 The graph of $y = x^3 - 2x^2 - 4x$ has been drawn on the grid given here. Use the graph to find estimates of the solutions to the equation

i $x^3 - 2x^2 - 4x = 0$

ii $x^3 - 2x^2 - 4x = 1$

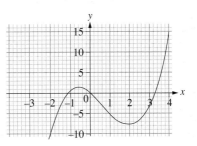

EDEXCEL, Question 27, Intermediate Paper 3, June 2000

6 $y = x^3 - 4x - 1$

a Complete the table of values.

b Draw the graph of $y = x^3 - 4x - 1$.

x	–2	–1	0	1	2	3
y		2				

c By drawing a suitable straight line on the grid, solve the equation $x^3 - 4x - 3 = 0$.

ULEAC, Question 12, Specimen Paper 3, 1998

7 a Complete the following table for $y = x^2 - 3x$.

x	–2	–1	0	1	2	3	4	5
y		4	0		–2	0		10

b On a pair of axes, draw the graph of $y = x^2 - 3x$.

c Use your graph to find the two solutions of the equation $x^2 - 3x = -1$.

d Using your graph, or otherwise, solve the inequality $x^2 - 3x < 0$.

MEG, Question 12, Specimen Paper 4, 1998

8 a i Complete the table for the graph of $y = x^2 - 7$:

x	–3	–2	–1	0	1	2	3
y	2	–3	–6				2

ii Draw the graph on a suitable grid.

b Use your graph to solve the equation $x^2 - 7 = 0$

c Use your graph to state the minimum value of y.

AQA (North), Question 10, Intermediate Paper 1, June 2000

9 a Complete the table below which gives the values of $y = x^2 + 3$ for values of x from –4 to 4.

x	–4	–3	–2	–1	0	1	2	3	4
$y - x^2 + 3$	19		7		3		7		19

b On graph paper draw the graph of $y = x^2 + 3$ for values of x from –4 to 4.

WJEC, Question 6, Intermediate Paper 2, June 1999

10 **a** Complete the table which gives the values of $y = 3x^2 - 4x - 2$ for values of x ranging from -2 to 2.5

x	-2	-1	0	0.5	1	2	2.5
$3x^2 - 4x - 2$	18		-2	-3.25		2	6.75

b On graph paper, draw the graph of $y = 3x^2 - 4x - 2$ for values of x ranging from -2 to 2.5

c Draw the line $y = 5$ on the same graph paper and write down the x-values of the points where your two graphs intersect.

d Write down the equation in x whose solutions are the x-values you found in **c**

WJEC, Question 19, Intermediate Paper 1, November 1999

Summary

How well do you grade yourself?

To gain a grade **E**, you need to be able to plot co-ordinates to draw a simple nonlinear graph of the form $y = ax^2 + b$.

To gain a grade **D**, you need to be able to plot any nonlinear graph of the form $y = ax^2 + bx + c$, $y = ax^3$ or $y = \dfrac{a}{x}$ using a table of values.

To gain a grade **C**, you need to be able to recognise and plot any quadratic, cubic or reciprocal graph using a table or any other method, and to use these graphs to solve quadratic or cubic equations.

To gain a grade **B**, you need to be able to sketch any quadratic, cubic or reciprocal graph using its properties and to know how the shape of the graph varies with different coefficients.

What you should know after you have worked through Chapter 25

- How to find co-ordinates using a variety of methods and how to use these co-ordinates to draw nonlinear graphs.

- How to draw graphs of a variety of functions such as $y = ax^2 + bx + c$, $y = ax^3$ and $y = \dfrac{a}{x}$.

- How to solve quadratic and cubic equations using graphs.

- How to recognise quadratic, cubic and reciprocal graphs, and how to sketch graphs of these functions according to their coefficients.

26 Dimensional analysis

Length

When we have an unknown length or distance in a problem, we represent it by a single letter, followed by the unit in which it is measured. For example,

    t centimetres x miles y kilometres

Example 1   A stick of rock is made up of equal lengths of green, red and orange rock. If it is z cm long, how long is each individual colour?

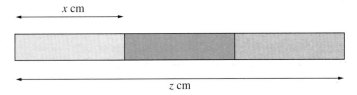

Let each piece be x cm long. Hence

    $3x = z$

$\Rightarrow$ $x = \dfrac{z}{3}$ cm

Example 2   Find the perimeters of these shapes.

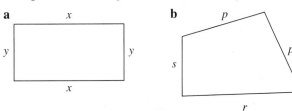

Shape **a** is a rectangle. Its perimeter is

$$P = x + y + x + y = 2x + 2y$$

Shape **b** is irregular. Its perimeter is

$$P = p + p + r + s = 2p + r + s$$

In Examples 1 and 2, each letter is a length and has the **dimension** or measure of length, e.g. centimetre, metre, kilometre, etc. The numbers (coefficients) written before the letters are **not** lengths and therefore have **no** dimensions. So, for example, $2x$, $2y$ or $2p$ has the **same** dimension as x, y or p respectively.

When just one length is involved in a calculation or formula, the calculation or formula is said to have **one dimension** or **1D**, which is represented by the symbol **[L]**.

EXERCISE 26A

Find an expression for the perimeter of each of these shapes.

1

2
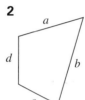

3

4
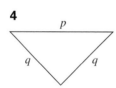

5
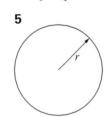

6
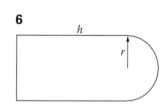

Area

Look at these four examples of formulae for calculating area.

$A = lb$ gives the area of a rectangle

$A = x^2$ gives the area of a square

$A = 2ab + 2ac + 2bc$ gives the surface area of a cuboid

$A = \pi r^2$ gives the area of a circle

These formulae have one thing in common. They all consist of terms that are the product of two lengths. We recognise this by counting the number of letters in each term of the formula. The first formula has two (l and b). The second has two (x and x). The third has three terms, each of two letters (a and b, a and c, b and c). The fourth also has only two letters (r and r) because π is a number (3.14159…) which has no dimension.

Hence, we can recognise formulae for area because they only have terms that consist of two letters. That is, two lengths multiplied together. They therefore have **two dimensions** or **2D**, represented by the symbol $[\mathbf{L} \times \mathbf{L}]$ or $[\mathbf{L^2}]$. Here, again, numbers not defined as lengths have no dimensions.

This confirms the units in which area is usually measured. For example,

> square metres (m × m or m²)   square inches (in × in or in²)
> square centimetres (cm × cm or cm²)

Example 1   What is the area of each of these shapes?

a

b

a This is a rectangle. Its area $A = x \times y = xy$

b This is a semicircle. Its area $A = \dfrac{1}{2} \times \pi \times r^2 = \dfrac{\pi r^2}{2}$

Example 2   What is the area of each of these shapes?

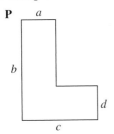 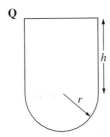

Shape P will have to be split into two separate rectangles.

The first has an area of ab.
The second has an area
of $d(c - a)$.

Total area $A = ab + d(c - a)$
$\qquad\qquad = ab + cd - ad$

Shape Q will have to be split into two separate shapes.

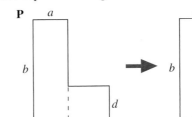

The first is a rectangle with an area of $2r \times h = 2rh$.

The second is a semicircle with an area of $\dfrac{\pi r^2}{2}$ (see previous example).

Total area $A = 2rh + \dfrac{\pi r^2}{2}$

EXERCISE 26B

1 Find a formula for each of these areas.

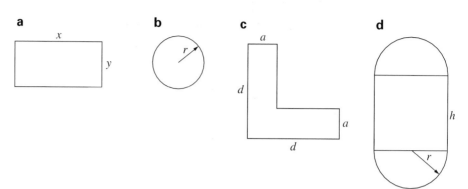

a   b   c   d

2 Find an expression for the area of each of these shapes.

a 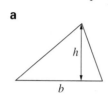   b 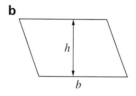   c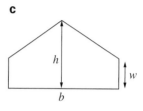

d 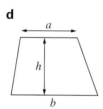   e 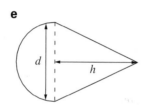   f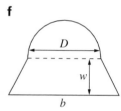

Volume

Look at these three examples of formulae for calculating volume.

$V = lbh$ gives the volume of a cuboid

$V = x^3$ gives the volume of a cube

$V = \pi r^2 h + \dfrac{4}{3}\pi r^3$ gives the volume of a cylinder with hemispherical ends

Again, these formulae have one thing in common. They all consist of terms that are the product of three lengths. We recognise this by counting the number of letters in each term of the formula. The first formula has three (l, b and h). The second has three (x, x and x). The third has two terms, each of three letters (r, r and h; r, r and r). Remember, π has no dimension.

Hence, we can recognise formulae for volume because they only have terms that consist of three letters. That is, three lengths multiplied together. They therefore have **three dimensions** or **3D**, represented by the symbol $[\mathbf{L} \times \mathbf{L} \times \mathbf{L}]$ or $[\mathbf{L^3}]$. Once more, numbers not defined as lengths have no dimensions.

This confirms the units in which volume is usually measured. For example,

cubic metres (m × m × m or m³)   cubic inches (in × in × in or in³)
cubic centimetres (cm × cm × cm or cm³)

Example Find the volume of each of these shapes.

a

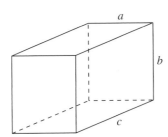

b

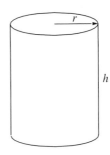

a This is a cuboid, so its volume $V = a \times b \times c = abc$

b This is a cylinder, so its volume V = area of circular end × height
$$= \pi r^2 \times h = \pi r^2 h$$

EXERCISE 26C

Find a formula for each of these volumes.

1

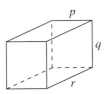

2

3

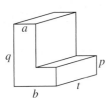

4

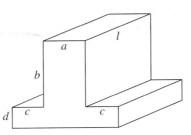

5

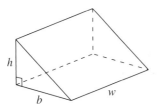

6

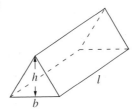

EXERCISE 26D

1   Indicate by L, A, V or [L], [L²], [L³] whether the following quantities are lengths, areas or volumes, or none of these (N).

a	1 mile	**b**	$5\,cm^3$
c	$3x$ centimetres	**d**	$65\,cm^2$
e	$4\pi\,cm$	**f**	$10\,km$
g	$4\pi\,cm^3$	**h**	$3\,m^3$
i	$6\,mph$	**j**	Diameter of a circle
k	Mass of the moon	**l**	Region inside a square
m	Space inside a football	**n**	Surface of a cone
o	Amount of air in a room	**p**	Amount of pop in a can
q	Value of an antique painting	**r**	18 inches
s	3 acres	**t**	7 litres
u	Rise and fall of the tide	**v**	Wattage of a light bulb
w	Noise made by a radio	**x**	Bearing of a ship from a harbour
y	Altitude of an aircraft	**z**	8 tonnes

2   Each of these represents a length, an area or a volume. Indicate by writing L, A or V which it is.

a	x^2	**b**	$2y$	**c**	πa	**d**	πab
e	xyz	**f**	$3x^3$	**g**	x^2y	**h**	$2xy$
i	$4y$	**j**	$3ab^2$	**k**	$4xz$	**l**	$5z$
m	abc	**n**	$ab + bc$	**o**	$abc + d^3$	**p**	$2ab + 3bc$
q	$a^2b + ab^2$	**r**	$a^2 + b^2$	**s**	πa^2	**t**	$\dfrac{abc}{d}$
u	$\dfrac{(ab + bc)}{d}$	**v**	$\dfrac{ab}{2}$	**w**	$(a + b)^2$	**x**	$4a^2 + 2ab$
y	$3abc + 2abd + 4bcd + 2acd$			**z**	$4\pi r^3 + \pi r^2 h$		

Consistency

One way in which scientists and mathematicians check complicated formulae to see whether they are correct is to test for **consistency**. That is, check that every term is of the same **order** (dimension) and represents the same **unit**. We are only concerned with lengths, areas and volumes, so it is easy for us to test for consistency.

Each term in a formula must have the correct number of dimensions. It is not possible to have a formula with a mixture of terms, some of which have, for example, one dimension and some two dimensions. When terms are found to be mixed, the formula is said to be **inconsistent** and is rejected.

Example

i Which of these formulae are consistent?

ii If any are consistent, do they represent a length, an area or a volume?

a	$a + bc$	**b**	$\pi r^2 + ab$	**c**	$r^3 + 2\pi r^2$
d	$a(b + c)$	**e**	$\dfrac{(ab^2 + a^2b)}{2}$	**f**	$\dfrac{\pi(R^2 + r^2)}{x}$

Formula **a** is inconsistent because the first term has one letter (order 1), and the second has two letters (order 2). Hence, it is a mixture of length and area. So it has no meaning, i.e. $[L] + [L^2]$ is not possible.

Formula **b** is consistent because the first term has two letters (r and r) multiplied by a dimensionless number (π), and the second term also has two letters (a and b). Hence the formula could represent an area, i.e. $[L^2] + [L^2] = [L^2]$ is true.

Formula **c** is inconsistent because the first term is of order 3 and the second term is of order 2. It is a mixture of area and volume, so it has no meaning, i.e. $[L^3] + [L^2]$ is not possible.

Formula **d** is consistent. If we multiply the bracket out, it produces two terms of order 2. Because the bracket is consistent, the whole expression must be. It could represent an area, i.e. $[L] \times [L] = [L^2]$.

Formula **e** is consistent. Each term is of order 3 and the whole expression could represent a volume, i.e. $[L^3] + [L^3] = [L^3]$ is true.

Formula **f** is also consistent. There are two terms of order 2 on the top line and one term of order 1 on the bottom. One dimension can be cancelled to give two terms of order 1. Hence the formula could represent a length, i.e. $[L^2]/[L] = [L]$ is true.

EXERCISE 26E

1 Indicate whether each of these formulae is consistent (C) or inconsistent (I).

   a $a + b$ **b** $a^2 + b$ **c** $a^2 + b^2$ **d** $ab + c$

   e $ab + c^2$ **f** $a^3 + bc$ **g** $a^3 + abc$ **h** $a^2 + abc$

   i $3a^2 + bc$ **j** $4a^3b + 2ab^2$ **k** $3abc + 2x^2y$ **l** $3a(ab + bc)$

   m $4a^2 + 3ab$ **n** $\pi a^2(a + b)$ **o** $\pi a^2 + 2r^2$ **p** $\pi r^2 h + \pi rh$

   q $\pi r^2(R + r)$ **r** $\dfrac{(ab + bc)}{d}$ **s** $a(b^2 + c)$ **t** $\pi ab + \pi bc$

   u $(a + b)(c + d)$ **v** $\pi(a + b)(a^2 + b^2)$ **w** $\pi(a^2 + b^2)$ **x** $\pi^2(a + b)$

   y $\pi r^2 h + \pi r^3$

2 Write down whether each formula is consistent (C) or inconsistent (I). When it is consistent, say whether it represents a length (L), an area (A) or a volume (V).

   a $\pi a + \pi b$ **b** $2\pi r^2 + h$ **c** $\pi r^2 h + 2\pi r^3$ **d** $2\pi r + h$

   e $2\pi rh + 4\pi r^3$ **f** $\dfrac{\pi r}{6} + \pi a^2$ **g** $r^2 h + \pi rh^2$ **h** $\pi r^2(r + h)$

   i $\pi r^2 h + 2r^3 + \dfrac{h^2 r}{6}$ **j** $2\pi r^3 + 3\pi r^2 h$ **k** $4\pi a + 3x$ **l** $3\pi r^2 a + 2\pi r$

   m $\dfrac{\pi r^2 h}{3} + \dfrac{\pi r^3}{3} + x^3$

3 What power * would make each formula consistent?

   a $\pi abc + a^* b$ **b** $\dfrac{\pi r^* h}{2} + \pi h^* + \dfrac{rh^2}{2}$

   c $\pi a(b^* + ac)$ **d** $a^* b + ab^* + c^3$

4 Kerry has worked out a volume formula as $V = \dfrac{(2hD^2 + hd)}{4}$

   It is wrong. Why?

Examination questions

1   Taking l, b h and r to be lengths, complete the table to show which of the formulae 1, 2, 3, 4, or 5 denotes length, area or volume.

	Formula
Length	
Area	
Volume	

Formulae: 1 $h^2(l + b)$

2   $\pi r(l + r)$

3   $4(l + b)^2$

4   $\pi\sqrt{(h^2 - b^2)}$

5   $b^2(\dfrac{h}{3} + l)$ *NICCEA, Question 11, Paper 3, June 1995*

2   r, a and b are all lengths.

Which of the following expressions could be a volume?

$\dfrac{ar}{2}(4b + \pi r)$ $2(ab)^2 + \pi r^2 b$ $4a^2b + rb^3$ $2abr + \dfrac{\pi ar^2}{2}$

OCR, Question 17, Intermediate (B) Paper 4, June 2000

3   Here are 3 expressions:

Expression	Length	Area	Volume	None of these
$3rl$				
$\dfrac{2(r + l)^2}{h}$				
$\dfrac{4\pi r^2 l}{3}$				

r, l and h are lengths.

π, 2, 3 and 4 are numbers and have no dimension.

Put a tick in the correct column to show whether the expression can be used for length, area, volume or none of these.

EDEXCEL, Question 26, Intermediate Paper 3, June 2000

4   The letters f, g and h all represent lengths.

For each of the following expressions, state whether it could represent a length, an area, a volume or none of these.

a $f^2(h + g)$

b $\sqrt{(h^2gf)}$

c $\pi(3f + 2g)$

OCR, Question 15, Intermediate (A) Paper 3, June 2000

5 Some pills are in the form of elliptical prisms, *L* mm long, *W* mm wide and *H* mm thick.

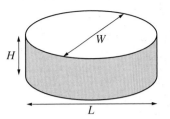

  a Explain why the formula
  $V = 0.8(L + W + H)$ cannot be used to estimate the volume of a pill.

  b One of the following formulae may be used to estimate the volume of a pill.
  $$V = 0.8LWH \quad V = 0.8LW + H \quad V = 0.8(L + W)H \quad V = 0.8L + WH$$
  Which is the correct formula?

  WJEC, Question 22, Intermediate Paper 2, June 1999

6 This diagram shows the cross-section of a warehouse.

The top of the roof is *H* metres above the floor. The side walls are *W* metres high. The width of the warehouse is *L* metres.

An estate agent wants to estimate the area of cross-section of the warehouse.

  a Explain why the formula
  $$A = \frac{(8H + 2W + L)}{10}$$
  cannot be a suitable formula for him to use.

  b Look at these formulae.

  i $A = \dfrac{8WHL}{10}$ **ii** $A = \dfrac{L(8H + 2W)}{10}$ **iii** $A = \dfrac{LW + 8H}{10}$

  One of these formulae can be used to estimate the area of cross-section. Which is it? Give a reason for your answer.

  WJEC, Question 18, Paper 2, June 1995

7 The diagram shows a child's play brick in the shape of a prism. The following formulae represent certain quantities connected with this prism.

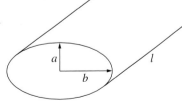

  $\pi ab \quad \pi(a + b) \quad \pi abl \quad \pi(a + b)l$

  Which of the formulae represent areas?

  SEG, Question 18, Paper 4, 1995

Summary

How well do you grade yourself?

To gain a grade **E**, you need to be able to calculate areas and volumes of simple shapes and know the units used to measure them.

To gain a grade **C**, you need to be able to calculate lengths, areas, and volumes of plane shapes and right prisms.

To gain a grade **B**, you need to be able to recognise whether a formula is dimensionally consistent and whether it represents a length, an area or a volume.

What you should know after you have worked through Chapter 26

- How to recognise whether a formula is 1D, 2D or 3D.

- How to recognise when a formula is not consistent and state the reasons why.

27 Proof

This chapter is going to ...

introduce you to the proofs of certain mathematical results which you have already met and used. It will then explain the important difference between the numerical verification of a result and rigorously proving it.

What you should know

The mathematical results in this book, such as:
✔ The interior angles in a triangle add up to 180°.
✔ The sum of any two odd numbers is always an even number.
✔ The theorems concerning circles.
✔ Pythagoras's theorem.

Can you **prove** any of the above results?

The method of mathematical proof is to proceed in logical steps, establishing a series of mathematical statements by using facts which are already known to be true. With few exceptions, a proof will also require the use of algebraic manipulation.

On this page and the next two, we prove three standard results: Pythagoras's theorem, the sum of the interior angles of a triangle is 180°, and the sum of any two odd numbers is always an even number. Follow them through, making sure that you understand each step in the process.

Proof of Pythagoras's theorem

Draw a square of side c inside a square of side $(a + b)$, as shown.

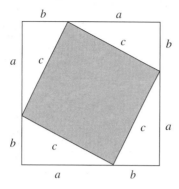

The area of the exterior square is $(a + b)^2 = a^2 + 2ab + b^2$.

The area of each small triangle around the shaded square is $\frac{1}{2}ab$.

The total area of all four triangles is $4 \times \frac{1}{2}ab = 2ab$.

Subtracting the total area of the four triangles from the area of the large square gives the area of the shaded square:
$$a^2 + 2ab + b^2 - 2ab = a^2 + b^2$$

But the area of the shaded square is c^2, so
$$c^2 = a^2 + b^2$$

which is Pythagoras's theorem.

The sum of the interior angles of a triangle is 180°

One of your earlier activities in geometry may have been to draw a triangle, to cut off its corners and to stick them down to show that they make a straight line.

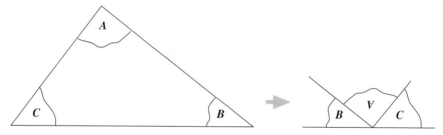

Does this prove that the interior angles make 180° or were you just lucky and picked a triangle that worked? Was the fact that everyone else in the class managed to pick a triangle that worked also a lucky coincidence?

Of course not! But this was a demonstration, not a proof. You would have to show that this method worked for **all** possible triangles (there is an infinite number!) to say that you have proved this result.

Your proof must establish that the result is true for **all** triangles.

Look at the following proof.

Start with triangle ABC with angles α, β and γ (figure **i**).

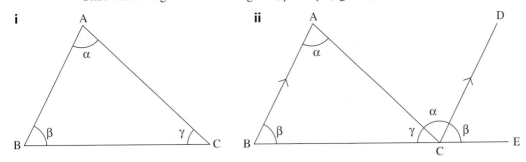

On figure **i** draw a line CD parallel to side AB and extend BC to E, to give (figure **ii**) where

$\angle ACD = \angle BAC = \alpha$ (alternate angles)

$\angle DCE = \angle ABC = \beta$ (corresponding angles)

BCE is a straight line, so $\alpha + \beta + \gamma = 180°$.

This proof assumes that alternate angles are equal and that corresponding angles are equal. Strictly speaking, we should prove these results, but we have to accept certain results as true. We call these results our **assumptions**.

The sum of any two odd numbers is always an even number

If you try this with numbers, you can see that the result is true. For example, $3 + 5 = 8$, $11 + 17 = 28$. But this is not a proof. Once again, we may have been lucky and found some results that work. Until we have tried an infinite number of different pairs, we cannot be sure.

Look at the following algebraic proof.

Let n be any whole number.

Whatever whole number is represented by n, $2n$ has to be even. So, $2n + 1$ represents any odd number.

Let one odd number be $2n + 1$, and let the other odd number be $2m + 1$.

The sum of these is
$$(2n + 1) + (2m + 1) = 2n + 2m + 1 + 1$$
$$= 2n + 2m + 2$$
$$= 2(n + m + 1)$$

which must be even.

EXERCISE 27A

In some questions, a numerical example is used to give you a clue which will help you to write down an algebraic proof.

1 **a** Choose any odd number and any even number. Add these together. Is the result odd or even? Does this always work for any odd number and even number you choose?

   b Let any odd number be represented by $2n + 1$. Let any even number be represented by $2m$, where m and n are integers. Prove that the sum of an odd number and an even number always gives an odd number.

2 Prove the following results.

   a The sum of two even numbers is even.

   b The product of two even numbers is even.

   c The product of an odd number and an even number is even.

   d The product of two odd numbers is odd.

   e The sum of four consecutive numbers is always even.

   f Half the sum of four consecutive numbers is always odd.

3 **a** Show that the triangle ABC (figure **i**) is isosceles.

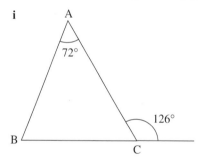

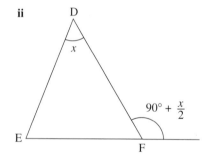

   b Prove that the triangle DEF (figure **ii**) with one angle of x and an exterior angle of $90° + \dfrac{x}{2}$ is isosceles.

4 Prove that a triangle with an interior angle of $\dfrac{x}{2}$ and an exterior angle of x is isosceles.

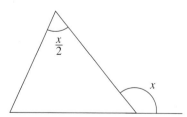

5 a Using the theorem that the angle subtended by an arc at the centre of a circle is twice the angle subtended by the same arc at the circumference, find the values of angles DAB and ACB in the circle shown in figure **i**.

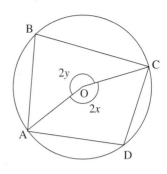

b Prove that the sum of the opposite angles of a cyclic quadrilateral is 180°. (You may find figure **ii** useful.)

6 A Fibonacci sequence is formed by adding the previous two terms to get the next term. For example, if we start with 3 and 4, the series is

$$3, 4, 7, 11, 18, 29, 47, 76, 123, 199, \ldots$$

a Continue the Fibonacci sequence below up to 10 terms.

$$1, 1, 2, \ldots$$

b Continue the Fibonacci sequence below up to 10 terms.

$$a, b, a + b, a + 2b, 2a + 3b, \ldots$$

c Prove that the the difference between the 8th term and the 5th term of any Fibonacci sequence is twice the sixth term.

7 The nth term in the sequence of triangle numbers 1, 3, 6, 10, 15, 21, 28, … is given by

$$\tfrac{1}{2}n(n + 1)$$

a Show that the sum of the 11th and 12th terms is a perfect square.

b Explain why the $(n + 1)$th term of the triangular number sequence is given by

$$\tfrac{1}{2}(n + 1)(n + 2).$$

c Prove that the sum of any two consecutive triangle numbers is always a square number.

8 a The triangle ABC is isosceles. BCD and AED are straight lines. Find the value of the angle CED, marked x, in figure **i**.

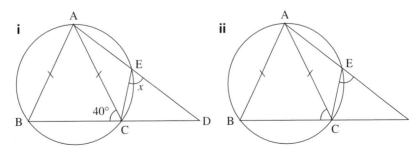

b Prove that angle ACB = angle CED in figure **ii**.

9 The diagram shows part of a 10×10 'hundred square'.

12	13	14	15
22	23	24	25
32	33	34	35
42	43	44	45

a One 2×2 square is marked.

   i Work out the difference between the product of the bottom left and top right values and the product of the top left and bottom right values:

$$22 \times 13 - 12 \times 23$$

   ii Repeat this for any other 2×2 square of your choosing.

b Prove that this will always give an answer of 10 for any 2×2 square chosen.

c A calendar grid (where the numbers are arranged in rows of seven) is

1	2	3	4	5	6	7
8	9	10	11	12	13	14
15	16	17	18	19	20	21
22	23	24	25	26	27	28
29	30	31				

Prove that you always get a value of 7 if you repeat the procedure in part **a i**.

d Prove that in a number square that is arranged in rows of n numbers then the difference is always n if you repeat the procedure in part **a i**.

10 Prove that if you add any two-digit number from the 9 times table to the reverse of itself (i.e. swap the tens and units digits), the result will always be 99.

Algebraic proof

There are three levels of 'proof':

   Verify that …,

• This means all you have to do is to substitute numbers into the result to show that it works.

   Show that …,

• This means you have to show that both sides of the result are the same algebraically.

   Prove that ….

• This means you have to manipulate the left-hand side of the result to become its right-hand side.

The following example demonstrates these three different procedures.

Example You are given that

$$n^2 + (n + 1)^2 - (n + 2)^2 = (n - 3)(n + 1)$$

a Verify that this result is true.

b Show that this result is true.

c Prove that this result is true.

a Choose a number for n, say $n = 5$.

Put this value into both sides of the expression, which gives

$$5^2 + (5 + 1)^2 - (5 + 2)^2 = (5 - 3)(5 + 1)$$
$$25 + 36 - 49 = 2 \times 6$$
$$12 = 12$$

Hence, the result is true.

b Expand the LHS and the RHS of the expression to get

$$n^2 + n^2 + 2n + 1 - (n^2 + 4n + 4) = n^2 - 2n - 3$$

Collect like terms on each side, which gives

$$n^2 + n^2 - n^2 + 2n - 4n + 1 - 4 = n^2 - 2n - 3$$
$$n^2 - 2n - 3 = n^2 - 2n - 3$$

That is, both sides are algebraically the same.

c Expand the LHS of the expression to get

$$n^2 + n^2 + 2n + 1 - (n^2 + 4n + 4)$$

Collect like terms, which gives

$$n^2 + n^2 - n^2 + 2n - 4n + 1 - 4 = n^2 - 2n - 3$$

Factorise the collected result

$$n^2 - 2n - 3 = (n - 3)(n + 1)$$

which is the RHS of the original expression.

EXERCISE 27B

1 Speed Cabs charges 45 pence per kilometre for each journey. Evans Taxis has a fixed charge of 90p plus 30p per kilometre.

   a **i** Verify that Speed Cabs is cheaper for a journey of 5 km.

   ii Verify that Evans Taxis is cheaper for a journey of 7 km.

   b Show clearly why both companies charge the same for a journey of 6 km.

   c Show that, if Speed Cabs charges a pence per kilometre, and Evans Taxis has a fixed charge of £b plus a charge of c pence per kilometre, both companies charge the same for a journey of

   $$\frac{100b}{(a - c)} \text{ kilometres}$$

2 You are given that

   $$(a + b)^2 + (a - b)^2 = 2(a^2 + b^2)$$

   i Verify that this result is true for $a = 3$ and $b = 4$.

   ii Show that the LHS is the same as the RHS.

   iii Prove that the LHS can be simplified to the RHS.

3 Prove that $(a + b)^2 - (a - b)^2 = 4ab$.

4 The rule for converting from degrees Fahrenheit to degrees Celsius is to subtract $32°$ and then to multiply by $\frac{5}{9}$.

Prove that the temperature that has the same value in both scales is $-40°$.

5 The sum of the series

$$1 + 2 + 3 + 4 + \ldots + (n - 2) + (n - 1) + n$$

is given by $\frac{1}{2}n(n+1)$.

a Verify that this result is true for $n = 6$.

b Write down a simplified value, in terms of n, for the sum of the two series

$$1 + 2 + \quad 3 + \quad \ldots + (n - 2) + (n - 1) + n$$
$$\text{and} \quad n + (n - 1) + (n - 2) + \ldots + 3 + \quad 2 + \quad 1$$

[**Hint**: Add together the first term in each series, the second term in each series, and so on.]

c Prove that the sum of the first n integers is $\frac{1}{2}n(n + 1)$.

6 The following is a 'think of a number' trick.

- Think of a number.
- Multiply it by 2.
- Add 10.
- Divide the result by 2.
- Subtract the original number.

The result is always 5.

a Verify that the trick works when you pick 7 as the original number.

b Prove why this works.

7 The following process is from the AQA coursework called Round and Round.

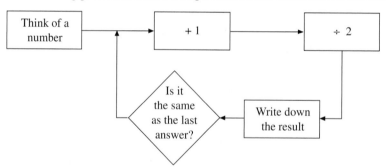

a Start with 6. Verify that the sequence starts, 3.5, 2.25, 1.625, 1.3125, ….

b Start with 1. What happens?

c Prove that 1 gives the same answer each time.

d Prove that the number $\dfrac{a}{b - 1}$ gives the same result for the process below.

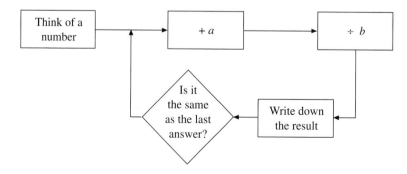

8 You are told that

> When two numbers have a difference of 2, the difference of their squares is twice the sum of the two numbers.

   a Verify that this is true for 5 and 7.

   b Prove that the result is true. [**Hint**: Use a and $a + 2$ as the numbers.]

   c Prove that when two numbers have a difference of n, the difference of their squares is n times the sum of the two numbers.

9 Four consecutive numbers are 4, 5, 6 and 7.

   a Verify that their product plus 1 is a perfect square.

   b Complete the multiplication square and use it to show that

   $$(n^2 - n - 1)^2 = n^4 - 2n^3 - n^2 + 2n + 1$$

	n^2	$-n$	-1
n^2	n^4		$-n^2$
$-n$		n^2	
-1			

   c Let four consecutive numbers be $(n - 2)$, $(n - 1)$, n, $(n + 1)$. Prove that the product of four consecutive numbers plus 1 is a perfect square.

10 Here is another mathematical trick to try on a friend.

   - Think of two single-digit numbers.
   - Multiply one number (your choice) by 2.
   - Add 5 to this answer.
   - Multiply this answer by 5.
   - Add the second number.
   - Subtract 4.
   - Ask your friend to state his or her final answer.
   - Mentally subtract 21 from his or her answer.

   The two digits you get are the two digits your friend first thought of.

   Prove why this works.

EXERCISE 27C

You may not be able algebraically to prove all of these results. Some of them can be disproved by a counter-example. You should first try to verify each result, then attempt to prove it – or at least try to demonstrate that the result is probably true by trying lots of examples.

1 T represents any triangle number. Prove that

   a $8T + 1$ is always a square number

   b $9T + 1$ is always another triangle number.

2 Lewis Carroll, who wrote *Alice in Wonderland*, was also the mathematician Charles Dodgson. In 1890, he suggested the following results.

  a For any pair of numbers, x and y, if $x^2 + y^2$ is even, then $\frac{1}{2}(x^2 + y^2)$ is the sum of two squares.

  b For any pair of numbers, x and y, $2(x^2 + y^2)$ is always the sum of two squares.

  c Any number whose square is the sum of two squares is itself the sum of two squares.

  Can you prove these statements to be true or false?

3 For all values of n, $n^2 - n + 41$ gives a prime number. True or false?

4 For any integer n, $2n$, $n^2 - 1$ and $n^2 + 1$ form three numbers that obey Pythagoras's theorem. Can you prove this?

5 Waring's theorem states that

  Any whole number can be written as the sum of not more than four square numbers.

  For example, $27 = 3^2 + 3^2 + 3^2$ and $23 = 3^2 + 3^2 + 2^2 + 1^2$.

  Is this always true?

6 Take a three-digit multiple of 37, e.g. $7 \times 37 = 259$. Write these digits in a cycle.

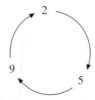

  Take all possible three-digit numbers from the cycle, e.g. 259, 592 and 925.
  Divide each by 37 to find that

  $259 = 7 \times 37$

  $592 = 16 \times 37$

  $925 = 25 \times 37$

  Is this true for all three-digit multiples of 37?
  Is it true for a five-digit multiple of 41?

7 Prove that the sum of the squares of two consecutive integers is an odd number.

8 PQRS is a parallelogram.

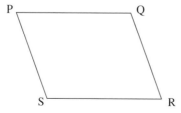

  Prove that triangles PQS and RQS are congruent.

9 OB is a radius of a circle, centre O. C is the point where the perpendicular bisector of OB meets the circumference.

Prove that triangle OBC is equilateral.

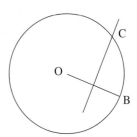

Summary

How well do you grade yourself?

To gain a grade **C**, you need to be able to verify results by substituting numbers into them, and be able to understand the proofs of simple theorems such as an exterior angle of a triangle is the sum of the two opposite interior angles.

To gain a grade **B**, you need to be able to show that an algebraic statement is true, using both sides of the statement to justify your answer.

What you should know after you have worked through Chapter 27

- The meaning of the terms 'verify that', 'show that' and 'prove that'.
- How to prove some standard results in mathematics, such as Pythagoras's theorem

Appendix: Coursework guidance

During your GCSE course, you will need to do at least two coursework tasks. One of the tasks will cover content from Number and Algebra and/or Shape and Space (Ma1 task), and the other will cover content from Handling Data (Ma4 task). The tasks will be assessed and marked by your teacher or by the examination board. Each task will carry 10% of the total marks for the examination. Each task has three strands, with a maximum mark of 8 in each strand. The two tables which follow will give you some idea of what each strand means and what you need to do in order to obtain a particular mark in each strand.

Ma1 task

Strand i: Decisions This is about how you decide to solve a particular problem and then to ask your own questions in order to extend the problem. This corresponds to column **i** in the coursework examples.

Strand ii: Presentation This is about how you present your work mathematically. It involves making tables of results, drawing graphs, using algebraic notation or using computer software. This corresponds to column **ii** in the coursework examples.

Strand iii: Reasons This is about finding solutions to problems and drawing conclusions. You need to find patterns, rules or formulae and to explain how you obtained them. This corresponds to column **iii** in the coursework examples.

Mark	Strand i: Making and monitoring decisions to solve problems	Strand ii: Communicating mathematically	Strand iii: Developing skills of mathematical reasoning
1	Show that you understand the problem by giving examples.	Explain how you intend to solve the problem by giving examples or drawing diagrams.	Find easy examples that fit the problem.
2	Plan a suitable method to help to solve the problem further.	Write out your results clearly and carefully in a list or in a table.	Look for any patterns in your results.
3	Identify the necessary information and check that your results are sensible.	Show your results in clearly labelled tables or with diagrams and symbols.	Explain the pattern, or find a rule for your results.
4	Break down the problem into easier and more manageable stages.	Link your tables, diagrams or graphs with a clear explanation.	Test another example to show that your pattern or rule works.
5	Introduce some questions of your own to extend the problem to give a fuller solution.	Explain how you have improved the presentation of your work to make it clearer.	Explain why your rule or formula works by using simple algebra, graphs or computer software.
6	Develop the problem further by introducing questions that involve different mathematical techniques.	Develop the problem by introducing algebra or other forms of mathematical notation.	Comment constructively on your solution to show that you have fully understood the problem.
7	Analyse a complex problem by considering approaches which use three features or variables.	Show you can present an accurate and convincing mathematical solution.	Give reasons why you are considering using approaches which use three features or variables.
8	Introduce new content or an area of mathematics that is unfamiliar into a complex problem.	Use mathematical techniques efficiently to give a complete and concise solution.	Provide a full proof in your solution to a complex problem.

Ma4 task

Strand i: Planning This is about how you decide to design the problem by specifying your aims and planning an overall strategy. This corresponds to column **i** in Coursework Example 4

Strand ii: Collection and presentation of data This is about the methods you use to collect the data for the problem and how you use statistical calculations, diagrams or computer software to illustrate the data. This corresponds to column **ii** in Coursework Example 4

Strand iii: Interpretation This is about how you interpret and summarise the results based on your statistical calculations and diagrams. This corresponds to column **iii** in Coursework Example 4.

Mark	Strand i: Specify the problem and plan	Strand ii: Collect, process and represent data	Strand iii: Interpret and discuss results
1–2	Clearly state your overall plan and aims. The structure of the report should be related to your aims.	Use simple statistical calculations based on your data. Present your results in a clear and organised way.	Comment on any patterns in the data. Attempt to summarise any results you notice in the data.
3–4	Use simple statistical techniques which are linked to your overall plan and aims. Decide how to collect your data and use an appropriate sample size.	Use relevant statistical calculations for the problem, such as mode, median, mean and range. Present your data in a variety of forms, such as graphs and pie charts, and link them with a relevant explanation.	Comment on patterns and any exceptions you find in the data. Interpret any graphs and calculations used and draw sensible conclusions.
5–6	In more complex problems, write your aims in statistical terms. Consider how to overcome any practical problems when choosing your sample.	Ensure that your data is relevant and reliable, and use more complex statistical calculations, such as the mean for grouped data. Use appropriate diagrams, such as frequency graphs or scatter diagrams, and give clear reasons for your choice of presentation.	Give reasons for any patterns you find in the data, and draw conclusions from your diagrams and calculations. Make relevant comparisons and show that the nature of the sampling method used may have some significance on your results.
7–8	Plan and look for practical problems that you might encounter, and consider how to avoid bias, modifying your method of data collection in light of this. Use other suitable data collection techniques and refine these to enhance the problem.	Ensure that all practical problems are dealt with, and use effectively a wide range of statistical calculations to present a convincing argument. Use a range of diagrams, such as histograms, to help you to summarise the data and show how the variables are related.	All diagrams and calculations should be correctly interpreted in order to appreciate the significance of the results. Explain why any possible bias might affect your conclusions, and make suggestions on how you could make an improvement.

In the coursework examples in this book, you can see how the marks are awarded at each stage of the solution. For example, 5 in column **ii** means that a mark of 5 has been awarded in Strand **ii**. By carefully studying these examples, you should be able to improve your coursework marks.

Answers

Exercise 1A

1 12138   **2** 45612   **3** 29988   **4** 20654   **5** 51732   **6** 25012   **7** 19359   **8** 12673   **9** 19943   **10** 26235
11 31535   **12** 78399   **13** 17238   **14** 43740   **15** 66065   **16** 103320   **17** 140224   **18** 92851   **19** 520585
20 78660

Exercise 1B

1 25   **2** 15   **3** 37   **4** 43   **5** 27   **6** 48   **7** 53   **8** 52   **9** 32   **10** 57   **11** 37 rem 15   **12** 25 rem 5
13 34 rem 11   **14** 54 rem 9   **15** 36 rem 11   **16** 17 rem 4   **17** 23   **18** 61 rem 14   **19** 42   **20** 27 rem 2

Exercise 1C

1 6000   **2** 312   **3** 68   **4** 43 rem 11p   **5** 57.6 km   **6** 60200   **7** 5819 l **8** £428.40   **9** 22 rem 10p   **10** 8
11 £1.75   **12** £190.08   **13 a** 14p   **b** £2.70   **14** £344.50

Exercise 1D

1 a 8   **b** 3   **c** 15   **d** 12   **e** 15   **f** 12   **g** 2, 6   **h** 3, 3, 3   **i** 4, 4, 12   **j** 6, 6, 12   **k** 3, 3, 9   **l** 5, 5, 25
m 2, 2, 14   **n** 4, 4, 24   **o** 5, 5, 40   **2 a** 4, 6, 4, 5, 12   **b** 6, 9, 4, 5, 18   **c** 8, 12, 12, 15, 24   **d** 10, 15, 8, 10, 30
e 14, 21, 12, 15, 42   **3 a** $\frac{5}{6}$ **b** $\frac{3}{5}$ **c** $\frac{1}{8}$ **d** $\frac{2}{3}$ **e** $\frac{7}{10}$ **4 a** $3 \div 8$ **b** $2 \div 7$ **c** $5 \div 12$ **d** $7 \div 8$ **e** $9 \div 11$

Exercise 1E

1 a 2, 3   **b** 4, 5   **c** 5, 7   **d** 18, 6, 6, 2, 3   **e** 25, 5, 3, 5   **f** 30, 3, 3, 7, 10   **2 a** $\frac{2}{3}$ **b** $\frac{1}{3}$ **c** $\frac{2}{3}$ **d** $\frac{3}{4}$ **e** $\frac{1}{3}$ **f** $\frac{1}{2}$
g $\frac{7}{8}$ **h** $\frac{4}{5}$ **i** $\frac{1}{2}$ **j** $\frac{1}{4}$ **k** $\frac{4}{5}$ **l** $\frac{1}{5}$ **m** $\frac{5}{7}$ **n** $\frac{2}{3}$ **o** $\frac{2}{5}$ **p** $\frac{2}{5}$ **q** $\frac{1}{3}$ **r** $\frac{7}{10}$ **s** $\frac{1}{4}$ **t** $\frac{2}{3}$ **u** $\frac{2}{3}$ **v** $\frac{1}{3}$ **w** $\frac{3}{4}$ **x** $\frac{2}{3}$ **y** $\frac{2}{7}$
3 a 4, 6, 8   **b** 4, 30, 40   **c** 21, 70, 70   **d** 24, 25, 32   **4 a** $\frac{7}{8}$ **b** $\frac{3}{5}$ **c** $\frac{3}{4}$ **d** $\frac{7}{10}$ **5 a** >   **b** =   **c** >   **d** <   **e** <
f >   **g** <   **h** >   **i** >   **j** <   **k** =   **l** <   **m** <   **n** =   **o** <   **p** >

Exercise 1F

1 a 18   **b** 10   **c** 18   **d** 28   **e** 15   **f** 18   **g** 48   **h** 45   **2 a** £1800   **b** 128 g   **c** 160 kg   **d** £116   **e** 65 l
f 90 min   **g** 292 d   **h** 21 h   **i** 18 h   **j** 2370 miles   **3 a** $\frac{5}{8}$ of £40   **b** $\frac{3}{4}$ of 280   **c** $\frac{4}{5}$ of 70   **d** $\frac{5}{6}$ of 72   **e** $\frac{2}{5}$ of 95
f $\frac{3}{4}$ of 340   **4** £6080   **5** £3150   **6** 23000   **7** 52 kg   **8 a** 856   **b** 200186   **9** Both the same

Exercise 1G

1 $2\frac{1}{3}$ **2** $2\frac{2}{3}$ **3** $2\frac{1}{4}$ **4** $1\frac{1}{3}$ **5** $2\frac{2}{3}$ **6** $1\frac{1}{5}$ **7** $2\frac{3}{4}$ **8** $3\frac{3}{4}$ **9** $3\frac{1}{3}$ **10** $2\frac{1}{7}$ **11** $2\frac{5}{6}$ **12** $3\frac{3}{5}$ **13** $4\frac{3}{4}$ **14** $3\frac{1}{7}$
15 $1\frac{3}{11}$ **16** $1\frac{1}{11}$ **17** $5\frac{3}{4}$ **18** $2\frac{3}{5}$ **19** $5\frac{3}{5}$ **20** $8\frac{2}{5}$ **21** $2\frac{1}{10}$ **22** $2\frac{1}{2}$ **23** $1\frac{2}{3}$ **24** $3\frac{1}{8}$ **25** $2\frac{3}{10}$ **26** $2\frac{1}{11}$ **27** $7\frac{3}{5}$
28 $5\frac{2}{3}$ **29** 5   **30** 2   **31** $\frac{10}{3}$ **32** $\frac{35}{6}$ **33** $\frac{9}{5}$ **34** $\frac{37}{7}$ **35** $\frac{41}{9}$ **36** $\frac{17}{5}$ **37** $\frac{5}{2}$ **38** $\frac{13}{3}$ **39** $\frac{43}{6}$ **40** $\frac{29}{5}$ **41** $\frac{19}{2}$
42 $\frac{89}{9}$ **43** $\frac{59}{7}$ **44** $\frac{16}{5}$ **45** $\frac{35}{4}$ **46** $\frac{28}{3}$ **47** $\frac{26}{5}$ **48** $\frac{11}{4}$ **49** $\frac{30}{7}$ **50** $\frac{49}{6}$ **51** $\frac{26}{5}$ **52** $\frac{37}{6}$ **53** $\frac{61}{8}$ **54** $\frac{13}{5}$ **55** $\frac{71}{8}$
56 $\frac{73}{9}$ **57** $\frac{61}{8}$ **58** $2\frac{1}{21}$ **59** $\frac{17}{16}$ **60** $\frac{19}{4}$

Exercise 1H

1 a $\frac{8}{15}$ **b** $\frac{7}{12}$ **c** $\frac{3}{10}$ **d** $\frac{11}{12}$ **e** $\frac{7}{8}$ **f** $\frac{1}{2}$ **g** $\frac{1}{6}$ **h** $\frac{1}{20}$ **i** $\frac{1}{10}$ **j** $\frac{1}{8}$ **k** $\frac{1}{12}$ **l** $\frac{1}{3}$ **m** $\frac{1}{6}$ **n** $3\frac{5}{14}$ **o** $10\frac{1}{5}$ **p** $2\frac{1}{6}$
2 a $\frac{7}{9}$ **b** $\frac{5}{8}$ **c** $\frac{3}{8}$ **d** $\frac{1}{15}$ **e** $1\frac{13}{24}$ **f** $\frac{59}{80}$ **g** $\frac{22}{63}$ **h** $\frac{37}{54}$ **i** $3\frac{31}{45}$ **j** $4\frac{47}{60}$ **k** $\frac{41}{72}$ **l** $\frac{29}{48}$ **m** $1\frac{43}{48}$ **n** $1\frac{109}{120}$ **o** $1\frac{23}{30}$ **p** $1\frac{31}{84}$
3 $\frac{1}{20}$ **4** $\frac{1}{6}$ **5** $\frac{13}{15}$ **6** $\frac{1}{3}$ **7** 124   **8** 260   **9** three-quarters of 68 = 51   **10** £51   **11** 18   **12** 7 min

Exercise 1I

1 a $\frac{1}{6}$ **b** $\frac{1}{10}$ **c** $\frac{3}{8}$ **d** $\frac{3}{14}$ **e** $\frac{3}{8}$ **f** $\frac{1}{5}$ **g** $\frac{2}{7}$ **h** $\frac{3}{10}$ **i** $\frac{3}{32}$ **j** $\frac{1}{2}$ **k** $\frac{2}{5}$ **l** $\frac{3}{8}$ **m** $\frac{7}{20}$ **n** $\frac{16}{45}$ **o** $\frac{3}{5}$ **p** $\frac{5}{8}$
2 a $\frac{5}{12}$ **b** $2\frac{1}{12}$ **c** $6\frac{1}{4}$ **d** $2\frac{11}{12}$ **e** $3\frac{9}{10}$ **f** $3\frac{1}{3}$ **g** $12\frac{1}{2}$ **h** 30   **3** 3 km   **4** $\frac{1}{12}$ **5** $\frac{3}{8}$ **6** $\frac{3}{8}$ **7** 21 t   **8** $\frac{2}{5}$ of $6\frac{1}{2} = 2\frac{3}{5}$
9 £5   **10** £30   **11** £10.40

Exercise 1J

1 a $\frac{3}{4}$ **b** $1\frac{1}{2}$ **c** $1\frac{1}{15}$ **d** $1\frac{1}{14}$ **e** 4   **f** 4   **g** 5   **h** $1\frac{5}{9}$ **i** $\frac{4}{9}$ **j** $1\frac{3}{5}$ **2** 18   **3** 40   **4** 15   **5** 16   **6 a** $2\frac{2}{15}$
b 38   **c** $1\frac{7}{8}$ **d** $\frac{9}{32}$ **e** $\frac{1}{16}$ **f** $\frac{256}{625}$ **7 b i** $\frac{3}{5}$ **ii** $\frac{5}{8}$ **iii** $\frac{8}{13}, \frac{13}{21}$ **c** $\frac{21}{34}$

Exercise 1K

1 a −8   **b** −10   **c** −11   **d** −3   **e** 2   **f** −5   **g** 1   **h** 4   **i** 7   **j** −8   **k** −5   **l** −11   **m** 11   **n** 6   **o** 8
p 8   **q** −2   **r** −1   **s** −9   **t** −5   **u** 5   **v** −9   **w** 8   **x** 0   **2 a** 3 °C   **b** 0 °C   **c** −3 °C   **d** −5 °C
e −11 °C   **3 a** 10 °C   **b** 7 °C   **c** 9 °C   **4** −9 −6 −5 −0.5 1 1.8 3 8   **5 a** −3   **b** −4   **c** −2   **d** −7
e −14   **f** −6   **g** −12   **h** −10   **i** 4   **j** −4   **k** 14   **l** 11   **m** −4   **n** −1   **o** −10   **p** −5   **q** −3   **r** 5   **s** −4
t −8   **6 a** 2   **b** −3   **c** −5   **d** −7   **e** −10   **f** −20   **7 a** 2   **b** 4   **c** −1   **d** −5   **e** −11   **f** 8   **8 a** 13   **b** 2
c 5   **d** 4   **e** 11   **f** −2   **9 a** −10   **b** −5   **c** −2   **d** 4   **e** 7   **f** −4   **10** For example: 0 + 1, 2 + (−1), 3 + (−2),
4 + (−3), 5 + (−4), 6 + (−5), 7 + (−6), 8 + (−7), 9 + (−8), 10 + (−9)   **11** For example: 0 − (−1), −1 − (−2), −2 − (−3), −3 − (−4)
−4 − (−5), −5 − (−6), −6 − (−7), −7 − (−8), −8 − (−9), −9 − (−10)

Exercise 1L

1 a −15 **b** −14 **c** −24 **d** 6 **e** 14 **f** 2 **g** −2 **h** −8 **i** −4 **j** 3 **k** −24 **l** −10 **m** −18 **n** 16 **o** 36 **p** −4 **q** −12 **r** −4 **s** 7 **t** 25 **u** 18 **v** −8 **w** −45 **x** 3 **y** −40 **2 a** −9 **b** 16 **c** −3 **d** −32 **e** 18 **f** 18 **g** 6 **h** −4 **i** 20 **j** 16 **k** 8 **l** −48 **m** 13 **n** −13 **o** −8 **p** 0 **q** 16 **r** −42 **s** 6 **t** 1 **u** −14 **v** 6 **w** −4 **x** 7 **y** 0 **3 a** −2 **b** 30 **c** 15 **d** −27 **e** −7 **4 a** 4 **b** −9 **c** −3 **d** 6 **e** −4 **5 a** −9 **b** 3 **c** 1 **6 a** 16 **b** −2 **c** −12 **7 a** 24 **b** 6 **c** −4 **d** −2 **8** For example: $1 \times (-12)$, -1×12, $2 \times (-6)$, $6 \times (-2)$, $3 \times (-4)$, $4 \times (-3)$ **9** For example: $4 \div (-1)$, $8 \div (-2)$, $12 \div (-3)$, $16 \div (-4)$, $20 \div (-5)$, $24 \div (-6)$ **10 a** 21 **b** −4 **c** 2 **d** −16 **e** 2 **f** −5 **g** −35 **h** −17 **i** −12 **j** 6 **k** 45 **l** −2 **m** 0 **n** −1 **o** −7 **p** −36 **q** 9 **r** 32 **s** 0 **t** −65

Exercise 1M

1 a 20 **b** 60 **c** 80 **d** 50 **e** 100 **f** 110 **g** 650 **h** 40 **i** 1000 **j** 1020 **2** Elsecar 750, 849; Hoyland 1150, 1249; Jump 550, 649 **3 a** 75, 84 **b** 115, 124 **c** 185, 194 **4 a** 200 **b** 600 **c** 800 **d** 500 **e** 1000 **f** 100 **g** 600 **h** 400 **i** 1000 **j** 1000 **5 a** 2000 **b** 6000 **c** 8000 **d** 5000 **e** 10000 **f** 1000 **g** 6000 **h** 4000 **i** 9000 **j** 2000 **6 a** 11500, 12499 **b** 16500, 17499 **c** 4500, 5499 **d** 27500, 28499 **e** 18500, 19499 **f** 9500, 10499 **7 a i** 3470 **ii** 3500 **iii** 3000 **b i** 1030 **ii** 1000 **iii** 1000 **c i** 8760 **ii** 8800 **iii** 9000 **d i** 12650 **ii** 12600 **iii** 13000 **e i** 10000 **ii** 10000 **iii** 10000 **f i** 1990 **ii** 2000 **iii** 2000 **g i** 1210 **ii** 1200 **iii** 1000 **h i** 1000 **ii** 1000 **iii** 1000 **i i** 12990 **ii** 13000 **iii** 13000 **j i** 350 **ii** 300 **iii** 0 **8 a** 25 min **b** 55 min **c** 20 min **d** 55 min **e** 10 min **f** 10 min **g** 45 min **h** 35 min **i** 5 min **j** 0 min **9** Microwave needs to be precise. **10 a** 30 min **b** 1 h 30 min **c** 2 h **d** 1 h 30 min **e** 5 h 30 min **f** 4 h **11 a** True **b** False **c** True **d** True **e** True **f** False **12 a** Man Utd v Liverpool **b** Bolton v QPR **c** 17 000, 31 000, 21 000, 34 000, 29 000, 26 000, 25 000, 33 000, 35 000 **d** 17 400, 31 000, 21 000, 34 100, 29 500, 25 600, 25 300, 33 100, 34 900 **e** 251 890 **f** 252 000 **g** 251 000 **h** No

Exercise 1N

1 a 4.8 **b** 3.8 **c** 2.2 **d** 8.3 **e** 3.7 **f** 46.9 **g** 23.9 **h** 9.5 **i** 11.1 **j** 33.5 **k** 7.1 **l** 46.8 **m** 0.1 **n** 0.1 **o** 0.6 **p** 65.0 **q** 213.9 **r** 76.1 **s** 455.2 **t** 51.0 **2 a** 5.78 **b** 2.36 **c** 0.98 **d** 33.09 **e** 6.01 **f** 23.57 **g** 91.79 **h** 8.00 **i** 2.31 **j** 23.92 **k** 6.00 **l** 1.01 **m** 3.51 **n** 96.51 **o** 0.01 **p** 0.07 **q** 7.81 **r** 569.90 **s** 300.00 **t** 0.00 **3 a** 4.6 **b** 0.08 **c** 45.716 **d** 94.85 **e** 602.1 **f** 671.76 **g** 7.1 **h** 6.904 **i** 13.78 **j** 0.1 **k** 4.002 **l** 60.0 **m** 11.99 **n** 899.9959 **o** 0.0 **p** 0.01 **q** 0.0 **r** 78.393 **s** 200.00 **t** 5.1 **u** 0.10

Exercise 1P

1 a 50000 **b** 60000 **c** 30000 **d** 90000 **e** 90000 **f** 50 **g** 90 **h** 30 **i** 100 **j** 200 **k** 0.5 **l** 0.3 **m** 0.006 **n** 0.05 **o** 0.0009 **p** 10 **q** 90 **r** 90 **s** 200 **t** 1000 **2 a** 65, 74 **b** 95, 149 **c** 950, 1499 **3** Elsecar 750, 849; Hoyland 1150, 1249; Barnsley 164 500, 165 499 **4** Huddersfield 10 500, 11 499; Leeds 27 450, 27 549; Middlesborough 15 000, 24 999 **5 a** 56000 **b** 27000 **c** 80000 **d** 31000 **e** 14000 **f** 5900 **g** 1100 **h** 850 **i** 110 **j** 640 **k** 1.7 **l** 4.1 **m** 2.7 **n** 8.0 **o** 42 **p** 0.80 **q** 0.46 **r** 0.066 **s** 1.0 **t** 0.0098 **6 a** 60000 **b** 5300 **c** 89.7 **d** 110 **e** 9 **f** 1.1 **g** 810 **h** 5000 **i** 67 **j** 1 **k** 9 **l** 9.75 **m** 13 **n** 20 **o** 870 **p** 30 **q** 0.074 **r** 0.010 **s** 0.09 **t** 0.0709 **u** 9.8

Exercise 1Q

1 a 35000 **b** 15000 **c** 960 **d** 12000 **e** 1000 **f** 4000 **g** 4 **h** 20 **i** 1200 **j** 50 **k** 20 **l** 6 **m** 5 **n** 4 **o** 20 **p** 30 **2 a** 14 **b** 10 **c** 1.1 **d** 1 **e** 5 **f** $\frac{2}{3}$ **g** 4 **h** $\frac{1}{2}$ **i** $\frac{1}{2}$ **j** 20 **k** 1 **l** 2 **m** 2 **n** 5 **o** 1 **p** 1 **3 a** £3000 **b** £2000 **c** £1500 **d** £700 **4 a** £15000 **b** £18000 **c** £18000 **5** 8 **6** £21000 **7** 8p **8** 25 **9** 30 kg **10 a** 40 **b** 10 **c** £70 **11 a** 10000 **b** 30000 kg (30 t) **12** 1200 **13 a** 30 **b** 120 **c** 1440 **14** 400 **15 a** 3 kg **b** 200 **16** 25 min

Exercise 1R

1 a 1.7 m **b** 6 min **c** 240 g **d** 80 °C **e** 35000 **f** 600 **g** 16 miles **h** 284519 **i** 14 m² **2** 82 °F, 5.3 km, 110 min, 43 000 people, 6.289 s, 67th, 1788, 15, 4.67 s **3** 40 **4** 40 min **5 a** £2500 **b** £600 **c** £90 **6** 60 **7** 70 mph **8** 70 **9** 300 **10** 80000 kg (80 t)

Examination questions (Chapter 1)

1 13 boxes, 32 left over **2** e.g. $\frac{3}{10}, \frac{1}{3}, \frac{5}{12}$ **3 a i** 500 **ii** 8 **b** $40 \times 0.03 = 1.2$ **4** 9*l* **5 a** −5 °C, −1 °C, 2 °C **b** 7 °C **6** 5 **7 a** $\frac{5}{24}$ **b** $\frac{5}{12}$ **c** $\frac{2}{3}$ **8 a** 9 °C **b** −6 °C **9 a** 34650 **b** 34749

Exercise 2A

1 a $\frac{2}{25}$ **b** $\frac{1}{2}$ **c** $\frac{1}{5}$ **d** $\frac{1}{20}$ **e** $\frac{1}{10}$ **f** $\frac{3}{4}$ **g** $\frac{1}{4}$ **h** $\frac{17}{20}$ **i** $\frac{3}{5}$ **j** $\frac{2}{5}$ **k** $\frac{7}{20}$ **l** $\frac{9}{10}$ **m** $\frac{1}{25}$ **n** $\frac{3}{10}$ **o** 1 **2 a** 0.27 **b** 0.85 **c** 0.13 **d** 0.06 **e** 0.08 **f** 0.02 **g** 0.346 **h** 0.125 **i** 0.984 **j** 2.0 **k** 1.25 **l** 1.75 **m** 0.34 **n** 0.268 **o** 1.12 **3** 150 **4** 0 **5** 19 **6 a** 77% **b** 39% **c** 63% **7** 27% **8** 61.5% **9 a** 50% **b** 20% **c** 90% **10 a** $87\frac{1}{2}$%, 75%, $62\frac{1}{2}$%, 50%, 25% **b** $12\frac{1}{2}$%, 25%, $37\frac{1}{2}$%, 50%, 75%

Exercise 2B

1 a £45 **b** £6.30 **c** 128.8 kg **d** 1.125 kg **e** 1.08 h **f** 37.8 cm **g** 12p **h** 2.94 m **i** £7.60 **j** 33.88 min
2 96 **3** £1205 **4** 221 **5** 8520 **6** 197 **7** Each team 22 500, referees association 750, other teams 7500,
FA associates 15 000, celebrities 29 250 **8 a** 72 **b** 48 **c** 49 to 71 **9** 749, 757, 772, 733, 694 **10** Lead 150 g, tin 87.5 g,
bismuth 12.5 g **11 a** £3.25 **b** 2.21 kg **c** £562.80 **d** £6.51 **e** 42.93 m **f** £24 **12** Nitrogen 480 cm^3, oxygen 120
cm^3 **13** 13 **14** £270

Exercise 2C

1 a £62.40 **b** 12.96 kg **c** 472.5 g **d** 599.5 m **e** £38.08 **f** £90 **g** 391 kg **h** 824.1 cm **i** 253.5 g **j** £143.50
2 £29 425 **3** 1 690 200 **4 a** Bob £17 325, Jean £20 475, Anne £18 165, Brian £26 565 **b** No **5** £411.95 **6** 7600
7 575 g **8** 918 **9** 60 **10** TV £287.88, microwave £84.60, desk £135.13, rug £22.91 **11** 35 970

Exercise 2D

1 a £9.40 **b** 23 kg **c** 212.4 g **d** 339.5 m **e** £4.90 **f** 39.6 m **g** 731 m **h** 83.52 g **i** 360 cm **j** 117 min
2 £5525 **3 a** 52.8 kg **b** 66 kg **c** 45.76 kg **4** Mr Speed £56, Mrs Speed £297.50, James £126.50, John £337.50 **5** 448
6 703 **7** £18 975 **8 a** 66.5 mph **b** 73.5 mph **9** Sweatshirt £16.72, tracksuit £22.88 **10** 524.8 units

Exercise 2E

1 a i 10.5 kg **ii** 11.03 kg **iii** 12.16 kg **iv** 14.07 kg **b** 9 **2** 12 years **3 a** £9592.84 **b** 20 years **4 a i** 2550
ii 2168 **iii** 1331 **b** 7 years **5 a** £6800 **b** £3481.60 **c** £1140.85 **6 a i** 1.9 million litres **ii** 1.6 million litres
iii 1.2 million litres **b** 10 August **7 a** £475.24 **b** £564.63 **c** £670.84 **8 a i** 51 980 **ii** 84 752
iii 138 185 **b** 2010 **9 a** 21 yrs **b** 21 yr **10** 30 yr

Exercise 2F

1 a 25% **b** 60.61% **c** 46.35% **d** 12.5% **e** 41.67% **f** 60% **g** 20.83% **h** 10% **i** 1.92% **j** 8.33%
k 45.5% **l** 10.5% **m** 31.25% **n** 40% **o** 2.19% **p** 8.33% **q** 7.2% **r** 0.05% **s** 0.09% **t** 12.5%
2 a 48.3% **b** 64.3% **c** 10.5% **d** 81.8% **e** 26.3% **3** Maths 74.7%, English 76.7%, science 65%, French 53.8%,
geography 84.4%, history 85% **4** 11.1% **5** 4.9% **6 a** Olives 7.8%, currants 3.0%, figs 0.9% **b** Olives 6.5%, currants
2.5%, figs 1.4% **c** Olives −1.3%, currants −0.5%, figs +0.5% **7** 2.2% **8** 33.7% **9** 90.5% **10** Commonwealth 20.9%,
USA 26.5%, France 10.3%, other 42.3%

Exercise 2G

1 a 210 kg **b** £225 **c** 800 g **d** 12 h **e** £460 **f** 250 m **g** 60 cm **h** £3075 **i** £200 **j** 480 g **k** £400
l 920 m **2** 80 **3** T-shirt £8.40, tights £1.20, shorts £5.20, sweater £10.74, trainers £24.80, boots £32.40 **4** £20 **5** £833.33
6 £78 **7** £2450 **8** 1.25 kg **9** 4750 **10** £25.85 **11** 0.25% less

Examination questions (Chapter 2)

1 3.48%. Lost deposit. **2** £360.50 **3 a** £2366 **b** £11.05 **4** 0.59 0.6 65% $\frac{2}{3}$ **5** 30% **6 a** 1728 **b** 2 250 000
7 a £20 905 **b** £5066.25 **8 a** 5% **b** 18 **c** $\frac{1}{6}$ **9 a** £5.53 **b** 7.1% **10 a** 3407 **b** 1999 **11** £1.40
12 £6348 **13 a** £12.42 **b** £14.60

Exercise 3A

1 a 1 : 3 **b** 3 : 4 **c** 2 : 3 **d** 2 : 3 **e** 2 to 5 **f** 2 to 5 **g** 5 to 8 **h** 25 to 6 **i** 3 : 2 **j** 8 : 3 **k** 7 to 3 **l** 5 to 2
m 1 to 6 **n** 3 to 8 **o** 5 to 3 **p** 4 to 5 **2 a** 1 to 3 **b** 3 to 2 **c** 5 to 12 **d** 8 : 1 **e** 17 to 15 **f** 25 to 7 **g** 4 to 1
h 5 to 6 **i** 1 to 24 **j** 48 to 1 **k** 5 : 2 **l** 3 : 14 **m** 2 : 1 **n** 3 : 10 **o** 31 : 200 **3** $\frac{7}{10}$ **4** $\frac{2}{5}$ **5 a** $\frac{2}{9}$ **b** $\frac{1}{3}$
c Twice as many **6 a** $\frac{1}{2}$ **b** $\frac{7}{20}$ **c** $\frac{3}{20}$ **7** James $\frac{10}{23}$, John $\frac{8}{23}$, Joseph $\frac{5}{23}$ **8** Sugar $\frac{5}{22}$, flour $\frac{3}{11}$, margarine $\frac{2}{11}$, fruit $\frac{7}{22}$ **9 a** $\frac{1}{10}$
b 25.5% **10 a** 78.1% **b** 12.5%

Exercise 3B

1 a 160 g, 240 g **b** 80 kg, 200 kg **c** 150, 350 **d** 950 m, 50 m **e** 2 h 55 min, 2 h 5 min **f** £20, £30, £50 **g** £36, £60, £144
h 50 g, 250 g, 300 g **i** £1.40, £2, £1.60 **j** 120 kg, 72 kg, 8 kg **2 a** 160 **b** 37.5% **3 a** 28.6% **b** 250 kg **4 a** 21
b 94.1% **5 a** Miss Mott : No, Mrs Wright : Yes, Mr Brennan : No, Ms Smith : No, Mr Kaye : Yes
b Waist 26 hips 30; waist 31, hips 38; waist 33, hips 37 **6 a** 1 to 400 000 **b** 1 to 125 000 **c** 1 to 250 000 **d** 1 to 25 000
e 1 to 20 000 **f** 1 to 40 000 **g** 1 to 62 500 **h** 1 to 10 000 **i** 1 to 60 000 **7 a** 1 to 1 000 000 **b** 47 km **c** 8 mm
8 a 1 to 250 000 **b** 2 km **c** 4.8 cm **9 a** 1 to 20 000 **b** 0.54 km **c** 40 cm **10 a** 1 : 1.6 **b** 1 : 3.25
c 1 : 1.125 **d** 1 : 1.44 **e** 1 : 5.4 **f** 1 : 1.5 **g** 1 : 4.8 **h** 1 : 42

Exercise 3C

1 a 3 : 2 **b** 32 **c** 80 **2 a** 160 **b** 48 **3** Lemonade 20 l, ginger 0.5 l **4 a** 13.9% **b** 75 **5 a** 11 **b** 32%
6 Kevin £2040, John £2720 **7** 5.5 l **8** 1 kg **9** 10 125 **10 a** 14 min **b** 75 min **c** 60%

Exercise 3D

1 18 mph **2** 280 miles **3** 52.5 mph **4** 1.19 pm **5** 4 min 10 s **6 a** 75 mph **b** 6 h 30 min **c** 175 miles **d** 240 km
e 63.5 km/h **f** 325 km **g** 4 h 18 min **7 a** 170 km **b** 48.6 km/h **8 a** About 36 min **b** About 6 mph **9 a** 10 m/s
b $3\frac{1}{3}$ m/s **c** $16\frac{2}{3}$ m/s **d** $41\frac{2}{3}$ m/s **e** $20\frac{5}{6}$ m/s **10 a** 90 km/h **b** 43.2 km/h **c** 14.4 km/h **d** 108 km/h **e** 1.8 km/h
11 a 64.8 km/h **b** 27.8 s **c** About 8.07 **12 a** $6\frac{2}{3}$ m/s **b** 66 km **c** 5 min **d** $133\frac{1}{3}$ m

Exercise 3E

1 0.75 g/cm³ **2** $8\frac{1}{3}$ g/cm³ **3** 32 g **4** 120 cm³ **5** 156.8 g **6** 3200 cm³ **7** 2.72 g/cm³ **8** 36 800 kg (36.8 t)
9 1.79 g/cm³ **10** 1.6 g/cm³

Examination questions (Chapter 3)

1 13 790 kg (13.79 t) **2** 9, 3, $1\frac{1}{2}$, 225, 15 **3** 30 cm **4** £396, £324, £252 **5** Anne £250, Bill £150 **6 a** 5 km **b** 30
km/h **7** 42 mph **8 a** £735 **b** £196 **9 a** 70 mph **b** 89.6 mph **10** 211 s **11 a** Ruth £100, Ben £80 **b** 60%

Exercise 4A

1 a 17.6 cm, 17.4 cm² **b** 23.2 cm, 30.75 cm² **c** 152 mm, 1083 mm² **d** 48.4 cm, 91.65 cm² **2 a** 34 cm, 52 cm²
b 10 cm, 50 cm² **c** 8 cm, 48 cm² **d** 7 cm, 22 cm² **e** 6 cm, 22 cm² **f** 2.1 cm, 6.3 cm² **g** 5.3 cm, 18.6 cm² **3 a** 71 cm,
166.5 cm² **b** 57 cm, 130.34 cm² **c** 62 cm, 135.7 cm³ **4 b** 100 **c** 500 **5 b** 10000 **c** 60000 **d** 1 000 000
6 a 400 mm² **b** 80 000 cm² **c** 3 000 000 m² **7 a** 390 m **b** 6750 m² **8 a** 920 m **b** 1 h 52 min **9** £839.40
10 40 cm **11 a** 20 min **b** 4.2 kg **12 a** 40.32 m² **b** 252 **13** close to 500 cm² **14** 24 m² **15 a** 26 packs **b** 129
c 117 whole tiles, 9 tiles each cut to 30 cm × 50 cm, 13 tiles each cut to 20 cm × 50 cm, 1 tile cut to 20 cm × 30 cm (Answer not unique)

Exercise 4B

1 a 15.7 cm **b** 25.8 cm **c** 25.1 cm **d** 36.4 cm **e** 37.7 m **f** 56.5 m **g** 4.1 cm **h** 23.2 m **i** 11.9 cm **j** 14.5 mm
k 18.2 m **l** 5.0 cm **2 a** 188.5 cm **b** 26 526 **3** 8.8 m **4 a i** 1.5 mm **ii** 8.8 cm **iii** 211 cm **b i** 4.7 mm
ii 79.2 cm **iii** 0.08 mm **5 a** 201 m, 207 m, 214 m, 220 m, 226 m **b** 88.9% **6 a** 440 cm **b** 5 **7 a** 9.42 cm
b 15.4 cm **8** 38.6 cm **9** 36.0 cm **10** 181 436 **11 a** Sue 62.8 cm, Julie 69.1 cm, Dave 75.4 cm, Brian 81.7 cm
b The difference between the distances round each waist of two people is 2π times the difference between their radii **c** 6.28 m
12 a 3770 cm **b** 2653

Exercise 4C

1 a 6 cm², 12 cm **b** 120 cm², 60 cm **c** 24 cm², 24 cm **d** 30 cm², 30 cm **2 a** 21 cm² **b** 55 cm² **c** 155 cm²
3 146.5 m² **4 a** 1875 cm² **b** 300 cm² **5** 40 cm² **6** 8.64 cm² **7 a** 64 cm² **b** 49 cm² **c** 36 cm²
8 Triangle *c*, 75 cm²

Exercise 4D

1 16 cm **2 a** 28 cm² **b** 8 cm **c** 4 cm **d** 3 cm **e** 6.6 cm **f** 45.5 cm² **3 a** 40 cm² **b** 65 cm² **c** 80 cm² **4 a**
65 cm² **b** 50 m² **5** First triangle: base 10 cm, vert ht 10 cm. Second triangle : base 20 cm, vert ht 5 cm
6 a 133.5 cm² **b** 14.4% **7 a** 24 cm, 23.85 cm² **b** 31 m, 38.35 m² **c** 32 cm, 45 cm² **8 a** 74 cm² **b** 63.75 m²

Exercise 4E

1 a 30 cm² **b** 77 cm² **c** 24 cm² **d** 42 cm² **e** 40 m² **f** 6 cm **g** 3 cm **h** 10 cm **i** 3 cm **j** 2.5 cm **k** 12 cm
2 a 27.5 cm, 36.25 cm² **b** 33.4 cm, 61.2 cm² **c** 38.5 m, 86.4 m² **3 a** 57 m² **b** 702.5 cm² **c** 84 m² **4 a** 47 m²
b 51 m² **c** 86 m² **5** Any pair of lengths that add up to 10 cm. For example: 1 cm, 9 cm; 2 cm, 8 cm; 3 cm, 7 cm; 4 cm, 6 cm;
4.5 cm, 5.5 cm **6** Shape *c*, 25.5 cm² **7** Shape *a*, 28 cm² **8** 80.2% **9** 1 100 000 km² **10 a** 30 m, 48 m²
b 52 cm, 150 cm²

Exercise 4F

1 a 5 cm, 10 cm, 31.4 cm, 78.5 cm² **b** 4.5 cm, 9 cm, 28.3 cm, 63.6 cm² **c** 4 cm, 8 cm, 25.1 cm, 50.3 cm² **d** 3.50 cm, 7.00 cm,
22 cm, 38.5 cm² **e** 2.9 m, 5.8 m, 18.2 m, 26.4 m² **f** 17.5 m, 35.0 m, 110 m, 963 m² **g** 3.8 m, 7.6 m, 23.9 m, 45.4 m²
h 19.3 m, 38.5 m, 121 m, 1170 m² **i** 0.08 mm, 0.16 mm, 0.503 mm, 0.0201 mm² **2 a** 201.1 cm² **b** 63.6 m² **c** 530.9 cm²
d 0.8 m² **e** 380.1 m² **f** 3525.7 m² **3** 1p : 3.1 cm², 2p : 5.3 cm², 5p : 2.3 cm², 10p : 4.5 cm **4 a** 56.5 cm² **b** 19.6 cm²
c 115.5 cm² **5 a** 49.1 m² **b** 54.9 cm² **c** 16.8 cm² **6** 201 m² **7 a** 50.3 m² **b** 44.0 cm² **c** 28.3 cm² **8 a** 15
b 33.7% **9** 158 **10 a** 31.4 cm **b** 58.9 cm²

Exercise 4G

1 a 4π **b** 20π **c** 15π **d** 4π **2 a** 16π **b** 25π **c** 9π **d** 81π **3** $\frac{50}{\pi}$ **4** $\frac{10}{\sqrt\pi}$ **5** 2, 2π, π; $\frac{1}{2}$, π, $\frac{\pi}{4}$; 100, 200π,
10000π; 100, 100π, 2500π; $\frac{5}{\pi}$, $\frac{10}{\pi}$, $\frac{25}{\pi}$; $\frac{6}{\sqrt\pi}$, $\frac{12}{\sqrt\pi}$, $12\sqrt\pi$ **6 a** 12.5π **b** 16π **c** $\frac{363\pi}{4}$ **7** $16\pi + 80$ **b** $50\pi + 80$ **c** 21π **8** $\frac{25}{\pi}$
9 $16\sqrt\pi$ **10 a** $\frac{5}{\sqrt\pi}$ **b** $\frac{7}{\sqrt\pi}$ **c** $\frac{20}{\sqrt\pi}$

Examination questions (Chapter 4)

1 $37\,\text{m}^2$ **2** $214\,\text{cm}$ (3 sf) **3** $201\,\text{cm}^2$ (3 sf) **4** $2.58\,\text{m}^2$ **5 a** $188\,\text{cm}$ (3 sf) **b** 3 **6** $34.2\,\text{cm}^2$ **7** $30.9\,\text{cm}^2$ **8 a** $400\,\text{m}$
b $10\,100\,\text{m}^2$ **9 a** 16π **b i** $32\,\text{cm}^2$ **ii** $48\pi - 8$

Exercise 5A

1 $108\,\text{cm}^3$, $84\,\text{cm}^3$, $165\,\text{cm}^3$ **2 a** $180\,\text{cm}^3$ **b** $5\,\text{cm}$ **c** $6\,\text{cm}$ **d** $10\,\text{cm}$ **e** $81\,\text{cm}^3$ **3 a** $72\,\text{cm}^3$ **b** $162\,\text{cm}^3$
c $1200\,\text{cm}^3$ **4 a** $108\,\text{cm}^2$ **b** $225\,\text{cm}^2$ **c** $700\,\text{cm}^2$ **5 a** $160\,\text{cm}^3$ **b** $480\,\text{cm}^3$ **c** $150\,\text{cm}^3$ **6 a i** $64\,\text{cm}^3$
ii $343\,\text{cm}^3$ **iii** $1000\,\text{cm}^3$ **iv** $2.74\,\text{m}^3$ **v** $176\,\text{m}^3$ **b i** $96\,\text{cm}^3$ **ii** $294\,\text{cm}^2$ **iii** $600\,\text{cm}^2$ **iv** $11.8\,\text{m}^2$ **v** $188\,\text{m}^2$
7 $10\,000$ **8** 100 **9** $1\,000\,000$ **10** 86 **11** $148\,\text{cm}^3$, $468\,\text{cm}^3$, $260\,\text{cm}^3$ **12** $16.8\,\text{g}$ **13** $972\,\text{g}$ **14** $0.9\,\text{g/cm}^3$
15 $8294\,\text{kg}$ (8.3 t) **16** $1.02\,\text{g/cm}^3$ **17** $4.8\,\text{m}$ **18** $159\,\text{cm}$ **19** $48\,\text{m}^2$ **20** $62.5\,\text{kg}$ **21 a** $3\,\text{cm}$ **b** $5\,\text{m}$ **c** $2\,\text{mm}$
d $1.13\,\text{m}$ (3 sf)

Exercise 5B

1 a $251\,\text{cm}^3$ **b** $445\,\text{cm}^3$ **c** $2150\,\text{cm}^3$ **d** $24.9\,\text{m}^3$ **2 a** $226\,\text{cm}^3$ **b** $14.9\,\text{cm}^3$ **c** $346\,\text{cm}^3$ **d** $1060\,\text{cm}^3$ **3** £80
4 $1228\,\text{kg}$ **5** $3.02\,\text{cm}$ **6** $3.99\,\text{cm}$ **7** $332\,l$ **8** $1.71\,\text{g/cm}^3$ **9 a** $3691\,\text{cm}^3$ **b** $29.2\,\text{kg}$ **10** $0.461\,\text{mm}$ **11** $7.78\,\text{g/cm}^3$
12 $270\,\text{km}$ **13** $340\,\text{km}$ **14 i** $396\pi\,\text{cm}^3$ **ii** $300\pi\,\text{cm}^3$

Exercise 5C

1 i a **b** **c** **d** **e** **f**

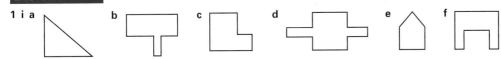

ii a $21\,\text{cm}^2$ **b** $48\,\text{cm}^2$ **c** $36\,\text{m}^2$ **d** $108\,\text{m}^2$ **e** $25\,\text{m}^2$ **f** $111\,\text{m}^2$ **iii a** $63\,\text{cm}^2$ **b** $432\,\text{cm}^3$ **c** $324\,\text{m}^3$ **d** $432\,\text{m}^3$
e $225\,\text{m}^3$ **f** $1332\,\text{m}^3$ **2** $525\,\text{m}^3$ **3** $146\,\text{cm}^3$ **4 a** $21\,\text{cm}^3$, $210\,\text{cm}^3$ **b** $54\,\text{cm}^2$, $270\,\text{cm}^2$ **5** $7.65\,\text{m}^3$ **6** $19\,600\,\text{m}^3$
7 $327\,l$ **8** $1.024\,\text{t}$ **9** Solid b heaviest ($2880\,\text{g}$), solid a lightest ($2851\,\text{g}$) **10** $905\,\text{g}$ **11** $2450\pi\,\text{cm}^3$

Examination questions (Chapter 5)

1 a $300\,\text{cm}^3$ **b** $13.0\,\text{cm}^3$ **2 a** $9.8\,\text{m}^3$ **b** $6860\,\text{kg}$ **3 a** $27\,\text{cm}$ **b** $64\,800\,\text{cm}^3$ **c** $64.8\,l$ **4 a** $5\,l$ **b** $26.1\,l$
5 a $38.5\,\text{cm}^2$ **b** $323\,\text{cm}^3$ **7** $12.1\,\text{cm}$ **8**

3 cm
4 cm
4 cm

Exercise 6A

1 a $x + 2$ **b** $x - 6$ **c** $x + k$ **d** $x - t$ **e** $3 + x$ **f** $m + d$ **g** $b - y$ **h** $p + t + w$ **i** $8x$ **j** hj **k** $\dfrac{x}{4}$ **l** $\dfrac{2}{x}$ **m** $\dfrac{y}{t}$
n wt **o** a^2 **p** g^2 **2 a** $10x + 2y$ **b** $7x + y$ **c** $6x + y$ **3 a** $5a$ **b** $4b$ **c** $6c$ **d** $5d$ **e** $9e$
f $6f$ **g** $3g$ **h** h **i** $4i$ **j** $4j$ **k** $7k$ **l** $5l$ **m** $2m$ **n** 0 **o** $34x$ **p** $18p$ **q** $3q$ **r** 0 **s** $3s$ **t** $15t$ **u** $3u$
v $-v$ **w** $-w$ **x** $6x$ **y** $5y$ **z** 0 **4 a** $7x$ **b** $6y$ **c** $3t$ **d** $2m$ **e** $8k$ **f** $-2x$ **g** $-3t$ **h** $-5x$ **i** $-5k$ **j** $4x$
k $9a$ **l** $5t$ **m** $2m$ **n** 0 **o** f **5 a** $5x + 9y$ **b** $2m + 5p$ **c** $7x + 5$ **d** $5x + 6$ **e** $5p$ **f** $5x + 6$ **g** $4p - 6$
h $6x + 2y$ **i** $5p + t + 5$ **j** $8w - 5k$ **k** $3 - 2x$ **l** 5 **m** c **n** $8k - 6y + 10$ **6 a** $3a + 2b$ **b** $2b + 3c$ **c** $2c + 3d$
d $5d + 2e$ **e** $5e + 7f$ **f** $f + 3g + 4h$ **g** $g + 2h$ **h** $h + j$ **i** $2i + 3k$ **j** $3j + 7k$ **k** $2k + 9p$ **l** $3k + 2m + 5p$
m $7m - 7n$ **n** $6n - 3p$ **o** $20x + 4y$ **p** $17p + 9q$ **q** $16q - 6r$ **r** 0 **s** $7s - 4t$ **t** $10t + 5s$ **u** $6a - 3v$ **v** $2v$
w $2w - 3y$ **x** $11x - 5y$ **y** $-y - 2z$ **z** $-z - x$ **7 a** $8x + 6$ **b** $3x + 16$ **c** $2x + 2y + 8$ **8 a** $2f + 6$ **b** $3k - 12$
c $4t + 4$ **d** $6d + 9$ **e** $12t - 8$ **f** $10m + 6$ **g** $20 + 8w$ **h** $6 - 8x$ **i** $12 + 15p$ **j** $10t + 15w$ **k** $12m - 8d$ **l** $6x + 15y$
m $8f + 6$ **n** $40 - 10t$ **o** $12g + 6t$ **9 a** 75 pence **b** $15x$ pence **c** $4A$ pence **d** Ay pence **10** $£A - £B$ **11** $£\tfrac{1}{5}A$
12 $72 + x$, $T + x$ **13 a** $\tfrac{1}{2}T$ yr **b** $\tfrac{1}{2}T + 4$ yr **c** $T - x$ yr **14 a** £t **b** £$(4t + 3)$ **15 a** $8x$ **b** $12m$ **c** $18t$

Exercise 6B

1 i 8 **ii** 17 **iii** 32 **2 i** 3 **ii** 11 **iii** 43 **3 i** 9 **ii** 15 **iii** 29 **4 i** 9 **ii** 5 **iii** -1 **5 i** 13 **ii** 33
iii 78 **6 i** 10 **ii** 13 **iii** 58 **7 i** 4 **ii** 7.2 **iii** 26.4 **8 i** 6.5 **ii** 0.5 **iii** -2.5 **9 i** 1 **ii** -3 **iii** 6
10 i -7 **ii** -10 **iii** 6.5 **11 i** 0 **ii** -12 **iii** 18 **12 i** 12 **ii** 14 **iii** 4.4 **13 i** 13 **ii** -3 **iii** 5
14 i 15.4 **ii** -20 **iii** -0.5 **15 i** 13.5 **ii** -16 **iii** $2\tfrac{2}{3}$ **16 i** 5 **ii** 12.6 **iii** $6\tfrac{1}{2}$ **17 i** 2 **ii** 8 **iii** -10
18 i 3 **ii** 2.5 **iii** -5 **19 i** 6 **ii** 3 **iii** -2 **20 i** -4.8 **ii** 48 **iii** 32

Exercise 6C

1 a 2.2 **b** 2.125 **c** 1.3 **2 a** 1.4 **b** 1.4 **c** -0.4 **3 a** 1.8 **b** 3 **c** $1\tfrac{7}{9}$ (Accept 1.78) **4 a** 9 **b** 25
c 1.44 **5 a** 2.375 **b** -19.5 **c** 6.02 **6 a** 13 **b** 74 **c** 17 **7 a** 27 **b** 5 **c** 0 **8 a** 4 **b** -3 **c** 1.5
9 a 75 **b** 8 **c** -6 **10 a** 75 **b** 22.5 **c** -30 **11 a** 9.08 **b** 63.6 **c** 191 **12 a** 6.84 **b** 5 **c** 7.17
13 a 0.889 **b** 1.4 **c** 0.2 **14 a** ±3.32 **b** ±2.24 **c** ±4.06 **15 a** ±7.75 **b** ±8.75 **c** ±7.62

Exercise 6D

1 2 **2** 13 **3** 13 **4** 6 **5** 1 **6** 3 **7** 12 **8** 1 **9** 9 **10** 56 **11** 2 **12** 5 **13** 3 **14** 4 **15** 2.5
16 3.5 **17** 2.5 **18** 4 **19** 4 **20** 4.5 **21** 1.5 **22** 3.5 **23** 1.2 **24** 1.8

Exercise 6E

1 15 **2** 6 **3** 28 **4** 16 **5** 40 **6** 24 **7** 8 **8** 16 **9** 30 **10** 21 **11** 72 **12** 56 **13** 10 **14** 6 **15** 12
16 6 **17** 10.5 **18** 12.5 **19** −0.4 **20** −1.4

Exercise 6F

1 −1 **2** −3 **3** −2 **4** −3 **5** −1 **6** −2 **7** −3 **8** −6 **9** −10 **10** 7 **11** 17 **12** −4 **13** 7 **14** 2.8
15 1.75 **16** 7 **17** 6 **18** 1 **19** 11.5 **20** 0.2

Exercise 6G

1 3 **2** 7 **3** 5 **4** 3 **5** 4 **6** 6 **7** 8 **8** 1 **9** 1.5 **10** 2.5 **11** 0.5 **12** 1.2 **13** 2.4 **14** 4.5 **15** 3.5
16 2 **17** −2 **18** −1 **19** −2 **20** −2 **21** −1 **22** −4 **23** −2 **24** −1.5

Exercise 6H

1 a 2 and 3 **b** 4 and 5 **c** 5 and 6 **d** 7 and 8 **2 a** 3.1 **b** 4.5 **c** 6.3 **d** 7.9 **3 a** 3.42 **b** 4.12 **c** 5.65
d 8.43 **4 a** 3.8 **b** 4.2 **c** 5.6 **5 a** 2 and 3 **b** 3 and 4 **c** 8 and 9 **6 a** 3.1 **b** 3.6 **c** 4.2
7 a 2.7 **b** 3.1 **c** 1.7 **8 a** 4.4 **b** 3.1 **c** 4.2

Exercise 6I

1 7.8 cm × 12.8 cm **2** 19.0 m × 29.0 m **3** 5.68 m × 6.68 cm **4** 10.3 cm × 9.3 cm **5** 7.8 cm × 7.8 cm × 7.8 cm
6 7.1 cm **7** 3.5 cm **8** 1.80 cm **9 a** 2.3 **b** 3.1 **c** 1.4 **10** 2.6

Examination questions (Chapter 6)

1 a $F = 2C + 30$ **b i** 138 **ii** 12 **2** $4(l + b + h)$ **3 a** $x = 8$ **b** $y = 1.5$ **c** $z = 5$ **4** $x = 6$ **5 a i** $8y$ **ii** $6y + 6$
b 3 **c** 6 cm^2 **6 a** $4x + 20$ **b** $9x + 5 = 4x + 20$ **c** 3 kg **7 a i** 3.5 **ii** 6 **iii** 7 **b i** $16q$ **ii** $8n + 4p$
8 a i 24 cm^2 **ii** 35 cm^2 **b** 4.7 cm **9 a** 6.375, 7.296 **b** 1.5, 1.6 **c** 1.6 **10 a** 150 cm **b** 24 cm **c** $f = -6\frac{2}{3}$ cm,
which is impossible because length of George's forearm cannot be negative, i.e. < 0 **11** 2.5 **12 i** 2, 3 **ii** 2.7
13 a 60 in **b** 80 in **c** $\frac{f-32}{0.6}$ **14 a** 51 m/s **b** 7.5 s

Exercise 7A

1 a 40° **b** 30° **c** 35° **d** 43° **e** 100° **f** 125° **g** 340° **h** 225°

Exercise 7B

1 a 50° **b** 145° **c** 30° **d** 5° **2 a** $x = 60°, y = 120°$ **b** $x = 145°, y = 35°$ **c** $x = 101°, y = 79°$ **3 a** $x = 100°$
b $x = 110°$ **c** $x = 30°$ **4 a** $x = 55°$ **b** $x = 45°$ **c** $x = 12.5°$ **5 a** $x = 50°, y = 50°$ **b** $x = 40°, y = 100°$ **c** $x = 20°$,
$y = 80°$ **6 a** $x = 70°$ **b** $x = 110°$ **c** $x = 30°$ **d** $x = 95°$ **7 a** $x = 50°, y = 80°$ **b** $x = 65°, y = 60°$ **c** $x = 78°$,
$y = 102°$ **8 a** $x = 50°, y = 66°$ **b** $x = 25°, y = 45°$ **c** $x = 94°, y = 33°$ **9** 40°, 60°, 80° **10** 50°, 55°, 75°

Exercise 7C

1 a $a = 40°$ **b** $b = 70°, c = 70°$ **c** $d = 75°, e = 105°, f = 105°$ **d** $g = 50°, h = 130°, i = 130°$ **e** $j = 70°, k = 70°, l = 70°$
f $n = 80°, m = 80°$ **2 a** $a = 50°, b = 130°$ **b** $c = 65°, d = 65°, e = 115°, f = 115°$ **c** $g = 65°, h = 115°, i = 65°$ **d** $j = 72°$,
$k = 72°, l = 108°$ **e** $m = 105°, n = 105°, o = 105°, p = 105°$ **f** $q = 125°, r = 125°, s = 125°$ **3** $a + b, a + d, b + c, c + d, e + f,$
$e + h, f + g, h + g, a + h, a + g, b + f, b + h, c + f, c + h, d + e, d + g$ **4** $a = 95°, b = 66°, c = 114°$ **5 a** $x = 30°, y = 120°$
b $x = 25°, y = 105°$ **c** $x = 30°, y = 100°$ **6 a** $x = 50°, y = 110°$ **b** $x = 25°, y = 55°$ **c** $x = 20°, y = 140°$
7 a **b** **c**

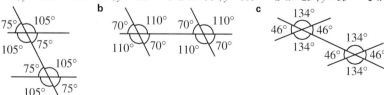

8 a 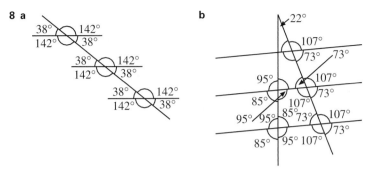 **b**

9 Use alternate angles to see *b*, *a* and *c* are all angles on a straight line, and so equal 180°

1 a 1440° **b** 2340° **c** 17 640° **d** 7740° **2 a** 150° **b** 162° **c** 140° **d** 174° **3 a** 9 **b** 15 **c** 102 **d** 50
4 a 15 **b** 36 **c** 24 **d** 72 **5 a** 12 **b** 9 **c** 20 **d** 40 **6 a** 130 **b** 95 **c** 130 **7 a** 50° **b** 40°
c 59° **8** Hexagon **9** 75°, 55°, 120°, 110° **10 a** Octagon **b** 89° **11 a** Pentagon **b** 54°, 63°, 72°, 81°, 90°

1 $a = b = 70°$, $c = 50°$, $d = 80°$, $e = 55°$, $f = 70°$, $g = h = 57\frac{1}{2}°$ **2 a** 75° **b** 50° **c** 62° **d** 40°
3   **4** 40°, 40°, 100° **5** $a = b = 65°$, $c = d = 115°$, $e = f = 65°$, $g = 80°$, $h = 60°$,
$i = 60°$, $j = 60°$, $k = 20°$ **6 a** 108° **b** 36° **c** 72° **7 a** 120° **b** 90°
c 60° **8 a** 135° **b** 67.5° **c** 22.5°

Triangle 1: 50°, 65°, 65°
Triangle 2: 80°, 50°, 50°

1 $a = 110°$, $b = 55°$, $c = 75°$, $d = 115°$, $e = 87°$, $f = 48°$ **2** $a = c = 105°$, $b = 75°$, $d = f = 70°$, $e = 110°$, $g = i = 63°$, $h = 117°$
3 $a = 135°$, $b = 25°$, $c = d = 145°$, $e = f = 94°$ **4** $a = c = 105°$, $b = 75°$, $d = f = 93°$, $e = 87°$, $g = i = 49°$, $h = 131°$ **5** $a = 58°$,
$b = 47°$, $c = 141°$, $d = 39°$, $e = g = 65°$, $f = 115°$ **6** $a = 40°$, $b = 75°$, $c = 15°$, $d = 75°$, $e = 75°$, $f = 105°$, $g = 105°$, $h = 10°$, $i = 95°$,
$j = 35°$ **7 a** $x = 60°$, $y = 30°$ **b** $x = 7°$, $y = 40°$ **8 a** $x = 25°$, $y = 15°$ **b** $x = 8$, $y = 17°$ **c** $x = 7°$, $y = 31°$ **9 a** $x = 65°$
b $x = 73°$ **c** $x = 55°$ **10 a** $w = 25°$, $x = 15°$, $y = 65°$ **b** $x = 23°$, $y = 88°$ **c** $a = 65°$, $b = 45°$, $c = 135°$, $d = 25°$, $e = 45°$,
$f = 70°$, $g = 135°$, $x = 20°$ **11 a** $x = 50°$: 60°, 70°, 120°, 110° – trapezium **b** $x = 60°$: 50°, 130°, 50°, 130° – parallelogram
c $x = 30°$: 20°, 60°, 140°, 140° – kite **d** $x = 20°$: 90°, 90°, 90°, 90° – square

1 a 45° **b** 135° **2 i** Trapezium **ii** Both base angles are acute **3 a** $a = 56°$, $b = 124°$ **b** $c = 60°$, $d = 120°$
c $e = 102°$ **d** Corresponding angles **4 a** 90° **b i** 72° **ii** 108° **5 a** 80° **b i** Rhombus **ii** All sides equal,
opposite angles equal **6 a** 60° **b** 120° **c** On a straight line (120° + 60° = 180°) **d** 60° **e** Parallel (alternate angles
equal) **7 i** 20° **ii** Alternate angle to 32° **iii** 48° **8 a i** 109° **ii** Angles on a line add up to 180° **b i** 24°
ii It is alternate angle with RSQ

1 a −4 **b** −10 **c** −3 **d** −7 **e** +4 **f** −12 **g** −20 **h** +12 **i** −5 **j** +4 **2 a** 7000 **b** 450 **c** 0.06
d 0.0097 **e** 3.8 **f** 0.29 **g** 0.0 **h** 9.92 **3 a** 6900 **b** 7935 **c** 10 494 **4 a i** 25.1 cm **ii** 50.3 cm²
b i 37.7 cm **ii** 113.1 cm² **5** 49.5 cm², 60 cm², 16 m² **6 a** 160 : 200 **b i** 200 ml **ii** 7.1431 **7** 2.681 kg
8 $-7x + 30y$ **9 a** $x = 3$ **b** $x = 6$ **10** $x = 2.5$ **11** 120 cm³ **12 b** 540° **c i** 10-sided polygon with equal sides and
interior angles **ii** 36° **iii** 144° **13 a** 60% **b** Boys 41.9%, girls 58.1%. Increased because higher proportion boys.
14 a 155° **b** 132° **c** 61°

1 a Congruent **b** Congruent **c** Not congruent **d** Congruent **e** Not congruent **f** Congruent **2 a** Triangle *ii*
b Triangle *iii* **c** Sector *i* **3 a** Yes **b** Yes **c** No **d** No **e** Yes **f** Yes **g** Yes **h** Yes
4 P   Q   PQR to QRS to RSP to SPQ,
                    SXP to PXQ to QXR to RXS
       X
  S   R

5 E   F   EGF to FHE to GEH to HFG,
                    EFX to HGX, EXH to FXG
       X
  H   G

6 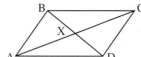 ABC to ACD,
BDC to BDA,
BXA to CXD,
BXC to AXD

7 AXB to AXC

1 a i $\begin{pmatrix} 1 \\ 3 \end{pmatrix}$ **ii** $\begin{pmatrix} 4 \\ 2 \end{pmatrix}$ **iii** $\begin{pmatrix} 2 \\ -1 \end{pmatrix}$ **iv** $\begin{pmatrix} 5 \\ 1 \end{pmatrix}$ **v** $\begin{pmatrix} -1 \\ 6 \end{pmatrix}$ **vi** $\begin{pmatrix} 4 \\ 6 \end{pmatrix}$ **2**

b i $\begin{pmatrix} -1 \\ -3 \end{pmatrix}$ **ii** $\begin{pmatrix} 3 \\ -1 \end{pmatrix}$ **iii** $\begin{pmatrix} 1 \\ -4 \end{pmatrix}$ **iv** $\begin{pmatrix} 4 \\ -2 \end{pmatrix}$ **v** $\begin{pmatrix} -2 \\ 3 \end{pmatrix}$ **vi** $\begin{pmatrix} 3 \\ 3 \end{pmatrix}$

c i $\begin{pmatrix} -4 \\ -2 \end{pmatrix}$ **ii** $\begin{pmatrix} -3 \\ 1 \end{pmatrix}$ **iii** $\begin{pmatrix} -2 \\ -3 \end{pmatrix}$ **iv** $\begin{pmatrix} 1 \\ -1 \end{pmatrix}$ **v** $\begin{pmatrix} -5 \\ 4 \end{pmatrix}$ **vi** $\begin{pmatrix} 0 \\ 4 \end{pmatrix}$

d i $\begin{pmatrix} 3 \\ 2 \end{pmatrix}$ **ii** $\begin{pmatrix} -4 \\ 2 \end{pmatrix}$ **iii** $\begin{pmatrix} 5 \\ -4 \end{pmatrix}$ **iv** $\begin{pmatrix} -2 \\ -7 \end{pmatrix}$ **v** $\begin{pmatrix} 5 \\ 0 \end{pmatrix}$ **vi** $\begin{pmatrix} 1 \\ -5 \end{pmatrix}$

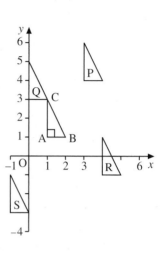

3 a $\begin{pmatrix} -3 \\ -1 \end{pmatrix}$ **b** $\begin{pmatrix} 4 \\ -4 \end{pmatrix}$ **c** $\begin{pmatrix} -5 \\ -2 \end{pmatrix}$ **d** $\begin{pmatrix} 4 \\ 7 \end{pmatrix}$ **e** $\begin{pmatrix} -1 \\ 5 \end{pmatrix}$ **f** $\begin{pmatrix} 1 \\ 6 \end{pmatrix}$ **g** $\begin{pmatrix} -4 \\ 4 \end{pmatrix}$ **h** $\begin{pmatrix} -4 \\ -7 \end{pmatrix}$

4 $10 \times 10 = 100$ (including $\begin{pmatrix} 0 \\ 0 \end{pmatrix}$)

1
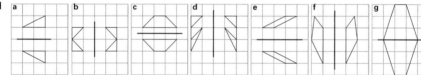

2
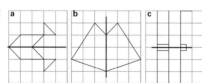

3 a–e 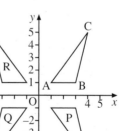 **f** Reflection in y-axis

4 c Always a reflection in y-axis

5
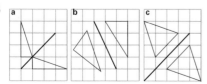

6
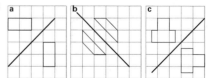

7 a–i

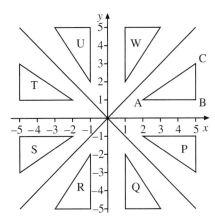

j Reflection in $y = x$ **8 c** Always a reflection in $y = x$
9 c iii x-co-ordinates stay the same, y-co-ordinates change sign
($+$ to $-$, $-$ to $+$)   **iv** Yes   **10 c iii** y-co-ordinates stay the same, x-co-ordinates change sign ($+$ to $-$, $-$ to $+$)   **iv** Yes
11 c iii x and y-co-ordinates change over   **iv** Yes
12 c iii x and y-co-ordinates change over and change sign
iv Yes

Exercise 8D

1 a

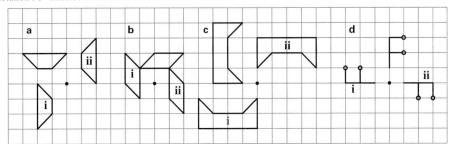

b Rotation 90° anticlockwise *or* rotation 270° clockwise
2 a

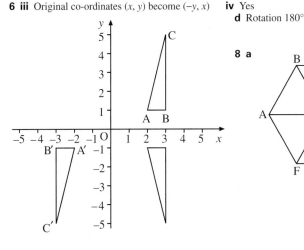

b i Rotation 90° clockwise   **ii** Rotation 270° anticlockwise   **3 a** 90° anticlockwise   **b** 270° anticlockwise   **c** 300° clockwise
d 260° clockwise   **4 c iii** Original co-ordinates (x, y) become $(y, -x)$ **iv** Yes   **5 iii** Original co-ordinates (x, y) become $(-x, -y)$
iv Yes   **6 iii** Original co-ordinates (x, y) become $(-y, x)$ **iv** Yes
7 a–c   **d** Rotation 180°   **e** Yes   **f** Yes

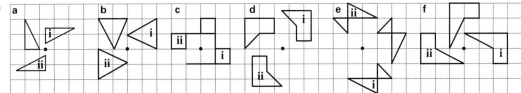

8 a

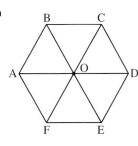

b i Rotation 60° clockwise about O
ii Rotation 120° clockwise about O
iii Rotation 180° about O
iv Rotation 240° clockwise about O.
c i Rotation 60° clockwise about O
ii Rotation 180° about O
9 a i Rotation 72° clockwise about O
ii Rotation 72° clockwise about O   **b i** BOC, COD, DOE, EOA
iii BDE, CAE, DAB, EBC

Exercise 8E

1

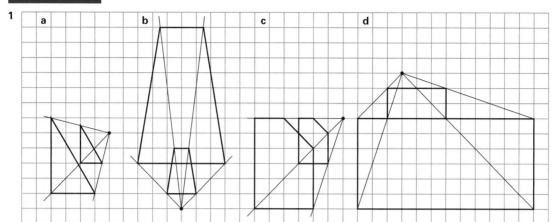

2

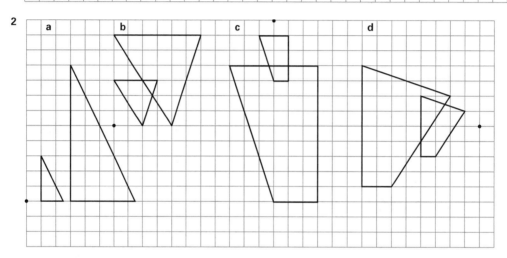

3 d All shapes the same

4

5

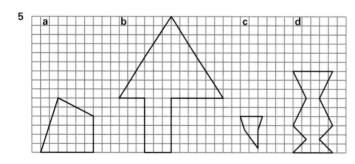

6 a Shape moves ('opposite' to centre of enlargement) **b** Shape and size of enlargement.

Exercise 8F

1 A translation $\begin{pmatrix} 1 \\ -2 \end{pmatrix}$, B reflection in y-axis, C rotation 90° clockwise about (0, 0), D reflection in $x = 3$, E reflection in $y = 4$, F enlargement by scale factor 2, centre (0, 1)   **2 a** T_1 to T_2: rotation 90° clockwise about (0, 0)   **b** T_1 to T_6: rotation 90° anticlockwise about (0, 0)   **c** T_2 to T_3: translation $\begin{pmatrix} 2 \\ 2 \end{pmatrix}$ **d** T_6 to T_2: rotation 180° about (0, 0)   **e** T_6 to T_5: reflection in y-axis

f T_5 to T_4: translation $\begin{pmatrix} 4 \\ 0 \end{pmatrix}$ **3 a–c**   **d** T_d to T: rotation 90° anticlockwise about (0, 0)

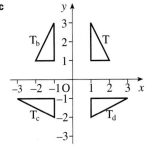

4 (–4, 3)   **5 a** (–5, 2)   **b** Reflection in y-axis   **6** (3, 1)   **7** Reflection in x-axis, translation $\begin{pmatrix} 0 \\ -1 \end{pmatrix}$, rotation 90° clockwise about (0, 0)   **8** Translation $\begin{pmatrix} 0 \\ -8 \end{pmatrix}$, reflection in x-axis, rotation 90° clockwise about (0, 0)

Examination questions (Chapter 8)

1

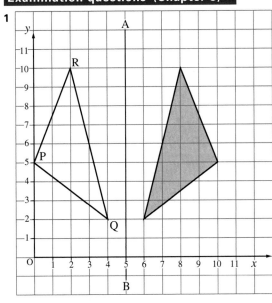

2 a Rotation of 180° about (0, 0) (or an enlargement of scale factor –1, centre of enlargement (0, 0))

b

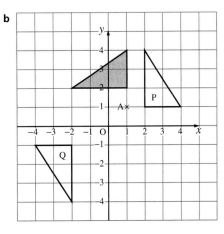

3 a i (6, –5) **ii** $\begin{pmatrix} 4 \\ -6 \end{pmatrix}$ **b i** (11, –1) **ii** $y = 3$ **4 a** (2, 4) **b–c**

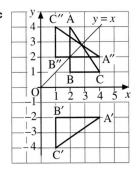

d Reflection in $y = x$

5 a Reflection in $y = -x$

b–c

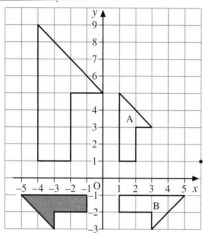

6 a x one of 3 equal angles around a point, totalling 360°

b

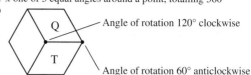

Angle of rotation 120° clockwise

Angle of rotation 60° anticlockwise

7

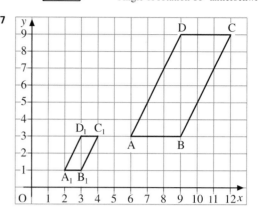

8 a 60° angles in equilateral triangle **b**

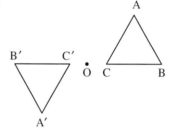

9 a (10, 11) **b** (−3, 4) **c** (8, 6)
10 BDE, CEA, DAB, EBC

Exercise 9A

1 a

Sheffield 205° from Rotherham **b**

Hope 350° from Castleton

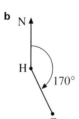

c

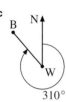

Wadebright 130° from Bude **d**

Manchester 085° from Liverpool

2

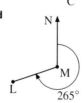

3 305° **4 a** ≈ 120° **b** ≈ 250° **c** ≈ 090° **d** ≈ 270° **e** ≈ 130° **f** ≈ 255° **5 a** West, south, east; east, south, west **b** 040°, 130°, 220°, 310°; 040°, 310°, 220°, 130°

Exercise 9B

1 a BC = 2.9 cm, ∠B = 53°, ∠C = 92° **b** EF = 7.4 cm, ED = 6.9 cm **c** ∠G = 105°, ∠H = 29°, ∠I = 46° **d** ∠J = 48°, ∠L = 32°, JK = 4.3 cm **e** ∠N = 55°, ON = OM = 6.9 cm **f** ∠P = 51°, ∠R = 39°, QP = 5.7 cm **2 b** ∠ABC = 44°, ∠BCA = 79°, ∠CAB = 57° **3 a** 5.9 cm **b** 18.88 cm² **4** 3.9 cm, 10 cm **5** 11 cm² **7** 28.5 m **8** 141 km **9** 14° **10 a** 242 km **b** 102° **11** 5.9 m **12** 45 m above ground **13 a** 20.2 m **b** 20.5 m **14** 13 m

Exercise 9D

4 a i Construct 60° angle and bisect it   **ii** Bisect 30° angle   **iii** Construct 90° angle and bisect it to get 45°. Bisect 45° angle
iv Construct 45° angle on upper arm of 30° angle   **8 b** AC = 5.2 cm, BC = 6.3 cm   **9 b** PR = 5.9 cm, RQ = 4 cm

Examination questions (Chapter 9)

1 43 m   **2**

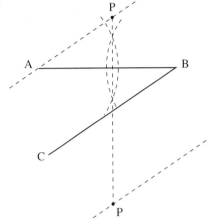

3

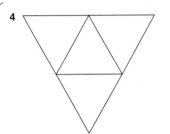

4

5 83 m

Exercise 10A

1 a

b

c

d

e

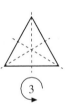

f

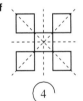

g

h

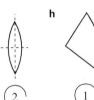

2 a No lines F G J L N P Q R S Z, one line A B C D E K M T U V W Y,
two lines H I X, infinite number O   **b** No rot symm A B C D E F G J K
L M P Q R T U V W Y, rot symm order 2 H I N S X Z, infinite rot symm O
3 See **2a**   **4 a** 3, 3   **b** 6, 6   **c** 4, 4   **d** 1, 0   **e** 8, 8   **f** ∞, ∞
g 1, 0   **5** Line of symmetry is perpendicular bisector of triangle's base
6 Same value

7 a

b

c

d

e

f

8 a Line symmetry   **b** Line symmetry
c Impossible   **d** Impossible   **9 a**

b

10 a i Example: **ii** Impossible   **iii** Impossible   **iv** Impossible   **b i** Example:

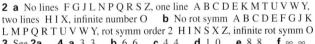

ii Example: **iii** Impossible   **iv** Impossible   **11 b** Order 2   **c** Always 2   **12 a** Yes   **b** One shape is mirror image of other. So all corresponding lengths and angles are the same.   **13** Most have rotational and line symmetry   **14 a** Impossible   **b** Impossible   **c** Impossible   **d** Square

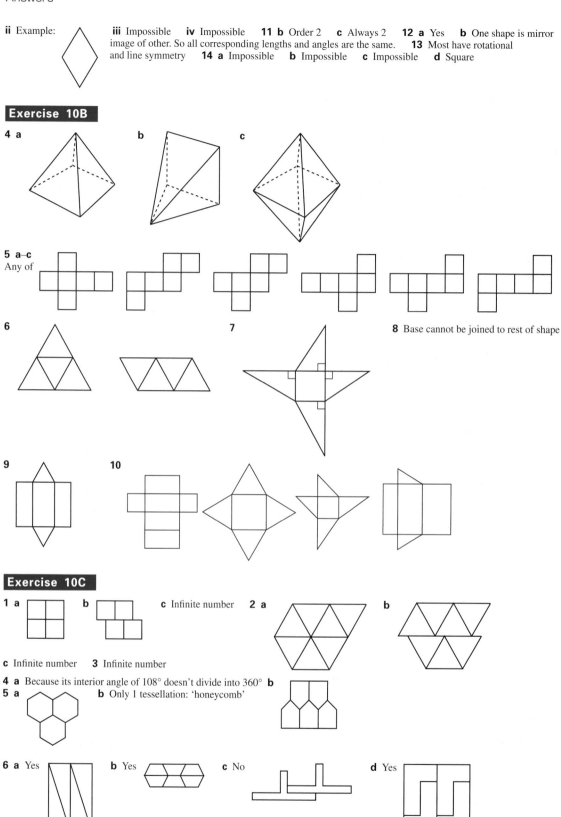

Exercise 10B

4 a   **b**   **c**

5 a–c
Any of

6   **7**   **8** Base cannot be joined to rest of shape

9   **10**

Exercise 10C

1 a   **b**   **c** Infinite number   **2 a**   **b**

c Infinite number   **3** Infinite number

4 a Because its interior angle of 108° doesn't divide into 360°   **b**
5 a   **b** Only 1 tessellation: 'honeycomb'

6 a Yes   **b** Yes   **c** No   **d** Yes

e Yes   **7** No straight sides to give exact fit without gaps

8 Yes **9** 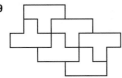 **10** or

---

1 Square-ended cuboid has 5 planes of symm: ACHF, BDEG, TRLJ, ONMP, QSIK; and 5 axes of symm: XV, YW, UZ, SK, QI.
Triangular prism has 4 planes of symm: BJTF, DNKC, AIGE; and 4 axes of symm: RO, SH, PL, QM   **2 a** 2 planes of symm
b 7 planes of symm, 7 axes of symm   **3 a** Infinite number of planes of symm, 1 axis of symm   **b** Infinite number of planes of
symm, 1 axis of symm   **c** Infinite number of planes of symm, infinite number of axes of symm   **4 a**
b None
5 a None   **b** None   **c** None   **d** None   **e** Infinite number   **f** None
6 Planes: BHD, BIA, BJC, DFA, DEC, CGA; axes: AM, CK, BN, DL
7 a Larger cuboid   **b** Cuboid   **c** Longer cylinder   **d** Sphere
8 a 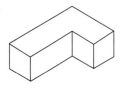   **b** Equilateral triangular prism   **9** Because it tessellates in space

10 a Yes, about the longitudinal vertical plane through its centre   **b** No   **c** No

---

1 a x one of 3 equal angles around a point, totalling 360°   **b i**   **ii** 120°   **c i** 2   **ii** 6   **d** Cube

2 a 6   **b i** ∠AOB = 60°   **ii** Equilateral

3 a   **b** ABC isosceles triangle   **c** ∠CBD = 143°   **4**   **5**

(other cuboids possible)

6 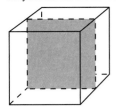   **7** You should have shown at least 5 full shapes to show how the shapes are fitting together.

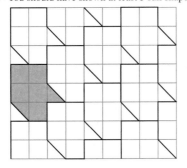

8 Both answers have more than one correct answer,
but your answer should look something like these.

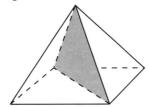

9 a Eight ways.   **b** Pane could be turned round (inner
face becomes outer face) and each face has 4 positions

11 a

b 3   **c** 3   **12 a** or   **b** 4   **c** 1, order 4

1 a 3, 6, 9, 12, 15   **b** 7, 14, 21, 28, 35   **c** 9, 18, 27, 36, 45   **d** 11, 22, 33, 44, 55   **e** 16, 32, 48, 64, 80   **2 a** 12, 24, 36
b 20, 40, 60   **c** 15, 30, 45   **d** 18, 36, 54   **e** 35, 70, 105   **3 a** 1, 2, 5, 10   **b** 1, 2, 3, 6, 9, 18   **c** 1, 5, 25   **d** 1, 2, 3, 5,
6, 10, 15, 30   **e** 1, 2, 3, 4, 6, 8, 12, 24   **f** 1, 2, 4, 8, 16, 32   **g** 1, 17   **h** 1, 2, 4, 5, 8, 10, 20, 40   **i** 1, 3, 5, 9, 15, 45   **j** 1, 2,
4, 8, 16   **4** 17 prime   **5** Square   **6** 2, 3, 5, 7, 11, 13, 17, 19   **7** 1, 4, 9, 16, 25, 36, 49, 64, 81, 100   **8** 1, 3, 6, 10, 15, 21, 28,
36, 45, 55, 66, 78, 91, …   **9** 4 packs of sausages and 5 packs of buns, or any multiple of these   **10** 24s   **11** 30s
12 After 12 min: Fred 3 laps, Debbie 4 laps   **13 a** 12   **b** 9   **c** 6   **d** 13   **e** 15   **f** 14   **g** 16   **h** 10   **i** 18
j 17   **k** 8   **l** 21   **14** $1 + 3 + 5 + 7 + 9 = 25$, $1 + 3 + 5 + 7 + 9 + 11 = 36$, $1 + 3 + 5 + 7 + 9 + 11 + 13 = 49$,
$1 + 3 + 5 + 7 + 9 + 11 + 13 + 15 = 64$

1 a $84 = 2 \times 2 \times 3 \times 7$ **b** $100 = 2 \times 2 \times 5 \times 5$ **c** $180 = 2 \times 2 \times 3 \times 3 \times 5$ **d** $220 = 2 \times 2 \times 5 \times 11$ **e** $280 = 2 \times 2 \times 2 \times 5 \times 7$
f $128 = 2 \times 2 \times 2 \times 2 \times 2 \times 2 \times 2$ **g** $50 = 2 \times 5 \times 5$ **h** $1000 = 2 \times 2 \times 2 \times 5 \times 5 \times 5$ **i** $576 = 2 \times 2 \times 2 \times 2 \times 2 \times 2 \times 3 \times 3$
j $650 = 2 \times 5 \times 5 \times 13$ **2 a** $2^2 \times 3 \times 7$ **b** $2^2 \times 5^2$ **c** $2^2 \times 3^2 \times 5$ **d** $2^2 \times 5 \times 11$ **e** $2^3 \times 5 \times 7$ **f** 2^7 **g** 2×5^2
h $2^3 \times 5^3$ **i** $2^6 \times 3^2$ **j** $2 \times 5^2 \times 13$ **3** $1 \times 23, 2 \times 3, 2^2, 5, 2 \times 3, 7, 2^3, 3^2, 2 \times 5, 11, 2^2 \times 3, 13, 2 \times 7, 3 \times 5, 2^4, 17, 2 \times 3^2, 19, 2^2 \times 5,$
$3 \times 7, 2 \times 11, 23, 2^3 \times 3, 5^2, 2 \times 13, 3^3, 2^2 \times 7, 29, 2 \times 3 \times 5, 31, 2^5, 3 \times 11, 2 \times 17, 5 \times 7, 2^2 \times 3^2, 37, 2 \times 19, 3 \times 13, 2^3 \times 5, 41,$
$2 \times 3 \times 7, 43, 2^2 \times 11, 3^2 \times 5, 2 \times 23, 47, 2^4 \times 3, 7^2, 2 \times 5^2$ **4 a** Double each time   **b** 64, 128   **c** 81, 243   **d** 256, 1024, 4096
e $3, 3^2, 3^3, 3^4, 3^5, 3^6; 4, 4^2, 4^3, 4^4, 4^5$

1 a 2^4 **b** 3^5 **c** 7^2 **d** 5^3 **e** 10^7 **f** 6^4 **g** 4^1 **h** 1^7 **i** 0.5^4 **j** 100^3 **2 a** $3 \times 3 \times 3 \times 3$ **b** $9 \times 9 \times 9$ **c** 6×6
d $10 \times 10 \times 10 \times 10 \times 10$ **e** $2 \times 2 \times 2 \times 2 \times 2 \times 2 \times 2 \times 2 \times 2 \times 2$ **f** 8   **g** $0.1 \times 0.1 \times 0.1$ **h** 2.5×2.5 **i** $0.7 \times 0.7 \times 0.7$
j 1000×1000 **3 a** 16   **b** 243   **c** 49   **d** 125   **e** 10 000 000   **f** 1296   **g** 4   **h** 1   **i** 0.0625   **j** 1 000 000
4 a 81   **b** 729   **c** 36   **d** 100 000   **e** 1024   **f** 8   **g** 0.001   **h** 6.25   **i** 0.343   **j** 1 000 000   **5 a** 1   **b** 4   **c** 1
d 1   **e** 1   **6** Always 1   **7** 10^6 **8** 10^6 **9 a** 1   **b** -1 **c** 1   **d** 1   **e** -1 **10 a** 1   **b** -1 **c** -1 **d** 1   **e** 1
(even powers give 1, odd powers give -1)   **11** $2^2, 2^3, 2^4, 2^5, 2^6, 2^7, 2^8, 2^9$; 4, 8, 16, 32, 64, 128, 256, 512   **12** $2^0, 2^1$; 1, 2
13 $2^{-2}, 2^{-1}, 2^0, 2^1$; 0.25, 0.5, 1, 2   **14** $10^{-3}, 10^{-2}, 10^{-1}, 10^0, 10^1$; $10^4, 10^5, 10^6, 10^7, 10^8$. 0.001, 0.01, 0.1, 1 10, 10000, 100000,
1 000 000, 10 000 000, 100 000 000. Six. 10^6 Top row: consecutive numbers differ by factor of 10; bottom row: consecutive powers
differ by 1

1 a 5^4 **b** 5^{10} **c** 5^5 **d** 5^3 **e** 5^{15} **f** 5^9 **g** 5^2 **h** 5^3 **i** 5^{-5} **2 a** 6^3 **b** 6^5 **c** 6^1 **d** 6^0 **e** 6^1 **f** 6^{-2}
g 6^6 **h** 6^{-7} **i** 6^2 **3 a** 4^6 **b** 4^{15} **c** 4^6 **d** 4^{-6} **e** 4^6 **f** 4^0 **4 a** a^3 **b** a^5 **c** a^7 **d** a^4 **e** a^2 **f** a^1
5 a $6a^5$ **b** $20a^4$ **c** $8a^3$ **d** $9a^2$ **e** 15   **f** $8a^6$ **g** $-6a^4$ **h** $8a^8$ **i** $-10a^{-3}$ **6 a** $3a$ **b** $4a^3$ **c** $3a^4$ **d** $6a^{-1}$
e $4a^7$ **f** $5a^{-4}$ **7 a** $8a^5b^4$ **b** $10a^3b$ **c** $30a^{-2}b^{-2}$ **d** $2ab^3$ **e** $8a^{-5}b^7$ **8 a** $3a^3b^2$ **b** $3a^2c^4$ **c** $8a^2b^2c^3$

1 a 31   **b** 310   **c** 3100   **d** 31 000   **2 a** 65   **b** 650   **c** 6500   **d** 65 000   **3** Factors of 10 are the same, e.g. $100 = 10^2$
4 a 7.3×10 **b** 7.3×10^2 **c** 7.3×10^3 **d** 7.3×10^5 **5 a** 0.31   **b** 0.031 **c** 0.0031   **d** 0.000 31   **6 a** 0.65
b 0.065   **c** 0.0065   **d** 0.000 65   **7** Factors of 10 are the same, e.g. $1000 = 10^3$ **8 a** $7.3 \div 10$ **b** $7.3 \div 10^2$ **c** $7.3 \div 10^3$
d $7.3 \div 10^5$ **9 a** 250   **b** 34.5   **c** 4670   **d** 346   **e** 207.89   **f** 56 780   **g** 246   **h** 0.76   **i** 76   **j** 89 700   **k** 865
l 10 050   **m** 999 000   **n** 23 456   **o** 98 765.4   **p** 43 230 000   **q** 7867.9   **r** 2036.7   **s** 764.3   **t** 3 457 800   **u** 345.78
v 6000   **w** 56.7   **x** 560 045   **y** 9090.7   **z** 70 086   **10 a** 0.025   **b** 0.345   **c** 0.004 67   **d** 3.46   **e** 0.207 89
f 0.056 78   **g** 0.0246   **h** 0.0076   **i** 0.000 076   **j** 0.000 008 79   **k** 0.000 865   **l** 1.005   **m** 0.000 000 999   **n** 2.3456
o 0.098 765 4   **p** 0.000 4323   **q** 0.786 79   **r** 20.367   **s** 7.643   **t** 0.000 345 78   **u** 0.000 000 034 578   **v** 0.000 000 000 06
w 0.000 000 567   **x** 0.005 560 045   **y** 0.000 090 907   **z** 0.070 086   **11 a** 60 000   **b** 120 000   **c** 10 000   **d** 42 000
e 21 000   **f** 300   **g** 150   **h** 1400   **i** 100 000   **j** 200 000   **k** 28 000   **l** 900   **m** 400   **n** 8000   **o** 160 000
p 4500   **q** 8000   **r** 250 000   **s** 10 000   **t** 600   **u** 3000 **v** 60 000   **w** 4 000 000   **x** 360 000 **y** 48 000 000 000
z 1 200 000 000   **12 a** 5   **b** 50   **c** 25   **d** 30   **e** 7   **f** 300   **g** 6   **h** 30   **i** 4   **j** 5   **k** 2   **l** 100   **m** 40
n 200   **o** 20   **p** 20   **q** 2   **r** 1   **s** 16   **t** 150   **u** 12   **v** 15   **w** 40   **x** 5   **y** 40   **z** 320   **13 a** 230   **b** 57
8 900   **c** 4790   **d** 57 000 000   **e** 216   **f** 10 500   **g** 0.000 32   **h** 9870   **14 a** True   **b** True   **c** True
d Depends on model. Most cannot display this form

Exercise 11F

1 a 0.31 **b** 0.031 **c** 0.0031 **d** 0.00031 **2 a** 0.65 **b** 0.065 **c** 0.0065 **d** 0.00065 **3 a** $9\,999\,999 \times 10^{99}$
b 0.000001×10^{-99} (Depends on number of digits displayed) **4 a** 31 **b** 310 **c** 3100 **d** 31000 **5 a** 65 **b** 650
c 6500 **d** 65000 **6 a** 250 **b** 34.5 **c** 0.00467 **d** 34.6 **e** 0.020789 **f** 5678 **g** 246 **h** 76 **i** 7600
j 897000 **k** 0.00865 **l** 100.5 **m** 0.00000999 **n** 234.56 **o** 9876.54 **p** 4323000 **q** 0.078679 **r** 0.20367
s 76.43 **t** 0.000034578 **u** 345780 **v** 60000000 **w** 0.000567 **x** 56004.5 **y** 90907 **z** 0.0070086
7 a 2.5×10^2 **b** 3.45×10^{-1} **c** 4.67×10^4 **d** 3.4×10^2 **e** 2.078×10^5 **f** 5.678×10^{-4} **g** 2.46×10^3 **h** 7.6×10^{-2}
i 7.6×10^{-4} **j** 8.97×10^{-1} **k** 8.65×10^3 **l** 1.005×10^2 **m** 9.99×10^{-1} **n** 2.3456×10^2 **o** 9.87654×10
p 4.323×10 **q** 7.8679×10^3 **r** 2.0367×10^2 **s** 7.643×10 **t** 3.4578×10 **u** 3.4578×10^{-3} **v** 6×10^{-4}
w 5.67×10^{-3} **x** 5.60045×10 **y** 9.0907×10^{-1} **z** 7.0086×10 **8** $7.2 \times 10, 1.5 \times 10^3, 5.7 \times 10^4$ **9** 2.7797×10^4
10 $2.81581 \times 10^5, 3 \times 10, 1.382101 \times 10^6$ **11** $1.298 \times 10^7, 2.997 \times 10^9, 9.3 \times 10^4$ **12 a** 5.67×10^3 **b** 2.346×10^5
c 6×10^2 **d** 3.46×10^{-1} **e** 7×10^{-4} **f** 5.6×10^2 **g** 6×10^5 **h** 7×10^3 **i** 3.5×10^{-6} **j** 1.6 **k** 1 **l** 1×10^3
m 2.3×10^7 **n** 3×10^{-6} **o** 2.56×10^6 **p** 1.08×10^9 **q** 4.8×10^2 **r** 1.12×10^2 **s** 2.7×10^2 **t** 6×10^{-1}
u 2.8×10^6

Exercise 11G

1 a 2.8×10^{16} **b** 3.5×10^{13} **c** 2.4×10^{14} **d** 1.05×10^{16} **e** 4.5×10^{11}
f 4.2×10^9 **g** 1.5×10^{11} **h** 2.7×10^{31} **i** 1.8×10^2 **j** 4.2×10^5
2 a 3×10^4 **b** 3×10^3 **c** 4×10^4 **d** 1.8×10^{-13} **e** 4×10^6
f 3.5×10^{15} **g** 1.2×10^3 **h** 6×10^6 **i** 5×10^6 **j** 1.4×10^{-1}
3 a 2×10^2 **b** 4×10^2 **c** 9×10^{11} **d** 4×10^{10} **e** 6×10^0 **f** 8×10^2
4 a 1.6×10^{13} **b** 4×10^{-2} **c** 2.08×10^7 **d** 1.92×10^7 **e** 2.5×10^1
5 a 2×10^{-4} **b** 8×10^0 **c** 4.5×10^{-2} **d** -3.5×10^{-2} **e** 1.25×10^{-1}
6 a 4×10^{13} **b** 1.6×10^{-2} **c** 5.08×10^7 **d** 4.92×10^7 **e** 6.25×10^1
7 a 9×10^{-5} **b** 5×10^0 **c** 2.4×10^{-2} **d** -1.6×10^{-2} **e** 2×10^{-1}

Examination questions (Chapter 11)

1 a 540 **b** 50 **2 i** 6561 **ii** 0.04 **3 a i** 1, 4, 9, 16, 25, 36, 49 **ii** 2, 4, 5, 10, 20, 25 **iii** 5, 10, 15, 20, 25, 30, 35, 40, 45
iv 2, 3, 5, 7, 11, 13, 17, 19, 23, 29, 31, 37, 41, 43, 47 **b** 49, 2, 42 **4 a** $\frac{1}{9}$ **b** 2^{-6} **c i** 1.8×10^{10} **ii** 4×10^3
5 a 7.75×10^8 **b** 1833 **6 a i** 3.9×10^5 **ii** 390000 **b i** 6.7×10^{-3} **ii** 0.0067 **7 a i** 7.348×10^8 **ii** 5.7×10^{-4}
b i 2.02122×10^{-6} **ii** 6.295302×10^{-11} **8** 4.23 light years **9 a** 1.6×10^8 **b** 28000

Exercise 12A

1 $x = 4, y = 1$ **2** $x = 1, y = 4$ **3** $x = 3, y = 1$ **4** $x = 5, y = 2$ **5** $x = 7, y = 1$ **6** $x = 5, y = \frac{1}{2}$ **7** $x = 4, y = 2$
8 $x = 2, y = 4$ **9** $x = 3, y = 5$ **10** $x = 2.25, y = 6.5$ **11** $x = 4, y = 3$ **12** $x = 5, y = 3$

Exercise 12B

1 $x = 2, y = 3$ **2** $x = 7, y = 3$ **3** $x = 4, y = 1$ **4** $x = 2, y = 5$ **5** $x = 4, y = 3$ **6** $x = 1, y = 7$ **7** $x = 2, y = 1$
8 $x = 3, y = 5$ **9** $x = 6, y = 3$ **10** $x = 8, y = 2$ **11** $x = 1, y = 5$ **12** $x = 4, y = 3$

Exercise 12C

1 $x = 2, y = 5$ **2** $x = 3, y = 4$ **3** $x = 1, y = 4$ **4** $x = 6, y = 2$ **5** $x = 7, y = 3$ **6** $x = 4, y = 3$ **7** $x = 5, y = 1$
8 $x = 3, y = 8$ **9** $x = 9, y = 1$ **10** $x = 7, y = 3$ **11** $x = 4, y = 2$ **12** $x = 6, y = 5$

Exercise 12D

1 $x = 3, y = -2$ **2** $x = 2, y = \frac{1}{2}$ **3** $x = -\frac{3}{7}, y = 3\frac{2}{7}$ **4** $x = 1.5, y = 4$ **5** $x = 3.5, y = 1.5$ **6** $x = -2, y = -3$ **7** $x = -1, y = 2.5$
8 $x = -3, y = -2$ **9** $x = 2.5, y = -0.5$ **10** $x = -1.5, y = 4.5$ **11** $x = -2.5, y = -3.5$ **12** $x = -0.5, y = -6.5$

Exercise 12E

1 Amul £7.20, Kim £3.50 **2** £1.49 **3** £2.25 **4** 84p **5** 10.3 kg **6** £4.40 **7** £62.00 **8** £1.21 **9** £195
10 2 h 10 min

Exercise 12F

1 a $x < 3$ **b** $t > 8$ **c** $p \geq 10$ **d** $x < 2$ **e** $y \leq 3$ **f** $t > 5$ **g** $x < 6$ **h** $y \leq 15$ **i** $t \geq 18$ **j** $x < 7$ **k** $x \leq 3$ **l** $t \geq 5$
m $x \geq -6$ **n** $t \leq \frac{8}{3}$ **o** $y \leq 4$ **p** $x \geq -2$ **q** $w \leq 5.5$ **r** $x \leq \frac{14}{5}$ **2 a** $x \leq 8, x = 1, 2, 3, 4, 5, 6, 7, 8$ **b** $x < 7, x = 2, 4, 6$
c $x < \frac{47}{3}, x = 1, 4, 9$ **d** $x < \frac{23}{5}, x = 1, 3$ **e** $x < 9, x = 2, 3, 5, 7$ **3 a** $x \leq 2$ **b** $x > 38$ **c** $x < 6\frac{1}{2}$ **d** $x \geq 7$ **e** $t > 10$
f $y \leq \frac{7}{5}$ **g** $t < \frac{43}{4}$ **h** $x > 17$ **4 a** $3 < x < 6$ **b** $2 < x < 5$ **c** $-1 < x \leq 3$ **d** $1 \leq x < 4$ **e** $2 \leq x < 4$ **f** $0 \leq x \leq 5$
g $2 \leq x \leq 4$ **h** $1 \leq x < 6$

Exercise 12G

1 a $x > 1$ **b** $x \leq 3$ **c** $x < 2$ **d** $x \geq -1$ **e** $x \leq -1$ **f** $x < 1$ **g** $x > -1$ **h** $x \geq 1$ **I** $x \leq 2$

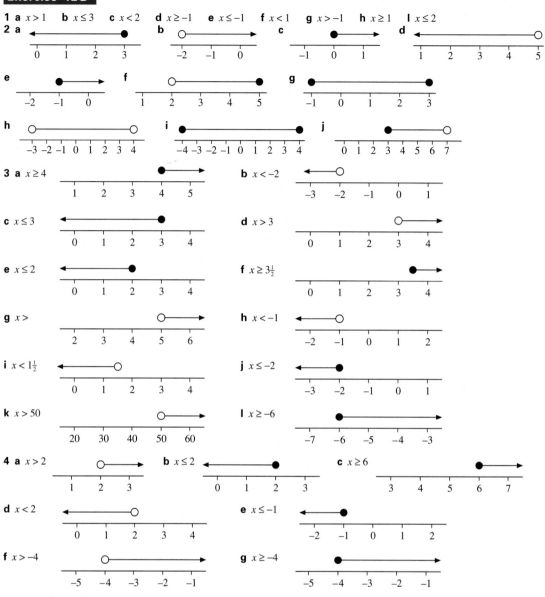

3 a $x \geq 4$ **b** $x < -2$

c $x \leq 3$ **d** $x > 3$

e $x \leq 2$ **f** $x \geq 3\frac{1}{2}$

g $x >$ **h** $x < -1$

i $x < 1\frac{1}{2}$ **j** $x \leq -2$

k $x > 50$ **l** $x \geq -6$

4 a $x > 2$ **b** $x \leq 2$ **c** $x \geq 6$

d $x < 2$ **e** $x \leq -1$

f $x > -4$ **g** $x \geq -4$

h $x \leq -5$

Exercise 12H

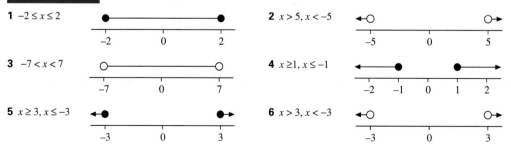

1 $-2 \leq x \leq 2$ **2** $x > 5, x < -5$

3 $-7 < x < 7$ **4** $x \geq 1, x \leq -1$

5 $x \geq 3, x \leq -3$ **6** $x > 3, x < -3$

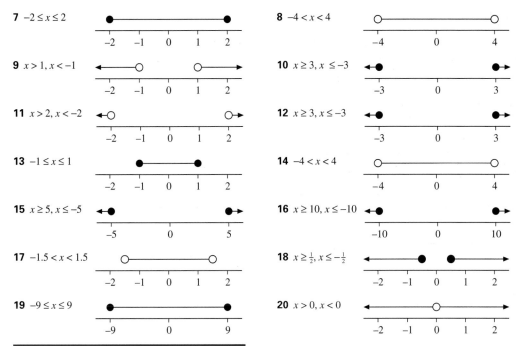

7 $-2 \le x \le 2$

8 $-4 < x < 4$

9 $x > 1, x < -1$

10 $x \ge 3, x \le -3$

11 $x > 2, x < -2$

12 $x \ge 3, x \le -3$

13 $-1 \le x \le 1$

14 $-4 < x < 4$

15 $x \ge 5, x \le -5$

16 $x \ge 10, x \le -10$

17 $-1.5 < x < 1.5$

18 $x \ge \frac{1}{2}, x \le -\frac{1}{2}$

19 $-9 \le x \le 9$

20 $x > 0, x < 0$

Examination questions (Chapter 12)

1 i $x + y = 40, 2x + 3.5y = 92$ **ii** $x = 32, y = 8$ **2** $x = 3, y = -0.5$ **3** $x = 7, y = 0.5$ **4** $-3 < x < 3$
5 $n < -2$ **6** $x > -3.6$ **7** $a = 1.5, b = 0.5$ **8** $x = 3, y = -2$ **9 a** $x > 2$ **b** $x > 4$ and $x < -4$
10 a $n < 2.5$, 2, greatest

Exercise 13A

1 a i 1   **ii** 2   **iii** 2.2   **iv** 3   **b i** 11   **ii** 10   **iii** 9.6   **iv** 4   **c i** 4   **ii** 9   **iii** 8.6   **iv** 11   **d i** 3   **ii** 4
iii 5   **iv** 9   **e i** 15   **ii** 11   **iii** 12   **iv** 14   **f i** 23   **ii** 25.7   **iii** 25   **iv** 9   **2 a i** 4   **ii** 5.4   **b i** 8   **ii** 6.1
c i 13   **ii** 13.7   **d i** 5   **ii** 6.2   **e i** 4   **ii** 6.2   **f i** 23   **ii** 5.7   **3 a i** 6   **ii** 6   **b i** 4   **ii** 4   **c i** 4   **ii** 5
d i 5   **ii** 4.2   **e i** 4.5   **ii** 4.3   **f i** 3.5   **ii** 4.3   **g i** 6   **ii** 5.8   **h i** 3.5   **ii** 4.4   **4** No, $\bar{x} = 31.5$ **5 a** 29
b 28   **c** 27.1   **d** 14   **6 a** 150   **b** 20   **7 a** £18 000, £24 000, £23 778   **b** 6% rise   **8 a** Median   **b** Mode
c Mean   **9 a i** 6   **ii** 16   **iii** 26   **iv** 56   **v** 96   **b** Units are the same   **c i** 136   **ii** 576   **iii** 435   **iv** 856
10 a i 5.6   **ii** 15.6   **iii** 25.6   **iv** 55.6   **v** 95.6   **c i** 135.6   **ii** 575.6   **iii** 435   **iv** 855.6   **11** 11.6   **12** 42.7 kg

Exercise 13B

1 a i 7   **ii** 6   **iii** 6.4   **b i** 4   **ii** 4   **iii** 3.7   **c i** 8   **ii** 8.5   **iii** 8.2   **d i** 0   **ii** 0   **iii** 0.3   **2 a** 668   **b** 1.9
c 0   **d** 328   **3 a** 2.2, 1.7, 1.3   **b** Better dental care   **4 a** 0   **b** 1.0   **5 a** 7   **b** 6.5   **c** 6.5   **6 a** 1   **b** 1
c 1.0   **7 a** Roger 5, Brian 4   **b** 3, 8   **c** 5, 4   **d** 5.4, 4.5   **e** Roger, smaller range   **f** Brian, better mean   **8 a** 34
c $x = 10, y = 24$ **d** 2.5

Exercise 13C

1 a i 31–40   **ii** 29.9   **b i** 0–100   **ii** 158.6   **c i** £5.01–£10   **ii** £9.44   **d i** 7–9   **ii** 8.4   **2 a** 81–90 g
b 8617.5 g   **c** 86.2 g   **3 a** 207   **b** 19–22 cm   **c** 20.3 cm   **4 a** 41–50   **b** 49.8   **c** 13.4%   **5 a** 160   **b** 52.6 min
c Modal group   **d** 65%   **6 a** 5.25 min   **b** Modal group   **c** Yes, 50% were over 5 min late   **7 a** 176–200 h   **b** 31%
c 193.6 h   **d** No   **8** Average price increases: Soundbuy 17.7p, Springfields 18.7p, Setco 18.2p

Exercise 13D

1 iii 140.9 cm   **2 ii** Boys 12.9, girls 13.1   **3 ii** 1.9   **4 ii** 6.2 goals   **5 ii** Mon 28.9, Wed 21.4, Fri 21.8 min   **6 i** Boys
ii 111   **v** Boys 4.8 kg, girls 4.5 kg   **7 i** 1.8   **8 i** Age 16–17: £13.31, age 18–20: £16.21   **9 ii** 45.8 words/min   **iii** $33\frac{1}{3}$%
10 i 63   **ii** 2.9

Exercise 13E

4 c 23.8 g   **5 a i** 40   **ii** 15   **iii** 25   **b** 15%   **6 a** 55°   **b** 22   **c** $33\frac{1}{3}$%   **7 a i** 333°   **ii** 5°
8 d Girls £2.30, boys £2.52

Examination questions (Chapter 13)

1 a 31　**b** 1, 6, 11, 2　**c** 281 to 290　**d** Your pie chart should be labelled and have the following angles of sectors as 18°, 108°, 198° and 36°

2 a This is an example of a good observation sheet; it is not unique.

What use have you made of a computer in your coursework?				
	Boys	F	Girls	F
Word processing				
Spreadsheets				
Both word processing and spreadsheets				
Something else				
None				

You should have included word processing, spreadsheets, both and the possibility of none at all.
b 0.95

3 a 69　**b** 15　**c** Increases　**4 a** $\frac{1}{4}$　**b i** 170°　**5 a** 150–155 litres　**b** 155.8 litres　**c** Mean　**7** 98.8 grams
8 a 12.55 m　**9 a** 1500　**b** August　**c** 7000　**d** 3333　**12 a i** 50.1 s　**ii** 40–50 s　**b** Mean　**10 a** Here are a few types of questions you could have included: Do you do any exercise? Do you play football? How often do you do exercise?
b It is biased towards sporty people. It is only asking girls.　**c i** It is a leading question.　**ii** There is no response for a NO answer.
11 a The upper limit of the age 49 is one second younger than 50, so it can be estimated as 50, hence the midpoint is really between 40 and 50, which is $90 \div 2$, which is 45.　**b** 41.6　**c** 20 – 29

d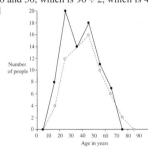

e There are a number of valid comments to be made, including:
there are more women than men,
the women tend to be younger than the men.
The distribution of the women is bimodal (having two peaks).
The range of the men's ages is greater than that of the women.

Exercise 14A

1 $6t$　**2** $12y$　**3** $15y$　**4** $8w$　**5** $3t^2$　**6** $5b^2$　**7** $2w^2$　**8** $15y^2$　**9** $8p^2$　**10** $6t^2$　**11** $12m^2$　**12** $15t^2$　**13** $2mt$
14 $3wy$　**15** $5qt$　**16** $6mn$　**17** $6qt$　**18** $12fg$　**19** $10hk$　**20** $21pr$　**21** y^3　**22** t^3　**23** $3m^3$　**24** $4t^3$　**25** $6n^3$
26 $20r^3$　**27** t^4　**28** h^5　**29** $12n^5$　**30** $10t^7$　**31** $6a^7$　**32** $4k^7$　**33** t^3　**34** $6y^2$　**35** $12d^3$　**36** $15p^6$
37 $3mp^2$　**38** $6t^2y$　**39** $6m^2n$　**40** $8m^2p^2$

Exercise 14B

1 $6 + 2m$　**2** $10 + 5l$　**3** $12 - 3y$　**4** $20 + 8k$　**5** $6 - 12f$　**6** $10 - 6w$　**7** $3g + 3h$　**8** $10k + 15m$　**9** $12d - 8n$
10 $t^2 + 3t$　**11** $m^2 + 5m$　**12** $k^2 - 3k$　**13** $3g^2 + 2g$　**14** $5y^2 - y$　**15** $5p - 3p^2$　**16** $3m^2 + 12m$　**17** $4t^2 - 4t$
18 $8k - 2k^2$　**19** $8g^2 + 20g$　**20** $15h^2 - 10h$　**21** $15t - 12t^2$　**22** $6d^2 + 12de$　**23** $6y^2 + 8ky$　**24** $15m^2 - 10mp$
25 $y^3 + 5y$　**26** $h^4 + 7h$　**27** $k^3 - 5k$　**28** $3t^3 + 12t$　**29** $4h^4 - 4h$　**30** $5g^4 - 10g$　**31** $12m^3 + 4m^2$　**32** $10k^4 + 5k^3$
33 $15d^3 - 3d^4$　**34** $6w^3 + 3tw$　**35** $15a^3 - 10ab$　**36** $12p^4 - 15mp$　**37** $5m^2 + 4m^3$　**38** $t^4 + 2t^4$　**39** $5g^2t - 4g^4$
40 $15t^3 + 3mt^2$　**41** $12h^3 + 8gh^2$　**42** $8m^3 + 2m^4$

Exercise 14C

1 a $7t$　**b** $9m$　**c** $3y$　**d** $9d$　**e** $3e$　**f** $2g$　**g** $3p$　**h** $2t$　**i** $5t^2$　**j** $4y^2$　**k** $5ab$　**l** $3a^2d$　**2 a** $22 + 5t$
b $21 + 19k$　**c** $10 + 16m$　**d** $16 + 17y$　**e** $22 + 2f$　**f** $14 + 3g$　**g** $10 + 11t$　**h** $22 + 4w$　**3 a** $2 + 2h$　**b** $9g + 5$
c $6y + 11$　**d** $7t - 4$　**e** $17k + 16$　**f** $6e + 20$　**g** $7m + 4$　**h** $3t + 10$　**4 a** $4m + 3p + 2mp$　**b** $3k + 4h + 5hk$
c $3n + 2t + 7nt$　**d** $6pq + 3p + 7q$　**e** $6h + 6j + 13hj$　**f** $21ty + 6t + 8y$　**g** $24p + 12r + 13pr$　**h** $20k - 6m + 19km$
5 a $13t + 9t^2$　**b** $5y + 13y^2$　**c** $18w + 5w^2$　**d** $14p + 23p^2$　**e** $7m + 4m^2$　**f** $22d - 9d^2$　**g** $10e^2 - 6e$　**h** $14k^2 - 3kp$
6 a $17ab + 12ac + 6bc$　**b** $18wy + 6ty - 8tw$　**c** $16gh - 2gk - 10hk$　**d** $10ht - 3hp - 12pt$　**e** $ab - 2ac + 6bc$
f $12pq + 2qw - 10pw$　**g** $14mn - 15mp - 6np$　**h** $8r^3 - 6r^2$

Exercise 14D

1 $6(m + 2t)$　**2** $3(3t + p)$　**3** $4(2m + 3k)$　**4** $4(r + 2t)$　**5** $m(n + 3)$　**6** $g(5g + 3)$　**7** $2(2w - 3t)$　**8** $2(4p - 3k)$
9 $2(8h - 5k)$　**10** $2m(p + k)$　**11** $2b(2c + k)$　**12** $2a(3b + 2c)$　**13** $y(3y + 2)$　**14** $t(4t - 3)$　**15** $2d(2d - 1)$　**16** $3m(m - p)$
17 $3p(2p + 3t)$　**18** $2p(4t + 3m)$　**19** $4b(2a - c)$　**20** $4a(3a - 2b)$　**21** $3t(3m - 2p)$　**22** $4at(4t + 3)$　**23** $5bc(b - 2)$
24 $2b(4ac + 3ed)$　**25** $2(2a^2 + 3a + 4)$　**26** $3b(2a + 3c + d)$　**27** $t(5t + 4 + a)$　**28** $3mt(2t - 1 + 3m)$　**29** $2ab(4b + 1 - 2a)$
30 $5pt(2t + 3 + p)$　**31** Not possible　**32** $m(5 + 2p)$　**33** $t(t - 7)$　**34** Not possible　**35** $2m(2m - 3p)$　**36** Not possible
37 $a(4a - 5b)$　**38** Not possible　**39** $b(5a - 3bc)$

Exercise 14E

1 $x^2 + 5x + 6$ **2** $t^2 + 7t + 12$ **3** $w^2 + 4w + 3$ **4** $m^2 + 6m + 5$ **5** $k^2 + 8k + 15$ **6** $a^2 + 5a + 4$ **7** $x^2 + 2x - 8$
8 $t^2 + 2t - 15$ **9** $w^2 - 2w - 3$ **10** $f^2 - f - 6$ **11** $g^2 - 3g - 4$ **12** $y^2 + y - 12$ **13** $x^2 + x - 12$ **14** $p^2 - p - 2$
15 $k^2 - 2k - 8$ **16** $y^2 + 3y - 10$ **17** $a^2 + 2a - 3$ **18** $t^2 + t - 12$ **19** $x^2 - 5x + 4$ **20** $r^2 - 5r + 6$ **21** $m^2 - 4m + 3$
22 $g^2 - 6g + 8$ **23** $h^2 - 8h + 15$ **24** $n^2 - 5n + 4$ **25** $x^2 + 9x + 20$ **26** $18 - 3t - t^2$ **27** $15 - 2b - b^2$ **28** $y^2 - 6y + 5$
29 $p^2 - p - 6$ **30** $7k - k^2 - 10$ **31** $x^2 - 9$ **32** $t^2 - 25$ **33** $m^2 - 16$ **34** $t^2 - 4$ **35** $y^2 - 64$ **36** $p^2 - 1$
37 $25 - x^2$ **38** $49 - g^2$ **39** $x^2 - 36$

Exercise 14F

1 $6x^2 + 11x + 3$ **2** $12y^2 + 17y + 6$ **3** $6t^2 + 17t + 5$ **4** $8t^2 + 2t - 3$ **5** $10m^2 - 11m - 6$ **6** $12k^2 - 11k - 15$
7 $6p^2 + 11p - 10$ **8** $10w^2 + 19w + 6$ **9** $6a^2 - 7a - 3$ **10** $8r^2 - 10r + 3$ **11** $15g^2 - 16g + 4$ **12** $12d^2 + 5d - 2$
13 $8p^2 + 26p + 15$ **14** $6t^2 + 7t + 2$ **15** $6p^2 + 11p + 4$ **16** $6 - 7t - 10t^2$ **17** $12 + n - 6n^2$ **18** $6f^2 - 5f - 6$
19 $12 + 7q - 10q^2$ **20** $3 - 7p - 6p^2$ **21** $4 + 10t - 6t^2$ **22** $8r^2 - 10r + 3$ **23** $8x^2 - 22x + 5$ **24** $17m - 12m^2 - 6$
25 $4x^2 - 1$ **26** $9t^2 - 4$ **27** $25y^2 - 9$ **28** $16m^2 - 9$ **29** $4k^2 - 9$ **30** $16h^2 - 1$ **31** $4 - 9x^2$ **32** $25 - 4t^2$
33 $36 - 25y^2$

Exercise 14G

1 $x^2 + 10x + 25$ **2** $m^2 + 8m + 16$ **3** $t^2 + 12t + 36$ **4** $p^2 + 6p + 9$ **5** $m^2 - 6m + 9$ **6** $t^2 - 10t + 25$ **7** $m^2 - 8m + 16$
8 $k^2 - 14k + 49$ **9** $9x^2 + 6x + 1$ **10** $16t^2 + 24t + 9$ **11** $25y^2 + 20y + 4$ **12** $4m^2 + 12m + 9$ **13** $16t^2 - 24t + 9$
14 $9x^2 - 12x + 4$ **15** $25t^2 - 20t + 4$ **16** $25r^2 - 60r + 36$ **17** $x^2 + 2xy + y^2$ **18** $m^2 - 2mn + n^2$ **19** $4t^2 + 4ty + y^2$
20 $m^2 - 6mn + 9n^2$

Exercise 14H

1 $(x + 2)(x + 3)$ **2** $(t + 1)(t + 4)$ **3** $(m + 2)(m + 5)$ **4** $(k + 4)(k + 6)$ **5** $(p + 2)(p + 12)$ **6** $(r + 3)(r + 6)$
7 $(w + 2)(w + 9)$ **8** $(x + 3)(x + 4)$ **9** $(a + 2)(a + 6)$ **10** $(k + 3)(k + 7)$ **11** $(f + 1)(f + 21)$ **12** $(b + 8)(b + 12)$
13 $(t - 2)(t - 3)$ **14** $(d - 1)(d - 4)$ **15** $(g - 2)(g - 5)$ **16** $(x - 3)(x - 12)$ **17** $(c - 2)(c - 16)$ **18** $(t - 4)(t - 9)$
19 $(y - 4)(y - 12)$ **20** $(j - 6)(j - 8)$ **21** $(p - 3)(p - 5)$ **22** $(y + 6)(y - 1)$ **23** $(t + 4)(t - 2)$ **24** $(x + 5)(x - 2)$
25 $(m + 2)(m - 6)$ **26** $(r + 1)(r - 7)$ **27** $(n + 3)(n - 6)$ **28** $(m + 4)(m - 11)$ **29** $(w + 4)(w - 6)$ **30** $(t + 9)(t - 10)$
31 $(h + 8)(h - 9)$ **32** $(t + 7)(t - 9)$ **33** $(d + 1)^2$ **34** $(y + 10)^2$ **35** $(t - 4)^2$ **36** $(m - 9)^2$ **37** $(x - 12)^2$
38 $(d + 3)(d - 4)$ **39** $(t + 4)(t - 5)$ **40** $(q + 7)(q - 8)$ **41** $(p + 2)(p - 1)$ **42** $(v + 7)(v - 5)$ **43** $(t + 1)(t + 3)$
44 $(m + 1)(m - 4)$ **45** $(x + 2)(x - 3)$ **46** $(x + 3)(x - 3)$ **47** $(t + 5)(t - 5)$ **48** $(m + 4)(m - 4)$ **49** $(3 + x)(3 - x)$
50 $(7 + t)(7 - t)$ **51** $(k + 10)(k - 10)$

Exercise 14I

1 $-2, -5$ **2** $-3, -1$ **3** $-6, -4$ **4** $-3, 2$ **5** $-1, 3$ **6** $-4, 5$ **7** $1, -2$ **8** $2, -5$ **9** $7, -4$ **10** $3, 2$ **11** $1, 5$
12 $4, 3$ **13** $-4, -1$ **14** $-9, -2$ **15** $2, 4$ **16** $3, 5$ **17** $-2, 5$ **18** $-3, 5$ **19** $-6, 2$ **20** $-6, 3$ **21** $-1, 2$
22 $-6, -4$ **23** $2, 16$ **24** $-6, 4$ **25** $-9, 6$ **26** $-10, 3$ **27** $-4, 11$ **28** $-8, 9$ **29** $8, 9$ **30** 1

Exercise 14J

1 $k = \dfrac{T + 2}{3}$ **2** $m = \dfrac{P - 7}{2}$ **3** $y = \dfrac{X + 1}{5}$ **4** $p = \dfrac{Q - 3}{8}$ **5** $r = \dfrac{A + 9}{4}$ **6 i** $n = \dfrac{W - t}{3}$ **ii** $t = W - 3n$

7 i $y = \dfrac{x + w}{5}$ **ii** $w = 5y - x$ **8 i** $m = \dfrac{p - t}{7}$ **ii** $t = p - 7m$ **9 i** $k = \dfrac{t + f}{2}$ **ii** $f = 2k - t$

10 i $m = \dfrac{g - v}{6}$ **ii** $v = g - 6m$ **11** $m = \sqrt{t}$ **12** $p = \sqrt{k}$ **13** $b = \sqrt{(a - 3)}$ **14** $h = \sqrt{(w + 5)}$ **15** $p = \sqrt{(m - 2)}$

16 i $t = u^2 - v$ **ii** $u = \sqrt{(v + t)}$ **17 i** $m = k - n^2$ **ii** $n = \sqrt{(k - m)}$ **18** $r = \sqrt{\left(\dfrac{T}{5}\right)}$ **19** $t = \sqrt{\left(\dfrac{P}{3}\right)}$ **20 i** $w = K - 5n^2$

ii $n = \sqrt{\left(\dfrac{K - w}{5}\right)}$

Examination questions (Chapter 14)

1 a 51 **b** $t = \dfrac{v - u}{g}$ **c** 7.5 **2 a** $150\,\text{cm}$ **b** $f = \dfrac{h - 90}{3}$ **3** $\sqrt{(5y - 4)}$ **4** $p = \dfrac{7r - 12}{4}$
5 a $x^2 + 2x - 15$ **b** $3a(2a - 3b)$ **6 a** $3x(2x - 3y)$ **b i** $(x - 2)(x - 6)$ **ii** $x = 2$ and $x = 6$ **7 a** $a(2b - 1)$ **b i** 6 **ii** $2, 3$
8 a $6x^2 + x - 12$ **b** $\sqrt{(6d/b)}$ **9 a** $4\frac{1}{2}$ **b ii** 7 **10 a** $7x + 7y - xy$ **b** $2p(3p - 4)$ **c** $2x^2 + 7x - 15$

Answers

Revision paper (Chapters 1–14)

1 a −10 **b** 18 **c** −5 **d** 4 **2 i** 55.25 litres **ii** 39.9 litres **3 a** 75 mph **b** 2.6 h **c** 315 miles **4 a** 22 cm, 28 cm²
b 27.4 cm, 31.5 cm² **c** 26.8 cm, 42 cm² **5** 191 m **6 a i** 3.5 **ii** 2.8 **b** 4.6 **7 a** 36° **b** 24
8 d Reflection in $y = x$ **11 i** 7.03×10^3 **ii** 1.95×10^{13} **iii** 1.92×10^4 **iv** 3.61×10^{-10} **12** $x = 9\frac{1}{2}, y = 2$ **13** 58.2
14 a $x^2 - 2x - 15$ **b** −2, −3

Exercise 15A

1 a i $8\frac{1}{4}$ kg **ii** $2\frac{1}{4}$ kg **iii** 9 lb **iv** 22 lb **b** 2.2 lb **2 a i** 10 cm **ii** $22\frac{1}{2}$ cm **iii** 2 in **iv** $8\frac{3}{4}$ in **6** $2\frac{1}{2}$ cm
3 a i $320 **ii** $100 **iii** £45 **iv** £78 **b** $3.2 **4 a i** £120 **ii** £82 **b i** 32 **ii** 52 **c** Initial charge
5 a i £100 **ii** £325 **b i** 500 **ii** 250 **c** Initial charge **6 a i** £70 **ii** £29 **b i** £85 **ii** £38 **7 a i** 26.5 cm
ii 27.51 cm **b i** 5.5 kg **ii** 16.5 kg **c** 25.375 cm **8 a i** 40 km **ii** 16 km **iii** 25 miles **iv** $9\frac{1}{2}$ miles **b** 8 km
9 a i 95 °F **ii** 68 °F **iii** 10 °C **iv** 32 °C **b** 32 °F **10 a i** 3 m³ **ii** $8\frac{1}{4}$ m³ **iii** 13 yd³ **iv** $6\frac{3}{4}$ yd³ **b** 1.3
11 b 2.15 pm **12 b** £50

Exercise 15B

1 a i 9 am **ii** 10 am **iii** 12 noon **b i** 40 km/h **ii** 120 km/h **iii** 40 km/h **2 a i** 125 km **ii** 125 km/h
b i Between 2 and 3 pm **ii** Between 15 and 25 km/h **3 a** 30 km **b** 40 km **c** 67 km/h **4 a i** 250 m/min **ii** 15 km
b 500 m/min **c** Paul, 1 min **5 a** He fell **c i** 400 m/min **ii** 20 km/h **6 a** Ravinder – car, Sue – bus, Michael – cycle
b 4.00 pm, 4.20 pm, 4.35 pm **c** 0.4 km/min **d** 14.4 km/h **7 a** 30 min **b** 80 km/h **c** 20 km/h
d i 20 km/h **ii** 6.00 pm **8 b** 1.67 m/s **ii** 6 km/h

Exercise 15C

1 a 1.5 **b** 0.5 **c** −0.5 **d** −1 **c** 0.6 **f** 3 **g** $\frac{4}{3}$ **h** 0.2 **i** −1 **2 a** $\frac{15}{2}$ **b** 3 **c** $\frac{5}{4}$ **d** $\frac{2}{25}$ **e** $\frac{6}{35}$ **f** $\frac{1}{2}$ **g** $-\frac{4}{5}$
h 25 **i** $-\frac{25}{9}$ **j** $\frac{25}{6}$ **k** $\frac{25}{18}$ **l** $\frac{2}{3}$ **m** $\frac{4}{5}$ **n** 4 **p** −4 **3 a** 1.2 **b** By reading up from Price before VAT **4 a** $\frac{5}{2}$
b 2.5 cm **5 a** $\frac{5}{16}$ **b** 31p **6 a** $\frac{8}{5}$ **b** 1.6 **7 a** 35 **b** 35 ft³ **8 a** $\frac{9}{2}$ **b** $4\frac{1}{2}$ litres

Exercise 15D

1 a 32 °F **b** $\frac{9}{5}$ (Accept 1.8) **c** $F = 1.8C + 32$ **2 a** £1 + £2/km **b** £3 + £1/km **c** £1.50 + £1.50/km **3 a** 0.07 **b** £10
c Charge = £10 + 7p/unit **4 a** $\frac{5}{2}$ **b** £20 **c** Charge = £20 + £2.50/day **5 a** $\frac{1}{2}$ **b** £50 **c** Charge = £50 + 50p/person
6 a $\frac{1}{10}$ **b** 25.4 cm **c** 1 mm **d** Length = 25.4 cm + 1 mm/kg

Examination questions (Chapter 15)

1 a 33 miles **b** 45 mph **c** 10.40–11.50 **2 b i** £82 **ii** 333 **3 a i** 1300 **ii** 20 km/h
b
4 a y, 12, 8, 6, 4, 3, (2.4), 2 **b**
c 3.2 hours **d** 27 gallons

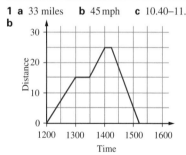

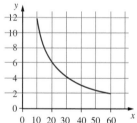

5 b i 32.5 °C **ii** 68 g **c i** $w = 50 + 0.4t$ **ii** 88 g **6 b** 51 mph **c** 25 min **d** Gradient of line **f** ≈ 8 miles

Exercise 16A

1 2, 3 **2** Sf = 4, not similar **3 a** Enlargement **b** 1 : 3 **c** Angle R **d** AB **4 a** Sides in same ratio **b** 2 : 1
c Angle Q **5 a** Sides in same ratio **b** Angle P **c** PR **6 a** Sides in same ratio **b** Angle Q **c** AR **7 a** 8 cm
b 7.5 cm **c** 3.5 cm **d** 12 cm, 10 cm **e** $6\frac{2}{3}$ cm, $13\frac{1}{2}$ cm **f** 24 cm, 13 cm **g** 10 cm, 6 cm **h** 4.2 cm
8 a Sides in same ratio **b** 1 : 3 **9** 4.8 m

Exercise 16B

1 a 9 cm **b** 6 cm **2 a** 9 cm **b** 5 cm **c** 14 cm **d** 5 cm **e** 60 cm, 75 cm **f** 56 cm, 24 cm **g** 45 cm, 60 cm
h 10 cm, 8 cm **3** 82 m **4** 220 ft **5** 15 m **6** 8 cm, 10 cm, 16 cm **7** 3.09 m **8** 6 m

Exercise 16C

1 5cm **2** 6cm **3** 10cm **4** 16cm **5** 6cm, 7.5cm **6** 8cm, 11.2cm **7** 15cm, 21cm **8** 3cm, 2.4cm

Examination questions (Chapter 16)

1 7.5cm **2** 1.125m **3** 27cm **4** 280m **5 a** 24cm **b** 40.5cm **6 a** All corresponding angles equal **b** 3.75m
7 2.8m **8 a** Triangles ABC and ADE **b i** 6cm **ii** 20cm

Exercise 17A

5 a 85 **b** 181 **c** 100 **d** 128 **e** 74 **f** 34 **6 a** 32 **b** 40 **c** 39 **d** 104 **e** 120 **f** 75 **7 a** 130
b 120 **c** 88 **d** 45.3 **e** 95 **f** 394 **8** Square 13, square 5 and subtract answers to obtain 144 (side of 12cm)

Exercise 17B

1 10.30cm **2** 5.92cm **3** 8.49cm **4** 20.62cm **5** 18.60cm **6** 17.49cm **7** 32.2cm **8** 2.42m **9** 500m
10 707.11m **11** 6.73cm **12** 1.06cm

Exercise 17C

1 a 15cm **b** 14.66cm **c** 6.33cm **d** 18.33cm **e** 5.40cm **f** 217.94m **g** 0.44cm **h** 8m **2 a** 19.85m
b 15.49cm **c** 15.49m **d** 12.38cm **e** 22.91m **f** 19.85m **g** 7.14m **h** 0.64m **i** 16.61m **j** 10.20m
k 4.53m **l** 10.04cm

Exercise 17D

1 20cm **2** 34cm **3** 100cm **4** 120cm **5** 32cm **6** 32m **7** 90m **8** 10m **9** 52cm **10** 25cm **11** 85cm
12 150cm **13** 27cm **14** 60cm **15** 35cm **16** 45cm

Exercise 17E

1 6.63m **2** 2.06m **3** 10.82m **4** 11.31m **5** 9.22m **6** 19.21km **7** 147.05km **8** 2.37km **9 a** 127m
b 99.62m **c** 27.38m **10** 12ft **11 a** 3.87m **b** 1.74m **12** 3.16m **13** 5.10 **14 a** 4.74 **b** 4.54m
15 16.47cm^2 **16** 58.59km **17** 192.35 **18** 120.01m **19** $25^2 = 24^2 + 7^2$: therefore, right-angled **20** 7.21

Exercise 17F

1 32.25cm^2, 2.83cm^2, 49.99cm^2 **2** 22.25cm^2 **3** 15.59cm^2 **4** 27.71 **5 a**

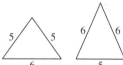

b Triangle with 6cm, 6cm, 5cm **6 a** **b** 166.26cm^2

7 259.81cm^2 **8 a** 8.25cm **b** 11.66cm **c** 5.72cm

Examination questions (Chapter 17)

1 AB = 8.20m **2 a** LE = 119.27km **b** 330km/h **3 a** **b** 270° **c** 16.12km
4 a 1 : 25000 **b** 24.41km **5 a** 86.64cm^2 **b** 45.6cm
6 7.85m **7** 8.9km **8 a** 38.1m **b** 697.5m^3
9 a 10.3m **b** 43.9m **10** Kevin, because $14^2 \neq 11^2 + 9^2$

H ——— 14 miles ——— B

8 miles

K

Exercise 18A

1 a 0.682 **b** 0.829 **c** 0.922 **d** 1.00 **e** 0.707 **f** 0.342 **g** 0.375 **h** 0.00 **i** 0.574 **j** 0.966 **k** 1.0
l 0.946 **2 a** 0.731 **b** 0.559 **c** 0.388 **d** 0.00 **e** 0.707 **f** 0.940 **g** 0.927 **h** 1.00 **i** 0.819 **j** 0.259
k 0.017 **l** 0.326 **3** 45° **4 a i** 0.574 **ii** 0.574 **b i** 0.208 **ii** 0.208 **c i** 0.391 **ii** 0.391 **d** Same
e i sin 15° is the same as cos 75° **ii** cos 82° is the same as sin 8° **iii** sin x is the same as cos $(90° - x)$ **5 a** 4.532
b 4.459 **c** 3.508 **d** 0.624 **e** 6.000 **f** 0.000 **g** 3.508 **h** 1.871 **6 a** 5.612 **b** 7.075 **c** 19.940 **d** 4.483
e 6.000 **f** 10.000 **g** 12.548 **h** 43.288 **7 a** 7.727 **b** 48.627 **c** 2.279 **d** 15.187 **e** 28.430 **f** 6.725
g 21.459 **h** 16.935

Exercise 18B

1 a 30° **b** 51.7° **c** 39.8° **d** 61.3° **e** 87.4° **f** 45.0° **g** 5.9° **h** 46.2° **i** 62.6° **j** 11.5° **k** 44.4° **l** 48.6°
2 a 60° **b** 38.3° **c** 50.2° **d** 28.7° **e** 2.6° **f** 45.0° **g** 84.1° **h** 43.8° **i** 27.4° **j** 78.5° **k** 45.6° **l** 41.4°
3 a 53.1° **b** 41.8° **c** 44.4° **d** 56.4° **e** 2.4° **f** 22.6° **g** 73.7° **h** 14.5° **4 a** 36.9° **b** 48.2° **c** 45.6°
d 33.6° **e** 87.6° **f** 67.4° **g** 16.3° **h** 75.5° **5** Error message, largest value 1, smallest value −1 **6 a i** 17.5°
ii 72.5° **iii** 90° **b** Yes

Exercise 18D

1 a 0.933 **b** 1.483 **c** 2.379 **d** Infinite **e** 1.000 **f** 0.364 **g** 0.404 **h** 0.000 **i** 0.700 **j** 3.732 **k** 57.290
l 2.904 **2 a** 0.956 **b** 0.899 **c** 2.164 **d** 0.999 **e** 0.819 **f** 0.577 **g** 0.469 **h** 0.996 **i** 0.754 **j** 0.956
k 0.191 **l** 5.145 **3** Has values > 1 **4 a** 10.723 **b** 5.402 **c** 3.669 **d** 14.114 **e** Infinite **f** 0.000 **g** 39.250
h 1.913 **5 a** 1.463 **b** 7.774 **c** 17.893 **d** 14.372 **e** 0.401 **f** 7.151 **g** 8.152 **h** 19.801 **6 a** 29.856
b 44.761 **c** 20.329 **d** 2.376 **e** 16.710 **f** 7.032 **g** 17.791 **h** 194.311 **7 a** 3.564 **b** 8.960 **c** 14.375
d 9.900 **e** 28.356 **f** 8.912 **g** 66.261 **h** 2.622 **8 a** 6.568 **b** 12.803 **c** 57.870 **d** 9.697 **e** 1.555 **f** 7.779
g 7.927 **h** 16.984 **9 a** 6.973 **b** 19.940 **c** 14.432 **d** 12.051 **e** 15.681 **f** 28.954 **g** 21.139 **h** 4.659

Exercise 18E

1 a 17.5° **b** 22.0° **c** 32.2° **2 a** 5.288 cm **b** 5.755 cm **c** 13.248 cm **3 a** 4.573 cm **b** 6.860 cm **c** 100.4 cm
4 a 5.119 cm **b** 9.766 cm **c** 6.292 cm **d** 15.53 cm **e** 9.506 cm **f** 10.199 cm **g** 17.058 cm **h** 22.17 cm
5 a 47.2° **b** 5.416 cm **c** 13.681 cm **d** 38.0° **e** 14.153 cm **f** 51.1° **g** 6.698 cm **h** 44.0°

Exercise 18F

1 51.3°, 75.5°, 51.3° **2** 6.474 cm, 32.640 cm, 136.941 cm **3 a** 5.353 cm **b** 14.833 cm **c** 12.041 cm **d** 8.619 cm
e 12.306 cm **f** 5.871 cm **g** 4.767 cm **h** 43.415 cm **4** 7.325 cm, 39.066 cm, 134.817 cm **5 a** 5.592 cm **b** 46.6°
c 4.264 cm **d** 40.1° **e** 13.268 cm **f** 40.4° **g** 11.873 cm **h** 56.918 cm

Exercise 18G

1 33.7°, 36.9°, 52.1° **2** 5.094 cm, 30.353 cm, 1119.6 cm **3** 8.242 cm, 61.971 cm, 72.794 cm **4 a** 9.020 cm **b** 7.507 cm
c 7.143 cm **d** 8.895 cm **e** 13.083 cm **f** 8.104 cm **g** 11.301 cm **h** 50.780 cm **5 a** 13.738 cm **b** 48.4°
c 7.032 cm **d** 41.2° **e** 8.360 cm **f** 19.845 cm **g** 58.2° **h** 5.236 cm

Exercise 18H

1 a 12.586 **b** 59.588 cm **c** 74.724 **d** 15.973 **e** 67.881 **f** 20.054 **g** 20.128 **h** 9.139 **i** 1.545 **2 a** 44.4°
b 39.8° **c** 44.4° **d** 49.5° **e** 58.7° **f** 38.7° **g** 48.2° **h** 36.9° **i** 66.4° **3 a** 67.4° **b** 11.326 **c** 133.512
d 28.1° **e** 39.725 **f** 263.459 **g** 50.2° **h** 51.3° **i** 138.198 **j** 22.776

Exercise 18I

1 65.4° **2** 2.05–3.00 m **3** 44.4° **4** 6.82 m **5** 7.03 m **6** 31° **7** 5.657 cm **8** 25.3° **9** 19.6°, 4.776 m
10 0.498 m **11** 42.45 m **12** 21.138 m

Exercise 18J

1 10.101 km **2** 21.8° **3** 428.9 m **4** 156.26 m **5** 222.4 m, 42° **6 a** 21.46 m **b** 17.79 m **7** 13.4 m **8** 19.5°

Exercise 18K

1 a 73.36 km **b** 15.59 km **2 a** 14.72 km **b** 8.5 km **3** 120.3° **4** 58.69 km **b** 12.47 km **5 a** 15.89 km
b 24.11 km **c** 31.185 km **d** 37.7° **6** 2.28 km **7 a** 66.22 km **b** 11.74 km **c** 13.14 km **d** 260.4°
8 43.29 km, 101.5°

Exercise 18L

1 5.786 cm **2** 48.2° **3** 7.416 cm **4** 81.63 cm **5** 9.9 m **6 a** 36.40 cm² **b** 115.44 cm² **c** 90.6 cm² **d** 159.93 cm²

Examination questions (Chapter 18)

1 a 12.26 cm **b** 78.2° **2 a** 36 m **b** 7.1° **3 a** 13.6 cm **b** 14.5 cm **c** 69.8° **4** 116 cm **5 a** 29.544
b ii 40 **iii** 26.14% **6 a** 1.9° **b** 450 m **c** ≈ 0.9 km/h **7 a** 4.494 cm **b** 35.952 cm² **8 a** LE = 119 km
b 33° **c** 333 km/h **9 a** 7.846 m **b** 18° **10** 83.6°

Exercise 19A

1 Metres **2** Kilometres **3** Centimetres **4** Kilograms or grams **5** Litres **6** Kilograms **7** Tonnes **8** Millilitres **9** Centilitres **10** Metres **11** Kilograms **12** Litres **13** Grams **14** Centilitres **15** Millimetres

Exercise 19B

1 1.25 m **2** 8.2 cm **3** 0.55 m **4** 2.1 km **5** 2.08 cm **6** 1.24 m **7** 14.2 cm **8** 3.56 km **9** 3.55 m **10** 0.94 m **11** 0.65 km **12** 0.045 m **13** 80.5 cm **14** 12.5 m **15** 2.06 km **16** 4.2 kg **17** 5.75 t **18** 8.5 cl **19** 2.58 l **20** 3.4 l **21** 0.6 t **22** 0.755 kg **23** 8 l **24** 2 l **25** 63 cl **26** 1.02 t **27** 4.5 l **28** 2.04 kg **29** 4.5 l **30** 0.055 l **31** 8.4 m³ **32** 35 cm³ **33** 1.035 m³ **34** 0.53 m³ **35** 530 cm **36** 34 000 m **37** 3400 mm **38** 135 mm **39** 67 cm **40** 7030 m **41** 7.2 mm **42** 25 cm **43** 5 cm **44** 640 m **45** 110 mm **46** 2400 ml **47** 590 cl **48** 84 ml **49** 5200 l **50** 580 g **51** 3750 kg **52** 74 cl **53** 0.000 94 l **54** 45 800 g **55** 12 500 ml **56** 2160 cl **57** 15 200 g **58** 14 000 l **59** 1560 kg **60** 0.19 ml

Exercise 19C

1 24 in **2** 12 ft **3** 3520 yd **4** 80 oz **5** 56 lb **6** 6720 lb **7** 40 pt **8** 48 in **9** 36 in **10** 30 ft **11** 64 oz **12** 5 ft **13** 70 lb **14** 12 yd **15** 224 oz **16** 5 miles **17** 120 pt **18** 5280 ft **19** 8 ft **20** 7 st **21** 7 gal **22** 2 lb **23** 5 yd **24** 5 tons **25** 63 360 in **26** 8 lb **27** 9 gal **28** 10 st **29** 3 miles **30** 35 840 oz

Exercise 19D

1 20 cm **2** 13.2 lb **3** 48.3 km **4** 67.5 l **5** 2850 ml **6** 10 gal **7** 12 in **8** 31.25 miles **9** 5.455 kg **10** 3.070 pt **11** 160 km **12** 150 cm **13** 123.2 lb **14** 180 l **15** 1140 ml **16** 93.75 miles **17** 90.9 kg **18** 39.37 in **19** 4.04 pt **20** 22.2 gal **21** 4500 ml **22** 1093 yd **23** 30 cm **24** 6.364 kg **25** 8.89 pt **26** 2200 lb **27** 90 cm **28** 0.61 km **29** 1.018 kg **30** 0.9 m **31** Ton **32** Metre **33 a i** 1000 g **ii** 1 kg **iii** 35.56 oz **b i** 4560 g **ii** 4.560 kg **iii** 162.15 oz **34 a** 6480 cm³ **b** 2513 cm³ **c** 9.425 ft³ **35 a** 130 miles **b** 50 mph **c** 2 h 36 min

Exercise 19E

1 $69.45 **2** DM 249.24 **3** € 121.53 **4** BFr 7681.2 **5** SKr 1813.5 **6** ¥ 401 754 **7** SFr 1353.24 **8** L 5 225 800 **9** £30.81 **10** £140.70 **11** £10 **12** £2.24 **13** £16.27 **14** £14.47 **15** £123.43 **16** £41.23 **17** $236.13 **18** L 218 254 **19** BFr 31 364.9 **20** £325.31 **21** £236.14 **22** £2.46 **23** SKr 785.85 **24** £71.59 **25** SFr 2174.85 **26** DM 1557.75 **27** £248.29 **28** € 498.27 **29** ≈ £27 **30** Britain, Germany, Japan, France, Italy **31 a** FFr 18 029.11 **b** £71.27

Exercise 19F

1 a Large jar **b** 600 g tin **c** 5 kg bag **d** 75 ml tube **e** Large box **f** Large box **g** 400 ml bottle **2 a** 2 lb bag **b** 5 lb packet **c** 1 lb jar **d** 1 l carton **3 a** Large tin **b** 1 large and 2 small tins

Examination questions (Chapter 19)

1 a 70 kg **b** 480 **c** 300 **2** Enough potatoes, not enough milk **3** Costsave **4 a** 41.28 francs **b** £2.68 **5 a** 4950 **b i** 945 **ii** £90 **6 a** 707.5 DM **b** £45.94 **c** 54 mph **7 a** 27 cm **b** 64 800 cm³ **c** 64.8 l **8 a** 1960 FFr **b** £2.50 **9** £40.15 **10** Yes (speed of 56 km per hour or 31.25 mph limit)

Exercise 20A

1 Circle with radius **a** 2 cm **b** 4 cm **c** 5 cm **3** Circle with radius 4 m **4**

5 a

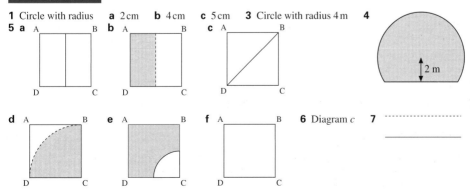

6 Diagram *c* **7**

Exercise 20B

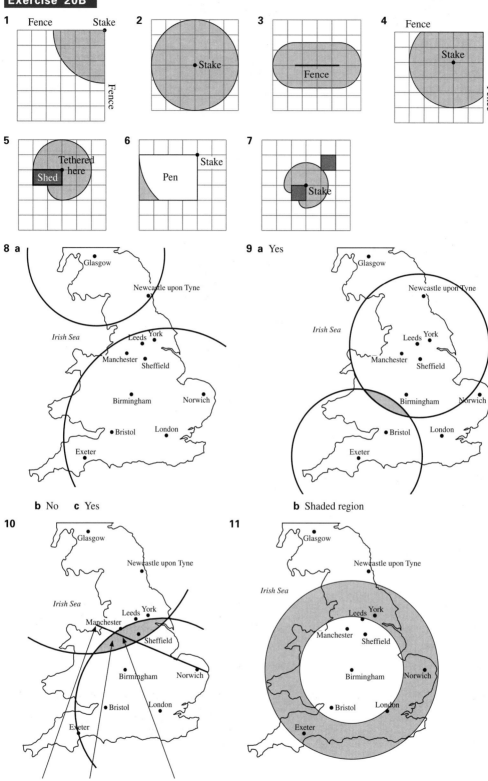

1 Fence Stake / Fence

2 Stake

3 Fence

4 Fence Stake / Fence

5 Tethered here / Shed

6 Stake / Pen

7 Stake

8 a
Glasgow
Newcastle upon Tyne
Irish Sea
Leeds York
Manchester
Sheffield
Birmingham
Norwich
Bristol
London
Exeter

b No **c** Yes

9 a Yes
Glasgow
Newcastle upon Tyne
Irish Sea
Leeds York
Manchester
Sheffield
Birmingham
Norwich
Bristol
London
Exeter

b Shaded region

10
Glasgow
Newcastle upon Tyne
Irish Sea
Leeds York
Manchester
Sheffield
Birmingham
Norwich
Bristol
London
Exeter

a The line **b** The region **c** This part of line

11
Glasgow
Newcastle upon Tyne
Irish Sea
Leeds York
Manchester
Sheffield
Birmingham
Norwich
Bristol
London
Exeter

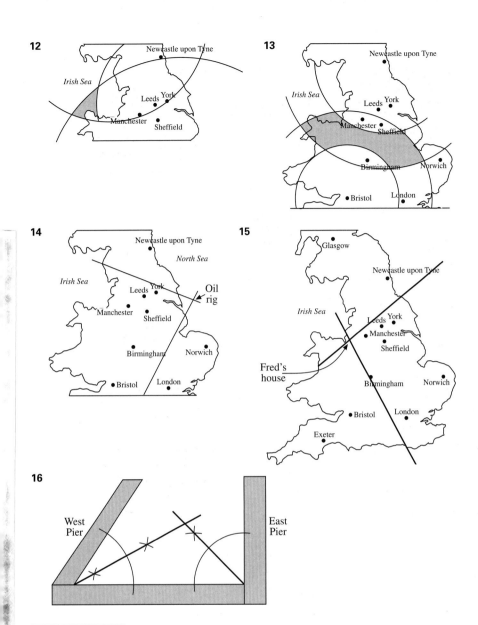

12

13

14

15

16

1 a 56°   **b** 62°   **c** 105°   **d** 115°   **e** 55°   **f** 45°   **g** 30°   **h** 60°   **i** 32°   **j** 145°   **k** 133°   **l** 24°   **2 a** 55°
b 52°   **c** 50°   **d** 24°   **e** 39°   **f** 80°   **g** 34°   **h** 30°   **3 a** 41°   **b** 49°   **c** 41°   **4** 109°   **5 a** 72°   **b** 37°
c 72°   **6** 68°   **7 a** $x = y = 40°$ **b** $x = 131°, y = 111°$ **c** $x = 134°, y = 23°$ **d** $x = 32°, y = 19°$ **e** $x = 59°, y = 121°$
f $x = 155°, y = 12\frac{1}{2}°$

Exercise 20D

1 a $a = 50°, b = 95°$ **b** $c = 92°, x = 90°$ **c** $d = 110°, e = 110°, f = 70°$ **d** $d = 99°, e = 105°$ **e** $j = 89°, k = 89°, l = 91°$
f $m = 120°, n = 40°$ **g** $p = 44°, q = 68°$ **h** $x = 40°, y = 34°$ **2 a** $x = 64°, y = 128°$ **b** $x = 48°, y = 78°$ **c** $x = 137°$,
$y = 47°$ **d** $x = 36°, y = 72°$ **e** $x = 55°, y = 125°$ **f** $x = 35°$ **g** $x = 48°, y = 45°$ **h** $x = 66°, y = 38°$ **3 a** $x = 49°$,
$y = 49°$ **b** $x = 70°, y = 20°$ **c** $x = 80°, y = 100°$ **d** $x = 100°, y = 75°$ **4 a** $x = 50°, y = 62°$ **b** $x = 92°$ **c** $x = 93°$,
$y = 42°$ **d** $x = 55°, y = 75°$ **5 a** $x = 95°, y = 138°$ **b** $x = 14°, y = 62°$ **c** $x = 32°, y = 48°$ **d** 52°   **6 a** 71°   **b** $125\frac{1}{2}°$

Exercise 20E

1 a 38°   **b** 110°   **c** 15°   **d** 45°   **2 a** 6 cm   **b** 10.8 cm   **c** 0.47 cm   **d** 8 cm   **3 a** $x = 12°, y = 156°$ **b** $x = 100°$,
$y = 50°$ **c** $x = 62°, y = 28°$ **d** $x = 30°, y = 60°$ **4 a** 62°   **b** 66°   **c** 19°   **d** 20°   **5** 191.6 cm^2 (radii are 6, 4, 3 cm)
6 64.1 cm^2 **7** 19.5 cm

Answers

1   **2** 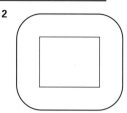 **3** 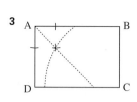 **4 c** $\sqrt{3}$ m

5

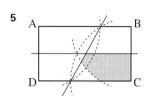

1 a −12 **b** $1\frac{1}{8}$ **c** 5.66 **2 a** £483.84 **b** 12.5% **c** £314.93 **3** 8.9 g/cm^3 **4** 199 cm^2 **5** 12 m^3, 78 750 cm^3
6 a 53.6 **b** $x = 1.53$ or −6.53 **7 a** 99° **b** 128° **c** 85° **11 a** 6.708×10^3 **b** 5 **12** 9.22 am, 50 miles from both
stations **14 a** £6 **b i** $N = 4(C-3)$ **ii** 20 **15 a** 1 **b** $-\frac{3}{2}$ **16 a** Triangles ACE and BCD **b i** 5 cm
ii 2.4 cm **17 a** 13.2 cm **b** 14.97 cm **c** No **18 a** 11.5 cm **b** 3.5 cm **c** 55.1° **19** Large packet

1 Values of y: −4, −2, 0, 2, 4 **2** Values of y: −2, 0, 2, 4, 6 **3** Values of y: −6, −4, −2, 0, 2 **4** Values of y: −1, 0, 1, 2, 3
5 Values of y: −6, −5, −4, −3, −2 **6 a** Values of y: −7, −6, −5, −4, −3; −8, −6, −4, −2, 0 **b** (−1, −6)
7 a Values of y: −8, −4, 0, 4, 8, 12; 2, 4, 6, 8, 10, 12 **b** (6, 12) **8 a** Values of y: −7, −4, −1, 2, 5 and 2, 3, 4, 5, 6 **b** (2, 5)

6 b (−1, −1) **7 b** (−4, −11) **8 b** (6, 1) **9 b** No, lines parallel **10 b** (−1, −1)
c The other two symmetrical about $y = x$

1 a 2 **b** $\frac{1}{3}$ **c** −3 **d** 1 **e** −2 **f** $-\frac{1}{3}$ **g** 5 **h** −5 **i** $\frac{2}{5}$ **j** $-\frac{3}{4}$ **3 a** 1 **b** −1 Symmetrical about both axes
4 a $\frac{1}{2}$ **b** $\frac{2}{5}$ **c** $\frac{1}{5}$ **d** $\frac{1}{10}$ **e** 0 **5 a** $\frac{5}{3}$ **b** 2 **c** 3 **d** 10 **e** Infinite

2 b (2, 7) **3 b** (−4, 1) **4 b** (3, 6)

1 a $y = \frac{3}{2}x - 2$ **b** $y = x + 1$ **c** $y = 2x - 3$ **d** $y = \frac{1}{2}x + 3$ **e** $y = x$ **f** $y = \frac{3}{2}x - 1$ **g** $y = 2x$ **h** $y = \frac{1}{5}x + 3$ **i** $y = \frac{3}{2}x + 1$
2 a i $y = 2x + 1, y = -2x + 1$ **ii** Reflection in y-axis **iii** Different sign **b i** $y = \frac{2}{5}x - 1, y = -\frac{2}{5}x - 1$
ii Reflection in y-axis **iii** Different sign **c i** $y = x + 1, y = -x + 1$ **ii** Reflection in y-axis **iii** Different sign **3 a** $y = -2x$
b $y = -\frac{1}{2}x$ **c** $y = -x + 1$ **d** $y = -\frac{2}{5}x - 1$ **e** $y = -\frac{3}{2}x - 3$ **4 a i** $y = 1 - 2x, y = \frac{1}{2} - \frac{1}{2}x$ **ii** Lines reflected in $y = x$ (also
applies to **b** and **c**) **iii** One gradient reciprocal of the other (also applies to **b** and **c**) **b i** $y = 2.5x + 2.5, y = 0.4x - 1$
c i $y = 2, x = 2$

2 b (2, 0) **3 b** (2, 2) **4 b** (4, 2)

1 4, 1 **2** 2, 3 **3** 3, 10 **4** 5, 5 **5** 1, 5 **6** 3, 16 **7** −2, 6 **8** −6, −9 **9** 1, −1 **10** 2, 6 **11** 2, 8 **12** $7\frac{1}{2}$, $3\frac{1}{2}$

Exercise 21H

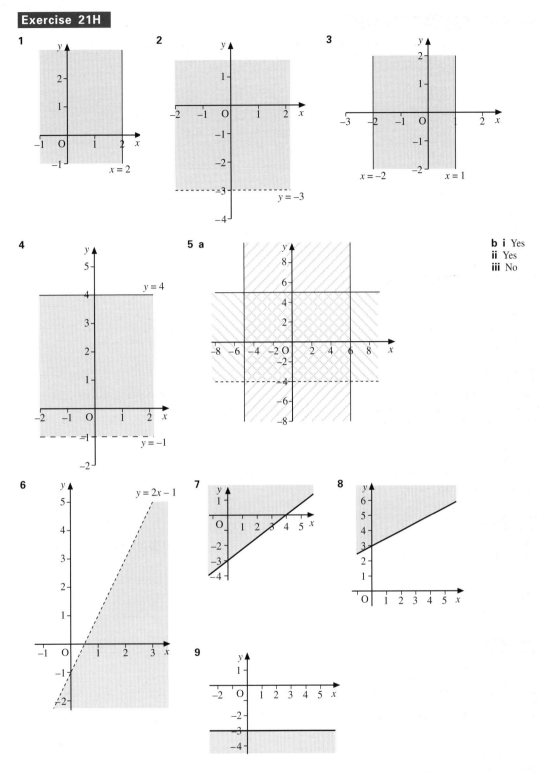

1

$x = 2$

2

$y = -3$

3

$x = -2$ $x = 1$

4

$y = 4$

$y = -1$

5 a

b i Yes
ii Yes
iii No

6

$y = 2x - 1$

7

8

9

10 e i No   **ii** Yes   **iii** Yes   **11 g i** No   **ii** No   **iii** No   **12 b i** No   **ii** Yes   **iii** Yes   **iv** No   **13 b i** No
ii No   **iii** Yes   **14 b i** Yes   **ii** Yes   **iii** No   **iv** No

Examination questions (Chapter 21)

1 b $x = 1\frac{1}{2}, y = 3$ **2 a i** Not on the straight line **c** $x = -\frac{1}{2}, y = 2\frac{1}{2}$ **3 b ii** 32.5°C **iii** 68 g **c i** $a = 0.4, b = 50$ **iii** 88 g
4 b $x < 6$ **5 b** $x = 2.5, y = 4$ **7 b** 60p

Exercise 22A

1 a Positive correlation **b** Negative correlation **c** No correlation **d** Positive correlation **2** A person's reaction time increases as more alcohol is consumed **3** As people get older, they consume less alcohol **4** No relationship between temperature and speed of cars on M1 **5** As people get older, they bank more money **6 c** ≈ 20 cm/s **d** ≈ 35 cm
7 b Greta **c** ≈ 70 **d** ≈ 72 **8 c** Yes, usually (good correlation) **9 c** ≈ £75 000 **d** Locality, improvements
e Yes, positive correlation **10 b** No correlation **c** No **11 c** ≈ 20 tonnes/acre **12 c** ≈ 53 ml/l

Exercise 22B

1

9.3	9.1	9.0	9.1	8.7	8.6	9.1	9.0	9.4	9.7	9.7
9.9	10.1	9.7	9.9	9.4	9.9	10.0	10.0	9.9	10.1	10.6

2 b

356	390	429	465	504	534
566	593	613	643	666	700
719	752	781	781	788	800
800	786	784	784	784	784
784	772	751	732	706	674
661					

c It gradually increases, has a peak in the fourth week, then slowly decreases

3 a

108	107	108	106	110	111	113	119
119	120	120	123	124			

4 a

51	50	51	54	51	53	48	51	51

b It has remained pretty stable.

5 a

14.4	14.4	13.9	13.6	13	12.4	12.4	12.3	12.1	12.1	12
12.1	12.1	11.9	11.9	11.9	12	12	11.6	11.4	11.6	11.4

b A gradual reduction is seen.

6 b

80	81	82	83	82	85	87	90
94	92	91	89	86			

c There was a sudden jump, which could have been when they started using email.

7 a

12.3	13	13	10	10.3	10	13.7	13	13.7	13	13
13	13	13.3	13	13.7	13.3	13.3	13.7	14.3	13.7	13.3

b The trend is a slight improvement in sales.

8 a

44.5	42.2	41	41.3	42.3	44.5	45.8

b There was a dip in collections in the middle of the collection time.

9 a

Video	3.7	3.6	3.3	2.8	2.5
DVD	0.6	1.1	1.4	2.1	2.8

b The video sales are going down while the DVD sales are increasing.

Exercise 22C

1 c 53 s, 16 s **2 c** 56 s, 17 s **d** Children: lower median **3 c** 67 °F, 17 °F **4 c** 605, 277 **d** 37/38 **5 c** 48, 43
d 18% **6 c** £2.25, £1.08 **7** 1187 g, 142 g, 10

Exercise 22D

1 a

Time (minutes)

b Both distributions have the same interquartile range but the students' median and upper quartile are 1 min 30 s higher. The students are much slower than the pensioners. Even though the fastest person was a student, the slowest was also a student.

2 a

Size (numbers of pupils)

b Schools are much bigger in Rotherham than in Dorset. The Dorset distribution is symmetrical but the Rotherham distribution is negatively skewed. This means that most schools in Rotherham are large.

3 a The medians of both resorts are about the same but Resort B has a much wider temperature range. The greatest extremes are reached in Resort B.   **b** Resort A: weather is likely to be good as the data is highly consistent.

4 a

b Both distributions have a similar interquartile range but the men's median is greater. The men also have a wider range in salaries due to some high salaries. The difference between the lower quartile and the median for women, and the upper quartile and the median for men is about the same and indicates that the men are better paid.

Examination questions (Chapter 22)

1 b The higher the birth rate, the higher the life expectancy.   **2 a** 25   **d** ≈ 22 **e** Positive correlation   **3 c** 16
4 a Amanda – D, Mark – A, Julie – B   **b** 'I watched a lot of TV, so I didn't do much homework'   **c** Negative correlation
5 b 6 days   **d** 23 or 24 grams   **6 b** 11 minutes   **7 a** 1050   **c** 53   **8 b i** 235   **ii** 44   **iii** 51   **9 b** 53, 45, 60, 15
c 51   **10 a** 18, 28, 40, 48, 53, 60   **c** 30 years

Exercise 23A

1 a $\frac{1}{5}$, $\frac{2}{25}$, $\frac{1}{10}$, $\frac{21}{200}$, $-\frac{37}{250}$, $-\frac{163}{2000}$, $\frac{329}{2000}$ **b** 6   **c** 1   **d** $\frac{1}{6}$ **e** 1000   **2 a** $\frac{19}{200}$, $\frac{27}{200}$, $\frac{4}{25}$, $\frac{53}{200}$, $\frac{69}{200}$ **b** 40   **c** No   **3 a** 32,
b Yes   **4 a** $\frac{1}{5}$, $\frac{1}{4}$, $\frac{39}{100}$, $\frac{21}{50}$, $\frac{77}{200}$, $\frac{1987}{2000}$ **b** 8   **5 a** 0.429, 0.326, 0.294, 0.289, 0.303, 0.306   **b** 0.286, 0.168, 0.190, 0.152,
0.202, 0.201   **c** 0.5, 0.3, 0.2   **d** 1   **e** Red 10, white 6, blue 4   **6 a** 6   **7 a** B   **b** B   **c** C   **d** A   **e** B   **f** A
g B   **h** A   **8 a** Caryl   **b** $\frac{107}{275}$, $\frac{169}{550}$, $\frac{91}{550}$, $\frac{38}{275}$ **c** Yes   **9 a** Not likely   **b** Impossible   **c** Not likely
d Certain   **e** Impossible   **f** 50–50 chance   **g** 50–50 chance   **h** Certain   **i** Quite likely

Exercise 23B

1 a $\frac{1}{6}$ **b** $\frac{1}{6}$ **c** $\frac{1}{2}$ **d** $\frac{1}{13}$ **e** $\frac{1}{4}$ **f** $\frac{1}{2}$ **g** $\frac{1}{3}$ **h** $\frac{1}{26}$ **i** $\frac{1}{13}$ **j** 0   **2 a** $\frac{1}{2}$ **b** $\frac{1}{2}$ **c** $\frac{1}{2}$ **d** $\frac{1}{52}$ **e** $\frac{4}{13}$ **f** $\frac{1}{52}$ **3 a** 0
b 1   **4 a** $\frac{1}{10}$ **b** $\frac{1}{2}$ **c** $\frac{2}{5}$ **d** $\frac{1}{5}$ **e** $\frac{2}{5}$ **5 a** $\frac{1}{3}$ **b** $\frac{1}{3}$ **c** $\frac{2}{3}$ **6 a** $\frac{6}{11}$ **b** $\frac{5}{11}$ **c** $\frac{6}{11}$ **7 a** $\frac{1}{5}$ **b** $\frac{1}{2}$ **c** $\frac{1}{2}$ **d** $\frac{7}{10}$
8 a $\frac{7}{15}$ **b** $\frac{1}{15}$ **c** $\frac{8}{15}$ **d** 0   **e** $\frac{8}{15}$ **9** $\frac{1}{50}$ **10 a** AB, AC, AD, AE, BC, BD, BE, CD, CE, DE   **b** 1   **c** $\frac{1}{10}$ **d** 6   **e** $\frac{6}{10}$
f $\frac{3}{10}$
11 a $\frac{2}{5}$ **b i** 3   **ii** 9   **c i** $\frac{1}{3}$ **ii** $\frac{2}{3}$ **12 a** $\frac{1}{3}$ **b** $\frac{1}{3}$ **c** $\frac{5}{6}$ **d** 0   **e** 1   **13 a** $\frac{1}{4}$ **b** $\frac{3}{8}$ **c** $\frac{1}{4}$ **d** $\frac{3}{8}$ **e** $\frac{1}{2}$ **f** $\frac{3}{4}$
14 a 2   **b** 5   **c i** $\frac{5}{9}$ **ii** $\frac{4}{9}$ **15 a** $\frac{1}{13}$ **b** $\frac{1}{13}$ **c** $\frac{1}{2}$ **d** $\frac{2}{13}$ **e** $\frac{7}{13}$ **f** $\frac{1}{26}$

Exercise 23C

1 a Yes   **b** Yes   **c** No   **d** No   **e** Yes   **f** Yes   **2** Events **a** and **f**   **3** $\frac{3}{5}$ **4 a i** $\frac{3}{10}$ **ii** $\frac{3}{10}$ **iii** $\frac{3}{10}$ **b** Events i,
ii and iv **c** iv **5 b i** $\frac{1}{10}$ **ii** $\frac{3}{10}$ **iii** $\frac{3}{10}$ **iv** $\frac{7}{10}$ **c** Events i and ii **d** Event ii **6 a** $\frac{3}{8}$ **b** $\frac{1}{8}$ **c** Events i and iv
d Outcomes overlap   **7** $\frac{3}{20}$ **8** Not mutually exclusive events   **9 i** a and b **ii** c, 9   **iii** c, 6   **iv** c, 36   **v** c, 12
vi c, 1   **vii** c, 10   **viii** c, 15   **ix** a **x** c, 12

Exercise 23D

1 25   **2** 1000   **3 a** 260   **b** 40   **c** 130   **d** 10   **4** 5   **5** 400   **6 a** 150   **b** 100   **c** 250   **d** 0   **7 a** 167
b 833   **8** 1050   **9 a** 10, 10, 10, 10, 10, 10   **b** 3,5   **c** Find the average of the scores ($\frac{21}{6}$)

Exercise 23E

1 a $\frac{1}{6}$ **b** $\frac{1}{6}$ **c** $\frac{1}{3}$ **2 a** $\frac{1}{4}$ **b** $\frac{1}{2}$ **c** $\frac{1}{2}$ **3 a** $\frac{2}{11}$ **b** $\frac{4}{11}$ **c** $\frac{6}{11}$ **4 a** $\frac{1}{3}$ **b** $\frac{6}{15}$ **c** $\frac{11}{15}$ **d** $\frac{11}{15}$ **e** $\frac{1}{3}$ **5 a** 0.6
b 120   **6 a** 0.8   **b** 0.2   **7 a** $\frac{17}{20}$,   **b** $\frac{2}{5}$ **c** $\frac{3}{4}$ **8** Probability cannot exceed 1

Exercise 23F

1 a 7   **b** 2 and 12   **c** $P(2) = \frac{1}{36}$, $P(3) = \frac{1}{18}$, $P(4) = \frac{1}{12}$, $P(5) = \frac{1}{9}$, $P(6) = \frac{5}{36}$, $P(7) = \frac{1}{6}$, $P(8) = \frac{5}{36}$, $P(9) = \frac{1}{9}$, $P(10) = \frac{1}{12}$, $P(11)$
$= \frac{1}{18}$ $P(12) = \frac{1}{36}$ **d i** $\frac{1}{12}$ **ii** $\frac{1}{3}$ **iii** $\frac{1}{2}$ **iv** $\frac{7}{36}$ **v** $\frac{15}{36}$ **vi** $\frac{5}{18}$ **2 a** $\frac{1}{6}$ **b** $\frac{11}{36}$ **c** $\frac{1}{6}$ **d** $\frac{5}{9}$ **3 a** $\frac{1}{36}$ **b** $\frac{11}{36}$ **c** $\frac{5}{18}$
4 a $\frac{5}{18}$ **b** $\frac{1}{6}$ **c** $\frac{1}{9}$ **d** 0   **e** $\frac{1}{2}$ **5 a** $\frac{1}{4}$ **b** $\frac{1}{2}$ **c** $\frac{3}{4}$ **d** $\frac{1}{4}$ **6 a** $\frac{1}{8}$ **b** $\frac{3}{8}$ **c** $\frac{7}{8}$ **d** $\frac{1}{8}$ **7 a** 16   **b** 32   **c** 1024
d 2^n
8 c i $\frac{1}{16}$ **ii** $\frac{1}{4}$ **iii** $\frac{15}{16}$ **iv** $\frac{1}{16}$ **9 a** $\frac{1}{12}$ **b** $\frac{1}{4}$ **c** $\frac{1}{6}$ **10 a** 6   **b i** $\frac{4}{25}$ **ii** $\frac{13}{25}$ **iii** $\frac{1}{5}$ **iv** $\frac{3}{5}$

Exercise 23G

1 a $\frac{1}{4}$ **b** $\frac{1}{2}$ **c** $\frac{3}{4}$ **2 a** $\frac{2}{3}$ **b** $\frac{1}{2}$ **d i** $\frac{1}{6}$ **ii** $\frac{1}{2}$ **iii** $\frac{5}{6}$ **e** 15   **3 a** $\frac{2}{5}$ **b i** $\frac{4}{25}$ **ii** $\frac{12}{25}$ **4 a** $\frac{1}{13}$ **b** $\frac{12}{13}$ **c i** $\frac{1}{169}$
ii $\frac{25}{169}$ **5 a i** $\frac{2}{5}$ **ii** $\frac{3}{5}$ **b i** 4   **ii** 1   **c i** 4   **ii** 2   **e i** $\frac{2}{5}$ **ii** $\frac{7}{10}$ **6 a** $\frac{1}{8}$ **b** $\frac{3}{8}$ **c** $\frac{7}{8}$ **7 a** 0.14   **b** 0.41
c 0.09   **8 a** $\frac{2}{5}$ **c i** $\frac{1}{3}$ **ii** $\frac{7}{15}$ **iii** $\frac{8}{15}$ **9 a** $\frac{1}{4}$ **b** 0   **d i** $\frac{1}{2}$ **ii** $\frac{1}{2}$ **iii** 0   **10 a** 1   **b** 1   **c**

$$\begin{array}{ccc} & \boxed{\frac{1}{4}} & \boxed{\frac{1}{4}} \\ & & \boxed{\frac{1}{10}} \\ \boxed{\frac{3}{5}} & \boxed{\frac{1}{3}} & \boxed{\frac{3}{5} \times \frac{1}{3}} \\ \boxed{\frac{2}{3}} & \boxed{\frac{2}{3}} & \boxed{\frac{3}{5} \times \frac{2}{3}} & \boxed{\frac{2}{3}} \end{array}$$

Exercise 23H

1 a $\frac{4}{9}$ **b** $\frac{4}{9}$ **2 a** $\frac{1}{169}$ **b** $\frac{2}{169}$ **3 a** $\frac{1}{221}$ **b** $\frac{8}{663}$ **4 a** $\frac{1}{4}$ **b** $\frac{1}{2}$ **5** $\frac{1}{216}$ **6 a** $\frac{4}{25}$ **b** $\frac{12}{25}$ **7 a** $\frac{3}{20}$ **b** $\frac{1}{2}$ **8 a** 0.08
b 0.32 **c** 0.48 **9 a** 0.336 **b** 0.452 **c** 0.024 **10 a** $\frac{1}{6}$ **b** 0 **c i** $\frac{2}{3}$ **ii** $\frac{1}{3}$ **iii** 0

Examination questions (Chapter 23)

1 a
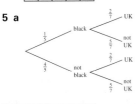

2	3	4	5	6
3	4	5	6	7
4	5	6	7	8
5	6	7	8	9
6	7	8	9	10

b i $\frac{1}{25}$ **ii** 0 **iii** $\frac{5}{25}$ **2 a** 0.91 **b** 3 **c i** 0.0081 **ii** 0.1638 **3 a** $\frac{1}{500}$ **b** $\frac{3}{10}$
c Proportion of girls not known **4 a** 0.09 **b** P(same) = 0.46, P(different) = 0.54: Sarah wins

5 a

(tree diagram: first branches $\frac{1}{5}$ black, $\frac{4}{5}$ not black; black splits $\frac{2}{7}$ UK, $\frac{5}{7}$ not UK; not black splits $\frac{2}{7}$ UK, $\frac{5}{7}$ not UK)

b i $\frac{2}{35}$ (0.057) **ii** $\frac{13}{35}$ (0.37) **6 a** 0.2, 0.6, 0.4 **b i** 0.48 **ii** 0.52
7 a i 0.2 **ii** 0.5 **iii** 0.7 **b** 20 **8 a** $\frac{1}{18}$ **b** $\frac{1}{6}$
9 a $\frac{7}{12}$ **c i** $\frac{1}{4}$ **ii** $\frac{31}{60}$

Exercise 24A

1 $11111 \times 11111 = 123454321$, $111111 \times 111111 = 12345654321$
2 $99999 \times 9999 = 999980001$, $999999 \times 999999 = 999998000001$ **3** $7 \times 8 = 7^2 + 7$, $8 \times 9 = 8^2 + 8$
4 $50 \times 51 = 2550$, $60 \times 61 = 3660$ **5** $1+2+3+4+5+4+3+2+1 = 25 = 5^2$, $1+2+3+4+5+6+5+4+3+2+1 = 36 = 6^2$
6 $21+223+25+27+29 = 125 = 5^3$, $31+33+35+37+39+41 = 216 = 6^3$
7 $1+6+15+20+15+6+1 = 64$, $1+7+21+35+35+21+7 = 128$
8 $12345679 \times 45 = 555555555$, $12345679 \times 54 = 666666666$
9 $1^3 + 2^3 + 3^3 + 4^3 = (1+2+3+4)^2 = 100$, $1^3 + 2^3 + 3^3 + 4^3 + 5^3 = (1+2+3+4+5)^2 = 225$
10 $36^2 + 37^2 + 38^2 + 39^2 + 40^2 = 41^2 + 42^2 + 43^2 + 44^2$, $55^2 + 56^2 + 57^2 + 58^2 + 59^2 + 60^2 = 61^2 + 62^2 + 63^2 + 64^2 + 65^2$
11 12345678987654321 **12** 999999998000000001 **13** $12^2 + 12$ **14** 8190 **15** $81 = 9^2$ **16** $512 = 8^3$ **17** 512
18 999999999 **19** $(1+2+3+4+5+6+7+8+9)^2 = 2025$

Exercise 24B

1 a 9, 11, 13: add 2 **b** 10, 12, 14: add 2 **c** 80, 160, 320: double **d** 81, 243, 729: multiply by 3 **c** 28, 34, 40: add 6
f 23, 28, 33: add 5 **g** 20 000, 200 000, 2 000 000: multiply by 10 **h** 19, 22, 25: add 3 **i** 46, 55, 64: add 9 **j** 405, 1215,
3645: multiply by 3 **k** 18, 22, 26: add 4 **l** 625, 3125, 15 625: multiply by 5 **2 a** 16, 22 **b** 26, 37 **c** 31, 43
d 46, 64 **e** 121, 169 **f** 782, 3907 **g** 22 223, 222 223 **h** 11, 13 **i** 33, 65 **j** 78, 108 **3 a** 21, 34: add previous 2 terms
b 49, 64: next square number **c** 47, 76: add previous 2 terms **4** 15, 21, 28, 36 **5** 61, 91, 127 **6 a** 48, 96, 192
b 33, 39, 45 **c** 29, 47, 76 **d** 38, 35, 32 **e** 37, 50, 65 **f** 26, 33, 41 **g** 14, 16, 17 **h** 19, 22, 25 **i** 28, 36, 45
j 5, 6, 7 **k** 0.16, 0.032, 0.0064 **l** 0.0625, 0.031 25, 0.015 625

Exercise 24C

1 a 3, 5, 7, 9, 11 **b** 1, 4, 7, 10, 13 **c** 7, 12, 17, 22, 27 **d** 1, 4, 9, 16, 25 **e** 4, 7, 12, 19, 28 **2 a** 4, 5, 6, 7, 8 **b** 2, 5,
8, 11, 14 **c** 3, 8, 13, 18, 23 **d** 0, 3, 8, 15, 24 **e** 9, 13, 17, 21, 25 **3** 0, $\frac{1}{3}$, $\frac{2}{4}$, $\frac{3}{5}$, $\frac{4}{6}$, $\frac{5}{7}$ **4 a** 1, 3, 6, 10, 15, 21
b Triangle numbers **5 a** 24, 120, 720 **b** 69

Exercise 24D

1 a $2n+1$ **b** $4n+1$ **c** $5n+3$ **d** $6n-4$ **e** $3n+2$ **f** $7n-5$ **g** $4n-3$ **h** $4n-1$ **i** $3n-1$ **j** $10n-8$
k $4n+4$ **l** $5n-1$ **2 a** 151 **b** 105 **c** 248 **d** 197 **e** 394 **f** 54 **g** 251 **h** 395 **i** 148 **j** 168 **k** 355
l 393 **3 a** 33rd **b** 30th **c** 100th = 499 **4 a i** $4n+1$ **ii** 401 **iii** 101 **b i** $2n+1$ **ii** 201 **iii** 99 or 101
c i $3n+1$ **ii** 301 **iii** 100 **d i** $2n+6$ **ii** 206 **iii** 100 **e i** $4n+5$ **ii** 405 **iii** 101 **f i** $5n+1$ **ii** 501
iii 101 **g i** $3n-3$ **ii** 297 **iii** 99 **h i** $6n-4$ **ii** 596 **iii** 98 **i i** $8n-1$ **ii** 799 **iii** 103 **j i** $2n+23$
ii 223 **iii** 99 or 101 **5 a** $\dfrac{2n+1}{3n+1}$ **b** Terms decrease **c i** 0.667 774 … **ii** 0.666 777 74…
d 0.666 677 7774 and 0.666 666 777 777 74 **6 a** $\dfrac{4n-1}{5n-1}$ **b** Terms increase **c i** 0.7964… **ii** 0.799 64…
d 0.799 9 64… and 0.799 999 64…

Exercise 24E

1 b $4n-3$ **c** 97 **d** 50th diagram **2 b** $2n+1$ **c** 121 **d** 49th set **3 a** 18 **b** $4n+2$ **c** 12 **4 b** $2n+1$
c 101 **d** 149th diagram **5 a i** 24 **ii** $5n-1$ **iii** 224 **b** 25 **6 a i** 20 cm **ii** $(3n+2)$ cm **iii** 152 cm **b** 332
7 a i 14 **ii** $3n+2$ **iii** 41 **b** 66 **8 a i** 20 **ii** 162 **b** 79.8 km **9 a i** 10 **ii** $2n+2$ **iii** 20 **b** 14
10 a i 5 **ii** n **iii** 18 **b** 20

Exercise 24F

1 a i 35, 48 **ii** $n^2 - 1$ **b i** 38, 51 **ii** $n^2 + 2$ **c i** 39, 52 **ii** $n^2 + 3$ **d i** 34, 47 **ii** $n^2 - 2$ **e i** 35, 46
ii $n^2 + 10$ **2 a i** 37, 50 **ii** $(n+1)^2 + 1$ **b i** 35, 48 **ii** $(n+1)^2 - 1$ **c i** 41, 54 **ii** $(n+1)^2 + 5$ **d i** 50, 65
ii $(n+2)^2 + 1$ **e i** 48, 63 **ii** $(n+2)^2 - 1$ **3 a i** 30, 42 **ii** $n(n-1)$ **b i** 60, 84 **ii** $2n(n-1)$ **c i** 56, 72
ii $(n+1)(n+2)$ **d i** 15, 21 **ii** $\frac{1}{2}n(n-1)$ **e i** 54, 70 **ii** $n(n+3)$ **4 a i** $n^2 + 4$ **ii** 2504 **b i** $3n + 2$ **ii** 152
c i $(n+1)^2 - 1$ **ii** 2600 **d i** $(n+2)^2 - 4$ **ii** 2700 **e i** $n^2 + 2$ **ii** 2502 **f i** $5n - 4$ **ii** 246

Examination questions (Chapter 24)

1 a i 13 **ii** Add previous 2 terms: 21 **b** $3n - 2$ **2 a i** 78 **ii** 7 **b i** Add 4 each time **ii** $4n + 1$ **3 a** 23, 27
b Add 4 **c** $4n - 1$ **4 a** 41 **b** $n + 1$ **c** 126 **d** $3n + 6$ **5 a** $3n$ **b** $4n + 1$ **6** $6n - 4$ **7 a** n^2 **b** $n(n+1)$
8 a $10n + 2$ **b** $10n + 12$ **9 a** 31, 63 **b** $5n + 2$ **c** $n(n+1)$ **10 a** 21, 28 **b** C2 = B2 + B1, C3 = B3 + B2,
C4 = B4 + B3 etc **c i** 400 **ii** $Cn = n^2$

Exercise 25A

1 a Values of y: 27, 12, 3, 0, 3, 12, 27 **b** 6.8 **c** 1.8 or −1.8 **2 a** Values of y: 27, 18, 11, 6, 3, 2, 3, 6, 11, 18, 27 **b** 8.3
c 3.5 or −3.5 **3 a** Values of y: 40, 28, 18, 10, 4, 0, −2, −2, 0, 4, 10 **b** 1.75 **c** 4.2 or −1.2 **4 a** Values of y: 27, 16, 7, 0, −
5, −8, −10, −8, −5, 0, 7 **b** −8.8 **c** 3.4 or −1.4 **5 a** Values of y: 18, 10, 4, 0, −3, −2, 0, 4 **b** 6.8 **c** 0.2 or 4.8
6 a Values of y: 2, −1, −2, −1, 2, 7, 14 **b** 0.25 **c** 0.7 or −2. **e** (1.1, 2.6) and (−2.6, 0.7) **7 a** Values of y: 18, 11, 6, 3, 2, 3, 6
b 2.25 **c** 2.4 or −0.4 **e** (−1, 6) **8 a** Values of y: 18, 12, 8, 6, 6, 8, 12 **b** 9.75 **c** 2 or −1 **d** Values of y: 14, 9, 6, 5, 6, 9, 14
e (1, 6) **9 a** Values of y: 4, 1, 0, 1, 9, 16 **b** 7.3 **c** 0.4 or −2.4 **e** (1, 4) and (−1, 0)
10 a Values of y: 15, 9, 4, 0, −3, −5, −5, −3, 0, 4, 9 **b** −0.5 and 3

Exercise 25B

1 a Values of y: 12, 5, 0, −3, −4, −3, 0, 5, 12, **b** 2 and −2 **2 a** Values of y: 7, 0, −5, −8, −9, −8, −5, 0, 7 **b** 3 and −3
3 c Values of y: 15, 8, 3, 0, −1, 0, 3, 8, 15 **d** Values of y: 11, 4, −1, −4, −5, −4, −1, 4, 11 **e** 1 and −1, 2.2 and −2.2
4 a Values of y: 5, 0, −3, −4, −3, 0, 5, 12 **b** −4 and 0 **5 a** Values of y: 16, 7, 0, −5, −8, −9, −8, −5, 0 **b** 0 and 6
6 a Values of y: 10, 4, 0, −2, −2, 0, 4, 10, 18 **b** −3 and 0 **7 c** Values of y: 10, 4, 0, −2, −2, 0, 4, 10 **d** Values of y: 6, 0, −4,
−6, −6, −4, 0, 6, 14 **e** 0 and 3, −5 and 0 **8 a** 9, 4, 1, 0, 1 **b** 2 **c** Only 1 root **9 a** Values of y: 10, 3, −2, −5, −6, −5,
−2, 3, 10 **b** 0.6 and 5.4

Exercise 25C

1 a Values of y: 10, 5, 4, 2.5, 2, 1.33, 1, 0.67, 0.5 **b i** 0.8 **ii** −1.6 **2 a** Values of y: 10, 8, 5, 4, 2, 1, 0.8, 0.5, 0.4
b i 0.7 **ii** −0.7 **3 a** Values of y: 10, 5, 3.33, 2, 1.25, 1, 0.33, 0.2, 0.1, 0.07 **b i** 0.13 **ii** −0.25 **4 a** Values of y: 10, 5,
2.5, 2, 1.25, 1, 0.5, 0.33, 0.25 **b i** −0.67 **ii** 25 **5 a** Values of y: 10, 5, 2.5, 2, 1, 0.5, 0.4, 0.25, 0.2 **c** 4.8 and 0.2
6 a Values of y: 25, 12.5, 10, 5, 2.5, 1, 0.5, 0.33, 0.25 **c** 0.48 **7 a** Values of y: 0.5, 0, −0.33, −1, −1.5, −3, −4, −9, 11, 6, 5, 3.5,
3, 2.33, 2, 1.5 **b** Values of y: −3.5, −4, −4.33, −5, −5.5, −7, −8, −13, 7, 2, 1, −0.5, −1, −1.67, −2, −2.5 **c** These 2 graphs are
translations of $y = \frac{2}{x}$

Exercise 25D

1 a Values of y: −24, −12.63, −5, −0.38, 2, 2.9, 3, 3.13, 4, 6.38, 11, 15.63, 30 **b** 4.7 **2 a** Values of y: −54, −31.25, −16, −6.75,
−2, −0.25, 0, 0.25, 2, 6.75, 16, 31.25, 54 **b** 39.4 **3 a** Values of y: 27, 15.63, 8, 3.38, 1, 0.13, 0, −0.13, −1, −3.38, −8, −15.63, −
27 **b** 0.2 **4 a** Values of y: −36, −23.13, −14, −7.88, −4, −1.63, 0, 1.63, 4, 7.88, 14, 23.13, 36 **b** 0.6 **5 a** Values of y: −45,
−26.88, −14, −5.63, −1, 0.63, 0, −0.63, −5, −7.88, −10, −10.63, −9 **b** −9.3 **6 a** Values of y: −17, −7.13, −1, 2.13, 3, 2.38, 1, −
0.38, −1, −0.13, 3, 9.13, 19 **b** −1.9, 0.3, 1.5 **7 a** Values of y: −19, −9.13, −3, 0.13, 1, 0.375, −1, −2.38, −3, −2.13, 1, 7.13, 17
b 3.2 **8 a** Values of y: −7, 1.38, 6, 7.63, 7, 4.88, 2, −0.88, −3, −3.63, −2, 2.63, 11 **b** −2.7, 0.5, 2.1 **9 a** Values of y: −16, −
5.63, 1, 4.63, 6, 5.88, 5, 4.13, 4, 5.38, 9, 15.63, 26 **c** −1.6, −0.4, 1.9 **10 a** Values of y: −20, −9.63, −3, 0.63, 2, 1.88, 1, 0.13, 0,
1.38, 5, 11.63, 22 **c** −1.9, 0.4, 1.5 **11 a** Quadratic **b** Linear **c** Reciprocal **d** Reciprocal **e** None **f** Cubic
g Linear **h** None **i** Quadratic

Examination questions (Chapter 25)

1 a 1, 2, 5, 10, 17, 26, 37, 50 **c** 6.6 **2 a** 1, −2, −3, −2, 1, 6, 13 **c** (2.8, 5) **3 a** Graph C **b** $v = kr^2$
4 a 3.3 **b ii** 3.3, −0.3 **5 a i** −1.3, 0, 3.3 **ii** −1, −0.3, 3.4 **6 a** −1, 2, −1, −4, −1, 14 **c** −1.8, −0.2, 2.1 **7 a** 10, 4, 0,
−2, −2, 0, 4, 10 **c** 0.4 and 2.6 **d** $0 < x < 3$

8 a i $-7, -6, -3$ **ii** 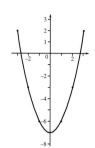 **b** $2.6, -2.6$ **c** -7

9 a $12, 4, 4, 12$ **b** 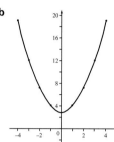 **10 a** $5, -3$ **b** 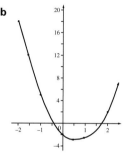 **c** -1 and 2.3
d $3x^2 - 4x - 2 = 5$

Exercise 26A

1 $P = a + b$ **2** $P = a + b + c + d$ **3** $P = 4x$ **4** $P = p + 2q$ **5** $P = 2\pi r$ **6** $P = 2h + (2 + \pi)r$

Exercise 26B

1 a $A = xy$ **b** $A = \pi r^2$ **c** $A = 2ad - a^2$ **d** $A = 2rh + \pi r^2$ **2 a** $A = \frac{1}{2}bh$ **b** $A = bh$ **c** $A = \frac{1}{2}bh + \frac{1}{2}bw$
d $A = \frac{1}{2}h(a + b)$ **e** $A = \frac{1}{8}\pi d^2 + \frac{1}{2}dh$ **f** $A = \frac{1}{8}\pi D^2 + \frac{1}{2}w(b + D)$

Exercise 26C

1 $V = pqr$ **2** $V = \pi r^2 h$ **3** $V = aqt + bpt - apt$ **4** $V = abl + adl + 2cdl$ **5** $V = \frac{1}{2}bhw$ **6** $V = \frac{1}{2}bhl$

Exercise 26D

1 a L **b** V **c** L **d** A **e** L **f** L **g** V **h** V **i** N **j** L **k** N **l** A **m** V **n** A **o** V **p** V **q** N
r L **s** A **t** V **u** L **v** N **w** N **x** N **y** L **z** N **2 a** A **b** L **c** L **d** A **e** V **f** V **g** V
h A **i** L **j** V **k** A **l** L **m** V **n** A **o** V **p** A **q** V **r** A **s** A **t** A **u** L **v** A **w** A **x** A
y V **z** V

Exercise 26E

1 a C **b** I **c** C **d** I **e** C **f** I **g** C **h** I **i** C **j** I **k** C **l** C **m** C **n** C **o** C **p** I **q** C
r C **s** I **t** C **u** C **v** C **w** C **x** C **y** C **2 a** C,L **b** I **c** C,V **d** C,L **e** I **f** I **g** C,V
h C,V **i** C,V **j** C,V **k** C,L **l** I **m** C,V **3 a** 2 **b** 2,3 **c** 2 **d** 2,2 **4** Inconsistent

Examination questions (Chapter 26)

1 Length: 4, area: 2, 3, volume: 1, 5 **2** $\frac{ar}{2}(4b + \pi r)$ and $2abr + \frac{\pi ar^2}{2}$
3

Expression	Length	Area	Volume	None of these
$3rl$		✓		
$\frac{2(r + l)^2}{h}$				✓
$\frac{4\pi r^2 l}{3}$			✓	

4 a Volume **b** Area **c** Length **5 a** Because the lengths are added, giving a one-dimensional formula. If they were to
represent volume, they would all need to be multiplied to each other. **b** $0.8LWH$ **6 a** [L] units **b** Formula *ii*: [L^2] units
7 πab, $\pi(a + b)l$

Index